# International Organizations

THIRD EDITION

# International

# Organizations

## The Politics and Processes
## of Global Governance

Margaret P. Karns
Karen A. Mingst
Kendall W. Stiles

LYNNE
RIENNER
PUBLISHERS

BOULDER
LONDON

Published in the United States of America in 2015 by
Lynne Rienner Publishers, Inc.
1800 30th Street, Boulder, Colorado 80301
www.rienner.com

and in the United Kingdom by
Lynne Rienner Publishers, Inc.
3 Henrietta Street, Covent Garden, London WC2E 8LU

**Library of Congress Cataloging-in-Publication Data**
Karns, Margaret P.
  International organizations : the politics and processes of global
governance / Margaret P. Karns, Karen A. Mingst, and Kendall W. Stiles. —
Third edition.
    pages cm
  Includes bibliographical references and index.
  ISBN 978-1-62637-151-4 (alk. paper)
1. International agencies. 2. International organization.  I. Mingst,
Karen A., 1947–  II. Stiles, Kendall W. III. Title.
  JZ4850.K37 2015
  341.2—dc23

                                        2015020506

**British Cataloguing in Publication Data**
A Cataloguing in Publication record for this book
is available from the British Library.


Printed and bound in the United States of America

 The paper used in this publication meets the requirements
of the American National Standard for Permanence of
Paper for Printed Library Materials Z39.48-1992.

5

*To Chadwick F. Alger—*
*teacher, mentor, and pioneer in the field—*
*and to the next generation of students of international*
*organizations and global governance*

# Contents

## 8   Global Economic Governance                                                   379

Case Study: The Global Financial Crisis of 2008, 379
An Evolving Global Economy, 382
Governance of Global Finance, 387
Governance of Trade: From GATT to the WTO, 396
Macroeconomic Policy Coordination:
     The Roles of the OECD, G-7, and G-20, 404
The Key Roles of Functional Institutions and Regimes, 408
Private Governance, 410
The Regionalization of Economic Governance, 412
Critics of Governance Institutions in Finance and Trade, 420

## 9   Promoting Economic Well-Being and Human Development                          425

Case Study: Economic Globalization and Africa, 425
Evolution of the Idea of Development, 427
Alternative Strategies to Achieve Development, 431
Actors in Promoting Development, 432
Evolving Varieties of Development-Related Governance, 456

## 10   Protecting Human Rights                                                      467

Case Study: Human Trafficking, 467
The Roots of Human Rights and Humanitarian Norms, 470
The Key Role of States: Protectors and Abusers
     of Human Rights, 474
International Human Rights Institutions and Mechanisms, 475
The Processes of Human Rights Governance, 486
Global Human Rights and Humanitarian Governance in Action, 510
The Globalization of Human Rights and
     the Role of the United States, 525

## 11   Protecting the Environment                                                  529

Case Study: Climate Change, 529
Relating Environmental Problems to Security, Economics,
     and Human Rights, 535
Emergence of the Environment as an Issue Area, 536
The Evolution of Global Environmental Governance, 537
Global Environmental Regimes and Institutions, 544

# Illustrations

**Tables**

**Figures**

# Preface

**The politics and processes of global governance have become** increasingly complex in recent years as the varieties and actors have multiplied and challenges have mounted. Many of the ideas we tried to express in the first edition of this book had a long period of gestation. They have continued to develop since that edition appeared in 2004 and the second edition in 2010. The world has changed, and there has been an astonishing amount of new scholarship in several areas over the past decade. Throughout, we have continued to be inspired by three scholars who contributed significantly to the study of international organizations, the late Inis L. Claude Jr., Harold K. Jacobson, and Chadwick F. Alger. It is to them, and to the next generation of students of international organizations and global governance, that we dedicate this book.

This third edition has been thoroughly updated to take into account new developments, shifting power relations, and current scholarship on global governance. It includes newer theoretical approaches, such as critical feminism, the English School, and securitization, and it highlights the increasing importance of regional organizations. We have divided the material on economic relations into two chapters, one covering trade and monetary governance primarily among developed countries and the other examining developing states' quest for human development, including governance relating to health and food security. New case studies include the governance dilemmas posed by the Libyan and Syrian civil wars, Islamic extremism, human trafficking, LGBT rights, and climate change. Particular attention is paid to newer forms of governance, including partnerships and private governance. The book continues to be informed by familiar and emerging theories of international organization.

As we wrote in the preface to the first edition of *International Organizations,* when Lynne Rienner calls and invites you to write a book, the invitation is hard to resist, particularly when it comes with passion, enthusiasm, and encouragement. Lynne was patient then, and continued to be so through the second edition and now this third edition. We thank her for all the support that she has provided throughout our work on the book.

It was with Lynne's encouragement and support also that we welcomed Ken Stiles as a coauthor for this third edition, and some of the changes in the book reflect his fresh thinking. Coordination among three authors can be a challenge, and in keeping with the book's subject, we have had to develop new "habits of cooperation."

We have incurred a debt to our students who have tested pieces of the book and given us feedback on what worked and what did not. We are grateful to the many colleagues around the world who have contributed ideas and feedback, helping us to refine our thinking and improve the book, particularly those who participated in a panel discussion on teaching international organization at the International Studies Association meetings in 2012. To all of those who have participated in discussions of our ideas but are not named here, we also say thanks.

Portions of Chapters 3–4 and 7–12 are drawn from Karen A. Mingst and Margaret P. Karns, *The United Nations in the 21st Century,* 4th ed. (Boulder: Westview Press, 2012). Those sections are included with permission of Westview Press.

No project like this is possible without the support of families, who bear the burden of long hours, weeks, and months of concentrated labor. Special thanks to Ginger Stauffer for the "thankless" task of merging and compiling the revised reference list. We are grateful to our spouses—Ralph Johnston, Robert Stauffer, and Rebecca Stiles—for all the love, support, and encouragement they provided, as well as to Ginger and Brett Stauffer, Paul Karns, Kristen Waters, Penelope Isaksen, Renee and Alexander Stiles, and Christina Harrison. We are also grateful to our grandchildren—Quintin Stauffer, Anna Karns, Zachary and Ian Waters, Olivia and Sophia Stumpe, Chase, Brandon, Cayden, and Callie Isaksen, Oscar Stiles, and Addilyn Harrison—who represent the next generations.

# 1

# The Challenges of Global Governance

Growing evidence of climate change, along with the continuing threat of global terrorism, pandemics, the resurgence of ethnonationalism, and memories of the meltdown of financial markets in 2008, has brought home to people around the world the complex problems we face today. These also include the dangers of nuclear weapons proliferation, large-scale humanitarian crises and intractable conflicts in Africa and the Middle East, the persistence of deep poverty, the continuing growth of international migration both legal and illegal, and failed states.

None of these problems can be solved by sovereign states acting alone. All require cooperation of some sort among states and the growing number of nonstate actors; many require the active participation of ordinary citizens; some demand the establishment of new international mechanisms for monitoring or the negotiation of new international rules; and most require the refinement of means for securing states' and other actors' compliance. Many contemporary problems are also requiring new types of partnerships—some between existing organizations such as the United Nations (UN) and the North Atlantic Treaty Organization (NATO) in Libya or the African Union (AU) in Somalia; others involve public-private partnerships such as between the UN and the Bill and Melinda Gates Foundation to address various international health issues. In short, there is a wide variety of cross-border issues and problems that require governance. Sometimes the need is truly global in scope, as with pandemics or climate change. In other cases, the governance problem is specific to a region of the world or group of countries, as with the need to manage an international river or regional sea. Sometimes, a problem cannot be neatly classified, as with the Arctic, where the nexus of issues posed by climate change affects not just states and peoples but significant parts of the world. As Bruce Jentleson (2012: 145) has noted, "The need for global governance is not an if question. It is a how question." But what do we mean by "global governance," and why is the need for it increasing?

1

## What Is Global Governance?

In 2005, two international relations scholars noted: "The idea of global governance has attained near-celebrity status. In little more than a decade the concept has gone from the ranks of the unknown to one of the central orienting themes in the practice and study of international affairs (Barnett and Duvall 2005: 1). Sometimes the term *global governance* has been used as just a synonym for international organizations. More often, however, it is used to capture the complexity and dynamism of the many collective efforts by states and an increasing variety of nonstate actors to identify, understand, and address various issues and problems in today's turbulent world. In 1995 the Commission on Global Governance, an independent group of prominent international figures, published a report on what reforms in modes of international cooperation were called for by global changes following the Cold War's end. The commission defined governance as "the sum of the many ways individuals and institutions, public and private, manage their common affairs. It is a continuing process through which conflicting or diverse interests may be accommodated and cooperative action may be taken. It includes formal . . . as well as informal arrangements that people and institutions have agreed to or perceive to be in their interest" (Commission on Global Governance 1995: 2).

How does governance relate to government? While clearly related, the two concepts are not identical. As James Rosenau (1992: 4) put it:

> Both refer to purposive behavior, to goal-oriented activities, to systems of rule; but government suggests activities that are backed by formal authority, by police powers to insure the implementation of duly constituted policies, whereas governance refers to activities backed by shared goals that may or may not derive from legal and formally prescribed responsibilities and that do not necessarily rely on police powers to overcome defiance and attain compliance. Governance, in other words, is a more encompassing phenomenon than government. It embraces governmental institutions, but it also subsumes informal, nongovernmental mechanisms whereby those persons and organizations within its purview move ahead, satisfy their needs, and fulfill their wants.

Thus, global governance is not global government; it is not a single world order; there is no top-down, hierarchical structure of authority, but both power and authority in global governance are present in varying ways and to varying degrees. Reviewing the evolution of the concept, Thomas Weiss and Rorden Wilkinson (2014:211) conclude, "We understand global governance as the sum of the informal and formal ideas, values, norms, procedures, and institutions that help all actors—states, IGOs, civil society, and TNCs—identify, understand, and address trans-boundary problems." It therefore encompasses international law and international organizations created by states, but goes well beyond them, because today's world is far more complex and far less state-centric, with a wide variety of actors and governance mechanisms. It is "the collective effort by sovereign states, international organizations, and other nonstate actors to address common challenges and seize opportunities than transcend national frontiers. . . . [It is] an ungainly patchwork of formal and informal institutions" (Patrick 2014b: 59).

The concept of global governance has ancient roots, but contemporary conceptions are very much a product of developments since the Cold War's end. Analyzing the varieties of global governance and the actors in the politics and processes that have shaped them is the central purpose of this book. In doing this, we show why, if one wants to understand collective global efforts to solve those "problems without passports," it is no longer enough to look just at international organizations created by states. Although states retain their sovereignty and still exercise coercive power, global governance increasingly rests on other bases of authority. Thus, Emmanuel Adler and Steven Bernstein (2005: 302) note that "the decoupling of coercive force and legitimate rule is the most striking feature of contemporary global governance." The study of this phenomenon therefore requires exploring not only the forms that it can take, the politics and processes by which it has developed, the actors who play various roles, and the relationships among them, but also the forms and patterns of both power and authority. As the title of one book conveys, "Who governs the globe?" is an essential question to answer, as are also the questions of "who get what," "who benefits," and with what consequences (Avant, Finnemore, and Sell 2010b). Part of the value, then, of the concept "global governance" is the way that it enables us to look at international organization (IO)—the long-term process of organizing collective efforts to deal with shared problems—past, present, and future (Claude 1964: 4). Global governance is incredibly complex and no one book can cover it all. For the sake of manageability, we have chosen to focus primarily on interstate varieties of global governance, and particularly on intergovernmental organizations (IGOs), while also showing where and how various types of nonstate actors (NSAs) play important roles. We introduce networks, forms of private governance, and public-private partnerships, but leave these to others to elaborate. Because global governance is also dynamic, the study of it is the study of how changes have occurred in efforts to deal with shared transboundary problems, how changes are occurring, and even how changes could or should occur in the future.

## Why the Growing Need for Global Governance Now?

The emergence of the concept of global governance in the 1990s accompanied the growing awareness of the rapid pace of a number of systemic changes taking place in the world, as well as the rapid proliferation of issues and actors and the inadequacy of existing international organizations to provide solutions to many problems. These changes include globalization, technological advances, the Cold War's end, and the growth of transnationalism. Separately and collectively, they have fundamentally altered global politics at the same time that they have contributed to the increased need for global governance.

### Globalization

Since the late 1980s, what had initially appeared to be simply growing interdependence among states and peoples has become something much more fundamental—a complex multidimensional process of economic, cultural, and social change. Particularly noticeable is the rapid pace of change, the compression of time and space, and the scale and scope of interconnectedness. There are many definitions of globalization, some of which focus primarily on its economic dimensions, namely the "integration of national economies into the international economy through trade, direct foreign investment (by corporations and multinationals), short-term capital flows, international flows of workers and humanity generally, and flows of technology" (Bhagwati 2004: 3). More broadly, however, globalization can be defined as "a historical process involving a fundamental shift or transformation in the spatial scale of human social organization that links distant communities and expands the reach of power relations across regions and continents" (McGrew 2008: 19).

In its contemporary form, globalization is unprecedented in the degree to which economic markets, cultures, peoples, and states have become linked, thanks to improvements in transportation and communications that speed the movement of ideas, goods, news, capital, technology, and people, and to deregulation and privatization of businesses, finance, and services in many countries. Globalization has spurred the proliferating networks of nongovernmental organizations (NGOs) and financial markets, linking likeminded people and investors, as well as the unwelcome, often illegal actors—terrorists and drug traffickers. It has contributed to the homogenization of culture with the global spread of ideas and popular culture. It has also contributed to heterogeneity, with the reassertion of ethnicity and nationalism in many parts of the world in reaction to globalization. The ways in which global events can have local consequences and vice versa mean that crises in one region can affect jobs, production, personal savings, and investment in other regions, as, for example, ripples from the 1998 Asian financial crisis could be felt in Ohio and Washington state as well as in Bangkok and Jakarta. Civil wars and conflicts in some of the world's poorest regions, such as Somalia and Mali, ripple outward through the flows of asylum seekers and illegal migrants to richer countries.

The effects of globalization change the significance of the borders of states and the very nature of world politics. They mean that states no longer have a monopoly on power and authority. They increase the recognition of transnational problems that require global regulation in some form. The consequence has been a huge growth in transnational, regional, and global forms of public and private rulemaking and regulation since the early 1990s. This includes expanded jurisdiction of existing IGOs like the International Maritime Organization, networks of cooperation among government agencies such as the Financial Action Task Force that link government experts on money laundering, as well as private standard-setting initiatives such as that by the Forest Stewardship Council.

While globalization affects all spheres of human activity—economic, social, cultural, technological, environmental, and political—not all peoples or areas of the world are equally affected. Some critics charge that globalization has deepened global inequality between the haves and have-nots, especially those living on less than a dollar a day (Stiglitz 2002). Undoubtedly, globalization has created winners and losers between countries and also within countries. Given both the detrimental and the beneficial effects of globalization, the question is *how* globalization will be governed. As then–UN Secretary-General Kofi Annan put it at the turn of the millennium: "The central challenge we face today is to ensure that globalization becomes a positive force for all the world's people, instead of leaving billions of them behind in squalor" (2000: 6). Yet it is also important to recognize that further globalization is not inevitable. Many of the changes of the past two decades are reversible. With the failure of the World Trade Organization (WTO) to conclude a new multilateral trade agreement, for example, regional and bilateral free trade agreements have proliferated, potentially undermining the liberal WTO-based global trade system that has been a core element of economic globalization.

Globalization has both coincided with and contributed to the growth of transnationalism and the deregulation and privatization shift, all of which can be linked to the revolution in global communications and transport.

## Technological Changes

Globalization would not have been possible without major technological changes in both transport and communications that permit the movement of people and goods rapidly over great distances and move information, images, written words, and sound by telephone, Internet, television networks, and various forms of social media. Today's container ships and tankers carry many times the tonnage faster and at lower cost than ever before. The ease and lower cost of contemporary jet travel have contributed to the flow of international tourists. In 2012, the number of tourists worldwide passed the 1 billion mark for the first time; by contrast, the figure was just 25 million in 1952.

Moving people and goods more cheaply and easily is facilitated by the technological advances in communication. From the mid-nineteenth-century development of the telegraph, through to the telephone, radio, film, television, photocopying, satellite communications, faxing, cell phones, the Internet, e-mail, and social media, the advances have had an enormous impact on global politics and governance. In 2013, the International Telecommunication Union (ITU) reported that the number of cell or mobile phone subscriptions in the world had reached 6.8 billion—accounting for 96 percent of the world's population, including 89 percent of the people in developing countries. In comparison, a substantially smaller number of people, 2.8 billion, had access to the Internet in 2013, representing about 40 percent of the world's population (see www.itu.int). The technological revolution in communications also gives more people access to major international news sources such as CNN and Al Jazeera. They and other sources provide twenty-four-hour instantaneous and often eyewitness coverage of all types of events. The ramifications of these developments are hard to overstate. Transnational communications allow citizens all over the world to exchange ideas and information and to mobilize like-minded people in support of a particular cause in virtual real time. The cascade of events from Tunisia to Egypt to Yemen, Jordan, Bahrain, Morocco, Libya, and Syria during the Arab Spring in 2011 owed much to people's use of Internet-based social media such as Facebook and Twitter and the inability of authoritarian governments to block the flow of images and information. Both the transportation revolution and the communications revolution have aided the formation of transnational groups, social movements such as those on behalf of women, and networks.

### The Cold War's End

The end of the Cold War was brought about by the collapse of Soviet-supported communist governments in Central Europe, symbolized by the fall of the Berlin Wall in 1989, and the disintegration two years later of the Soviet Union itself into fifteen separate, independent states. The fax machine and television were important in transmitting images and information across the Iron Curtain into Poland, Czechoslovakia, Hungary, East Germany, and other countries. The Cold War's end marked the ending of one historical era and the beginning of another. The international system shifted from a bipolar structure to a post–Cold War structure that was simultaneously unipolar, dominated by a single superpower (the United States), and a nonpolar, networked system of a globalized world.

Although the Cold War's end contributed to the so-called third wave of democratizations in formerly communist states, Latin America, and Asia, it also removed the support of one or the other superpower from many weak states in Asia and Africa, unleashing a long string of deadly conflicts in the former Yugoslavia, Somalia, Afghanistan, and elsewhere. At the same time, it opened new political space for states and nonstate actors—space for pursuing new types of cooperation in ending those very conflicts, expanding the scope and reach of human rights norms, and reducing barriers to trade and investment. In short, it produced a series of new governance challenges as well as possibilities for developing new forms of governance.

### Expanding Transnationalism

Contributing to the Cold War's end and benefiting from increased democratization, accelerating globalization, and the advances in technology and transport is the growth of transnationalism—the processes through which individuals and various types of nonstate actors work together across state borders. It is exhibited in the activities of global civil society, NGOs, transnational advocacy networks, and transnational social movements.

Civil society comprises more than just NGOs; it is broader, encompassing all organizations and associations that exist outside the state and the market (i.e., government and business). It includes advocacy groups and associations of professionals such as doctors, lawyers, labor unions, chambers of commerce, religious groups, ethnic associations, and sporting associations. The key distinction between NGOs and civil society groups is their links to citizens. Many NGOs are elite-run groups with tenuous links to citizens on whose behalf they claim to act. Like NGOs, civil society is neither inherently good nor inherently bad. People work together to advance both nefarious and worthy ends.

The spread of democracy has bolstered the growth of civil society in countries where restrictions on citizens' groups have been lifted. Civil society groups communicate with each other domestically and cross-nationally, creating new coalitions from the local to the global. These transnational civil society groups permeate numerous issue areas, including the environment, human rights, economic development, and security. Their demands for representation in processes of global governance contribute to the increased need to reform existing international institutions and to find new ways to incorporate nonstate actors into global governance. Various types of transnational groups are discussed further in Chapter 6.

Systemic changes inevitably have a variety of consequences for states and for state sovereignty. The increased need for global governance magnifies the importance of multilateralism as a core process as well as the importance of leadership and different strategies used by states and nonstate actors. As Deborah Avant, Martha Finnemore, and Susan Sell (2010c: 7) note, however, "knowing global needs is rarely enough to explain how and why a particular governance outcome was chosen."

## Actors in Global Governance

The complexity of global governance is a function not only of its many forms, but also of its many actors. To be sure, states are central actors in IGOs and in many other forms of global governance, but IGO bureaucracies, treaty secretariats, NGOs, multinational corporations (MNCs), scientific experts, civil society groups, international credit-rating agencies, think tanks, major foundations, networks, partnerships, private military and security companies, as well as transnational criminal and drug-trafficking networks are among the many nonstate actors (see Figure 1.1). As one pair of scholars put it, "In essence, global governance implies a multiactor perspective on world politics" (Dingwerth and Pattberg 2006: 191). Still, "the novelty is not simply the increase in numbers but also the ability of nonstate actors to take part in steering the political system" (Biermann and Pattberg 2012: 6). Thus, studying actors in global governance means examining the nature and degree of various actors' participation as well as their relative power and authority.

### States

States continue to be key actors in global governance. States alone have sovereignty, which has historically given them authority not only over their own territory and people, but also over powers delegated to international institutions. To be sure, today's reality is that sovereignty is compromised by many states' own weaknesses, by globalization, the Internet, and social media, by conditionality on international aid, and by the influences of international norms and NSAs such as banks, global financial markets, and NGOs. Traditionally, states have been the primary sources of IGOs' funding and of military capabilities for multilateral peacekeeping and peace enforcement. They create international law and norms and determine their effectiveness through their compliance or failure to comply. States are also still a primary locus of people's identities.

Because the more than 190 states in the international system vary so dramatically, however, their relative importance in global governance

---

**Figure 1.1  Actors in Global Governance**

- States and their subnational and local jurisdictions
- IGOs and their bureaucracies
- NGOs
- Experts and epistemic communities
- Networks and partnerships
- Multinational corporations
- Private foundations

varies. Large, powerful states are more likely to play greater roles than are smaller, less powerful states. With significant shifts in the relative power of major states now under way, however, patterns that have prevailed in the past are changing, making the future difficult to predict.

Historically, the United States used its dominant position after World War II to shape much of the structure and rules of the postwar international system, including the liberal international economic order. Because it used both its hard material power and its soft power of attraction and persuasion to promote the principles of multilateralism and compromise as well as to promote liberal ideas, scholars refer to US hegemony in characterizing the US role. IGOs offered a way to create structures compatible with American notions of political order and through which to promote US political and economic interests as well as ideas and values. Although domestic support for such institutions was not necessarily ensured, governmental and public commitment were generally strong both in the United States and many other countries. The predominance of Americans in many secretariats and the relatively large share of operating and program funding contributed by the United States reinforced US influence over the policies and programs of many IGOs.

Nonetheless, the history of the United States and international commitments is a mixed one, as shown by the rejection of membership in the League of Nations in 1921, of the proposed International Trade Organization in 1948, of the UN Convention on the Law of the Sea in 1982, and of the International Criminal Court (ICC) in 1998. Since 1972, the United States has used its veto in the UN Security Council more than any of the other four permanent members. The US Congress withheld full payment of US dues to the UN from 1985 to 2000 and has held up reform of the International Monetary Fund (IMF) since 2010.

To be sure, US hegemony was challenged throughout the Cold War by the Soviet Union and its allies and by the rise of nationalism among states in Africa, Asia, and the Caribbean that gained their independence from European colonial rule in the 1950s and 1960s. It has also been challenged by the country's own quasi-imperial overstretch and wars in Vietnam, Iraq, Afghanistan, and the global war on terror, which have drained resources and cost the United States legitimacy among friends and allies. Yet the international order that US hegemony created persists.

Today, however, the United States cannot shape global governance alone. As one journalist commented in 2011: "The United States still has formidable strengths. . . . But America will never again experience the global dominance it enjoyed in the 17 years between the Soviet Union's collapse in 1991 and the financial crisis of 2008. Those days are over" (Rachman 2011: 63).

Emerging powers such as China, India, and Brazil increasingly challenge US and Western dominance. China's rise in particular raises questions about the future. As the second largest economy in 2013 (and largest in late 2014 by the IMF's recalculation of gross domestic product [GDP]), a major donor to the World Bank, a major investor in Asia, Latin America, and Africa, and the world's largest emitter of carbon dioxide, it will inevitably be a key actor. China, however, as one scholar notes, is "a least-likely" case of compliance with international norms and rules given its history, cultural traditions, and power (Kent 2007). Yet, since 2010, it has shown increasing confidence and assertiveness due to its economic growth and the perception of US weakening. Russia, too, seeks to restore its position as a major player following the Soviet Union's dissolution and the collapse of Russia's economy in the 1990s, which diminished its power. India and Brazil are among the other assertive emerging powers. Together with China, they blocked continuation of the WTO Doha negotiations in 2008 on the issue of the right of developing countries to resist liberalization of trade in agricultural products. Both Brazil and India are active contenders for permanent seats on the UN Security Council. India has long refused to participate in treaties and other arrangements, such as the Nuclear Non-Proliferation Treaty, that it regards as favoring the more powerful states. Likewise, Brazil has worked to build the Common Market of the South (Mercosur) as a trading bloc in South America and resisted US efforts to create the Free Trade Area of the Americas. China, India, and Brazil are now among the major contributors to UN peacekeeping operations. The BRICS (Brazil, Russia, India, China, and South Africa) are home to 40 percent of the world's population, and account for 20 percent of world GDP, 15 percent of world trade, and for two-thirds of world economic growth (Thakur 2014). They are challenging the liberal international economic order, including the dominant position of the US dollar and the World Bank's role in development funding, as they create a BRICS development bank based in Shanghai. A further challenge comes from the Asian Infrastructure Investment Bank created in 2014 with substantial initial funding from China.

Middle-power states have traditionally played a particularly important role in international institutions, often acting in concert in the UN and other IGOs, taking initiatives on arms control, human rights, and other issues. Argentina, Australia, Canada, the Netherlands, Nigeria, Norway, and Sweden, for example, are known for their commitment to multilateralism, ability to forge compromises, and support for reform in the international system. The Nordic countries (Denmark, Finland, Iceland, Norway, and Sweden), together with the Netherlands, for example, have traditionally been major contributors to UN peacekeeping operations; they have met or exceeded development assistance targets; and they have provided about 10 percent of all UN leadership positions. Although they have exemplified Western values, "their effectiveness and reputation within the UN have rested on a perception . . . as being *different* from the rest of the West (or

North)" (Laatikainen 2006: 77). The essence of the role of middle powers lies in the importance of secondary players as both followers and leaders.

For the large number of less developed, small, and weak states, power and influence generally come only insofar as they are able to form coalitions that enlarge their voices and offer opportunities to set global agendas and link issues of importance to them. IGOs provide valuable arenas for this and also for international recognition and legitimacy. Through their collective efforts, small and developing countries have endeavored to shape the agendas, priorities, and programs of many IGOs with varying degrees of success. The Group of 77 (G-77) has been a major vehicle for developing countries to push their interests since the mid-1960s. Similarly, the thirty-nine member Alliance of Small Island States has been able to gain a voice on the issue of global climate change. Small states also often pick and choose the issues of highest priority around which to focus their limited resources. For example, Malta made its mark in the late 1960s by urging adoption of the norm of the seabed and other common areas as "the common heritage of mankind." By analyzing the roles of small states in global governance, one can discover how skillful use of multilateral diplomacy and networks can alter the power equation, leading to outcomes that serve the interests of people, groups, and states that are not generally considered powerful.

Although states are still regarded as central to maintaining order in the world, since 1990 an increasing number of states have been sources of disorder due to their inability to perform most basic functions. Hence, problems emanating from weak, failing, and failed states have become twenty-first-century global governance challenges. They include spillover in the form of refugees from civil wars and conflicts as well as groups such as the Taliban that use neighboring states as sanctuaries; terrorist groups such as al-Qaeda in Mahgreb that exploit the weakness of states surrounding the Sahara; weak states such as the Democratic Republic of Congo (DRC), the Central African Republic (CAR), and Mali that are unable to protect their own citizens; and states such as Somalia that are unable to control piracy emanating from their territory. State capability, however, also includes the ability to comply with international rules, to track infectious diseases, to limit sex, drug, and arms trafficking, and to promote human well-being so that people do not feel compelled to migrate elsewhere in search of a better life.

States themselves, however, may not act with one voice in global governance. Increasingly, provincial, state, and local governments, especially in democratic countries with federal forms of government, are involved in international economic negotiations, and in implementing environmental regulations and human rights initiatives, acting independently and occasionally at odds with their respective national governments. Mayors of large cities now meet periodically at global conferences, for example, becoming subnational actors in global governance. Similarly, transgovernmental networks of government officials—police investigators, financial regulators, judges, and legislators—provide a means of exchanging information, tracking money laundering and terrorist financing, coordinating cross-border law enforcement, expanding the reach of environmental and food safety regulations, and providing training programs and technical assistance to counterparts (Slaughter 2004: 2–4). Such networks are part of the multilevel character of global governance. As Frank Biermann and Philipp Pattberg (2012: 13) put it, "Global standards need to be implemented and put into practice locally, and global norm setting requires local decision-making and implementation . . . with the potential of conflicts and synergies between different levels of regulatory activity." Chapters 10 and 11 examine some examples.

In short, states "are sharing powers—including political, social, and security roles at the core of sovereignty—with businesses, with international organizations, and with a multitude of citizens groups. . . . The steady concentration of power in the hands of states that began in 1648 with the Peace of Westphalia is over, at least for a while" (Mathews 1997: 50).

### Intergovernmental Organizations

IGOs are organizations that include at least three states as members, that have activities in several states, and that are created through a formal intergovernmental agreement such as a treaty, charter, or statute. They also have headquarters, executive heads, bureaucracies, and budgets. In 2013–2014, the *Yearbook of International Organizations* identified about 265 IGOs ranging in size from 3 members (the North American Free Trade Agreement [NAFTA]) to more than 190 members (the Universal Postal Union [UPU]). Members may come primarily from one geographic region (as in the case of the Organization of American States [OAS]) or from all geographic regions (as in the case of the World Bank). Although some IGOs are designed to achieve a single purpose (such as the Organization of Petroleum Exporting Countries [OPEC]), others have been developed for multiple tasks (such as the United Nations). The majority of IGOs are regional or subregional, with a commonality of interest motivating states to cooperate on issues directly affecting them. Among the universe of IGOs, most are small in membership and designed to address specific functions. Most have been formed since World War II, and Europe, among the different regions, has the densest concentration of IGOs (see Figure 1.2).

IGOs are recognized subjects of international law, with separate standing from their member states. In a 1949 advisory opinion, *Reparations for Injuries Suffered in the Service of the United Nations,* the International Court of Justice (ICJ) concluded: "The Organization [the United Nations]

**Figure 1.2   Classifying Types of IGOs**

| Geographic Scope | Examples |
| --- | --- |
| Global | UN<br>WHO<br>WTO |
| Regional | ASEAN<br>AU<br>EU |
| Subregional | ECOWAS<br>GCC |

| Purpose | Examples |
| --- | --- |
| General | OAS<br>UN |
| Specialized | ILO<br>WHO<br>WTO |

was intended to exercise and enjoy, and is in fact exercising and enjoying, functions and rights which can only be explained on the basis of international personality and the capacity to operate upon an international plane. It is at present the supreme type of international organization, and it could not carry out the intentions of its founders if it was devoid of international personality."

International relations scholars have long viewed IGOs primarily as agents of their member states and focused on their structural attributes, decisionmaking processes, and programs. After all, IGOs are formed by states, and states grant IGOs responsibilities and authority to act. Yet, increasingly, IGOs have also been seen as actors in their own right, because their secretariat members play key but often invisible roles in persuading states to act, coordinating the efforts of different groups, providing the diplomatic skills to secure agreements, and ensuring the effectiveness of programs (Mathiason 2007). These include senior officials such as the UN Secretary-General (UNSG) and his or her under- and assistant secretaries-general as well as the UNSG's special representatives (SRSGs); the directors-general of organizations such as the World Health Organization (WHO) and World Trade Organization (WTO); the UN High Commissioners for Refugees and Human Rights (UNHCR and UNHCHR); the president of the World Bank; the executive director of the International Monetary Fund; and the president of the European Commission. These individuals "will generally possess an identity that is distinct from that of any other entity and an interest in promoting the well-being of the organization and its membership" (Duffield 2007: 13). Stories are legion about the roles secretariat officials have played in achieving international trade agreements, cease-fires in wars, governments' agreement to revise their development strategies to meet international guidelines, and organizational reforms.

Like other bureaucracies, IGO secretariats often do much more than their member states may have intended. Because many, but not all, IGO bureaucrats are international civil servants rather than individuals seconded to a secretariat from national governments, they tend to take their responsibilities seriously and work hard "to promote what they see as 'good policy' or to protect it from states that have competing interests" (Barnett and Finnemore 2004: 5). IGO bureaucracies also tend to develop their own organizational cultures—sometimes based on the professional backgrounds of many staff (e.g., public health, finance)—and this can influence how they define issues and what types of policy solutions they recommend. They must respond to new challenges and crises, provide policy options for member states, determine how to carry out vague mandates, reform themselves, and formulate new tasks and procedures. For example, the UN Secretariat created peacekeeping at the height of the Cold War, and later devised postconflict peacebuilding operations that include a wide variety of tasks from electoral assistance to police and court reform. IGOs have resources, including money, food, weapons, and expertise. Many IGO bureaucracies play important roles in analyzing and interpreting information, giving it meaning that can prompt action. To some extent, therefore, IGOs "help determine the kind of world that is to be governed and set the agenda for global governance" (Barnett and Finnemore 2004: 7).

Thus, IGO bureaucracies are not just tools of states. They are also purposive actors that have power to influence world events. Their authority, and that of bureaucracies generally, "lies in their ability to present themselves as impersonal and neutral—as not exercising power but instead serving others" (Barnett and Finnemore 2004: 21). The need to be seen in this way is crucial to the credibility of the UN Secretariat or the EU Commission, for example. Yet there is also significant evidence of IGOs doing something that "wasn't specifically tasked to them . . . [and] outside any reasonable notion of delegated discretion" (Oestreich 2012: 11). This theory of IGO agency and its implications is discussed further in Chapter 2.

To be sure, not all IGOs are alike, as we shall examine in subsequent chapters. Their authority and autonomy as actors in global governance vary significantly in kind and degree. Like domestic bureaucracies, international bureaucracies may use inaction as a way to avoid doing something they oppose. IGOs may also act against the interests and preferences of strong or weak states (and their secretaries-general may suffer retaliation as a result);

they may form partnerships with nonstate actors, other IGOs, and select states to pursue or protect certain policies; and they may attempt to persuade states to change their behavior—for example, by reducing corruption, eliminating food subsidies, or turning over war criminals for prosecution by the International Criminal Court.

In addition to IGO secretariats, there are secretariats for a large number of international treaties, particularly in global environmental governance, where there is no strong, central IGO. The size of these secretariats varies; that of the UN Framework Convention on Climate Change is quite large; others have just a few staff members. Their roles as autonomous actors include generating and disseminating knowledge, framing the definitions of problems and identifying solutions, influencing negotiations through their ideas and expertise, and aiding states with treaty implementation (Biermann and Siebenhüner 2013: 149–152). The autonomous influence of the international secretariats of both IGOs and treaty regimes varies widely, as it does with all bureaucracies. A major study of environmental bureaucracies has found that the type of problem is a key factor; people and procedures are two other important factors (Dicrmann and Siebenhüner 2009. 149–132).

## Nongovernmental Organizations

Like IGOs, nongovernmental organizations are key actors in global governance, playing a number of roles. The growth of NGOs and NGO networks since the 1980s has been a major factor in their increasing involvement in governance at all levels, from global to local. Increasingly, global governance is marked by various types of interactions between IGOs and NGOs.

NGOs are private voluntary organizations whose members are individuals or associations that come together to achieve a common purpose. Some organizations are formed to advocate a particular cause such as human rights, peace, or environmental protection. Others are established to provide services such as disaster relief, humanitarian aid in war-torn societies, or development assistance. Some are in reality government-organized groups (dubbed GONGOs). Scholars and analysts distinguish between not-for-profit groups (the vast majority) and for-profit corporations; it is also common to treat terrorist, criminal, and drug-trafficking groups—the "dark side" of NGOs—separately, as discussed further in Chapter 6.

NGOs are increasingly active today at all levels of human society and governance, from local or grassroots communities to national and international politics. Many national-level groups, often called interest or pressure groups, are now linked to counterpart groups in other countries through networks or federations. International nongovernmental organizations (INGOs), like IGOs, may draw their members from more than one country, and they may have very specific functions or be multifunctional. It is the big international NGOs, along with transnational advocacy networks (TANs) such as the Coalition to Ban Landmines, that bring together many smaller NGOs that are among the most visible NGO actors in global governance. Their roles have been particularly important in expanding human rights and humanitarian and environmental law.

The estimates of numbers of NGOs vary enormously. The 2013–2014 *Yearbook of International Organizations* identifies over 8,500 nongovernmental organizations that have an international dimension in terms of either membership or commitment to conduct activities in several states. Exclusively national NGOs number in the millions. Many large international NGOs (INGOs) are transnational federations involving formal, long-term links among national groups. Examples include the International Federation of Red Cross and Red Crescent Societies, Oxfam, Médecins Sans Frontières (Doctors Without Borders), the World Wildlife Fund, Transparency International (the leading NGO fighting corruption worldwide), Human Rights Watch, and Amnesty International.

The majority of the thousands of grassroots groups that exist in countries around the world are not part of formal networks, but may have informal links to large international human rights and development NGOs like Human Rights Watch and CARE, from which they obtain funding for local programs or training assistance. The links between grassroots and international NGOs are key to activities such as promoting population control, empowerment of women, health care, respect for human rights, and environmental protection. Because these relationships often involve large, Northern-dominated NGOs and Southern grassroots groups, there is a concern about the dependence they foster. Since the early 1990s, the Internet, e-mail, fax, and, more recently, various forms of social media have been valuable tools for NGO mobilization and autonomy, enabling them to access areas that governments and IGOs may be slow to reach.

NGOs are key sources of information and technical expertise on a wide variety of international issues, from the environment to human rights and corruption. They frequently are key actors in raising awareness of and helping to frame issues. Thus, landmines came to be seen as a humanitarian rather than an arms control issue, for example (Thakur and Maley 1999). They lobby for policy changes by states, IGOs, and corporations; along with civil society groups, they mount mass demonstrations around major international meetings such as Group of Seven (G-7) summits and the annual World Economic Forum in Davos. They contribute to international adjudication by submitting friend-of-the-court briefs to international criminal tribunals such as those for the former Yugoslavia and Rwanda, as well as to trade and investment tribunals (Charnovitz 2006: 353–354). Many NGOs have participated at least indirectly in UN-sponsored global conferences and international negotiations, raising issues and submitting documents. In some instances, they have contributed treaty language, such as with the Convention to Ban Landmines and the Rome Statute of the International Criminal Court. They also play important roles in monitoring states' and corporations' implementation of human rights norms and environmental regulations.

We explore the diversity and global governance activities of NGOs and other nonstate actors in Chapter 6, as well as in the issue chapters.

## Experts and Epistemic Networks

In a world whose problems seem to grow steadily more complex, knowledge and expertise are critical to governance efforts. There is a need to understand the science behind environmental problems such as climate change, ozone depletion, and declining fish stocks in order to consider policy options. Cost-effective alternatives must be developed for fuels that emit carbon dioxide if there is to be political support for making policy changes and new rules. Thus, experts from governmental agencies, research institutes, private industries, and universities around the world have increasingly been drawn into international efforts to deal with various issues. For example, in the UN's early years, statisticians and economists developed the System of National Accounts, which provides the basis for standardizing how countries calculate GDP and other core statistics that serve as a means of measuring economic performance (Jolly, Emmerij, and Weiss 2009: 42). The technical committees of the International Organization for Standardization (ISO), for example, are entirely composed of experts. Often experts may be part of transnational networks and participate in international conferences and negotiations, laying out the state of scientific knowledge, framing issues for debate, and proposing possible solutions. Since 1988, hundreds of scientists from around the world have participated on the Intergovernmental Panel on Climate Change (IPCC), whose policy-neutral reports have provided key inputs for global climate change negotiations and sought to raise awareness of the rapid climate-related changes taking place and their likely effects in the future. Scholars have coined the phrase "epistemic communities" to identify such networks of knowledge-based experts.

## Networks and Partnerships

Networks have become ubiquitous since the 1970s, when Robert Keohane and Joseph Nye (1971) first pointed out the importance of regular interactions of governmental and nongovernmental actors across national boundaries. Subsequently, other scholars, such as Thomas Risse-Kappen (1995), James Rosenau (1997), Kathryn Sikkink (2009), and Anne-Marie Slaughter (2004), have explored the existence of various types of networks, and their power, roles, and policy impact.

Analytically, networks can be examined as both actors and structures. As actors, they may be defined as an organizational form consciously created by any set of actors that pursue "repeated, enduring exchange relations with one another . . . [yet] lack a legitimate organization authority to arbitrate and resolve disputes that may arise during the exchange" (quoted in Kahler 2009: 5). Networks are distinguished by their voluntary nature, the central role of information and learning, their ability to generate trust among participants, and their lack of hierarchy (Sikkink 2009: 230). Networks' success depends on their ability to promote and sustain collective action, add new members, and adapt. Their effectiveness will also vary by issue area. As noted previously, TANs are one particular form of network active in global governance, for example in setting and monitoring human rights standards; illicit networks such as transnational criminal organizations are targets of governance efforts to control money laundering and other illegal activities; while transgovernmental networks allow government officials to share regulatory approaches, provide technical assistance, and harmonize approaches to problems.

Some networks also provide forms of governance. For example, the Active Learning Network for Accountability and Performance was created in 1997 by major donor organizations to foster learning and provide better accountability and information on the performance of humanitarian organizations following problems that surfaced following the 1994 genocide in Rwanda. The network includes UN agencies, national donor agencies, and humanitarian NGOs; has established standardized categories of analysis and evaluation; and maintains an online evaluation reports database.

Partnerships have also become increasingly common as actors and particularly as forms of governance. Catia Gregoratti (2014: 311) notes, for example, how partnerships between the UN and businesses have "refashioned not only ideas of how development should be achieved and who should deliver it but also the institutional architecture of the UN itself." Such partnerships involve UN agencies and private corporations and have become widespread throughout the UN system, particularly in areas of development, health, women, and children. Their functions range from advocacy, developing standards of conduct, and business development in less developed countries (LDCs), to providing funding, goods, and services.

### Multinational Corporations

MNCs are a particular form of nonstate actor organized to conduct for-profit business transactions and operations across the borders of three or more states. They are companies based in one state with affiliated branches or subsidiaries and activities in other states and can take many different forms, from Aflack selling insurance in Japan and Levis subcontracting jean production to Nepalese factories, to Royal Dutch Shell's operations in Nigeria and Goldman Sachs's global operations. By choosing where to invest or not to invest, MNCs shape the economic development opportunities of individual communities, countries, and entire regions such as Africa, where for a long time little foreign investment took place. Now, thanks in part to heavy Chinese investment, many parts of Africa are experiencing rapid growth for example, where in the 1990s it was investment in China that contributed to its rapid economic growth. Still, the share of worldwide foreign direct investment going to less developed countries has remained just 1.8 percent of the total, with much of it going to a few oil- and mineral-rich countries (Essoungou 2011: 15).

Since the 1970s, MNCs have "profoundly altered the structure and functioning of the global economy" (Gilpin 2001: 290). They control resources far greater than those of many states and have taken an active and often direct role in influencing international environmental decisionmaking (Biermann and Pattberg 2012: 8). Globalization of markets and production in industries such as banking and automobiles has challenged corporate leaders and managers to govern these complex structures, and posed problems for states and local governments losing connection to and control of these larger corporate networks. Corporate choices about investment have also changed the landscape of development assistance. Far more funding for development today comes from private investment capital than from bilateral, government-to-government aid, or from multilateral aid through the UN and other IGOs.

In short, MNCs are important global governance actors whose activities have long raised a number of questions. How can they best be regulated—through new forms of international rules or codes of conduct, or through private, industry-developed mechanisms? How can they be mobilized for economic development in collaboration with international agencies and NGOs? How can less developed countries be assured that powerful MNCs will not interfere in their domestic affairs, challenge their sovereignty, destroy their resources and environment, and relegate them to permanent dependency? MNCs are particularly important actors in addressing trade, labor, and environmental issues such as ozone depletion and global warming. It was in recognition of the need both to regulate corporate behavior and to engage MNCs as positive contributors to global governance that UN Secretary-General Kofi Annan initiated the UN Global Compact on Corporate Responsibility in 1999, which now encompasses more than 10,000 companies in more than 130 countries, an innovation that is discussed further in Chapter 9.

* * *

The various actors in global governance cannot be analyzed in isolation from one another. They play varying roles, with varying degrees of power, authority, and effectiveness. Sometimes, they compete with each other for scarce resources, international standing, and legitimacy. At other times, their activities complement one another. Increasingly, they are linked in complex networks and partnerships. Subsequent chapters will explore these roles and relationships further.

## Processes of Global Governance: Multilateralism Matters

Multilateral negotiations are a key part of global governance, constituting "the diplomatic bargaining processes through which the international community confers political legitimacy or comes to accept . . . [generalized] principles" (Hampson 1995: 3). Understanding the nature of multilateral diplomacy, therefore, is essential to understanding how IGOs and informal groupings of states function, how nonstate actors have become involved in governance processes, and how different kinds of outcomes come about.

John Ruggie (1993a: 8) has stated: "At its core, multilateralism refers to coordinating relations among three or more states in accordance with certain principles." Thus relationships are defined by agreed-upon rules and principles, and perhaps by organizations. Participants expect that outcomes will yield "diffuse reciprocity" (Keohane 1984) or roughly reciprocal benefits over time. For example, the principle of nondiscrimination governing the global trade system—most-favored-nation status—prohibits countries from discriminating against imports from other countries that produce the same product. In collective security arrangements, participants must respond to an attack on one country as if it were an attack on all. By contrast, bilateralism is expected to provide specific reciprocity and roughly balanced (but not necessarily equal) exchanges by each party at all times. Kishore Mahbubani (2013: 248, 254–255), former Singaporean ambassador to the UN, describes how when he walks into a multilateral setting, he expects to encounter "three voices: reason, power, and charm. The voice of charm has been underestimated," he says. "But neither reason nor charm can override the voice of power, which remains the single strongest factor in multilateral diplomacy and international relations."

### Complex Diplomacy

Prior to the twentieth century, there was very little multilateralism. As we will discuss in Chapter 3, the nineteenth century was marked by the development of a number of public international unions and river commissions. The Concert of Europe provided a series of periodic gatherings of great (European) powers. Out of these evolved many of the norms for multilateral diplomacy. The twentieth century saw the accelerated trend from bilateral to multilateral diplomacy and institutions, especially formal organizations, and the growth of conference diplomacy focused on specific global issues.

What makes multilateralism in the twenty-first century different from multilateralism at the end of World War II, then, is its complexity. There are now literally scores of participants. States alone have almost quadrupled in number since 1945. The first sessions of the UN General Assembly now look like cozy, intimate gatherings. Other types of actors add to the complexity, as do various coalitions of states. As one observer notes: "Large numbers . . . introduce a qualitatively different kind of diplomacy in international politics. The hallmark of this diplomacy is that it occurs between groups or coalitions of state actors" (Hampson 1995: 4). In addition, a central issue for many IGOs today is how to do a better job of incorporating NGOs, civil society groups, and other nonstate actors into processes of global governing, since "securing agreement of government officials is not enough to permit the smooth running of these institutions" (O'Brien et al. 2000: 208). And, diplomats—the representatives of states—need to engage in "network diplomacy" with this variety of players, not just with fellow diplomats, with diplomacy itself becoming an exercise in "complexity management" (Heine 2013: 62).

Greater numbers of players (and coalitions of players) mean multiple interests, with multiple rules, issues, and hierarchies that are constantly in flux. These all complicate the processes of multilateral diplomacy and negotiation—of finding common ground for reaching agreements on collective action, norms, or rules. Managing complexity has become a key challenge for diplomats and other participants in multilateral settings. For example, UN-sponsored conferences have several thousand delegates from 193 member countries, speaking through interpreters in English, French, Russian, Chinese, Spanish, and Arabic. There are hundreds of NGOs and numerous private citizens interested in what happens and active around the official sessions trying to influence delegates.

Although the universe of multilateral diplomacy is complex, there is actually a high degree of similarity in the structures of most IGOs and in the types of decisionmaking processes used. Let us look at key patterns in how decisions get made in IGOs and other settings.

### How Do Decisions Get Made?

Historically, since IGOs are created by states, the principle of sovereign equality has dictated one-state, one-vote decisionmaking. Indeed, until well into the twentieth century, all decisions had to be unanimous, as states would not accept the concept of majority decisionmaking. This is often cited as one of the sources of failure for the League of Nations.

An alternative principle accords greater weight to some states on the basis of population or wealth and results in weighted or qualified voting. In the IMF and World Bank, for example, votes are weighted according to financial contribution. In the EU's Council of Ministers, qualified majority voting applies to issues where the EU has supranational authority over member states. The number of votes for each state is based on population; the number of votes required to pass legislation ensures that the largest states must have support of some smaller states; and neither the smaller states alone nor fewer than three large states can block action. Another form of qualified majority voting prevails in the UN Security Council, where the five permanent members each possess a veto and all must concur (or not object) for decisions to be taken.

Since the 1980s, much of the decisionmaking in the UN General Assembly, Security Council, and other bodies, as well as in global conferences, the WTO, and many other multilateral settings such as the various "Gs" (informal groupings of states such as the G-7 and G-20), has taken the form of consensus that does not require unanimity. It depends on states deciding not to block action and it often means that outcomes represent the least common denominator—that is, more general wording and fewer tough demands on states to act. "Pressure toward consensus," Courtney Smith (1999: 173) notes, "now dominates almost all multilateral efforts at global problem solving." The puzzle, he suggests, is "how an organization that is composed of 185 [*sic*] member states, influenced by numerous nongovernmental organizations, lobbied by multinational corporations, and serviced by an international secretariat reconciles all of these potentially diverse interests in search of a consensus on the most pressing issues of the day." Key variables in consensus building are leadership; small, formal negotiating groups; issue characteristics (including issue salience to different actors); various actor attributes such as economic or military power or ability to serve as brokers; the amount and quality of informal contacts among actors; and personal attributes of participants such as intelligence, tolerance, patience, reputation, negotiating skills, creativity, and linguistic versatility. Let us look briefly at two of these: leadership and actor strategies.

## Leadership

Leadership in multilateral diplomacy can come from diverse sources: powerful and not-so-powerful states, a coalition of states, an NGO or coalition of NGOs, a skillful individual diplomat, or an IGO bureaucrat. Leadership can involve putting together a winning coalition to secure agreement on a new international trade agreement; it may involve the skill of negotiating a treaty text acceptable to industry, NGOs, and key governments. It may be the efforts of a coalition of NGOs and college students publicizing an issue such as sweatshops and pressuring companies to change their behavior. It may involve a government's (or any other actor's) willingness to act first—to commit monetary resources to a program or military forces for enforcement, to change trade laws, or to commit to significant carbon dioxide emissions reductions. Leadership in multilateral diplomacy can also come from a prominent official such as the UN Secretary-General or the WTO's director-general, who prods various actors to do something.

Historically, the United States provided much of the leadership for multilateralism after World War II, using its position as the dominant, hegemonic power to shape the structure of the system, including through the establishment of many IGOs, such as the UN, the Bretton Woods institutions, the International Atomic Energy Agency (IAEA), and the liberal international trade regime centered first in the General Agreement on Tariffs and Trade (GATT) and later in the WTO. This enabled the United States to use IGOs as instruments of its national policies and to create institutions and rules compatible with its interests and values. The wisdom of this approach as then–US senator Barack Obama put it in 2007 was to recognize that "instead of constraining our power, these institutions magnified it" (Obama 2007).

As geopolitical shifts are taking place, the United States has found itself stretched thin and has been less willing and able to lead at the same time that rising powers such as the BRICS are insisting on greater voice in multilateral institutions. As Bruce Jentleson (2012: 141) notes, "While it remains generally true that most countries believe that global problems are most likely to be resolved or at least effectively managed if the United States plays a constructive role, there is much less deference to US preferences and privileges." The result is that, even more than in the past, leadership in global governance may come from disparate sources or be absent altogether.

### Actor Strategies

The nature of multilateral arenas means that actors cannot just present their individual positions on an issue and then sit down. Delegates must actively engage in efforts to discern the flexibility or rigidity of their respective positions. They must build personal relationships in order to establish the trust that is essential to working together. Some states, NGOs, and other actors will take a stronger interest in particular topics than others; some will come with specific proposals; some will be represented by individuals with greater expertise than others on a topic; some will be represented by individuals with little or no experience in multilateral diplomacy while others have long experience and great skill in negotiating across cultures, which is an inherent part of multilateral diplomacy; and some actors' positions will matter more than those of others, because of their relative power in the international system, in a given region, or on a particular issue. The face-to-face interactions of the individuals representing participating states (and groups) are what caucusing is all about, even in an age of Skype and teleconferencing. It may take place at the back of the General Assembly hall, in the delegates' dining room, at diplomatic receptions, in the restrooms, or in the corridors surrounding the official meeting place. In short, those actors that pursue well-thought-out strategies for taking advantage of multilateral arenas and diplomacy are more likely to be successful in securing their aims.

One actor strategy that is a hallmark of multilateral diplomacy is the formation of groups or coalitions of states. States can pool their votes, power, and resources to try to obtain a better outcome than they might by going it alone. Early in the UN's history, for example, regional groups formed to elect nonpermanent members of the Security Council and other bodies. The Cold War produced competing groups under the leadership of the Soviet Union and United States, plus the Non-Aligned Movement. Latin American, African, and Asian states formed the G-77 in 1964. As a result, group diplomacy is pervasive throughout much of the UN system as well as in regional organizations and the WTO.

Group members must negotiate among themselves to agree on a common position, maintain cohesion, prevent defections to rival coalitions, and choose representatives to bargain on their behalf. Small states or middle powers often play key roles in bridging the positions of different groups of states. For example, during the Uruguay Round of international trade negotiations in the early 1990s, a group of countries called the Cairns Group, led by Canada, Australia, and Argentina, helped to resolve sharp disagreements between the United States and the European Union (EU) over agricultural trade. A variation on coalition building, especially for nonstate actors, is the creation of networks to expand their reach and link diverse groups with shared concerns and awareness that common goals cannot be achieved on their own. Networking has been used extensively by TANs for a variety of issues and problems, from promoting the rights of women and stopping the construction of large dams to addressing the governance challenges of HIV/AIDS.

The proliferation of international forums means that states and nonstate actors can often choose where to take certain issues—an option called "forum shopping." Although some issues logically belong only within the relevant specialized IGO, the increasing interrelatedness of many issues makes the neat compartmentalization of these IGOs often outdated. Thus, for example, a labor issue could be raised in the International Labour Organization (ILO), the WTO, or the EU. Health issues could be raised in the WHO, the World Bank, the UN Joint Programme on HIV/AIDS (UNAIDS), the Bill and Melinda Gates Foundation, the Global Health Security Initiative (of the Group of Eight [G-8]), or the Global Fund to Fight AIDS, Tuberculosis, and Malaria.

In general, states and nonstate actors will select forums where they believe they will get the best reception. Despite consensus that African states should resolve regional conflicts in an African organization, such as the African Union, some African states have preferred to take disputes to the UN, where they hope to gain more support for their cause. With regional bodies such as the EU, AU, and NATO gaining greater experience in different types of peace operations in different places ranging from Afghanistan, the Congo, and Somalia to Libya, Mali, and the Central African Republic, they represent choices for states and new ways of partnering for the UN.

## The Varieties of Global Governance

Global governance encompasses a variety of cooperative problem-solving arrangements and activities that states and other actors create in an effort to resolve conflicts, serve common purposes, and overcome inefficiencies in situations of interdependent choice. These forms include IGOs and NGOs; less formal groupings of states ("Gs"), clubs, friends groups, and the BRICS; international rules, regulations, standards, and laws, as well as the norms or "soft law"; international regimes in which the rules, norms, and structures in a specific issue area are linked together; ad hoc arrangements and conferences; private governance arrangements; and public-private partnerships such as the UN Global Compact and Partnerships for Sustainable Development (see Figure 1.3). The varieties are rapidly proliferating, complicating efforts to create neat categories. IGOs are collaborating with other IGOs such as in the joint UN-AU peacekeeping operations in Darfur and Somalia. IGOs now subcontract many projects to NGOs, particularly in the areas of development and humanitarian relief. Some of the many interactions may be characterized as networks, others as partnerships, and some as simply "interactions." Where scholars in the past identified international regimes governing issues such as nuclear nonproliferation, now there are a number of "regime complexes"—"networks of three or more international regimes that relate to a common subject matter" such as food security (Orsini, Morin, Young 2013: 29). Let us look briefly at these varieties of global governance.

### Intergovernmental Organizations

IGOs provide the central core of formal multilateral machinery that constitutes the "architecture of global governance" (Cooper and Thakur 2014: 265). Over the past century, more and more IGOs have been created to perform more and more tasks. They serve many diverse functions, including collecting information and monitoring trends (as in the case of the United Nations Environment Programme [UNEP]), delivering services and aid (the UNHCR), providing forums for intergovernmental bargaining (the EU) and adjudicating disputes (the ICJ). They have helped states form stable habits of cooperation through regular meetings, information-gathering and analy-

---

**Figure 1.3    Varieties of Global Governance**

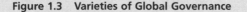

- International structures and mechanisms (formal and informal)
    IGOs: global, regional, other
    NGOs
- International rules and laws
    Multilateral agreements; customary practices; judicial decisions,
    regulatory standards
- International norms or "soft law"
    Framework agreements; select UN resolutions
- International regimes
- Ad hoc groups, arrangements, and global conferences
- Private and hybrid public-private governance

---

sis, and dispute settlement, as well as operational activities (see Figure 1.4). They enhance individual and collective welfare. They have provided modes of governance in the evolution of the world economy since 1850 (Murphy 1994). They also "construct the social world in which cooperation and choice take place" and "help define the interests that states and other actors come to hold" (Barnett and Finnemore 2005: 162). A further function of IGOs and particularly of the UN has been the development of key ideas and concepts about security and economic and social development. As the authors of the final volume of the United Nations Intellectual History Project (UNIHP) conclude, ideas are among the most significant contributions the UN has made to the world and to human progress. The UN has generated ideas, provided a forum for debate, given ideas legitimacy, promoted their adoption for policy, generated resources for implementing and monitoring progress, and has sometimes even served to bury ideas (Jolly, Emmerij, and Weiss 2009: 34–35).

Yet how IGOs serve their various functions varies across organizations. Organizations differ in membership. They vary by the scope of the subject and rules. They differ in the amount of resources available and by level and degree of bureaucratization as well as in their effectiveness.

Why do states join such organizations? Why do they choose to act and to cooperate through formal IGOs? Kenneth Abbott and Duncan Snidal (1998: 4–5) suggest that IGOs "allow for the centralization of collective activities through a concrete and stable organizational structure and a supportive administrative apparatus. These increase the efficiency of collective activities and enhance the organization's ability to affect the understandings, environment, and interests of states." Thus, states join to participate in a stable negotiating forum, permitting rapid reactions in times of crisis. They join IGOs to negotiate and implement agreements that reflect their

---

**Figure 1.4   IGO Functions**

- Informational: gathering, analyzing, and disseminating data
- Forum: providing place for exchange of views and decisionmaking
- Normative: defining standards of behavior
- Rule creation: drafting legally binding treaties
- Rule supervision: monitoring compliance with rules, adjudicating disputes, taking enforcement measures
- Operational: allocating resources, providing technical assistance and relief, deploying forces
- Idea generation

---

own interests and those of the larger community. They participate to provide mechanisms for dispute resolution. They join to take advantage of centralized organization in the implementation of collective tasks. By participating, they agree to shape international debate on important issues and forge critical norms of behavior. Yet states still maintain their sovereignty and varying degrees of independence of action.

IGOs not only create opportunities for their member states, but also exercise influence and impose constraints on their member states' policies and processes. IGOs affect member states by setting international and hence national agendas, and forcing governments to take positions on issues. They subject states' behavior to surveillance through information-sharing. They encourage the development of specialized decisionmaking and implementation processes to facilitate and coordinate IGO participation. They embody or facilitate the creation of principles, norms, and rules of behavior with which states must align their policies if they wish to benefit from reciprocity. For example, as described in Chapter 8, China's admission to the WTO affected its national policies and required extensive governmental reforms.

Most countries perceive that there are benefits to participating in IGOs even when it is costly. South Africa never withdrew from the UN over the long years when it was repeatedly condemned for its policies of apartheid. Iraq did not withdraw from the UN when it was subjected to more than a decade of stringent sanctions. China spent fourteen years negotiating the terms of its entry into the international trade system and undertaking changes in laws and policies required to bring itself into compliance with WTO rules. Twelve countries joined the EU between 2004 and 2007, despite the extensive and costly changes required.

Although the earliest IGOs were established in the nineteenth century, there was a veritable explosion of IGOs in the twentieth century, as discussed in Chapter 3. Major-power wars (especially World Wars I and II), economic development, technological innovation, and the growth of the state system, especially with decolonization in the 1950s and 1960s, provided impetus for creating many IGOs. Since the 1960s, there has also been a growing phenomenon of IGOs creating other IGOs. One study found that IGO birthrates "correlate positively with the number of states in the international system," but found death rates of IGOs low (Cupitt, Whitlock, and Whitlock 1997: 16). Of thirty-four IGOs functioning in 1914, eighteen were still operational at the end of the twentieth century. The Cold War's end brought the death of the Warsaw Treaty Organization and the Council of Mutual Economic Assistance, both Soviet-bloc institutions. The creation of the UN in 1945 led to the demise of the League of Nations. The authoritative source for all data on international organizations, both IGOs and NGOs, is the Union of International Associations (UIA), located in Brussels, and its *Yearbook of International Organizations.*

### Nongovernmental Organizations

The governance functions of NGOs parallel many functions provided by IGOs. In general, however, NGOs can be divided into service and advocacy groups. The latter provide processes at many levels to pressure or persuade individuals, governments, IGOs, corporations, and other actors to improve human rights, protect the environment, tackle corruption, ban landmines, or intervene in conflicts such as Syria's civil war. The Geneva Conventions delegate legal responsibility for humanitarian law to the International Committee of the Red Cross (ICRC). Some IGOs, such as the International Labour Organization, the World Tourism Organization, and the UN Joint Programme on HIV/AIDS, provide for NGO roles in their governance. As a result of global trends to privatize activities previously controlled by governments, services once provided by governments or IGOs are now often contracted out to NGOs. They deliver disaster relief, run refugee camps, administer development programs, strive to contain the international spread of disease, and work to clean up the environment. They are important forms of global governance because of the ways they enable individuals to "act publicly" (Kaldor 2003: 585). Likewise, their "voluntary, local, and issue-specific character . . . [and the networks they create] make them a useful link between the subnational community and national and international communities and institutions" (Ku and Diehl 2006: 171). In this sense, they function as transmission belts among multiple levels of governance.

### Rule-Based Governance: International Rules and Law

The scope of what is generally known as public international law has expanded tremendously since the 1960s. Although the statute of the International Court of Justice recognizes five sources of international law (treaties or conventions, customary practice, the writings of legal scholars, judicial decisions, and general principles of law), much of the growth has been in treaty law. Between 1951 and 1995, 3,666 new multilateral treaties were concluded (Ku 2001). At the conclusion of the twentieth century, according to Douglas Johnston (1997), there were a total of 82,000 publicized international agreements, including the Vienna Convention on Treaties, conventions on ozone, climate change, and whaling, law of the sea, humanitarian law (the Geneva Conventions), human rights law, trade law, and intellectual property law, as well as arms control agreements. By far the largest number of new multilateral agreements deals with economic issues. Treaty-based law has been particularly valued, because the process of negotiation now involves all affected countries. Nonetheless, customary practice persists as an important source of new law, particularly because of the long time it takes to negotiate and bring into effect agreements involving large numbers of countries.

For purposes of global governance, one major limitation of public international law is that it applies only to states, except for war crimes and crimes against humanity. At present, only EU treaties can be used directly to bind individuals, multinational corporations, NGOs, paramilitary forces, terrorists, or international criminals. They can, however, establish norms that states are expected to observe and, where possible, enforce against nonstate actors.

Another problem in the eyes of many is the absence of international enforcement mechanisms and the role of self-interest in shaping states' decisions about whether or not to accept treaties and other forms of international rules. International law traditionally left states to use "self-help" to secure compliance. Both the UN Charter and EU treaties, however, provide enforcement mechanisms, primarily in the form of sanctions, although the threat of sanctions is not necessarily a strong motivator for states to comply with international rules.

Abram Chayes and Antonia Chayes (1995), instead, cite efficiency, interests, and norms as key factors, and treaty ambiguity and lack of capability as principal sources of noncompliance. States often value a reputation for law-abiding behavior and desire the benefits of reciprocity ("I'll scratch your back if you'll scratch mine"); they are generally inclined to comply with international law. Peer pressure from other states and domestic or transnational pressures from NGOs may induce compliance. For weaker and developing states, failure to comply can be a consequence of inadequate local expertise, resources, or governmental capacity to do what is required for compliance. In short, the "force" of international law often comes from the "felt need to coordinate activities . . . and to ensure stable and predictive patterns of behavior," and the reality is "imperfect, varied, and changing implementation and compliance," with many factors affecting the extent to which states meet legal commitments (Jacobson and Weiss 1995: 122).

International and regional organizations, too, incorporate different levels of legal commitments. The EU has its own legal system that lies between traditional national legal systems and international law, with the European Court of Justice to interpret it and enforce judgments against member states. The body of EU law includes the various EU treaties, regulations, and directives. The EU can be categorized as having a high level of legal obligation (i.e., states are legally bound by rules); relatively high levels of precision (rules are definite); and high levels of delegation (authority granted to third parties for implementation). These legal obligations do not refer to all areas of EU policies, however, as is discussed in Chapters 5, 8, and 11. Other IGOs and regional integration arrangements lie between the extremes of legalization, where actors combine and invoke varying degrees of obligation, precision, and delegation to create subtle blends of politics and law (Abbott et al. 2000).

### International Norms or "Soft Law"

Scholars have increasingly recognized the importance of norms in international relations. These are shared expectations or understandings regarding standards of appropriate behavior for various actors, particularly states. They range from the norm that states are obligated to carry out treaties they ratify (*pacta sunt servanda*) to the expectation that combatants will not target civilians. Norms vary in strength, and determining whether one exists involves ascertaining whether states perceive that a certain practice is obligatory or expected. Some norms are so internalized in states that they are difficult to recognize unless a violation occurs. Still others are weak, contested, or "emerging."

Many international legal conventions set forth nonbinding obligations for states that are in fact norms and sometimes referred to as "soft law." Examples include human rights and labor rights norms, the concept of the global commons applied to the high seas, outer space, and polar regions, as well as the concept of sustainable development. Generally, "the degree of formalization determines the strength of a rule, especially when it is made legally binding" (Duffield 2007: 10).

Soft law can take a number of forms when a formal agreement is not possible or desirable. In 2005, for example, the final document of the UN-sponsored World Summit endorsed the emerging norm of responsibility to protect (R2P), which is seen as the soft-law basis for humanitarian interventions when states fail to protect peoples at risk of genocide, ethnic cleansing, or other major human rights violations. Other forms of soft law include codes of conduct, world conference declarations, and certain UN General Assembly resolutions.

In environmental law, an initial framework convention often sets forth norms and principles that states agree on, such as those for ozone depletion and global climate change, but no concrete actions. As scientific understanding of the problem improves, the political environment changes, and technology provides new possible solutions (such as substitutes for ozone-depleting chemicals or carbon dioxide–producing energy sources), leading states, key corporations, and other interested actors may agree on specific, binding steps to be taken. Protocols are used to supplement the initial framework convention and form the "hard" law. The Kyoto Protocol, for example, was the first attempt to give effect to general principles in the 1992 UN Framework Convention on Climate Change. Negotiations under way seek to produce a successor agreement in 2015—a hard-law agreement—that establishes state obligations to take urgently needed action to reduce emissions. Soft law is easier to negotiate and more flexible, and leaves open the possibility of negotiating hard law in the future. Soft law can also be a means of linking international law to private entities, including individuals and MNCs, such as through codes of practice of corporate social responsibility.

### International Regimes and Regime Complexes

Scholars have used the concept of international regimes to understand governance where principles, norms, rules, and decisionmaking procedures are linked to one another in a particular issue area. Where international regimes exist, such as for nuclear weapons proliferation, whaling, European transboundary air pollution, and food aid, participating states and other international actors recognize the existence of certain obligations and feel compelled to honor them. Because this is "governance without government," they comply based on an acceptance of the legitimacy of the rules and underlying norms, and the validity of the decisionmaking procedures. They expect other states and actors also to comply and to utilize dispute settlement procedures to resolve conflicts.

International regimes encompass rules and norms, as well as the practices of actors that show both how their expectations converge and their acceptance of and compliance with rules. IGO decisionmaking procedures, bureaucracy, budget, headquarters, and legal personality may be required (or established) within a given issue area, but individual IGOs, by themselves, do not constitute a regime. Some issues, such as nuclear accidents that trigger widespread nuclear fallout, do not need a formal organization that functions regardless of whether there is an accident. Ad hoc arrangements for decisionmaking and taking action when an accident occurs can be coupled with rules and norms. The regime for nuclear weapons proliferation, however, includes the inspection machinery and safeguard systems of the International Atomic Energy Agency (IAEA) and the export controls of the Nuclear Suppliers Group, as well as the Nuclear Non-Proliferation Treaty (NPT), the Comprehensive Test Ban Treaty (CTBT) (which is observed even though it is not yet fully in effect), the UN Security Council's enforcement powers, and the IAEA's technical assistance programs to non–nuclear weapon countries for developing peaceful uses of nuclear energy. In issue areas where regimes exist, they are key types of global governance.

Recently, scholars have identified a number of "regime complexes." These are "networks of three or more international regimes that relate to a common subject matter; exhibit overlapping membership; and generate substantive, normative, or operative interactions recognized as potentially problematic whether or not they are managed effectively." A key characteristic of regime complexes is the "divergence regarding the principles, norms, rules, or procedures of their elemental regimes" (Orsini, Morin, and Young 2013: 29). The food security regime complex, explored further in Chapter 9, is one example. Its three elemental regimes include the agriculture/food regime based around the Food and Agriculture Organization (FAO), the WTO-based international trade regime, and the human rights regime and norms dealing with the right to food. Other examples include the human mobility, maritime piracy, and international forest regime complexes.

### Groups, Arrangements, and Global Conferences

As multilateralism has become the dominant practice in international affairs, other less formal, institutionalized forms of global governance have emerged. These include various intergovernmental arrangements and groups ("Gs") that lack the legal formality of charters or treaties such as UN-sponsored global conferences, panels, forums, and commissions.

The first of the "Gs" was the G-77, formed by developing countries of Africa, Asia, and Latin America in 1964 in conjunction with the establishment of the United Nations Conference on Trade and Development (UNCTAD). For many years, it operated as a unified bloc constituting more than two-thirds of the UN's membership. It is still active today, but less cohesive, as member country interests have diverged.

The Group of Seven (G-7) began in the mid-1970s when summit meetings of governmental leaders were not yet common practice and major changes in international economic relations suggested the value of periodic, informal gatherings. These later evolved into a regular arrangement, including annual summits, but not a formal IGO. The G-7's agenda also grew well beyond macroeconomic policy coordination, as discussed further in Chapter 8. From 1992 to 2014, Russia joined the group for noneconomic discussions, thus creating the Group of Eight (G-8), which dealt with issues surrounding the Cold War's end, the rising threat of terrorism, and so on.

Two groups that have assumed increasing importance in global governance are the Group of 20 (G-20) and the BRICS. Like the G-7/8, they are not formal IGOs. The G-20 originated in 1999 as a forum for economic policy discussions among the finance ministers and central bank governors of advanced and emerging market countries. It includes nineteen states and the EU, with the World Bank and IMF participating on an ex officio basis. Today, the G-20 members represent 90 percent of world GDP, 80 percent of world trade, and two-thirds of world population. Little known until the 2008–2009 global financial crisis, when US president George W. Bush convened the first summit meeting, it now convenes annually at the summit level and like the G-7/8 does not have a permanent secretariat. The 2008–2009 crisis also prompted Brazil, Russia, India, and China to convene their own first summit in Moscow in 2009 to explore how they could exert more influence over the global financial system and reduce the dominance of the United States. South Africa became the capital "S" in BRICS in 2011. Although the BRICS hold the potential to outstrip the rest of the world economically in coming years, as a group they lack unifying values, goals, and even interests, leading to skepticism about their potential impact (Cooper and Thakur 2013). Both groups are discussed further in Chapter 8.

Beginning in the 1970s the United Nations convened many global conferences and, more recently, summits on topics ranging from the environment, food supply, population, and women's rights to water supplies, children, and desertification. There was a large cluster of these conferences in the 1970s and another in the 1990s, with a lull in the 1980s and a deliberate effort to scale back since 2000. These conferences have spawned complex multilateral diplomacy, with NGOs, scientific experts, corporations, and interested individuals trying to influence outcomes, but often have been disappointing because their outcomes represent the least common denominator of agreement among the large number of participants, of whom only states, however, actually have a formal say.

Conferences like the Summit for Children (New York, 1990), the Earth Summit (Rio, 1992), and the Fourth World Conference on Women (Beijing, 1995) have been important global political processes for addressing interdependence issues. Cumulatively, the conferences have also bolstered understanding of the linkages among issues such as environmental protection, equal rights (especially for women), poverty elimination, and participation of local communities. They are discussed further in Chapter 4.

### Private Governance

Private governance is a growing phenomenon, yet one that only recently has received much attention. Although the meaning of the term is disputed, private governance involves authoritative decisionmaking in areas where states have not acted, or have chosen not to exercise authority, or where states have themselves been ineffective in the exercise of authority. Examples include international accounting standards; the private bond-rating agencies, such as Moody's Investors Service and Standard & Poor's Ratings Group, whose rules can shape government actions through the threatened drop in a country's rating; International Chamber of Commerce rules and actions; private industry governance, such as the Worldwide Responsible Apparel Manufacturing Principles and the Forest Stewardship Council, through which major corporations and advocacy groups collaborate; and labor standards within a single multinational firm such as Nike or Ford. The International Organization on Standardization, a nongovernmental organization that sets voluntary standards for many industries, has set almost 20,000 standards since its founding in 1927. In 2013, two groups of retail companies—one US, the other European—agreed on joint inspection standards for garment factories in Bangladesh as part of an effort to improve workplace safety there following the Rana Plaza building collapse in April 2013, in which more than 1,100 workers died. This private governance initiative, put together with the assistance of the International Labour Organization, provides for inspections and assistance in paying for needed safety upgrades (Greenhouse 2013: B3).

Private authorities are neither inherently good nor inherently bad. "What is evident, though," Debora Spar (1999: 48) says, "is that private entities will play an ever-increasing role in the development and management of electronic interaction. . . . They will assume quasi-governmental functions in many instances, regulating activity in their particular spheres through a combination of formal and informal rules, administrative and technical means."

### Public-Private Partnerships

Since the late 1980s, the variety of public-private partnerships involving the UN and most of its specialized agencies, funds, and programs, including the UN Development Programme (UNDP), the World Bank, the UN Children's Fund (UNICEF), and the UN Environment Programme (UNEP), has mushroomed with the recognition that such partnerships can contribute to achieving internationally agreed development goals. UN Secretary-General Kofi Annan's Global Compact initiative, noted earlier, was an important milestone, as was the 2002 Johannesburg World Summit on Sustainable Development, which called for the creation of partnerships for sustainable development, several hundred of which have now been created. Such partnerships have become a major source of funding and have influenced ideas of how development should be achieved and who should deliver it, as well as the architecture of the UN itself (Gregoratti 2014: 311). Some are large, institutionalized, multistakeholder arrangements; others are more temporary with fewer actors. Not all are about donating money, as they may also involve mobilizing corporate knowledge, personnel, and expertise to achieve policy objectives.

Although the new varieties of forms of global governance vary in scope, effectiveness, and durability, as discussed in subsequent chapters, those that do not involve states have begun to raise troubling questions of legitimacy. We explore this issue in Chapter 12.

## The Politics and Effectiveness of Global Governance

The politics of global governance reflects "struggles over wealth, power, and knowledge" in the world (Murphy 2000: 798) as well as over "the global structures, processes, and institutions that shape the fates and life chances of actors around the world" (Barnett and Duval 2005: 7–8). Thus, although power relationships among states still matter, so do the resources and actions of a host of nonstate actors. Among the central issues in the politics of global governance, then, are who gets to participate in decision-making, whose voice gets heard, who gets excluded at what price, and whose interests do certain institutions privilege. Power matters as do the authority and legitimacy of global governance arrangements that increasingly depend on the accountability and transparency of multilateral institutions. And, as with all types of governance, effectiveness, or the ability to deliver public goods and to make a difference, matters.

### Power: Who Gets What? Who Benefits? Who Loses?

At one time, the politics of global governance seemed to be about US power and hegemony. To be sure, US power and preferences shaped, and continue to influence, many pieces of global governance, including the UN and the liberal international economic system. Following the Cold War's end and the dissolution of the Soviet Union, the United States emerged as the sole superpower; its economy drove globalization, and democracy seemed to be spreading everywhere. Yet, especially since the invasion of Iraq in 2003, US power and influence in the world have declined substantially. Even before then, the unilateralist policies of the George W. Bush administration were leading small, middle-power, and larger states to take initiatives without US participation, let alone leadership, such as with the International Criminal Court, the Kyoto Protocol, and the convention banning antipersonnel landmines. Today, there are many indicators that the United States is no longer at the center of global politics in the same way it once was, and that there are "more states with more relations with one another on a wider range of issues than ever before" (Jentleson 2012: 135). As discussed earlier, that emerging powers such as China, India, and Brazil, as well as smaller states such as Qatar, are taking on bigger roles, and that nonstate actors, networks, and private authorities are becoming key governance actors, make for a world in which the politics of different issues and of governance is pluralized. And there are more IGOs taking on duties and responsibilities. Thus, it may be surprising that many of the definitions of global governance "mask the presence of power" (Barnett and Duvall 2005: 6).

Global governance arrangements exist because states and other actors create them and imbue them with power, authority, and legitimacy and deem them valuable for performing certain tasks and serving certain needs and interests. Yet IGOs are not just passive structures and agents of states. As Michael Barnett and Martha Finnemore (2005: 162) argue, they have power "both because of their form (as rational-legal bureaucracies) and because of their (liberal) goals" as well as the authority that derives from goals that are "widely viewed as desirable and legitimate." They can exercise "compulsory power" through the use of material resources such as debt relief, food, money, guns, and sanctions, as well as normative resources such as naming and shaming, spreading global values and norms, or inculcating "best practices." IGO secretariats' ability to set agendas of meetings and conferences, to structure options for Security Council debates, and to classify and organize information whether on types of economies, what is a genocide, or who is a refugee all constitute "institutional power." A third type of IGO power, "productive power," is that of determining the existence of a problem such as internally displaced persons (as differentiated from refugees who cross national borders), defining it, proposing solutions, and persuading other actors to accept those solutions (Barnett and Finnemore 2005).

As for the power of nonstate actors, that also can be derived from various material resources as well as symbolic and normative resources. Transnational advocacy groups, civil society organizations, and NGOs of all stripes have shown the many ways in which they can marshal the resources inherent in naming and shaming to pressure multinational corporations as well as governments of targeted states to change their behavior.

Power, whether in global or local governance, is intimately linked to authority and to legitimacy. IGOs can exercise power in large part because they are generally recognized to have legitimate authority, just as states whose governments are recognized as legitimate are recognized by other states and accepted as members of IGOs. Understanding the nature and types of authority and legitimacy in global governance is part of the puzzle.

## Authority and Legitimacy: Who Governs and On What Basis?

Historically, states were the only entities thought to have authority in international politics, due to their sovereignty, and the only authority IGOs had was assumed to be that delegated by states and, hence, was subject to withdrawal. In recent years, however, more attention has focused on the issues of authority and legitimacy. There is gradual recognition of the varied bases of authority and legitimacy in global governance.

In their book *Who Governs the Globe,* Avant, Finnemore, and Sell (2010b: 9–10) define authority as "the ability to induce deference in others. Authority is thus a social relationship, not a commodity; it does not exist in a vacuum. Authority is created by the recognition, even if only tacit or informal, of others." David Lake (2010: 592, 597) adds that authority "ultimately rests on the collective acceptance or legitimacy of the governor's right to rule" and is "always contested and . . . negotiated." Although, traditionally, capacity for enforcement (particularly with force) has been assumed to be essential for the exercise of authority, more recent thinking has emphasized that enforcement can take a variety of forms and that the essential indicator is others' compliance.

Five bases of authority in global governance articulated by Avant, Finnemore, and Sell (2010c) are: institutional, delegated, expert, principled, and capacity-based. The first is derived from the rules and purposes of an institution, whether an IGO such as the IMF or a credit-rating agency such as Moody's. The second is the primary basis of IGO authority: delegated authority from member states for certain tasks such as peacekeeping. The third derives from the need for certain tasks to be done by those with specialized knowledge about them. And, while expertise may make an IGO authoritative, the institution will also be shaped by that expertise in how staff see the world and define issues, what policy options are considered, and the very culture of the institution. The fourth base—principled or moral authority—reflects the fact that many IGOs and NGOs are created precisely to serve or protect a set of principles, morals, or values such as peace, women's rights, disarmament, or environmental protection. Finally, demonstrated ability to accomplish set tasks such as alleviating extreme poverty is a further basis of authority.

Yet why do the powerful and not-so-powerful actors in global governance decide to cooperate? Why do actors obey rules in the absence of coercion or change their behavior when shamed by a transnational advocacy group or accept the authority of the ICJ or a private credit-rating agency? The decision to comply with rules, norms, and law fundamentally rests on legitimacy: "the belief by an actor that a rule or institution ought to be obeyed" (Hurd 2007: 30). Such a belief affects behavior, Ian Hurd adds, because "the decision whether to comply is no longer motivated by the simple fear of retribution or by a calculation of self-interest but instead by an internal sense of rightness and obligation."

A key aspect of legitimacy in the international system is membership in the international community, whose system of multilateral, reciprocal interactions helps to validate its members, institutions, and rules. IGOs, like the UN, for example, are perceived as legitimate to the extent that they are created and function according to certain principles of right process, such as one-state, one-vote. The UN Security Council's legitimacy as the core institution in the international system imbued with authority to authorize the use of force derives from the widespread acceptance of that role, as we will examine in Chapter 4.

As political theorists have long noted, flags and rituals are important symbols of legitimate authority. Thus, when peacekeeping forces wear UN blue helmets, they symbolize the international community's desire to preserve a cease-fire in hostilities and, since their coercive power is severely limited, it is their token presence that often (but not always) induces states and other actors to comply. When the Security Council refused to approve the US military operation in Iraq in 2003, it denied the United States the symbols of legitimacy and affected how the mission was regarded by much of the world. The very first such symbol of legitimate international authority was the red cross (and later the red crescent)—the emblem adopted by the International Committee of the Red Cross after its founding in 1863 as the first emergency humanitarian organization. As Thomas Franck (1990: 205) states, "It is because states constitute a community that legitimacy has the power to influence their conduct." Today, we could add that it is because there is a growing sense of common humanity and of an international community or global village that legitimacy is such an important variable in global governance.

Legitimacy is also increasingly tied to whether nonstate actors and civil society have a voice and can participate in global governance. Steve Charnovitz (2006: 366) asserts, "Intergovernmental consultation with NGOs can enhance the legitimacy of international decision-making, but it is the consultation itself that makes the contribution, not the quantity of NGO support obtained." In Chapters 4 and 6, we explore the issue of NGO participation.

We borrow from Ronnie Lipschutz (1997: 83) a useful set of questions to bear in mind regarding the politics of governance: "Who rules? Whose rules? What rules? What kind of rules? At what level? In what form? Who decides? On what basis?" And, who benefits? Answers to these questions will emerge in subsequent chapters, but first we examine two critical challenges for global governance: accountability and effectiveness.

### Accountability

As a result of the diffusion of domestic democratic norms into the international arena, global governance actors, including IGOs, NGOs, MNCs, experts, and private governors, have faced growing demands for greater accountability and transparency. Some of these demands come from NGOs and civil society groups; others come from democratic governments, major donors, and major borrowers. There is no single, widely accepted definition of accountability, however. At its core is the idea of account-giving—reporting, measuring, justifying, and explaining actions. For some, account-

ability involves a set of standards for evaluating the behavior of public entities. How responsive and responsible are they? Do they act in a fair and
equitable manner? For others, accountability is defined in terms of mechanisms that involve obligations to explain and justify conduct (Schillemans
and Bovens 2011: 4–5).

The question is, therefore, to whom, for what, and by what mechanisms
various global governance actors are accountable. Are IGOs accountable
only to their member states, for example? To their major donors? To development aid recipients? Trying to satisfy both donors and recipients may satisfy neither. Tamar Gutner (2010), for example, has shown that the system
set up by the IMF reduced the ability of anyone to hold it accountable. To
whom are NGOs accountable? Clifford Bob (2010: 200), for example,
argues that advocacy groups are held accountable in democratic states primarily by the domestic laws that regulate their activities, since dissatisfied
members can simply leave the organization. What about expert groups or
private governance arrangements? The fact that many global governance
actors and certainly most IGOs have multiple constituencies, are responsible for multiple tasks, and face multiple demands and points of view makes
them vulnerable to what some scholars have termed "multiple accountabil-
ities disorder" (Schillemans and Bovens 2011).

Ruth Grant and Robert Keohane (2005) have identified seven accountability mechanisms that operate in world politics, ranging from hierarchical
and fiscal accountability to peer and public reputational accountability.
They add, however, that international accountability is relatively haphazard
and less likely to constrain more powerful actors. Central to having
accountability is ensuring transparency. With respect to IGOs, Alexandru
Grigorescu (2007: 626) asserts that "information about an organization's
deliberations, decisions, and actions needs to be made available to determine if government representatives and IO officials are acting in the public's interest"; without transparency, "officials cannot be held accountable
for their actions." Transparency is also important for assessing an organization's performance, and hence mechanisms for regular review and question-
ing as well as investigation of possible wrongdoing and failure are key
(Koppell 2011: 59).

For IGOs, issues of accountability and transparency frequently turn on
whether conferences and meetings are closed to the public and operate
more like private clubs. The UN Security Council, along with the World
Bank, WTO, and IMF, for example, have all been charged with operating in
secrecy. There is also an active debate over the "democratic deficit" in EU
institutions, as discussed in Chapter 5.

Some institutions may have established mechanisms for accountability,
such as the World Bank's Inspection Panel and the UN's Office of Internal
Oversight Services. In other situations, an ad hoc body may be created to

investigate a particular problem, as in the case of the independent inquiry committee (the Volcker Committee) that investigated the UN's Oil-for-Food Programme. NGOs and member states play key roles in pushing for such IGO accountability and transparency.

Lack of transparency may adversely affect not only legitimacy and compliance, but also the efficacy of all kinds of institutions. An ongoing challenge for global governance in the future, then, is how to increase transparency and accountability of the varieties of governance without undermining the very conditions that enable deal-making and cooperation.

### Effectiveness: Measuring Success and Failure

The second critical challenge involves the effectiveness of governance and the success or failure of different approaches to addressing needs and problems. What are the outcomes of rules and actions? How are people actually affected? Is security increased, are health and well-being improved, is poverty reduced, is environmental degradation slowed? The task of assessing effectiveness is one of the central challenges in public policymaking.

P. J. Simmons and Chantal de Jonge Oudraat (2001: 13–14) remind us: "Effectiveness goes beyond formal compliance; parties may come into compliance with agreements effortlessly for a time and without undertaking any measures that change behavior or contribute to solving the problem. Agreements themselves may not be ambitious enough to provide more than temporary or cosmetic relief of global problems." The key questions are: What works? And, for whom does it work? Who does what to translate agreements into action, including incorporating norms into domestic laws? Which techniques or mechanisms work best to get actors to change their behavior, and what are the reactions to noncompliance? What types of incentives or technical assistance to developing countries will enable them to comply with environmental rules? How and when are diplomacy or public shaming, economic sanctions, or military force most likely to secure compliance? When are particular types of peace operations most likely to secure, keep, or build conditions of lasting peace? We address these issues particularly in Chapters 7 through 12.

\* \* \*

The challenges of global governance, then, include a wide variety of international policy problems and issues that require governance, not all of which are necessarily global in scope. Rather, what we see are multilevel, often diffuse varieties of governance with many different actors playing key roles alongside states. The need for more governance is clearly rising; the processes are complex; the politics is an ongoing struggle to influence "who gets what" and "who benefits"; and the issues of legitimacy, accountability, and effectiveness require constant attention. Most important, we should not assume that all global governance is necessarily good. As Inis Claude (1988: 142) noted many years ago, "I must question the assumption of the normative superiority of collective policy, the view that one can have greater confidence in the wisdom and the moral quality of decisions made by a collectivity concerning the use of power and other resources than in the quality of policies set and followed by individual states."

## Suggested Further Reading

Avant, Deborah D., Martha Finnemore, and Susan K. Sell, eds. (2010) *Who Governs the Globe?* New York: Cambridge University Press.

Barnett, Michael, and Raymond Duvall, eds. (2005) *Power in Global Governance.* New York: Cambridge University Press.

Chayes, Abram, and Antonia Handler Chayes. (1995) *The New Sovereignty: Compliance with International Regulatory Agreements.* Cambridge: Harvard University Press.

Hale, Thomas, and David Held, eds. (2011) *The Handbook of Transnational Governance: Institutions and Innovations.* Malden, MA. Polity.

Johnson, Tana. (2015) *Organizational Progeny: Why Governments Are Losing Control over the Proliferating Structures of Global Governance.* New York: Oxford University Press.

Slaughter, Anne Marie. (2004) *A New World Order.* Princeton: Princeton University Press.

Weiss, Thomas G. (2014) *Governing the World? Addressing "Problems Without Passports."* Boulder: Paradigm Publishers.

Weiss, Thomas G., and Rorden Wilkinson, eds. (2014) *International Organizations and Global Governance.* New York: Routledge.

# 2

# The Theoretical Foundations of Global Governance

## Why Theory Matters

Scholars use theories to describe, explain, and predict various aspects of international relations. Each is based on a set of key ideas about the nature and roles of individuals, conceptions of the state, sovereignty, and interactions among states and other actors, as well as conceptions about the international system.

The principal goal of theory is to simplify and clarify what matters most. Although scholars may disagree about what to include and what to leave out, they leave it to the consumers of theoretical work to decide whether the choices are reasonable and whether they help explain real-world events.

An important debate in international relations (IR) theory generally is whether one should focus on measuring and explaining human behavior and institutions objectively, through positivist or rationalist theory, or whether one should instead focus on interpreting the language and symbols of social interaction through constructivist or nonrationalist theory. This is especially relevant to global governance, since values, rules, and identities play an important role alongside more traditional factors such as economic and military capability and interests. Although the debate tends to polarize scholars, each approach and method provides a useful lens through which to study global governance (Fearon and Wendt 2002).

Rationalist theories identify links between antecedents, called independent variables, and outcomes, referred to as dependent variables. From theory, propositions are hypothesized and tested by observations in the real world. For example, functionalist theory proposes that international organizations tend to grow from a more narrow and technical focus to broader and more political undertakings. This insight can be tested against the development of European regionalism or the history of the creation of UN specialized agencies through careful tracing of processes, detailed case studies of particular institutions, or perhaps a statistical test that covers multiple cases.

In contrast, constructivism and most critical theories are not testable in the same ways. Rather they are critiqued with reference to whether the propositions are internally logical or help to elucidate the true nature of international institutions. For example, since many social constructivists argue that actors' identities and interests are the product of debate and inter-action, one could study the evolution of a legal principle, such as the prohi-bition against the use of force in international relations, to explore whether this dynamic occurs.

In this chapter, we briefly discuss five major theories—liberalism, real-ism, social constructivism, the English School, and critical theories—with particular attention to what each says about global governance and interna-tional cooperation.

## Liberalism

Liberal theory in the classical tradition holds that human nature is basically good, social progress is possible, and human behavior is malleable and per-fectible through institutions. Injustice, aggression, and war are, according to liberals, products of inadequate or corrupt social institutions and of mis-understanding among leaders. They are not inevitable, but rather can be eliminated through collective or multilateral action and institutional reform. The expansion of human freedom is a core liberal belief that can be achieved through democracy and market capitalism.

The roots of liberalism are found in the seventeenth-century Grotian tradition, the eighteenth-century Enlightenment, nineteenth-century politi-cal and economic liberalism, and twentieth-century Wilsonian idealism. The Grotian tradition developed from the writings of Hugo Grotius (1583–1645), an early Dutch legal scholar. Just prior to the European states' challenge to universal religious authority in the Peace of Westphalia (1648), Grotius asserted that all international relations were subject to the rule of law—both the law of nations and the law of nature. He rejected the idea that states can do whatever they wish and that war is the supreme right of states. Grotius believed that states, like people, are basically rational and law-abiding.

The Enlightenment's contribution to liberalism rests on Greek ideas that individuals are rational human beings and have the capacity to improve their condition by creating a just society. If a just society is not attained, then the fault rests with inadequate institutions. The writings of Immanuel Kant (1724–1804) reflect these core Enlightenment beliefs with their exten-sive treatment of the relationship between democracy and peace. Kant was among the first thinkers to articulate this connection and the possibility of "perpetual peace" among democratic states. The liberal theory of democratic peace does not mean that democratic states would refrain from war in their relations with nondemocratic states, but Kant did argue that in a "pacific union," free, democratic states would retain their sovereignty while working to avoid war.

Nineteenth-century liberalism linked the rationalism of the Enlightenment, and the growing faith in modernization through the scientific and industrial revolutions, to promoting democracy and free trade. Adam Smith and Jeremy Bentham believed that free trade would create interdependencies that would raise the cost of war and reward fair cooperation and competition with peace, prosperity, and greater justice. This strand of liberalism forms the basis for economic liberalism, examined in Chapters 8 and 9. To stimulate individual (and therefore collective) economic growth and to maximize economic welfare, free markets must be allowed to develop and governments must permit free economic intercourse.

The beliefs of US president Woodrow Wilson, captured best in the "Fourteen Points," on which the Versailles Treaty (ending World War I) and the Covenant of the League of Nations were based, formed a core of twentieth-century liberalism. Wilson envisioned that creating a system of collective security, promoting self-determination of peoples, and eliminating power politics could prevent war. The League of Nations illustrated the importance that liberals place on international institutions for collective problem solving. Early-twentieth-century liberals were also strong advocates of international law, arbitration, and courts to promote cooperation and guarantee peace. Because of their faith in human reason and progress, they were often labeled "idealists." With the League of Nations' failure to prevent World War II and the Cold War, liberalism and idealism came under intense criticism from realist theorists.

For liberals, while individual human beings are key actors, states are the most important collective actors, but they are pluralistic not unitary actors. That is, moral and ethical principles, power relations among domestic and transnational groups, and changing international conditions shape states' interests and policies. There is no single definition of states' national interests; rather, states vary in their goals, and their interests change. Liberals also recognize the roles of nonstate actors and transnational and transgovernmental groups.

Liberals believe that cooperation is possible and will grow over time for two reasons. First, they view the international system as a context within which multiple interactions occur and where various actors "learn" from their interactions, rather than a structure of relationships based on the distribution of power among states and a fixed concept of state sovereignty. Power matters, but it is exercised within this framework of rules and institutions, which also makes international cooperation possible. Second, liberals expect mutual interests to increase with greater interdependence, knowledge, communication, and the spread of democratic values. This will promote greater cooperation and thereby peace, welfare, and justice.

Liberals view international organizations as arenas where states interact and cooperate to solve common problems. International law is viewed as one of the major instruments for framing and maintaining order in the international system, although it represents horizontal rather than hierarchical authority. As Louis Henkin (1979: 22) explains:

> If one doubts the significance of this law, one need only imagine a world in which it were absent. . . . There would be no security of nations or stability of governments; territory and airspace would not be respected; vessels could navigate only at their constant peril; property—within or without any given territory—would be subject to arbitrary seizure; persons would have no protection of law or diplomacy; agreements would not be made or observed; diplomatic relations would end; international trade would cease; international organizations and arrangements would disappear.

For liberals, international organizations play a number of key roles, including contributing to habits of cooperation and serving as arenas for negotiating and developing coalitions. They are a primary means for mitigating the danger of war, promoting the development of shared norms, and enhancing order. They carry out operational activities to help address substantive international problems, and may form parts of international regimes. They can be used by states as instruments of foreign policy or to constrain the behavior of others. Andrew Moravcsik (1997), for one, uses liberal theory to show the links between domestic politics within states and intergovernmental cooperation.

Finally, a new strain of liberal theory has developed since the 1990s that draws attention to the role of women in global governance as both an independent and dependent variable. Positivist feminist theorists argue that most of international relations theory, including liberal theory, has ignored the place of women. For international organization scholars, this means paying more attention to the role of women in international institutions as leaders, staffers, and lobbyists. Historically women have been poorly represented in the halls of power; they were virtually absent from the League of Nations and only recently have they held senior positions at the United Nations.

Liberal feminists also call for increased attention to developing organizational policies that affect women, especially the role of women in economic development, women as victims of crime and discrimination, and women in situations of armed conflict. For too long, these issues have been neglected.

Core liberal beliefs in the roots of cooperation and roles of international institutions have been challenged since the 1970s by so-called neoliberal institutionalists. Their ideas form an important variant on liberal theory.

### Neoliberal Institutionalism or Neoliberalism

In the 1970s, liberalism experienced a revival following the preeminence of realism during the Cold War. Increasing international interdependence and heightened awareness of the sensitivities and vulnerabilities that characterize interdependence were major factors boosting this revival. Robert Keohane and Joseph Nye's book *Power and Interdependence* (1977), which outlined how international institutions constituted an important response to conditions of complex interdependence, also had a major impact. Neoliberal institutionalists argue that "even if . . . anarchy constrains the willingness of states to cooperate, states nevertheless can work together and can do so especially with the assistance of international institutions" (Grieco 1993: 117). They therefore take a more state-centric view of international relations and believe that states are rational actors in a generally anarchic world. States have incentives to cooperate because they seek to maximize absolute gains. As a result, cooperation is a common occurrence, not the rare exception. Through institutions, states can solve collective action problems.

Some neoliberal institutionalists, such as Robert Axelrod and Robert Keohane (1986), have drawn on game theory and particularly the Prisoners' Dilemma game to illustrate how cooperation is in the individual state's self-interest. The Prisoners' Dilemma is the story of two prisoners, each being held and interrogated separately for an alleged crime. The interrogator tells each prisoner that if one of them confesses and the other does not, the one who confesses will go free and the one who keeps silent will get a long prison term. If both confess, both will get somewhat reduced prison terms. If neither confesses, both will receive short prison terms based on lack of evidence. In the first play, both prisoners will confess and each will serve a longer sentence than if they had cooperated and kept silent. The self-serving behavior of each player leads to bad outcomes for both players. If the game is repeated, however, or the environment is changed, for instance, by allowing communication, the possibility of joint gains provides incentives to cooperate by remaining silent. Neoliberals have drawn a number of conclusions from studying Prisoners' Dilemma games. They have shown that if states use a tit-for-tat strategy of reciprocating each other's cooperation, they are likely to find this mutually beneficial over the long term, especially if the costs of verifying compliance and sanctioning cheaters are relatively low compared to the costs of joint action (Grieco 1993: 122).

They have also shown that the applicability of the Prisoners' Dilemma varies between economic and security issues when there are shared norms, and if issues are linked. Finally, use of the Prisoners' Dilemma has helped neoliberals demonstrate that although states may be independent actors, their policy choices tend to be interdependent.

The 1970s and early 1980s presented a puzzle for neoliberals. Given the major international economic dislocations resulting from the collapse of the Bretton Woods arrangements for international monetary relations, increasing third world debt, and the decline in US economic power relative to Europe and Japan, why did the post–World War II institutions for economic cooperation (such as the IMF and GATT) not collapse? Keohane's influential book *After Hegemony* (1984) answered this question by emphasizing the cooperation that states achieved through international institutions and the effects of institutions and practices on state behavior.

Thus, according to neoliberal institutionalists, states that have continuous interactions with each other choose to cooperate, because they realize that they will have future interactions with the same actors. Continuous interactions also serve as the motivation for states to create international institutions, which in turn moderate state behavior, provide a context for bargaining and mechanisms for reducing cheating by monitoring behavior, and facilitate transparency of the actions of all. International institutions provide focal points for coordination and serve to make state commitments more credible by specifying what is expected, thereby encouraging states to establish reputations for compliance. They are an efficient solution to problems of coordination because they provide information that aids decision-making and reduces the transaction costs for achieving agreement among large numbers of states (Keohane and Martin 1995). States benefit because institutions do things for members that cannot be accomplished unilaterally. Thus, institutions have important and independent effects on interstate interactions, both by providing information and by framing actions, but they do not necessarily affect states' underlying motivations.

Neoliberals recognize that not all efforts to cooperate will yield good results. Cooperation can aid the few at the expense of the many, and accentuate or mitigate injustice. Unlike earlier liberals, some neoliberals have been more willing to address issues of power. To explain the creation, for example, of the post–World War II network of international economic institutions and shared standards for liberalizing trade and capital flows, neoliberal institutionalists such as Robert Keohane (1984) and John Gerard Ruggie (1982) have focused on the role of the United States as a hegemonic state, the particular character of the order it created (embedded liberalism), and the joint gains it offered the Europeans and Japanese for cooperating.

Liberalism and neoliberalism have spawned several middle-level theories that provide additional dimensions for explaining international cooperative behavior. These include functionalism, regime theory, rational design, and collective goods theory.

## Functionalism

Functionalism is rooted in the belief that governance arrangements arise out of the basic, or functional, needs of people and states. Thus, it explains the origin and development of many IGOs. Functionalists, however, assert that international economic and social cooperation is a prerequisite for political cooperation and eliminating war, whose causes (in their view) lie in ignorance, poverty, hunger, and disease.

As articulated by David Mitrany in *A Working Peace System* (1946: 7), the task of functionalism is "not how to keep the nations peacefully apart but how to bring them actively together." He foresaw "a spreading web of international activities and agencies, in which and through which the interests and life of all nations would be gradually integrated" (14). Not all functionalists share this vision, but they do share a belief that it is possible to bypass political rivalries of states and build habits of cooperation in nonpolitical economic spheres. Increasing amounts of such cooperation will expand these cooperative interactions and build a base of common values, eventually spilling over into cooperation in political and military affairs. A key aspect of this process is the role of technical experts and the assumption that these experts will lose their close identification with their own states and develop new sets of allegiances to like-minded individuals around the globe. The form that specific functional organizations take is determined by the problem to be solved; form follows function.

Functionalism is applicable at both regional and global levels and has been important in explaining the evolution of the European Union as a process of integration. The "father of Europe," Jean Monnet, believed that nationalism could be weakened and war in Europe made unthinkable in the long run by taking practical steps toward economic integration that would ultimately advance European political union. The success of the European Coal and Steel Community, proposed by Monnet, led to the creation of the European Atomic Energy Community to manage peaceful uses of atomic energy and to the creation of the European Economic Community, with its common market and many facets of practical cooperation.

Functional theory fell short in its prediction that such cooperation would spill over in a deterministic fashion from the economic area into areas of national security. Although most analysts would credit European integration with making the region a "zone of peace," achieving common foreign and security policy has proved particularly difficult for EU members. In fact, neofunctionalists theorized that the process and dynamics of cooperation are not automatic. At key points, political decisions are needed and these may or may not be taken (Haas 1964). The evolution of European integration has borne this out (see Chapter 5).

Functionalist theory also helps us understand the development of early IGOs such as the Universal Postal Union and Commission for Navigation on the Rhine River, as well as the specialized agencies of the UN system such as the World Health Organization, UN Children's Fund, Food and Agriculture Organization, and International Labour Organization. These are discussed further in Chapter 3 and subsequent chapters.

Harold Jacobson, William Reisinger, and Todd Mathers (1986) tested key propositions of functionalism as an explanation for the phenomenon of IGO development and found that the overwhelming number of IGOs could be classified as functional. That is, they have specific mandates, links to economic issues, and limited memberships, often related to geographic region. The majority of those created since 1960 have been established by other IGOs and show increasing differentiation of functions. Yet this trend toward greater specialization "has not yet radically transformed this system, as functionalism hoped would happen" (157).

Functionalism fails to address a number of key questions. If the ultimate goal is elimination of war, and war is not caused just by economic deprivation, illiteracy, hunger, and disease, then how can the other causes of war be alleviated? How can political and nonpolitical issues be distinguished? Will habits of economic and social cooperation transfer to political areas? In fact, the European integration process since 1950 has shown the degree to which functionalists underestimated the strength of state sovereignty and national loyalties. Despite these limitations, functionalism has proven a useful theoretical approach for understanding IGOs and the cooperation many IGOs foster in economic and social issue areas.

### International Regimes

A second important middle-level theory within liberalism emerged from international law. In the 1970s, legal scholars began to use the concept of international regimes, introduced in Chapter 1. They recognized that international law consists not only of formal authoritative prohibitions, but also of more informal norms and rules of behavior that over time may become codified and sometimes institutionalized. By referring to the totality of these norms and rules of behavior as "regimes," these scholars emphasized the governance provided for specific issue areas. International relations scholars have found regime theory particularly useful for examining many aspects of governance. According to the most widely used definition, a regime includes "sets of implicit or explicit principles, norms, rules, and decisionmaking procedures around which actors' expectations converge in a given issue area" (Krasner 1982: 1).

Regime theory has been shaped not only by liberalism and especially neoliberalism, but also by realism and neorealism. Some regime theorists focus on the role of power relations among states in shaping regimes, particularly the role of a hegemonic state such as the United States (or Great Britain in the nineteenth century). Others recognize how common interests aid states in enhancing transparency and reducing uncertainty in their environment. Regime theorists have also used constructivist approaches to focus on social relations and the ways in which the strong patterns of interaction often found in an international regime actually affect state interests (Hasenclever, Mayer, and Rittberger 2000). Explaining how regimes are created and maintained, and how, why, and when they change, are key tasks for regime theorists.

Regime theory has shown how states create these frameworks to coordinate their actions with those of other states, if and when necessary for achieving their national interests. Regimes can provide information to participants and reduce uncertainty. Over time, coordination may lead to a partial convergence of interests and values among the parties in a regime.

Regime theorists have focused on IGO roles in the creation and maintenance of regimes, while being careful not to equate an IGO with the existence of a regime. By themselves, IGOs do not constitute a regime, but their charters may incorporate principles, norms, rules, decisionmaking processes, and functions that formalize these aspects of a regime. An IGO's decisionmaking processes may then be used by member states for further norm and rule creation, for rule enforcement and dispute settlement, for the provision of collective goods, and for supporting operational activities. Thus, IGOs are one way that habits of cooperation are sustained and expanded.

Identifying international regimes in different issue areas enables scholars to discuss the interaction not only between states and IGOs, but also between various IGOs, between IGOs and NGOs, and among noninstitutionalized rules and procedures that have developed over time. Regimes enable scholars to examine informal patterns and ad hoc groupings that enhance international cooperation. As Andreas Hasenclever, Peter Mayer, and Volker Rittberger (2000: 3) succinctly summarize:

> Regimes are deliberately constructed, partial international orders on either a regional or a global scale, which are intended to remove specific issue areas of international politics from the sphere of self-help behaviour. By creating shared expectations about appropriate behaviour and by upgrading the level of transparency in the issue area, regimes help states (and other actors) to co-operate with a view to reaping joint gains in the form of additional welfare or security.

There is now a substantial body of literature explaining the formation, persistence, and decline of international regimes, as well as their specific properties and openness to change (Rittberger 1993; Young 1989). There is also a growing examination of issue areas where regimes have not developed. In the areas of global deforestation and small arms, the absence of regimes can be explained by the absence of recognized interdependence of issues or perceived need for collective action (Dimitrov et al. 2007). In recent years, some scholars have also begun to explore regime complexes in issue areas where multiple regimes overlap, often with conflicting norms, rules, and procedures, such as in food security and human mobility, as discussed in Chapter 9. Despite inherent ambiguities, the study of international regimes and regime theory has helped link international institutions and governance by establishing that governance and order are embedded in norms and involve more than just organizational structures.

### Rational Design

During the 1990s there was considerable debate among regime theorists and other liberal international scholars regarding the reasons why certain types of organizations had particular distinguishing characteristics. A response came from those scholars versed in the rational choice approach to decisionmaking, a simplified and abstract description of players' goals and constraints to predict types of agreements. Barbara Koremenos, Charles Lipson, and Duncan Snidal (2001) offer propositions linking different characteristics of organizations. For example, where the issue at stake involves distributing benefits and costs fairly, organizational membership is apt to be larger. When there are doubts about what other states will do in the future, organizational decisionmaking will tend to be centralized; it will be more decentralized when a few states are negotiating over a narrow range of issues. Likewise, compliance with rules will be easier to enforce if organizations are narrowly focused.

Rational design theorists applaud the theory's parsimony; it can explain many outcomes with a small number of independent variables—one of the goals of positivist theory. The theory holds up fairly well when tested against actual events. For example, participation in the nuclear nonproliferation regime requires states to accept inspections, a deliberate strategy to reduce uncertainty and defection. Rational design theory has also shown why institutions like the Marshall Plan and the European Common Market were heavily centralized but flexible (Oatley 2001).

Critics of rational design raise many questions, however. Who participated in the negotiations to create the institution? What was their status and rank? Was it not the product of preexisting rules and the powers that be (Ruane 2011: 51)? In the UN Security Council, for example, why does

France have veto power while Germany has no permanent seat? This is explained by the state of the world in 1945. During negotiations leading to the creation of a new institution, critics argue that it is nested in larger political structures and arrangements that are themselves the products of other decisions. It is not easy to know where to start and which decisions matter most or where the application of raw power matters most (Duffield 2003). In rational design, there is little accounting for historical contingencies, accidents, miscalculations, or future possibilities.

One recent variant of rational design incorporates elements of functionalism, in what Jonas Tallberg and colleagues (2013) call rational functionalism, to address the relationship between states, international organizations, and transnational actors. They argue that states and IGO bureaucracies are rational actors that make deliberate choices about nonstate actor access based on their assessments of what "functional benefits" those actors may be able to bring to the organization" (29).

### Collective or Public Goods Theory

Still another approach within liberalism to explaining governance and cooperation has involved the application of collective or public goods theory. Biologist Garrett Hardin, in his article "The Tragedy of the Commons" (1968), tells the story of a group of herders who share a common grazing area. Each herder finds it economically rational to increase the size of his own herd, allowing him to sell more in the market and hence return more profits. Yet if all herders follow what is individually rational behavior, then the group loses; too many animals graze the land and the quality of the pasture deteriorates, which leads to decreased output for all. As each person rationally attempts to maximize his own gain, the collectivity suffers, and eventually all individuals suffer. What Hardin describes—the common grazing area—is a collective good available to all members of the group, regardless of individual contribution.

Collective or public goods may be tangible or intangible. In the global context, they include the "natural commons" such as the high seas, atmosphere, ozone shield, and polar regions. They also include "human-made global commons" (Kaul 2000: 300) such as universal norms and principles and the Internet, as well as "global conditions" ranging from peace and financial stability to environmental sustainability and freedom from poverty.

The use of collective goods involves activities and choices that are interdependent. Decisions by one state have effects for other states; that is, states can suffer unanticipated negative consequences as a result of the actions of others. For example, a decision by developed countries in the 1980s to continue the production and sale of chlorofluorocarbons would have affected all countries through long-term depletion of the ozone layer. With collective goods, market mechanisms are inadequate and alternative forms of governance are needed. A central concern in collective or public goods theory, therefore, revolves around the question of who provides the public goods. Without some kind of collective action mechanisms, there is a risk that such goods will not be adequately provided. Once they are, however, the goods exist and all can enjoy them, which creates the problem of "free-riding."

Collective goods are easier to provide in small groups than in large groups. Mancur Olson, in *The Logic of Collective Action* (1968: 35), argues that "the larger the group, the farther it will fall short of providing an optimal amount of a collective good." Free-riding and defection are harder to conceal and easier to punish if the group is small. With larger groups, the fraction of the group that benefits will decline and organizational costs will increase. Smaller groups can more effectively monitor each other and exert pressure, and collective pressure can be more effectively mobilized.

Another alternative is to force nations or peoples to govern collective goods by establishing organizations with effective police powers that coerce states or individuals to act in a mutually beneficial manner. Such an organization could, for example, force people to limit the number of children they have in order to stop the population explosion. Elinor Ostrom (1990), however, suggests that the most effective management may be self-governance, with private agents acting as enforcers. Individuals or groups make binding contracts to commit themselves to cooperative strategies, and use the enforcers to monitor each other and report infractions.

Finally, public goods theory suggests that those confronted with a collective action problem could seek to restructure actors' preferences through rewards and punishments. For example, mechanisms could be established to offer positive incentives for states to refrain from destroying the polar regions and to tax or threaten to tax those who fail to cooperate.

Collective goods theory can be used to explain the role of international agreements, IGOs, as well as international regimes in producing (or underproducing) various goods. It can also be used to investigate the gaps in international efforts to deal with policy issues. Collective goods theory is especially useful for examining those global commons areas such as the high seas or ozone layer over which no state can claim sovereignty because these have been designated as the common heritage of humankind.

Thus, collective or public goods theorists, along with other liberal theorists, see international organizations, international law, and international regimes playing positive roles in facilitating cooperation and managing public goods. They believe, for example, that the UN has helped to check power politics, create some degree of shared interests in place of national interests, and provide a forum for international cooperation. These views stand in opposition to those of realists, who are primarily interested in states' exercise of power and pursuit of national interests.


## Realism

A product of a long philosophical and historical tradition, realism in its various forms is based on the assumption that individuals act rationally to protect their own interests. Within the international system, realists see states as the primary actors, entities that act in a unitary way in pursuit of their national interest, which is generally defined in terms of maximizing power and security relative to other states. States coexist in an anarchic international system characterized by the absence of an authoritative hierarchy. As a result, states must rely primarily on themselves to manage their own insecurity through balance of power and deterrence. Because each state is concerned with acquiring more power relative to other states, competition between states is keen and there is little basis for cooperation.

To most realists, in the absence of international authority there are few rules or norms that restrain states, although Hans Morgenthau, generally regarded as the father of modern realism, did include chapters on international morality, law, and government in his pathbreaking textbook *Politics Among Nations*. In his view (1967: 219–220): "The main function of these normative systems has been to keep aspirations for power within socially tolerable bounds. . . . [M]orality, mores, and law intervene in order to protect society against disruption and the individual against enslavement and extinction." Yet Morgenthau suggested that there had been a weakening of these moral limitations from earlier times, when there was a cohesive international society bound together through elite ties and common morality. Thus, international law and government, in his view, are largely weak and ineffective. For Morgenthau, international organizations are a tool of states to be used when desired; they can increase or decrease the power of states, but they do not affect the basic characteristics of the international system; because they reflect the distribution of power among states, they are no more than the sum of their member states. In fact, they are susceptible to great-power manipulation. Thus, international organizations have no independent effect on state behavior or world politics in general.

Most realist theorists do not claim that international cooperation is impossible, only that there are few incentives for states to enter into international arrangements. Since international institutions and agreements have no enforcement power, they have no authority and hence no real power (Gruber 2000). Realists do not acknowledge the importance or influence of nonstate actors such as NGOs and MNCs in international politics and governance, nor do they accept the idea of IGOs as independent actors. To most realists, deterrence and balance of power have proven more effective in maintaining peace than have international institutions.

## Neorealism or Structural Realism

Among the variants of realism, the most powerful is neorealism, or structural realism, which owes much to Kenneth Waltz's *Theory of International Politics* (1979). The core difference between traditional realists and neorealists lies in the emphasis placed on the structure of the international system for explaining world politics. The system's structure is determined by the ordering principle, namely the absence of overarching authority (anarchy), and the distribution of capabilities (power) among states. What matters are states' material capabilities; state identities and interests are largely given and fixed. Anarchy poses a severe constraint on state behavior. But how it is defined, and how much of a constraint it imposes on the possibilities for cooperation and international order, are matters of dispute and some confusion among both neorealists and neoliberals (Baldwin 1993). This has important implications for theorizing about global governance, since most definitions involve questions of government, authority, and governance in some way. Likewise, the way in which the power distribution shapes state behavior and provides order in international politics, either through balances of power or through a hierarchy of relations between states with unequal power, underscores that order is a product less of state actions, much less of international institutions, than of system structure.

In neorealist theory, the possibilities for international cooperation are logically slim, though not impossible. As Waltz (1979: 105) posits:

> When faced with the possibility of cooperating for mutual gain, states that feel insecure must ask how the gain will be divided. They are compelled to ask not "Will both of us gain?" but "Who will gain more?" If an expected gain is to be divided, say, in the ratio of two to one, one state may use its disproportionate gain to implement a policy intended to damage or destroy the other. Even the prospect of large absolute gains for both parties does not elicit their cooperation so long as each fears how the other will use its increased capabilities.

In contrast to this neorealist emphasis on relative gains from cooperation, neoliberals stress that actors with common interests try to maximize their absolute gains (Stein 1982: 318). Relative gains may be more important in security matters than in economic issues, making cooperation more difficult to achieve, harder to maintain, and more dependent on states' power (Lipson 1984: 15–18). Since anarchy fuels insecurity, states are wary of becoming too dependent on others, preferring greater control and increased capabilities.

Many neorealists do recognize the emergence of international regimes and institutions, but believe their importance has been exaggerated. Others such as John Mearsheimer are not just skeptical about international institutions, but also outright disdainful. In his view, institutions are merely arenas for pursuing power relationships. They have "minimal influence on state behavior and thus hold little promise for promoting stability in the post–Cold War world" (1994–1995: 7). While not all neorealists would go as far as Mearsheimer, it is clear that many believe that international institutions do not have independent effects worth studying. Although there are many criticisms of neorealism's inability to explain system change and failure to incorporate variables other than the structure of the international system, it continues to have a strong influence on IR scholars. One middle-level theory derived from realism that has addressed issues of international cooperation more directly is strategic or rational choice.

### Strategic or Rational Choice Theory
Strategic or rational choice theory has enjoyed wide usage in other fields of political science as well as in economics. It assumes that preferences are deduced from objective and material conditions of the state. Predicated on the view that markets are the most efficient mechanism of human behavior, strategic choice theorists often use the language of microeconomic theory to explain state choices. Yet they also acknowledge that market imperfections may arise. Information may be incomplete, or transaction costs may be too high. Then, organizations and institutions can play key roles. They may also act as constraints on choice.

Lloyd Gruber (2000) is intrigued by the fact that states find it rational to take part in international arrangements, even though they would prefer the original, precooperation status quo. He argues that states fear being left behind; they want to join the bandwagon, even when it is not directly in their best interest. States come to believe that the status quo—not participating in such agreements—is not an option, and thus they may be forced to conform to the rules of the game.

Key to rational or strategic choice theory is the assumption that state actions are based on rational calculations about subjective expected utility. Such calculations incorporate estimates of others' capabilities and likely intentions. From this perspective, then, Keohane (1993: 288) suggests, "international institutions exist largely because they facilitate self-interested cooperation by reducing uncertainty, thus stabilizing expectations." Hence an analysis of rational state action within Europe, for example, must take Europe's many international institutions into account.

### Theories of Hegemonic Stability and Great-Power Concerts
Middle-level hegemonic stability theory is rooted in the realist tradition, but like international regime theory draws from other traditions. It was developed in the 1970s and 1980s to answer the question of how an open

world economy is created and maintained. The theory's answer is that these occur through the power and leadership of a dominant or hegemonic state that uses its position in a liberal international economy in particular ways. As Robert Gilpin (1987: 72) notes, "Hegemony without a liberal commitment to the market economy is more likely to lead to imperial systems and the imposition of political and economic restrictions on lesser powers."

Hegemonic stability theory is based on the premise that an open market economy is a collective or public good (Kindleberger 1973) that cannot be sustained without the actions of a dominant economy. When there is a predominant state with "control over raw materials, control over sources of capital, control over markets, and competitive advantages in the production of highly valued goods" (Keohane 1984: 32), it has the means to exercise leadership over other economies as well as to use its economic power for leverage over other states. If such a dominant power is committed to an open, liberal world economy based on nondiscrimination and free markets, it can use its position to guarantee provision of the collective good—an open trading system and stable monetary system. In so doing, it must perform several roles, including the creation of norms and rules, preventing cheating and free-riding, encouraging others to share the costs of maintaining the system, managing the monetary system, using its own dynamism as an engine of growth for the rest of the system, and responding to crises. As strategic choice theorists would argue, the hegemon may also be engaging in behavior that serves to perpetuate its power and position.

There are, to date, only two examples of such hegemonic leadership. The first occurred during the nineteenth century, when Great Britain used its dominant position to create an era of free trade among major economic powers. The second occurred after World War II, when the United States established the Bretton Woods system to promote international trade and investment. An important part of its role was the willingness to pay the costs to make its vision of a liberal economic order a reality.

Some have questioned whether a theory based on two cases is sufficient to explain why a dominant state would undertake a leadership role or be committed to liberal values. These depend, as Ruggie (1982) has noted, on the hegemon's "social purpose" and commitment to "embedded liberalism."

The persistence of international economic regimes in the face of the economic dislocations of the 1970s and 1980s led Keohane (1984), as noted earlier, to explore the consequences of declining hegemony. He found that, in a view compatible with the institutionalist position, cooperation may persist, even if the hegemon's power declines and it is not performing a leadership role. A residue of common interests and the norms of the regime help to maintain it, for "regimes are more readily maintained than established" (Kindleberger 1986: 8). Such views have contributed significantly to understanding the bases of states' choices and the role of power, especially hegemonic power, in the creation of international regimes.

The role of power, particularly the economic power of preeminent states, also plays a key role in Daniel Drezner's book *All Politics Is Global* (2007). Like other realists and hegemonic stability theorists before him, Drezner posits that preeminent states (those with the largest internal markets and least vulnerability to external shocks) are the dominant actors in the global economy, but unlike realists, Drezner links state preferences to the domestic economies. Similar to neoliberal institutionalists, he also argues that other actors—IGOs, NGOs, global civil society actors—influence the processes of governance. States make the ultimate choices, however, among the different forums and institutions of global governance. Drezner's studies show that most cooperation will occur when there is a concert among the great powers, which may then be institutionalized in groups of the like-minded or even in universal IGOs, but if there is no agreement, rival standards may deadlock IGOs. If interests of great powers and other states diverge, then club groups are convened or preeminent states shop for the most convenient venue.

Although most realists have little to say about the varieties of global governance, more recent work on hegemonic stability and great-power behavior evidences cross-fertilization among different theories. These approaches lead researchers to look at the role of dominant states in global governance outcomes, and how other actors affect governance processes. The benefits of cross-fertilization become equally as evident when we examine the contribution of constructivism to global governance.

## Social Constructivism

Social constructivism has become increasingly important for studying global governance, particularly the role of norms and institutions. While there are many variants, all constructivists agree that the behavior of individuals, states, and other actors is shaped by shared beliefs, socially constructed rules, and cultural practices. They argue that what actors do, how they interrelate, and the way that others interpret their behavior create and can change the meaning of norms. The approach has strong roots in sociology and social theory.

At the core of constructivist approaches is a concern with identity and interests and how these can change—a belief that ideas, values, norms, and shared beliefs matter, that how individuals talk about the world shapes practices, and that humans are capable of changing the world by changing ideas. Whereas realists treat states' interests and identity as given, constructivists believe they are socially constructed—that is, influenced by culture, norms, ideas, and domestic and international interactions. Thus, Germany after World War II reoriented its identity to multilateralism, embedding itself in the North Atlantic Treaty Organization and European institutions with the encouragement of the United States. Russia, too, struggled to redefine its identity in the aftermath of the collapse of the Soviet Union and is currently further redefining it. For constructivists, then, states do not have identities or national interests prior to interactions with others. As Alexander Wendt (1995: 81) explains, "the social construction of international politics is to analyze how processes of interaction produce and reproduce the social structures—cooperative or conflictual—that shape actors' identities and interests and the significance of their material contexts."

Constructivists place a great deal of importance on institutions as embodied in norms, practices, and formal organizations. The most important institution in international society is sovereignty, since it determines the identity of states. Yet constructivists criticize those who see sovereignty as unchanging and point to various transformations in understandings of sovereignty since Westphalia. To illustrate how sovereignty determines the identity of states, however, one need only consider how failed states such as Somalia retain their statehood and continue to be members of IGOs.

Among the key norms affecting state behavior is multilateralism. In *Multilateralism Matters,* Ruggie (1993b) and others examine how the shared expectations surrounding this norm affect the behavior of states. Several other studies have examined the impact of norms and principled beliefs on international outcomes, including the evolution of the international human rights regime (Risse, Ropp, and Sikkink 1999), the end of apartheid in South Africa (Klotz 1995), the spread of weapons taboos (Tannenwald 2007), and humanitarian intervention (Finnemore 2003).

In examining international organizations, constructivists seek to uncover the social content of organizations and the dominant norms that govern behavior and shape interests, and to decipher how these interests in turn influence actors. IOs then may serve as agents of social construction, as norm entrepreneurs trying to change social understandings (Finnemore and Sikkink 2001). They can be teachers as well as creators of norms, socializing states to accept new values and political goals (Finnemore 1996b). The UN Educational, Scientific, and Cultural Organization (UNESCO), for example, "taught" developing states the relevance of establishing science bureaucracies as a necessary component of being a modern state. The World Bank put the concept of poverty alleviation on international and national agendas in the late 1960s as it "sold" poverty alleviation to members through a mixture of persuasion and coercion, redefining in the process what states were supposed to do to ameliorate the situation.

For constructivists, then, IGOs in particular have real power. Michael Barnett and Martha Finnemore (2005: 162) argue that IGOs "construct the social world in which cooperation and choice take place. They help define the interests that states and other actors come to hold and do so in ways compatible with liberalism and a liberal global order. These are important exercises of power." In addition, Barnett and Finnemore note with respect to the role of IGO bureaucracies that the authority of these organizations and their secretariats "lies in their ability to present themselves as impersonal and neutral—as not exercising power but instead serving others" (2004: 21). Yet, as the same authors explore in case studies, the perception of IGOs as servants of their member states may be deceiving.

Constructivists are also concerned with the potential of international organizations to socialize individual policymakers and states. Jeffrey Checkel (2005) explores the different mechanisms, including strategic calculation, role-playing, and normative suasion, that connect organizations to socializing outcomes. When the norms of the institution become deeply rooted and thus internalized, actors' identities can be transformed and interests changed. Most of this research focuses on the socializing effects of EU membership on candidate members.

Thus, to constructivists, international organizations are purposive actors with independent effects on international relations. They have been important to the processes of changing understandings and behavior with respect to poverty, humanitarianism, colonialism, slavery, and other problems. Although most constructivists have focused on positive outcomes such as decolonization, human rights norms, and poverty alleviation, others have made us mindful that international organizations may also be dysfunctional and act in ways contrary to the interests of their constituents. They may pursue particularistic goals, competing over turf, budgets, and staff. Such dysfunctional behavior may create a bureaucratic culture that tolerates inefficient practices, lack of accountability, and mission-defeating behaviors (Barnett and Finnemore 1999).

## The English School

Emerging in the 1930s and rediscovered in the 1980s, the English School merges realism, liberalism, and constructivism. Its proponents argue that while the world is at its core a system of autonomous, sovereign states, these states are not always mutually antagonistic. Rather, they have developed a shared system of rules and procedures to deal with many issues. Much like drivers on a highway, they have come to agree on the "rules of the road," even though they do not necessarily trust each other to always comply with them.

Beginning with European states a few hundred years ago and gradually expanding to include all states, the end result can be called a "society"

(Bull 1977). The word is carefully chosen, since it falls somewhere between anarchy and community, even though some English School authors express doubts whether community is possible (Mayall 1982). Power plays a very important role in this society, but even the most powerful have accepted (however grudgingly) that there are limits to what they can do. States are ultimately linked and bound by a shared belief that international rules apply to all (Linklater and Suganami 2006: 51). The result is an orderly, albeit competitive, international environment.

For English School scholars, the "master," primary, or fundamental institutions include sovereignty, balance of power, international law, diplomacy, territoriality, and great-power management, but there is no firm definition (Buzan 2004; Wilson 2012). International organizations are intervening variables, defined, shaped, and constrained by the "master" institutions, especially international law. Law establishes the identity and role of the key players—in this case states—and establishes their rights and duties. Duties are paramount, since they constrain state behavior. These are found in such documents as the Charter of the United Nations and the Treaty of Rome, and in such rules as the prohibition on the use of force and the right of self-defense. For some, international organizations like the UN might be able to lead states to adopt a more universalist approach, perhaps even including a "responsibility to protect" civilians in other states from gross violations of human rights law committed by their own governments. In this sense, English School scholars agree with constructivists that identities and rules are ever-evolving, although usually at a glacial pace.

Criticism of the English School comes primarily from realists who argue that the approach gives too much primacy to rules and norms and not enough to power. Others find problematic the absence of a clear definition of institutions and a confused picture of the relationship between institutions and practices (Wilson 2012).

## Critical Theories

Critical theories comprise a diverse group of overarching theories of international relations that challenge conventional wisdom and provide alternative frameworks for understanding the world. Among the most prominent are Marxist and neo-Marxist theories, and their derivative, dependency theory. They challenge realism's focus on the primacy of power and the existing order, and liberalism's optimism about the benefits of expanding markets for peace and stability. Those rooted in Marxism share a historicism that drives questions of how the present international order came into being and what forces are at work to change it. Understanding how structural changes occur and the role of social forces is central.

## Marxist and Neo-Marxist Theories

Although Marxism was discredited with the demise of the Soviet Union and the triumph of capitalism, it is still an important perspective for describing the hierarchy in the international system and the role of economics in determining that hierarchy. It still influences the thinking of many in the developing world whose colonial past and experience with capitalism are characterized by poverty and economic disadvantage. Marxist and neo-Marxist critical theories contribute important perspectives to understanding IR and global governance through the frameworks they provide for linking politics, economics, social forces, and structures of order.

Like realism and liberalism, Marxism comprises a set of core ideas that unite its variants. These include a grounding in historical analysis, the primacy of economic forces in explaining political and social phenomena, the central role of the production process, the particular character of capitalism as a global mode of production, and the importance of social or economic class in defining actors. The evolution of the production process also is a basis for explaining the relationship between production, social relations, and power. According to Karl Marx, a clash would inevitably occur between the capitalist class (the bourgeoisie) and the workers (the proletariat). From that class struggle would come a new social order. Interpreting this in the context of international relations, Robert Cox (1986: 220) noted: "Changes in the organization of production generate new social forces which, in turn, bring about changes in the structure of states and . . . [alter] the problematic of world order."

Marxist views of the structure of the global system, and hence of global governance, are rooted in these ideas about the relationships of class, the capitalist mode of production, and power. The hierarchical structure is a byproduct of the spread of global capitalism that privileges some states, organizations, groups, and individuals, and imposes significant constraints on others. Thus, developed countries have expanded economically (and in an earlier era politically, through imperialism), enabling them to sell goods and export surplus wealth that they could not absorb at home. Simultaneously, developing countries have become increasingly constrained and dependent on the actions of the developed.

Variants of Marxism emphasize the techniques of domination and suppression that arise from the uneven economic development inherent in the capitalist system. The influence of an Italian Marxist, Antonio Gramsci (1891–1937), on critical theorists and some neoliberal institutionalists, however, has been considerable, given Gramsci's particular interpretation of hegemony as a relationship of consent to political and ideological leadership, not domination by force. Thus Cox (1992b: 140) argued that the foundation of hegemonic order "derives from the ways of doing and thinking of the dominant social strata of the dominant state or states . . . [with] the acquiescence of the dominant social strata of other states."

These views have important implications for neo-Marxist theorizing about contemporary global governance. For example, in Craig Murphy's view (2000: 799), global governance is "a predictable institutional response not to the interests of a fully formed class, but to the overall logic of industrial capitalism." Cox (1986) and Stephen Gill (1994) have emphasized the importance of "globalizing elites" in the restructuring of the global political economy, and hence in global governance. These elites are found in the key economic institutions (the IMF, WTO, and World Bank), in finance ministries of G-7 countries, in the headquarters of MNCs, in private international relations councils (e.g., the Council on Foreign Relations and Trilateral Commission), and in major business schools. True, however, to a classical Marxist dialectical process, transnational social forces backing neoliberalism are increasingly challenged by those resisting globalization, as well as by environmental, feminist, and other social movements that in Murphy's view (2000) constitute a new locus for class analysis and a potential source of future change.

Marxists and neo-Marxists view international law and organizations as products of dominant states, dominant ideas, and the interests of the capitalist class. Some view them as instruments of capitalist domination imposed on others. The Gramscian view sees international organizations as a means to get others to consent to domination through shared ideas. Murphy (1994) argues that they have been instrumental in the development of the modern capitalist state by facilitating industrial change and the development of liberal ideology. Cox (1992a: 3) also sees them as being concerned with "longer-term questions of global structural change and . . . how international organizations . . . can help shape that change in a consensually desirable direction."

Marxists and neo-Marxists are almost uniformly normative in their orientation. They see capitalism as "bad," its structure and mode of production as exploitative. They have clear positions about what should be done to ameliorate inequities. Thus they are proponents of major structural change in international relations.

## Dependency Theory

Dependency theorists, particularly those writing in the 1950s from Latin America, such as Raul Prebisch, Enzo Faletto, Fernando Henrique Cardoso, and Andre Gunder Frank, sought to understand why development was benefiting rich Northern countries, rather than the poorer South, and why that gap was widening. They hypothesized that the basic terms of trade were unequal between the developing and the developed world, partially as a consequence of the history of colonialism and neocolonialism, and partly because multinational corporations and international banks based in developed countries were hamstringing dependent states. The latter organizations were seen as helping to establish and maintain dependency relations. They were also viewed as agents of penetration, not benign actors as liberals would characterize them, nor as marginal actors as realists believe. Dependency theorists argue that public and private international organizations are able to forge transnational relationships with elites in the developing countries (the "comprador class"), linking domestic elites in both exploiter and exploited countries in a symbiotic relationship.

Many dependency theorists argued that the solution was to disengage national economies from the international economy, to foster industrial growth in the South through import substitution, to protect internal markets from competition, and to seek major changes in international economic institutions. Only when countries in the South had reached a certain level of development could they participate fully in the international economy. These views had strong appeal and shaped the agenda of developing countries in the United Nations during the 1960s and 1970s. In essence, dependency theorists argued that development could not take place without fundamental changes in international economic relations in order to redress inequalities of power and wealth.

Dependency theorists share the view of other Marxist-derived theories that international organizations are generally the tools of capitalist classes and states. Multinational corporations are, likewise, instruments of capitalist exploitation and mechanisms of domination that perpetuate underdevelopment.

Even with the demise of the Soviet Union, Marxism and its variants did not disappear. Some aspects of these critical theories have resurfaced in the debates over globalization, particularly among opponents of globalization, including those who oppose corporate control over the economy and those who are trying to strengthen protection for workers, small farmers, poor people, and women. Stagnating economic and social conditions and the widening gap between rich and poor globally have also fueled renewed interest in the perspectives that critical theories offer.

### Critical Feminism

Among the strains of critical theory are feminists who argue that studying gender involves more than just counting women in elite positions or cataloging programs targeting women. Rather, gender permeates all international structures. International relations, with its emphasis on states and international organizations engaged in diplomacy and war, denigrates the role of homes, families, and communities. Studying international relations as exclusively the public domain means that a whole range of private human activity is simply ignored, even though it is at the heart of development, human rights, human security, and identity (Peterson 2003).

Critical feminists are especially interested in highlighting how contemporary international economic rules—as enforced by the wealthiest states, the IMF, private bond-rating agencies such as Standard & Poor's, and private investors generally—create a unique burden on women. They argue that a neoliberal capitalist model of economic governance puts pressure on states to reduce social spending and reduce protections on local goods from foreign competition, with the immediate result that the poor are exposed to the ravages of global competition.

Critical theorists see women as particularly vulnerable to exploitation when the public sector fails to provide essential services or is adversely affected by globalization. They point to the fact that the overwhelming majority of trafficked persons are women. Women experience a double-exploitation due to the way the world economy is defined and managed. Even the "mainstreaming of women" in development programs, as advocated by liberal feminists, is too often overwhelmed, they argue, by the grand strategy of promoting economic liberalization and austerity (True 2011).

Critics, including other feminists, have challenged the misandrogynistic tone of some critical feminist writing, arguing that the exploitative structures they describe are not automatically the fault of men, but that both women and men are part of the problem and part of the solution. In particular, neoliberal economists emphasize the importance of market forces as a means of disciplining profligate states and promoting the efficient use of resources, both of which will benefit all citizens, including women. These are issues discussed in subsequent chapters.

### Securitization Studies

A new approach to global governance is primarily a critique of the increasing role of security in public policy generally. It began with criticisms of the "military-industrial complex" in the 1940s, arguing that states were exaggerating security threats in order to feed the financial needs of those involved in producing weapons (Lasswell 1941).

Since the terrorist attacks of September 11, 2001, however, there has been a sense on the part of many radical and constructivist scholars that governments and international organizations are defining almost every problem as a security issue, hence the term "securitization" (not to be confused with its use in finance and insurance). Although certain issues clearly have a security dimension, securitization scholars assert that states and international organizations seek to exercise increasing control over their political environment by proclaiming the issue as a matter of security. In so doing, they remove the object from traditional political constraints and exert extraordinary powers in its defense (Buzan, Waever, and de Wilde 1998).

The most obvious use of this authority involves control by states over telecommunications. The US National Security Agency's monitoring of transnational cell phone and e-mail communication, as revealed in 2013, was justified by governmental authorities as necessary to protect national security. The same was true of Great Britain's ubiquitous use of closed-circuit television cameras justified in the name of national security. Border controls, likewise, have been tightened for security reasons, even though the vast majority of migration occurs for economic reasons. This critique is especially relevant to global governance and international organization with the emergence of the human security umbrella for discussing a myriad of issues.

Proclaiming an issue a matter of security demands a person with legal or moral authority and a capacity to act on the statement. Yet some may be skeptical of that claim or reject it altogether. In the case of the Iraq War, members of the United Nations were skeptical of the US claim that the world's security depended on removing the Saddam Hussein regime from power. The George W. Bush administration largely failed to paint the situation as an existential threat. Likewise, although governments and international organizations have portrayed the effort to limit human and drug trafficking in some parts of the world as a way to promote security, the rhetoric has not always been accepted by local authorities (Jackson 2006).

Determining what is a threat to security also involves defining what it is that is threatened (the territory? the constitution? the leader?) and how societies should respond to such threats (buying bonds? volunteering for the military? debating?).

## Theories of Organizational Interactions

Interstate relations are not the only interactions that are important for understanding international cooperation and global governance. Relevant middle-level theories that provide insights relevant to studying interactions both among the various global governance actors and within specific organizations can also be found in sociology and economics. These theories see organizations as making choices and interacting with their environments.

### Interorganizational Processes

The proliferation of actors in global governance has made it imperative to study interorganizational relations. Sociologists have long contended that for all types of organizations, the most important part of the environment is their cooperative and conflictual relations with other organizations. Organizational interdependence emerges from the shared need for resources (money, specialized skills, and markets), overlapping missions, or the desire to add new specialties at reduced cost. In response, organizations may innovate to exclude rivals or increase coordination and cooperation. Thus, interorganization theorists examine how and why organizations, often working within the same environment or on the same type of problems, may both clash and cooperate.

Interorganization theorists are also interested in the dependence of one organization on another. For example, the UN Security Council needs both resources and information to fulfill its mission, and such dependence limits its autonomy. Similarly, the regional development banks may depend on the World Bank for cofinancing large projects, for setting development priorities, and for technical expertise. In the 1980s, for example, the African Development Bank found itself subservient to the World Bank, having fewer economic resources and a less visible field presence, and being the last to be repaid. This dependence was reinforced by the attitude of the African countries themselves (Mingst 1987: 291).

Coordination problems between and among IGOs, such as those among economic and social agencies within the UN system, or among NGOs such as the humanitarian relief groups, form another group of interorganizational problems. Chapter 4 explores how the UN's Economic and Social Council was intended to play a central, coordinating role for the system but has lacked the resources and clout to do so effectively. Humanitarian crises in the 1990s and the problem of too many groups trying to help led to the creation of the UN's Office for Coordination of Humanitarian Affairs (OCHA) in 1998 as the lead humanitarian agency coordinating efforts in the field.

### Networks

Part of understanding how organizations interact is recognizing that they may interact not just with each other, but also within broader social networks. The concept of networks comes from sociology, but has been appropriated into thinking about global governance. Harold Jacobson was the first to identify the relevance of networks for the field, as reflected in the title of his pathbreaking textbook *Networks of Interdependence: International Organizations and the Global Political System* (1984). The sociological literature on networks examines the various links between organizations and individuals (both private and public), domestically and internationally. Often there is a linchpin organization in the network, an organization able to mobilize coalitions on particular issues or control the process of bargaining. Such organizations have seldom been delegated such authority, but are able to legitimize their actions with respect to the specific issue area (Jönsson 1986).

Various types of networks, as introduced in Chapter 1, are examined throughout this book. Anne Marie Slaughter (2004), for example, looks at networks of government officials, judges, legislators, and police that make up what she calls the "new world order." Miles Kahler (2009: 3) examines networks as both structures and actors in global governance and networked politics as "new forms of governance in international relations." Anna Ohanyan (2012: 372, 377) links network theory and sociological institutionalism in a theoretical approach for studying NGOs and their positive or negative agency that she terms "network institutionalism." She argues that the network approach "is a useful bridge between the NGO studies and dominant IR theories that generally treat NGOs as inconsequential and marginal in world politics" (372). Network structure, she notes, matters in "shaping the extent of NGO autonomy and agency . . . [while] network institutionalism focuses on the network position of an NGO as an important variable that can explain the extent of NGO agency in world politics" (377).

Transnational advocacy networks have become increasingly important to global governance, as discussed in Chapter 6. Such networks share "the centrality of values or principled ideas, the belief that individuals can make a difference, the creative use of information, and the employment by nongovernmental actors of sophisticated political strategies in targeting their campaigns." They are "bound together by shared values, a common discourse, and dense exchanges of information and services" (Keck and Sikkink 1998: 2). These networks also try to set the terms of international and domestic debate, to influence international and state-level policy outcomes, and to alter the behavior of states, international organizations, and other interested parties. The International Campaign to Ban Landmines is one prominent example of a transnational advocacy network from the late 1990s. The human rights, environmental, and women's movements further illustrate the phenomenon. Network analysis encompasses both international and domestic actors and processes, and examines how individuals and groups are linked and what strategies they use to promote their goals.

## Principal-Agent Interactions

Economists' work on the theory of the firm has been expanded by those studying US government bureaucracies, and more recently has been adapted to the study of IGOs and NGOs. Principal-agent theorists posit that principals (in politics, decisionmakers) delegate authority to an agent (e.g., a bureaucracy), empowering the agent to act on behalf of the principals. Principals delegate such authority for a number of reasons: to benefit from the agent's specialized knowledge, enhance certitude, resolve disputes, or enhance their own credibility. Yet principals need to be careful of agent autonomy—that is, of the agents taking independent actions that the principals do not want taken. Much of the principal-agent literature discusses ways in which principals control agents (establishing rules, monitoring and reporting, inserting checks and balances) and ways in which agents can become independent, autonomous actors.

Scholars of international organizations (both IGOs and NGOs) have turned to principal-agent theory to examine how states as collective principals delegate authority and control to IGOs and the ways that the agents (both IGOs and NGOs) can exert autonomy (Hawkins et al. 2006; Oestreich 2012). The theory has been used to show how agents interpret mandates, reinterpret rules, expand permeability to third parties, and create barriers to principals' monitoring. Much of this literature to date has focused on a few IGOs, including the IMF, World Bank, and EU.

In using principal-agent theory, some writers have found that NGOs may be crucial intermediaries between states and IGOs, but not independent actors that change preferences (Lake and McCubbins 2006: 341, 368). Other writers suggest the ways that NGOs have agency—the ability to choose among different courses of action, learn from experience, and effect change, which may be both independent from states and also dysfunctional (Cooley and Ron 2002).

Like social constructivists, then, principal-agent theorists are concerned with examining the degree of independence and autonomy of international organizations. Although social constructivists explain autonomy by reference to authoritative bureaucracies, principal-agent theorists find that principals limit their agents and that agents act rationally and strategically to try to expand their authority.

### Intraorganizational Processes

Another group of middle-level theories focuses on what happens within organizations themselves. Two have particular relevance for the study of global governance actors: theories of organizational culture, and theories of organizational adaptation and learning.

*Organizational culture.* Over time, organizations tend to develop cultures of their own, independent from and different than the cultures of their individual members. During the 1970s, sociologists and anthropologists began to study these cultures rather than seeing organizations only as technical, rational, impersonal mechanisms. During the 1980s, it became popular to think of organizations as autonomous sites of power, with their own particular cultures, norms, and values. Thus, organizations might become agents themselves, not just structures through which actors operate. Organization theorists, therefore, created typologies of organizational cultures and showed how these can change over time (Hawkins 1997). Some IR scholars have borrowed the notion of organizational culture, suggesting that bureaucracies develop cultures that influence state preferences. This counters the realist view that preferences are exogenously determined.

International organization scholars, particularly constructivists, have also seized upon the notion of organizational culture, believing that "the rules, rituals, and beliefs that are embedded in the organization (and its subunits) . . . [have] important consequences for the way individuals who inhabit that organization make sense of the world" (Barnett and Finnemore 1999: 719). For example, the practice of UN peacekeeping includes sets of rules designed to maximize the probability of success. Those rules, including requirements of consent and impartiality, were embedded in the peacekeeping culture of the UN and have provided one explanation why the UN Secretariat misperceived the unfolding genocide in Rwanda in 1994 (Barnett and Finnemore 2004). The World Bank has also been shown to have a distinctive organizational culture, since over half of its professional staff have graduate degrees in economics or finance from US or British institutions (Weaver 2008: 77). Organizational cultures, then, explain some organizational behaviors, although those cultures are subject to slow change.

*Organizational adaptation and learning.* Organization theorists have also been particularly interested in examining how organizations evolve. Ernst Haas (1990) delineates two such processes. In the first, organizations adapt by adding new activities to their agendas without actually examining or changing underlying bases of the organization and its values. The organization muddles through and change occurs incrementally. Such was the case when the UN took on added peacekeeping tasks in the early 1990s, including election monitoring, humanitarian aid delivery, and protection of populations threatened by ethnic cleansing and genocide. Only with the failures in Somalia and Bosnia did the UN Secretariat and UN member states look seriously at the lessons to be learned from the incremental, unplanned changes.

The second kind of change process is based on the premise that organizations can, in fact, learn. With learning, members or staff question earlier beliefs and develop new processes. Thus, learning involves redefinition of organizational purposes, reconceptualization of problems, articulation of new ends, and organizational change based upon new, underlying consensual knowledge. Such has been the case with the evolution of World Bank programs from an initial emphasis on infrastructure projects to poverty alleviation and good governance, discussed in Chapter 9, as well as with the evolution of UN peacekeeping, as discussed in Chapter 7. Other examples abound.

Organizational theories from both sociology and economics enable us to probe deeper within specific institutions of global governance by helping us understand both the interorganizational and intraorganizational processes. Increasingly, scholars are using multiple theoretical perspectives, enhancing our knowledge in new ways.

## IR Theory and Global Governance

One of the unanswered puzzles is that despite the fact that multilateral diplomacy and institutions became dominant forms of interaction in the twentieth century, multilateralism is generally neglected in IR theory (Caporaso 1993: 51). As we have seen, neoliberals and neorealists, in particular, have attempted to explain cooperation and the conditions under which cooperation becomes multilateral and institutionalized through international regimes. Constructivist approaches that look at processes of persuasion, discussion, and argumentation contribute further to these understandings. Constructivists have also contributed to our knowledge about how norms, ideas, and beliefs affect outcomes. Critical theories provide perspectives on contemporary structures of global governance; they and neorealist theory share a concern for the role of power and powerful actors. Liberalism and its middle-level derivatives, however, form the foundation for much global governance theorizing.

Subsequent chapters utilize these various theories when appropriate. In Chapters 3 and 5, functionalism explains much of the history of specialized organizations and the EU. In Chapters 7 through 11, specific international regimes are examined, along with their major principles, rules, and decisionmaking processes. In Chapter 7, realist theory helps us understand the difficulties that international institutions have in addressing threats to peace and security. Chapters 8 and 9 consider how hegemonic stability, great-power concert theories, and critical perspectives have affected efforts to address economic issues. In Chapter 10, liberal theory and constructivism contribute to understanding the evolution of human rights norms. In Chapter 11, collective goods theory forms a central focus for international efforts to address environmental problems. Throughout the book, middle-level interorganizational and intraorganizational theories help us understand how different organizations function and the connections among different actors and their roles.

## Suggested Further Reading

Baldwin, David A., ed. (1993) *Neorealism and Neoliberalism: The Contemporary Debate*. New York: Columbia University Press.
Barnett, Michael, and Martha Finnemore. (2004) *Rules for the World: International Organizations in Global Politics*. Ithaca: Cornell University Press.

Buzan, Barry. (2004) *From International to World Society? English School Theory and the Social Structure of Globalisation.* Cambridge: Cambridge University Press.

Hawkins, Darren G., David A. Lake, Daniel L. Nielson, and Michael J. Tierney, eds. (2006) *Delegation and Agency in International Organizations.* Cambridge: Cambridge University Press.

Rittberger, Volker, ed., with Peter Mayer. (1993) *Regime Theory and International Relations.* Oxford: Clarendon.

Sinclair, Timothy J. (2012) *Global Governance.* Cambridge: Polity.

Wendt, Alexander. (1995) "Constructing International Politics." *International Security* 20, no. 1 (Summer): 71–81.

# 3

# IGOs and the Foundations of Global Governance

**Political communities throughout history have tried to** establish norms and rules for interacting with their neighbors. The Greek city-states, for example, sought to establish permanent protective alliances to address conflict issues and to follow established rules. The Hanseatic League (1200s–1400s) was formed to facilitate trade and the interaction among a group of Northern European cities on the Baltic and North Seas. Similarly, the Kingdom of Naples and Sicily, the Papal States, and the city-states of Florence, Venice, and Milan established a system for regularizing diplomacy and commercial interaction in the fourteenth and fifteenth centuries. Many of these early practices persisted as the contemporary state system evolved, providing some foundation for the later development of other, more institutionalized forms of governance.

## The State System and Its Weaknesses: The Process of International Organization

International relations scholars date the contemporary state system from 1648, when the Treaty of Westphalia ended the Thirty Years War. Although most of the more than 100 articles of the treaty dealt with allocating the spoils of war, other provisions proved pathbreaking. Articles 64, 65, and 67 established several key principles of a new state system: territorial sovereignty; the right of the state (prince or ruler) to choose its religion and determine its own domestic policies; and the prohibition of interference from supranational authorities like the Catholic Church or Holy Roman Empire. The treaty marked the end of rule by religious authority in Europe and the emergence of secular states. With secular authority came the principle of the territorial integrity of states that were legally equal and sovereign participants in the international system.

Sovereignty was the core concept in this state system. As French philosopher Jean Bodin (1530–1596) stated, sovereignty is "the distinguishing mark of the sovereign that he cannot in any way be subject to the commands of another, for it is he who makes law for the subject, abrogates law already made, and amends obsolete law" (1967: 25). Although there is no supreme arbiter among states, Bodin acknowledged that sovereignty may be limited by divine law or natural law, by the type of regime, or even by promises to the people.

It was during this period that Hugo Grotius, the early Dutch legal scholar discussed in Chapter 2, rejected the concept that states have complete freedom to do whatever they wish. Thus, even in the seventeenth century, the meaning of state sovereignty was contested. More recently, Stephen Krasner (1993: 235) has argued: "The actual content of sovereignty, the scope of authority that states can exercise, has always been contested. The basic organizing principle of sovereignty—exclusive control over territory—has been persistently challenged by the creation of new institutional forms that better meet specific national needs." Although breaches of sovereignty occur continuously through treaties, contracts, coercion, and imposition, Krasner asserts that there is no alternative conception of international system organization. Other scholars such as James Rosenau (1997: 217–236) see states as vulnerable to demands from below—decentralizing tendencies including domestic constituencies and nonstate actors—and from above, including globalization processes and international organizations. They have to contend with a variety of new actors and processes that confound and constrain them, limiting authority and challenging the whole notion of state sovereignty, and hence the state system based on the principle. Even then–UN Secretary-General Kofi Annan said in his 1999 address to the UN General Assembly, "State sovereignty, in its most basic sense, is being redefined by the forces of globalization and international cooperation" (Annan 1999). As yet another scholar, Kalevi Holsti (2004: 138), has pointed out, however: "State capacity in the contemporary world varies greatly from the very weak to the very strong. But that does not make them less or more sovereign."

As described in Chapter 2, the nature of the contemporary state system and state sovereignty is a matter of dispute among IR theorists. Yet the weaknesses of the state system became increasingly apparent during the nineteenth century with growing international trade, migration, democratization, technological innovation, and other developments that increased interdependence and highlighted the limitations imposed by states' sovereignty. These changes gave rise to the process of international *organization*—the historical process that "represents a secular trend toward the systematic development of an enterprising quest for political means of making the world safe for human habitation" (Claude 1964: 405). The concrete manifestations of that process, which continues today, have been the creation of international *organizations* and particularly intergovernmental organizations.

This chapter provides a historical overview of that process of international organization since the mid–nineteenth century. It is a process that has been propelled and shaped not only by the weaknesses of the state system but also by major power wars, technological changes, economic development and growing interdependence, and now globalization, the decolonization process that ended European imperial rule over much of Latin America, Asia, and Africa, and the emergence of a host of governance challenges in the late twentieth and early twenty-first centuries. Subsequent chapters provide greater depth on the United Nations system, regional organizations, and nongovernmental organizations.

## Early Governance Innovations:
## The Legacy of the Nineteenth Century

In the nineteenth century, the process of international organization was stimulated by a number of key trends. The defeat of Napoleon in 1815 ended the upheavals that followed the French Revolution and Napoleon's effort to create a French empire in Europe. The emergence of five major European powers—Austria-Hungary, Britain, France, Prussia, and Russia—ushered in an era of relative peace that lasted for almost a century. Industrialization, beginning in England, spread to all parts of the continent, resulting in expanded commerce and trade among the European countries and between European states and their colonies. Technological innovations such as the telegraph gave rise to practical problems in interstate relations and the need to establish common standards. State-to-state interactions became more frequent and intense while the spread of democratic ideas empowered people to organize nongovernmental groups to address humanitarian needs, workers' rights, and private business interests.

In a pioneering textbook on international organization, *Swords Into Plowshares,* Inis Claude (1964) describes three major innovations of governance that emerged in the nineteenth century: the Concert of Europe, public international unions, and the Hague Conferences.

### The Concert of Europe

The first innovation was the Concert of Europe, established in 1815—a concert of major European powers making systemwide decisions by negotiation and consensus. Members agreed to coordinate behavior based on certain rights and responsibilities, with expectations of diffuse reciprocity. They still operated as separate states and societies, but within a framework of rules and consultation without creating a formal organization.

The concert system involved the practice of periodic multilateral meetings among the major European powers for the purpose of settling problems and coordinating actions. Meeting over thirty times in the century preceding World War I, the major powers constituted a club of the like-minded, dictating the conditions of entry for other would-be participants. They legitimized the independence of new European states such as Belgium and Greece in the 1820s. At the last of the concert meetings, which took place in Berlin in 1878, they divided up the previously uncolonized parts of Africa, extending the reach of European imperialism.

Although these concert meetings were not institutionalized and included no explicit mechanism for implementing collective action, they solidified important practices that later international organizations followed. These included multilateral consultation, collective diplomacy, and special status for "great powers." As Claude (1964: 22) summarizes, "The Concert system was the manifestation of a rudimentary but growing sense of interdependence and community of interest among the states of Europe." Such a community of interest was a vital prerequisite for modern international organizations and broader global governance.

The concert idea of mutual consultations among major powers and special responsibilities, necessitated by a growing community of interests, was the inspiration for the League of Nations Council as well as the UN Security Council and particularly for the concept of five permanent members with the special privilege of veto power. It can be seen in management of the international gold standard and in the Group of Seven, established in the 1970s initially to coordinate the macroeconomic policies of the major developed states and later broadened with Russia's inclusion (with the G-7 becoming the G-8) to encompass a range of issues from terrorism to Africa's lagging development.

### Public International Unions

Public international unions were the second important nineteenth-century organizational innovation. Agencies were initially established among European states to deal with problems stemming from the industrial revolution, expanding commerce, communications, and technological innovation. These functional problems involved such concerns as health standards for travelers, shipping rules on the Rhine River, increased mail volume, and the cross-boundary usage of the newly invented telegraph.

Many of these practical problems of expanding international relations among states proved amenable to resolution with intergovernmental cooperation. The International Telegraph Union (ITU) was formed in 1865 and the Universal Postal Union (UPU) in 1874; each was instrumental in facilitating communication, transportation, and hence commerce. With growing levels of interdependence, the European states had found it necessary to cooperate on a voluntary basis to accomplish nonpolitical tasks. Almost immediately, these began to include non-European states (and some colonial territories such as India).

Because the ITU and UPU were among the first IGOs to be established, they set a number of precedents. Both were based on international conventions that called for periodic conferences of parties to the convention. The delegates, however, came from telegraph and postal administrations of the parties, not ministries of foreign affairs—establishing the pattern of involving technical experts when dealing with technical matters. Thus, multilateral diplomacy was no longer the exclusive domain of traditional diplomats. Both organizations, along with subsequent public international unions, established international bureaus or secretariats composed of permanent staff hired from a variety of countries. They also created councils consisting of representatives of a few selected members to function as policy directorates on behalf of the organization in the intervals between general conferences. As Claude (1964: 32) notes, "Thus was established the structural pattern of bureau, council, and conference which, with many elaborations but few deviations, serves as the blueprint of international organization today." In addition, the public unions developed the techniques for multilateral conventions—lawmaking or rulemaking treaties—through the periodic revisions of the telegraph and postal regulations. Thus, public international unions and organizations dedicated to defined nonpolitical tasks gave rise to functionalism and specialized IGOs helping states deal with practical problems in their international relations, as discussed in Chapter 2.

## The Hague System

The third governance innovation in the nineteenth century was the concept of generalized conferences in which all states were invited to participate in problem solving. In 1899 and 1907, Czar Nicholas II of Russia convened two conferences in The Hague (Netherlands), involving both European and non-European states, to think proactively about what techniques states should have available to prevent war and under what conditions arbitration, negotiation, and legal recourse would be appropriate (Aldrich and Chinkin 2000). Exploration of such issues in the absence of a crisis was a novelty.

The Hague Conferences led to the Convention for the Pacific Settlement of International Disputes, ad hoc international commissions of inquiry, and the Permanent Court of Arbitration. The institutionalization of the latter was the culmination of the widespread practice of inserting clauses into treaties calling for arbitration should disputes arise among parties. The Permanent Court of Arbitration (1899), composed of jurists selected by each country from which members of arbitral tribunals are chosen, remains in existence and has been used extensively for handling boundary, investment, and other disputes involving states, corporations, and other nonstate actors.

The Hague Conferences also produced several major procedural innovations. This was the first time that participants included both small and non-European states, with all given equal voice. Twenty-six states participated in the first conference, including China, Siam, the Ottoman Empire, Mexico, and Japan. The second conference had forty-five participating states, adding almost all the Latin American states and thereby establishing the twin principles of universality and legal equality of states. What had been largely a European state system until the end of the nineteenth century became a truly international system at the beginning of the twentieth century. For the first time, participants utilized such techniques as electing chairs, organizing committees, and taking roll call votes, all of which became permanent features of twentieth-century organizations. The Hague Conferences also promoted the novel ideas of common interests of humankind and the codification of international law.

With the outbreak of World War I in 1914, a third Hague Conference was never convened. Yet the first two, along with numerous other conferences held during the nineteenth century, represented the first collective efforts to address problems of war, emergencies, and issues arising from new technologies and greater commerce on a regular, universal basis.

Nineteenth-century innovations, therefore, served as vital foundations for the development of twentieth century IGOs and the broader notion of global governance in the twenty-first century. States established new approaches to dealing with problems of joint concern, including the great-power multilateralism of the concert system, the functional and specialized public international unions, and the broader legalistic institutions of the Hague system. Innovative organs were created, innovative procedures were developed, and participation was broadened beyond the European states.

Alongside the development of these foundations for intergovernmental organizations, there were also important nongovernmental initiatives. These included the establishment of international peace societies, the International Committee of the Red Cross, the international labor movement, and the International Chamber of Commerce. This history is discussed further in Chapter 6.

Despite these developments, the institutional arrangements of the nineteenth century proved inadequate for preventing war among the major European powers. High levels of interdependence and cooperation in numerous areas of interest proved insufficient to prevent the outbreak of World War I, pointing vividly to the weaknesses and shortcomings of the nineteenth-century arrangements and the state system itself. Yet the war had barely begun when private groups and prominent individuals in both

Europe and the United States began to plan a more permanent framework to prevent future wars. NGOs such as the League to Enforce Peace, in the United States, and the League of Nations Society and Fabians, in Great Britain, played active roles in pushing for the creation of a new international organization and drafting plans for it. There were also French and British government committees appointed to consider the form of a new institution. US president Woodrow Wilson based his own proposal for a permanent international organization on some of these plans. The League of Nations expanded those foundations and set many important precedents.

## The League of Nations

*League principles.* The League of Nations first and foremost reflected the environment in which it was conceived. Ten of the League Covenant's twenty-six provisions focused on preventing war. Two basic principles were paramount: member states agreed to respect and preserve the territorial integrity and political independence of states; and members agreed to try different methods of dispute settlement, but failing that, the League was given the power under Article 16 to enforce settlements through sanctions. The second principle was firmly embedded in the proposition of collective security: that aggression by one state should be countered by all acting together as a "league of nations."

Although the Covenant's primary focus was on maintaining peace, it also recognized the desirability of economic and social cooperation, but established no machinery for carrying out such activities except in the provision for one or more organizations to secure "fair and humane conditions of labour for men, women and children" (Article 23). The Covenant also envisioned the desirability of bringing all public international unions under the League's direction, but this did not happen.

*League organs.* The Covenant of the League of Nations established three permanent organs—the Council, Assembly, and Secretariat—as well as two autonomous organizations, the Permanent Court of International Justice (PCIJ) and the International Labour Organization (ILO). The Council was composed of four permanent members (Great Britain, France, Italy, and Japan) and four elected members. Because the Covenant permitted the Council and Assembly to change both categories of membership, membership varied between eight and fifteen states. Germany, for example, gained permanent Council membership when it joined the League in 1926, as did the Soviet Union in 1934. The failure of the United States to ratify the Treaty of Versailles meant that it never assumed its seat. The Council was to settle disputes, enforce sanctions, supervise mandates, formulate disarmament plans, approve Secretariat appointments, and implement peaceful settlements. League members agreed to submit disputes to arbitration, adjudication, or the Council if they could not reach negotiated agreements. They agreed also to register all treaties with the League Secretariat (thus eliminating secret agreements). If states resorted to war, the Council had the authority under Article 16 to apply diplomatic and economic sanctions. Although the requirement of unanimity made action very difficult to achieve, the Council was clearly a lasting remnant of the European concert system.

The League's Assembly was a quasi-legislative body that met annually and consisted of representatives of all member states (sixty at the peak), each with one vote. It was authorized to admit new members, approve the budget, elect the nonpermanent members to the Council, and act on matters referred by the Council. Beginning with its first session in 1919, the Assembly established a number of precedents, such as requiring the League's Secretary-General to submit an annual report on the activities of the organization, engaging in general debate involving speeches by heads of delegations, and creating six committees to consider important matters between annual sessions (all practices continued by the UN General Assembly). Decisions within committees were by majority, in contrast to decisions within the Assembly itself, which required unanimity. Strict unanimity was tempered, however, by special procedures requiring less-than-majority votes. In practice, states generally preferred to abstain rather than block action. In addition to the main committees, the Assembly set up various other advisory committees dealing with health, drug traffic, slavery, trafficking in women, child welfare, transit, economics and finance, and intellectual cooperation. At the time, the League's Assembly was considered quite revolutionary and over time its activities drew even more attention than the Council.

The Covenant established the Secretariat but provided few instructions on its responsibilities. More a clearinghouse for relevant information, the Secretariat had little independent authority. Still, it became the first truly international civil service, with its members independent of the member states. The first League Secretary-General, Sir Eric Drummond (1919–1933), was considered an excellent administrator, but he chose not to undertake political initiatives and, by playing a limited role, avoided the kinds of political pressures to which later UN Secretaries-General have been subject. The Secretariat provided coordination for some twenty organizations that were affiliated with the League to some degree, including the Health Organization, the Mandates Commission, the ILO, and the PCIJ.

*Successes and failures.* The League did enjoy a number of successes, many of them concerned with European territorial issues. It conducted plebiscites in Silesia and the Saar and then demarcated the German-Polish border. It settled a number of territorial disputes, including those between Finland and Russia, and Bulgaria and Greece. In the latter case, the Council agreed to send military observers to oversee a cease-fire and troop withdrawal and established a commission of inquiry to recommend terms of settlement.

The League was successful in establishing and overseeing the mandate system under which former German colonies in Africa and the Pacific and non-Turkish territories of the former Ottoman Empire were administered by Great Britain, France, South Africa, Belgium, Australia, New Zealand, and Japan under the League's supervision. The League's Mandates Commission, composed of nongovernmental representatives, reviewed annual reports submitted by the colonial powers about conditions in the mandates.

Most important, the League was the first permanent international organization of a general political nature with continuously functioning political, economic, social, judicial, and administrative machinery. It embodied the twentieth-century idea that the international community could and should act against international lawbreakers and promote cooperation on a wide range of international problems.

Overall, the League fell far short of expectations, in large part because it was based on the principle of voluntary cooperation and because the sovereignty of its member states remained intact. As LeRoy Bennett (1995: 41) puts it, "As long as all members realized mutual advantages through cooperation, the League provided them with a useful avenue for achieving their common goals." When first Japan, then Italy and Germany, challenged the status quo, "the League mirrored the lack of cooperative will among its members." The failure to act when Japan invaded Manchuria in 1931 pointed to the organization's fundamental weaknesses: the Council's refusal to take decisive action, and the unwillingness of either Great Britain or France to institute military action or economic sanctions. The Council's delayed response to Italy's invasion of Ethiopia, a League member, in 1935, further undermined its legitimacy. Fifty of the fifty-four members of the League Assembly concurred with cutting off credit to the Italian economy and stopping arms sales, but these measures were insufficient to make Italy retreat, and by 1936 all sanctions against Italy were abandoned. The League neither intervened in the Spanish civil war nor opposed Hitler's remilitarization of the Rhineland and occupation of Austria and Czechoslovakia. With the great powers unwilling to uphold the League's principles, the institution's power and legitimacy deteriorated.

The League of Nations was also unable to respond to the economic depression of the 1930s. Proposals to reorganize the League's structures to address the economic and social issues did not come to fruition, although they did influence the League's successor: the United Nations.

In sum, the League enjoyed a number of successes but failed in some critical respects. Its close association with the unjust peace of World War I and the Treaty of Versailles hamstrung the organization from the outset. While absence of the United States from League membership proved a critical weakness, it was the unwillingness of other major powers, most notably Britain and France, to uphold the League's principles and to respond to overt aggression by Japan, Italy, and Germany that doomed the League as an instrument of collective security. Some would also argue that the very idea of collective security was impractical and overly idealistic in a world of sovereign states. The Covenant itself contained a number of gaps, although none that could be considered fatal flaws.

Between 1935 and 1939, many members withdrew, and the League was silent during the six years of World War II, from 1939 to 1945. Its members convened one final time, in April 1946, to terminate the organization and transfer its assets to the new United Nations.

### The Emergence of a Common Core of IGO Structures

Despite its shortcomings, the League of Nations represented an important step forward in the process of international organization and in global governance. Thus, early in World War II, many people recognized the need to begin planning for a new organization, albeit one whose scope was far greater than the League's. This planning began shortly after the United States entered the war in 1941 and built on the lessons of the League in laying the groundwork for its successor, the United Nations (Grigorescu 2005). Even before the war ended, a number of other specialized international organizations were established, including the Food and Agriculture Organization (FAO), the UN Relief and Rehabilitation Agency (UNRRA), the World Bank, and the International Monetary Fund (IMF). Shortly after World War II, still other IGOs were established in a number of regions around the world.

Over time, it became evident that one of the major trends of the twentieth century was the development of numerous international organizations, both small and large, general purpose and specialized, governmental and nongovernmental, global, regional, and transregional, to serve disparate goals and manage disparate needs, as shown in Figure 3.1.

Cumulatively, precedents set by the Concert of Europe, the public international unions, the Hague Conferences, and the League of Nations established the basic structural forms for the majority of international organizations and particularly IGOs. These include a limited membership council; an assembly of all member states wherein each state has one vote—signifying the internationalization of the democratic principle of equal representation of all members, regardless of size, wealth, or power; and a secretariat to provide administrative services, implement programs, and serve as institutional continuity. The councils in some IGOs, such as the

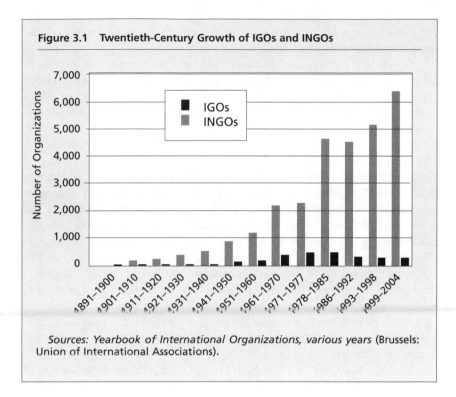

Figure 3.1    Twentieth-Century Growth of IGOs and INGOs

Sources: *Yearbook of International Organizations, various years* (Brussels: Union of International Associations).

UN Security Council, the European Union Council, and the executive boards of the World Bank and IMF, do not operate on the principle of one-state, one-vote, but have provisions for weighted or qualified voting such as Security Council permanent members' veto power. Not all full membership entities labeled "assembly" or "general assembly" or "conference" are alike. Although many are like the League Assembly in being made up of representatives of all member states, some are like the African Union's Assembly of Heads of State and Government—an entity that functions at the summit level only. Among regional organizations, only the Organization of American States has a general assembly modeled on the League and UN assemblies. A number of regional organizations have parliamentary bodies, although they differ in fundamental ways—e.g. NATO, the EU, Mercosur, and the AU. A number also have judicial bodies as discussed later in the chapter.

Thus, as one studies various IGOs, one sees commonalities in structures, decisionmaking processes, and some functions such as assemblies approving organizational budgets and electing executive heads. Yet one also must be attuned to the differences between and among organizations. As illustrated earlier, use of the term "assembly" does not necessarily mean that two entities with the same name in different organizations will have the same composition or functions.

Subsequent sections of this chapter will briefly examine the establishment of the United Nations, the expansion of functional and specialized organizations both within and outside the UN system, and the growth of international courts. The emergence of regional and transregional organizations is the subject of Chapter 5.

### The United Nations System

The establishment of the United Nations in the closing days of World War II was an affirmation of the desire of war-weary nations for a general international organization that could help them avoid future conflicts and promote international economic and social cooperation. In many important ways, the structure of the UN was patterned after that of the League of Nations, with changes made where lessons had been learned. For example, the League's Council could act only with unanimous agreement; the UN Security Council, while requiring the support of all five permanent members, requires only a majority of the nonpermanent members to take action. The UN Charter also built on lessons from the public international unions, conference diplomacy, and Hague Conference dispute settlement mechanisms.

The Atlantic Charter of August 14, 1941—a joint declaration by US president Franklin Roosevelt and British prime minister Winston Churchill calling for collaboration on economic issues and a permanent system of security—was the foundation for the "Declaration by the United Nations" in January 1942. Twenty-six nations affirmed the principles of the Atlantic Charter and agreed to create a new universal organization to replace the League of Nations. The UN Charter was then drafted in two sets of meetings between August and October 1944 at Dumbarton Oaks in Washington, DC. The participants agreed that the organization would be based on the principle of the sovereign equality of members, with all "peace-loving" states eligible for membership, thereby excluding the Axis powers—Germany, Italy, Japan, and Spain. It was further agreed (though not without some strong dissension) that decisions on security issues would require unanimity of the permanent members of the Security Council, the great powers. There was also consensus on broadening the scope of the new organization beyond that of the League, and President Roosevelt early on sought to ensure domestic support for US participation.

When the United Nations Conference on International Organization convened in San Francisco on April 25, 1945, delegates from the fifty participating states modified and finalized what had already been negotiated among the great powers. On July 28, 1945, with Senate approval, the United States became the first country to ratify the UN Charter. It took only three months for a sufficient number of countries to ratify the document. As one conference participant noted after the UN Charter was signed: "One of the most significant features was the demonstration of the large area of agreement which existed from the start among the 50 nations. . . . Not a single reservation was made to the charter when it was adopted. . . . The conference will long stand as one of the landmarks in international diplomacy" (Padelford 1945).

The UN Charter and the core principles that it incorporates as well as the major organs and their functioning are discussed in Chapter 4. Four of the UN's principal organs were patterned after those of the League of Nations: the Security Council, General Assembly, Secretariat, and International Court of Justice. The UN Charter remedied a major gap in the League Covenant by creating the Economic and Social Council (ECOSOC) and it carried the mandates system forward under the Trusteeship Council. As Chapter 4 also explores in depth, the UN is a complex system with many parts and many functions, making it the centerpiece of global governance since its inception, despite its many weaknesses. Other IGOs have been created within the UN system, such as the UN Conference on Trade and Development, and the International Atomic Energy Agency, as well as countless programs and committees. It has sponsored global conferences and summits; it serves as a catalyst for global policy networks and partnerships with nonstate actors.

Among the core elements of the UN system are nineteen specialized agencies, including the first two public international unions: the ITU and UPU. The number and nature of such specialized and functional organizations has greatly expanded over the course of the past century and many are not linked to the UN system.

## The Expansion of Functional
## and Specialized Organizations

The establishment of single-function IGOs to address specific issues such as health, economics, trade, labor issues, and environmental threats mirrors a pattern carried over from national governments. Over time, other organizations have been created to address still more specialized problems in response to the emergence of new issues and unmet needs. Thus the numbers of functional and specialized IGOs have increased exponentially since the mid–nineteenth century.

In line with functionalist theory, functional organizations were once perceived to be nonpolitical, with technical experts in a given field working out solutions to problems among the member states. Staying above politics, however, is not always possible, since the issues such IGOs deal with are not merely technical, but can touch at the core of state sovereignty and deeply political concerns, especially as rules and regulations expand. Nonetheless, they retain their functional, specialized character and are important elements of global governance, forming the institutional core for governance activities on a given set of issues.

The founders of the UN envisaged that functional agencies would play key roles in activities aimed at economic and social advancement. Therefore, Articles 57 and 63 of the UN Charter call for the affiliation with the United Nations of various specialized organizations established by separate intergovernmental agreements with "wide international responsibility" in economics, health, food, educational, and cultural fields. Today, the nineteen specialized agencies formally affiliated with the UN through agreements with ECOSOC and the General Assembly, like the UN itself, have global rather than regional responsibilities, but have separate charters, memberships, budgets, and secretariats as well as their own interests and constituencies. (See Chapter 4 for further discussion and Figure 4.2 for a full list of UN specialized agencies.) There are also a significant number of functional organizations within the UN system that are not classified as specialized agencies, as they have been established by the UN itself and report to the Security Council or General Assembly. And there are a wide variety of other specialized, functional organizations. Some are regional in scope; others have been formed by countries with shared interests in specific issues. Figure 3.2 illustrates the variety of functional organizations.

The evolution of governance and core functional IGOs in six major areas of activity are discussed here, with others discussed in subsequent chapters. Efforts to address health, communications, and labor issues began in the nineteenth century, while those for economic, refugee, agriculture, and food issues developed during the twentieth century. This evolutionary process continues, as later chapters detail.

### Health and the World Health Organization

One of the oldest areas of functional activity is health, an issue that respects no national boundaries. In medieval times, as trade expanded between Europe and East Asia, epidemics followed trade routes. European discovery of the Americas brought diseases like smallpox, measles, and yellow fever to the Western Hemisphere. Increased trade and travel in nineteenth-century Europe accelerated the spread of deadly diseases across national borders and populations. Clearly, no one state could solve health problems alone. Cooperation was required.

In response to a cholera outbreak in Europe, the first International Sanitary Conference was convened in Paris in 1851 to develop a collective response based on increased knowledge about public health and medicine and improvements in sanitation. Between 1851 and 1903, a series of eleven

---

**Figure 3.2    Functional Intergovernmental Organizations (representative)**

---

- *Functional Organizations Related to the United Nations*
  Food and Agriculture Organization
  International Atomic Energy Agency
  International Civil Aviation Organization
  International Labour Organization
  International Maritime Organization
  International Telecommunications Union
  UN High Commissioner for Refugees
  Universal Postal Union
  World Health Organization
  World Meteorological Organization

- *Other Functional Organizations*
  International Coffee Organization
  International Whaling Commission
  Northwest Atlantic Fisheries Organization
  Organization of Petroleum Exporting Countries
  World Trade Organization

- *Regional Functional Organizations*
  African Development Bank
  Arab Monetary Fund
  Economic Community of West African States
  Mekong River Commission
  Pan American Health Organization

---

such conferences developed procedures to prevent the spread of contagious and infectious diseases.

In 1907 the Office International d'Hygiène Publique (OIHP) was created, with a mandate to disseminate information on communicable diseases such as cholera, plague, and yellow fever. More than a decade later, at the request of the League of Nations Council, an international health conference met to prepare for a permanent international health organization. The OIHP did not become part of this new health organization, but remained a distinct organization with its own secretariat.

In 1948, a single health organization, the World Health Organization (WHO), came into being as a UN specialized agency. The principal decisionmaking body is the World Health Assembly (WHA), which is composed of three delegates from each member state, the majority of whom are medical doctors or come from health or related government ministries. This reflects the pattern set by the ITU and UPU as the first public international unions and gives meetings a professional atmosphere that differs greatly from that of the UN General Assembly. Typical of most IGOs, each country has one vote and decisions are made either by simple majority or by a two-thirds majority in the case of important questions. The WHA meets annually in contrast to the assemblies and conferences of many other functional organizations. As the legislative body of the WHO, it approves international regulations concerning sanitary and quarantine requirements and standards for diagnostic procedures as well as for biological, pharmaceutical, and other products; it controls the WHO's budget, appoints the director-general, elects members of the executive board, and sets policies. The WHA has occasionally adopted more symbolic resolutions that urge member states to take certain types of actions. Examples include the resolutions initiating WHO campaigns to eradicate smallpox (1959) and polio (1988). The executive board is a smaller group of thirty-four technically qualified individuals elected by the WHA for three year terms. By "gentlemen's agreement," at least three of the UN Security Council members are supposed to be represented. The board sets WHA agendas and resolutions to be considered and oversees implementation of WHA decisions and policies.

The WHO is close to being a quintessential functionalist organization and is one of the largest of the UN specialized agencies in terms of both membership (194 members), staff (8,000), and budget ($4 billion annually), a sign of the universality of health concerns. It is also one of the more decentralized functional organizations, having six regional offices. The WHO secretariat, located in Geneva, is highly technical, with the director-general, other officials, and many delegates being medical doctors. The medical and allied communities form a strong epistemic community based on their technical expertise and training.

Two aspects of WHO activities are discussed here: disease containment found in the International Health Regulations, and some of the policy areas. Some of the WHO's activities relating to development are examined in Chapter 9. The WHO's primary area of activity, expanded from that of its predecessor organizations, is providing security against the spread of communicable diseases. In 1951, the WHO passed the International Health Regulations (known as the International Sanitary Regulations prior to 1971), reaffirming this traditional emphasis. Under these regulations, states are required to report outbreaks of four communicable diseases (yellow fever, cholera, plague, smallpox) and take effective measures without impeding international commerce. Although the regulations are considered binding on all members unless a member notifies the WHO's director-general of its rejection or reservation within a given period of time, the regulations proved to be a weak instrument. States did not always see them as legally binding, and only a narrow set of diseases was covered. Notification reports were received only by governments, which often blocked the dissemination of information, fearing the economic consequences.

Globalization has had a dramatic effect, however, on the transmission, incidence, and vulnerability of individuals and communities to disease through migration, air transport, trade, and troop movements, including of

UN peacekeepers. During the 1980s and 1990s, new diseases emerged that were not covered under the International Health Regulations, such as Ebola, West Nile virus, and HIV/AIDS. Older diseases thought to be under control, such as tuberculosis, reemerged in different, often drug-resistant, forms. New threats to health arose with incidents of bioterrorism, such as the Tokyo sarin nerve gas attack in 1995 and the US anthrax scare in 2001. In short, the range of threats to health has broadened. At the same time, the Internet, cell phones, and other technologies have facilitated faster and better information about outbreaks that states might once have been able to hide, although the 2014 Ebola outbreak in West Africa demonstrated how difficult it can be to track and contain outbreaks in remote areas and countries with weak public health systems.

The emergence of new health threats and new technologies has brought new actors into health governance. A private initiative, ProMED (Program for Monitoring Emerging Diseases), was formed in 1994 to electronically connect health professionals concerned with new health threats. In 1997, the Global Public Health Intelligence Network was formed, at Canada's initiative and with WHO collaboration, to monitor health threats via worldwide information sources.

In 2007, after ten years of work, newly revised International Health Regulations took effect. They brought institutional changes to the WHO and committed states to notify the WHO command center within twenty-four hours of any emerging global health threat. The WHO, in turn, can now utilize the Internet to publicize potential problems, even over state objections. In the words of one expert: if this succeeds, it could lead to a "good-governance revolution" in disease prevention (Fidler 2007: 67). Yet the regulations did not come with financial resources to support implementation and, as some critics have charged, they perpetuated the link between health and an "absence of disease" framework rather than promoting a broader concept of health and the factors that support it (Youde 2012: 128–129).

Over time, the WHA has taken up various health-related issues as part of establishing global priorities and long-term work programs for the WHO. A number of these have pitted the WHO against large multinational corporations. In 1978, for example, the WHA mandated that the WHO develop a code of marketing practices as part of its Action Program on Essential Drugs to address the problem of lower-quality drugs being sold in developing countries—an issue that is discussed further in Chapter 9. In 1981 the WHA approved the International Code of Marketing Breast-Milk Substitutes. In 2003 it approved the Framework Convention on Tobacco Control. Not surprisingly, the WHO's campaign against tobacco encountered stiff opposition from the large tobacco companies and initially from the United States. The story of the choice to negotiate a framework convention and the extensive NGO activity on the issue is discussed in Chapter 6. The convention bans advertising of tobacco products, requires health warnings on packaging, and creates broader liability for manufacturers. It took effect in 2005 and had been ratified by 180 parties as of early 2015. The convention is the first global health treaty and has subsequently been complemented by the Protocol to Eliminate Illicit Trade in Tobacco Products, concluded in 2012. In spring 2015, Bloomberg Philanthropies and the Bill and Melinda Gates Foundation announced the creation of a global fund to fight tobacco industry challenges to anti-smoking laws and to help countries draft legislation to avoid such challenges.

Although the WHO has thus expanded the international health agenda well beyond the issues of controlling the spread of disease and remains the central international health institution, it now acts within a network of overlapping actors and of public, private, and multistakeholder structures that constitute contemporary global health governance.

### Telecommunications

Like health issues, telecommunication services have changed dramatically, from the invention of the telegraph and telephone in the nineteenth century to radio, computers, satellites, and Internet in the twentieth century and various social media in the early twenty-first century. The founding of the International Telegraph Union in 1865 enabled individuals to communicate through one international network. But as that network has changed and new types of communication devices have developed, the successor organization, the ITU, which merged with the International Radio Union in 1932, rests on informal understandings rather than formal legal edicts. These include open access to outer space and the radio spectrum of airspace, and the principle of prior use. States must respect use of specific frequencies and not transmit on them, but states also have a right to exclude foreign firms from their telecommunications industries, establishing the basis of a legal monopoly. Most telecommunications norms must be deduced from various agreements, statements, and the behavior of state and industry officials.

As in the health area, where multiple governance structures interact, the ITU is only one among many public and private bodies focusing on communications. It devotes significant attention to ensuring technical standards for diverse technologies and preventing interference in radio transmissions. The ITU works with the International Organization for Standardization and the International Electrotechnical Commission, both of which are nongovernmental entities, and with a group of regional bodies under the Global Standards Cooperation Group in setting these technical standards.

The exponential growth of the Internet has played a major role in globalization and the diffusion of ideas, culture, and technology. The Internet has also raised a host of new governance issues and the need for new sets of rules and new types of authorities to enforce those rules. What makes it a striking case in global governance is the predominance of private authorities and modes of governance. During the Internet's early years, the rules were really the product of a small epistemic community of technologically sophisticated users. Internet governance once involved just one key actor, the Internet Corporation for Assigned Names and Numbers (ICANN), which beginning in 1998 was a California-based, nonprofit group that managed the Internet's address system, allocating domain names, establishing rules for reallocation of names, and setting regulations for selling domain names.

Very quickly, states and IGOs came to play an increasing role. Beginning in 2001, the ITU succeeded in linking promotion of information and communication technology to the UN Millennium Declaration based on the argument that funding for telecommunication infrastructure was essential for developing countries to bridge the global digital divide. The UN convened the World Summit on the Information Society (WSIS) in 2003 and 2005, bringing together all the key stakeholders to address a broad range of Internet-related issues.

The WSIS stimulated two developments. Civil society actors fought to broaden the issue of Internet infrastructure and governance to questions of development and equity for developing countries. States and IGOs like the ITU sought a greater role in Internet governance more generally, challenging ICANN. The final outcome was the creation of the Internet Governance Forum, a multistakeholder arena within the UN system. That forum includes an advisory group with members from IGOs, the commercial private sector, and public civil society organizations whose task is to discuss issues of Internet governance. The ITU coordinates a number of WSIS follow-up activities, including the maintenance of a database of information and communication technology initiatives. What began in the nineteenth century as a state and IGO activity has been transformed in the twenty-first century into an increasingly global area of multistakeholder governance.

As discussed earlier, the ITU along with the UPU pioneered a number of structures for specialized, functional IGOs, namely the predominance of technical experts among the member state delegates to periodic conferences as well as in the bureau (secretariat). ITU administrative conferences, held every three to four years, deal with technical issues, while plenipotentiary conferences, held every four years, establish budgets and elect administrative council members, the secretary-general and deputy secretary-general, sector bureau directors, and members of the Radio Regulations Board. They may also revise the ITU Convention, approve strategic plans, and deal with any other questions that arise.

The origins, functions, and nature of other functional organizations tend to reflect the nature of the issues they were established to address. In that regard, the history of the International Labour Organization is quite different from that of either the WHO or the ITU.

## Labor Issues and the International Labour Organization

The origins of the ILO can also be traced to the nineteenth century, when growing problems with industrialization drove two industrialists, Welshman Robert Owen and Frenchman Daniel Legrand, to advocate an organization to protect workers from abuses. Long factory hours, poor working conditions, and low wages led to the formation of labor unions to advance the rights of workers. In 1913, the International Federation of Trade Unions was founded to address these grievances on a transnational basis. With the expansion of the right to vote in many European countries, labor assumed growing political importance, and Owen and Legrand's ideas led to adoption of the ILO constitution in 1919 by the Paris Peace Conference, based on the belief that world peace could only be accomplished by attention to social justice (see Murphy 1994). Thus the ILO became an autonomous organization within the League of Nations structure, an institutional model utilized for other functional organizations related to the United Nations.

Important principles articulated in the preamble to the ILO constitution detail the humanitarian, political, and economic motivations for its establishment. The first is based on the humanitarian recognition that "conditions of labour exist involving . . . injustice, hardship and privation to large numbers of people." Such persistent injustices pose a political threat, with the potential to upset international peace and harmony. Second, there is an economic implication that "the failure of any nation to adopt humane conditions of labour is an obstacle in the way of other nations which desire to improve the conditions in their own countries." Yet ironically, organized labor, while agreeing with the general goals, actually opposed the establishment of the ILO, believing that the proposed organization was too weak and lacked the capacity to set labor standards.

Setting standards for treatment of workers through the conclusion of international conventions is the ILO's major activity. Between 1919 and 1939, the ILO approved sixty-seven conventions, covering such issues as hours of work, maternity protection, minimum age, and old-age insurance, and in 1926 it was the first international organization to establish procedures for monitoring human rights within states—in this case, workers' rights. In 1926 it also instituted the system of annual meetings of the Committee of Experts to examine state reports on treaty implementation.

As of 2014, the ILO had concluded more than 190 conventions and supplementary protocols, of which 155 have received sufficient ratifications to come into force. It has also made more than 200 nonbinding recommendations. Among the eight conventions designated "fundamental" are those concerning elimination of forced and compulsory labor, freedom of association and the right to collective bargaining, elimination of discrimination in employment, and the abolition of child labor. More than 138 states have ratified all of these conventions; the United States has ratified but two: the conventions banning forced labor and child labor. Four conventions are also designated as "priority" instruments and referred to as "governance" conventions because of their importance to the international labor standards system.

The ILO, headquartered in Geneva, Switzerland, became a UN specialized agency in 1946. It accomplishes its work through three major bodies—the International Labour Conference, the Governing Body, and the International Labour Office—each of which includes a tripartite representation structure involving government officials, employers, and workers. This integration of governmental and nongovernmental representatives is a unique approach not duplicated in any other IGO. During the Cold War, this tripartite structure was controversial, since in communist states there was no clear differentiation between government, management, and labor. Since the 1990s, the tripartite structure has become controversial again with the declining numbers of individuals in labor unions and the increasing number of NGOs advocating on behalf of non-unionized workers, offering policy advice, and playing key monitoring roles. Yet NGOs have no official position in the tripartite structure and the labor unions do not want to share power. Thus, while the tripartite structure provides greater representation, tensions between different parts of civil society remain.

The International Labour Conference is the ILO's main decisionmaking body. It meets annually, with each member state represented by four individuals: two government officials, and one each from labor and management. The conference, with each individual voting independently, sets international labor standards, adopts the budget, and hears compliance reports compiled by the Committee of Experts.

The Governing Body, the executive arm of the ILO, establishes programs and the budget and elects the director-general. It is composed of fifty-six members representing twenty-eight governments, fourteen employers, and fourteen worker groups. Ten "states of chief industrial importance" (Brazil, China, France, Germany, India, Italy, Japan, Russia, the United Kingdom, and the United States) are ensured governmental seats; the other government members are elected by the International Labour Conference every three years. Employer and worker members are elected by their constituent groups.

The International Labour Office forms a permanent secretariat under the leadership of the director-general, who serves for a five-year renewable term. While the ILO employs about 2,700 officials, more than one-third are located outside of Geneva in its forty field offices.

Among functional organizations, the ILO is regarded as having the most effective system of monitoring, with the potential for enforcement. Governments report on practices covered under the various ILO conventions; ILO staff then prepare comments for the Committee of Experts and may use direct contacts, reports of other UN bodies, and reports from both employer and worker groups to supplement government reports. The findings of the Committee of Experts, although not binding on states, are then conveyed to a conference committee for a final report. In some cases, the ILO may form a commission of inquiry consisting of three independent members to undertake an investigation of a complaint of persistent non-compliance and to recommend measures to be taken to address the problem. Eleven such commissions have been established over the ILO's history. For example, in 1998, a commission of inquiry found that Myanmar had not complied with the forced labor conventions, which led to condemnation and denial of ILO development funds. In 2000, Article 33 was invoked for the first time with a request to the International Labour Conference to take measures against Myanmar. The norm, however, is not to utilize coercive measures, but to work with the country in question and offer technical assistance programs to facilitate compliance. A more recent complaint, in 2010, concerns Zimbabwe's failure to comply with the conventions on freedom of association and right to organize and collective bargaining.

While ILO processes have not substantially changed over time, the organization's jurisdiction has broadened. Initially, standards to improve the working conditions of male wage labor were the dominant focus. Standards then were expanded to include occupational health and safety. In recent years, the ILO has approved conventions for previously unrepresented and often nonorganized workers: women, migrant and domestic workers, and indigenous and tribal peoples. The platform of action labeled "Decent Work" aims to address the inequalities resulting from globalization by focusing on job creation, rights at work, social protection and dialogue, and gender quality.

The ILO continues to be the primary specialized, functional organization devoted to labor issues and standards. Increasingly, however, those issues overlap with trade issues and the work of the World Trade Organization (WTO). A number of states and many NGOs argue that trade rules and labor standards should be linked. Since the WTO has more "teeth" than the ILO, namely the power to impose sanctions, they want the WTO to be used for promoting labor standards (Elliott 2000). Yet, arguing that there is no direct link between trade and labor standards, many developing countries do not want to erode their competitive advantage, namely cheap labor. To them, the proper forum for dealing with labor issues is the ILO. Still, two major regional organizations have demonstrated the links between

trade and labor issues: the European Union, which has a long and successful history of addressing labor rights, and the North American Free Trade
Agreement, which has a side agreement on labor issues, the North American Agreement on Labor Cooperation.

Although there is a long history of international governance efforts on
labor issues, other areas of economic activity have only been the subject of
international cooperation since the end of World War II. Here, we look at
the foundations of international economic governance laid in the 1940s.

### The Origins of the Bretton Woods Institutions

As the industrial revolution expanded, the need for managing increased
trade, capital flows, and price fluctuations in raw materials grew. Some
initiatives were private, some public. During the 1920s and early 1930s,
industry-based cartels were created to coordinate product outputs and
hence control prices; many became successful at price-fixing and market-
allocation schemes. Agreements were reached for industrial products as
well as for various commodities, including tin, natural rubber, and wheat.
Generally, these were private initiatives, different from the government-
organized cartels of the 1960s such as the Organization of Petroleum
Exporting Countries (OPEC). Yet these earlier cartel arrangements were
sometimes signed by governments, as their promoters realized that secure
arrangements could be enforced only through state-to-state cooperation.

Neither private cartels nor governments were able to control the effects
of the worldwide Great Depression of the 1930s, however. Not only were
millions of people out of work and impoverished in the United States and
Europe, but the prices of most raw materials also plummeted, causing the
people in Europe's African and Asian colonies and in the independent countries of Latin America to suffer greatly. Governments, starting with the
United States in its Smoot-Hawley Tariff Act of 1930, adopted "beggar thy
neighbor" policies, raising barriers to imports and causing world trade to
collapse. But as noted earlier in the chapter, the League of Nations was not
set up to deal with economic issues. Efforts to initiate international cooperation as the depression unfolded failed, at least in part because of unwillingness by the United States to participate.

Faced with economic collapse, a number of US and British economists
realized during the 1930s that international institutions were needed to help
countries with balance-of-payments difficulties, to provide stable exchange
rates and economic assistance, and to promote nondiscrimination in and
reciprocal lowering of barriers to trade. The lesson was amplified by the
realization in 1944–1945 that recovery and rebuilding after World War II
would require more capital than war-ravaged countries alone could expect
to raise. The idea of an international institution to mobilize foreign assistance to support economic development of poorer countries came from Chi-

nese political leader Sun Yat-sen's writings, Latin American officials, and US policymakers (Helleiner 2014). The decolonization process and the tripling of the number of states in the 1950s and 1960s would make development assistance the major priority for the World Bank. The dual role envisaged for the World Bank is still reflected in its official name: the International Bank for Reconstruction and Development (IBRD).

Recognizing the importance of reducing barriers to the flow of goods and capital and the value of international economic cooperation for its own well-being, the United States furnished the vision of an open international economy, the leadership to establish institutions, and the money to assist others. Henry Dexter White, chief international economist at the US Treasury from 1942 to 1944, and British economist John Maynard Keynes presented competing plans for economic governance at a conference held in Bretton Woods, New Hampshire, in 1944. In an effort to provide an independent, countervailing balance to US economic power, Keynes proposed a world central bank capable of regulating the flow of credit; he also favored the creation of a new international currency to facilitate lending to countries experiencing liquidity problems. White argued for a weaker agency that would promote the growth of international trade but preserve the central role of the US dollar in the international economy.

White's plan prevailed. The newly formed International Monetary Fund (IMF) would not be a world central bank, but would promote economic growth by providing financial stability for countries facing short-term balance-of-payments difficulties and thereby stimulating international trade. Over time, the US view about conditionality for assistance would also prevail and be greatly strengthened in the 1980s, as discussed in Chapter 8.

Ideas about how governance of trade should proceed likewise differed. At the Bretton Woods meetings, a comprehensive body, the International Trade Organization, was proposed to provide a general framework for trade rules and a venue for ongoing trade discussions. One contentious issue concerned the special problem of commodities. The British, under Keynes's influence, argued for international government-controlled buffer stocks of commodities to reduce detrimental price volatility. The United States opposed all such schemes. The details were left to the Havana Conference in 1948, when the charter for the proposed International Trade Organization was to be approved.

At the Havana Conference, other major differences surfaced. The United States favored extensive trade liberalization, while the Europeans, including the British, were more concerned with retaining their special preferential arrangements with their colonies and former colonies. Many developing countries, absent from earlier negotiations, took a strong stance in favor of schemes protecting commodity exporters. Cuba, Colombia, and

El Salvador each played a key role, advocating such policies as unilateral producer actions. The efforts of the developing countries failed, however, and the industrialized countries won, agreeing only to limited producer and consumer schemes in which voting power was equally balanced. Absent, too, was any discussion of the idea that trading schemes should be used as a way to transfer economic resources from the rich to the poor countries. Such key differences, coupled with major opposition from a coalition of protectionists and free-traders in the US Congress and lack of enthusiasm in other industrialized countries, led to the failure of the ITO before it was established. The Havana Charter was never ratified.

Trade governance then took on a different character as twenty-three of the participants in the ITO negotiations developed the General Agreement on Tariffs and Trade (GATT) as a temporary arrangement. Despite its lack of organizational character, GATT became the major venue for trade negotiations from 1949 to 1995, with an interim committee for coordinating international commodity policy and a small secretariat of 200 persons. The World Trade Organization succeeded GATT in 1995 as the world's comprehensive trade organization, with infrastructure for dispute settlement that goes far beyond anything envisaged in the 1940s.

The three Bretton Woods institutions were designed to address systemic weaknesses in economic governance and promote a liberal economic order. The World Bank and IMF are UN specialized agencies, but until the late 1990s they operated largely independent of the UN system. The WTO has not become a specialized agency, but has an arrangement whereby its director-general participates in the UN Chief Executives Board—the entity for coordinating the disparate agencies within the UN system. The evolving governance roles of the World Bank, IMF, and GATT/WTO and their institutional structures are discussed in depth in Chapters 8 and 9, along with other elements of global economic governance.

## The Food and Agriculture Organization and International Food Regime

Efforts to create an international organization for food and agriculture first began in the late nineteenth century. An international conference was held in 1905 in Rome that led to creation of the International Institute for Agriculture, patterned after other early IGOs with a general assembly of member states (forty), a bureau, a secretary-general, and bureaus of Agriculture Intelligence and Plant Diseases, General Statistics, and Economic and Social Institutions. The institute published the first agricultural census in 1930 and provided crop reports and statistics on imports and exports that affected the prices of agricultural staples. Recognizing the importance of rebuilding agriculture and food supplies at the end of World War II, the United States hosted the UN Food and Agricultural Conference in 1943 (even before the UN's own creation), which then led to the creation of the Food and Agriculture Organization (FAO) as one of the first UN specialized agencies in 1945.

The FAO's purposes include increasing agricultural productivity to eliminate hunger and improve nutrition, addressing problems of surpluses and shortages, establishing common standards, and harmonizing national agricultural policies with free trade principles. Based in Rome, it carries out basic research to enhance technical assistance in agriculture and acts as an information center for agricultural activities, including fisheries and forestry. During the 1960s, the FAO supported the development and dissemination of high-yield strains of rice and other grains, along with fertilizers, pesticides, and technical assistance, producing the "green revolution" for developing countries.

Two other food organizations are also UN specialized agencies and form additional parts of the international food regime: the World Food Programme (WFP), created in 1961, and the International Fund for Agricultural Development (IFAD), established in 1977. Since the 1980s, the programmatic thrust of the UN system's food and agricultural organizations has been to promote sustainable agricultural practices, rural development, and alleviation of acute and chronic hunger. These food institutions are discussed further in Chapter 9.

The WFP is the UN's operational arm in food assistance, delivering half of all food aid and the majority of emergency food aid in a given year. To accomplish this task, it enjoys extensive relationships with both civil society and private sector actors. Initially supported largely by the United States and Canada, the WFP's activities have grown exponentially as the need for emergency food supplies and development projects has soared. In 2012, the WFP spent $1.10 billion, distributing 3.5 million tons of food to 90 million people in 80 countries, with a staff of over 13,000 employees, 90 percent of whom were in the field. The scale of humanitarian crises and food demands in late 2014 forced the WFP to temporarily suspend food aid for almost 2 million Syrian refugees. Because much of its work involves providing food aid in humanitarian crises, both conflict situations and natural disasters, the WFP works closely with the UN High Commissioner for Refugees (UNHCR) and the UN Office for the Coordination of Humanitarian Affairs (OCHA).

The FAO, IFAD, and WFP, like the WHO, have become connected to a large number of organizations—some global, some regional, some general-purpose, many very specialized, and some private—that are engaged in activities related to food and agriculture. These include the Agriculture and Development Assistance Committee, of the Organization for Economic Cooperation and Development (OECD), as well as the WTO and the WHO, all of which have specific interests and responsibilities that link them to the food regime. The Codex Alimentarius Commission, established by the FAO in 1961, sets guidelines, international standards, and codes of practice relating to food safety and pesticide residues to protect consumers' health and ensure fair practices in international agricultural trade.

In addition, there are private actors such as international and national research institutes and foundations as well as a host of NGOs. For example, the Consultative Group on International Agricultural Research (CGIAR), created in 1972, coordinates and oversees the work of fifteen research centers, such as the International Rice Research Institute, based in the Philippines. Both the Bill and Melinda Gates Foundation and the Howard G. Buffett Foundation are funding the WFP to buy surplus crops from poor farmers in Africa and Central America in order to feed WFP recipients facing hunger and starvation. This "purchase for progress" project is intended to help developing-country farmers produce more food and sell it in some of the poorest regions of the world. It is being tested in over twenty-one countries and represents a new public-private partnership (Wroughton 2000).

World food conferences and summits in 1974, 1996, 2002, and 2009 have brought together various constituencies and forged new principles of cooperation to eradicate hunger. At the 2009 World Food Summit, for example, participants pledged to increase investment in agriculture, to improve governance of global food issues in partnership with a variety of stakeholders, and to be proactive in addressing the effects of climate change on food security.

The multiplicity of organizations in the food regime has produced much overlap in responsibilities and some confusion, hence the calls for improving global governance for food security. The resulting "regime complex" is discussed further in Chapter 9.

A very different type of functional IGO first emerged at the end of World War I to address what we would now call humanitarian crises, namely the problems created by large numbers of people fleeing their homelands to escape war, religious persecution, famine, and revolution. Although displaced people have been a feature of international relations since time immemorial, until the twentieth century there had never been a notion of any international responsibility for helping refugees, including resettling them in new homelands.

### The UNHCR and the International Refugee Regime
The end of World War I led to unprecedented numbers of displaced people as millions fled their homelands during the war or were left stateless with the breakup of the Austro-Hungarian, Russian, and Ottoman empires, the

Russian Revolution and ensuing civil war, and the creation of new nation-states in Central Europe. By 1920, it was evident that something more orga-nized than private voluntary relief efforts was needed, particularly as states also had begun to introduce laws restricting immigration as well as national passports and other barriers to entry. It was also evident that the size of the refugee populations threatened regional security in Europe. As a result and under pressure from NGOs, the League of Nations established the Office of the High Commissioner for Refugees in 1921. The first commissioner, Fridtjof Nansen, a renowned Norwegian polar explorer, was mandated by the League to aid Russian refugees only, to spend League funds only for administration and not on actual relief, and to provide only temporary assis-tance. Limited as its mandate was, this was the first international organiza-tion formed to assist refugees and to define populations in need. Like many counterparts in early IGOs, Nansen used his post in innovative ways to expand the mandate by advocating for refugees, developing mechanisms to ensure their legal protection (e.g., the "Nansen passport," an internationally recognized document to facilitate travel), and cooperating with other inter-national agencies.

Still, the efforts to adopt a universal definition of "refugee" and a con-vention failed in the early 1930s, and governments kept the mandate of the high commissioner limited. Budgetary restrictions and lack of cooperation as well as strong anti-immigration bias in most countries and high unem-ployment levels during the Great Depression meant there was little support for responding to refugee and human rights crises in the 1930s, particu-larly Jews fleeing persecution in Europe (Loescher, Betts, and Milner 2008: 9).

To address the problem of millions of displaced people during World War II, the Allied powers established the United Nations Relief and Rehabil-itation Administration (UNRRA) in 1943 to provide emergency assistance in liberated areas. Its mandate, however, was limited to emergency assistance and promoting repatriation. It did not deal with the more complex problems arising from people fearing persecution if they were repatriated to countries that had come under Soviet occupation, or people needing resettlement in third countries. The UNRRA was abolished in 1947 as a result of heavy pressure from the United States, which was its primary funder, and was suc-ceeded first by the International Refugee Organization (also heavily sup-ported by the United States) and then by the UN High Commissioner for Refugees in 1950. Two important steps were accomplished during this short transition: the recognition of refugees' right not to be repatriated against their will (known as "non-refoulement") and the adoption of a universal def-inition of refugee that for the first time was linked to an individual's circum-stances rather than membership in a particular group (Loescher, Betts, and

Milner 2008: 11). The UN Convention on the Status of Refugees was ratified a year later, in 1951, and along with the 1967 protocol to the convention
has provided the basis for the UNHCR's mandate to protect refugees from
forced repatriation and from exploitation in the host state.

A variety of developments have forced the UNHCR to adapt this mandate over time. For one, while the problem of refugees was once thought to
be a temporary product of the end of World War II, the number of refugees
has only increased over time and the UNHCR's scope of responsibilities
has expanded from refugees fleeing communism in Eastern and Central
Europe, China, Korea, and Vietnam, to African, Latin American, and Asian
refugees fleeing war, civil unrest, authoritarian regimes, genocide, famine,
and dire economic conditions. Where much of the UNHCR's early role
involved ensuring refugees' legal protection under the convention, the
growth in numbers of refugees in the 1980s forced it to take on a greater
role in providing assistance to refugees in camps and protracted situations.
Since the Cold War's end, conflicts in the former Yugoslavia, Afghanistan,
Iraq, the Democratic Republic of Congo, Darfur, South Sudan, Syria, and
elsewhere have all displaced seemingly ever larger numbers of people.
These movements of peoples have included not only refugees under the
terms of the convention, but also internally displaced persons (IDPs) who
do not fall under the definition of refugees per se but have come under ad
hoc UNHCR aegis since the late 1990s, and so-called economic and environmental refugees, who do not qualify either. The scale of the problem of
displaced peoples now is extraordinary and a severe global governance
challenge.

To address the large and ongoing demands for protection and humani-
tarian relief, the UNHCR works with UN specialized agencies such as the
WFP and UNESCO, as well as with the International Committee of the Red
Cross and numerous NGOs that are equipped to meet humanitarian needs.
The UNCHR has become the public advocate for all displaced peoples. As
Michael Barnett and Martha Finnemore (2004: 120) note, not only can the
UNHCR, with its expanded authority, "shape how the world understands
refugees and their circumstances," but it can also, potentially, "control their
lives and determine their fates." Chapter 10 explores further the governance
challenges and dilemmas of the current refugee crisis.

As illustrated by the creation of the WHO, the ILO, the Bretton Woods
institutions, the international food regime, and the UNHCR, the development of specialized and functional organizations has been a key trend in the
evolution of elements of global governance. Similarly, institutions for international adjudication were first created by the Hague Conferences of 1899
and 1907 and thus began another trend, one that has led to the creation of
a growing variety of international courts for dispute settlement.

## International Courts
## for Adjudication and Dispute Settlement

The second Hague Conference, in 1907, established the Permanent Court of Arbitration as discussed earlier in the chapter—the first standing institution to settle international disputes through binding decisions based on international law. This laid the foundations for both the Permanent Court of International Justice (PCIJ) under the League of Nations, and its successor, the International Court of Justice (ICJ). Over the century since, there has been an increasing legalization of international issues, a corresponding increase in international courts, and an increased willingness by developing countries and nonstate actors, especially since the Cold War's end, to use international judicial bodies. There are now more than twenty permanent judicial institutions and approximately seventy other international institutions that exercise judicial or quasi-judicial functions (see the website of the Project on International Courts and Tribunals, www.pict-pcti.org). This represents a substantial shift in what Karen Alter (2014: 4–5) refers to as the "new international judicial architecture," wherein courts are not only resolving interstate disputes, but also assessing state compliance with international law and reviewing the legal validity of state and international legislative and administrative acts. Many of what she calls "new-style" courts have compulsory jurisdiction and allow nonstate actors to initiate litigation. That makes them "new political actors on the domestic and international stage" who because of their international nature are able to "circumvent domestic legal and political barriers and to create legal change across borders." Their legal nature allows them to "provoke political change through legal reinterpretation and . . . to harness multilateral resources to knit together broader constituencies of support." Equally significant is the volume of binding rulings issued by the growing number of international courts—some 37,000, more than 90 percent of which have been issued since 1990.

Both older-style international courts and newer ones are characterized by the independence of their judges, whose power comes from their mandate to interpret international law. They adjudicate disputes between two or more entities, at least one of which is a state or IGO, using established rules of procedure, and provide a legally binding ruling (Alter 2014: 70). Figure 3.3 illustrates both the number and the variety of contemporary international courts.

### From the PCIJ to the ICJ

The Covenant of the League of Nations, in Article 14, established the Permanent Court of International Justice. Judges representing major world legal systems were elected by the League's Council and Assembly. Unlike arbitral tribunals, the PCIJ was permanent, rules were fixed in advance, judgments were binding on parties, and proceedings were public. It could provide advisory opinions as well as binding decisions. The PCIJ, however,

---

**Figure 3.3 Selected International and Regional Courts**

---

- *Courts with Universal Scope*
  International Court of Justice
  International Criminal Court
  International Tribunal for the Law of the Sea
  Permanent Court of Arbitration
  World Bank Centre for the Settlement of Investment Disputes
  World Trade Organization Dispute Settlement Unit (includes the Dispute
     Settlement Body and the Appellate Body)

- *Ad Hoc Criminal Tribunals*
  International Criminal Tribunal for Rwanda
  International Criminal Tribunal for the Former Yugoslavia

- *Regional Courts*
  African Court of Justice
  Caribbean Court of Justice
  Central American Court of Justice
  Court of Justice of the Andean Community
  Court of Justice of the European Union and General Court
  Economic Community of West African States Court of Justice

- *Specialized Regional Courts*
  African Court on Human and Peoples' Rights
  Court of Justice of the Benelux Economic Union
  Court of Justice of the Common Market for Eastern and Southern Africa
  Court of Justice of the European Free Trade Association
  European Court of Human Rights
  Inter-American Court of Human Rights

- *Private International Arbitration*
  International Chamber of Commerce International Court of Arbitration
  London Court of International Arbitration

---

was never integrated into the League. States could participate in one and not the other. Thus, the United States was a party to the PCIJ beginning in 1931, but not a League member. Between 1922 and 1940, the PCIJ decided twenty-nine contentious cases between states and handed down twenty-seven advisory opinions. Hundreds of treaties and conventions conferred jurisdiction upon it to settle disputes among parties. Many PCIJ decisions helped to clarify key issues of international law and laid a solid foundation for its successor, the International Court of Justice, which refers directly to PCIJ decisions and procedures in conducting its business.

The International Court of Justice, with fifteen justices headquartered in The Hague, Netherlands, is a major organ of the United Nations. All members of the United Nations are, therefore, parties to the ICJ Statute. As the judicial arm of the United Nations, the ICJ shares responsibility with the other major organs for ensuring that the principles of the UN Charter are followed. Like the PCIJ, the International Court of Justice affords member states an impartial body for settling legal disputes and gives advisory opinions on legal questions referred to it by international agencies. The ICJ is discussed in more detail in Chapter 4.

## Regional Courts

With the growth of regional organizations, discussed in Chapter 5, there has been a corresponding proliferation of regional courts and judicial-like bodies, most of which deal with economic or human rights issues. The European Court of Justice (ECJ) is a key part of the European Union—the most legalized of all IGOs—and a key actor in Europe's process of integration over almost six decades. It has the power to interpret the various EU treaties and secondary legislation, as well as to rule on disputes between individuals, corporations, states, and EU institutions. The ECJ is one of the most active international courts, issuing hundreds of binding rulings each year. It is discussed further in Chapter 5.

As Figure 3.3 makes clear, Africa, Latin America, and Europe all have a variety of regional courts. All three regions have human rights courts; and all have multiple economic courts. The absence of courts in either the Middle East or Asia is noteworthy.

Many regional courts fit the description of "new-style" international courts, as they have compulsory jurisdiction and provide access for nonstate actors such as private litigants and supranational prosecutorial bodies (Alter 2014: 82). The former has been accomplished by making jurisdiction a condition of community membership rather than an opt-in or opt-out choice as it is for the ICJ. And, as Alter (2014: 86) notes, many of these courts have undergone significant design changes since 1990. For example, the Economic Community of West African States (ECOWAS) Court of Justice was originally established to address economic issues, but in 2005 gained jurisdiction over human rights violations and now provides direct access for private litigants.

## Specialized Courts and Tribunals

Among the specialized international courts are the ad hoc criminal tribunals for the former Yugoslavia and Rwanda, established by the UN Security Council in the 1990s, and the International Criminal Court, which came into existence in 2002. These are both discussed in Chapter 10. Some special courts and tribunals are tied to UN specialized agencies, such as the ILO's Administrative Tribunal and the World Bank's International Centre for the Settlement of Investment Disputes (ICSID). The International Tribunal for the Law of the Sea was established by the UN Convention on the Law of the Sea to adjudicate disputes relating to that particular convention. It is open to both state parties to the convention and nonstate entities such as IGOs and state and private enterprises. In 2014 the Permanent Court of International Arbitration ruled that the Philippines could take its case disputing China's territorial claims in the South China Sea to the Law of the Sea Tribunal, despite China's refusal to participate in legal proceedings.

The ICSID and the WTO's Dispute Settlement Body are particularly noteworthy. The former is an autonomous World Bank entity that provides facilities for dispute arbitration between member countries and investors who are citizens of other member countries. Submission of disputes is voluntary, but once the parties agree to arbitration, neither may withdraw its consent. Often agreements between host countries and investors include a provision stipulating that disputes will be sent to the ICSID. In recent years, the number of cases submitted to the ICSID has increased significantly and its activities have expanded to include consultations with governments on investment and arbitration law. The WTO's dispute settlement procedures are discussed in Chapter 9.

### Private International Adjudication

As economic globalization has broadened and deepened, cross-border trade and investment disputes have become more common. Although there are intergovernmental institutions for settlement of such disputes, such as the ICSID, the growth of such disputes has led to the establishment of private settlement approaches. There are upward of a hundred different forums, with caseloads doubling every year.

Generally, private arbitration procedures are flexible, with rules established for each case. Naturally, proceedings are held in private and the awards are confidential. The London Court of International Arbitration is one of the oldest such bodies, established in 1892. Its main function is to select arbitrators for private parties requesting arbitration. Among such groups, the most active is the International Chamber of Commerce's International Court of Arbitration, dating from 1923. It has handled more than 19,000 cases since then, involving parties and arbitrators from 180 countries. In 2012, almost 500 cases were adjudicated by arbitrators drawn from 76 countries. Increased international and regional adjudication reflects several trends: (1) international law's expansion into domains previously subject only to state jurisdiction; (2) state and nonstate actors' willingness to expand the availability and jurisdiction of courts and tribunals; (3) the growth of regional economic arrangements and transactions that require adjudication; and (4) massive human rights violations in post–Cold War conflicts that drove creation of arrangements for dealing with war crimes and crimes against humanity. As one legal analyst, Cesare Romano (1999: 709), concludes, "The enormous expansion and transformation of the international judiciary is the single most important development of the post–Cold War age."

\* \* \*

The foundations of contemporary institutions of global governance have evolved over time, from states themselves and a rudimentary set of international rules to an increasingly complex network of international organizations. As we have explored in this chapter, the nineteenth century set a series of precedents for the development of intergovernmental organizations. The twentieth century was marked by the rapid proliferation of IGOs and international adjudicatory institutions. The twenty-first century is already noted for the further evolution and proliferation of these and new types of institutions to meet the growing needs for global governance. The center for much of that activity is still the United Nations system. It is to this we turn in Chapter 4.

## Suggested Further Reading

Alter, Karen J. (2014) *The New Terrain of International Law: Courts, Politics, Rights*. Princeton: Princeton University Press.

Betts, Alexander, Gil Loescher, and James Milner. (2012) *The United Nations High Commissioner for Refugees (UNHCR): The Politics and Practice of Refugee Protection Into the Twenty-First Century*. 2nd ed. New York: Routledge.

Claude, Inis L., Jr. (1964) *Swords Into Plowshares: The Problems and Progress of International Organization*. 3rd ed. New York: Random House.

Harman, Sophie. (2012) *Global Health Governance*. London: Routledge.

Helleiner, Eric. (2014) *Forgotten Foundations of Bretton Woods: International Development and the Making of the Postwar Order*. Ithaca: Cornell University Press.

Mazower, Mark. (2013) *Governing the World: The History of an Idea, 1915 to the Present*. New York: Penguin.

Murphy, Craig N. (1994) *International Organization and Industrial Change: Global Governance Since 1850*. New York: Oxford University Press.

Northledge, F. S. (1986) *The League of Nations: Its Life and Times, 1920–1946*. New York: Holmes and Meier.

Steil, Benn. (2014) *The Battle of Bretton Woods: Keynes, White, and the Making of a New World Order*. Princeton: Princeton University Press.

## Internet Resources

Food and Agriculture Organization: www.fao.org
International Centre for the Settlement of Investment Disputes: www.icsid.world bank.org
International Labour Organization: www.ilo.org
International Telecommunication Union: www.itu.int
Project on International Courts and Tribunals: www.pict-pcti.org
UN High Commissioner for Refugees: www.unhcr.org
UN system: www.unsystem.org
Universal Postal Union: www.upu.int
World Food Programme: www.wfp.org
World Health Organization: www.who.org

# 4

# The United Nations: Centerpiece of Global Governance

**Since World War II, the United Nations has been the center-**piece of global governance. It is the only IGO with global scope and nearly universal membership, and its agenda encompasses the broadest range of governance issues. The UN is, in fact, a complex system with many pieces. Among its functions are the creation of international law, norms, and principles; it has created other IGOs within the UN system such as the UN Environment Programme, as well as countless other committees and programs; it has sponsored global conferences and summits. It serves also as a catalyst for global policy networks and partnerships with other actors. The UN, in short, is the central site for multilateral diplomacy, and the UN General Assembly is center stage. Its three weeks of general debate at the opening of each fall assembly session draw foreign ministers and heads of state from small and large countries to take advantage of the opportunity to address all the nations of the world and to engage in intensive diplomacy.

The UN Security Council is the core of the global security system and is the primary legitimizer of actions dealing with threats to peace and security. This is what made the 2002–2003 debate over war against Iraq so important. Would the Council endorse a US-led preventive war or not? Since the Cold War's end, the Council has redefined security threats to include systematic human rights violations, genocide, massive refugee flows, and HIV/AIDS. It has acted as an international regulatory and legislative authority in its imposition of sanctions, creation of war crimes tribunals, and responses to terrorism, all of which have created obligations for member states. In 2011, when the Council authorized the use of force to protect Libyan civilians, many observers cheered what they thought to be a greater willingness to intervene in humanitarian crises. Its failure to adopt any resolution, however, during the first three years of the Syrian civil war, with its huge loss of civilian lives and outflow of refugees into neighboring countries, made clear that inconsistency on intervention issues was still the norm.

The UN's importance, and especially the relative importance of the Security Council and General Assembly, have risen and fallen over the years as world politics affected the organization. The unprecedented Millennium Summit in 2000 and awarding of the 2001 Nobel Peace Prize to the organization and to Secretary-General Kofi Annan symbolized the UN's continuing role as the centerpiece of global governance. Yet the UN struggles today to meet the many ongoing challenges of threats to peace and security, lagging development, human rights violations, and environmental degradation.

## The UN Charter and Key Principles

The UN Charter expresses both hopes and aspirations of the UN's founders for a better world, lessons from the League of Nations, and the realities states were able to agree on in 1945. As discussed in Chapter 3, several key principles undergird the UN's structure and operation and represent fundamental legal obligations of all members. These are contained in Article 2 of the Charter as well as in other provisions (see Figure 4.1).

The most fundamental principle is the sovereign equality of member states, which means that states do not recognize any higher governing authority. Equality refers to states' legal status, not their size, military power, or wealth, making Russia, Lithuania, China, and Singapore equals. This is the basis for each state having one vote in the General Assembly. Inequality is also part of the UN framework, embodied in the permanent membership and veto power of five states (the P-5) in the Security Council.

Closely related to the UN's primary goal of maintaining peace and security are the twin principles that all member states shall (1) refrain from the threat or use of force against the territorial integrity or political independence of any state, or in any manner inconsistent with UN purposes; and (2) settle their international disputes by peaceful means. Many times since the UN's founding, states have failed to honor these principles and have often failed even to submit their disputes to the UN for settlement. Members also accept the obligation to support enforcement actions such as economic sanctions and to refrain from giving assistance to states that are the objects of UN preventive or enforcement action. They have the collective responsibility to ensure that nonmember states act in accordance with these principles as necessary for the maintenance of international peace and security. A further key principle is the obligation of member states to fulfill in good faith all the obligations assumed by them under the Charter. This affirms a fundamental norm of all international law and treaties: *pacta sunt servanda*—treaties must be carried out. Among these obligations is payment of assessed annual contributions (dues) to the organization.

---

**Figure 4.1    Key UN Charter Provisions**

---

*Chapter I: Purposes and Principles*
Art. 2(3): All Members shall settle their international disputes by peaceful
    means.
Art. 2(4): All Members shall refrain in their international relations from the
    threat or use of force against the territorial integrity or political
    independence of any state.
Art. 2(7): Nothing contained in the present Charter shall authorize the
    United Nations to intervene in matters which are essentially within the
    domestic jurisdiction of any state.

*Chapter VI: Pacific Settlement of Disputes*
Art. 33(1): The parties to any dispute . . . shall, first of all, seek a solution by
    negotiation, enquiry, mediation, conciliation, arbitration, judicial
    settlement, resort to regional agencies or arrangements, or other
    peaceful means of their own choice.

*Chapter VII: Action with Respect to Threats to the Peace, Breaches of the
Peace, and Acts of Aggression*
Art. 39: The Security Council shall determine the existence of any threat to
    the peace, breach of the peace, or act of aggression.
Art. 41: The Security Council may decide what measures not involving the
    use of armed force are to be employed. . . . These may include complete
    or partial interruption of economic relations . . . and other means of
    communication, and the severance of diplomatic relations.
Art. 42: Should the Security Council consider that measures provided for in
    Article 41 would be inadequate or have proved to be inadequate, it may
    take such action by air, sea, or land forces as may be necessary to
    maintain or restore international peace and security.
Art. 51: Nothing in the present Charter shall impair the inherent right of
    individual or collective self-defence if an armed attack occurs against a
    Member of the UN.

*Chapter VIII: Regional Arrangements*
Art. 52: Nothing in the present Charter precludes the existence of regional
    arrangements or agencies for dealing with such matters relating to the
    maintenance of international peace and security.
Art. 53: The Security Council shall . . . utilize such regional arrangements or
    agencies for enforcement action under its authority. But no enforcement
    action shall be taken under regional arrangements or by regional
    agencies without the authorization of the Security Council.

---

The final principle in Article 2 addresses the limits on the jurisdiction
of the UN and underscores the long-standing norm of nonintervention in
the domestic affairs of states, but provides a key exception for enforcement
actions. Yet who decides what is an international and what is a domestic
problem? Since the UN's founding in 1945, the scope of what is considered
"international" has broadened with UN involvement in human rights, development, and environmental degradation. Since the Cold War's end, many
UN peacekeeping operations have involved intrastate rather than interstate
conflicts, in other words conflicts *within* rather than *between* states. The

UN's founders recognized the tension between the commitment to act collectively against a member state and the affirmation of state sovereignty represented in the nonintervention principle. They could not foresee the dilemmas that changing definitions of security, ethnic conflicts, humanitarian crises, failed states, and terrorism would pose. Human rights might well be seen as a matter of domestic jurisdiction, but the Preamble and Article 1 of the UN Charter both contain references to human rights and obligate states to show "respect for the principle of equal rights and self-determination of peoples." Hence, discussions of human rights have always been regarded as legitimate international, rather than solely domestic, concerns. Actions to promote or enforce human rights norms have been much more controversial.

In Article 51, the Charter affirms states' "right of individual or collective self-defence" against armed attack. Thus, states are not required to wait for the UN to act before undertaking measures in their own (and others') defense. They are obligated to report their responses under Chapter VIII, Article 52, and they may create regional defense and other arrangements. The self-defense principle, not surprisingly, has led to many debates over who initiated hostilities and who was the victim of aggression. For example, in the Arab-Israeli conflict, was it Israel or the Arab states that first used force? In the debate over going to war against Iraq in 2003, did Iraq possess weapons of mass destruction (WMD), and did these pose a sufficient threat to the United States and other countries to justify war? A special committee labored for many years over the problem of defining aggression before concluding that the UN Security Council has the ultimate responsibility to determine what are acts of aggression.

## The Principal Organs of the United Nations

The structure of the United Nations as outlined in the Charter includes six principal bodies: the General Assembly, the Security Council, the Economic and Social Council, the Secretariat, the International Court of Justice, and the Trusteeship Council. Each organ has changed over time, responding to external realities, internal pressures, and interactions with other organs. Because the United Nations is a complex system of organizations, it extends well beyond these six organs. Among the affiliated organizations are the nineteen independently established specialized agencies, ranging from the World Health Organization, Food and Agriculture Organization, and International Labour Organization to the International Monetary Fund and World Bank (but not the World Trade Organization), as introduced in Chapter 3. In addition, the General Assembly, Security Council, and ECOSOC have used their powers to create a large number of subsidiary bodies, programs, and funds, illustrating the phenomenon of "IGOs creating other IGOs" (Jacobson 1984: 39). Figure 4.2 captures the complexity of the UN system. In the sections that follow, we discuss how the six major UN organs have evolved in practice and some of their political dynamics.

## The General Assembly

The UN General Assembly, like the League of Nations Assembly, was designed as the general debate arena where all UN members would be equally represented according to a one-state, one-vote formula. It is the organization's hub, with a diverse agenda and the responsibility for coordinating and supervising subsidiary bodies but with power only to make recommendations to members, except on internal matters such as elections and the budget. It has exclusive competence over the latter, giving it a measure of surveillance and control over all UN programs and subsidiary bodies. The Assembly also has important elective functions: admitting states to UN membership; electing the nonpermanent members of the Security Council, ECOSOC, and the Trusteeship Council; appointing judges to the ICJ; and appointing the UN Secretary-General on the recommendation of the Security Council. It also grants observer status to nonmember states and international organizations, such as for the Holy See (Vatican) and the Palestine Liberation Organization, as well as to many regional and other IGOs. In 2012, reflecting the frustration of a majority of UN members as well as the Palestinian people at the failure of efforts to negotiate an end to the Israeli-Palestinian conflict and create an independent Palestinian state, the Assembly voted to upgrade the Palestinian Authority's status from "nonmember observer entity" to "nonmember observer state," a recognition of de facto sovereign statehood.

In many ways, the General Assembly comes closer than any other international body to embodying what is often called the "international community." To paraphrase Shakespeare, if "all the world's a stage," the UN General Assembly is center stage—a stage particularly important for small states such as Costa Rica, Fiji, Malta, Singapore, and Zambia.

The General Assembly can consider any matter within the purview of the UN Charter (Article 10); although its recommendations are nonbinding, the number of items on the Assembly's agenda has continually grown over the years, from 46 in 1946 to more than 150 in recent years. Many items, however, are repeated year after year with no effort at review. They range from various conflict situations, such as the Israeli-Palestinian conflict, to arms control, development, poverty eradication, global resource management, human rights, advancement of women, international justice and law, reports from other UN organs, follow-up to prior UN-sponsored conferences, administrative matters, and the UN's finances. Resolutions may be aimed at individual member states, nonmembers, the Security Council or other organs, the Secretary-General, or even the Assembly itself.

114

Figure 4.2    The United Nations System

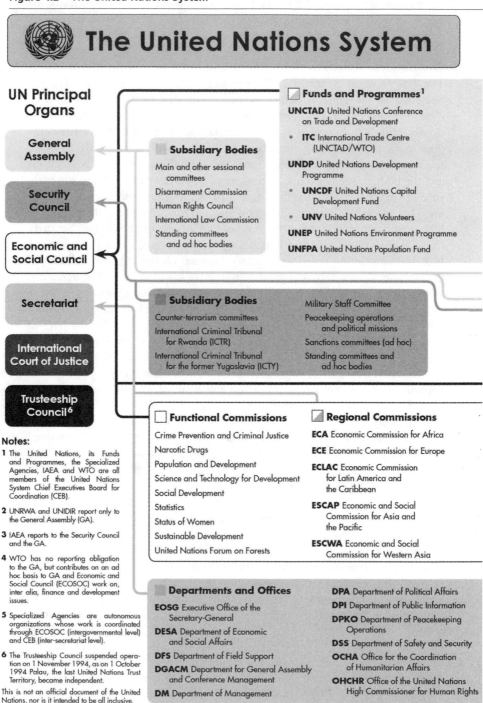

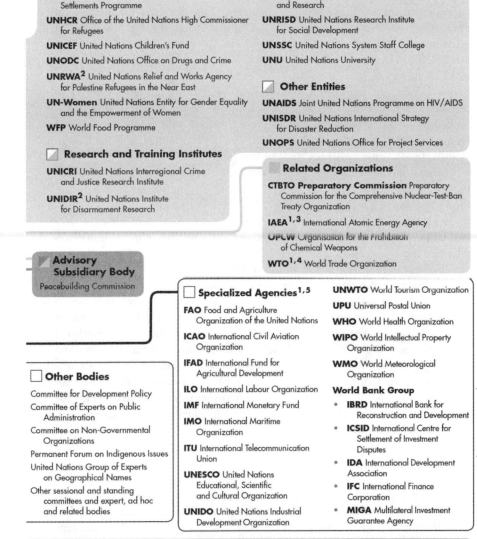

**UN-HABITAT** United Nations Human Settlements Programme

**UNHCR** Office of the United Nations High Commissioner for Refugees

**UNICEF** United Nations Children's Fund

**UNODC** United Nations Office on Drugs and Crime

**UNRWA**[2] United Nations Relief and Works Agency for Palestine Refugees in the Near East

**UN-Women** United Nations Entity for Gender Equality and the Empowerment of Women

**WFP** World Food Programme

### Research and Training Institutes

**UNICRI** United Nations Interregional Crime and Justice Research Institute

**UNIDIR**[2] United Nations Institute for Disarmament Research

**UNITAR** United Nations Institute for Training and Research

**UNRISD** United Nations Research Institute for Social Development

**UNSSC** United Nations System Staff College

**UNU** United Nations University

### Other Entities

**UNAIDS** Joint United Nations Programme on HIV/AIDS

**UNISDR** United Nations International Strategy for Disaster Reduction

**UNOPS** United Nations Office for Project Services

### Related Organizations

**CTBTO Preparatory Commission** Preparatory Commission for the Comprehensive Nuclear-Test-Ban Treaty Organization

**IAEA**[1,3] International Atomic Energy Agency

**OPCW** Organisation for the Prohibition of Chemical Weapons

**WTO**[1,4] World Trade Organization

### Advisory Subsidiary Body
Peacebuilding Commission

### Other Bodies

Committee for Development Policy

Committee of Experts on Public Administration

Committee on Non-Governmental Organizations

Permanent Forum on Indigenous Issues

United Nations Group of Experts on Geographical Names

Other sessional and standing committees and expert, ad hoc and related bodies

### Specialized Agencies[1,5]

**FAO** Food and Agriculture Organization of the United Nations

**ICAO** International Civil Aviation Organization

**IFAD** International Fund for Agricultural Development

**ILO** International Labour Organization

**IMF** International Monetary Fund

**IMO** International Maritime Organization

**ITU** International Telecommunication Union

**UNESCO** United Nations Educational, Scientific and Cultural Organization

**UNIDO** United Nations Industrial Development Organization

**UNWTO** World Tourism Organization

**UPU** Universal Postal Union

**WHO** World Health Organization

**WIPO** World Intellectual Property Organization

**WMO** World Meteorological Organization

**World Bank Group**

- **IBRD** International Bank for Reconstruction and Development
- **ICSID** International Centre for Settlement of Investment Disputes
- **IDA** International Development Association
- **IFC** International Finance Corporation
- **MIGA** Multilateral Investment Guarantee Agency

**OIOS** Office of Internal Oversight Services

**OLA** Office of Legal Affairs

**OSAA** Office of the Special Adviser on Africa

**SRSG/CAAC** Office of the Special Representative of the Secretary-General for Children and Armed Conflict

**SRSG/SVC** Office of the Special Representative of the Secretary-General on Sexual Violence in Conflict

**UNODA** Office for Disarmament Affairs

**UNOG** United Nations Office at Geneva

**UN-OHRLLS** Office of the High Representative for the Least Developed Countries, Landlocked Developing Countries and Small Island Developing States

**UNON** United Nations Office at Nairobi

**UNOV** United Nations Office at Vienna

Published by the United Nations Department of Public Information DPI/2470 rev.3—13-38229—August 2013

Although the Security Council is the primary organ for dealing with threats to international peace and security, the Assembly can make inquiries and studies with respect to conflicts (Articles 13–14); it may discuss a situation and make recommendations if the Security Council is not exercising its functions (Articles 11–12); and it has the right to be kept informed by the Security Council and the Secretary-General (Articles 10–12). The "Uniting for Peace" resolution, passed during the Korean War in 1950, however, ignited controversy over the respective roles of the two bodies. Under the resolution, the General Assembly claimed authority to recommend collective measures when the Security Council was deadlocked by a veto. It was subsequently used to deal with crises in Suez and Hungary (1956), the Middle East (1958, 1967, 1980, 1982), and the Congo (1960). In all, ten emergency special sessions of the Assembly have dealt with threats to international peace when the Security Council was deadlocked. The tenth emergency special session, originally convened during the Palestinian-Israeli crisis in 1997, has reconvened annually since then. In 1962, the ICJ, in the *Certain Expenses of the United Nations* case (ICJ Advisory Opinion 1962), was asked to give an advisory opinion on whether the General Assembly had the authority it claimed to authorize peacekeeping operations (the opinion was affirmative). Since the early 1990s, however, the permanent members of the Security Council have tacitly agreed that only the Security Council should authorize the use of armed force. Still, when the Security Council fails to act because of one or more P-5 vetoes, the General Assembly can give voice to international sentiment, as it did in February 2012 with a resolution demanding that the Syrian government cease violence against civilians and commit to a political process. In general, however, the Assembly is a cumbersome body for dealing with delicate situations of peace and security. It is most useful for the symbolic politics of agenda-setting and mustering large majorities in support of resolutions.

The UN Charter also entrusted the General Assembly with an important role in the development of international law (Article 13). Although the Assembly is not a world legislature, its resolutions may lay the basis for new international law by articulating new principles, such as one that called the seas the "common heritage of mankind," and new concepts such as sustainable development. These are often the basis for "soft law"—norms that represent a widespread international consensus but may not (yet) be embodied in "hard" or treaty form—and may (or may not) then be embodied in multilateral norm- or law-creating treaties and conventions drafted under General Assembly authorization. For example, the "common heritage" principle was incorporated into the 1967 Treaty on Outer Space and 1982 Convention on Law of the Sea. The 2005 World Summit endorsed the emerging norm of states' responsibility to protect their own people and the international community's responsibility to act when governments fail to protect vulnerable people. This R2P ("responibility to protect") norm, as it has become known, was the basis for the Security Council's 2011 decision to authorize the use of force to protect Libya's civilian population. Over time, the General Assembly has produced a large number of multilateral lawmaking treaties, including the 1961 Vienna Convention on Diplomatic Relations, the 1969 Vienna Convention on the Law of Treaties, the 1968 Treaty on the Non-Proliferation of Nuclear Weapons, the 1994 Convention on the Safety of United Nations and Associated Personnel, and the 2013 Arms Trade Treaty. Assembly resolutions have also approved all the major international human rights conventions, although most were drafted in the former Commission on Human Rights, which functioned under ECOSOC and was replaced in 2006 by the Human Rights Council, which reports to the General Assembly.

Finally, the General Assembly shares responsibilities for Charter revision with the Security Council. The Assembly can propose amendments with a two-thirds majority; two-thirds of the member states, including all the permanent members of the Security Council, must then ratify the changes. The General Assembly and Security Council together may also call a general conference for the purpose of Charter review. There have to date, however, been only two instances of Charter amendment, both enlarging the membership of the Security Council and ECOSOC.

*How the General Assembly functions.* Regular annual meetings of the General Assembly are held for three months each fall (or longer) and begin with a "general debate" period when heads of state, prime ministers, and foreign ministers by the score come to New York to speak before the Assembly. In addition, there have been twenty-eight special sessions called to deal with specific problems (e.g., financial and budgetary problems in 1963, development and international economic cooperation in 1975, disarmament in 1978, HIV/AIDS in 2001, and the follow-up to the Programme of Action of the International Conference on Population and Development in 2014). These special sessions should not be confused with the emergency special sessions convened under a "Uniting for Peace" resolution.

The bulk of the General Assembly's work occurs in six functional committees: the Disarmament and International Security Committee (the First Committee); the Economic and Financial Committee (the Second Committee); the Social, Humanitarian, and Cultural Committee (the Third Committee); the Special Political and Decolonization Committee (the Fourth Committee); the Administrative and Budgetary Committee (the Fifth Committee); and the Legal Committee (the Sixth Committee). All six are committees of the whole, exact duplications of the plenary Assembly. The Assembly also has created other, smaller committees to carry out specific tasks such as studying a question (e.g., the ad hoc Committee on International Terrorism) or framing proposals and monitoring (e.g., the Committee on Peaceful Uses of Outer Space, the Disarmament Commission). The Sixth Committee and the International Law Commission, an elected group of thirty-four jurists nominated by UN member states, have responsibility for drafting international conventions to carry out the Assembly's mission of "encouraging the progressive development of international law and its codification" (Article 13).

Each year, the General Assembly elects a president and seventeen vice presidents who serve for that year's session. By tradition, presidents tend to come from small and middle-power states, and often from developing countries. Only on three occasions (1953, 1969, and 2006) has a woman been elected. The president's powers are limited, but allow much to be accomplished through personal influence and political skills in guiding the work of the Assembly, averting crises, bringing parties into agreement, ensuring that procedures are respected, and accelerating the cumbersome agenda.

Key to the General Assembly's functioning are member states' own delegations. The UN Charter provides that each member can have no more than five representatives in the Assembly, but Assembly rules have permitted five alternates and unlimited advisers and technical experts. The practice of establishing permanent missions and ambassadors began with the League of Nations. Although missions are mandatory for Security Council members, who must be able to meet immediately in the event of an emergency, the practice became commonplace for most member states with the establishment of UN headquarters in New York in 1948. Missions vary in size from about 150 personnel (the US mission) to a single person of diplomatic rank. Small and poor states often combine their UN mission with their embassy in Washington, DC, to save money; most states' missions grow significantly during the fall Assembly sessions, sometimes including a few parliamentarians or legislators. (The US House and Senate alternate in having representatives on the US delegation to the General Assembly each year.)

Delegates attend General Assembly and committee sessions, participate in efforts to shape agendas and debate, and represent national interests. Expertise and skill in multilateral diplomacy matter, and enable some delegates to be more influential than others. Because almost all states of the world are represented at the annual Assembly sessions, there are many opportunities for informal bilateral and multilateral contacts, which countries may use to deal with issues outside the Assembly's agenda. UN diplomats have to deal with a huge spectrum of issues and many different viewpoints and policies. During the regular Assembly sessions, the social obligations of endless receptions, which would be politically incorrect not to attend, can be exhausting. Because it can take a long time for a new delegate to learn the ropes and become effective, it is not uncommon for some delegates to serve a long time. The United States, however, tends to rotate its foreign service officers at the UN mission frequently, demonstrating that experience in multilateral diplomacy is not valued highly.

Ties between UN missions and home governments vary from loose to tight. Some delegations have considerable autonomy in dealing with the various issues on Assembly agendas and determining how best to represent their countries' interests. Others operate on a "tighter leash" and must seek instructions from their capitals on what strategies to use and how to vote on given resolutions.

*Decisionmaking in the General Assembly.* Early in the UN's history, states from the same geographic region or with shared economic or political interests formed coalitions to shape common positions on particular issues and to control blocs of votes. Several factors led to the development of such groups. First, the Charter itself specified that in electing the nonpermanent members of the Security Council, the General Assembly give consideration to "equitable geographical distribution," but offered no guidance on how to do so or what the appropriate geographic groups should be. The five recognized regional groups of states are: Western European and Other (includes the United States, Israel, Japan, and Canada), Eastern European, African, Latin American and Caribbean, and Asian. Each regional group determines the rules and procedures for selecting candidates for Security Council or ECOSOC seats, and which candidates to support for the ICJ or for Secretary-General. Israel was excluded from all regional groups until 2000, for example, which had the effect of precluding it from being a candidate for the Security Council and other elected UN bodies.

A second factor in the emergence of caucusing groups is the one-state, one-vote principle. General Assembly decisions are made by a majority (either simple or two-thirds under specified circumstances such as elections and questions of peace and security). As a result, a stable coalition of states comprising a majority of members, like a majority political party or coalition of parties in a parliament, can control most decisions. Coalitions within the UN have tended to persist for long periods and to correspond with major substantive divisions in the General Assembly. The two longest-standing divisions have been the East-West one, defined largely by Cold War issues, and the North-South division, related to development issues.

During the Cold War, Eastern European states voted consistently with the Soviet Union, as did many nominally nonaligned states. The Western European, Latin American, and British Commonwealth states voted closely with the United States on Cold War–related issues and often on human rights and internal UN administration. Colonial and economic questions, however, produced fragmentation in this US-dominated coalition. By 1960, the United States could no longer muster a simple majority because of the influx of new African and Asian states. Since the Cold War's end, Russia and other Eastern European states have tended to vote with the Western European states or a larger "Northern" group.

The North-South issue division has centered on economic inequalities and development, colonialism and decolonization, and great-power military capabilities. In the 1950s, developing countries were fragmented into the Afro-Asian group, the Latin American group, and the Non-Aligned Movement (NAM). With the creation of the UN Conference on Trade and Development in 1964, they formed the Group of 77, and UNCTAD's own system of group negotiation reinforced their tendency to operate as a unified bloc that constituted more than two-thirds of the UN's membership. Beginning in the early 1970s, the G-77 "could, and did, steer the United Nations in directions that it wanted to move, it could, and did, commit the United Nations to principles that it wanted to legitimize, and it could, and did, demand global actions conducive to its interests. The Group of 77 ultimately could not enforce compliance with its demands, but it could bring attention to them and impressively argue for their rectitude" (Puchala and Coate 1989: 53).

Although the North-South divide persists, the G-77's cohesion began to erode in the late 1980s, making common policy positions difficult to forge. The South is now splintered between a number of more developed countries, such as Brazil, China, India, Malaysia, Mexico, and South Africa, a large number of very poor countries, and others in between. The developed countries, however, have never been as cohesive as the countries of the South. Many European states have been more supportive of developing countries' concerns than has the United States, weakening the North's ability to operate as a coalition in responding to the South.

Other caucusing groups within the UN include the Afro-Asian group, French-speaking and English-speaking African countries, the Association of Southeast Asian Nations (ASEAN), the NAM, the Organisation of Islamic Cooperation (OIC), the Alliance of Small Island States, and the European Union (see Figure 4.3). The level of activity and cohesion within these groups depends on the issue, as do the processes by which they formulate common positions. The EU has a formalized process of continual consultation and for delegating responsibility for enunciating common policies. Other groups rely on formal and informal meetings of delegates. The Alliance of Small Island States, a grouping of thirty-nine small island and low-lying coastal developing states that share similar development challenges and concerns about effects of climate change, has created its own NGO (Islands First) to assist with research and lobbying, and operates out of its chairman's permanent mission.

Although coalitions and blocs emerged in response to the UN's provisions for elections and voting, most General Assembly decisionmaking is

---

**Figure 4.3    Caucusing Groups in the United Nations (number of member states)**

---

- *Regional Groups*
  African states (53)
  Asian states (52)
  Eastern European states (21)
  Latin American and Caribbean states (33)
  Western European and Other states (29)

- *Other Multilateral Groups*
  Alliance of Small Island States (39)
  ASEAN (10)
  European Union (27)
  Group of 77 (133)
  Non-Aligned Movement (114)
  Organisation of Islamic Cooperation (57)

---

done by consensus—that is, by acclamation or acquiescence without any formal vote. In this case, the Assembly president consults with delegations and then announces that a resolution is adopted. Consensus, therefore, refers to a decision "supported by, or at least not objectionable to, all parties involved" (Smith 2006: 218). When the Assembly does vote, Article 18, paragraph 2, of the UN Charter specifies that it use a simple majority of those states "present and voting" to decide all questions other than "important questions" dealing with peace and security, elections, budget, and admission or suspension of members. Only one-third of Assembly decisions between the first and sixty-fourth sessions, however, involved recorded votes with the highest percentage of these occurring in the 1980s on Middle East issues (Hug 2012). Coalitions and blocs are as active in trying to forge consensus as in marshaling votes, but the outcome is less divisive because states' individual positions are not revealed as in a roll call vote.

*The General Assembly's shifting agendas and relevance.* Politics within the General Assembly mirrors world politics, but not always the realities of power, given the principle of one-state, one-vote. The Assembly is *the* place to set the agendas of world politics, to get ideas endorsed or condemned, actions taken or rejected. Any state can propose an agenda item. In the 1960s, UN membership increased dramatically (see Figure 4.4) with the end of European colonial rule in Africa and Asia, a process of largely peaceful transformation in which the UN played a significant role. The membership change had a particular impact on the General Assembly's agendas and voting patterns. From the early 1960s to the mid-1980s, the G-77 endeavored to use its two-thirds majority in the Assembly to achieve a number of third world goals, especially the proposed New International Economic Order, which is discussed in Chapter 9. That pattern shifted in the mid-1980s, however, with the eroding consensus within the G-77, with changes in Soviet and US policies that increased the Security Council's role, and with the increased importance of the IMF and World Bank for dealing with debt and development issues. The result has been a steady decline in the Assembly's role.

Today, the North-South divide persists around issues of economic inequality and development, self-determination (particularly for Palestine), and great-power military capabilities. But human security issues, including human rights, development, international security, global inequalities, and the environment, are often very divisive, as are questions of political rights, state sovereignty, and UN intervention. On these issues, while the North-South divide is still salient, there are more crosscutting currents. On the human rights and state sovereignty issues that the European Union and United States pushed successfully in the 1990s, support has dropped from 70 percent to less than 50 percent, and many Islamic countries now try to limit freedom of speech in the name of religion (Gowan and Brantner 2008).

Many criticisms of the UN are really criticisms of the General Assembly. The number of resolutions passed by the Assembly has steadily increased over time, from about 119 annually during the first five years to a peak of 360 per year during 2001–2002, when efforts to reduce the number began. The 68th Assembly, in 2013, approved 303 resolutions, many passed with little concern for implementation. Many resolutions are "ritual resolutions" that appear annually on agenda items such as the right to development or the situation in the Palestinian territories. Many are formulated in very general terms, thus masking dissent that would be evident if the wording were more specific.

Since the Cold War's end, the General Assembly has been marginalized as the epicenter of UN activity shifted to the Security Council and Secretariat, much to the dismay of the South, which would like more consultation between the General Assembly and Security Council on peace and security issues. Should tensions between Western powers, Russia, and China persist, however, the General Assembly could well once again be an alternative forum for marshaling international opprobrium on issues such as the Syrian civil war, conflict in the South China Sea, and Ukraine, with the Security Council stymied by Russian and Chinese vetoes.

Unquestionably, the General Assembly needs reform and revitalization. There has been some progress since the mid-1980s in reducing the agenda and number of resolutions as well as requiring explicit renewal of programs or funds based on continuing relevance and effectiveness. Changes, however, require the concurrence of a majority of states.

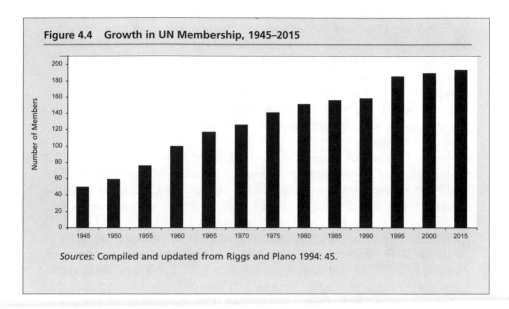

**Figure 4.4   Growth in UN Membership, 1945–2015**

*Sources:* Compiled and updated from Riggs and Plano 1994: 45.

### The Security Council

Under Article 24 of the UN Charter, the Security Council has primary responsibility for maintenance of international peace and security and the authority to act on behalf of *all* members of the United Nations. Provisions for carrying out this role are spelled out in Chapters VI and VII (see Figure 4.1). Chapter VI provides a wide range of techniques to investigate disputes and help parties achieve peaceful settlement. Chapter VII specifies the Security Council's authority to commit all UN members to take enforcement measures such as sanctions or military force. Prior to 1990, the Security Council used its enforcement powers under Chapter VII on only two occasions, relying on the mechanisms in Chapter VI to respond to conflicts during the Cold War years. For example, prior to 1992, all UN peacekeeping forces were authorized under Chapter VI. Since then, the Security Council's use of Chapter VII, including its provisions for economic sanctions and military enforcement action, has increased dramatically, and most peacekeeping operations now carry Chapter VII authority, as discussed further in Chapter 7.

The Security Council was kept small in order to facilitate more efficient (i.e., swifter) decisionmaking in dealing with threats to international peace and security. It is also the only UN body that has both permanent and nonpermanent members. The five permanent members—the United States, the United Kingdom (UK), France, Russia (successor state to the seat of the Soviet Union in 1992), and the People's Republic of China (PRC, which replaced the Republic of China in 1971)—are key to Security Council decisionmaking, since each has veto power. The nonpermanent members, originally six in number and expanded to ten in 1965, are elected by the General Assembly for staggered two-year terms after nomination by one of the five regional groups. At least four nonpermanent members must vote in favor of a resolution for it to pass. Under current rules, no country may serve successive terms as a nonpermanent member. Five of the nonpermanent seats go to Africa and Asia, two each to Latin America and Western Europe, and one to Eastern Europe.

The designation of permanent members reflected the distribution of military power in 1945 and the desire to ensure the UN's ability to respond quickly and decisively to any aggression. Neither the United States nor the Soviet Union would have accepted UN membership without veto power. The veto also reflected a realistic acceptance by others that the UN could not undertake enforcement action either against its strongest members or without their concurrence, but the veto has always been controversial among small states and middle powers. Since the Security Council represents less than 8 percent of the total UN membership, its composition is clearly outdated and discussion of "equitable representation" is a major reform issue.

The Security Council differs from the General Assembly and ECOSOC in that it has no regular schedule of meetings or agenda; historically, it has met and acted only in response to specific conflicts and crises. Any state, including non-UN members, has the right to bring issues before the Security Council, although there is no guarantee of action. The Secretary-General can also bring a matter to the Council's attention. In 2000, however, the Security Council initiated so-called thematic meetings to address broader issues such as HIV/AIDS as a threat to peace, child soldiers, cooperation between the UN and regional organizations under Chapter VIII of the Charter, the role of women in peace and security, protection of civilians, and small arms. This approach will become more important with efforts to address problems before they become crises and to support more preventive diplomacy by the Secretary-General.

Nonmembers may attend formal meetings and address the Council upon request when they have an interest in a particular issue. This practice has become routinized and nonmembers are often invited to private and informal meetings as well (Hurd 2002: 42). States that contribute peacekeeping troops now regularly participate in informal consultations with the Council, as do the heads of the International Committee of the Red Cross, other NGOs, and other nonstate actors. In short, "the Security Council is not a sealed chamber, deaf to voices and immune to pressure from beyond its walls" (Johnstone 2008: 88–89).

Much of the diplomacy and negotiation relating to the Council's work takes place in various informal consultations such as those among the P-5, with troop contributors, Secretariat officials, and nonstate actors. In fact, the *Security Council Report* (2014b) noted that the Council has increasingly tended to operate as two subgroups, with a significant gap between the P-5 and the ten nonpermanent members, resulting in a problem of internal transparency. And, although there have long been complaints about the Council's working methods, in actuality the Council has "continued to be the most adaptable international body, at times capable of modifying its methods of work literally on the spot" (*Security Council Report* 2014b). The Council presidency rotates monthly among the fifteen members, and presidents play an active role in facilitating discussions and consensus building, determining when the members are ready to reach a decision and, hence, to convene a formal meeting. The Council's president also confers regularly with the Secretary-General, with relevant states, and with other actors that are not represented on the Council.

With the extensive use of targeted sanctions since the early 1990s, the work of the Security Council also occurs in fourteen sanctions committees whose tasks include monitoring reports, managing exemptions, and managing designation lists. The committee chairs are typically a permanent representative from one of the ten nonpermanent member states. Decisionmaking is on a consensus basis. The committees are often assisted by panels or groups of experts and monitoring groups that are recruited from lists maintained by the Secretariat. In addition to managing sanctions regimes, the Council's work includes overseeing all UN peacekeeping operations, of which there were sixteen in 2014, plus one political mission (Afghanistan), and a number of working groups.

In addition to its responsibilities under the Charter for maintaining international security, the Council participates in the election of the Secretary-General, justices to the International Court of Justice, and new UN members in collaboration with the General Assembly. During the 1940s the Council held approximately 130 meetings a year. This frequency diminished during the Cold War; in 1959, for example, only five meetings were held. Since the early 1990s, the frequency of meetings has steadily risen, with 262 formal sessions in 2014; often the number of informal consultations is even greater. As of mid-2014, the Council had approved over 2,100 resolutions since its inception and issued hundreds of presidential statements that summarized the outcomes of meetings where no resolutions were acted upon. The majority of both have come since 1990.

The veto power of the permanent members has long been controversial. It was a particular problem during the Cold War, when the Soviet Union employed it frequently not only to block action on many peace and security issues but also to block admission of Western-supported new members and nominees for Secretary-General. The United States did not exercise its veto until the 1970s, reflecting its early dominance and many friends. Since then, however, the United States has used its veto more than any other permanent member. (See Table 4.1 for a summary of vetoes cast and note how infrequently the veto has been used since 1995.) The majority of US vetoes have been cast on resolutions relating to the Arab-Israeli-Palestinian conflict and in defense of Israel. China took advantage of the precedent that allowed abstentions not to be counted as negative votes (i.e., vetoes) to abstain a total of twenty-seven times between 1990 and 1996 on a series of enforcement measures (including those against Iraq), thus registering its disagreement but not blocking action. More recently, however, Russia and China exercised their vetoes on three occasions in 2011 and 2012 to block Council action on the civil war in Syria and worsening humanitarian crisis there, with more than 200,000 civilians killed and almost half the country's population displaced by the end of 2014. Russia exercised its veto once in early 2014 on the crisis in Ukraine. The data in Table 4.1 do not include the large number of vetoes exercised over the years regarding the election of a Secretary-General.

Although much of the literature on the UN has long emphasized the P-5 members' veto power as an important part of decisionmaking in the Security Council, the reality is that in recent years the Council has been divided on only a limited number of issues and otherwise operates largely by consensus. Presidential statements and press statements reflect Council agreement; the sanctions committees as well as working groups operate by consensus; and even most resolutions are adopted by consensus—93.5 percent between 2000 and 2014. Much of the change is a result of China abstaining on resolutions far less often since 2000. The *Security Council Report* (2014b) concludes that although there may be a premium on consensus, the downside is that "in pursuing resolutions with strict consensus . . . stronger language is lost."

**Table 4.1    Vetoes in the Security Council, 1946–2014**

|           | China[a] | France | United Kingdom | United States | USSR/ Russia | Total |
|-----------|----------|--------|----------------|---------------|--------------|-------|
| 1946–1955 | 1        | 2      |                |               | 80           | 83    |
| 1956–1965 |          | 2      | 3              |               | 26           | 31    |
| 1966–1975 | 2        | 2      | 10             | 12            | 7            | 33    |
| 1976–1985 |          | 9      | 11             | 34            | 6            | 60    |
| 1986–1995 |          | 3      | 8              | 24            | 2            | 37    |
| 1996–2008 | 4        |        |                | 12            | 3            | 19    |
| 2009–2014 | 4        |        |                | 1             | 6            | 11    |

*Source:* Global Policy Forum, www.globalpolicy.org; *Security Council Reports.*
*Note:* a. From 1946 to 1971, the Chinese seat on the Security Council was occupied by the Republic of China (Taiwan).

The Cold War made Security Council actions on peace and security threats extremely problematic. It resulted in some conflicts, such as the French and US wars in Vietnam, and Soviet interventions in Czechoslovakia and Hungary, not being brought to the UN at all. A UN response to the North Korean invasion of South Korea in 1950 was possible only because the Soviet Union was boycotting the Security Council at the time. As noted earlier, the General Assembly stepped in to address some crisis situations with recommendations and also the innovation of peacekeeping operations (discussed further in Chapter 7). Although Cold War politics often sidelined the Security Council, it has been recognized at least since the mid-1960s that the Council has the power of "collective legitimation" on behalf of a large part of the international community (Claude 1967; Voeten 2005).

In the late 1980s, the Security Council's activity, power, and prestige increased dramatically. Major shifts in Soviet foreign policy led to closer P-5 cooperation and a succession of breakthroughs in regional conflicts, including the Iran-Iraq War and conflicts in Afghanistan, Central America, Namibia, and Cambodia. The number of Security Council meetings per year rose and the Council also initiated the practices of informal, private consultations and decisionmaking by consensus. In the confrontation with Iraq following its invasion of Kuwait in 1990, the strength of agreement among both the P-5 and the nonpermanent members of the Council was unprecedented.

Since 1990, the Security Council has taken action on more armed conflicts (particularly intrastate conflicts), made more decisions under Chapter VII of the UN Charter, authorized more peacekeeping operations, and imposed more types of sanctions in more situations than ever before. It took the unprecedented step of creating ad hoc war crimes tribunals to prosecute individuals responsible for genocide and war crimes in Rwanda, the former Yugoslavia, and Sierra Leone, and has made referrals to the International Criminal Court, established in 2002. It authorized NATO bombing against Bosnian Serb forces in Bosnia in 1995. It authorized UN-administered protectorates in Kosovo and East Timor. It expanded definitions of threats to peace to include terrorism even before the 9/11 attacks and thereafter approved Resolution 1373, which requires all member states to adopt antiterrorism measures outlined in the International Convention for the Suppression of the Financing of Terrorism. It has attempted to prevent Iran, North Korea, and other actors from acquiring nuclear weapons, and approved Resolution 1540 (2004), which obligates states to establish domestic controls to prevent proliferation of weapons of mass destruction to state or nonstate actors. It has attempted to support democratization in Haiti and Côte d'Ivoire and to promote the roles of women in peace and security and the protection of civilians. It authorized military action to the latter end in Libya and for cross-border humanitarian assistance in Syria.

Unquestionably, however, the inability of Security Council members to agree on action to halt the conflict in Syria or even for a long period to agree on a humanitarian assistance mission demonstrates the Council's impotence in the face of great-power opposition.

The creation of various monitoring bodies since 1990, such as the sanctions committees, the Counter-Terrorism Committee, and the 1540 Committee has marked a sharp departure from earlier actions of the Security Council and also demonstrated a degree of learning regarding how best to frame and target sanctions, for example, and how to improve their effectiveness (*Security Council Report* 2013b). The use of such regulative and legislative authority *over* UN members, and the Council's intrusive sanctions and weapons inspection regimes for Iraq (discussed in Chapter 7), led Canadian diplomat David Malone (2006: 173) to call this "a movement toward a regulatory approach to international peace and security." Likewise, the Council's overall activism since Iraq's invasion of Kuwait in 1990 has led UN member states to view it as "the most relevant international institution for granting or withholding collective legitimation for international war" and for the use of armed force more generally (Hurd 2007: 124). The case of war against Iraq in 2003 shows, Ian Hurd (2008b: 35) argues, "that even powerful states were forced to frame their policies around the existence of the Council. Both coalitions of states, pro- and anti-invasion . . . accepted that Council approval was a powerful resource for states, and so they fought to either win it or withhold it from the other." Despite concerns at the time that the Council was a failed body, both sides clearly saw the legitimacy of its authority at stake.

Still, there continues to be vigorous debate inside and outside the UN about the Security Council's power, authority, and legitimacy. Clearly, the Charter endows the Council with a great deal of formal power; it also gives it "primary authority in the international system over questions of international peace and security." Yet the use of that authority is problematic given the "contradiction between international commitment and state sovereignty," particularly the traditional assumption that international obligations are binding only with states' consent (Hurd 2007: 5). The Council's authority exists only "when actors believe that a rule or hierarchy is *legitimate* and thereby contributes to their perceptions of their interests" (Hurd 2008b: 27). Searching for evidence of the Council's authority for the post–9/11 antiterrorism actions mandated in Resolution 1373, for example, Bruce Cronin and Ian Hurd (2008: 201) confirm: "It is not the act of issuing these mandatory declarations that offers evidence of increased authority, but, rather, the fact that most member states accepted the *right* of the Council to do so."

The passage of time has thus shown that the Council's authority and legitimacy remain strong. The reality that the Council refused to approve the US war against Iraq in 2003 reinforced the Council's perceived authority and thus others saw the war as illegal and illegitimate and refused to support it. Russia's about-face, however, when the Council-authorized NATO intervention in Libya turned into regime change rather than just protection of civilians, along with Russia and China's use of their veto power to block action in Syria, underscores the difficulty of addressing threats to *domestic* peace and security. In short, when there is P-5 consensus, action can be taken (usually with an effort to frame the problem as one of international peace and security); when the Security Council is divided, the result is stasis.

In short, the UN Charter gives the Security Council enormous formal power, but does not give it direct control over the means to use that power. The Council depends upon the voluntary cooperation of states and their willingness to contribute to peacekeeping missions, to enforce sanctions, to pay their dues, and to support enforcement actions either under UN command or by a coalition of the willing with sufficient highly trained military personnel and material. Most important, states' voluntary compliance depends on their perceptions of the legitimacy of the Council and its actions—its symbolic power (Hurd 2002: 35). As the Iraq case demonstrated, even powerful states may work hard to use that symbolic power to serve their interests.

The increased Security Council activity since 1990 has led many UN members to push strongly for reform in the Council's membership in order that it better reflect the world of the twenty-first century, not the world of 1945. This debate, which we take up later in the chapter, concerns how to make the Council function more effectively and how to ensure the continuing legitimacy of its authority.

### The Economic and Social Council

Although the sections of the UN Charter (Chapters IX and X) that deal with ECOSOC are short and very general, this is the most complex part of the UN system. ECOSOC is the UN's central forum for addressing international economic and social issues, and its purposes range from promoting higher standards of living to identifying solutions to economic, social, and health problems and "encouraging universal respect for human rights and fundamental freedoms." The activities it oversees encompass more than 70 percent of human and financial resources of the UN system. The founders of the UN envisaged that the various specialized agencies, ranging from the ILO, WHO, and FAO to the World Bank and IMF, would play primary roles in operational activities devoted to economic and social advancement, with ECOSOC responsible for coordinating those activities. Hence the Charter speaks of ECOSOC's functions in terms of that coordination, as well as in terms of undertaking research and preparing reports on economic and social issues, making recommendations, preparing conventions (treaties), convening conferences, and consulting with nongovernmental organizations. Of those tasks, coordination has proven the most problematic, since a myriad of activities lie outside the effective jurisdiction of ECOSOC. It is through consultative status with ECOSOC that many NGOs have official relationships with the UN and its activities. (See Chapter 6 for further discussion.)

ECOSOC's membership has been expanded through two Charter amendments. The original eighteen members were increased to twenty-seven in 1965 and to fifty-four in 1973. Members are elected by the General Assembly to three-year terms based on nominations by the regional blocs. Motivated by recognition that states with the ability to pay should be continuously represented, the five permanent members of the Security Council and major developed countries such as Germany and Japan have been regularly reelected. ECOSOC acts through decisions and resolutions, many of which are approved by consensus or simple majority votes. None are binding on member states or on the specialized agencies, however. Recommendations and multilateral conventions drafted by ECOSOC require General Assembly approval (and, in the case of conventions, ratification by member states).

ECOSOC holds one four-week substantive meeting in July each year, alternating between UN headquarters in New York and Geneva, where several of the specialized agencies and other programs are headquartered. It also holds many short sessions, panel discussions, and preparatory meetings throughout the year. The annual session is now divided into five segments: high-level, coordination, operational activities, humanitarian affairs, and general. The high-level segment includes the High-Level Political Forum on Sustainable Development (HLPF) established in 2012 to replace the Commission on Sustainable Development. The HLPF is responsible for the Annual Ministerial Review, created in 2007, to assess progress in implementing international development goals, including the Millennium Development Goals (MDGs). Each year, it focuses on a different theme; in 2013, the theme was science, technology, and development. In addition, the biennial Development Cooperation Forum brings together all relevant actors for dialogue on issues relating to development cooperation, such as financing, different types of partnerships, and accountability. Meetings include member states, all relevant UN institutions, civil society groups, and private institutions.

The economic and social activities that ECOSOC is expected to coordinate are spread among many subsidiary bodies (such as expert and working groups composed of independent experts and consultants), nine functional commissions, five regional commissions, and the nineteen specialized agencies. A number of entities created by the General Assembly, such as the UNDP, the UN Fund for Population Activities (UNFPA),

UNICEF, and the World Food Programme, report to both the General Assembly and ECOSOC, compounding the complexity and confusion. The scope of ECOSOC's agenda includes widely diverse topics, ranging from housing, literacy, and the environment to narcotic drug control, refugees, statistics, and the rights of indigenous peoples. Development is by far the largest subject area.

*The specialized agencies and their relationship to ECOSOC.* Several of the specialized agencies, including the ILO, UPU, and World Meteorological Organization (WMO), predate the UN itself, as discussed in Chapter 3. Article 57 of the UN Charter laid out the broad terms under which these agencies were to be brought into relationship with the UN. The first agreement, with the ILO, provided a model for others, although the system of weighted voting in the Bretton Woods institutions distinguishes them from other agencies. The agreements cover such things as exchange of information and documents, treatment to be given by agencies to recommendations from the UN organs, and cooperation in personnel, statistical services, and budgetary arrangements. Among the factors that have complicated the relationship of specialized agencies to ECOSOC is geographical dispersal. The ILO, ITU, World Intellectual Property Organization (WIPO), and WHO are headquartered in Geneva, but the FAO is in Rome, UNESCO is in Paris, the International Civil Aviation Organization (ICAO) is in Montreal, the IMF and World Bank are in Washington, DC, and the International Maritime Organization (IMO) is in London. In the field, each agency has often had its own separate building and staff. This dispersal affects efficiency, budgets, and coordination.

Historically, the specialized agencies and particularly the Bretton Woods institutions have operated quite independently of ECOSOC and the rest of the UN system. Since directors-general of the agencies have the same diplomatic rank as the UN Secretary-General, they have often perceived themselves as operating their own fiefdoms. How can one achieve an integrated international program when different agencies, each with its own administration and objectives, are carrying out similar activities? The ILO is illustrative. Its activities include employment promotion, vocational guidance, social security, safety and health, labor laws and relations, and rural institutions. These overlap with the FAO's concern with land reform, UNESCO's mandate in education, the WHO's focus on health standards, and the UN Industrial Development Organization's (UNIDO) concern with manpower in small industries. The result is constant coordination problems. Since 1998, ECOSOC has hosted annual meetings of finance ministers and officials from the World Bank, IMF, WTO, and UNCTAD to improve interactions among these institutions and coordinate financing for development. Likewise, in the late 1990s, resident directors of the World Bank and IMF began cooperating more with other UN agency personnel working in developing countries. In 2008, the high-level UN Development Group was merged into the Chief Executives Board for Coordination, which is discussed later.

*Functional commissions.* Part of ECOSOC's work is done in eight functional commissions: Social Development, Narcotic Drugs, the Status of Women, Science and Technology for Development, Population and Development, Crime Prevention and Criminal Justice, Statistics, and Forests. The Commission on Statistics reflects the importance of statistical studies and analysis to economic and social programs, and the major contribution the UN system makes annually to governments, researchers, and students worldwide through its statistical studies. The wide range of data on social and economic conditions that have been gathered over the years is vital to dealing with various world problems. For example, when the General Assembly inaugurated the First Development Decade in 1961, women were among the groups singled out for development funds, even though there were then no data on the economic status of women. Only with the publication in 1991 of the first edition of *The World's Women,* compiled under the auspices of the Commission on the Status of Women, were data finally available to inform policymaking on issues relating to women around the world. The importance of data collection and dissemination is discussed further in Chapter 9, but as Michael Ward (2004: 2) concludes in his book *Quantifying the World:* "The creation of a universally acknowledged statistical system and of a general framework guiding the collection and compilation of data according to recognized professional standards, both internationally and nationally, has been one of the great and mostly unsung successes of the UN organization."

The Commission on the Status of Women was established in 1946 to prepare recommendations and reports concerning the promotion of women's political, economic, social, and educational rights, and concerning any problems requiring immediate attention. It drafted a series of early conventions on women's political and marital rights as well as the Declaration on the Elimination of Discrimination Against Women, adopted by the General Assembly in 1967, and the Convention on the Elimination of All Forms of Discrimination Against Women (CEDAW), which was approved in 1979 and entered into force in 1981. After the 1995 Fourth World Conference on Women, in Beijing, the commission was given a central role in monitoring implementation of the Beijing Platform for Action under the broad mandate of achieving gender equality and empowerment of women. That mandate was broadened in 2000 to include follow-up to the Beijing+5 special session of the General Assembly. Sessions focus on specific themes such as gender equality; violence against girls; access of women and girls to education, science, and technology; empowerment of rural women; and caregiving in the context of HIV/AIDS. The commission has forty-five members, who are elected by ECOSOC for four-year terms, and meets annually, along with NGO representatives, for ten days.

Until 2006, one of the most active commissions was the Commission on Human Rights. All of the UN-initiated declarations and conventions on human rights up to then were products of this body's work. Following the 2005 World Summit, the General Assembly in 2006 created the Human Rights Council, which has assumed many of the former commission's responsibilities but reports to the Assembly rather than ECOSOC (see Chapter 10 for further details).

*Regional commissions.* Since 1947, ECOSOC has created five regional commissions. These are designed to stimulate regional approaches to development and are discussed in Chapter 9.

*Field activities.* One of the major factors in the proliferation of economic and social activities has been the growth of operational field activities, especially technical assistance. The UN, through various programs, including the UNDP, created in 1965, and through specialized agencies such as the WHO, the FAO, and UNESCO, disburses funds and expertise to developing countries to train people and introduce new technologies. Coordinating these activities in the field is a large part of ECOSOC's challenge.

Coordination is inherently difficult within any complex organization, and national governments have their own problems in this regard. Indeed, one analyst argues that ECOSOC's problems are attributable in part to "the absence of coordination at the national level in regard to international policies and programmes" (Taylor 2000: 108). The steady expansion of UN economic and social activities over more than seven decades has made ECOSOC's mandate almost impossible to fulfill, leading to persistent but largely unsuccessful calls for reform since the late 1940s, as discussed later.

## The Secretariat

The UN Secretariat comprises about 43,000 professional and clerical staff based in New York, Geneva, Vienna, Nairobi, and field operations around the world, not including the secretariats of the specialized agencies or military and civilian personnel in UN peace operations. These international civil servants are individuals who, though nationals of member countries, represent the international community. The earliest IGO secretariats were established by the UPU and ITU in the 1860s and 1870s, but their members were not independent of national governments. The League of Nations established the first truly international secretariat, which was responsible for carrying out the will of the League's members while remaining impartial or neutral in serving the organization as a whole. Member states were expected to respect the international character and responsibilities of the staff, regardless of their nationality. This practice carried over to the UN and the specialized agencies, with UN Secretariat members recruited from an ever-broader geographic base as the membership expanded. Secretariat members are not expected to give up their national loyalty, but to refrain from promoting national interests—a sometimes difficult task in a world of strong nationalisms.

While the General Assembly, Security Council, and ECOSOC provide arenas where member states debate issues and make recommendations and decisions, the UN Secretariat, including the Secretary-General and senior leadership, form the "second" UN. They wield significant influence within the UN itself and occasionally over member states. The Secretary-General in particular has thereby contributed to the emergence of the UN as an autonomous actor in global governance and world politics.

*The Secretary-General.* The position of the UN Secretary-General (UNSG) has been termed "one of the most ill-defined: a combination of chief administrative officer of the United Nations and global diplomat with a fat portfolio whose pages are blank" (Hall 1994: 22). The Secretary-General is manager of the organization, responsible for providing leadership to the Secretariat, preparing the UN's budget, submitting an annual report to the General Assembly, and overseeing studies conducted at the request of the other major organs. Article 99 of the UN Charter authorizes the Secretary-General to present to the Security Council issues that threaten international peace. This provides the legal basis for the Secretary-General's authority and ability to be an independent actor. The UNSG also commands moral authority as "the representative of the community's interests or the defender of the values of the international community" (Barnett and Finnemore 2004: 23).

Over time, UNSGs have often, but not always, come to play significant political roles as spokespersons for the organization; as conveners of expert groups, commissions, and panels to frame issues, marshal research, and outline choices; and as mediators drawing on the Charter's spirit as the basis for taking initiatives. Yet the Secretary-General must simultaneously meet the demands of two constituencies—member states and the Secretariat itself. States elect the UN's chief administrator and do not want to be either upstaged or publicly opposed by the person in that position. The Secretary-General also has to answer to Secretariat personnel working in programs and agencies across the UN system. As chief executive officer, the UNSG also has to have good personnel management and budgetary skills. The balancing act is not always easy.

The Secretary-General holds office for a five-year renewable term on recommendation by the Security Council and election by two-thirds of the General Assembly. The process of nomination is intensely political and

| Figure 4.5     UN Secretaries-General, 1946–present | | |
| --- | --- | --- |
| Secretary-General | Nationality | Dates of Service |
| Trygve Lie | Norway | 1946–1953 |
| Dag Hammarskjöld | Sweden | 1953–1961 |
| U Thant | Burma | 1961–1971 |
| Kurt Waldheim | Austria | 1972–1981 |
| Javier Pérez de Cuéllar | Peru | 1982–1991 |
| Boutros Boutros-Ghali | Egypt | 1992–1996 |
| Kofi Annan | Ghana | 1997–2006 |
| Ban Ki-moon | Republic of Korea | 2007–present |

secretive, with the P-5 having key input because of their veto power. For example, the United States strongly opposed the reelection of Boutros Boutros-Ghali in 1996, forcing member states to agree on an alternate candidate, Kofi Annan. Efforts to establish a better means of selecting this global leader have been unsuccessful thus far. Not surprisingly, those elected have tended to come from relatively small states (see Figure 4.5).

The UNSGs have been a key factor in the emergence of the UN as an autonomous actor in world politics, thereby making the UN something more than just a forum for multilateral diplomacy. The effectiveness of the Secretariat depends heavily on its leadership and on the "competence, capability, and general character of any Secretary-General" (Jonah 2007: 170). Hence, personality, experience, and skills matter. It has long been debated, however, to what extent the person holding the office is or should be a "secretary" or a "general"; in other words, to what extent the UNSG is primarily an administrator or an activist and initiator (Chesterman 2007). Kent Kille (2006), for example, describes three key leadership styles of Secretaries-General: manager, strategist, and visionary. From the standpoint of IR theories, UNSGs are generally analyzed as an agent, with member states (and sometimes the Secretariat itself) being the principals, but there is also ample evidence of them as autonomous actors, with that autonomy on occasion constrained.

Since 1945, successive Secretaries-General have taken advantage of opportunities for initiatives, applied flexible interpretations of Charter provisions, and sought mandates from UN policy organs as necessary. They have developed their own political roles as well as the role of the institution. Their personalities and interpretation of the Charter, as well as world events, have combined to increase the power, resources, and importance of the position.

The UNSG is well placed to serve as a neutral communications channel and intermediary for the global community. While representing the institution, he or she can act independently of the policy organs even when resolutions have condemned a party to a dispute, maintaining lines of communication and representing the institution's commitment to peaceful settlement and alleviation of human suffering. Over time, Secretaries-General have used various methods to maintain peace, from fact-finding and using their "good offices" to employing "groups of friends" (Whitfield 2007). For example, Dag Hammarskjöld articulated principles for UN involvement in peacekeeping and coined the phrase "preventive diplomacy." Javier Pérez de Cuéllar epitomized the ideal intermediary using a persistent, low-key approach to Israel's 1982 invasion of Lebanon, the Falklands/Malvinas War, the Iran-Iraq War, and the ongoing conflicts in Cyprus, Namibia, Afghanistan, and Central America. Increasingly, UNSGs have appointed special representatives (SRSGs) to fulfill various roles in conjunction with UN peace operations as well as to promote action on various thematic issues—a development that, as Manuel Fröhlich (2013: 232) notes, "underscores the fact or the ambition that, at times, IOs act in their own right."

Secretaries-General have also played the role of norm entrepreneurs. For example, both Boutros Boutros-Ghali and Kofi Annan encouraged the development of the UN's role in promoting democratic governance (Johnstone 2007; Haack and Kille 2012). Following NATO's intervention in Kosovo in 1999 without Security Council authorization but in support of the emerging norm of humanitarian intervention, Annan chose to speak directly to the meaning of state sovereignty, recognizing "rights beyond borders" (UN 1999a).

A key resource for UNSGs is the power of persuasion. The "force" of majorities behind resolutions may lend greater legitimacy to initiatives, though it may not ensure any greater degree of success. Autonomy is also key to the UNSG's influence. For example, during the Security Council's 2002–2003 debate over Iraq's failure to disarm and cooperate with UN inspections and whether to authorize a US-led war, Kofi Annan steered an independent course by pushing for Iraqi compliance, Security Council unity, and peace, preserving his own ability to serve as a neutral intermediary.

As U Thant stated: "The Secretary-General must always be prepared to take an initiative, no matter what the consequences to him or his office may be, if he sincerely believes that it might make the difference between peace and war" (quoted in Young 1967: 284). Annan put it more bluntly in saying: "I know some people have accused me of using diplomacy. That's my job" (quoted in Crossette 1999: A8). Secretary-General Boutros Boutros-Ghali pushed the boundaries of the office and demonstrated the limits of autonomy. As one commentator describes: "He saw an opening for the UN in the post–Cold War disarray and plunged: prodding the United States to send thousands of American soldiers to rescue Somalis from famine; urging the United Nations into new terrain in Cambodia, Bosnia and Haiti" (Preston 1994: 10–11). His activism and his antagonistic relationship with the United States led to his defeat for a second term in 1996.

Kofi Annan, who had served in the UN for thirty-five years, became the first Secretary-General from within the UN bureaucracy. He proved even more of an activist than his predecessor, earning the 2001 Nobel Peace Prize for himself and the organization. He carried out extensive administrative and budgetary reforms. He initiated steps to strengthen liaison with NGOs and regional IGOs, and dialogue with major business leaders. He was the first UNSG to make a special effort to build a better relationship with the US Congress, an important step given Congress's refusal to appropriate full funding for US dues to the UN for much of the 1990s. As he put it, "The United Nations needs the United States to achieve our goals, and I believe the United States needs the United Nations no less" (quoted in Gourevitch 2003: 54).

Annan was widely respected and was reelected by acclamation in 2001. He used his "bully pulpit" as UN head to take initiatives on a wide variety of issues, from HIV/AIDS and the Millennium Development Goals to the Global Compact on Corporate Responsibility. He took the unprecedented step of commissioning independent reports on the UN's failures in the 1995 massacre in the UN-declared safe area of Srebrenica, the 1994 Rwandan genocide, and the 2003 attack on UN personnel in Iraq. Those reports and the public acceptance of blame were "nothing short of revolutionary at the United Nations" (quoted in Crossette 1999: A8).

The latter part of Annan's tenure was marred by scandals over the Oil-for-Food Programme with Iraq (discussed later) and sexual misconduct of peacekeepers in the Democratic Republic of Congo. He devoted considerable energy to trying to secure reforms at the time of the UN's sixtieth anniversary in 2005, even though such initiatives usually come from member states (Luck 2005). Despite these missteps, "Annan expanded the secretary-generalship to its greatest possible dimensions. . . . The political space available to a secretary-general is a consequence both of his own ambition and skill and of the willingness of the members to have him play such a role. If that willingness disappears, diplomatic gifts avail nothing" (Traub 2006: 405).

Still, even activist Secretaries-General can find their influence limited. As Mark Malloch Brown (2008: 10), former administrator of UNDP and later *chef de cabinet* to Kofi Annan, remarked: "I found when it came to management and budgetary matters that the secretary-general was less influential than I had been as administrator of UNDP. Whereas I had had a cooperative board that was not infected by bitter political confrontation, he was hostage to intergovernmental warfare."

Ban Ki-moon, the Republic of Korea's former foreign minister and a career diplomat, succeeded Annan in January 2007 as the second Asian to lead the UN. He pledged to deliver more and work with all constituencies, including states, NGOs, and the business community. In the early years of his tenure, he took initiatives on climate change, Darfur, and preventive diplomacy. In pressing for management reform, he appointed three women from developing countries to senior posts in the UN Secretariat and instituted policies to eliminate patronage jobs and to foster competition for jobs internally. He reorganized the Departments of Peacekeeping Operations and Political Affairs. Yet in 2010, Inga-Britt Ahlenius, outgoing Undersecretary-General of the Office of Internal Oversight Services, wrote a scathing critique of Ban's management practices, particularly his efforts to undercut the independence of the internal investigations division (Lynch 2010: A14). He was criticized for his handling of the Sri Lankan civil war in 2009 and waited until a year into the fighting in Syria before speaking out about the atrocities and appointing a special representative. He refused to take responsibility on behalf of the institution for the cholera epidemic in Haiti that has been linked to UN peacekeepers. Nonetheless, Ban was reelected for a second term in 2012. As one journalist has remarked, however, "while Ban has been a letdown on many fronts, it's worth asking whether anyone else could have done better—at least on Syria. . . . The fact is that when the great powers squabble, there's little that anyone in the organization can accomplish, be they competent or not. . . . The big powers, tired of locking horns with Annan, wanted someone bland and pliable to replace him, and the colorless South Korean fit the bill" (Tepperman 2013).

Conflict-related SRSGs are now appointed in conjunction with all UN peace operations; from the earliest times, special representatives have also served as mediators exercising significant independent influence. Among the most notable have been Sergio Viera de Mello, who served successively in Lebanon, Kosovo, East Timor, and Iraq; Martti Ahtisaari, winner of the 2008 Nobel Peace Prize, who served as SRSG in Namibia and Kosovo; and Lakhdar Brahimi, who has served on thirteen occasions, including in Haiti, South Africa, Afghanistan, Iraq, and Syria.

In the case of thematic SRSGs, between 1997 and 2013, SRSGs were dealing with thirty-two different topics, ranging from the impact of armed conflict on children and HIV/AIDS in Africa to the Millennium Development Goals, the Global Compact on Corporate Responsibility, migration, and sexual violence in conflict. They represent the Secretary-General by "becoming a presence themselves—not necessarily with office space in New York, but certainly as a distinct voice and promoters of ideas in direct consultation with diplomats and the media as well as with governments, relevant agencies, and NGOs worldwide" (Fröhlich 2014: 186). In short, SRSGs have a degree of leeway for action that allows them to exercise leadership, speak for the UNSG, and help in the exercise of that office. But only under Ban Ki-moon and following the passage of Security Council Resolution 1325, on the roles of women in peace and security, have women been appointed more frequently as SRSGs (Fröhlich 2014: 179).

*Functions of the Secretariat.* The UN Secretariat and the secretariats of the specialized agencies share some of the characteristics of bureaucracies more generally. They derive authority from their rational-legal character and from their expertise; they derive legitimacy from the moral purposes of the organization and from their claims to neutrality, impartiality, and objectivity; they derive power from their missions of serving others. Their work often has little to do with the symbolic politics of the General Assembly or the high-politics debates of the Security Council. It involves the implementation of the economic, humanitarian, and social programs as well as peace operations, which represent much of the UN's tangible contribution to fulfilling the promises of its charter. The Secretariat is also responsible for gathering statistical data, preparing studies and reports, servicing meetings, preparing documentation, and providing translations of speeches, debates, and documents in the UN's six official languages.

The Secretariat is organized into a series of offices and departments, as shown in Figure 4.2. Each of these is headed by an undersecretary or assistant secretary-general, division head, or high commissioner. Among the various Secretariat reforms has been the creation of the post of deputy secretary-general in 1997 and a more cabinet-style of management in 2005. The Senior Management Group, chaired by the Secretary-General, brings together leaders of UN departments, offices, funds, and programs in regular meetings, including video conferences with UN offices around the world. It is a forum for policy-related matters, planning, and information-sharing with respect to emerging challenges and cross-cutting issues. The deputy secretary-general is tasked with many of the administrative responsibilities and management of Secretariat operations. In addition, the Chief Executives Board, which includes the executive heads of twenty-nine UN specialized agencies and programs, meets twice a year under the Secretary-General's chairmanship to facilitate coordination across the entire UN system. In place since 1946, it was originally known as the Administrative Committee on Coordination. With the name change in 2000, it was reorganized into three committees: the High-Level Committee on Management, the High-Level Committee on Programmes, and the UN Development Group (chaired by the UNDP head).

The different agencies and programs within the UN system as well as parts of the core Secretariat are staffed by technocrats—individuals with specialized training and knowledge who shape policy options consistent with that expertise and are also often active in generating, synthesizing, and disseminating knowledge. Their expertise influences "what problems are visible to staff and what range of solutions are entertained" (Barnett and Finnemore 2005: 174). The ways in which UN bureaucrats understand particular conflict situations, for example, can also influence how member states view them. During the 1994 Rwandan genocide, the UN Secretariat defined the situation as a civil war and failed to see that the unfolding genocide was something quite different from violence against civilians in other ethnic conflicts. Neither the Department of Peacekeeping Operations nor Secretary-General Boutros-Ghali made the case for intervention. Thus the UN's failure to stop the genocide in Rwanda was "the predictable result of an organizational culture that shaped how the UN evaluated and responded to violent crises" (Barnett and Finnemore 2004: 155).

The UN Secretariat has been criticized for lapses in its neutrality, duplication of tasks, slowness in advancing women and appointing them to leadership positions, and poor management practices. Member states share blame with UNSGs and staff for the problems. General Assembly and Security Council resolutions may be vague and unrealistic; objectives often depend on member governments' actions and other factors to be fulfilled; and since the UN is a political organization, the Secretariat is subject to interference from member states. Indeed, many member states do not necessarily want the UN to have an effective Secretariat and Secretary-General, since that could diminish their own ability to control what the UN does.

The lack of women in the Secretariat has long been noted. Since 1987, twenty women have held senior leadership positions in the UN. Thirteen UN agencies have had at least one woman leader; four organizations and the office of deputy secretary-general have been led by two women each (Haack 2014: 44). Only at the lowest levels of the Secretariat has gender balance actually been achieved, with women holding 60 percent of positions; at the highest level, women hold only 27 percent of positions (UN Women 2014). Furthermore, women predominantly hold positions relating to low politics and "soft" issues such as social welfare, human rights, the environment, and health rather than the "hard," high-politics issues of security, trade, finance, and agriculture, with the sole exception of Christine Lagarde, managing director of the IMF since 2011 (Haack 2014: 44, 48–51). Despite the efforts of a "triangular alliance" of women working in the Secretariat, women diplomats, and women's movements outside the UN, change has been difficult to achieve (Haack 2014: 42, 43). We discuss other aspects of Secretariat reform later in the chapter.

### The International Court of Justice
As the judicial arm of the United Nations, the ICJ shares responsibility with the other major organs for ensuring that the principles of the Charter are

followed. Its special role is providing states with an impartial body for settling legal disputes in accordance with international law (so-called contentious cases) and giving advisory opinions on legal questions referred to it by the General Assembly, Security Council, and specialized agencies.

The General Assembly and Security Council play a joint role in electing the fifteen judges, who serve nine-year terms (five are elected every three years). Judges must have qualifications befitting appointment to the highest judicial body in their home country and recognized competence in international law. Together they represent the major legal systems of the world, but act independently of their national affiliations, utilizing different sources of law set forth in Article 38 of the ICJ Statute as the basis for judgments. Their deliberations take place in private, their decisions are decided by majority vote, and decisions include the reasons on which they are based.

The ICJ has noncompulsory jurisdiction, meaning that parties to a dispute (states only) must all agree to submit a case to the court; there is no way to force a party to appear before the court, but once states agree to ICJ jurisdiction, they are legally bound to follow the decision. With no executive to enforce decisions, however, enforcement depends on voluntary compliance of states, the perceived legitimacy of the court's actions, and the "power of shame" if states fail to comply with an ICJ judgment.

The issue of the court's jurisdiction has been a particularly vexing one. Article 36.2 of the ICJ Statute—the Optional Clause—gives states the opportunity to declare that they recognize ICJ jurisdiction as compulsory. States that sign this clause agree to accept the court's jurisdiction in all legal disputes, or they may agree to accept the court's jurisdiction as compulsory only for disputes with other states that have also accepted compulsory jurisdiction. The clause was tested in 1984 when Nicaragua initiated proceedings against the United States for mining its harbors and undermining its government and economy (ICJ Contentious Case 1984b). The United States disputed the court's jurisdiction on the grounds that Nicaragua had not accepted compulsory ICJ jurisdiction and that even had it done so, the issues were political not legal. The ICJ ruled against the United States. In response, President Ronald Reagan terminated US acceptance of the court's compulsory jurisdiction in October 1985.

The ICJ had 130 contentious cases brought before it between 1946 and 2014. In the past, the court was never heavily burdened, but its caseload has increased substantially. In the 1970s it averaged one or two pending cases; between 1990 and 1997 that number increased to between nine and thirteen pending cases; and in 2014 there were fourteen cases on the docket. In addition, between 1946 and 2014 the court issued twenty-six advisory opinions. The increased caseload is a result in part of greater trust in the court by developing countries after the Nicaragua case showed that a small, developing country could win a judicial victory over a major power (the United States). An added factor has been the option of using a chamber of five justices to hear and determine cases by summary procedure, potentially speeding up what is often a very lengthy process. Noting that this option has been used for a number of complex territorial dispute cases such as that involving the Gulf of Maine (ICJ Contentious Case 1984a), J. G. Merrills (2011: 139) notes that "states also see the chambers procedures as a way of having cases which raise highly technical issues heard by small tribunals selected for their expertise."

Only rarely have ICJ cases dealt with major political issues of the day, since few states want to trust a legal judgment for settlement of a largely political issue. Several cases addressed decolonization questions, including in Namibia and Western Sahara (ICJ Advisory Opinions 1971, 1975). There have been a growing number of cases involving territorial disputes, including delimitation of the North Sea continental shelf, fisheries jurisdiction in the previously mentioned Gulf of Maine, and the maritime boundary between Cameroon and Nigeria (ICJ Contentious Cases 1969, 1984a, 2002). A number of pending cases concern maritime delimitation in the Caribbean Sea and Pacific Ocean. The court has also ruled on the legality of nuclear tests (ICJ Contentious Case 1974 [*Nuclear Tests Cases*]), as well as on hostage taking (ICJ Contentious Case 1980 [*Case Concerning US Diplomatic and Consular Staff in Tehran*]), environmental protection (ICJ Contentious Case 1997 [*Case Concerning the Gabcikovo-Nagymaros Project*]), and genocide (ICJ Contentious Case 2007 [*The Application of the Genocide Convention in the Conflict between Bosnia-Herzegovina and the former Yugoslavia*]). A 2014 decision concerning Japan's whaling in the Antarctic is discussed in Chapter 11.

On twenty-six occasions, the ICJ has issued advisory opinions on legal issues relating to the functioning of the UN. Among the more prominent of these are the opinion concerning reparation for injuries suffered during UN service, in which the UN's international legal personality was clarified; the opinion on the issue of reservations to multilateral treaties; the opinion that declared peacekeeping expenses to be part of the fiscal obligations of member states; and the immunity from legal process of a special rapporteur of the Commission on Human Rights (see, respectively, ICJ Advisory Opinions 1949, 1951, 1962, 1999). In the first, the United Nations was accorded the right to seek payment from a state held responsible for the injury or death of a UN employee. With this case, the ICJ also established that it had the power to interpret the UN Charter, which was not expressly conferred upon it either by the Charter or by the court's own statute or rules. Two more recent advisory opinions concerned the legal consequences of the construction of the barrier wall in the occupied Palestinian territories and the accordance with international law of Kosovo's unilateral declaration of independence (ICJ Advisory Opinions 2004, 2010). Both represented more political issues and were requested by the General Assembly.

When dealing with the UN Charter and the legality of acts of other UN organs, the ICJ, in the words of Justice Mohammed Bedjaoui, has shown "discretion, measure, modesty, restraint, caution, sometimes even humility" (quoted in Ramcharan 2000: 183). In the 1949 *Reparation for Injury* case cited above, the court took an activist approach to its powers, but in its 1971 advisory opinion on Namibia it took a narrower view that it did not have power to review actions by the General Assembly and Security Council. In 1992 the court also took a narrow view of its role when asked by Libya to authorize provisional measures after the Security Council threatened it with sanctions unless it extradited nationals accused of participation in the Lockerbie bombing of Pan Am Flight 103 (ICJ Contentious Case 1992).

The ICJ is limited by the fact that only states can bring contentious cases. This excludes the court from dealing with contemporary disputes involving states and nonstate actors such as terrorist and paramilitary groups, NGOs, and private corporations, and explains why Karen Alter (2014) refers to the ICJ as an "old style" court in contrast to the newer courts discussed in Chapters 1, 3, 10, and 11. In addition, what she calls "new style" international courts have far-reaching compulsory jurisdiction and may perform judicial roles other than dispute settlement, such as administrative review, enforcement, and constitutional review. Furthermore, while judicial decisions are sources of international law under the ICJ Statute, Article 38.1(d) also provides that the "decision of the Court has no binding force except as between the parties and in respect of that particular case." In other words, state sovereignty limits the applicability of ICJ judgments, unlike the judgments of national courts, which use precedents from prior cases to shape future judgments and hence the substance and interpretation of law. In reality, however, the ICJ has used many principles from earlier cases to decide later ones. This contributes to greater consistency in its decisions and more respect for its ability to contribute to the progressive development of international law. The ICJ also draws increasingly from decisions rendered by national and regional courts in an effort to give the impression of a unified field of international legal jurisprudence.

Past assessments of the court frequently dwelt on its relatively light caseload and slow processes, but others have stressed its contributions to "the process of systematizing, consolidating, codifying and progressively developing international law" (Ramcharan 2000: 177). Using the contentious case involving a territorial dispute between Qatar and Bahrain, Alter (2014: 177) notes how, despite lengthy proceedings, the ICJ could issue "a binding compromise under the guise of a legal solution" to address a long-standing dispute that had eluded resolution outside the ICJ. The outcome also benefited the economic development of both parties. Thus, the ICJ has been important to the constitutional development of global governance and complementary to the UN's political organs in its role.

### The Trusteeship Council

The UN Trusteeship Council was originally established to oversee the administration of the non-self-governing trust territories that carried over from the mandate system of the League of Nations. These were former German colonies, mostly in Africa, that were placed under the League-supervised control of other powers (Great Britain, France, Belgium, South Africa, and Japan) because they were deemed unprepared for self-determination or independence. After World War II, the mandates for Lebanon, Syria, Jordan, and Iraq were terminated and each country was granted independence. Great Britain turned the Palestine mandate over to the UN in 1947 when it was unable to cope with rising conflict between Arabs and Jews. The eleven UN trust territories also included Pacific islands that the United States liberated from Japan during World War II. The council's supervisory activities included reporting on the status of the people in the territories and conducting periodic visits to the territories.

At the initial Trusteeship Council session in 1947, Secretary-General Trygve Lie stated that the goal for the trust territories was full statehood. Thus, when the council terminated the agreement for the Trust Territory of the Pacific Islands in 1993, it no longer had any responsibilities. For almost fifty years, however, the council and its system of supervision provided a model for the peaceful transition to independence for other colonial and dependent peoples, thus playing a role in the remarkable process of decolonization during the 1950s and 1960s.

The Trusteeship Council no longer meets in annual sessions. Absent a UN Charter amendment abolishing it, there have been proposals for new functions such as giving the council responsibility for monitoring conditions affecting the global commons (seas, seabed, and outer space) and for providing policy guidance on long-term global trends.

### Global Conferences and Summits

Multilateral global conferences date back to the period after World War I when the League of Nations convened conferences on economic affairs and disarmament. Since the late 1960s, the UN has sponsored global conferences and summit meetings of heads of state and government on topics ranging from the environment, food supply, population, and women's rights, to children, water supplies, and racism, as shown in Table 4.2. Often, these are intended to focus international attention on new or persisting problems and bring together diverse constituencies to develop programs of action. They are ad hoc events, convened at the request of one or more

**Table 4.2  UN-Sponsored Global Conferences and Summits**

| Focus | Global Conferences | Summits |
|---|---|---|
| Aging | 1982, 2002 | |
| Agrarian reform and rural development | 1984 | |
| Children | | 1990 |
| Climate | 1979, 1990, 2007– | 2014 |
| Desertification | 1977 | |
| Education | 1990 | |
| Environment | 1972 | |
| Environment and development | 1992 | |
| Financing for development | | 2002, 2008 |
| Food | 1974, 2002 | 1996 |
| Habitat (human settlements) | 1976, 1996 | |
| Human rights | 1968, 1993 | |
| Illicit trade in small arms | 2001 | |
| Information society | | 2003, 2005 |
| Law of the Sea | 1958, 1973–1982 | |
| Least-developed countries | 1981, 1990, 2001 | |
| Millennium Development Goals | | 2010 |
| New and renewable sources of energy | 1981 | |
| Population | 1974, 1984 | |
| Population and development | 1994 | |
| Racism | 1987, 2001 | |
| Science and technology for development | 1979 | |
| Social development | | 1995, 2000 |
| Sustainable development | | 2002, 2012 |
| Sustainable development, small island states | 1994, 2005, 2014 | |
| UN reform, new-millennium challenges | | 2000, 2005 |
| Water | 1977 | |
| Women | 1975, 1980, 1985, 1995 | |
| World financial and economic crisis | | 2009 |

countries, and authorized by the General Assembly or ECOSOC, with all member states eligible to attend. Names can be deceiving and this is particularly true for those events since 1990 termed "summits" in which the sessions for heads of state and government last one or two days and may or may not be accompanied by a conference running from two to six weeks. There was a large cluster of global conferences in the 1970s and another in the 1990s, with a lull in the 1980s and a deliberate effort to scale back after 2000.

A second type of UN-sponsored global conference has been used for negotiating major law-creating treaties for states to subsequently ratify. Sometimes prompted by the drafting of a text by the International Law Commission—a body of legal experts that looks for patterns of law and tries to codify them—the first such conference was the UN Conference on the Law of the Sea, convened from 1973 to 1982 with over 160 governments engaged in complex negotiations. The Law of the Sea Convention, concluded in 1982, came into effect in 1994 and has since been ratified by

165 states. A similar treaty-negotiating process began in 2007 for a successor agreement to the 1997 Kyoto Protocol, on climate change, which expired in 2012. As with the Law of the Sea conference, these negotiations have been long and difficult, with the outcome still in doubt, as discussed in Chapter 11.

UN-sponsored global conferences and summits serve a variety of purposes. They "seek to raise global consciousness about a particular problem, hoping to change the dominant attitudes surrounding the definition of the issue"; educate publics and government officials; generate new information; provide opportunities to develop soft law, new norms, principles, and international standards; highlight gaps in international institutions by providing new forums for debate and consensus building; and "set in motion a process whereby governments make commitments and can be held accountable" (Schechter 2005: 9). The environmental and women's conferences, in particular, also led governments to create national bodies to address the issues.

Global conferences provide opportunities for developing transnational issue networks by inviting participation and input from scientific and other expert groups, NGOs, and private corporations. Most global conferences, but not necessarily summits, have involved two conferences in the same location—the official conference with UN member states and a parallel NGO-organized conference. Participation has varied widely, from the 1972 UN Conference on the Human Environment (UNCHE) in Stockholm, which included 114 UN member states and over 250 NGOs in the parallel Environment Forum, to the 2002 Johannesburg Summit on Sustainable Development, attended by approximately 21,000 accredited people, including representatives of 191 states and some 3,200 representatives of NGOs and other organizations. These parallel conferences contributed greatly to the growth of NGOs and civil society, raising important questions about who gets to participate in global governance; they have also helped to increase understanding of the links among issues as seemingly disparate as environmental protection, human rights (especially for women), poverty alleviation, and development and trade. But as we discuss further in Chapter 6, NGO participation in the intergovernmental global conferences has varied widely, as has their ability to propose measures and help shape specific outcomes.

Global conferences typically have involved extensive preparatory processes, including in-depth studies by experts and preparatory meetings, convened by committees known as "prepcoms" and involving NGOs and states. This is where decisions are made on many key agenda items, experts are brought in, and NGO roles at the conference itself are determined. There may also be regional meetings to help build consensus on proposed conference outcomes. By one estimate, at least 60 percent of the final conference outcomes are negotiated during the preparatory process (Schechter 2001: 189). The background studies can also serve as wake-up calls to the international community, such as when studies prior to the 1982 World Assembly on Aging showed that developing countries would face challenges of aging populations in less than fifty years.

The outcomes of global conferences generally include declarations and action plans. Several of the conferences in the 1970s also led to new institutions to meet conference goals, among them the UN Environment Programme (UNEP) and the UN Development Fund for Women (UNIFEM). The 1992 UN Conference on the Environment and Development (UNCED), held in Rio de Janeiro, charged NGOs with key roles in implementing goals. The Platform of Action approved at the 1995 Fourth World Conference on Women, in Beijing, called for "empowering women" through access to economic resources. Subsequent chapters analyze the outcomes of UN conferences in various issue areas, but many scholars agree with the assessment that the "conferences are one of the main devices . . . that are used to spawn, nurture, and massage new ideas as well as to nudge governments, international secretariats, and international civil service to alter their conceptions and policies" (Emmerij, Jolly, and Weiss 2001: 89).

Critics from across the political spectrum have argued that the large global conferences are too unwieldy, often duplicate the work of other bodies, and are an inefficient way to identify problems and solutions. They have questioned whether the conferences are just expensive media events whose declarations and programs of action have little value, citing as an example the 1995 Beijing Platform, with its 360 articles on steps to be taken (Fomerand 1996). By the late 1990s, the difficulties of monitoring what was actually being done and integrating implementation of conference outcomes with the main UN organs, especially ECOSOC, had become especially problematic, and the US Congress had joined the critics to impose a moratorium on US participation in UN global conferences, except for the Durban anti-racism conference scheduled for 2001. Even before the United States took its stand on future conferences, the UN began a systematic effort in 1995 to focus on crosscutting themes coming out of the conferences. ECOSOC convened a special session in 1998 on the challenge of integrating and coordinating implementation and follow-up to major conferences and summits. In 2003, the General Assembly voted to end the practice. As a result, a number of subsequent major UN-sponsored gatherings have been "summits," rather than global conferences, often convened for only one or two days immediately prior to the fall General Assembly session. For example, the Millennium Summit in 2000 focused on mobilizing agreement on the eight Millennium Development Goals, thus deliberately addressing the need to integrate the development-related goals of various separate conferences.

At the 2005 World Summit, various UN reform proposals were the central focus, with Secretary-General Kofi Annan putting forth his own program of action, *In Larger Freedom: Towards Development, Security, and Human Rights for All* (Annan 2005). Although leaders failed to act on Security Council reform, they did approve the creation of the Peacebuilding Commission and the Human Rights Council to replace the Commission on Human Rights, strengthened UN oversight capacity, and approved language endorsing the "responsibility to protect," condemned terrorism "in all its forms and manifestations," and recognized the serious challenge posed by climate change (Annan 2005). Yet another summit was convened in 2009 on the World Financial and Economic Crisis, and UNSG Ban Ki-moon convened the Climate Summit in 2014 to galvanize action on the problem of climate change.

The bottom line is that UN-sponsored conferences and summits are an integral part of global governance, not just stand-alone events tied to the United Nations. As part of broader political processes, the conferences in particular have mobilized energies and attention in a way that established institutions cannot. They have pushed different parts of the UN system, but the "record of policy and procedural implementation is spotty, varied, and obviously incomplete" (Schechter 2001: 185). Much depends on NGOs' ability to sustain pressure on governments to live up to commitments they have made, and to assist the UN in meeting the demands placed upon it. We will return to our assessment of this record in subsequent chapters.

## Persistent Organizational Problems and the Need for Reform

Over the UN's seven-decade history, there have been many efforts at reform. Indeed, one longtime observer has called this "a constant refrain . . . never finished, never perfected" (Luck 2007: 653). In the 1970s, the focus was on improving coordination of economic and social programs in the UN system; in the 1980s, calls for financial reforms dominated the agenda; since the early 1990s, managerial reforms, improvement of the UN's ability to support different types of peace operations, and Security Council reform have been among the major issues. The UN is still hamstrung by pre–Cold War structures, redundant agencies, inadequate personnel policies, lack of accountability and transparency, limited resources, and the inability to meet the needs of a changing world. As one former UN official has noted, "The world wants more of the UN, and the organization is only able to deliver less" (Brown 2008: 3).

How, then, can UN reform occur? Many changes can and have been accomplished without amending the UN Charter, demonstrating the Charter's flexibility and adaptability as well as the innovativeness of various bodies in creating new entities to meet new demands; addressing coordination, management, transparency, and accountability issues; and terminating bodies that have outlived their usefulness. In 1997, for example, Secretary-General Kofi Annan merged three departments into one, the Department of Economic and Social Affairs, and merged all of the Geneva-based human rights programs into the single office of the UN High Commissioner for Human Rights. He reduced the size of the UN Secretariat by almost 4,000 personnel; created the post of deputy secretary-general; grouped the central offices into five executive groups, with their heads forming a cabinet; and promoted the idea of UN "houses" in developing countries to bring UN development agencies and programs together. As valuable as these incremental changes were, they barely scratched the surface. His successor, Ban Ki-moon, restructured support for peacekeeping operations by creating a new Department of Field Support while retaining the planning and strategy functions in the Department of Peacekeeping Operations. He also oversaw the consolidation of four agencies dealing with gender issues into UN Women and the "Delivering As One" initiative to streamline all UN agency operations in a given country.

Changes in the major organs, however, require amending the UN Charter. This has happened only on two occasions: in 1963, when the membership of the Security Council was increased from eleven to fifteen, its voting majority was changed from seven to nine, and ECOSOC was enlarged from eighteen to twenty-seven members; and again in 1971, when ECOSOC was expanded to fifty-four members. Like many constitutions, the UN Charter is designed to be difficult to amend. Under Articles 108 and 109, any amendments must be approved and ratified by two-thirds of the UN member states, including all five permanent members of the Security Council. The principal reform that would require Charter amendment is changing the size and composition of the Security Council. It also is the most controversial.

The key ingredients for serious UN reform, as a former UN official notes, "will require major concessions from powerful and weak countries alike" and a willingness to "rise above their own current sense of entrenched rights and privileges and find a grand bargain" (Brown 2008: 6, 8). Nowhere is this more true than in Security Council reform.

## Structural Reform of the Security Council

Virtually everyone agrees that more states should be added to the Security Council. The permanent members underrepresent the majority of the world's population; Europe is overrepresented at the expense of Latin America, Africa, and Asia; China is the only third world and Asian country among the permanent members; both Germany and Japan contribute more financially than do Russia, China, the UK, and France, yet have no guaranteed role. In addition to geopolitical and systemic changes, there is greater normative value placed on diversity, equity, and representation today than in 1945. And, as Ian Hurd (2008a: 201) notes, "changing the formal membership, it is said, is a necessary step to increasing, or to halting the loss of, the legitimacy of the Council and of its resolutions." Thus the first key issue is the size and composition of the Council's membership. Yet if its size is increased to enhance its representativeness, it must still be small enough to ensure efficiency.

A second issue concerns whether or not to continue the distinction between permanent and nonpermanent members. Closely related is the question of whether new permanent members will have veto power. Some proposals would give no veto power to the new permanent members; others would limit veto power of all permanent members to Chapter VII decisions; still others would grant veto power comparable to what the P-5 currently enjoy; others would eliminate the veto entirely on the grounds that it is undemocratic. The latter is a nonstarter for all permanent members, and Britain and France are hardly eager to give up their seats. Having more permanent members with veto power, however, would likely increase the potential for blockage.

Resolving the issues of representation and permanent membership has proven impossible thus far. There is no agreement on what process or formula should be used to determine who would get new permanent seats. There are three likely African candidates, for example (Nigeria, Egypt, and South Africa). Countries such as Italy and Pakistan that know a rival is more likely to be a candidate (Germany and India respectively) tend to oppose adding permanent seats. The United States formerly supported permanent seats for both Germany and Japan, but came out in opposition to Germany when it condemned the US invasion of Iraq in 2003. China opposes seats for both Japan and India. Brazil, India, Germany, and Japan publicly campaigned for permanent seats in advance of the 2005 sixtieth-anniversary World Summit, and Secretary-General Annan also pushed hard for action, yet those efforts came to naught. Some observers have even suggested that any new Security Council members not be states at all but rather regional bodies. This could mean replacing France and Britain with a rotating EU seat (something the European Parliament has already endorsed) and including the African Union and other bodies. The issues in the debate over reforming the Security Council's composition are summarized in Figure 4.6.

In short, there is no agreement precisely because the issue of Security Council representation is so important. It testifies "to the divergent perspectives and interests among member states, and to the value capitals place on the work of the council" (Luck 2005: 410).

With respect to increasing the transparency and efficiency of the Security Council's work, however, there have been a number of changes, as dis-

---

**Figure 4.6     The Debate over Security Council Reform**

- *Representation*
  More permanent members to better reflect current geopolitical and
    economic realities
  Proposed additions: Germany and Japan, one to two members each
    from Africa, Asia, and Latin America; alternatively, replace France
    and the UK with an EU seat and add other regional bodies
  Eliminate all permanent seats

- *Veto Power*
  Eliminate entirely
  Reduce scope for its use to Chapter VII decisions
  Retain for current P-5, but don't give to new permanent members
  Give to all permanent members

- *Efficiency*
  Size should be large enough to allow greater representation, but small
    enough to preserve the ability to act
  Proposed size: twenty to twenty-five members

---

cussed earlier, including consultations with countries that contribute troops
and matériel to peacekeeping operations, and with NGOs. More meetings
are open, especially at early stages of deliberation, and the Security Council
cil now provides more information on the nature of discussions and what
resulted.

Yet even with representation issues unresolved, the Security Council
retains a high degree of legitimacy. With the sole exception of Saudi Arabia, which declined a seat in 2013 to protest the Council's failure to resolve
the Syrian crisis and Iranian nuclear situation, states want to become nonpermanent members. Participation is seen as a mark of status and prestige
for a state and its diplomats. And the Council continues to be called upon to
mount new peacekeeping operations and to address new security threats. As
discussed earlier, it continues to be seen as the most authoritative body
within the UN. Even if the composition of the Security Council were
changed, however, other persistent problems, namely coordination of the
array of different agencies and programs within the UN system and improving management, would still need to be addressed.

## Coordination and Management

The problem of multiple agencies engaged in similar tasks with no coordination has plagued the UN system almost from the beginning, in part
because the founders designed the organization to be decentralized, as this
would increase the capacity of different groups to participate while minimizing the potential for politicization. As John Ruggie (2003: 303) states,
"It is not designed as a matrix at all but as a set of deeply rooted columns

connected only by thin and tenuous rows. Nothing that has transpired since 1945 has transformed that fundamental reality." Yet, increasingly, as a result of globalization, issues no longer fit into clear sectoral or regional boundaries.

Despite the plethora of proposals over the years for improving ECOSOC's effectiveness as the main coordinating agency for economic and social programs, the issues persist and the global conferences of the 1990s compounded the problems. Each spawned a special commission to follow up on the program of action, yet because of zero-growth budgets at the time, there were fewer resources to meet greater demands. A major step toward coordination among the many UN entities that deal with economic and social development was taken with the Millennium Development Goals, as discussed in Chapter 9.

Coordination and management issues have also plagued UN efforts to deal with humanitarian crises since the early 1990s. Typically, there is a functional division of responsibilities: the UNHCR manages refugee camps, UNICEF handles water and sanitation, the WFP is responsible for food supplies, and the WHO handles the health sector. In a number of situations, peacekeeping forces have been mandated to safeguard relief workers and supplies. The presence of large numbers of NGOs often complicates the task of coordination. Initially, there was a significant lack of coordination, as each agency "had its own institutional dynamics, formulated its own priorities, and moved according to a timetable of its own devising" (Minear 1994: 28). Donor countries pushed the General Assembly in 1991 to appoint a humanitarian coordinator and a humanitarian affairs department to remedy the problems, but neither was given power over other agencies, nor over staff and resources. In 1997, a further reorganization produced the Office for the Coordination of Humanitarian Affairs, whose head now chairs the Executive Committee on Humanitarian Affairs, which is composed of some fifteen UN agencies and departments.

A different approach to coordination has been taken with regard to dealing with HIV/AIDS, as discussed in Chapter 9. Although the WHO was the logical agency for initial responses in the 1980s, awareness of the multifaceted nature of the problem led to the creation in 1996 of the United Nations Joint Programme on HIV/AIDS, which involves eight UN agencies, and in 2001 of the UN System Integrated Plan on AIDS, which links the work of twenty-nine UN funds, programs, and agencies.

## Secretariat Reform

The UN Secretariat grew almost constantly until the 1990s, from 300 persons in 1946 to 3,000 in 1964, 11,000 in 1974, and over 14,000 in 1994. Staffing rose to over 30,000 in 2006 (this figure included those on contracts of less than one year, who made up roughly one-sixth of the total). It has leveled off at around 43,000 since 2010 (or roughly 35,000 if contracts of less than one year are excluded). This growth stemmed from both the expansion of the UN's membership and the proliferation of programs and activities, ranging from peacekeeping missions to technical assistance. As the UN bureaucracy expanded, charges of political bias and administrative inefficiency surfaced. The United States was particularly vocal in this regard. The first five UNSGs paid little attention to internal management of the Secretariat and also had little incentive for change. Only in the 1990s did the UN implement management systems such as program reviews, internal audits, performance evaluations of staff, and effective recruitment and promotion practices. Even then, developed countries were more concerned than developing countries about effective management, financial control, and clear objectives. As Julius Nyerere, former president of Tanzania, said in 1995: "We all want to see the United Nations well managed. But it is not a business; its operations cannot be judged solely by 'efficiency' in money terms" (quoted in Beigbeder 2000: 207).

When Kofi Annan became Secretary-General in 1997, he was pressured by the United States in particular to reduce the size of the Secretariat by 25 percent and implement other reforms such as merging departments and cutting administrative costs. In his "quiet revolution," thirty departments were grouped into four sectoral areas (peace and security, humanitarian affairs, development, and economic and social affairs); his senior management group served as a cabinet; a think tank was established to provide analytical and research capacity independent of member governments; and human rights bodies were consolidated. These changes did not require Charter amendments.

At the beginning of the new millennium, several further reforms were undertaken. The Brahimi Report of 2000 called for strengthening the Secretariat's ability to support peacekeeping operations, and the General Assembly approved a 50 percent increase in staff for the Department of Peacekeeping Operations and more flexibility in administration (UN 2000). In 2002, a new system went into effect for recruiting, placing, and promoting staff that gave more emphasis to merit, competence, and accountability for results than to tenure and precedent.

The latter part of Kofi Annan's tenure as Secretary-General was marred by a series of scandals that raised issues of mismanagement and accountability, prodding still more reforms. As a result of the highly publicized scandals concerning the UN's management of its Oil-for-Food Programme, initiated in 1996 as an exception to the comprehensive sanctions imposed on Iraq in 1990, former US Federal Reserve chairman Paul Volcker chaired a UN investigation that examined contractor overcharges, violations of bidding rules, and insufficiently monitored contractors. Although the Secretary-General was found not guilty, his son was implicated, and others at the UN resigned or were fired. The scandal provided ammunition for UN critics, raising major questions about the UN's ability to manage large, long-term projects and about who was more responsible for the failures: the P-5 or the Secretariat. As a result, the Secretariat introduced measures to improve the performance of senior management, including monitoring of individual performance and policies covering fraud, corruption, financial disclosure, and procurement contracts. It also created a new Office of Internal Oversight Services, with operational independence. Pilot programs were developed in selected countries to attempt a unified UN budget under the "Delivering As One" initiatives in 2007 in the hope of adding coherence and efficiency to country-level projects.

In sum, ongoing Secretariat reform is necessary if the UN's bureaucracy is to grow in capacity, adapt its management and working procedures, and maintain its effectiveness and legitimacy. Proposals for further reform include improving the quality of UN staff, the representation of women as discussed earlier, the manner of selecting the Secretary-General, and the scope of that position. A number of observers have suggested that the UNSG cannot manage the UN system effectively while simultaneously serving as the world's chief diplomat (Fasulo 2009). In addition to separating the roles, Thomas Weiss (2009) has suggested that the Secretary-General should have more authority to hire, fire, and promote on the basis of merit rather than geography. At least, two or three candidates (rather than a single individual) should be nominated for senior posts and the choice left to the Secretary-General and agency heads (Weiss 2014b: 303). To raise the quality of candidates for junior posts, special recruitment efforts and expanded use of standardized examinations should be implemented.

Financing is another persistent problem for the UN. More than "mere housekeeping," one observer suggests, "some of the most contentious political struggles that have wracked and at times imperiled the organization have swirled around its financing" (Laurenti 2007: 675).

## Financing

Like the UN system itself, the UN's budget is complex. The regular budget covers its administrative machinery, major organs, and their auxiliary agencies and programs. It grew from less than $20 million in 1946 to $1.6 billion in 2008, but has remained relatively constant since the late 1990s due to the resistance of major donor states to increases in the budget. The two-year budget for 2014–2015 was $5.53 billion. Peacekeeping expenses constitute a separate budget ($7.06 billion in 2014–2015) and each of the specialized agencies also has a separate budget. The three types of budget expenditures are funded by member states' assessments according to a formula based on ability to pay. Many economic and social programs (such as UNICEF, the UNDP, the WFP, and the UNHCR) are funded by states' voluntary contributions, which frequently exceed the amounts of their assessments. Table 4.3 illustrates the relative size of each of these categories of budget expenditure based on assessed and voluntary contributions and changes between 1986 and 2013. The fluctuation of peacekeeping costs since 1990 is particularly notable. Also evident are the effects of the major powers' insistence on "no growth" in the UN's regular budget during the 1990s, despite developing countries' interest in increased UN social and economic activities. Prior to that time, UN budgets had grown with membership increases, new programs and agencies, inflation, and currency-rate fluctuations.

The formulas for member states' assessed contributions for both the regular budget and peacekeeping operations are reevaluated every three years. The General Assembly's Committee on Contributions considers national income, per capita income, any economic dislocations (such as from war), and members' ability to obtain foreign currencies. Initially, the highest rate (for the United States) was set at 40 percent of the UN budget. The minimum rate was 0.04 percent for states with the most limited means. Over time, these have been adjusted, with the US share reduced to 25 percent in 1972 and 22 percent in 1995, and the minimum reduced to 0.01 percent in 1978 and 0.0001 percent in 1997. Between 1985 and 2000, for example, Japan's share increased significantly, from 11.82 percent to 20.57 percent, while the Soviet/Russian figure declined from 11.98 percent to 1.15 percent, reflecting Russia's reduced size and economic difficulties. Between 1995 and 2005, China saw its assessment triple, from 0.72 to 2.05 percent. In 2014, it rose to 5.1 percent. Figure 4.7 shows the scale of assessments for major contributors and the majority of UN members for 2013–2015. Particularly striking is that all but eighteen UN members con-

Table 4.3   UN System Expenditures, 1986–2013 ($ millions)

| | Assessed Contributions | | | | Voluntary Contributions | | |
|---|---|---|---|---|---|---|---|
| | Regular | Peacekeeping | Agencies | Total Assessed | Organs | Agencies | Total Voluntary |
| 1986 | 725 | 242 | 1,142 | 2,109 | 3,075 | 951 | 4,026 |
| 1990 | 838 | 379 | 1,495 | 2,712 | 4,436 | 1,346 | 5,782 |
| 1995 | 1,181 | 3,281 | 1,847 | 6,309 | 5,778 | 1,159 | 6,937 |
| 2000 | 1,090 | 2,139 | 1,766 | 4,995 | 4,023 | 955 | 4,978 |
| 2004 | 1,389 | 3,645 | 2,000 | 7,034 | 9,529 | 2,165 | 11,694 |
| 2007 | 2,054 | 5,148 | 2,198 | 9,400 | 12,289 | 3,281 | 15,570 |
| 2013 | 2,606 | 7,258 | 3,390 | 13,254 | 1,440 | 27,296 | 28,736 |

*Sources:* For expenditures prior to 2013: www.globalpolicy.org/finance/tables/tabsyst.htm; www.globalpolicy.org/finance/tables/finvol.htm. For 2013 expenditures: www.un.org/ga/search/view _doc.asp?symbol=A/69/305.

tribute less than 1 percent of the budget each, while the top five contributors, representing just 5 out of 193 votes, are assessed 51 percent of the UN's costs. This creates a political problem, since budgets are voted on primarily by states who contribute little, fueling resentment on the part of wealthy states.

Not surprisingly, however, the UN has frequently experienced difficulties in getting states to pay their assessments. States may fail to pay because of budget technicalities, poverty, or politics, including unhappiness with the UN in general or with specific programs and activities. In 2012, for example, only twenty-six member states had paid their assessments in full by January 31 of that year—the last day allowed under financial regulations. The result has been periodic financial crises. The only sanction provided by the UN Charter, in Article 19, is denial of voting privileges in the General Assembly if a member falls more than two years in arrears.

The first UN financing crisis arose in the early 1960s over peacekeeping operations in the Congo and Middle East, with the Soviet Union, other communist countries, and France refusing to pay because, in their view, peacekeeping authorized by the General Assembly was illegal. The ICJ's *Certain Expenses* opinion (ICJ Advisory Opinion 1962) confirmed the

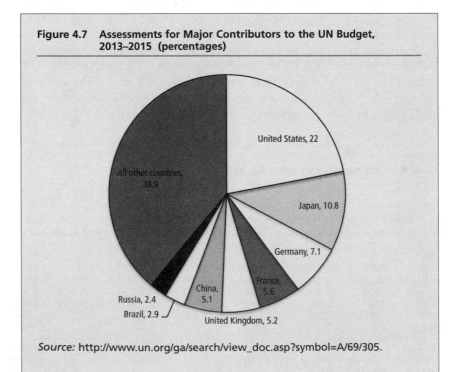

**Figure 4.7    Assessments for Major Contributors to the UN Budget, 2013–2015  (percentages)**

United States, 22

Japan, 10.8

Germany, 7.1

France, 5.6

United Kingdom, 5.2

China, 5.1

Brazil, 2.9

Russia, 2.4

All other countries, 38.9

*Source:* http://www.un.org/ga/search/view_doc.asp?symbol=A/69/305.

legality of the General Assembly's action and the obligation of members to pay. The second crisis arose in the 1980s, when the United States began withholding part of its dues. The Congress and the Ronald Reagan administration were unhappy with the politicization of many UN agencies, with General Assembly procedures that gave the United States, as the largest contributor, so little weight in budget decisions, with UN administration and management in general, and with the size of the US assessment relative to that of other wealthy states. The compromise worked out by a group of eighteen high-level intergovernmental experts appointed by the General Assembly gave the major donors increased power to review programs and establish priorities for use of financial resources through the Committee for Programme and Coordination, which operates by consensus. This became the model followed by almost all UN agencies.

In the late 1990s, the UN faced its most serious financial crisis. Member states owed the UN over $2.5 billion for current and past assessments to cover both regular and peacekeeping expenses. Only 100 of 185 members had paid in full. The United States owed $1.6 billion, or two-thirds of the total due. The arrearages (i.e., unpaid assessments or debts) threatened the organization's ability to fulfill the various mandates given it by member states, and illustrated the tension between demands for governance and institutional weakness arising from states' unwillingness (in the case of the United States) or inability (in the case of many states in economic crisis) to pay their assessed contributions. The crisis of the late 1990s was partially resolved by an agreement struck in the US Congress and the UN General Assembly to reduce the US assessments for the regular budget and peacekeeping, and for payment of all arrears by 2003, subject to certain conditions (Karns and Mingst 2002). Nonetheless, at the end of 2014, total arrearages stood at $3.5 billion, and the United States still owed 32 percent of the total.

There has been no shortage of proposals for changes to deal with the UN's persistent financing problems. All seek to provide a steady and predictable flow of resources for peacekeeping and economic and social activities—revenues that would be independent of states in particular. As Thomas Weiss (2009: 196) notes, "Allowing the UN to manage such independent revenues would alleviate the world organization's reliance on member-states' largesse and permit a more rational and less agency-driven agenda regarding priorities and resource availabilities." Among the ideas that have been mentioned are international taxes on arms sales, international air travel, international petroleum trade (carbon tax), and currency transactions ("Tobin tax"). Pledges from corporations such as Winterthur and Pfizer and private philanthropists such as Bill Gates and Ted Turner have provided resources for specific needs such as programs on children's health and the Global Fund to Fight AIDS, Tuberculosis, and Malaria, but such funds cannot be used to meet regular budget obligations. States are fundamentally reluctant, however, to see the UN's dependence on them for its financing reduced too much, because that would reduce their ability to control what the UN does.

### Integrating Nonstate Actors

The increasing involvement of NGOs and private businesses with UN programs and activities demonstrates another area of needed reform: how to better integrate nonstate actors into the UN system. Some of the initiatives that were undertaken in the 1990s in this regard are discussed elsewhere, such as changes in NGO participation, discussed in Chapters 6 and 9. Prior to the Millennium Summit of 2000, the People's Millennium Forum brought together representatives of more than a thousand NGOs based in more than a hundred countries. Its participants resolved to create a global civil society forum to deal with UN institutions, member states, and other institutions (Alger 2007). Nonstate actors now play a substantial role in supplementing the limited financial resources of the UN system. Thus, greater participation by nonstate actors is a persistent issue for the UN, as explored in Chapter 6.

While the UN is the centerpiece of global governance, there are many other pieces, among them regional organizations. But what is the relationship between the UN as a global IGO and various regional IGOs?

## The UN's Relationship to Regional Organizations

When the United Nations was created in 1945, there were virtually no regional IGOs in existence. The Organization of American States, the Council of Europe, NATO, and the Arab League were all created between 1945 and 1950, for example. Nonetheless, among the UN's founders there was a tension between the principles of globalism and regionalism, as mentioned in Chapter 1. The British Foreign Office was more interested in regional spheres of influence and order, while US president Franklin Roosevelt was an advocate of a universal or global organization. The debate was framed almost exclusively in terms of security, and as a result the provisions of Chapter VIII of the UN Charter refer to regional security arrangements. The Charter is silent on broader roles for regional organizations, such as promoting economic and social cooperation, and on how these might be linked to UN activities.

Although Article 52 legitimizes the existence and operation of regional alliances and encourages regional efforts to settle local disputes peacefully, it is very clear that the UN Security Council, under Articles 24, 34, and 35, has primary responsibility for maintenance of international peace and security. The Council has sole authority to authorize the use of force and to obligate member states to undertake sanctions, except in situations where states may exercise their right of self-defense, either individually or collectively (Article 51). The Council may also utilize regional security agencies for enforcement action under its authority, but "no enforcement action shall be taken under regional arrangements or by regional agencies without the authorization of the Security Council" (Article 53). Regional organizations are to inform the Security Council of any activities planned or undertaken to maintain international peace and security (Article 54).

The Charter does not define the regional entities referred to in Chapter VIII, nor does it indicate how such entities are to interrelate with the UN, thus leaving issues of responsibility and legitimacy unresolved. For much of the Cold War, this was unimportant. This changed dramatically when the UN became overburdened by post–Cold War regional, intrastate, and ethnic conflicts, as well as by collapsing states and demands for peace operations. The environment "both dictated and demanded greater regional involvement in the maintenance of peace and security" (Fawcett 2003: 16). By the late 1990s, regional organizations were actually supporting more peace operations than was the UN. As of 2008, twenty-two regional and other types of organizations were participating in high-level meetings with the Secretary-General and Security Council (Karns 2009). We discuss further the nature of the relationship between the UN and regional IGOs in dealing with post–Cold War conflicts in Chapter 7.

Beyond these security-related provisions of the UN Charter, ad hoc arrangements were created for coordinating the work of the regional development banks with UN development agencies and the World Bank. Recognizing the necessity of approaching many economic and social problems within regional contexts, as noted, ECOSOC early on created regional economic commissions and arrangements to mesh their work with that of other programs. Some of these arrangements are discussed further in Chapter 9.

Today, regionalism and globalism coexist with minimal friction outside the security area, and regional organizations have proliferated even more rapidly than global ones. They have become increasingly important pieces of the global governance puzzle.

## Suggested Further Reading

Chesterman, Simon, ed. (2007) *Secretary or General? The UN Secretary-General in World Politics*. New York: Cambridge University Press.
Cronin, Bruce, and Ian Hurd, eds. (2008) *The UN Security Council and the Politics of International Authority*. New York: Routledge.
Jolly, Richard, Louis Emmerij, and Thomas G. Weiss. (2009) *The United Nations: A History of Ideas and Their Future*. Bloomington: Indiana University Press.
Malone, David, ed. (2004) *The UN Security Council: From the Cold War to the 21st Century*. Boulder: Lynne Rienner.
Mingst, Karen A., and Margaret P. Karns. (2012) *The United Nations in the 21st Century*. 4th ed. Boulder: Westview.

Weiss, Thomas G., and Sam Daws, eds. (2007) *The Oxford Handbook on the United Nations*. New York: Oxford University Press.
Weiss, Thomas G., and Ramesh Thakur. (2010) *Global Governance and the UN: An Unfinished Journey*. Bloomington: Indiana University Press.

## Internet Resources

Academic Council on the United Nations System, UN Security Council Database: http://acuns.org/annotated-bibliography-topics
Global Policy Forum: www.globalpolicy.org
International Court of Justice: www.icj-cij.org
*Security Council Report:* www.securitycouncilreport.org
UN Association of the United States of America: www.unausa.org
UN Charter: www.un.org/en/documents/charter
UN home page: www.un.org
UN Millennium Development Goals: www.un.org/millenniumgoals
UN reform: www.un.org/reform
UN system: www.unsystem.org

# 5

# Regional Organizations

**Regions and regional organizations have emerged as major** forces in international politics. Hence the study of international organizations and global governance includes the many regional and subregional organizations in Europe, Asia, Africa, the Middle East, and the Americas; their efforts to address security, economic, environmental, and human rights issues; and the interactions between and among global and regional organizations.

Early political and economic communities were regional, given the limits of trade and communications. Chapter VIII of the UN Charter envisaged the creation of regional security arrangements, a number of which were created during the early years of the Cold War. Although there is no similar Charter provision with respect to regional economic and social cooperation, ECOSOC very early created regional economic commissions, and regional development banks were established in the 1950s and 1960s. Today there is a strong sense of regionalism as one level of governance in the world, along with the global and local, and of the potentially "productive partnership between these different levels" (Hurrell 2007: 141).

Regional organizations can be categorized along the same lines as global organizations: general-purpose, peace and security, economic, functional, and technical. Many are predominantly economic, created to improve economic growth, development, and well-being through the lowering of barriers to trade in goods and services as well as to capital flows. Regional trade agreements, in particular, have proliferated in recent years, and are discussed in Chapter 8. There are also regional human rights and environmental institutions.

Regions vary widely in terms of their scope, institutional forms, membership, and identity. The sharpest contrast is between Europe (especially the EU) and Asia. Europe has developed formal bureaucratic-legalistic institutions, including courts with enforcement powers, qualified majority voting procedures, extensive transparency and monitoring, a dense legal system of rules and regulations, and hence significant intrusions on the sovereignty of member states. Regionalism in Asia is more informal and non-legalistic, involving consensus decisionmaking, informal agreements, limited commitments by states, and strong adherence to the norm of noninterference in states' internal affairs. Africa has an extensive set of institutions, but they are relatively weak because of member states' limited resources and reluctance to accept intrusions on sovereignty. Regions also vary in the extent to which member states share a sense of identity. Studies of comparative regionalism analyze the causes of these variations, the dynamics of the processes by which regions rise and decline, and how differences in the context, scope, structures, and shared identity of regional governance arrangements correlate with effectiveness. Rationalist theories, particularly realism and liberalism, have long dominated theorizing on regionalism; constructivism has had a significant impact particularly since the mid-1990s. As Alice Ba (2014: 312) notes in a recent critique: "Theories have generally not been sufficiently inclusive of the world's full range of experiences and conditions and how such differences might bear on the form and purpose of regional organizations outside the Euro-American zone, as well as the analytic categories, concepts, and processes that theorists draw upon and highlight to understand and explain them."

This chapter examines some of the major factors and theories regarding the roots and dynamics of regionalism, as well as the major institutions and dynamics within five regions of the world: Europe, Latin America, Asia, Africa, and the Middle East. Regional organizations' activities with respect to security, economic well-being and development, human rights, and the environment are also discussed in the chapters dealing with each of these issue areas.

## The Roots and Dynamics of Regionalism

As Amitav Acharya (2012: 21) observes, "the study of regions has evolved considerably in the scholarly literature on international relations." The idea that states within a given geographic area can more easily and effectively address common economic and security problems because they are closer to the problems and are presumed to share some background and approaches is no longer considered sufficient for the development of regionalism, however. The latter is a dynamic process involving the development of intraregional interdependence, institution building, and creation of a degree of regional identity among states and peoples in a given area (26). It is not necessarily a one-way process, as the sense of region-ness, the degree of commitment to common policies, and effectiveness of institutions can easily decline over time. This begs the question of how regions are defined.

## Defining a Region

Traditional definitions of regionalism assumed that the participating states shared geographical proximity, some cultural, linguistic, and historical heritage, as well as a degree of mutual interdependence. The constructivist approach posits that a region is a social and political construction with various concepts, metaphors, and practices determining how the region is defined and who is included and excluded (Acharya 1997). This view emphasizes that regions are *made;* it is less static in that it acknowledges how identity, norms, and meaning can change over time. Still another approach defines regions in terms of nonterritorial, functional factors such as transnational capitalist processes, the environment (e.g., acid rain), or identity groups (Väyrynen 2003: 27).

The lack of agreement on the definition of regions means there is no single guide to identifying their boundaries. Rather, decisions as to what constitutes a particular region reflect the perceptions, prejudices, or desires of those states that constitute a core group for regional initiatives. They form in effect an "in-group" that subsequently determines whether to accept any "outsiders." What is now the EU began with six member states in western Europe. Today it has twenty-eight members that span the continent. Turkey's application for membership challenges the definition of "Europe," because Turkey is a predominantly Muslim country with a weak democratic system straddling both Europe and western Asia. Similarly, Australia and New Zealand do not fit neatly with all definitions of "Asia," and India has only recently sought inclusion in what are still predominantly southeastern and eastern Asian regional initiatives.

Most regions are marked today by multiple organizations with overlapping memberships. Where several organizations coexist in the same geographic and political space, they may be viewed as concentric circles or nested regimes (see, for example, Figures 5.1 and 5.4).

## Two Waves of Regionalism

There have been two waves of regionalism since World War II. The first wave accompanied the Cold War and the initial stages of European integration, lasting from the late 1940s to the mid-1970s. It generated rather Eurocentric theories of regionalism. Countries in several parts of the world tried to emulate the European experiment, but relatively few economic gains were realized and no other region has approached Europe's degree of integration.

The second wave of regionalism began in the late 1980s, coinciding with the European moves toward the single internal market and European Union in 1992, the Canada-US Free Trade Agreement, which subsequently was converted to NAFTA, and increasing globalization. It was spurred by global economic changes, the Cold War's end, uncertainty over the outcome of world trade negotiations, the "triumph" of liberal market economics, and new attitudes toward international cooperation. Where European regionalism was the model in the first wave, the second wave's "'new regionalism' is both global and pluralistic" (Söderbaum 2003: 4). Liberal market economic theories encouraged eliminating barriers to trade and creating larger markets through regional trade agreements. Transnational interdependence issues such as drug trafficking, environmental degradation, and terrorism have driven regional initiatives such as the Shanghai Cooperation Organization (SCO), and the Summits of the Americas.

One further feature of "new regionalism" is the growth of nonstate and civil society activities as part of the dynamics within regions. These include anti-Americanism in regions such as Latin America and Europe, anti-Japanese and anti-Chinese protests, and Chinese production networks in Asia. Such "societal resistance to regional powers," Acharya (2007a: 649) notes, "could be inspired by local resentment against their economic and political dominance. It could also represent a reaction led by civil society actors, against globalization (and its regional variant, regionalization)."

## Political Factors Driving Regionalism

Regardless of the theoretical approach one takes, then, regionalism does not just happen. Deliberate policy choices by states' leaders are key to expanding economic or political activity among a group of states in order to reap anticipated benefits. Among the political factors linked to the development of regionalism are power dynamics, identity (or shared perception of a definable region) and ideology, internal and external threats, domestic politics, and leadership.

*Power dynamics.* Power dynamics can play a significant role either through pivotal regional powers such as Indonesia in ASEAN and Egypt in the Arab League, or through the efforts of great or hegemonic powers to create and shape regional orders. Regionalism in Europe, Latin America, and Asia, for example, has been strongly influenced by US preferences. In the European case, the United States supported early regional initiatives as imperative to resisting communism. Latin American countries saw regionalism as a way to counter US influence. In the Asian case, the United States preferred bilateral relationships over multilateral regionalism. The creation of the ASEAN Regional Forum (ARF) in the 1990s was an effort by the Southeast Asian states to engage both China and the United States in "a system of regional order . . . thereby dampening not only their mutual rivalry but also their dominance over the weaker states of the region" (Acharya 2007a: 648). Future Asian regionalism will clearly be influenced by the rise of both China and India. While power dynamics matter, however, identity and ideology within the region are also important.

*Identity and ideology.* A number of studies have focused on identity, or shared perception of being part of a definable region, as a key factor in the definition of region and development of regionalism. Acharya (2012: 23) argues that "as with nation-states, regions may be 'imagined' and 'socially constructed.'" He stresses that "territorial proximity and functional interactions are by themselves inadequate to constitute a region in the absence of an 'idea of the region,' whether conceived from inside or out." In other words, he adds, "regional coherence and identity are not givens, but result primarily from self-conscious socialization among the leaders and peoples of a region." Thus, much of his and others' work has analyzed how the ASEAN states constructed their sense of regional identity through the elaboration of key ideas and processes often described as the "ASEAN Way." Yet as constructivists posit, national and regional identities are both subject to reinterpretation and change, making it "possible for former enemies to become friends and for security communities to replace historical patterns of anarchy and disorder" (Acharya 2007a: 636). The prime example of this phenomenon is Germany's transformation from enemy to core member of multiple European organizations.

Ideology can also be a factor that brings states together into a regional organization. Both NATO and the EU are based on liberal ideology, while third world regional organizations were and still are based on anticolonialism, nonintervention, and ideologies of pan-Arabism (the Arab League) and pan-Africanism (the Organization of African Unity [OAU] and the African Union). Like identity, however, ideologies can change. In the 1990s, for example, the Organization of American States (OAS) embraced liberal democracy, along with a shift from nonintervention to democracy promotion, and regional trade arrangements in many regions now embrace liberal economics. Still, shared identity or ideology alone cannot bring about a regional security community. Such entities, and other types of regional organizations, tend to arise out of external or internal threats.

*Internal and external threats.* A shared sense of external or internal threat can be a key political factor that drives states toward closer regional cooperation. The Cold War threat of communism, and especially of Soviet expansion, was a powerful impetus to regionalism in Western Europe in the 1950s and 1960s. It was directly responsible for the creation of NATO (1949) and part of the rationale behind the European Community's formation. Other Cold War regional alliances included the Rio Pact (1947), the Southeast Asian Treaty Organization (SEATO, 1954), and the Warsaw Treaty Organization (1955). European integration was also driven by the desire to contain German nationalism by enmeshing that country in tight links with France and other neighboring states. The heightened US presence in Southeast Asia during the Vietnam War and Vietnam's 1978 invasion of

Cambodia were external threats that played a major role in the formation and evolution of ASEAN. The Iranian Revolution of 1979 and the war between Iran and Iraq in the 1980s were both seen as threats by the tiny states of the Persian Gulf that established the Gulf Cooperation Council (GCC) in 1981.

The Cold War's end reshaped many regional organizations. Not only did Soviet-dominated institutions die, but the loss of the Soviet threat also required a fundamental rethinking of NATO's purpose and a redefinition of the memberships and activities of other European organizations. Thus threats or the absence of threats clearly overlap with power dynamics, since resistance to outside or regional powers often plays a role in regionalism. Fear of a resurgent Japan has been one of the deterrents to Asian regionalism, for example, while shared hostility to the state of Israel has been the primary source of unity for the Arab League. Unquestionably, rising anti-Americanism fueled by resentment of US dominance has contributed to challenges to the US role in Latin America, Asia, the Middle East, and Europe. This is evident in the EU's effort to create a self-defense force separate from NATO and in Venezuela's efforts to create a "Bank of the South" as an alternate regional financing institution to the Inter-American Development Bank (IDB), IMF, and World Bank, which are all seen as US-dominated. China's rise is likely to reshape both ASEAN and other Asia regional organizations, while Russia's seizure of Crimea and threats against Ukraine in 2014 refocused NATO's attention on European defense.

Economic crises are another form of threat that has increased countries' perceptions of the need for friendly neighbors. The 1997–1998 Asian financial crisis and China's increasing share of foreign direct investment, for example, contributed to a sharpened awareness that ASEAN needed to develop its capacity to deal with financial and monetary vulnerability. The failure to advance trade liberalization under the WTO since the late 1990s, and attendant fear that rival trade blocs would limit market access, have led to the proliferation of regional and bilateral free trade agreements, as discussed in Chapter 8. In Africa, the proliferation of conflicts, humanitarian disasters, pandemics, and political and economic failures led to the reorganization of the OAU into the African Union (AU) and efforts to strengthen regional institutions. Elsewhere, however, complex transnational threats such as terrorism, environmental degradation, drug trafficking, and crime have challenged traditional definitions of regions and of security itself and given rise to new conceptions of human and cooperative security.

*Domestic politics.* State structures and regime types matter with respect to regional governance initiatives. Where states in a region have similar types of political and economic institutions, it will be easier to reach agreement on regional arrangements, and such arrangements are likely to be more effective. The EU is a prime example of this, in that all member states are democracies. ASEAN's expansion in the 1990s illustrates the difficulty that regional organizations encounter when there are wide variations among members' political systems, from communist regimes (Vietnam and Laos), to states emerging from authoritarianism (Myanmar), to democratic states punctuated by military rule (Thailand). Peter Katzenstein (2005: 221) argues that "similarity in regime type facilitates a political-legal regionalism in Europe, dissimilarity an ethnic- and market-based one in Asia."

In addition to regime types, the nature of domestic coalitions and their strategies toward other states affect the structure of regional order (Solingen 1998). It takes a strong domestic political coalition, including strong export-oriented manufacturing industries, to support closer economic integration, for example, and to take the often tough decisions to open borders to trade and subject locally owned companies to outside competition. This was the case with South America's Common Market of the South (Mercosur). Pressures from a transnational coalition of European firms in favor of a European market were important to completing the EU single market in 1992. Protecting sovereignty, regime legitimacy, and domestic regimes are foremost among the concerns of domestic coalitions and individual leaders in Africa, Asia, and the Middle East, ensuring that regional institutions are weaker and often less effective.

Regional arrangements can also affect domestic politics, creating commitments that governments may find helpful in resisting demands of domestic groups. A preferential trade agreement, for example, can aid a government in locking in liberal economic reforms (Mansfield and Milner 1999: 605). It may also give a federal government enhanced power over its states and provinces, as NAFTA has done in Canada and the United States.

*Leadership.* Regionalism does not just happen. Deliberate policy choices by states and their leaders are key to increasing the flow of economic and political activities. Jean Monnet and Robert Schuman were among those visionary post–World War II Europeans who conceived of a united Europe, as well as leaders of France and West Germany who were each instrumental to the birth of post–World War II European regionalism. Indonesia played a lead role for ASEAN, while Australia and Japan did so for the Asia-Pacific Economic Cooperation (APEC), Egypt and Gamal Abdul Nasser for the Arab League, and Venezuela and Colombia for the Andean Pact. The United States provided leadership for both NATO and the OAS, but it was Canada, not the United States, that proposed the Canada-US Free Trade Agreement, the predecessor of NAFTA.

## *Economic Factors Driving Regionalism*

High levels of economic interdependence, most notably trade and investment flows, the complementarity of economies and policies, the availability of compensatory mechanisms for integration in developing countries, and the desire to stimulate trade and attract foreign investment through creation of a larger market are commonly linked to regional economic initiatives. Interdependence increases the costs generated by lack of coordinated national policies because it raises the sensitivity of economic events in one country to what is happening with trading partners. It is the foundation of the functionalist theory of regional integration. And, in many regions, regionalism has followed increases in intraregional trade flows, often stimulated by regional preferential trade agreements. This has been greatest in Western Europe and to a lesser degree within the Economic Community of West African States (ECOWAS).

Economic globalization has stimulated regional integration in a variety of ways. The globalization of foreign direct investment has deepened regional integration in Europe, for example. Elsewhere, states have adopted regionalism as a strategy to counter the adverse effects of globalization. The New Partnership for Africa's Development (NEPAD) represented an attempt to counter Africa's increasing marginalization in an era of globalization. Yet as our discussion shows, economic factors and prospects of higher material well-being alone have rarely sufficed as a basis for successful regional cooperation.

Economic interconnectedness, however, does not necessarily lead countries within a geographical area to see themselves as part of a region or to think in terms of regional cooperation. After reviewing the literature on how interdependence may affect states' perceptions of their identity, sense of community, and shared interests, John Ravenhill (2001: 14–15) concludes: "No clear correlation exists between levels of interdependence between specific economies, measured by the relative importance of bilateral trade flows, and the emergence of economic regionalism . . . [and] no critical threshold of regional economic interdependence exists below which regionalism never occurs and beyond which such collaboration always takes place." Until the 1980s, for example, interdependence was low among Asian countries, and although Asian intraregional trade has grown exponentially since 1990, most Asian countries, including Japan, still depend on North American markets for their exports. Consequently, they have insisted on "open regionalism" to keep regional trade arrangements open to outsiders (and preserve their own freedom to participate in other trade arrangements). This contrasts with the more closed regionalism of the European Union, NAFTA, and Mercosur, where trade advantages are limited to members.

## Comparing Regions

By examining some of the major regional organizations, we will see more clearly how history, culture, domestic politics, and other factors have facilitated or impeded the growth of regional institutions. Europe, where regionalism has progressed the furthest, can be used as a frame of reference.

## Europe's Regional Organizations

After World War II, European states established a dense network of regional organizations to address security, economic, and other needs. In the Cold War years, the Iron Curtain formed a sharp boundary line between two sets of organizations. In Eastern Europe, states under Soviet domination joined together in the Warsaw Pact for common defense and in the Council of Mutual Economic Assistance (COMECON) to manage their economic relations. In Western Europe, with strong encouragement from the United States, the Organization for European Economic Cooperation (OEEC) was established in 1948 to administer US Marshall Plan aid and to lower trade and currency barriers; NATO was established in 1949. The Europeans themselves created the Council of Europe in 1949, a multipurpose organization "to achieve a greater unity among its Members for the purpose of safeguarding and realizing the ideals and principles which are their common heritage and facilitating their economic and social progress" (Council of Europe, Statute 2, Article 1).

Very shortly, however, the perceived shortcomings of the OEEC and Council of Europe led six countries (France, West Germany, the Netherlands, Belgium, Luxembourg, and Italy) to begin a process of deeper integration through a new set of institutions, starting with establishment of the European Coal and Steel Community (ECSC) in 1952. The six countries then established the European Atomic Energy Community (Euratom) and European Economic Community (EEC, also known as the European Community [EC] or Common Market) in 1958. The integration process they initiated continues today as the European Union. The Western European Union was established in 1954 to provide a framework for German rearmament, and the European Free Trade Association (EFTA) was established in 1960 for states that chose not to join the Common Market. During the period of détente between East and West in the 1970s, the Conference on Security and Cooperation in Europe (CSCE, or Helsinki Conference) was established, bringing together countries from Eastern and Western Europe (plus the two superpowers).

The Warsaw Pact and COMECON disbanded in 1991 with the collapse of communist governments in Central and Eastern Europe and the dissolution of the Soviet Union itself. Ten former members are now members of

NATO, and ten have joined the EU. The Cold War's end transformed the landscape and regional organizations of Europe; Russia's efforts in recent years to recreate links with parts of the former Soviet Union continue to affect that landscape and its dense set of nested institutions, as shown in Figure 5.1. This section examines three of the European organizations: NATO, the OSCE, and the EU.

### The North Atlantic Treaty Organization

NATO is the most highly organized regional security organization in the world. It began as a Cold War military alliance, designed, in the words of its first secretary-general, Lord Ismay, "to keep the Americans in, the Russians out, and the Germans down" (quoted in Schimmelfennig 2007: 145). It has long been far more than just a treaty of alliance, and since the Cold War's end has undergone a major transformation. Since 1991, it has

**Figure 5.1    Nested European Institutions**

| OSCE | | |
|---|---|---|
| **NATO** | | Belarus<br>Holy See<br>Kazakhstan<br>Kyrgyzstan<br>Mongolia<br>Tajikistan<br>Turkmenistan<br>Uzbekistan |

*OSCE*

*NATO*

United States
Canada

| Albania<br>Iceland<br>Norway<br>Turkey | *EU*<br><br>Belgium Latvia<br>Bulgaria Lithuania<br>Denmark Luxembourg<br>Croatia Netherlands<br>Czech Republic Poland<br>Estonia Portugal<br>France Romania<br>Germany Slovakia<br>Greece Slovenia<br>Hungary Spain<br>Italy United Kingdom | *Council of Europe*<br><br>Andorra<br>Armenia<br>Azerbaijan<br>Bosnia-Herzegovina<br>Former Yugoslav<br>   Republic of<br>   Macedonia<br>Georgia<br>Liechtenstein<br>Moldova<br>Monaco<br>Montenegro<br>Russia<br>San Marino<br>Serbia<br>Switzerland<br>Ukraine |
|---|---|---|
| | Austria, Cyprus, Finland, Ireland,<br>Malta, Sweden | |

enlarged its membership to twenty-eight (see Figure 5.1), and created a number of partnerships with Mediterranean and Eurasian states, including Russia. During the Cold War years, NATO's focus was on collective defense and deterrence of the Soviet Union. Even as it debated its mission after the Cold War's end, NATO became involved in its first operations on the periphery of Europe—first in Bosnia and Herzegovina, then in Kosovo, and subsequently in Afghanistan, Iraq, Sudan, and Libya as well as in anti-piracy operations off Somalia. With Russia's annexation of Crimea in 2014 and President Vladimir Putin's claim of a right to intervene on behalf of Russian-speakers, NATO has been pushed to return to its priority of collective territorial defense of its European members, with Russia as the primary threat.

At the core of the 1948 North Atlantic Treaty is the agreement in Article 5 "that an armed attack against one or more of them [the parties to the treaty] in Europe or North America shall be considered an attack against them all," obligating all member states to assist the member attacked when the state consents. The first time this was invoked in more than fifty years, however, was following the September 11, 2001, terrorist attacks on the United States. Yet NATO is also firmly grounded in a liberal theory of peace, as the treaty's preamble states that members "are determined to safeguard the freedom, common heritage and civilization of their peoples, founded on the principles of democracy, individual liberty, and the rule of law."

*Structure.* NATO's principal organ is the North Atlantic Council, which meets at least twice yearly at the ministerial level (i.e., ministers of foreign affairs or defense) and weekly at the ambassadorial level at its headquarters in Brussels. Periodically, the council also meets at the summit level (i.e., heads of government and state) to provide strategic direction for the alliance, launch new initiatives, and build partnerships with non-NATO members. Decisions tend to be made on the basis of consensus, with members having a de facto veto. The NATO secretary-general chairs the council, in addition to preparing budgets, arranging meeting agendas, supervising the secretariat, and representing the organization in relations with governments and other international organizations. A large number of committees handle defense planning, political affairs, armaments, airspace, and communications. The NATO Parliamentary Assembly, comprising 248 legislators from member countries and partner states, though an independent body, links the alliance with legislatures and, through them, with citizens.

The NATO Military Committee, composed of chiefs of staff or their representatives from all member countries, oversees NATO's elaborate integrated military command structure and missions. Over all is the Supreme Allied Commander Europe, known as SACEUR, a position traditionally held by a senior US military officer. Supreme Headquarters Allied Powers Europe (SHAPE), located in Mons, Belgium, is responsible for all alliance operations. Whereas NATO's Cold War collective defense structure limited members' flexibility in responding to attacks, the broader, cooperative security focus of the post–Cold War NATO has given members more flexibility with respect to specific missions. The renewed sense of Russia as an adversary will force NATO members to agree on how to respond. NATO's post–Cold War operations were open to nonmembers, partners, and nonpartners with the result that twenty-two countries, including Russia, participated in the NATO-led operation in Bosnia in the 1990s, for example. Along with the integrated command structure, there is a complex structure of civilian and military consultation, cooperation, and coordination, as well as agreements on members' force levels and defense expenditures. Forces are maintained in Western Europe, the Atlantic, and the Mediterranean, and efforts have been made over many years to coordinate equipment specifications and training to ensure their interoperability (e.g., that Dutch, French, or German artillery can use US ammunition). Despite the integrated command structure, however, military forces remain under command of their national officers.

*Key issues.* There have been a number of persistent issues within NATO. A key issue has long been the US commitment to European defense and the degree to which the United States and Europe agree on security priorities. The US tendency to inform allies of policy changes only after decisions have been made, rather than consulting with them beforehand, has been a recurring source of tension. Burden-sharing has also been a persistent debate. The United States has frequently complained about the Europeans paying and doing too little to maintain their own defense capabilities (a classic free-rider problem).

In the first part of the 1990s, NATO was an organization in search of a new role, which prompted debate over NATO's enlargement and the scope and nature of its mission inside and outside Europe. Behind the post–Cold War issue of NATO enlargement was the belief that the values uniting the alliance for more than fifty years, namely democracy, the rule of law, and individual liberties, were keys to lasting peace and security in the Euro-Atlantic region stretching from Vladivostok to Vancouver. The goal, therefore, was to extend the zone of peace and stability eastward and to provide incentives for political and economic change in former Soviet-bloc countries. There was fierce debate, however, over the desirability of enlarging NATO versus strengthening other European security arrangements, such as the OSCE. Although NATO members worked hard to convince Russia that NATO expansion was not a threat, Russia fiercely opposed enlargement. In 1997, NATO admitted Poland, the Czech Republic, and Hungary as full members. In 2004, seven other Eastern European countries were admitted; Croatia and Albania joined in 2009. Yet NATO enlargement was not accompanied by either enhanced military capabilities or a new shared security vision.

An important corollary to NATO's enlargement between 1994 and 2014 was its efforts to build constructive relations with Russia. Alongside the 1997 decision on enlargement, the Founding Act on Mutual Relations, Cooperation, and Security between NATO and the Russian Federation was signed. This created the Permanent Joint Council, a mechanism for regular consultations and cooperation regarding a wide range of issues such as joint peacekeeping operations, transparency of military doctrines, defense conversion, and nuclear safety. In the West, the council was seen also as a mechanism for influencing Russian military reform and perceptions of NATO. In Russia, it was viewed as an institutionalized means of limiting the impact of NATO enlargement and ensuring Russian influence on NATO policies.

Realists saw NATO expansion as a means to achieve relative gains against Russia and further enhance Western security. Liberals viewed it as a means to strengthen democracy in former communist states and bring stability to crisis areas. Despite the efforts to establish mechanisms for consultation and cooperation, Russia continued to perceive NATO as an anti-Russian military alliance. NATO's intervention in Kosovo in 1999 over Russia's opposition (and without UN Security Council sanction) fed Russian fears, which were reinforced by US proposals to advance Georgia's and Ukraine's candidacy for NATO membership following Russia's invasion of Georgia in 2008. Russia's fears were one aspect of the crisis over Ukraine that began in 2014, although there was no move to bring Ukraine into NATO.

*New post–Cold War roles: Former Yugoslavia and the Balkans.* The conflicts in the former Yugoslavia in the early 1990s drew NATO into its first military operations beginning in 1992, first in enforcing an arms embargo and then a no-fly zone. In 1995, with UN Security Council authorization, NATO planes bombed Bosnian Serb installations, an action that helped shift the military balance in the Bosnian war and led to peace negotiations. Under the Dayton Accords, NATO then undertook major peacekeeping and peacebuilding responsibilities. NATO members provided the majority of Implementation Force (IFOR) troops, with twenty-two other countries, including Russia, also contributing. IFOR was succeeded by the Stabilization Force (SFOR) from 1996 to 2004, after which the EU took over. In 1999, NATO's seventy-eight-day bombing campaign against the Federal Republic of Yugoslavia (Serbia) and intervention in Kosovo marked yet another step in its post–Cold War role. NATO then provided the majority of troops for the Kosovo Force (KFOR) from 1999 to the present.

*Afghanistan and the war on terrorism.* The September 11, 2001, terrorist attacks led NATO members to express their solidarity with the United States by invoking Article 5 of the North Atlantic Treaty for the first time. With the US declaration of a global war against terrorism, NATO moved to adapt to this new security environment and sought to enhance its operational capabilities to act quickly and in different modes with a 25,000-member rapid reaction force. Commitments to this force have fallen short, however, as members have had difficulty keeping troops, planes, and helicopters at the necessary state of readiness on top of other alliance commitments in the Balkans, Afghanistan, and elsewhere.

In August 2003, NATO assumed command of the 5,000-member, UN-sanctioned International Security Assistance Force (ISAF) in Afghanistan. This marked NATO's first operation outside of Europe. Initially, NATO forces operated only around the capital and separately from the US forces. That changed in 2006, and by the end of 2008 NATO had over 50,000 troops in Afghanistan assisting the Afghan government in extending its authority throughout the country, conducting operations against the resurgent Taliban and al-Qaeda, and supporting the Afghan army. The mission has been controversial among the European allies, however, a number of which imposed restrictions on where and how their troops could operate in Afghanistan (primarily to minimize casualties). US officials repeatedly had to make the case for why European security was linked to NATO's success in stabilizing Afghanistan. With the official termination of ISAF in 2014, NATO and US forces will continue to provide training and assistance to the Afghan National Security Forces under the US-Afghan Bilateral Security Agreement and the NATO Status of Forces Agreement.

*Other operations: Iraq, Darfur, Somalia, Libya.* The 2003 Iraq War sharply divided the NATO allies, creating a crisis within the alliance. European members refused US requests for limited support; three countries blocked planning for NATO support of its own member, Turkey, and for any official NATO presence in Iraq. The alliance, however, had a role in training and assisting the Iraqi army from 2004 to 2011. It has supported African Union peacekeeping missions in the Darfur region of Sudan and in Somalia, principally by providing airlift for AU peacekeepers. In addition, NATO ships have patrolled waters off the Horn of Africa to combat piracy.

NATO's role in the toppling of the Muammar Qaddafi regime in Libya in 2011, however, was more extensive and controversial. Under UN Security Council Resolutions 1970 and 1973 (2011), NATO enforced a no-fly zone and arms embargo as well as undertaking air and naval strikes against Libyan forces attacking or threatening civilians and civilian-populated areas. By one set of measures, Operation Unified Protector saved tens of thousands of lives. "It conducted an air campaign of unparalleled precision, which, although not perfect, greatly minimized collateral damage. It enabled the Libyan opposition to overthrow one of the world's longest-ruling dictators . . . without a single allied casualty" (Daalder and Stavridis 2012: 2). By other measures, NATO's operation amounted to war, not a humanitarian intervention, in the eyes of many.

The Libyan operation, involving eighteen countries (fourteen NATO members and four partners), demonstrated NATO's unique ability to respond quickly and effectively to crises, thanks to its unified command structure and capability for planning and executing complex operations. It was also indicative, however, of tensions within the alliance in that fourteen member countries did not participate, including Germany and Poland, although they did not block the decision to act. Furthermore, the operation highlighted the ongoing problem of European underinvestment in defense capabilities in that the United States provided 75 percent of the intelligence and surveillance data; 75 percent of the refueling planes that made the operation possible; much of the ammunition; and military personnel to aid in targeting strikes (Daalder and Stavridis 2012: 6).

NATO presents the unusual case of an international organization whose original purpose disappeared, presenting the challenge of transforming itself, with a variation of the original purpose reappearing twenty years later. Members have had to negotiate in every case to determine whether to take a common response, particularly when the United States has pushed for new and greater activity outside Europe. For close to twenty years, NATO was seen by some as a transatlantic group of democratic states, not a military alliance, as its enlargement promoted and protected democracies. Although military action in Afghanistan could be justified as a matter of self-defense, the cooperation of European allies looked more like an ad hoc coalition of the willing than an alliance commitment. Beginning with events in Crimea and Ukraine in 2014, as noted previously, issues of alliance commitment became primary once again. They revived debate over how to interpret Russian actions and what they mean for NATO's future. They also prompted new attention to enhancing members' military capabilities, and to where troops and equipment should be stationed.

### The Organization for Security and Cooperation in Europe
The OSCE is the broadest organization in the European security architecture, with fifty-seven member states in Europe and Central Asia, plus the United States and Canada. As the successor to the Conference on Security and Cooperation in Europe, it has evolved since 1990 into an important instrument for broadly defined security cooperation and coordination, and conflict prevention and resolution.

The predecessor CSCE was the product of a Soviet Warsaw Pact proposal in the early 1970s to convene an all-European conference to resolve the outstanding issues from World War II, particularly territorial boundaries and the division of Germany. The Helsinki Final Act of 1975 contains a set of ten principles governing interstate relations, including refraining from the threat or use of force, inviolability of frontiers, peaceful settlement of disputes, respect for human rights and fundamental freedoms, self-determination of peoples, and cooperation among states. These form the normative core of what is now the OSCE-based European security regime. The Cold War's end and pressures for independence from groups and regions within the Soviet Union and Yugoslavia led to strengthening of CSCE-supported confidence-building measures, transparency, democratization, and minority rights protections.

Following approval of the Charter of Paris for a New Europe in 1990, the CSCE was gradually transformed into the OSCE. A secretariat, parliamentary assembly, and permanent council were established to supplement the annual ministerial meetings and biannual summits, along with the Conflict Prevention Center, the Office for Democratic Institutions and Human Rights, the Office of the High Commission on National Minorities, and the Office of the Special Representative and Coordinator for Combating Human Trafficking. The OSCE has played a major role in managing post–Cold War changes in Europe through a wide range of activities from arms control and counterterrorism to transnational crime and trafficking in drugs, arms, and people. It is particularly noted for its work in organizing, supervising, and monitoring all aspects of electoral processes as well as its efforts to protect and promote human rights and minority rights. It has trained police in Croatia, Serbia, Kyrgyzstan, and Azerbaijan; negotiated a cease-fire in Chechnya; mediated agreements between governments and secessionist regions in Moldova, Azerbaijan, Georgia, and Tajikistan; and undertaken conflict prevention activities and both election and cease-fire monitoring in Ukraine in 2014. Its largest and longest-running mission has been in Kosovo, where its responsibilities as part of the UN Mission in Kosovo (UNMIK) and alongside NATO's security force have included development of civil society, electoral assistance, human rights protection, police development, and reestablishing a judicial system. Despite its large membership, the OSCE has been able "to respond more rapidly than most other institutions and to adapt its responses more appropriately to the specific issues arising in particular cases" (Hopmann 2000: 601).

The OSCE has often come under fire, however, from Russia and other states for what is seen as too exclusive a focus on countries "east of Vienna" (i.e., the former Soviet Union and Yugoslavia), as well as for applying uneven standards in its election monitoring, paying too much attention to the human-dimension activities (such as human rights promotion), and operating without sufficient political control from the decision-making bodies (Ghébali 2005: 14). In 2007 and 2008, the OSCE decided not to send observers for Russia's parliamentary and presidential elections as a result of the restrictions Russia imposed. Yet it sent observers for the 2012 presidential election at Russia's request. Many Central Asian states, however, have limited OSCE election observation. The OSCE's roles in several conflict situations, including Ukraine, are discussed further in Chapter 7.

While the activities of the OSCE overlap with those of NATO, the Council of Europe, and the EU, it occupies a niche because of its broad membership and its long-term field missions in many parts of the former Soviet Union and Yugoslavia. There is both cooperation and competition with the European Union, the strongest regional organization.

### The European Union

The EU is a unique entity that has become deeply institutionalized and involves far more commitment than any other regional organization. Whereas the initial steps involved only six Western European states, today twenty-eight states are full members. The EU's development embodies a process of integration, where steps taken in one area have spilled over into others over time. It has exemplified both functionalism and neofunctionalism. It encompasses aspects of both supranationalism (sometimes also referred to as federalism) and intergovernmentalism. Its development has involved both the widening of membership and the deepening of ties among the member states, integrating economies and societies more closely, and expanding the authority of community institutions over the member states. Much of the policymaking in Europe today is common or EU policy, made in Brussels through EU institutions. The EU affects the daily lives of its more than 500 million citizens, most of whom can now move freely between member states and carry EU passports. The EU commands 18 percent of world GDP, and citizens in nineteen member countries use the euro, launched in 2002, as their currency.

The EU's development has transformed governance in Europe, influencing everything from regulations on the habitat of birds to voting in the World Trade Organization; with its own legal system, parliament, bureaucracy, currency, and court, its complex institutions resemble those of nation-states. It has also altered global politics and governance. The process of European integration is attributable to a complex set of factors, but is not irreversible, as calls in Britain for withdrawal and the success of anti-EU parties in the 2014 EU parliamentary elections demonstrate.

*Historical overview of European integration.* Regional political and economic integration in (Western) Europe began in part as an effort by European leaders to find ways to overcome the national rivalries that had led to two devastating world wars in the first half of the twentieth century. The United States was committed to promoting democracy and a more open international economic system to replace the protectionism, competitive currency devaluations, and other policies that had marked the rivalries among European powers (and excluded US businesses from European markets). The Soviet threat added impetus to strengthening the war-weakened countries, as did internal threats from strong communist parties in France and Italy. A desire to enmesh the Germans in international agreements that would prevent them from posing future threats to European security was another motivating factor. The United States added incentives through post–World War II Marshall Plan requirements that the European governments cooperate in developing a plan for utilizing aid, formulate a joint effort rather than submit a series of national requests, and create an international organization to administer the aid to the sixteen participating countries. There were also visionary Europeans such as Jean Monnet and Alcide De Gasperi who dreamed of the possibilities of a "United States of Europe." Security threats, economic incentives, and visions all played a part. So, too, did economic interests of powerful sectors, particularly in the French and German economies (notably heavy industry and agriculture), along with trends in the post–World War II international economy (notably rising trade and capital flows among the industrialized countries), which led governments to look for ways to respond to new opportunities for promoting economic gains.

*The European Coal and Steel Community.* The birth of European integration occurred in May 1950 with a proposal by then–French foreign minister Robert Schuman to place Franco-German coal and steel production under a common "high authority." This meant accepting recently defeated Germany as an economic equal and handing over authority for both countries' key coal and steel industries to a supranational authority. Schuman provided a concrete step for turning vague dreams into reality, but in the key economic sector that supported war-making capability (arms industries)—a strategy that accorded well with neofunctionalist theory. The result was the European Coal and Steel Community, established in 1951 with six member states (France, Germany, Italy, Belgium, Luxembourg, and the Netherlands). Great Britain rejected an invitation to join, because of strong sentiments in both major political parties against loss of sovereignty and national control over coal and steel.

Illustrating the classic dynamic of functionalism, the ECSC was successful enough in boosting coal and steel production that the six member states agreed in 1958 to expand their cooperation under the European Atomic Energy Community and the European Economic Community. The founding documents of these three organizations form the constitutional basis of the European Union. The governing institutions of the three have been merged. Two other integrating organizations were proposed in the 1950s but rejected: the European Defence Community and European Political Community.

*The Treaties of Rome: Euratom and the Common Market.* The Treaties of Rome represented recognition that the community could not develop the coal and steel sectors in isolation from other economic sectors. One treaty committed members to creating a common market over a period of twelve years through removal of all restrictions on internal trade; a common external tariff; reduction of barriers to free movement of people, services, and capital; the development of common agricultural and transport policies; and the establishment of the European Social Fund and European Investment Bank. The second treaty created Euratom to establish a common market for atomic energy.

Although there were certainly tensions among the members and between governments and the community institutions, there was remarkably rapid progress in taking significant steps toward achieving the desired common market. In 1962, the Common Agricultural Policy (CAP) came into existence, with a single market for farm products and guaranteed prices for farmers. In the 1960s also, the six members began the arduous process of harmonizing various health, safety, and consumer protection standards and regulations, as well as easing the barriers to movement of workers among member countries. In 1968, two years ahead of schedule, they completed an industrial customs union and had removed enough internal barriers to trade to agree on a common external tariff with nonmember countries and to form a single negotiating party in international trade talks. In 1969, governments agreed on the principles of economic and monetary union, both of which were regarded as essential to achieving political union, although the sovereignty that would be lost with monetary union was particularly difficult for them to contemplate at the time. Despite disagreement over whether economic or monetary union should come first, they did agree to begin efforts toward controlling exchange-rate fluctuations and coordinating their national economic policies.

*Enlargement.* Slow economic growth in the 1970s stalled any deepening of European integration, but there was movement on another front. In 1973, the community's first enlargement took place with the accession of Great Britain, Ireland, and Denmark (Norwegian voters rejected the accession agreement their government had signed). Later in the 1970s, a strong desire to bolster the new democracies in Greece, Spain, and Portugal provided political impetus for their accession. The addition of Ireland and the three southern European countries introduced a much wider disparity among members' levels of economic development than existed with the original six or with the UK and Denmark. In 1994, the decision was made to admit Finland, Sweden, and Austria. Then, in anticipation of further enlargements to former Soviet-bloc states in Eastern Europe, the European Council delineated conditions for new members, including respect for democracy, rule of law, and human rights, protection of minorities, a functioning market economy, and a demonstrated capacity to implement past and future EU rules and legislation. These so-called Copenhagen conditions have provided benchmarks for candidate countries as well as incentives for making the requisite changes in their economies, political systems, and laws. Three further enlargements, in 2004, 2007, and 2013, brought in eleven Eastern European and two Mediterranean countries. Table 5.1 details some consequences of the seven enlargements, which have increased the EU's influence as the world's largest economic bloc but complicated the community's decisionmaking processes.

The EU now encompasses much of the continent and far greater diversity. For the thirteen newer members, EU membership has meant adhering to 80,000 pages of EU laws and regulations accumulated over five decades of the integration process. Although all members won special concessions and extra time to phase in the EU's now extensive environmental legislation, they had to wait seven to ten years before getting full benefits such as free movement of labor and agricultural subsidies. Still, the requirements for accession provided a powerful incentive for governments to change, although once they became members, those incentives diminished. The implications of the latest enlargements for the EU itself are enormous. The disparities and tensions between older and newer members create a number of issues, including the need for reform of institutional structures.

*Deepening integration.* The process of deepening European integration has entailed completing the creation of a single market, expanding the range of common policies, the establishment of the European Union itself, and the monetary union and single currency. It has involved four additional treaties and a number of institutional changes. It is still widely viewed as an elite-driven process and this has proved increasingly controversial.

In 1987, European Community members took their most important step since the Treaty of Rome with their adoption of the Single European Act (SEA), which established the goal of completing a single market by the end of 1992. This meant a complicated process of removing all remaining physical, fiscal, and technical barriers to trade, harmonizing different national health, food-processing, and other standards, varying levels of indirect taxation such as value-added taxes, and removing barriers to movement of peoples such as professional licensing requirements (see Chapter 8 for fur-

**Table 5.1  EU Enlargements**

| | Original Members (1958) | First Enlargement (1973) | Second Enlargement (1981) | Third Enlargement (1986) | Fourth Enlargement (1995) | Fifth Enlargement (2004) | Sixth Enlargement (2007) | Seventh Enlargement (2013) |
|---|---|---|---|---|---|---|---|---|
| Member states | Belgium<br>France<br>Germany<br>Italy<br>Luxembourg<br>Netherlands | Britain<br>Denmark<br>Ireland | Greece | Portugal<br>Spain | Austria<br>Finland<br>Sweden | Cyprus<br>Czech Republic<br>Estonia<br>Hungary<br>Latvia<br>Lithuania<br>Malta<br>Poland<br>Slovakia<br>Slovenia | Bulgaria<br>Romania | Croatia |
| Population (million) | 185 | 273 | 287 | 338 | 370 | 450 | 493 | 506 |
| Number of seats in European Parliament | 142 | 273 | 287 | 338 | 370 | 732 | 785 | 751 |
| Number of member states | 6 | 9 | 10 | 12 | 15 | 25 | 27 | 28 |

ther discussion). The changes, however, allowed banks and companies to do business throughout the community; allowed EC residents to live, work, and draw pensions anywhere in the EC; and ended monopolies in sectors such as electricity and telecommunications. They also included a number of important institutional changes such as greater power for the European Parliament (EP).

Even before the SEA's 1992 deadline for completing the single market, the twelve members signed the Maastricht Treaty on European Union, calling for "an ever closer union among the peoples of Europe." The original European Community became one of three pillars of the new EU. The second pillar comprises Common Foreign and Security Policy (CFSP), while the third includes justice and home affairs—new areas of common policy. Both the second and third pillars, however, remain largely matters for individual governments or, at best, intergovernmental agreement. Maastricht also gave impetus to European monetary union with agreement to institute a single European currency in 1999, and created a nascent European citizenship with a common passport and rights to live and vote wherever citizens liked. It included further institutional changes as well. Ratification of the Maastricht Treaty encountered problems when Danish voters rejected it in a referendum; it was also put to a referendum in France, where it narrowly passed. Following agreement that Denmark could opt out of certain provisions in the treaty, Danish voters passed a second referendum. This, however, was a wake-up call to EU leaders that deepening integration was not accepted by all of Europe's citizens and prompted debate about the "democratic deficit" within the EU, whereby most decisions have been made by governmental leaders and bureaucrats without direct input from voters.

Three additional treaties have dealt with enlargement and institutional reform. The Treaty of Amsterdam, which was signed in 1997 and came into force in 1999, gave a green light to further enlargement and dealt with issues such as social policy, immigration, asylum, the environment, and consumer protection. In 2003, the Treaty of Nice entered into force, bringing changes important to an enlarged and more democratic EU such as increasing the number of seats in the European Parliament, modifying the weights in the EU's system of qualified majority voting, and limiting the number of commissioners to one per state. An EU constitution was then drafted in 2002–2003 to address more of the structural problems anticipated with the 2004 enlargement, but was rejected by referendums in France and the Netherlands in 2005, effectively killing it. The 2007 Lisbon Treaty incorporates many of the draft constitution's provisions designed to improve the efficiency of institutions and make them more democratic. It also provides the EU with international legal status, enabling it to sign international treaties or be a member of other IGOs, and made the EU Charter of Rights legally binding on members. The Lisbon Treaty was rejected by Ireland's voters in 2008 but approved in 2009 after changes were made. Figure 5.2 summarizes key parts of the European integration process.

*Structure.* The current structure of EU institutions, including the European Council, the European Commission, the Council of Ministers, the European Parliament, and the European Court of Justice, is shown in Figure 5.3.

*The European Commission.* The European Commission is the supranational, executive, and bureaucratic body of the EU and the engine for integration. It has the exclusive responsibility for initiating new community laws and for advancing the goals of the treaties. In this respect, it is "the conscience of the European Union because it is designed to look after the good of the whole, which no one government or group of governments could do alone" (Ginsberg 2007: 165). The Commission works with national bureaucracies to ensure that states implement policies and legislation; it represents the EU in international trade negotiations and at the UN, draws up the budget and spends funds approved, and can promulgate regulations on technical matters that are binding on states. The Commission also plays a key role in the enforcement of EU law, with the right to warn states when they are violating treaty obligations, to publicize states' failure to implement EU law, to initiate legal action in the European Court of Justice against them, and to impose sanctions or fines if law is not being implemented.

---

**Figure 5.2     Timeline of European Integration**

| | |
|---|---|
| 1951 | European Coal and Steel Community created (six members) |
| 1957 | Treaties of Rome establish European Economic Community and European Atomic Energy Community (six members) |
| 1962 | Common Agricultural Policy launched |
| 1968 | Completion of customs union |
| 1970 | Launch of European political cooperation |
| 1979 | First direct elections for European Parliament |
| 1986 | Single European Act launches single market |
| 1992 | Maastricht Treaty on European Union (three pillars) |
| 1997 | Treaty of Amsterdam authorizes further enlargement |
| 2002 | Launch of single currency (euro) |
| 2003 | Treaty of Nice brings institutional reforms |
| 2009 | Treaty of Lisbon authorizes constitutional changes |

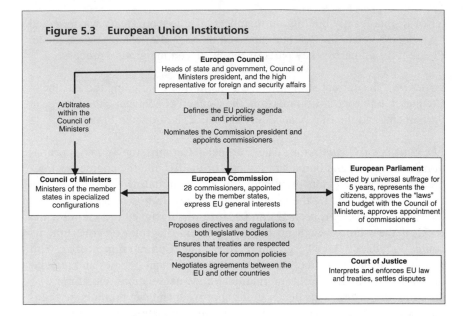

**Figure 5.3    European Union Institutions**

The Commission is led by a group of twenty-eight commissioners who are nominated by national governments (one per member state) in consultation with the Commission president for five-year renewable terms. They are not national representatives and may not be removed by their national governments. Rather, they are expected to act in the interests of the EU as a whole and according to the letter and spirit of the founding treaties. The Commission as a whole is approved by the European Parliament, which may also censure and thereby remove the entire Commission, but not individual commissioners, which the Parliament came close to doing in 1999. Most commissioners are responsible for one or more particular policy areas (known as directorates-general) and for supervising the work of some 33,000 civil servants ("Eurocrats"), aided by their respective personal staffs or cabinets. The directorates include all major policy areas of the EU, ranging from agriculture and the internal market to competition policy, justice and home affairs, external relations, regional policy, trade, and environment and energy. The Commission functions, therefore, much like a national government cabinet and on the basis of collective responsibility, making decisions by consensus or simple majority.

The president of the Commission functions as the EU's chief executive. He or she assigns the portfolios of other commissioners and can veto nominations for commissioners. The president represents the Commission in meetings with national governments and at summit meetings such as those of the G-7/8. Like other commissioners, the president is appointed for a renewable five-year term and is nominated by the European Council (the heads of member governments) and approved by the European Parliament. Recent Commission presidents have all been former prime ministers. Romano Prodi of Italy (1999–2004), for example, oversaw the euro's launch and the 2004 enlargement, while his successor, José Manuel Barroso of Portugal, had to deal with the European debt crisis (discussed in Chapter 8).

*The Council of Ministers (Council of the European Union).* The EU's Council of Ministers is made up of national government ministers who make decisions on law and policy. As such, it represents intergovernmentalism. The Council of Ministers must approve Commission proposals for new laws in conjunction with the European Parliament. Historically, it was far more powerful than the Parliament, but the Maastricht Treaty increased the Parliament's power so that the two share responsibility not only for accepting, modifying, or rejecting proposals for new laws, but also for approving the EU budget. In addition, the Council of Ministers has executive functions with respect to EU common foreign, security, and defense policy, coordination policies, judicial cooperation, and concluding treaties on the EU's behalf. It can also request the Commission to conduct studies and initiate proposals.

The Council of Ministers is made up of one government minister per state, with the composition changing based on the subject under consideration (foreign, economic, agriculture, competition policy, etc.). In effect, therefore, the Council of Ministers comprises multiple councils (ten in all) responsible for specific policy areas. The frequency and importance of council meetings depend upon the degree to which member states have transferred policymaking authority to the EU. Agriculture and fisheries ministers, for example, meet monthly to deal with issues of commodity prices and subsidy levels, while transport, education, and environment ministers meet only a few times a year, since these areas are still largely the domain of national governments. With efforts to increase common foreign, security, and defense policy since 1992, the foreign ministers have met more frequently.

The presidency of the Council of Ministers rotates every six months by country, and along with the Commission president, the Council of Ministers president represents the EU at many major international meetings. The two tend to form a co-executive. Continuity between presidents and support for the council are provided by the Committee of Permanent Representatives (COREPER), which comprises the ambassadors of member states in Brussels and other senior officials. COREPER actually negotiates agreements on all policy initiatives except the most contentious issues.

The Council of Ministers uses different voting systems depending on the policy areas and political sensitivity of the subject. Unanimity is required for foreign, security, and defense policy, as it is for changes to the treaties, enlargement, and taxation. Some fifty policy areas are decided by qualified majority voting—a complex system of weighting member states' votes that ensures that big countries cannot act without the cooperation of at least some of the smaller countries (or vice versa). As of 2014, the Lisbon Treaty's provision for a new system more akin to a double majority requiring 55 percent of the member states (currently fifteen) and representing at least 65 percent of the EU population came into effect. In reality, most Council decisions are taken by consensus, without a formal vote.

Because the members of the Council of Ministers are national political figures, the dynamics of the council are inevitably influenced by national interests, the stability of a national government, the ideology of various members, and their relative authority. As John McCormick and Jonathan Olsen (2014: 133) note, "the keys to understanding how it works are found in terms such as *compromise, bargaining,* and *diplomacy.*"

*The European Council or Summit.* The European Council came into existence in 1974 when member-state heads of state and government (prime ministers and presidents) agreed to hold regular summit meetings to give greater political impetus to the integration process and broad policy direction. The European Council convenes four or more times a year. Although it generally does not get involved in details of legislation and policymaking, it has become the key body for major EU initiatives such as concluding the single market, monetary union, enlargement, foreign policy issues, constitutional reform, and the European debt crisis. The Single European Act gave legal status to the European Council; the Lisbon Treaty created the post of president, elected by the European Council for a two-and-a-half-year term, renewable once, and responsible for organizing and hosting Council summits and working to build consensus among its members. Council makeup now includes the heads of state and government, one minister (usually foreign affairs) per member, the Council president, the president of the European Commission, and the high representative for foreign affairs and security policy. The advantages of the European Council include its flexibility given the lack of rules and separate bureaucracy; its informality and absence of formal agendas; and its ability to delegate to other institutions and focus on the big picture (McCormick and Olsen 2014: 179).

*The European Parliament.* The European Parliament (EP) is the voice of EU citizens in that it is the only EU body that is directly elected by voters in the member states (since 1979). Yet it is little known or understood. It consists of 751 members (MEPs) elected for five-year renewable terms, with seats allocated according to member states' population. This makes it one of the largest legislative bodies in the world, and unwieldy because of its size, twenty-three official languages, and cycle of perpetual motion among three venues: Strasbourg for plenary sessions, Brussels for committee meetings, and Luxembourg, where staff have their offices.

MEPs are seated by political group, not by national delegations. The rules of procedure strongly encourage the formation of these transnational political groups. Seven party groups plus the so-called nonattached members span the left-right ideological spectrum of European politics and range from pro- to anti-European. The three largest groups are the Socialist Group on the left, the European People's Party Group on the right, and the Alliance of Liberals and Democrats for Europe in the center. The growth of green and extreme-right parties in various European countries has been mirrored by their appearance in the EP since the mid-1980s. The 2014 EP elections saw anti-EU parties secure roughly a quarter of the vote in both France and Britain and about a hundred seats in Parliament, or close to one-third of the seats if one counts all anti-establishment party members. Despite ideological differences, however, party groups frequently share common interests on particular issues and in promoting the EP's influence in the EU legislative process.

The Parliament's role has expanded over time with the growth of EU membership and with MEPs using arguments about democratic accountability to gain greater legislative and supervisory responsibilities. Its input into the lawmaking process was successively expanded by the SEA, Maastricht, and Amsterdam treaties. The Lisbon Treaty widened the EP's legislative co-decision power with that of the Council of Ministers over some fifty areas, including the internal market and immigration, international agreements, and the budget. The Commission, however, still has the sole power to propose new laws and policies, and the Parliament still lacks sufficient credibility with voters "to fully exploit its advantages" (McCormick and Olsen 2014: 140). Turnout for EP elections has fallen steadily since 1979 (43 percent in 2014), and voter mistrust of the Parliament has risen.

In effect, the Council of Ministers and the European Parliament now constitute a bicameral (two-house) legislature. As a result, the Council of Ministers and the Commission must take the Parliament's opinions more seriously. EU-level interest groups pay more attention to the Parliament to influence the shape of legislation, whereas once they directed most of their efforts at the Commission.

From a weak advisory assembly whose members were appointed by national parliaments, the European Parliament has evolved into the only directly elected and accountable institution in the EU. It has steadily increased its powers. While it has narrowed the EU's democratic deficit and become a co-legislature with the Council of Ministers, the Parliament still is not a true legislature, since it cannot introduce new laws. Low voter turnout in EP direct elections underscores voters' sense that it still does not affect their lives very much.

*The European Court of Justice*. What makes the ECJ's role unique among international judicial bodies is that EU treaties are legally enforceable documents, unlike the UN Charter. They create legal obligations that the ECJ has the responsibility to interpret and enforce from its seat in Luxembourg. The ECJ also has the power to rule on the constitutionality of all EU law, provide advisory opinions to national courts in cases where there are questions about compatibility of national and EU law, and settle disputes involving other EU institutions, member states, individuals, or corporations. Member states are obligated to uphold European law and to enforce ECJ decisions.

The ECJ is composed of twenty-eight judges appointed by member states for six-year renewable terms, plus nine advocates-general who help ease the court's burden by reviewing cases coming to the court and providing what are, in effect, preliminary opinions that may be accepted or rejected by the full court. The ECJ itself may sit in full (*en banc*) or in smaller chambers. Court rules require that cases brought by member states be heard by the full court. In the civil law tradition, decisions are generally announced without indicating any dissenting opinions. There is no appeal. In 1989, to respond to a rising caseload and allow the judges to concentrate on fundamental tasks, the Court of First Instance (now called the General Court) was established to deal with all cases brought by individuals and companies, with the exception of cases dealing with trade defense issues such as antidumping. Thus this court hears competition cases and disputes over technical legislation and questions of fact. In 2005, the EU Civil Service Tribunal took over all cases involving disputes between the EU institutions and their staff, such as those involving gender discrimination and application of staff regulations.

ECJ cases fall into two broad categories: preliminary rulings in which the court is advising national courts and tribunals on how points of national law relate to EU law, and direct actions brought by an individual, corporation, member state, or EU institution. Direct actions include cases brought by the European Commission against a member state for failure to fulfill an obligation, as well as cases brought by individuals, corporations, member states, or an EU institution seeking to annul an EU law on the grounds that it is illegal, or seeking action against an EU institution for failure to act in accord with the treaties. Virtually every member state has been brought before the court at least once—and some several hundred times—for failure to fulfill obligations. A 1964 landmark case (*Flaminio Costa v. Enel*) established the supremacy of EU law over national law even when it conflicts with the latter (ECJ 1964).

The ECJ has had an essential role in promoting European regional integration and governance by determining the EU's character and extending the reach of EU law, especially in cases related to the single market, such as *Cassis de Dijon,* in which the court ruled that products meeting one country's standards could not be barred from sale in another (ECJ 1979). Since 1954, it has heard over 15,000 cases and issued more than 7,500 judgments. ECJ cases cover subjects from trade issues to agricultural policy questions, environmental law, consumer safety regulations, freedom of movement for workers, and equal treatment for women. In 1995, the court also upheld freedom of movement for workers by overturning Belgian soccer rules that made it difficult for a Belgian player to transfer to a French club (ECJ 1995). In 2014, the ECJ ruled that a 2006 Council of Ministers directive on retention of telephone and e-mail data was invalid because it interfered with fundamental rights to privacy protected by the EU Charter and data privacy rules (ECJ 2014).

The ECJ's success (together with the corresponding development of EU community law) has hinged on the willingness of national courts to seek and abide by preliminary rulings, and the court's efforts through direct actions to get member states to fulfill their legal obligations under the treaties. No member state has refused to accept a major ECJ ruling, but there have been many instances of delayed implementation. The court has the power to impose fines on states for refusing to act on its rulings, and the Commission may initiate infringement proceedings with the ECJ, which can lead to a fine or imposition of sanctions, measures that other international courts do not have the authority to undertake. Furthermore, states do criticize ECJ rulings that they view as hostile to their national interests. The court's success (and power) can also be attributed to its actions vis-à-vis other EU institutions. The ECJ, for example, helped expand the EP's powers by ruling that the latter could bring community acts for judicial review. Given the ECJ's unprecedented powers and success, it is not surprising that Karen Alter (2000: 491) concludes: "The ECJ is perhaps the most active and influential international legal body in existence, operating as a constitutional court of Europe." Representing supranationalism over the intergovernmentalism of the Council of Ministers, the ECJ plays a key institutional role in European regionalism and the development of the legal order that EU law represents.

EU law is more than the decisions of the ECJ, however. There are laws in the form of regulations issued by the Council of Ministers alone, by the Council and the Parliament together, or by the Commission alone (depending upon the applicable section of the treaties and date); directives issued by the Commission that specify results to be achieved, such as competition policy or air pollution standards, but leave the means to member states; and finally, decisions that are binding measures issued to specific parties, such as to block a merger between two companies. EU law represents a distinctive legal system, lying between traditional national (or municipal) legal systems and international law, with a powerful court to interpret the law and enforce judgments against member states. As William Phelan (2012: 375) points out, "all Member States must comply with all compulsory and automatically applied EU obligations addressed to them. . . . It is thus an obligation that is *not conditional* on other states' behavior." In sum, then, EU law represents the pooled sovereignty that characterizes the EU and is an important aspect of what makes the EU very different from other international organizations. Much the same can be said for many areas of common EU policy.

*Other EU Institutions.* In addition to the Commission, Council of the European Union, Council of Ministers, Parliament, and Court of Justice, the EU has a variety of specialized institutions and agencies that have been created over the years as the scope of European integration and needs have required. These include the European Police Office, or Europol, to facilitate police cooperation since the opening of borders between member states; the European Central Bank, created in 1998 in conjunction with the creation of the single currency and catapulted to greater visibility with the eurozone crisis after 2008 (see Chapter 8); and the European Investment Bank, set up in 1958 to provide long-term finance for capital development projects.

*EU common policies.* Beginning with trade and agriculture, the EU has moved progressively into more and more areas of policy, ranging from fisheries and food safety to transport, competition, social policy, regional development, monetary policy and common currency, environment, justice and home affairs, external relations, and human rights. Three different approaches have been used to advance common policies: mutual recognition of different national standards, community directives establishing standards frameworks, and harmonization of standards (the most difficult, since this requires agreeing on a new common set of standards). Chapter 8 addresses policies associated with the single market, agriculture, and monetary union, which are all supranational policies and part of the first EU pillar. EU environmental policy is discussed in Chapter 11. We focus here, then, on social policy, also part of the first pillar; on common foreign, security, and defense policy (the second pillar); and on justice and home affairs (the third pillar).

*Social policy.* EU social policy, along with regional development policy, aims to address social and economic inequalities within and among the member states. It arises from the long history of social welfare policies in most EU member countries and encompasses workers' rights, equal pay for men and women, workers' freedom of movement, and working and living conditions. The most active proponents have been European labor unions, social democratic parties, and the European Commission. The opponents include businesses and conservative political parties who argue that high labor costs reduce European company competitiveness.

The Commission actively promoted common social policy, beginning in the 1980s, because of concerns for the social dimensions of the single market, such as the consequences of workers' mobility and variations in social security benefits and wages. It became a key part of the Single European Act. A separate Charter of Social Rights was adopted in 1989 by eleven of the then twelve members and subsequently incorporated into the Maastricht Treaty with an opt-out provision for Great Britain, and into the Amsterdam Treaty with Great Britain as a participant. Provisions were added for EU action against discrimination based on age, gender, disability, ethnicity, belief, race, and sexual orientation. Efforts have also been under way since 1999 to make European university education more compatible and to encourage educational exchanges and the transfer of credits. These changes have greatly increased the mobility of European university students. Much of the attention since 1991, however, has been on the persistent problem of unemployment, an issue that has taken center stage during the eurozone crisis, as discussed in Chapter 8.

Social policy illustrates an area of policy where the EU's supranational powers are evident. EU Common Foreign and Security Policy (CFSP) and European Security and Defense Policy (ESDP) illustrate more intergovernmentalism.

*Common foreign, security, and defense policy.* After achieving the initial customs union and common external tariff in 1968, the European Community began negotiating as one entity in GATT and initiated foreign policy coordination in 1970 under the guise of European Political Cooperation (EPC). One of the earliest areas of cooperation was the situation in the Middle East, with the community speaking out on behalf of Palestinian rights and a two-state solution to the Israeli-Palestinian conflict.

The Single European Act (1987) and the Maastricht Treaty (1992) strengthened the bases for formulating and implementing CFSP, although the efforts at common policy have often been long on rhetoric and short on results. For example, the EU failed to prevent war in Yugoslavia in 1991–1992, despite having assumed primary responsibility for dealing with the situation with the blessing of the UN and the United States. The reluctance of the larger countries (Britain, France, and Germany) to give up their individual voices in world politics (let alone their Security Council permanent seats), and member states' divergent positions on specific issues, diminished the EU's potential influence as a collective entity. Since the

1999 European Council decision to create a defense capability independent of NATO, EU capabilities for humanitarian, peacekeeping, peace enforcement, and anti-piracy operations have enabled it to assume an increasingly active role in global politics and governance on a wide range of issues. Taking members' individual contributions and the EU contribution together, the EU is the largest contributor to the UN and contributes the majority of global development aid. It is also a major source of humanitarian relief aid through UN agencies and NGOs. With its rapid reaction force, the EU undertook peace enforcement in the Democratic Republic of Congo in 2003 under Security Council authorization; it has mounted a number of military, police, and civilian operations in Aceh (Indonesia), Bosnia, Chad, Georgia, Kosovo, and Moldova. It has been active in international election monitoring outside Europe, since the OSCE takes the lead within Europe. It has strongly supported both the International Criminal Court and the Kyoto Protocol, on global climate change (discussed in Chapters 10 and 11 respectively), and has emerged as a leading proponent of global environmental cooperation, democracy, human rights, nonproliferation of weapons of mass destruction, and antiterrorism efforts. Still, there have been significant disagreements such as whether to support the US-led invasion of Iraq in 2003 or to intervene in Libya and Syria in 2011–2012. In 2014, the EU overcame initial hesitation among a number of member states to join with the United States in imposing economic sanctions on Russia for its actions in Crimea and eastern Ukraine.

CFSP and ESDP are both intergovernmental areas of common policy, falling under the second EU pillar, over which member governments exercise a great deal of influence. Yet there is strong overlap with both the first and third pillars. Decisionmaking tends to take place either in the Council of Ministers or the European Council summits. A key player in policy formulation and implementation is the high representative for CFSP—the EU's foreign minister. The first person to hold that position, Catherine Ashton, for example, led the six-party negotiations with Iran over its nuclear program that began in 2010. A number of special representatives with ambassadorial rank hold posts in various trouble spots such as the Middle East, Africa's Great Lakes region, as well as Afghanistan, Bosnia, and Kosovo, and report to the high representative. Beyond consultation, the European Parliament is rarely involved in CFSP and ESDP, and the ECJ has no legal authority over either. The European Defence Agency has been established to support ESDP and facilitate coordination with NATO, including exchange of classified intelligence.

The EU has an extensive web of relationships with individual countries through its Neighborhood Policy and with other regional groupings such as ASEAN, NAFTA, Mercosur, and the AU. The Commission has missions in many capitals and at the United Nations. Other countries maintain diplomatic representatives in Brussels. The Commission's president participates in G-7/8 summits, and the EU has been a member of several "contact groups" such as those for the former Yugoslavia and the Israeli-Palestinian conflict. The EU's development assistance is now organized through the Cotonou Agreement, signed in 2000 by the seventy-eight African, Caribbean, and Pacific countries and the then EU-15. The agreement links development assistance to certain conditions—democracy promotion, respect for human rights, and an enhanced role for civil society and the private sector. The EU has begun to phase out trade preferences for these countries, however, and is eager to negotiate economic partnership agreements to establish free trade agreements with individual members.

The development of EU foreign policy has reflected some shared interests of EU members. It has also reflected the evolving habits of cooperation of the members, their learning from past mistakes such as in the former Yugoslavia, and their willingness to create new capabilities and procedures to make their policies more effective. Constructivists have helped illuminate these developments and the related effects of socialization (Checkel 2005). Similar habits and learning have shaped the evolution of justice and home affairs.

*Justice and home affairs.* The goal in adding police and judicial affairs—the third pillar—to EU policy competence was to establish common practices for all EU and legal non-EU residents regarding racism, xenophobia, corruption, and cross-border crimes such as terrorism, and trafficking in persons, illicit drugs, and arms. It has proved to be a particularly important area of EU cooperation, with the last three enlargements eastward, growing concerns with terrorism since 2001, and increasing illegal immigration, trafficking in persons and arms, and organized crime. Cooperation in these areas began long before their incorporation into the Maastricht Treaty. The 1985 Schengen Agreement was a milestone because it abolished internal EU border checks and permitted free movement of persons. Britain and Ireland have remained outside Schengen and newer members have had to have their external border checks certified as secure.

Decisionmaking for justice and home affairs is intergovernmental, since internal security, police, and judicial affairs are considered core areas of state sovereignty. Thus, the ECJ has no jurisdiction. The Amsterdam Treaty did shift free movement of persons and all border management (e.g., illegal immigration and asylum policy) from the third EU pillar, justice and home affairs, to the first, supranational pillar, where the Commission has the power of legislative initiative. Europol coordinates action against transnational crimes, while the EU's Counter-Terrorism Coordinator oversees implementation of its action plan. According to Roy Ginsberg (2007: 273), although there will be some delegation of authority by governments to the EU, "member governments are not ready to transfer sovereignty to the EU in areas where they have responsibilities to provide for the security of their citizens." This reluctance to delegate too much authority is well explained by principal-agent theory, as discussed in Chapter 2. And, large numbers of illegal immigrants and asylum seekers in recent years have illumined the tensions between rising anti-immigrant sentiments in many EU countries, the need for burden-sharing with destination countries such as Greece, Italy, and Spain that have been receiving thousands of illegal migrants and asylum seekers from Africa and the Middle East, and humanitarian impulses to save lives.

*Future directions of European integration: The challenges of widening and deepening.* The challenges of enlargement or widening of the community are matched by the challenges of deepening the integration of its members. Although states have made conscious choices in both, strong differences in states' positions persist. With respect to deepening, Denmark and Great Britain oppose more supranationalism or federalism and the European Monetary Union (EMU, which both opted out of). Both new- and old-member domestic resistance have increased the probabilities of disagreement over deepening, especially in light of the eurozone crisis, which has led to tensions over demands by the European Central Bank and German government for austerity, as discussed further in Chapter 8. The 2014 European Parliament elections demonstrated the rising opposition to the EU in all member states except the Netherlands. Britain, as noted, is scheduled to hold a referendum on its own membership in 2016. The 2014 referendum on Scottish independence, while it failed, nonetheless called attention to the fact that the EU has no provisions for the disintegration of its members, a number of whom face separatist movements.

With respect to enlargement, some suggest that the EU has reached the limits of its absorption capacity. Yet Albania, Iceland, Macedonia, Montenegro, Serbia, and Turkey are candidate countries; Bosnia-Herzegovina and Kosovo are potential candidate members. Turkey's candidacy, given its large Muslim population, challenges predominant conceptions of European identity, and several member states oppose its membership. The debate over Turkey's accession also underscores that although the EU constitutes an extraordinary achievement in regional integration, its further development cannot be taken for granted, since much will depend on the long-term effects of recent enlargements, success in implementing institutional reforms in the Lisbon Treaty, and the resolution of Turkey's candidacy. Expansion of regional organizations poses new burdens that impact effectiveness. It is also important, however, to recall that the EU is one of many European institutions and that while the former socialist states of Eastern and Central Europe chose to look westward after the fall of communism in

1990, Russia itself and other European and Eurasian parts of the former Soviet Union, with exceptions such as Georgia, Ukraine, and Moldova, have created their own regional initiatives on Europe's eastern fringe and these continue to evolve.

## Is Europe a Model for Other Regions?

Theories of regional organization have been heavily influenced by the European experience and European integration theory. The EU has served as "a laboratory in which to investigate a series of common political phenomena developed further in Europe than elsewhere on the globe" (Moravcsik 1998: 500). There is no question that countries in other regions of the world have often viewed developments in Europe as a potential model to follow. In 2015, with the EU in mind, for example, the Eurasian Union became operational with Russia, Belarus, Kazakhstan, Armenia, and Kyrgyzstan as members. Yet the circumstances that supported the development of European regional governance, and particularly European integration as it progressed from the ECSC to the EU, cannot be duplicated elsewhere. In fact, many Asian leaders strongly reject the European model as inappropriate. Nevertheless, people in many regions of the world continue to use the European experience as a benchmark and guide to one model of regional governance even as ferment in Europe itself challenges that model.

## Regional Organizations in the Americas

### Evolution of Regionalism in the Americas

Some of the oldest regional initiatives took place in the Western Hemisphere in the nineteenth century. In 1889, the first of nine International Conferences of American States created the International Union of American Republics (later renamed the Pan American Union). The last of these conferences, in 1948, established the Organization of American States (OAS) as the primary forum for inter-American cooperation. In a separate initiative, the Inter-American Treaty of Reciprocal Assistance (Rio Treaty) was signed in 1947. This is a far more limited collective defense arrangement than NATO, because the Latin American governments refused to accept joint command of military forces or any binding obligation to use force without their explicit consent (Article 20).

There have also been a variety of initiatives for subregional economic integration among groups of states in North, Central, and South America and the Caribbean to promote development. The Summit of the Americas process, begun in the 1990s, attempted to reinvigorate hemispheric regionalism and had some success in enhancing the OAS's authority and providing impetus for reform (Rosenberg 2001: 80).

These various initiatives embody two approaches to Latin American regionalism. One is the idea of hemispheric regionalism or pan-Americanism, encompassing the entire Western Hemisphere (or, with more recent initiatives, the Latin Americans alone). The other has promoted subregional cooperation and economic integration among Latin American countries as a strategy for development. Both approaches have eschewed EU-style supranationalism in favor of intergovernmentalism. Both are marked by the differing visions of the United States and the Latin American states. Whereas the United States has historically been interested in the security of its backyard, Latin Americans have seen unity as the most effective way to secure their interests, including protection against US dominance. Many Latin American nations historically opposed ceding any authority to an organization in which the United States was a member. The coexistence of these two approaches reflects the most significant characteristic of the Americas: the enormous disparity in size, power, and economic wealth between the United States and all other states—a disparity that has diminished in recent years with economic growth throughout much of Latin America and the rise of both Mexico and Brazil as significant regional if not global actors.

Regionalism in Latin America made a strong comeback with the Cold War's end, settlements of the Central American conflicts of the 1980s, and the end of ideological conflict. Key factors included the move from authoritarian regimes to democracy in all Latin American countries except Cuba; the acceptance by most governments of neoliberal market capitalism; the effects of globalization, including Latin American countries' fear of being marginalized in the world economy; and a new security agenda of transnational problems, including drug trafficking and environmental concerns. We look first at the hemispheric approach embodied in the OAS, then at the integrationist approach associated with subregionalism in NAFTA and Mercosur.

### Hemispheric Regionalism

Key to inter-American hemispheric regionalism has been the amount and type of attention given by the United States to Latin America. Historically, periods of US interest in the region have been followed by periods of neglect, when the United States put global interests above Latin American concerns. US hegemony was greatest during the 1950s and 1960s, when the United States got the Latin Americans to accept its anticommunist agenda and used the Rio Treaty to legitimize actions in Guatemala, Cuba, and the Dominican Republic. The United States supported many Latin military regimes in the 1960s and 1970s. Political and economic changes in Latin America and the Caribbean in the 1980s were seen as positive developments by the United States, leading to new hemispheric initiatives in the 1990s, particularly linked to democracy promotion. Since 2000, US attention to Latin America has been diverted, however, by the wars on terrorism and in Iraq and Afghanistan, with hemispheric concerns rarely getting high-level attention.

*The Organization of American States.* In 1948, twenty-one countries in the Western Hemisphere adopted the Charter of the Organization of American States and simultaneously signed the American Declaration of the Rights and Duties of Man, the first international document devoted to human rights principles. Fourteen other nations joined subsequently, including the Caribbean island states and Canada. Cuba was excluded from participation between 1962 and 2009 for its adherence to Marxist-Leninism and its alignment with the communist bloc. No other regional organization in the world includes as strong a North-South dimension as the OAS. The OAS Charter includes provisions for strengthening regional peace and security, common action against aggression, and limiting conventional weapons. It also calls for promoting representative democracy, seeking solutions for political, juridical, and economic problems, and promoting economic, social, and cultural cooperation, as well as for eradication of extreme poverty. In recent years, the OAS has devoted more attention to transnational criminal threats to hemispheric security (e.g., drugs, arms, terrorism, human trafficking, money laundering).

The primary organs of the OAS include the General Assembly, the Permanent Council, the General Secretariat, and the Inter-American Council for Integral Development. There are a variety of committees and other organs, including the Inter-American Committee on Terrorism, the Inter-American Commission on Human Rights, the Inter-American Court of Human Rights (discussed further in Chapter 10), and the Inter-American Development Bank (discussed further in Chapter 9).

The General Assembly, which meets annually and, when requested, in special session, is considered the OAS's highest decisionmaking body, with each member state having one vote. Like the UN General Assembly, it may consider any matter relating to friendly relations among American states, and most decisions are made by consensus or when necessary by majority vote, with certain matters such as approval of the budget requiring a two-thirds majority. The Permanent Council conducts much of the day-to-day business of the OAS, meeting regularly at headquarters in Washington, DC. Its activities include assisting in peaceful settlement of disputes and undertaking diplomatic initiatives under the Inter-American Democratic Charter in the event of an unconstitutional change of government. Permanent Council decisions require a two-thirds majority, but most decisions are taken by consensus. The council is alternately known as the Organ of Consultation under the Rio Security Treaty. When it meets in this mode, its members are usually the foreign ministers.

The OAS General Secretariat supports the work of the organization, including technical assistance projects. Since the mid-1990s, it has also served as secretariat for the Summit of the Americas process, even though the summits are not officially part of the OAS. The OAS secretary-general has traditionally come from one of the Latin American states. The election of Chilean José Miguel Insulza in 2005 signaled the erosion of US influence, however, as he was the first secretary-general not endorsed by the United States. The breadth of the OAS's agenda has severely strained its resources, with persistent budget shortfalls, staff cuts, and difficulty recruiting and retaining qualified personnel (Meyer 2014: 25).

The OAS, like the UN, has several specialized organizations, including the Pan American Health Organization, the Inter-American Drug Abuse Control Commission, and the Inter-American Indigenous Institute. The Inter-American Commission on Women, established in 1928, was the first IGO in the world to work for women's political and civil rights and support women's participation in governance. Today, it continues to support women's movements at the governmental level, through NGOs, and at the grassroots level, with a focus on the full range of women's rights.

The United States has historically viewed the OAS as an instrument for advancing its interests in the hemisphere and is the organization's largest financial contributor (41 percent in 2013). During the Cold War, the United States used the OAS to counter communist subversion and, after 1960, the spread of Cuba's communist revolution. In 1962, the Cuban government was excluded from participation and sanctions were imposed; however, in 2009, in a major shift, the OAS lifted the suspension, subject to conditions that Cuba must meet before it can return. (A 1975 resolution had released OAS members from their obligation to enforce the sanctions.) Latin American support for the US anticommunist agenda waned after the mid-1960s. In 1979, the United States failed to get OAS support for blocking the leftist Sandinistas from taking power in Nicaragua. In 1983, the United States invaded Grenada without consulting the OAS, but under the pretext of the Eastern Caribbean Defense Treaty. Since the Cold War's end, collective defense against aggression from outside has been less central to the OAS agenda, and US influence has declined. Particular concerns for the United States continue to be the reintegration of Cuba, the application of the Inter-American Democratic Charter (discussed later), reform of the human rights system, newer security issues such as counterterrorism and antidrug efforts, and the need for OAS reform. The US decision in late 2014 to reestablish diplomatic relations with Cuba after more than five decades was widely welcomed in Latin America, and is likely to affect the dynamics within the region and the OAS in coming years.

With regard to peaceful settlement, the OAS has played a role in numerous regional border and other disputes, such as the 1995 border war between

Ecuador and Peru, a dispute between Belize and Guatemala (2003), and another between Colombia and Ecuador (2008), but it had little success in dealing with Colombia's long-running civil war. Ad hoc groups such as the Contadora Group (Mexico, Venezuela, Panama, and Colombia) and the Rio Group (Mexico, Venezuela, Panama, Colombia, Brazil, Argentina, Peru, and Uruguay), which helped secure peace in Central America's conflicts in the 1980s, however, have often been more effective than the OAS. The OAS has undertaken joint peacekeeping missions with the UN in Haiti, El Salvador, and Nicaragua, and been involved in various peacebuilding activities such as disarmament, demobilization, reintegration, truth and reconciliation, and electoral assistance in Colombia, Guatemala, Haiti, Nicaragua, and Suriname.

Democratic government has been a goal of peoples in the Americas almost since independence. It was endorsed in declarations of inter-American conferences beginning in 1936 and incorporated into the Charter of the Organization of American States and into the Inter-American Convention on Human Rights, yet the OAS was largely silent during the 1960s and 1970s when right-wing dictatorships became the norm in most countries. The wave of democratizations throughout the region in the late 1980s and 1990s led the OAS to assume a major role in defending and promoting democracy.

The first step toward this new role occurred in 1979 with a resolution condemning the human rights record of the Anastasio Somoza regime in Nicaragua. From the mid-1980s to 2001, the OAS approved a set of legal norms and procedures for the defense of democracy. Promotion of democracy was declared "an indispensable condition for the stability, peace, and development of the region" in the Protocol of Cartagena de Indias (1985), a revision of the OAS Charter. The Unit for the Promotion of Democracy was established in 1990 to assist with elections, and in 1991 the OAS General Assembly approved a resolution (1080) requiring its organs to take "immediate action" in the event of a "sudden or irregular interruption of the democratic institutional process" of any member state. Such threats to democracy include military coups or leaders' self-coups to stay in power past a constitutional term limit, as well as flawed elections and constitutional crises. That resolution, Craig Arceneaux and David Pion-Berlin (2007: 4) conclude, "made longstanding commitments to democratic defense operable." Six years later, the 1997 Protocol of Washington gave the OAS the right to suspend a member whose democratically elected government is overthrown by force (with a two-thirds majority voting in favor). And in 2001, the General Assembly adopted the Inter-American Democratic Charter, which proclaims the peoples' right to democracy and their governments' obligation to promote and defend it (Article 12); governments failing to uphold this obligation can be suspended from the OAS. The charter was drafted and approved in a remarkably short period of time (nine months) for an organization noted for its slowness (Cooper 2004: 96–97).

Under the democracy mandate, the OAS has acted against coups or self-coups on ten occasions: Suriname (1990), Haiti (1991–1994, 2004), Peru (1992), Guatemala (1993), Paraguay (1996, 2000), Ecuador (2000), and Venezuela (1992, 2002). It has acted against election failures in four instances: the Dominican Republic (1994), Peru (2000), Haiti (2001), and Honduras (2009). These actions have included diplomatic, financial, economic, and military sanctions on Haiti, a mission to Venezuela headed by the OAS secretary-general, and the unprecedented step of suspending Honduras from membership following the 2009 coup in that country, with that suspension lifted in 2011.

Overall, however, the OAS's record on defending democracy is mixed, particularly since 2002. In many cases, it has taken weak or no action, leading Arceneaux and Pion-Berlin (2007: 24) to conclude that the OAS "remains reluctant to condemn democratic deficiencies when faced with either threats that are ambiguous or domestic constituencies united and adamant in their defense of sovereignty."

Inadequate resources limit what the OAS can do, just as limited finances have always constrained its role in fostering economic and social development. The Latin American countries, for example, have long sought more attention to development needs and preferential treatment in trade and finance, while the United States has preferred that the OAS not be heavily involved in development activities. As a result, the UN's Economic Commission for Latin America and the Caribbean (ECLAC) and other forums have played key roles in regional development, as discussed in Chapter 9. Liberalization of most Latin American countries' economic policies in the 1980s, however, led to the creation of the Council for Integral Development and other OAS initiatives to promote new and better cooperation among members to overcome poverty, benefit from the digital revolution, and advance social and economic development. The alternative subregional integration approach is still the dominant one for promoting development, however. Subregional organizations also have the advantage of promoting economic integration and political cooperation without the United States and Canada—their response to the persistent perception that the OAS is US-dominated. Yet the OAS "is unlikely to disappear any time soon. The OAS is still equipped to take on critical issues . . . that newer multilateral mechanisms seem years away from being able to handle adequately" (Shifter 2012: 61).

## Subregional Integration

The diversity of the subregions within the Americas, along with the small size and low levels of economic development of many countries, has long driven efforts at subregional integration as an approach to development and to dealing with US dominance. The "integration as road to development" approach emerged from initiatives by the UN-based Economic Commission for Latin America (ECLA, which became ECLAC after inclusion of the Caribbean countries) and its first secretary-general, Argentine economist Raul Prebisch. Both were closely associated with dependency theories of underdevelopment that attributed the lack of development to structural factors in the international system, most notably the dominance of the "center" in production of manufactured goods and unequal exchange of manufactured goods and raw materials. Since many national markets are small and a strategy of industrialization through import substitution had its limits, subregional integration was seen as a means to providing larger markets and economies of scale for industrialization. Based on these ideas, there were a number of subregional integration efforts in Central and South America in the 1950s and 1960s. These so-called first-wave schemes varied significantly, from loose trade arrangements (as in the Latin American Free Trade Association [LAFTA]) to more interventionist integration systems (the Andean Group), but most were little more than empty shells. The 1973–1974 oil crisis and severe economic difficulties in most Latin American countries, including huge debt burdens, ended much of the effort at regional integration and reinforced inward-looking attitudes from the early 1970s until the 1990s.

Although the first wave of initiatives was largely unsuccessful, the second wave, beginning in the 1990s, has been more so as a result of learning, domestic political and economic changes, and changes in the global environment. It included five new subregional integration efforts: the North American Free Trade Agreement (NAFTA, comprising the United States, Canada, and Mexico); the Common Market of the South (Mercosur, comprising Argentina, Brazil, Uruguay, and Paraguay); the Andean Community (Venezuela, Ecuador, Peru, Colombia, and Bolivia); the Central American Common Market (CACM); and the Caribbean Community (CARICOM). The shared interests exhibited in these communities stemmed from a "common sense of vulnerability" among the many still fragile democracies whose small economies make them susceptible to financial crises, instability, subversion, and drug trafficking (Hurrell 1995: 257).

More recently, in 2004, Venezuela and nine other left-leaning countries launched the Bolivarian Alliance for the Peoples of Our America (ALBA) and its Peoples Trade Treaty to counter the US-led Free Trade Agreement of the Americas (FTAA). In 2008, under the leadership of Brazil, the South American countries initiated the twelve-member Union of South American Nations (UNASUR) and have been developing a formal organized structure, including a permanent secretariat. Yet despite the proliferation of regional integration initiatives, intraregional trade in South and Central

America amounted to just 27 percent of total trade in 2008, compared with 63 percent in the EU, and 52 percent in Asia. Clearly, economic interdependence is still not a major factor in Latin American subregional integration. We look here at two of the second-wave subregional initiatives: NAFTA and Mercosur.

*North America: NAFTA.* When the North American Free Trade Agreement was established in January 1994, few people thought of North America as a region. The United States accounted for more than 85 percent of the gross domestic product of the region, and Canada and Mexico had long endeavored to show their independence, if not resistance, to US domination. Yet both were heavily dependent on the United States economically and, in the protectionist climate of the late 1980s, feared possible interruptions in trade. Canada took the first step by concluding the US-Canada Free Trade Agreement in 1988. In 1990, Mexico's president proposed a free trade area with the United States and Canada, hoping to boost both trade and foreign investment. NAFTA was pushed by free trade advocates in all three countries and by business interests. It was opposed by labor, environmental, and other groups in all three. It not only marked a major shift in Mexican foreign and economic policies, but also had a major impact on hemispheric regionalism. At the time of its creation, NAFTA was unique in that it was the first free trade agreement involving two developed countries and a developing one.

In its early years, NAFTA sparked substantial growth in trade among the three countries and also accelerated "the flow of people, cultures, food, music, and sports across the two borders" (Pastor 2005: 217). Yet both economic competition from China and the 9/11 attacks on the United States had a significant dampening effect. In the latter case, increased border security between the United States and Canada slowed the growth of trade. Still, Gary Hufbauer, Cathleen Cimino, and Tyler Moran (2014: 2), in their assessment of NAFTA after twenty years, conclude that "the agreement can be credited with making important strides toward intraregional integration and higher living standards in all three countries," which has led to a "striking" degree of interdependence. They also credit NAFTA with creating a new foundation for US-Mexican relations, "dramatically" improving the dynamic of official and private relations (16). Former Mexican foreign minister Jorge Castañeda (2014: 134–137) credits NAFTA for helping to transform Mexico into a multiparty democracy with a competitive export economy and helping to "open Mexicans' minds."

NAFTA's institutional structures are relatively weak, with proponents of North American regional integration repeatedly calling for strengthening them. In contrast to the EU's strong institutions, the NAFTA Commission, composed of trade ministers from each country, is "neither seen nor heard, aside from a semi-annual meeting and joint statement" (Hufbauer and

Schott 2005: 61). Two other commissions, on labor cooperation and environmental cooperation, have had limited effects on issues such as water resources and migration. And, while NAFTA's six dispute settlement processes have had some success, the most politicized disputes, over Canadian softwood and Mexican trucking into the United States, proved too controversial for parties to accept the results of supposedly binding arbitration (Hufbauer and Schott 2005: 62). In addition, there are more than thirty working groups on goods, investment, services, rules of origin, agricultural subsidies, and other topics, plus a regional development bank and a small secretariat that supports the dispute settlement processes, working groups, and commissions. NAFTA clearly doesn't lack institutional structures; what it lacks is commitment from its members and commitment, particularly from the United States, to closer integration.

NAFTA's existence and particularly Mexico's decision to join with its North American neighbors have had a significant impact on other subregional initiatives in the hemisphere, complicating initiatives in Central America and stimulating arrangements farther south. In turn, NAFTA will likely be affected by future trade agreements that involve the three partners, such as the proposed transatlantic and transpacific partnerships.

*South America: Mercosur.* Mercosur (Mercado Común del Sur) illustrates what can happen in a region when long-standing interstate rivalries are reduced—much as was the case between France and Germany with the creation of the European Coal and Steel Community. Reconciliation between Brazil and Argentina during the 1980s led to a set of bilateral agreements on nuclear issues, energy cooperation, arms control, trade, integration, and development. In 1990, both renounced their nuclear programs, and in 1991 they signed the Treaty of Asunción with Paraguay and Uruguay, creating Mercosur. At that time, steps toward integration "aimed at reversing the dark ages of authoritarianism, intraregional antagonism, economic crisis, and international marginalization" (Hirst 1999: 36). Mercosur was also a response by the South American governments to discussions that would lead to NAFTA and the EU's single market, which they feared would cost them markets and influence.

When Mercosur was initially created in 1991, it included just the four countries. Similar to the process of European integration, it was driven by the chief executives of the member states, not business, civil society, or parliaments (Gardini 2010). In 2006, Venezuela began the process of becoming a member (completed in 2012); Bolivia followed in 2012; and as of 2014, there were six associate members (Chile, Colombia, Ecuador, Guyana, Peru, and Suriname).

Mercosur represents an approach somewhere between a common market along the lines of the EU and a free trade area such as NAFTA. Although economic integration is a central part of Mercosur, stimulating broad regional cooperation is also important, along with opening national and regional markets to the opportunities economic globalization offered, consistent with the Washington Consensus in the 1990s (see Chapters 8 and 9). Mercosur was also very much tied to a belief in the link between democracy, development, and regional integration. The need to consolidate democratic transitions in the Southern Cone, Andrea Oelsner (2013: 119) argues, "became a central, enduring, distinguishing, and cohesive attribute of the organization."

In contrast to NAFTA's detailed legal framework, Mercosur is a simpler intergovernmental agreement with a loose, evolving structure and set of rules. The original Treaty of Asunción has been supplemented by a number of protocols and its institutional structure has been enlarged over time. The Common Market Council is Mercosur's highest organ, composed of ministers of foreign affairs and economy with decisions made by consensus. The Common Market Group, effectively the executive body for Mercosur, initiates measures for trade opening, macroeconomic policy coordination, and negotiation of agreements with nonmember states and international organizations, and is composed of representatives from member state ministries. It, too, operates by consensus. Succeeding the initial Joint Parliamentary Committee, the Mercosur Parliament was formally inaugurated in 2007 as an oversight body with representatives from member parliaments; a shift to a proportional representation system and direct election approved in 2010 had only been ratified by Paraguay as of 2014. An interesting feature of the parliament is the provision for virtual sessions. Yet no sessions have been held since 2011 and the parliament's primary outputs have been declarations, recommendations, and requests for reports from other bodies. Other institutions include the Administrative Office, which services meetings; a series of working subgroups that conduct studies for the Common Market Council; the Consultative Economic and Social Forum; and the Permanent Review Tribunal. Overall, Mercosur is considered to be "'light' on institutions," and implementation depends on relations among the presidents, who are both "decision makers and dispute settlers" (Dominguez 2007: 109).

Like the EU, Mercosur sought the graduated achievement of a customs union and common external tariff as its initial goal. This stimulated a substantial growth in intraregional trade and investment in the 1990s, so that by 1995 it was the fourth largest trade bloc after the EU, NAFTA, and ASEAN. It also stimulated growth of networks among business, labor, and other groups, as well as supportive public opinion, creating conditions of more complex interdependence (Solingen 1998). As Oelsner (2013: 122) notes, "rather than being the result of interdependence, Mercosur sought to create interdependence." Mercosur survived the intertwined economic crises in Brazil and Argentina between 1999 and 2003, as well as other problems, through bilateral interexecutive negotiations and because of the socialization among executive officials within Mercosur that changed perceptions of strategic interests and provided positive incentives to foster regional cooperation (Mera 2005).

On the democracy front, Paraguay has posed the most problems. After intervening in political crises there in 1996 and 1999, Mercosur adopted a clause similar to that of the OAS in 1997, requiring all members to be constitutional democracies. This provided the basis for suspending Paraguay's membership in 2012 after the ouster of its president. Oelsner (2013: 121) argues that while "democracy as a political identity" is still central, this attribute "has gradually lost in cohesion capacity."

Assessments of Mercosur's record overall are decidedly mixed. On the positive side, tariff barriers on goods have been lowered, intrabloc trade has grown, democracy has been defended, and a community of interests has been forged, notably between traditional rivals Brazil and Argentina. On the negative ledger, no agreement on a common external tariff has been forged after more than two decades, and exports to countries outside the community have expanded much more rapidly than internal trade, although the latter rebounded significantly after the 2008 global financial crisis. Mercosur has not achieved its core economic objective of becoming the common market of the South, as its name implies, however, nor have its members necessarily formed a cohesive bloc in extraregional and international trade negotiations. On other issues, there has been little harmonization of policies, and the majority of decisions taken have not been enforced (Dominguez 2007: 110). Furthermore, Brazil's ambitions to be a global power and its initiative to create a Union of South American Nations have had a tendency to undercut the importance of Mercosur.

The European experience teaches us that regional integration is a long-term process "marked by waves and undercurrents. Although scholars of regionalism take notice of the waves . . . often ignored are the undercurrents, the daily actions of the countless smaller actors who keep the project moving forward in response to the waves" (Mace et al. 1999: 36). Such is certainly the case with the undercurrents of both the inter-American hemispheric approach and the various subregional initiatives. There is no question that "the kaleidoscope of regional organizations in the Americas" is undergoing substantial change with the diminished influence of the United States, Brazil's rise, shifts in regional alignments, and new regional architecture (Shifter 2012: 56).

## Asia's Regional Organizations

Unlike the overarching organizations for Europe, Latin America, and Africa, there is no pan-Asian organization (save for the Asian Development

Bank), due to "diversity, ideological polarization, as well as competing national and sub-regional identities" (Acharya 2007b: 24). Instead, there are multiple regional constructions in what is a still-unfolding process in different parts of Asia that will be increasingly influenced by China and India's rise as global and regional powers. The oldest and strongest of these has been the Association of Southeast Asian Nations, established by five Southeast Asian nations in 1967. In the 1990s, ASEAN played an important role in establishing the ASEAN Regional Forum (ARF) and also created the ASEAN Plus Three (APT), linking the ten ASEAN members with China, Japan, and South Korea, thus linking Southeast and Northeast Asia. In 2001, the first Central Asian organization—the Shanghai Cooperation Organization (SCO)—came into being, under Chinese and Russian leadership. The East Asian Summit (EAS), initiated in 2005, engages all the major powers in Asia, including the United States. There is also the South Asian Association for Regional Cooperation, as well as the Northeast Asia Six Party Talks, which focus exclusively on the issue of North Korea's nuclear weapons. Established in 1989, the Asia-Pacific Economic Cooperation (APEC) is unusual in that it spans the Pacific Rim from Asia to the Americas, including seven ASEAN members, several countries of North and South America, plus Australia, New Zealand, China, Russia, Japan, South Korea, Hong Kong, and Taiwan (the inclusion of the latter two explains why APEC members are referred to as "economies" not countries). Created primarily to promote "open regionalism" and particularly regional trade, APEC also provided the only institutionalized forum for heads of government from all Pacific Rim countries until the initiation of the East Asian Summit in 2005. Its importance has diminished in recent years. None of these Asian regional institutions have collective defense or security functions comparable to those of the OAS and NATO, since the United States as a hegemonic leader preferred a system of bilateral security guarantees for key Asian allies (Acharya 2013).

Defining different parts of the region and building regional identity have been major challenges for Asian states. Over time, choices about whom to include or exclude have shaped these definitions. The coexistence of ASEAN, APEC, the ARF, and the SCO can be viewed as a set of overlapping circles, as illustrated in Figure 5.4.

Asia's regionalism is often compared to that of Europe and particularly the EU. The two could not be more different, however. The legalization and bureaucratization of the EU contrast sharply with Asian and Asia-Pacific regional institutions, which tend to be more informal, having few specific rules or binding commitments, small secretariats, consensus decisionmaking, and a strong emphasis on process over substance and outcomes. Informal processes include extensive meetings, consultations, and dialogues; informal outcomes typically refer to agreements on general principles and

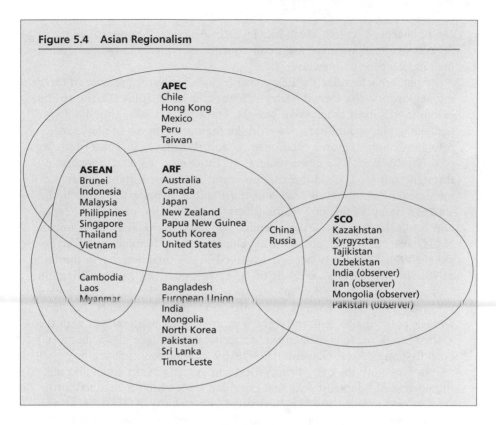

Figure 5.4   Asian Regionalism

nonbinding codes of conduct. Where EU members have been willing to cede sovereignty, Asian states have generally been what some call "sovereignty protectionist."

A number of factors have influenced the development of Asian regionalism. Japanese imperialism prior to World War II left a wariness of regional cooperation that might involve new forms of Japanese domination. In recent years, tensions rooted in this legacy and unresolved territorial disputes have risen between China and Japan as well as South Korea. Since many Asian countries gained their independence only after World War II, they have been strongly nationalist, attached to state sovereignty, and suspicious of other forms of dependency or perceived domination. As a result, the norm of nonintervention in states' internal affairs is a strong component of Asian regionalism. Furthermore, the Cold War divided the region. That division persists on the Korean peninsula, and there are still four communist states in the region (China, Vietnam, Laos, and North Korea). Other factors include the diversity of cultures, levels of development, and distribution of wealth; limited experience with cooperation; and the absence of a clear concept of region. Much like in Latin America, the patterns of interdependence that now exist are a consequence of regional initiatives, rather than having been an impetus.

Another factor affecting East Asian regionalism is the presence of three major powers—the United States, China, and Japan (plus Russia, to the extent it sees itself as an Asian power). The United States, long the dominant economic and military power in the region, continues to play a major role in shaping regional relationships and dynamics. In contrast to its post–World War II encouragement of European regional cooperation through both NATO and the EU, however, the United States never promoted multilateralism in Asia and the Pacific. It preferred a "hub and spokes system" of bilateral relationships with key allies, particularly Japan and South Korea, and never intended the short-lived SEATO to mirror NATO as a collective defense arrangement in Asia (Hemmer and Katzenstein 2002). China only became involved in regional activity in the late 1990s, in large part as a result of ASEAN initiatives and socialization (Johnston 2003; Ba 2006). Now, its increasing assertion of a great-power role is creating new tensions and shifts in regional alignments. Japanese foreign policy has consistently given priority to its bilateral ties with the United States and long maintained "an ambivalent attitude to whether it [is] actually part of Asia" (Ravenhill 2007a: 390). That, too, is changing.

In fact, until the early twenty-first century, it was the small and middle powers of Southeast Asia that provided leadership for regional initiatives based on their shared insecurity and vulnerability. ASEAN began as a coalition of weak states under Indonesian leadership—a factor that helped it to build trust with China and other actors. In the 1990s, Australia and Japan provided leadership for APEC's creation. Since the late 1990s, however, China has increasingly been the driver of East and Central Asian institution building. The future of Asian regionalism may well depend on the degree and nature of leadership by China, Japan, and India, and on the extent of US engagement. For the present, ASEAN maintains its position of centrality that results from its structural position as the central node in networks of East Asian regional institutions, and its position bridging those networks despite its lack of material power.

Domestic politics has also been a factor influencing the evolution of Asian regionalism. For example, ruling coalitions have seen ASEAN as a way to sustain themselves and maintain access to both export markets and foreign investment (Solingen 1998, 2008). Yet because most states in the region have had authoritarian governments, concern for political legitimacy also explains their reluctance to create strong regional institutions (Narine 2004: 424).

Transnational links in the form of networks of business leaders, economists, and security specialists from university centers and think tanks, along with government officials acting in their private capacity, historically have also been drivers of Asian regionalism (Woods 1993; Evans 2005). Except in ASEAN and the SCO, where intergovernmental cooperation came first, these so-called track-two interactions, along with commercial networks (both Japanese and US), have played important roles in building confidence among countries with little history of intergovernmental cooperation, and have provided venues for the formation of epistemic communities, which have been a key source of ideas. Various track-two dialogues have sought to generate agreement on regional solutions for problems such as trade, crime, maritime navigation, health and environmental threats, and security threats, including North Korea's nuclear program. These networks have contributed to the gradual process of regionalization—knitting the countries and elites of East and Southeast Asia in particular into increasingly dense linkages (Katzenstein 2005; Ravenhill 2007b). NGOs and civil society groups such as professional and business associations have been part of this process, gradually becoming sources of bottom-up regionalization, but have generally been less important than corporate and track-two networks.

Finally, a set of "triple shocks" has had a major impact on Asian regionalism: the Cold War's end, the 1997–1998 Asian financial crisis, and the September 11, 2001, terrorist attacks on the United States. The first opened political space for developing regional economic and security ties through ASEAN, the ARF, and APEC. The second demonstrated the vulnerability of Asian economies in an era of globalization, and the weakness of both ASEAN and APEC, providing impetus for a number of steps toward more formal institutional commitments. The third highlighted new types of nontraditional security threats, spurring a broadening of APEC's focus and the creation of the SCO, among other developments. The rise and increasing assertiveness of China, India's rise, the new tensions between the United States and Russia, and the uncertainties about US commitment to and defense capabilities in Asia may well provide future "shocks" for Asian regionalism. We look here in more detail at ASEAN and its related institutions and the SCO.

### The Association of Southeast Asian Nations

ASEAN was established in 1967 by Indonesia, Singapore, Malaysia, the Philippines, and Thailand to promote political stability, regime security, and economic growth. Profound historical, cultural, and economic circumstances divided them, but concerns about the outcome of the war in Vietnam, the future of the US commitment to regional security, Chinese-supported communist insurgencies, and separatist movements united them. External threats, therefore, were a key impetus, since the founding states wanted to minimize the possibility of intervention and domination by the

United States and China and to find "regional solutions to regional problems" (quoted in Acharya 2012: 173).

ASEAN's core norm is nonintervention, derived from the international norm and a series of Asian conferences held between 1947 and the 1955 Asian-African Conference at Bandung, where the ideas of the third world and nonalignment were born. Other important norms are peaceful settlement of disputes, avoidance of military alliances, consultation, and seeking common responses to common problems. ASEAN's norms were meant to guide members' interactions, protect their authoritarian regimes, and keep outside powers from intervening. Yet these norms have impeded collective responses to many problems, particularly since the mid-1990s.

The so-called ASEAN Way encompasses these core norms and the process of informal consultation and consensus building, derived from Malay culture, through which decisions are made. It involves avoiding legalistic procedures and voting, a preference for nonbinding resolutions, and an emphasis on "process over product" (Acharya 2001). If there is no consensus, the members agree to disagree. If there is an intractable dispute, members set it aside and focus on cooperation in other areas. The ASEAN Way has been adopted by other regional groupings, including APEC, the APT, and the ARF. Understanding of the ASEAN Way and ASEAN's unique characteristics has largely been the result of constructivists' analyses and their focus on norms and ideas, which has "shed light on processes and security contributions that realist and liberal theorists had considered non-phenomena" (Ba 2014: 297).

One of ASEAN's major tasks has been identity building—defining the region of Southeast Asia—and this task has in part centered on the issue of membership. Between 1967 and 1995, ASEAN admitted only one new member—Brunei (1984). It rejected inclusion of India, Sri Lanka, Australia, and Papua New Guinea, then accepted Vietnam in 1995, Laos and Myanmar (Burma) in 1997, and Cambodia in 1999—completing what was referred to as "the ASEAN ten." This enlargement increased ASEAN's political and economic diversity and magnified the challenges of consensus decisionmaking, however. All four newer members are less developed than the existing members; two have communist regimes (Laos and Vietnam); one (Cambodia) has been highly unstable and increasingly close to China; Myanmar (then a military dictatorship) was admitted despite protests from the United States, the European Union, and human rights NGOs. ASEAN has undergone dramatic political changes since 2010, although the process of democratization is still under way. Because of these differences, ASEAN has become a two-tiered organization wherein accommodating differences means allowing countries to opt out or push ahead on certain issues (referred to as the "ASEAN minus X" practice). There have been problems in socializing the newer members, and their weaker commitments complicate efforts to reform ASEAN to deal with newer regional problems. There has also been growing tension between Indonesia and the Philippines and other members over how much to promote liberalization and democratization. As a result of these differences, there is no assurance that other countries such as Timor Leste will be allowed to become full members.

*Structure.* A distinctive feature of ASEAN has been the slow development of the types of organizational structures found in many IGOs. Rather than centralized decisionmaking institutions, the ASEAN Way led to an extremely dense pattern of formal and informal meetings of ministers, heads of government, other senior officials, and diplomats from member governments. These provide regular processes for consultation and searching for accommodation, along with numerous ad hoc and permanent committees. Initially, only foreign ministers met. The 1975 communist victory in Vietnam and US withdrawal prompted the first summit meeting, in 1976. Following the 1997–1998 Asian financial crisis, members' finance ministers began to meet regularly. Similarly, the haze generated by forest fires in Indonesia in the late 1990s (see Chapter 11) prompted environmental ministers to initiate meetings. In 1976 a small permanent secretariat was established in Jakarta, Indonesia, to coordinate activities, and in 1993 the post of secretary-general was added, but with only limited powers and capabilities.

Since the mid-1990s, ASEAN has taken a number of steps that have begun to change its character as a regional organization. The first step was the agreement in 1992 to create an ASEAN Free Trade Area (AFTA); a second was the ASEAN Surveillance Process, created to monitor capital flows and regional economic developments in the wake of the 1997–1998 Asian financial crisis; two others include the 2003 Bali Declaration of ASEAN Concord II and the 2007 ASEAN Charter, which was ratified by all ten members in 2008. The former set in motion a process to create the ASEAN Community, based on three "pillars"—the ASEAN Economic Community, the ASEAN Security Community, and the ASEAN Socio-Cultural Community. Taken together, these three proposed communities aim to enhance the structures for cooperation if ASEAN's members can move beyond the rhetoric of well-meaning phrases (Ravenhill 2008; Narine 2008). For example, the ASEAN secretariat, although still very small, has been given more authority to monitor compliance and settle trade disputes. The charter for the first time gave ASEAN international legal personality; set out a framework for institutional accountability and a compliance system; included a commitment to promoting democracy, human rights, and human security (albeit with no definitions of these terms); and called for creation of a regional human rights body (albeit with no provision for intervening in a members' affairs in the event of gross violations of rights). The Intergovernmental Commission on Human Rights is discussed further in Chapter 10. As Jörn Dosch (2008: 542) notes, "for an organization that had strictly avoided any discourse on political order in its 40-year history, even the most reluctant embrace of core democratic norms and values is a major step forward." The charter also renamed and somewhat enhanced the weak ASEAN Inter-Parliamentary Assembly, whose members are delegates from ruling parties. Still, giving ASEAN legal personality is an achievement, although the actual significance of that step remains to be seen.

There are no guarantees that ASEAN's ambitious goals will be met, and timetables have continually slipped. Unlike the EU, ASEAN's secretary-general has no authority to negotiate on behalf of the organization and "drive" the processes of institutional development, which continue to depend on consensus decisionmaking. Resources are limited, as all members are assessed equally, based on what the poorest members agree to pay, and there is little encouragement of voluntary contributions. The four newer members have proven to be a conservative influence, resisting changes in the noninterference principle and lagging in their ability and willingness to commit to new forms of cooperation.

*Evaluating ASEAN's roles: Maintaining regional peace and security.* During its first twenty years, ASEAN's primary focus was regional peace and stability. The 1967 ASEAN Declaration aimed to halt member states' interventions against each other's regimes. In 1971, members created the Zone of Peace and Neutrality to help them resist external Cold War pressures. After the communist victory in Vietnam and US withdrawal, members concluded the Treaty of Amity and Cooperation (1976). This made political cooperation a formal part of the ASEAN agenda and codified rules of conduct, including the nonuse of force, peaceful settlement (or deferral) of disputes, and common responses to regional problems. The 1978 Vietnamese invasion of Cambodia was seen as a major threat to the authoritarian governments in other states and to the norm of nonintervention. ASEAN successfully campaigned for more than a decade to block the Vietnamese-backed Cambodian regime from taking Cambodia's UN seat, and turned a blind eye to Thailand's military assistance to the Khmer Rouge and treatment of refugees from Cambodia, violating its core norm of nonintervention. Yet the Cambodian issue was central to ASEAN members' development of greater unity in the 1980s, and they also devised many of the core elements of the 1991 Paris Peace Accords.

The Cold War's end, globalization, and other developments of the 1990s created uncertainties for ASEAN members, requiring a redefinition of the group's purpose. The responses included several security and economic initiatives, including the establishment of the ASEAN Regional Forum in 1994 to promote multilateral security dialogue, the agreement to create AFTA, membership in APEC, admission of the four new members, the initiation of dialogues with outside powers, and the 1995 Bangkok Treaty, which created the Southeast Asian Nuclear Weapon–Free Zone.

There have been a few cases of mediation in some of the region's numerous territorial disputes, such as Thailand's involvement in the Malaysian-Philippine conflict over Sabah. In the long-running border dispute over the Temple Preah Vihear between Thailand and Cambodia—despite the ASEAN Treaty of Amity and Cooperation, which commits members to resolve conflicts without armed force; two International Court of Justice rulings; and ample warnings—ASEAN failed to avert violent clashes in 2011. The effort by Indonesia as ASEAN chair at the time to get agreement to send observers to monitor a cease-fire faltered when Thailand retracted permission, underscoring the organization's weakness in the face of conflicts between members. With respect to the disputes over demarcation of exclusive economic zones as well as several islands, disputes that involve many members, ASEAN reached consensus in 1992 on the Declaration on the South China Sea and in 2002 concluded a code-of-conduct agreement with China. China made clear beginning in 2012, however, that it does not feel bound by that agreement and rejects any role for ASEAN in resolving territorial disputes, insisting on bilateral talks. The disputes between China and Vietnam as well as between China and the Philippines escalated in 2014, but ASEAN members failed to reach agreement on a unified strategy.

In the 1999–2000 East Timor crisis, ASEAN persisted in its longstanding solidarity with Indonesia and its adherence to the principle of nonintervention, leaving initiative to Australia and the UN. Only Thailand supplied troops for the UN peacekeeping operation. That adherence has not been unbending, however, as demonstrated by ASEAN's successful efforts to persuade Myanmar to accept international humanitarian assistance following the devastation of Cyclone Nargis in 2008 when the country's initial reaction was to refuse all outside aid. Likewise, Myanmar was not permitted to take its turn as the ASEAN chair in 2006 because of the military junta's crackdown on peaceful protests (Tan 2013: 254, 256).

With regard to newer, nontraditional security threats, particularly threats to human security from epidemics, transnational crime, environmental degradation, and natural disasters, ASEAN's responses have been hampered by the nonintervention norm and the requirement that all decisions be taken by consensus. Members have also been unable to put together a collaborative strategy for dealing with the smog and haze from fires caused by logging and land-clearing in Indonesia that have blanketed the region virtually every year since the late 1990s. The SARS crisis in 2003, for example, revealed how little institutionalized regional cooperation existed in public health policy. Although that crisis and the avian flu pandemic in 2005 led to strengthening of monitoring mechanisms and a division of responsibility among ASEAN's original five members for vaccination procedures, emergency preparedness, public awareness, and surveillance systems, this left out the four less developed members of ASEAN, all of which have weak health systems. Nonintervention, in short, has inhibited ASEAN's development and made it difficult to cope with newer transnational threats.

*ASEAN and economic cooperation.* Unlike regional groupings in Latin America, ASEAN member states adopted an outward orientation of integration into the global economy rather than subregional integration as their strategy for growth. They were among the first developing countries to embrace export-led growth and to liberalize trade and investment. Four members (Indonesia, Malaysia, Singapore, and Thailand) made great economic and social strides, and ASEAN itself was "widely regarded as the developing world's most successful subregional institution" (Soesastro and Morrison 2001: 58).

Globalization in the 1990s and China's rapidly increasing draw of investment persuaded ASEAN leaders that regional trade integration, similar to what was taking place in the EU and NAFTA, was the appropriate approach to stimulate economic growth. Yet ASEAN's ability as an organization to promote economic cooperation was inhibited by the outward orientation of most ASEAN economies and the low levels of dependence on trade with other members; members' resistance to meaningful integration, including to mechanisms for monitoring or enforcing agreements; and the disparity between the four newer members and the other six. The 1997–1998 Asian financial crisis highlighted all these weaknesses and members' vulnerability to global economic trends. Although not set up to deal with financial and monetary relations, ASEAN suffered a loss of confidence as the press and scholarly journals lamented its failure, disarray, and loss of direction. The crisis clearly highlighted ASEAN's institutional weaknesses and the limits of the ASEAN Way, particularly the drawbacks to the ASEAN practice of not criticizing or even commenting on members' domestic policies. In the aftermath, finance ministers began meeting regularly, the ASEAN Surveillance Process was created, and the APT meetings at various levels with Japan, China, and South Korea were initiated.

A number of changes were also made in AFTA after the financial crisis, including rules for trade liberalization, a dispute settlement mechanism (1996), and protocols for notification of changes in commitments agreed earlier (1998 and 2000). Original targets were revised downward, but AFTA was successfully concluded among the six more developed members in late 2002, with the remaining four given longer periods to complete the process.

Although the significance of AFTA remains a matter of debate, the goal of creating the ASEAN Economic Community (AEC), with free flow of goods, services, investment, and skilled labor, by 2020, aims to build on AFTA's foundation. A 2014 report by the Asian Development Bank and Institute of South-East Asian Studies in Singapore, however, concludes that there is "no prospect of coming close to . . . [a] single market by . . . 2020 or 2025" (*The Economist* 2014b: 42). Furthermore, while ASEAN has been successful in freeing most categories of goods in intraregional trade from tariffs, the report notes that "non-tariff barriers have replaced tariffs as protective measures for domestic industries" and ASEAN's small secretariat has no powers to force compliance. Plus, the disparities among ASEAN's members, far greater than the inequalities among members of other regional organizations, are an important variable affecting efforts to foster economic cooperation and integration. Those "vast differences in the openness of member states' economies—from Singapore . . . to heavily protected and closed economies like Laos and Cambodia—have arguably retarded the creation of the ASEAN Free Trade Area" (Kurlantzick 2012: 12). Instead, states have increasingly moved to conclude bilateral free trade agreements.

*ASEAN, ASEAN Plus Three, ASEAN Regional Forum, and ASEAN's dialogue partners.* In keeping with its emphasis on building and maintaining relationships, one of the notable features of ASEAN is its extensive set of dialogues with other countries on issues of common concern, together with the consultative institutions that it has initiated. As of 2014, ASEAN had dialogue partnerships with China, Japan, South Korea, the European Union, India, Australia and New Zealand, Canada, the United States, Russia, and Pakistan. The ASEAN Plus Three meetings were established in 1999 and cover a range of concerns, from economic, trade, and financial cooperation to security, terrorism, environment, human trafficking, piracy, and energy. After the 1997–1998 financial crisis, for example, the APT approved the Chiang Mai Initiative in 2000 to provide a regional financing facility, funded by China and Japan, to help support currencies in future crises and protect members from a volatile international financial system (Khong and Nesadurai 2007: 33).

In 2005, the APT initiated the first East Asian Summit, which included Australia, New Zealand, and India. Among its outcomes was the Declaration on Avian Influenza Prevention, Control, and Response, to strengthen national and regional capacity to combat avian flu. More recent summit declarations have dealt with energy and food security. The EAS summits now include eighteen countries, with Russia and the United States first participating in 2011. Topics generally include financial and nontraditional security issues.

ASEAN was also responsible for creating the first Asia-Pacific multilateral security institution—the ASEAN Regional Forum—in 1994, after the Cold War's end. The idea for such an institution based on the norm of cooperative security came out of exchanges among Asian and Western security scholars and policymakers through the network of ASEAN Institutes for Strategic and International Studies (ASEAN-ISIS) (Katsumata 2006). The idea required acceptance by China, Japan, and the United States, however, and among these China posed the biggest problem. China was wary of any security organization, partly for fear that its neighbors might "gang up" against it on the Taiwan issue or territorial disputes, and partly because the Chinese military was hostile to sharing information on its doctrine and deployment. ASEAN members were also initially reluctant to participate in security dialogue. Their reversal reflected a conscious decision to take the lead in order to dominate such a dialogue. By doing so and by proposing that the ARF adopt the ASEAN Way as its modus operandi, they helped persuade China to participate. Thus the ARF is an anomaly—a security institution spearheaded by small states and middle powers.

Today the ARF has twenty-seven participants, including the ASEAN members, China, Japan, the United States, Russia, India, Canada, the European Union, North Korea, and Mongolia (see Figure 5.4). In keeping with the ASEAN Way, the ARF relies on consensus decisionmaking and only in 2004 was a support unit created within the ASEAN secretariat. Its core includes complex official and unofficial (track-one and track-two) processes, with an ASEAN member always serving as chair. The ministerial-level meetings (track one) involve foreign ministers, not defense ministers. The ASEAN-ISIS network continues to be a key part of the track-two process, along with the Council for Security Cooperation in the Asia-Pacific (CSCAP), a federation of security research organizations that forms a regular, nongovernmental forum on Asia-Pacific security (Ball and Guan 2010). Its working groups create a research base for ARF security dialogues.

The ARF's goals include confidence building, preventive diplomacy, and conflict resolution. Dialogue topics have included the South China Sea islands disputes, denuclearization, maritime security, illegal migration, drug trafficking, counterterrorism, confidence-building measures such as notification of military exercises, regional maritime and air surveillance regimes, and exchanges of defense policy white papers. In 2007, Yuen Khong and Helen Nesadurai (2007: 37) concluded that "years of patient confidence building" had facilitated the gradual acceptance of the norms of regional conduct and a degree of trust among countries with long histories of mutual suspicion and conflict. Beyond track-two discussions, however, the ARF could do little about North Korea's nuclear program. The action in that case has fallen to the Six-Party Talks, led by China and the United States, and including both North and South Korea, Japan, and Russia. Nor does the ARF have much traction for dealing with crises in either the East or South China Seas. Still, as Mely Caballero-Anthony (2014: 569–570) notes: "None of the major powers—China, India, Japan, or the United States—

would tolerate one of their number, or any other major power, taking the lead in the region. The only viable alternative . . . was and still is ASEAN." Based on her use of network analysis, she adds that ASEAN's role as "the first architect or builder of regional security community institutions in Asia has enhanced and reinforced its centrality. Higher betweenness allows it to act as a bridge between the ARF, APT and EAS and to facilitate the access of one node . . . to another."

In sum, ASEAN has "punched above its weight" in many ways in developing its own regional identity and fostering Asian regionalism. The cumulative effect of hundreds of ASEAN meetings each year in a region where personal relations are highly valued is to reinforce ASEAN's importance for regional identity building. Its approach of consensual multilateralism is predominant in all Asian regionalism and has prevented armed conflicts among its members and expanded relationships in a once divided region.

There are no guarantees that ASEAN's ambitious goals will be met in the future, however. With its still weak institutions and the divisions between its original and newer members, ASEAN's difficulty is "not one of lack of vision, ideas, or action plans. The problem is one of ensuring compliance and effective implementation" (quoted in Ravenhill 2008: 469).


### Shanghai Cooperation Organization

The Shanghai Cooperation Organization emerged out of the disintegration of the former Soviet Union and China's concerns about security along the more than 7,000-kilometer border it shares with Russia, Kazakhstan, Tajikistan, and Kyrgyzstan. Leaders of these five countries began annual summit meetings in 1996 to address the new security situation in Central Asia and their shared concerns about Islamic fundamentalism, as well as to sign a treaty on confidence-building measures in their shared border region. In 1997, they signed a second treaty on mutual reduction of military forces in the border region. Beginning in 1998, they expanded their agenda of security issues to address the triple threats of extremism, separatism, and terrorism, which China refers to as "the three evils." Some analysts saw these developments as an effort to counter NATO's expansion in Europe, but Russia and China have both repeatedly stressed over the years that the SCO is not a military alliance but the embodiment of a new security concept and new type of multilateral institution (Yuan 2010: 862). Although there were limited trade or economic relations among the five, they also decided to include economic cooperation and cultural exchanges, as well as nontraditional security issues of crime and drug trafficking. With each such addition, they added meetings of various ministers, including foreign affairs, defense, trade, economy, transportation, and law enforcement. In

1999, they created a joint monitoring group to oversee implementation of the confidence-building measures. With China's leadership, and despite the absence of any tradition of multilateralism among them, they turned the informal Shanghai Five meetings into a formal organization in 2001 and added Uzbekistan as a founding member, although it does not share a border with China. Observer states include Afghanistan, India, Pakistan, Iran, and Mongolia; dialogue partners are Belarus, Turkey, and Sri Lanka. Thus the SCO came about "more [as] an unintended result of practice rather than of design" (Wang 2008: 105).

The SCO's creation marked a broad shift in Chinese foreign policy toward Central Asia from bilateralism to multilateralism. This was the first time China played a leading role in creating a multilateral organization: the SCO was named after a Chinese city; its secretariat is based in a second Chinese city—Beijing; and a Chinese diplomat became the first secretary-general. The SCO also differs from other Asian organizations such as ASEAN and APEC in that it is driven by major powers—China and Russia—which each pay 24 percent of the budget. This makes SCO's own viability dependent on the relationship between the two, who do not view the SCO in the same way. Russia sees it more as a security body, while China is interested in its security and economic possibilities, particularly energy and promotion of a "new silk road" (McDermott 2012). Yet the presence of both China and Russia ensures that the agenda will not be dominated by either (Aris 2013: 8–9). In many ways, however, the SCO resembles ASEAN in that it is designed to facilitate intergovernmental cooperation at different levels and operates on the basis of informal discussion and consensus decisionmaking. There is no authority to enforce decisions and recommendations.

In 2002, SCO members approved a formal charter establishing both the permanent secretariat in Beijing, composed of officials from member governments, and the Regional Anti-Terrorism Structure, which is located in Tashkent, Uzbekistan. The organizational structure includes four councils— heads of state, heads of government (prime ministers), foreign ministers, and national coordinators. The latter coordinates the day-to-day activities of the SCO, whereas the secretariat provides technical and informational assistance for activities. There are also meetings of various other ministers and officials, working groups, a nongovernmental business council, an interbank association that coordinates major national banks to provide credit and funding for joint investment projects, and an SCO forum of nongovernmental experts and policy analysts. In short, the SCO has become highly institutionalized in a short period of time, with "multiple-layer, multiple area consulting mechanisms" (Wang 2008: 106).

Since the initial meetings, SCO security cooperation has expanded well beyond border management and confidence-building measures. The concerns with terrorism, extremism, and separatism have remained central, but the US military presence in Uzbekistan, Tajikistan, and Kyrgyzstan following the 9/11 attacks changed the geopolitics of the region. China and Russia both worried that this presence might become permanent. China, for one, saw the institutional development of the SCO as "an important way to strengthen cohesiveness and enhance the vitality of the organization" in order to counter that presence (quoted in Wang 2008: 110–111).

In light of their concerns about Islamic extremism and terrorism, SCO members have held joint antiterrorism military exercises. In 2014, one of the biggest antiterrorist exercises involved more than 7,000 personnel. In addition, they concluded the SCO Antiterrorism Convention in 2009 and a protocol on cooperation against illicit drug trafficking in 2010. The Regional Anti-Terrorism Structure, however, primarily functions as a means of sharing limited information about terrorist suspects and banned groups. "It is unclear," Roger McDermott (2012: 58) notes, "what level of multilateral intelligence sharing occurs, if any."

The SCO has defended member states' regimes in the face of outside criticism, such as the repression of uprisings in Uzbekistan (2005) and Kyrgyzstan (2010), stressing the sanctity of national sovereignty and the right of members to pursue whatever security policy they see fit (Aris 2013: 10). Since Kyrgyzstan actually appealed for assistance, however, and the SCO declined to intervene, questions have been raised about SCO's ability to respond to crises in the region. Following the 2008 Russian intervention in Georgia, Russia wanted SCO members to recognize the breakaway regions of South Ossetia and Abkhazia. Given the dangerous precedent that might be set in a region with such diversity and many separatist movements, however, members preferred a neutral stance, reflecting China's and the Central Asian states' overriding concern for territorial integrity and the norm of nonintervention. In short, ethnic separatism is a huge concern for all SCO members, along with terrorism, illicit arms and drug trafficking, illegal migration, and other transnational crimes. For China, however, there are particular challenges, since the region remains historically part of Russia's sphere of influence and therefore Central Asian states remain cautious with regard to China's growing presence (Yuan 2010: 860).

China has strong interests in increasing regional economic integration, gaining access to energy supplies, and improving better transportation routes to move Chinese goods to the region. Hence, much of the focus has been on infrastructure such as roads and railway, for which the SCO has worked collaboratively with the Asian Development Bank and the UN Economic and Social Commission for Asia and the Pacific. China has also been a major source of funding for these activities, particularly with its role in creating the Asian Infrastructure Investment Bank in 2014 and its "New Silk Road" initiative. There has been relatively little interest thus far in any free trade agreement, however, at least in part because of fear of China's dominance, and the economic gaps between member states remain wide. Thus, unlike the EU, where economic cooperation spilled over into the political and security areas, the SCO has turned functionalism upside down, moving from security cooperation to economic cooperation.

Recognizing the civilizational and religious diversity of Central Asia, another unique feature of the SCO is its cultural dialogues and exchanges. A perennial issue at SCO summits is the question of expanding membership. Should it admit Iran, a country under UN sanctions? What about India and Pakistan? Afghanistan? What is the organization's scope and aim? Is it limited to Central Asia with a clear agenda or does it aspire to become a larger pan-Asian umbrella with a wider agenda?

Asian regionalism is now a crowded field. Or, in the words of a leading Canadian participant in Asia's activities: "The noodle bowl of Asian regionalism . . . is not quite as thick or rich as its spaghetti-bowl counterpart in Europe. But . . . the noodle bowl is filling quickly" (quoted in Pempel 2005: 14). Wider and deeper institutionalization is taking place, with a stronger East Asian regionalism emerging, yet that too is still subject to definition. Overall, the Asian experience with regionalism has had a lot to do with identity construction and community building, processes that are still evolving, with the precise definition of the region uncertain. The future of Asian regionalism, however, will likely turn more on the dynamics among existing and rising major powers and on whether ASEAN is able to maintain its centrality.

Identity and community building are not significant issues for regional governance and cooperation efforts on the continent of Africa, where identity construction has not been as problematic and there are no major powers, but many other factors have impeded effective efforts.

## Africa's Regional Organizations

The ideal of unity among the inhabitants of the African continent was one prominent reaction to the enslavement, imperialism, and colonialism by Western European powers from the sixteenth century through the early twentieth. In the nineteenth century, the call for continental unity was largely based on unity of the nonwhite races, while in the twentieth century it was based on the notion that Africans should throw off domination by outside powers and receive independence. At the 1945 meeting of the Pan-African Congress in Manchester, England, participants issued the Declaration to the Colonial Peoples, supporting the right of political freedom and self-government.

In the late 1950s, under the initiative of Kwame Nkrumah, president of newly independent Ghana, a pan-African forum for independent countries began to take shape based on an underlying sense of continental unity. There were differences of opinion, however, between pan-Africanists and supporters of subregional approaches. Among the former, there were disagreements about how to achieve the pan-African ideal. Some preferred a very minimalist approach, with states agreeing to cooperate but not much more; others sought political union among the independent states. The group that prevailed opted for a loose, continent-wide organization of African states.

## From the Organization of African Unity to the African Union

In 1964 the leaders of thirty-one newly independent African states established the Organization of African Unity. It was conceived as a loose association based on voluntary cooperation, whose resolutions would carry moral rather than legal obligations. Three overriding principles guided the organization. First, all states were sovereign equals. Each state would have an equal say, with no greater weight given to larger or more powerful states. Second, states agreed not to interfere in the domestic affairs of fellow members. Third, territorial borders were sacrosanct, with no room for alteration in the status quo. No longer did states want to be dominated by outsiders, risk border changes that would unleash ethnic rivalries and invite outside intervention, or cause the independence leaders to lose their privileged positions. So at the outset, the OAU was designed as a voluntary organization limited by its founding principles.

Over time, each of these principles has been compromised. Although all states are legally equal, there was implicit recognition that some states are able to provide stronger leadership—such as Nigeria, Ghana, Kenya, Algeria, Egypt, or South Africa. The principle of noninterference in domestic affairs was also violated, most often during the 1990s, when human rights violations were condemned by other states. On a few occasions the OAU also supported changes in state boundaries, for example when Eritrea gained independence from Ethiopia.

Designed as a weak intergovernmental forum, the OAU did enjoy some notable successes. OAU members used the Assembly of Heads of State, in particular, as a forum for mediating disputes among states. The OAU sponsored for the first time an ad hoc, all-African military force to help establish law and order in Chad in 1981. At other times, members turned to the UN or to subregional organizations such as the Economic Community of West African States for dispute resolution or to organize regional military forces for a specific action. The OAU played a significant role in at least nine cases of securing troop withdrawals, using its diplomatic pressure to influence both African states and outside powers. The liberation of South Africa from white minority rule, a central OAU goal, was achieved in

1994. On economic and development issues, however, the OAU was largely silent, essentially deferring to the UN's Economic Commission on Africa. One area where it did take the initiative, through numerous conferences, was on the issue of HIV/AIDS, recognizing that health is a foundation for development.

Since the conditions under which the OAU was founded had changed and the organization's weakness contributed to Africa's marginalization in international politics, the OAU was replaced by the African Union in 2002, following two years of negotiations. Although unity remains an aspiration, the AU is designed to meet the challenges of a world characterized by economic globalization and democratization where African leaders need stronger institutions to respond to African problems (Makinda and Okumu 2008).

The AU carried over some of the OAU's overarching principles, including sovereign equality of states and respect for existing territorial borders. Additional principles found in its constitutive act strengthen the organization to respond more effectively to Africa's problems. First, AU members may intervene in the affairs of other states in "grave circumstances, namely war crimes, genocide and crimes against humanity." This is a radical departure from the OAU, although the vague language is open to varying interpretations. Second, to support democratization, AU members pledge support for good governance, democratic principles, and respect for human rights, explicitly rejecting political assassination and unconstitutional changes of regimes. Unlike the OAU, the AU can suspend or expel illegitimate governments and has done so, reinstating states when the governments are stabilized—a provision analogous to the OAS's democracy mandate discussed earlier. Third, resolving disputes peacefully and prohibiting use of force are a key principle. The AU Constitutive Act also links this peace and security principle with economic development, noting that the latter depends on the security of states and people. Fourth, achieving balanced social and economic development is a key principle, although the AU's role is only vaguely defined in its charter.

The principles behind the AU, then, are more progressive than those of the former OAU. Leaders pledge to hold free elections and to allow opposition parties to campaign freely; sovereignty is no longer a shield to hide gross misconduct. Yet while these objectives and pledges have been favorably received, their application has been uneven. As one scholar explains, these new principles "have been internalized unevenly by the AU's member states" and the move from nonintervention "to what is now commonly referred to as the doctrine of non-indifference" has been slow (Williams 2007: 256). That shift (states care and *may* act) has made it necessary for the AU to have operational capability to address cases of large-scale human rights violations and threats to democratic governments.

Several new organs were established to enable the AU to meet the new objectives and to provide added "teeth" (Williams 2011: 149–167). Consistent with the principle of sovereign equality, the annual Assembly of the African Union consists of the heads of state and government. It sets the policies, decides what actions to take, considers membership questions, and monitors the implementation of policies and decisions. It is the forum for informal dispute resolution, as under the OAU, but the AU's approach to security is much broader. As defined in the AU's Common African Defense and Security Policy (2004), security includes human rights, education, health, and rights to protection from poverty. Decisions are generally taken by consensus. It is the assembly that must approve calls for AU intervention and give directives to the Executive Council, which was established to execute the assembly's decisions regarding the outbreak of violence and other emergency situations.

The AU chairman (not a secretary-general) heads the African Union Commission, the secretariat that manages affairs between meetings of the other organs. With a bigger staff and more resources than under the OAU, the AU Commission has authority to take initiatives on behalf of the organization. It consists of commissioners responsible for different policy domains. For peace and security issues, the most relevant are the Department of Political Affairs (human rights, democratization, election monitoring) and the larger Peace and Security Directorate. Another directorate, along with the recognized subregional organizations, oversees the New Partnership for Africa's Development (NEPAD), the flagship economic program discussed in Chapter 9.

The Pan-African Parliament was created in 2004. Its 265 representatives, elected by member-state legislatures, implement the AU's policies and objectives, especially in the areas of democratization, good governance, and the rule of law. One of its first actions was to send a fact-finding mission to Darfur. The advisory Economic, Social, and Cultural Council was established in 2005 to give voice to members of civil society, including religious and social groups, reflecting the gradual democratization of the continent. The judicial arm of the AU has been reorganized several times— a subject addressed in Chapter 10.

The AU has undertaken several other measures to strengthen the democratization and governance agenda. In 2003 the African Peer Review Mechanism was created, a voluntary group of experts who work alongside governments and civil society groups to review the government's performance on democracy, good governance, and the rule of law. Following an investigation and a report, the expert panel makes recommendations for improvement. While states are not legally bound to implement the suggestions, and many states may not have the resources to do so, the process for those participating carries moral authority and signals commitment by

African states to the new agenda, with over a third of the AU's members participating. That commitment was reinforced in the AU Commission's 2009–2012 strategic plan and the 2011 summit, which emphasized Africans' "shared values." In addition, the Charter on Democracy, Elections and Governance entered into force in 2012, bringing together in one legal document members' commitments to democracy and governance.

Strengthening the AU's capacity to manage conflicts is the goal of the 2001 African Peace and Security Architecture. The Peace and Security Council (PSC), composed of fifteen members elected by the AU Assembly on a rotating basis, has broad authority to promote collective security. Not only can it use traditional peaceful settlement mechanisms such as mediation and conciliation, but it can also undertake both peace support operations and humanitarian actions. It also has the power to initiate sanctions. The PSC's ability to take such actions is limited, however, by both political and economic realities, notably its scant independent financial and material resources.

In addition to the PSC, the AU has created the Panel of the Wise, a consultative body to the PSC composed of five highly respected Africans, the Continental Early Warning System, and the African Standby Force. The latter is particularly important given the AU's growing role in responding to crises in different parts of the continent and since the AU, like the UN, has had to rely on ad hoc units, often without adequate funding and technical support. The AU's inability to respond to armed conflict in a timely way with African peacekeepers was evident in Mali in 2013, for example. France intervened initially with Operation SERVAL, forcing al-Qaeda in the Islamic Maghreb and related groups out of cities and paving the way for the African-led International Support Mission to Mali, organized by the Economic Community of West African States. After many delays, the African Standby Force, with both military and civilian components, is scheduled to become operational in 2015.

Of the many security issues facing the AU and its members, the conflicts in the Darfur region of Sudan and in Somalia have proven to be among the most challenging (Makinda and Okumu 2008: 83–89). With respect to Darfur, in 2003 the AU was called to mediate an end to a conflict between the Sudanese government and two rebel groups—the Sudanese Liberation Army and the Justice and Equality Movement—that had forced thousands to flee their homes and resulted in thousands of deaths that would later be labeled genocide by the United States and others. Those negotiations resulted in a cease-fire agreement in 2004 and the creation of an AU civilian and military monitoring force endorsed by the UN Security Council. Although the AU expressed concern about the humanitarian crisis, it did not declare the killing in Darfur a genocide. The AU force (the African Union Mission in Sudan [AMIS]) had few units trained in peace operations and lacked equipment and logistical support. NATO provided airlift for AU units and the EU provided funding, but AMIS's mandate and size precluded any peace enforcement. In 2007 the UN Secretary-General secured agreement to transform the AU force into a hybrid UN-AU force (the UN-AU Hybrid Mission in Darfur [UNAMID]) to protect civilians, provide security for humanitarian aid, and monitor compliance with a cease-fire agreement. UNAMID confronts many logistical and managerial problems, with both UNAMID personnel and humanitarian aid workers suffering casualties. In 2014, it (and the AU component in particular) faced renewed violence as well as charges of covering up sexual violence in Darfur and of being against prosecution of Sudanese president Omar Hassan al-Bashir, whose International Criminal Court investigation was suspended because no action had been taken in ten years.

In contrast, Somalia illustrates the AU's relative success in peacekeeping. Authorized by the UN Security Council in 2007, the African Union Mission in Somalia (AMISOM) has remained solely an AU operation, supplemented by NATO airlifts and supported by UN and EU funding. The AU has earned respect for its efforts in stabilizing the transitional government in Somalia and expanding the portions of the country under government control. It is discussed further in Chapter 7.

While enforcement continues to be a challenge for the AU, as it is for most regional organizations, the AU has enjoyed some other successes. In 2005 the AU imposed sanctions that helped to reverse a coup in Togo, and in 2008 it backed military intervention to restore democracy in the Comoros Islands. When Mauritania's military launched a coup against its democratically elected leader in 2008, the AU suspended Mauritania's membership, but failed to take additional measures. The Zimbabwean crisis further illustrates the problem. In 2007, an AU fact-finding mission to that country found widespread human rights abuses. A year later, an AU election-monitoring group labeled the Zimbabwean presidential election undemocratic and called for suspension from the organization. Yet Zimbabwe was allowed to take its seat at the 2008 summit, and the AU did not take stronger action, leaving most of the initiatives to another regional organization, the Southern African Development Community (SADC).

Fostering the conditions for continent-wide economic development is now on the agendas of all African organizations, and the AU is no exception. The AU has taken a holistic approach in conjunction with NEPAD, the African-generated self-help plan initiated in 2001 and endorsed by the G-7. For example, NEPAD's action plan adopted the neoliberal position that corruption hinders development and that curbing corruption requires cooperation among the African states and international donors. Although the AU has more authority across all issue areas than its predecessor had, the organization faces difficult tasks ahead.

## Subregional Integration Initiatives

Subregional groups have been formed all over Africa since the 1960s and continue to proliferate. Different colonial histories, diverse regional conditions, the weaknesses of the OAU and AU, and changing views about the relationship between regions and subregions all explain this proliferation. Although there is a debate over whether these subregional arrangements are the stepping-stones to broader regional integration or detract from continent-wide arrangements, there is widespread consensus that they produce "serious inefficiencies, duplication, unintended overlap, and even dissipating efforts" (Makinda and Okumu 2008: 53). We discuss two of these subregional initiatives, both of which have moved beyond their economic mandates into peace and security matters.

*The Economic Community of West African States.* Of the African subregional groupings, ECOWAS is one of the largest, with fifteen member states. ECOWAS was established in 1975 with the vision of becoming a single economic bloc organized into an economic and monetary union, but its members traded little intraregionally; their major trading partners were located outside of the ECOWAS area (in Europe or the United States); many of the states produced the same primary products and there was no viable transportation infrastructure linking the member states. Progress has been very slow in removing trading barriers, reducing tariffs, and eliminating nontariff barriers. In fact, some trade barriers and customs rules have actually increased, even as interstate roads have been constructed and telecommunication lines linked. Intraregional trade among ECOWAS members continues to average around 10 to 11 percent of total trade, as it has since ECOWAS's inception.

Dissatisfied with the progress toward the ambitious economic vision, the member states revised the ECOWAS Treaty in 2007 to give the organization supranational authority and stronger institutions. They transformed the ECOWAS secretariat into a commission with enhanced powers to implement policies and oversee projects in defined sectors. The ECOWAS Bank for Investment and Development provides financial resources. The Community Parliament has been given more administrative support, and new legal principles support enhanced supranationality. But creating more structures and reforming old ones does not guarantee that they will become effective or that economic activity will increase. Mistrust among members, fears of Nigerian domination, continuing armed conflicts, and the weak regional economies all limit further cooperation.

Absent progress on the economic dimension, ECOWAS assumed more of a security agenda in the 1990s. Under the standing mediation committee, a 4,000-person multinational force known as ECOMOG (ECOWAS Cease-Fire Monitoring Group) was formed in 1990 to intervene in the Liberian and Sierra Leonean civil wars. The force was largely operated and financed by Nigeria. It remained in place until 1998 and then was redeployed in 2003 after international mediation secured a cease-fire and before the UN's deployment of a peacekeeping mission. ECOMOG's forces were viewed as active participants in the civil strife rather than peacekeepers, however, and Nigeria itself was perceived as acting out of national interest rather than collective regional interest, which hampered ECOMOG's ability to be effective. Still, ECOMOG provided a buffer and some semblance of order. ECOMOG was better able to respond in Guinea-Bissau in 1999 and Côte d'Ivoire in 2002 thanks to a 1993 treaty revision. Yet ECOWAS's overall record is poor as a result of member states' disagreements, peacekeepers' participation in sexual exploitation and corruption, and its inability to successfully manage regional conflicts. Since 2000 the AU, working with the UN, has stepped in with stronger presence, as discussed in Chapter 7.

*The Southern African Development Community.* The end of apartheid in South Africa and its change of leadership in 1994 had a major impact on subregional institutions in southern Africa. Previously excluded from most African organizations, South Africa has become a leader particularly in the SADC, whose predecessor, the Southern African Development Coordination Conference (SADCC), was established to reduce economic dependency on South Africa's white minority regime. With its transformation in 1992 into SADC, a debate ensued (Hentz 2005: 22): Should the new regional organization be based on market cooperation? Should it focus on development? Should cooperation be ad hoc? Should it be primarily functional and project-oriented? SADC has tried to do all these things.

SADC, with a broad economic, social, and environmental agenda, now has fifteen member states and a population area of 277 million people. The SADC Summit, composed of heads of state and government, is the major policymaking institution, serving also as a legislative organ. Decisions taken by consensus at annual meetings are binding. A troika system, composed of the current, incoming, and outgoing chairs of the summit, provides continuity between sessions, as does the Council of Ministers (usually ministries of foreign affairs or finance). Both serve an advisory role to the summit, however, and even the council cannot make binding decisions. The SADC Secretariat provides executive functions. The SADC Treaty designates the SADC Tribunal to oversee implementation of the integration process, but the SADC Summit suspended the tribunal in 2010.

Originally organized as a development organization, SADC has embraced a free market approach and trade liberalization, becoming a free trade area in 2008, when 85 percent of intraregional trade among member states attached zero duty. The task of removing tariffs on sensitive products like textiles and clothing, however, is ongoing, and overall intra-SADC trade still remains at only 18 percent of total trade. SADC had hoped to create a customs union, a common market, and a monetary union, all of which have been delayed by members' overlapping memberships in other regional groups that either compete with or undermine SADC's objectives. Those include the Southern African Customs Union (SACU), the Common Market for Eastern and Southern Africa (COMESA), and the East African Community (EAC), illustrative of the "spaghetti bowl" of regional trade arrangements, discussed in Chapter 8.

SADC's development objectives have involved supporting functional projects among both SADC members and neighboring countries, such as transport, shared water resources, and hydroelectric power. In addition, SADC's agenda includes a range of other issues, from food, forestry practices, and mining activities to refugees and environmental conservation. Because many of its members, including Angola, Mozambique, Tanzania, Namibia, and South Africa, have recently become democratic, they are now united not only by their economic and social objectives, but also by the goal of promoting democratization.

Like ECOWAS, SADC has become involved with security issues, most notably in Lesotho in 1989 and the Democratic Republic of Congo from 1998 to 2002. In both cases, SADC members helped their friends by sending troops to support government authorities against insurgents. Although SADC was criticized for its prevarication in the Zimbabwean political crisis (2007–2008), it took the lead in mediating Madagascar's political crisis following a coup in 2009, reaffirming its commitment to constitutionality and acting in unison. In 2014, SADC sent an observer team to Lesotho to help restore security after a coup attempt, an affirmation of its political objectives.

## Regional Bottlenecks

The African states have established a large number of overlapping regional and subregional arrangements, many for economic purposes. They have approved grandiose agreements, often modeled after the EU experience, but they lack most of the factors that brought the European states together: high level of economic interactions, strong intraregional trade, complementarity of products, and relatively advanced transportation and infrastructure networks. The African states also lack regional economic hegemons that could play a key role in supporting and sustaining regional arrangements, although Nigeria and South Africa have exercised that role to some extent in ECOWAS and SADC.

It remains to be seen whether the strengthened African Union will be successful with political and security initiatives and whether that strength will reinvigorate the myriad of subregional groups. It also remains unclear whether the AU can be effective and exert greater influence in global arenas. The AU's experience in uniting around a common proposal for UN Security Council reform, for example, and in developing a continent-wide position during the 2009 UN Climate Change Conference, suggests that it will only see its positions adopted if it is realistic and enjoys support from influential states in Europe or elsewhere. As Martin Welz (2013: 437) reminds us, "the underlying problems of the AU, mainly the member states' reluctance to cede sovereignty which is a necessity to build a collective body, are deeply rooted."

## Regional Organizations in the Middle East

As the first *Arab Human Development Report* (UNDP 2002) suggested, "perhaps no other group of states in the world has been endowed with the same potential for cooperation, even integration, as have the Arab countries" (quoted in Solingen 2008: 279). Common language, history, and culture unite the Arab states, but much divides them, as has become increasingly apparent in recent years, and their efforts at regional cooperation have done little to remedy this. A variety of factors have influenced regional initiatives, among them the mix of different regime types (conservative monarchies, authoritarian regimes, and semi-democracies) with varying political agendas but shared interests in maintaining the domestic status quo rather than instituting significant political and economic structural reforms; the major disparities in wealth between rich states with small populations such as Qatar and poor states with high population densities such as Yemen; the low levels of intraregional trade; the similarity of states' imports and exports, reflecting a lack of complementarity; and the extensive involvement of outside powers, including bilateral alliances and economic and security dependencies (Legrenzi and Calculli 2013: 2–5). Twenty-two Middle Eastern states are members of the Arab League as of 2014, with two applicants (South Sudan and Chad); six member states also make up the Gulf Cooperation Council. These have been the primary regional and subregional institutions in the region. Both exclude the three non-Arab powers in the region: Turkey, Iran, and Israel.

### The League of Arab States

The League of Arab States, or Arab League, was formed in March 1945, seven months before the UN, and has been an important player in the Middle East as much for what it does not do as for what it has accomplished. The Arab League was created as a manifestation of pan-Arabism—the ideological and political project to unite all Arab people into a single Arab nation, to promote political and economic cooperation in a period when several Arab states were gaining independence. The League's charter, however, emphasizes state sovereignty, reflective of the colonial past and concerns about the security of its members' domestic (mostly authoritarian) regimes. Although the pan-Arab nationalism that helped to form the League has waned in the face of the divisions and rivalries within and among Arab states, the organization still promotes Arab unity, particularly in the conflict with Israel. It has largely failed, however, to achieve much more than ad hoc collaboration among its members. Part of the explanation rests with the fact that the League, for much of its history, has been a tool of Egypt's foreign policy, hence limiting its development (Maddy-Weitzman 2012: 71).

The Arab League is extensively, though weakly, institutionalized. According to its charter, the primary decisionmaking body is a council composed of the foreign ministers of each member state. It meets twice a year, but any two countries can call it into special session. Although not mentioned in the charter, periodic summit meetings of heads of state function as the de facto supreme decision body in place of the council and have occasionally been the source of significant outcomes. All member states have equal voice in all of the Arab League's bodies and most resolutions must pass by only a simple majority. A resolution is binding, however, only if a state votes for it. This provision has limited the power of the organization over its members. In addition to the council and summits, the Arab League has a variety of committees, a permanent secretariat and secretary-general based in Cairo, a joint defense council, a permanent military committee, and an economic council, as well as other agencies.

Economic, social, and cultural cooperation has been notably more successful than political and security cooperation, despite the League's higher visibility on these issues. Its economic initiatives have included steps toward creation of a common market (the Arab Economic Union), the Arab Development Bank, and the Greater Arab Free Trade Area, which came into being in 2005. Intraregional trade, however, remains low, as the Arab economies have long been heavily protected and had similar production patterns (Solingen 2008: 280).

The Arab League's primary focus has historically been its hostility to the state of Israel and its support for the Palestinian cause. On that issue and on decolonization issues, members have spoken with one voice in the United Nations. The League instituted a boycott of Israeli products in 1948, which remains in place today. Yet because of internal disputes among members, the League did not coordinate the wars with Israel in 1948, 1967, or 1973. It created the Palestine Liberation Organization (PLO) in 1964 and pushed its acceptance in 1974 as the legitimate representative of the Palestinian people. It expelled Egypt after the conclusion of the Camp David Accords with Israel in 1979. The restoration of relations with Egypt in 1989 represented the beginning of weakening the prohibition on diplomatic contact with Israel in the 1990s, as did Jordan's 1994 peace treaty with Israel, and contacts between Morocco, Qatar, and Israel. In 2002 the League endorsed Saudi Arabia's proposal to normalize relations with Israel in exchange for full Israeli withdrawal from the Occupied Territories—an initiative that it hoped would spur negotiations between Israel and the Palestinians and creation of an independent Palestinian state. The League stayed silent, however, during the conflict between Israel and Hamas in Gaza in 2014, despite widespread condemnation of Israel's extensive bombing and the large numbers of Palestinian civilian casualties. Concern about the spread of Islamist extremism overrode sympathy with the Palestinians.

With regard to other conflicts and threats to security in the region, the League has had a very mixed record. Joint military action was taken in 1961 to prevent Iraq from taking over Kuwait at the time of the latter's independence, and again in 1976 in the Lebanese civil war. The League failed to act in Yemen's civil wars in the 1960s and 1990s as well as the Iran-Iraq War in the 1980s, but did condemn Iraq's 1990 invasion of Kuwait. League members were divided over how to avert a US war against Iraq in 2003, with some members eager to pressure Saddam Hussein to disarm. The League did nothing, however, to contribute either to ending the conflict in Iraq or reintegrating Iraq into the Arab world. It supported the government of Sudan in the face of the genocide in the Darfur region of that country, opposing UN sanctions and International Criminal Court prosecution of Sudanese officials indicted for crimes against humanity.

The Arab League, however, showed greater relevance in response to the upheavals of the Arab Spring in 2011 and 2012, particularly the uprisings in Libya and Syria. In February 2011, at the initiative of Saudi Arabia and Qatar, the League condemned the Libyan government's violent crackdown on protesters and suspended it from participating in League meetings—an unprecedented intervention in the domestic affairs of a member state. In March 2011, a subsequent resolution called for the UN Security Council to impose a no-fly zone to protect Libyan civilians. This provided an important source of legitimacy for Security Council action and for US and NATO military intervention, even though Arab state support was not unanimous. Yet once it became evident that the intervention sought regime change, not just humanitarian protection, the League's secretary-general, Amr Moussa, "backtracked on the league's decision" (Maddy-Weitzman 2012: 74).

In the case of Syria, a League mediation mission, including the new secretary-general, Nabil al-Arabi, and ministers from Qatar, Algeria, Egypt, Oman, and Sudan, sought to get Syrian president Bashar al-Assad to take actions to defuse the crisis, including acceptance of a League monitoring mission. When that failed, Syria was suspended from League activities in November 2011, with eighteen of the twenty-two members voting in favor; the League subsequently imposed sanctions on Syria, including banning officials from traveling to other Arab countries, freezing Syrian assets in

Arab countries, and halting bank transactions. The League tried to send another monitoring mission to Syria only to have it turn into a farce in part because it was led by a Sudanese general linked to the genocide in Darfur. It later called for President Assad to step down, then for a joint Arab-UN peacekeeping force. Still later, in March 2012, it approved the appointment of former UN Secretary-General Kofi Annan as the UN–Arab League Special Representative (followed by Lakhdar Brahimi after Annan resigned, and by Staffan de Mistura in 2014). Despite this heightened activity, the Arab League proved to have very little leverage with Syria. The 2015 crisis in Yemen, combined with the threat from the extremist Islamic State (ISIS) in Iraq, Syria, and elsewhere, as well as continuing war in Syria and concerns about Iran's influence in the region, prompted the League to decide to create a joint military force. Only time will tell whether that comes to fruition as previous efforts at joint action have generally been unsuccessful.

In short, in its seventy years of existence, states in the Arab League have cooperated only periodically. The organization's problematic identity, leaders' fear of restrictions on sovereignty, and the weak institutional design explain that poor record (Barnett and Solingen 2007: 180–181). And, for all its rhetoric about social and economic development, the people of the region have seen very little improvement and the League continues to be known primarily for its limited political role.

### The Gulf Cooperation Council

Economically, politically, and culturally, Bahrain, Kuwait, Oman, Qatar, Saudi Arabia, and the United Arab Emirates are among the most homogeneous nations in the world. All are monarchies and oil-producing states. Despite these similarities, the Cooperation Council for the Arab States of the Gulf, or Gulf Cooperation Council (GCC), has been plagued by discord and competing visions that have hindered its effectiveness. Initially, Kuwait envisioned a common market among the six Gulf states, Oman sought a military alliance modeled after NATO, and Saudi Arabia sought an organization to provide a loose sense of collective security while allowing states to follow their own interests (Abdulla 1999). These ideas merged, and the GCC was created in 1981 in response to several new threats, including the Iranian Revolution of 1979, whose leaders threatened to sweep away their monarchies; the Soviet invasion of Afghanistan; and the war between Iran and Iraq. The GCC's charter calls for "coordination, integration, and cooperation among the member states in all fields." Its earliest action was to conclude an agreement to unify the economies of its member states, calling for a uniform system of tariffs, nondiscrimination with regard to capital and labor flows across their borders, harmonization of industrial development programs, a common investment policy, and coordination of oil industry policies (Lawson 2012: 6). Over time, however, both economic and security concerns have marked GCC activities. Historically, Saudi Arabia has been the dominant power among the six members, but since the Arab Spring in 2011, Qatar has emerged as an activist member in competition with Saudi Arabia. While Qatar funds Al Jazeera, the Saudis fund the rival Al Arabiya news network.

Institutionally, the primary organ of the GCC is the Supreme Council, which meets annually and is composed of the heads of state of the six member countries. Like ASEAN and the AU, all substantive decisions in the Supreme Council must be unanimous. While the Supreme Council finalizes decisions for the body, much of the work of the organization is handled by the Ministerial Council, which meets every three months and includes the foreign ministers. Although initially decisions were made on the basis of unanimity, the GCC now has a unitary veto system that requires each government's approval for negotiations and effectively maximizes Saudi Arabia's weight. Authority over some policies relating to regional infrastructure, however, is held by specialized agencies. The General Secretariat, located in Riyadh, supervises and supports implementation of policies. The Peninsula Shield Force, established in 1984, had 40,000 troops in 2014 based in Saudi Arabia.

Although the GCC has outlasted initial predictions of failure, its effectiveness as a regional organization has fluctuated over time. Politically, the GCC was ineffective in responding to the Iran-Iraq War and to Iraq's invasion of Kuwait, except in formally requesting US help in the latter case. Despite strong anti-American sentiment among citizens and high military spending, GCC members have relied on bilateral agreements with the United States for defense rather than on joint efforts. Five of the six members provide significant bases for US forces in the region. Saudi Arabia's base, for example, was used during the 1990–1991 Gulf War, and Kuwait's and Qatar's were used during the 2003 Iraq War, although Saudi Arabia requested that the United States give up its air base in that country in 2003. Bahrain and Qatar host US command headquarters. The GCC countries face a number of threats as a result of forces unleashed by the Arab Spring, Syrian civil war, continuing instability in Iraq, terrorism, and Iran's nuclear program.

Economically, the GCC has had duty-free trade among members since 1983 and a common market since 2008; efforts to create a customs union and single currency have repeatedly stalled, but the customs union came into effect in January 2015. Common citizenship allows citizens among the six states to move freely, but the huge populations of foreign workers are not accorded that privilege. A high commission established in 2009 is tasked with harmonizing rules of origin, and a GCC monetary council created the same year has guided the creation of a regional central bank. Among the major regional infrastructure projects are a unified pipeline network for natural gas, an integrated regional railway system, and a unified electrical power grid. There have also been regionalist initiatives "from below" by chambers of commerce and industry as well as private business to foster cross-border business and investment. As Fred Lawson (2012: 17) concludes, "By the second decade of the twenty-first century, the Gulf Cooperation Council had become transformed into a very different type of regionalist project from what it had been either in 1981 . . . or during the mid-1990s."

As the events of the Arab Spring unfolded in 2011, the GCC proved to be particularly cohesive and active. This was not surprising given the vulnerability of the six monarchies. Their responses focused particularly on Bahrain, Libya, and Yemen as well as on their own populations, pumping billions of dollars into neutralizing potential unrest. In the case of Bahrain, the Peninsula Shield Force (mostly Saudi troops) were deployed in Bahrain in March 2011 to quell the unrest of marginalized Shiite protesters. In Yemen, the GCC undertook prolonged mediation that ended with President Ali Abdullah Saleh stepping down from power in November 2011. In Libya, however, the GCC supported the uprising with the goal of ending Muammar Qaddafi's personal rule. To this end, as noted earlier, Saudi Arabia and Qatar pushed for Arab League action. In the case of Syria, these two GCC members supported rival Syrian opposition groups, motivated in part by the desire to end Iranian influence over Syria, but also reflecting their increasing competition (Maddy-Weitzman 2012). With the rise of Islamist groups in the region, the emergence of ISIS in 2014 as a potent force, the ongoing spillover from the civil war in Syria, and anarchy in Libya as well as the unresolved Israeli-Palestinian conflict, it remains to be seen whether regional organizations in the Middle East remain relatively impotent or develop new capabilities. In early 2015, some GCC countries joined a coalition with the United States to mount air strikes against ISIS in Iraq and Syria; some also joined Saudi Arabia in military action in Yemen.

## Assessing the Consequences of Regionalism

Regional organizations are among the key pieces of global governance and, since the Cold War's end, global regionalization has been a marked trend. Although in some quarters there is a tendency to see regionalism in competition with global efforts to address issues and problems, in most areas of governance, regional organizations and activities complement global ones through either shared or overlapping responsibilities. To be sure, regional free trade initiatives give rise to a fear of trade blocs and barriers to wider trade patterns. Indeed, the EU eliminated internal barriers to trade among its members and favored partners, but raised barriers to trade with others.

Its common policies, particularly in agriculture, for example, have provoked fierce trade wars, especially with the United States, and hampered efforts to open agricultural trade on a global basis. A regional human rights regime could compromise norms of universal human rights if it were to adopt a more restrictive view, say, of women's rights.

As this chapter has shown, regional organizations vary widely in the nature of their organizational structures, the types of obligations they impose on member states, their resources, and the scope of their activities, from the formality and supranationalism of the EU to the loose, informal political concertization of policies found in APEC and ASEAN. Generally, institutions in the developing world tend to be more "sovereignty-preserving than sovereignty-eroding" (Acharya and Johnston 2007: 262). Yet recent analysis has also shown that the differences between the EU and many other regional organizations can be overstated, particularly with respect to supranationalism and shared identity (Checkel 2007). Nonetheless, developments within the expanding universe of regional organizations are "crucial to understanding the many different directions in which governance is moving, the range of dilemmas being faced, and the different forms that regional politics . . . might take" (Hurrell 2007: 146).

## Moving Beyond Regionalism

Many issues and problems require more than regional cooperation, of course. Thus another trend is transregional partnerships such as the EU-ASEAN dialogue and the Asian summits. While these links may represent little more than the rituals of summit diplomacy, they also evidence awareness of the value of interactions among groups of nations in different regions and the potential for meaningful collaboration.

Transregional organizations have a long history, but since the early 1990s they have gained increasing urgency to address issues such as terrorism, drug trafficking, certain types of environmental degradation, and nontraditional security threats. Some, such as the Commonwealth and Francophonie, are the outgrowths of European colonialism, their memberships including the UK and many former British colonies in the former, and France and many of its former colonies in the latter. The Commonwealth, described as a "network of networks" (Shaw 2008), encompasses both the intergovernmental and nongovernmental bodies that grew out of the former British empire, and their shared histories and values. Other groups, such as the Alliance of Small Island States, the Non-Aligned Movement (NAM), and the Organisation of Islamic Cooperation (OIC) are coalitions of like-minded states. The NAM, for example, was born at the Bandung Conference in 1955, but convened its first summit conference, of twenty-five heads of state, in 1961. It has continued over the years to operate primarily through periodic summits without formal organizational structures, a constitution, or secretariat. Where NAM has long served to give voice to countries of the global South on political issues, the Group of 77 (G-77) has focused on economic development.

The Organisation of Islamic Cooperation (formerly the Organisation of the Islamic Conference) brings together states from several regions. When the OIC's charter was approved in 1972, it defined one of the organization's key objectives: "to co-ordinate efforts for the safeguarding of the Holy Places and support of the struggle of the people of Palestine, and help them to regain their rights and liberate their land." With charter amendments in 2008, the organization became more institutionalized, but key provisions remained: to respect self-determination and noninterference in members' domestic affairs. In neither document is there a provision for political unity. Today the OIC has fifty-seven member states.

Since its inception, the OIC has focused primarily on opposition to Israel, supporting the Palestinian cause, and promoting the unity of Islam. Yet it has accomplished very little. The US role in the Islamic world (including the 1990–1991 Gulf War and 2003 invasion of Iraq) has been a particular source of disunity within the OIC, which is polarized between those member states that view the United States as "the Great Satan" and those that host US troops (Akbarzadeh and Connor 2005: 82–83). Malaysia's colorful former prime minister Mahathir Mohamed captured the sense of frustration at the 2003 summit, stating: "We control 57 out of the 180 [*sic*] countries in the world. Our votes can make or break international organizations. . . . For well over half a century we have fought over Palestine. What have we achieved? Nothing? We are worse off than before" (quoted in Akbarzadeh and Connor 2005: 85).

Not only has the OIC failed to further its primary issue, but it has also found itself divided on the issue of terrorism. On the one hand, it has condemned terrorism, labeling attacks as "un-Islamic"; yet on the other hand, it has refrained from condemning Palestinian terrorism and suicide attacks. Thus, although the OIC adopted the Convention on Combating Terrorism in 1990, defining terrorism is problematic, since such actions are generally viewed as legitimate expressions of the Palestinian struggle for self-determination.

The Arab Spring caught the OIC by surprise, with many of its members, including Egypt, Yemen, Bahrain, Oman, Jordan, and Syria, confronted by pro-democracy movements. Instead of addressing these issues or calling a general meeting, the OIC Executive Committee focused on the humanitarian crisis in Libya. In 2011, then, the OIC joined with the Arab League in condemning the Libyan government's violent crackdown on protesters and in calling for UN Security Council action to impose a no-fly zone to protect Libyan civilians, but its response to the uprisings in other countries has not been consistent and member states have formulated their own policies. As Ishtiaq Hossain (2012: 308) concludes: "In terms of politics, security, and defense, the OIC has not succeeded. Although it is difficult the OIC should try to emulate the successes made by the GCC, the ASEAN and the APEC in the areas of economic, political and security."

Thus the landscape of regional and transregional organizations contains a large number of organizations, some much more important parts of global governance than others. Clearly, the processes of regionalization have varied widely in different parts of the world and will continue to evolve in response to the varying dynamics within the regions. Some of these processes have been shaped at least in part by nonstate actors, and it is to them that we turn in Chapter 6.

## Suggested Further Reading

Acharya, Amitav. (2012) *The Making of Southeast Asia: International Relations of a Region*. Ithaca: Cornell University Press.

Acharya, Amitav, and Alastair Ian Johnston, eds. (2007) *Crafting Cooperation: Regional International Institutions in Comparative Perspective*. Cambridge: Cambridge University Press.

Adler, Emanuel, and Michael Barnett, eds. (1998) *Security Communities*. Cambridge: Cambridge University Press.

Galbreath, David J. (2007) *The Organization for Security and Co-operation in Europe*. New York: Routledge.

Makinda, Samuel M., and F. Wafula Okumu. (2008) *The African Union: Challenges of Globalization, Security, and Governance*. London: Routledge.

McCormick, John, and Jonathan Olsen. (2014) *The European Union: Politics and Policies*. Boulder: Westview.

## Internet Resources

### Africa

African Union: www.africa-union.org
Common Market for Eastern and Southern Africa: www.comesa.int
Economic Community of West African States: www.ecowas.int
Southern African Development Community: www.sadc.int

### Asia

ASEAN Regional Forum: www.aseanregionalforum.org
Asia-Pacific Economic Cooperation: www.apecsec.org.sg
Association of Southeast Asian Nations: www.aseansec.org
Shanghai Cooperation Organization: www.sectsco.org

### Europe

Council of Europe: www.coe.int
European Court of Justice: www.curia.europa.eu/jcms/jcms/Jo2_6999/

European Union: www.europa.eu.int
North Atlantic Treaty Organization: www.nato.int
Organization for Security and Cooperation in Europe: www.osce.org

## Latin America
Mercosur: www.mercosur.org
North American Free Trade Agreement: www.nafta-sec.alena.org
Organization of American States: www.oas.org

## Middle East
Gulf Cooperation Council: www.gcc-sg.org
League of Arab States: www.arableagueonline.org

## Transregional Organizations
The Commonwealth: www.thecommonwealth.org
Non-Aligned Movement: www.nam.gov.za
Organisation of Islamic Cooperation: www.oic-oci.org

# 6

# Nonstate Actors: NGOs, Networks, and Social Movements

## Nonstate Actors in Action

### Take One: Nonstate Actors as Initiators of Policy Change

By the early-1990s, the tobacco market was changing, sales in developed countries were dropping due to increased government regulations and lawsuits that exposed the tobacco companies' knowledge of the dangerous effects of smoking. One result was a consolidation of tobacco companies; by 2000, 70 percent of cigarettes sold around the world came from just four firms. To compensate for the decline in developed-country markets, tobacco companies adopted a strategy to target consumers in developing countries where knowledge of the effects of smoking and government regulations were thin. Thus, by the early 1990s the number of smokers in the developing world surpassed those in the developed world despite the high cost of cigarettes relative to income.

In 1993, law professor Allyn Taylor and retired public health professor Milton Roemer approached Judith MacKay, leader of an Asian anti-tobacco NGO with close ties to the World Health Organization. They discussed lobbying WHO staff to propose a new binding treaty on tobacco regulation (MacKay 2003). The idea centered on drafting a set of clear principles that could attract nearly universal support; later amendments could be added on particular issues such as advertising, taxation, and anti-tobacco education programs. Initially, WHO staff were skeptical, leading one to recommend scaling back the proposal in favor of a mere voluntary "code of conduct" for tobacco firms (Roemer, Taylor, and Lariviere 2005)

At NGO conferences around the world, momentum built for moving forward. Experts and advocates lobbied their respective governments as well as personnel at the WHO itself. In 1998 the new WHO director-general, Gro Harlem Brundtland, named tobacco regulation one of her top two priorities.

Meanwhile, tobacco companies worked to establish behind-the-scenes ties with WHO staff to dissuade them from supporting the initiative. They also applied pressure on developing-country governments to resist changes to the status quo in the name of free trade, and filed lawsuits at the World Trade Organization. Despite these efforts, the Framework Convention on Tobacco Control came into effect in 2005. As of early 2015, the treaty had been ratified by 180 states covering 95 percent of the world's population. While some governments have lagged behind in enforcement, NGOs continue to perform an important monitoring role and lobby their respective governments to implement and enforce the treaty's provisions. Tobacco companies continue to press developing countries to resist tightening regulations.

### Take Two: The Dark Side of Nonstate Actors

Nonstate actors are no more likely than states to promote good causes, be altruistic, or be more cooperative. Indeed, opening borders between states has allowed not just do-gooders but also evil-doers to move more freely. Transnational nonstate actors such as terrorist groups, organized crime groups, and human traffickers have taken advantage of lower barriers to trade and travel. The 9/11 terrorists were able to obtain visas for entry into the United States at the US consulate in Riyadh, Saudi Arabia, by posing as tourists, although one was denied for being on a watch list. Human traffickers are generally able to enter Western countries with little difficulty, bringing their human products in tow. This is especially true in Western Europe, due to the 1995 Schengen Agreement, which largely eliminated border checks for those who gain entry into EU member states.

Human traffickers, terrorists, along with groups such as the Mafia, drug traffickers, pirates, and militias and paramilitary forces, are not new actors in international politics. What is new is the degree to which these groups have formed networks. Al-Qaeda is perhaps the best illustration of this dark side, with its networked character and many branches and affiliates, from al-Qaeda in Iraq and the Arabian peninsula to al-Shabab in Somalia, Jemaah Islamiah in Indonesia, Boko Haram in Nigeria, and the Islamic State spin-off. Both states and the international community, through formal and informal international organizations such as Interpol (International Criminal Police Organization), the UN, and the Financial Action Task Force, have waged war on this and other networks to fight crime, trafficking, and terrorism. The networks are decentralized and often skilled in using new technologies, take advantage of economic globalization for moving funds, and are able to adjust rapidly to new conditions, all of which makes them difficult to defeat. Our challenge is to understand the diverse character of these dark-side actors, the roles they play, the strategies they employ, and the ways in which their activities are reshaping international and domestic politics, as well as global governance.

## The Range of Nonstate Actors

Although 193 sovereign states are the major constituents of the international system, thousands of other actors are also part of global governance. These nonstate actors (NSAs) must work within the state-centric framework, although they are not sovereign and do not have the same kind of power resources as do states, nor in most cases do they have a territorial base (Islamic State being a prominent exception). NGOs (the acronym commonly used even for groups that are international) are the most common type of nonstate actors, but a variety of other terms are used to describe different types of NSAs. The International Campaign to Ban Landmines, for example, was a loose, transnational network of numerous NGOs from different parts of the world that did not even establish an address, bank account, and formal organizational identity until it was awarded the 1997 Nobel Peace Prize. The campaign against the OECD draft Multilateral Investment Agreement to regulate multinational corporations (MNCs) was also a loose transnational network of NGOs. Al-Qaeda may be variously described as a network of terrorist (nongovernmental) organizations, a civil society network among a committed group of Muslim believers, or a multinational enterprise generating revenue to finance its political goals and organized in a cluster of subsidiaries. Thus we need to examine the nature, activities, and roles of these nonstate actors. Figure 6.1 provides summary definitions of key terms used to describe different types of NSAs.

### *Nongovernmental Organizations*

NGOs are generally the most visible of the NSAs and participate as key members in coalitions and networks. As defined in Chapter 1, NGOs are voluntary organizations formed by individuals to achieve a common purpose, often oriented beyond themselves or to the public good. NGOs neither have a mandate from government nor want to share government power (Heins 2008: 17–18). There are differences of opinion, however, on whether those common purposes of NGOs must be in support of the public good (the UN criteria) or whether common purposes are sufficient in themselves, meaning that groups of the "dark side" should also be included. In this book, the emphasis is on the former.

Many NGOs are organized around a specific issue area, while others are organized to address broad issues such as human rights, peace, or the environment (Amnesty International, the Nature Conservancy). Some provide services, such as humanitarian aid (Catholic Relief Services) or development assistance (Grameen Bank), while many do both. Other NGOs are information-gathering and information-disseminating bodies (Transparency International). Millions of small local NGOs are active at the grassroots levels, while others operate nationally and internationally. Most international NGOs are headquartered in Northern and Western developed countries (Amnesty International in London; Oxfam in Oxford, UK; the Nature

**Figure 6.1    Types of Nonstate Actors**

- *NGOs/INGOs*
  Voluntary organizations formed and organized by private individuals, operating at the local, national, or international level, pursuing common purposes and policy positions; debate over whether activities need to be in support of a public good (e.g., Oxfam, Rotary, Doctors Without Borders).

- *Transnational Networks and Coalitions*
  Informal and formal linkages among NGOs and ad hoc groups on behalf of a certain issue (e.g., Third World Network, Landmine Survivors Network). Transnational advocacy networks are dedicated to promoting a specific cause (e.g., International Campaign to Ban Landmines).

- *Experts, Epistemic Communities*
  Experts drawn from governments, research institutes, international organizations, and nongovernmental community (e.g., experts on Mediterranean Sea or global climate change).

- *Multinational Corporations*
  Private actors doing business in three or more states whose goal is to make a profit (e.g., Nike, Shell Oil Company, Sony).

- *Social Movements*
  Large, generally informal coalitions of mass publics, individuals, and organizations dedicated to major social change (e.g., international human rights movement, women's movement).

- *Foundations and Global Think Tanks*
  Nonprofit organization funded by individuals, families, or corporations, established for charitable or community purposes (e.g., Ford Foundation, Bill and Melinda Gates Foundation, Wellcome Trust). Global think tanks provide research, analysis, and policy advice to governments and the public (e.g., Brookings Institution, Carnegie Endowment for International Peace).

- *Terrorist, Criminal, and Trafficking Groups and Networks*
  Transnational entities, often connected in networks that engage in crime, trafficking of drugs, arms, and people, as well as terrorism (e.g., Mafia, al-Qaeda).

Conservancy in Washington, DC) and receive funding from private donors and increasingly from governments and IGOs. Others have roots in the developing countries of the South, but receive some funding for local programs or training from international groups (Development Alternatives with Women for a New Era [DAWN]; Tostan, an NGO that addresses female genital mutilation in Africa). Some operate independently, while others are linked to counterpart groups through transnational networks or federations.

Yet NGOs are unique organizational entities. They, like multinational corporations, are subject to the laws and rules of the nation-state in which they operate. Thus, some states ban NGOs; today, numerous states, including the People's Republic of China, Russia, and states of Central Asia, impose strict governmental regulations. In Japan, NGOs operated under major legal and financial constraints until the 1990s. Still other countries, such as Bangladesh, Haiti, and Thailand, are known for having large and vigorous NGO communities with few restrictions. Under traditional international law, NGOs, unlike states and IGOs, have no independent international legal personality. Yet over time, they have been awarded responsibility for enforcing international rules in a few cases, and the right to bring cases in selected adjudicatory settings.

The variety of NGOs, the differences in their respective relationships to governments, and their funding sources have given rise to a variety of acronyms: GONGO (government-organized NGO), BINGO (business or industry NGO), and DONGO (donor-dominated NGO).

Among the internationally oriented NGOs, federations and networking are two important ways that NGOs are linked. The Vietnam Veterans of America, which was a key player in the 1990s campaign to ban landmines, illustrates a national NGO operating only within the United States for many of its goals, but linked to a global network to further the landmine campaign. In contrast, the Red Cross is officially the International Federation of Red Cross and Red Crescent Societies, headquartered in Geneva, Switzerland—a federation of national chapters. Oxfam International has been transformed from a British NGO into a transnational federation, with member chapters in Belgium, Canada, Hong Kong, New Zealand, Spain, the United Kingdom, and the United States, among others. These large, federated NGOs—Oxfam, World Wildlife Fund, Human Rights Watch, Save the Children—have shared overall goals, but leave most fundraising and activities to the individual country chapters. They differ in how much control they can exercise over chapters and how much they try to coordinate activities. Individual chapters, in many cases, may choose their own special interest. Most NGOs, whether federations of national organizations or not, maintain a secretariat that serves their members in different countries. How NGOs are organized makes a difference. Wendy Wong (2012), for example, finds that large grassroots human rights organizations with strong central leadership but decentralized implementation mechanisms are most effective.

Large numbers of NGOs are involved in humanitarian relief, from large, international NGOs to small, locally based groups. The Red Cross, Doctors Without Borders, the International Rescue Committee, and Oxfam are among the hundreds of international humanitarian relief organizations involved in complex emergencies such as the conflicts in Somalia, Congo, and Syria, the genocides in Rwanda and Darfur, and natural disasters such as the 2010 earthquake in Haiti and 2015 earthquake in Nepal.

Many humanitarian relief organizations, such as Oxfam, CARE, Catholic Relief Services, Save the Children, World Vision, and Doctors Without Borders, now integrate developmental components into relief work, focusing on agriculture, reforestation, and primary health care. Oxfam, for example, not only provides emergency relief in food crises, but also works at long-term development, helping Asian fishermen manage water resources. Doctors Without Borders has played a major role in addressing the HIV/AIDS epidemic and 2014 Ebola outbreak as well as helping to rebuild health infrastructure in conflict areas. Other NGOs concentrate exclusively on development, including thousands of small grassroots organizations along with larger organizations like the Grameen Bank, which provides microcredit loans to the poor.

In a few unusual cases, NGOs take the place of states, either performing services that an inept or corrupt government is not providing, or stepping in for a failed state. For many years, Bangladesh hosted the largest NGO sector in the world (more than 20,000 by one count), responding to what one Bangladeshi describes as "the failure of government to provide public goods and look after the poor, and the failure of the private sector to provide enough gainful employment opportunities" (quoted in Waldman 2003: A8). NGOs have taken on roles in education, health, agriculture, and microcredit, all of which originally were government functions. Some attribute the decline in Bangladesh's poverty rate since 1971, from 70 percent to 43 percent, to this nonstate sector. Increasingly, the government of Bangladesh has improved its capacity to take over the functions of some NGOs. While Bangladesh may be a unique case, the failed state of Somalia also witnessed an explosion of NGOs performing vital economic functions in the absence of a central government. And even though Somalia now has a partially functioning government, for more than two decades it has illustrated how nonstate actors (warlords, the Union of Islamic Courts, pirates) from the "dark side" flourish in the absence of an effective government.

NGOs engaged in advocacy are often more visible and vocal than the humanitarian relief and development providers. Whatever their focus, advocacy groups have become an important part of global governance. Often, they seek to change the policies and behavior of both governments and IGOs.

## Transnational Networks and Coalitions

NGOs seldom work alone for very long. The communications revolution, especially the advent of the Internet and social media such as Facebook and Twitter, has linked NGOs together with each other—sometimes formally, more often informally—and with states to block or promote shared goals.

Thus, transnational networks and coalitions create multilevel linkages between different organizations that each retain their separate organizational character and memberships, but through their linkages enhance power, information-sharing, and reach. International NGOs often are not in a position to work effectively with local people and groups. Grassroots groups need the help of other groups within their own country and often from transnational groups to have an impact on their own government or in addressing needs. This is where coalitions or networks become valuable. Anna Ohanyan (2012: 377–378) argues that NGOs "have used networks to increase their funding, expand issue areas of engagement, enhance their mobility worldwide, and improve their overall performance." Most important, she adds, through networks "NGOs have elevated their institutional position in local and/or global governance structures."

NGOs are remarkably flexible with respect to how they apply pressure to states and are willing to act directly through lobbying as well as through transnational NGO coalitions and networks (Willetts 2010). Transnational networks of NSAs are often supplemented by transgovernmental networks of substate actors, such as provincial and regional officials, mayors, judges, police, and local representatives of national governments, with the result that policy coordination may take place without the direct engagement of the central government—and sometimes without its knowledge (Slaughter 2004).

We can illustrate the differences in how NGO coalitions organize by examining two coalitions that have formed around the issue of protecting the elephant and banning trade in ivory. One coalition includes several of the major environmental and conservation international NGOs, such as the World Wildlife Fund (a branch of the World Wide Fund for Nature [WWF]), the International Union for the Conservation of Nature and Natural Resources (IUCN), and Trade Records Analysis of Flora and Fauna in Commerce (TRAFFIC). Most of the member organizations are based in the North, where they raise funds, conduct research, educate the public, and work with IGOs such as the UN Environment Programme (UNEP) and the secretariat of the Conference of Parties to the Convention on International Trade in Endangered Species of Wild Fauna and Flora (CITES). This particular coalition is highly integrated; its member organizations have large, professional staffs of scientists and program specialists who have a presence in countries with large elephant populations, such as Kenya, South Africa, Zimbabwe, and Botswana. They work with governments to manage protected areas, monitor wildlife population changes, engage in research, and fund special projects. They also work with major ivory consumers such as Japan, China, and Hong Kong. Their funding comes from governments, foundations, corporations, as well as individual members.

In contrast to this coalition of highly professional NGOs, another coalition formed in the 1980s to push for a ban on ivory trade was loosely composed of preservation and animal rights organizations, such as Friends of the Animals, Greenpeace, the Humane Society, and Amnistie pour les Éléphants. It was primarily geared toward raising public awareness and thereby influencing governmental decisions. Through a major media campaign in the late 1980s and early 1990s, it was instrumental in achieving a worldwide ban on ivory trade in 1989. Funding came almost exclusively from members, and there was no organizational structure to aid in implementing long-term solutions. It was not geared to work with governments of both ivory-consuming and elephant-host countries to promote an overall conservation strategy that would address underlying causes of elephant population decline (Princen 1995). As poaching and trafficking of ivory have mushroomed since 2008, due in part to both demand in Asia and the involvement of international criminal groups, many new groups have formed to press for new action on the problem. How CITES itself is implemented through TRAFFIC is discussed in detail in Chapter 11.

The second coalition just described illustrates a special type of network or coalition, often more visible and vocal, namely a transnational advocacy network (TAN). TANs bring new ideas into policy debates, along with new ways of framing issues to make them comprehensible and to attract support, new information, and resources. Although they come in all shades, organizational formats, sizes, and approaches, they share "the centrality of values or principled ideas, the belief that individuals can make a difference, the creative use of information, and the employment . . . of sophisticated political strategies in targeting their campaigns" (Keck and Sikkink 1998: 2). These campaigns focus advocacy efforts, target resources, and win public support typically with a topical focus, such as elephants, whales, the Amazon, or Africa's Great Lakes. Human rights campaigns have focused either on specific rights abuses such as torture, violence against women, child soldiers, and slavery, or on specific countries such as Argentina and South Africa. Peace groups have long focused on banning a particular type of weapon (nuclear weapons, landmines, small armaments, cluster munitions) and opposing wars (Vietnam, Iraq, Afghanistan, Syria, Israel/Hamas).

Key to the functioning of advocacy networks are the formal and informal connections among participating groups. Individuals, information, and funds move back and forth among them. Larger NGOs provide money and various kinds of services, such as help with organization building and training, to smaller NGOs. Small grassroots groups provide information about human rights violations or pending environmental disasters to NGOs, often including stories told by those whose lives have been adversely affected. By framing issues for broader appeal, advocacy networks seek to change the policies and behavior of *both* governments and IGOs, to secure changes in international and national laws, and to make a difference.

Over time, TANs have learned from each other (Clark, Friedman, and Hochstetler 1998). Close relationships between key players in women's rights and human rights groups led to the mainstreaming of women's rights into the human rights movement in the 1990s. Environmentalists seeking protection of public spaces used the language of human rights. The Cluster Munition Coalition has worked in tandem with the International Campaign to Ban Landmines and adopted many of its strategies.

The "dark side" networks, however, stand in contrast to the advocacy networks. Transnational criminal and terrorist networks have adapted networked business models of transnational enterprises. Goods produced in low-risk areas are trafficked to high-income areas through strategic alliances, subcontracting, and joint ventures. Their networks are ordered, self-repairing (branches can be easily replaced), and resilient. What is trafficked can be easily changed (drugs to human beings to organs to arms or ivory). The ties between different parts of a criminal network may be based on blood, neighborhood, past participation, ethnicity, or language (Madsen 2014: 401). Not surprisingly, global crime governance is also organized through a public-private network on the grounds that "it takes a network to defeat a network" (Madsen 2014: 404).

### Experts and Epistemic Communities

Experts on different subjects, drawn from government agencies, research institutes, private industry, and universities, are important actors in many global governance issues and often are drawn together into so-called epistemic communities. The sharing of knowledge by experts through transnational networks is critical to understanding the problems themselves, framing issues for collective debates, and proposing specific solutions. Epistemic communities, therefore, are networks of knowledge-based experts—professionals with competence in a particular issue domain. Although they may come from a variety of academic disciplines and backgrounds, they share normative beliefs, understanding about the causes of particular problems, criteria for weighing conflicting evidence, and a commitment to seeking policy solutions (Haas 1992: 3).

Epistemic communities are particularly important in addressing complex scientific, environmental, and health issues, but in principle could be influential in shaping policy outcomes in any issue area where shared knowledge is critical. For example, in the 1980s, amid growing concern that the Mediterranean Sea was dying, all eighteen governments in the region participated in negotiating the Med Plan under UNEP auspices. Critical to bringing together the states and securing agreement, however, was the network of ecologists in UNEP, the FAO, and several governments. They shared a common concern about the Mediterranean's health and the necessity of multilateral policies to regulate pollutants. Drawing on the expertise of regional marine scientists, they drafted the Barcelona Convention and Land-Based Sources Protocol to deal with land-based and marine-based sources of pollution. They pressed governments to regulate pollutants other than oil, including those transported by rivers. They encouraged governments to enforce policies for pollution control and to adopt more comprehensive measures. Not surprisingly, the strongest measures for pollution control were taken in countries where members of the epistemic community were entrenched in government agencies and influential (P. Haas 1990). The Med Plan became the model for arrangements for nine other regional seas.

Other examples of epistemic communities can be found among the scientific experts on whaling (cetologists), stratospheric ozone, and global climate change (e.g., the Intergovernmental Panel on Climate Change, discussed in Chapter 11). They can be found also among experts on nuclear proliferation and intellectual property as well as many other issues. Several epistemic communities are discussed in subsequent chapters.

### Foundations and Global Think Tanks

Private foundations, which are legal entities in most developed countries, are nonprofit organizations that serve charitable or community purposes. They are funded by individuals, families, or corporations, but they serve public purposes. With a philanthropic tradition and favorable tax provisions, foundations have a long history in the United States. Foundations such as the Ford Foundation, the Rockefeller Foundation, the Bill and Melinda Gates Foundation, and the Turner Foundation have played a key role in funding various international programs, from international peace to population control programs and health research. The Gates Foundation, for example, with resources of $60 billion, gives about $1 billion a year largely to international health programs such as childhood immunization programs, AIDS research, fighting the Ebola epidemic, and strengthening health delivery systems, making it the largest single donor to international health. The Gates Foundation and many others, including Britain's Wellcome Trust, often participate as multistakeholder actors in global governance, mobilizing financial resources, social capital, and expertise. Increasingly, foundations now work with MNCs and private enterprises.

Global think tanks are often thought of primarily as research institutions that produce scholarly-like work on policy problems both domestic and international. Some, however, have become global institutions utilizing local staff and scholars in offices on two or more continents and providing advice to both governments and international institutions. A few have also taken on other tasks. The International Peace Institute, for example, trains military and civilian personnel in peacekeeping; the Brookings Institution's project on internally displaced persons has played a major role in drawing attention to the growing problem of IDPs and working to help these populations in partnership with the London School of Economics (McGann 2014).

## Multinational Corporations

Multinational corporations are a special type of nongovernmental actor engaged in for-profit business transactions and operations across national borders. MNCs exist in various forms and are an important part of the global economy, as described in Chapters 8 and 9. As key actors, they have been for many years targets of international and state efforts to regulate their behavior. NGOs have linked labor violations with MNC behavior and pollution with MNC practices, targeting companies such as Nike, McDonald's, Starbucks, Walmart, Shell, and Apple and using the power of consumers to boycott the products of a given corporation, mobilizing campaigns to raise awareness, or initiating legal action to stop oil exploration in the case of Conoco and the Ecuadorean rainforest. In the competitive environment of today's global markets, a boycott is likely to lead the targeted corporation to terminate or modify its practices.

As a result of NGO-led campaigns to end sweatshops and child labor, protect rainforests, boycott blood diamonds, and prevent the scuttling of a North Sea oil rig, major corporations have responded by implementing codes of conduct, certifications that certain standards have been met, and monitoring mechanisms, all under the rubric of corporate social responsibility. Under pressure from NGO-led grassroots campaigns, these codes of conduct have had to be continually strengthened, with corporations making concessions that would have been unthinkable in the past.

The 1999 UN-sponsored Global Compact invites corporations around the world to commit to adopting a series of steps to minimize human rights and labor violations in connection with their economic activities. Participating firms are expected to submit annual reports on their progress in implementing the program and are permitted to use the Global Compact logo in their marketing. Direct enforcement is nonexistent; only when a firm has failed to report for four years in a row is it "de-listed." MNCs are among the nonstate actors that have increasingly been brought into the broader global governance framework, working in partnerships with other actors, including the UN, as discussed in Chapter 9.

## Partnerships

Partnerships among actors bring together those interested in or affected by an issue, including government agencies, IGOs, MNCs, professional groups, NGOs, private foundations, religious groups, and individuals in both formal and informal settings. They can take various forms and have sometimes been referred to as global policy networks or multistakeholder actors. As one analyst notes regarding the value of multiple stakeholders, they "can sort through conflicting perspectives, help hammer out a consensus, and translate that consensus into actions its members will be more inclined to support and implement" (Reincke 1999–2000: 47). The short-lived World Commission on Dams (WCD) illustrates this phenomenon. This special independent body, representing the supporters and opponents of big dams, was created in 1998 and conducted a global review of the effectiveness of large dams. Its work concluded in 2000 with the establishment of internationally accepted criteria for dam construction.

Other examples of partnerships include the Roll Back Malaria Partnership, which was launched in 1998 by the WHO, UNICEF, the UNDP, and the World Bank, and later joined by NEPAD, the G-8, Japan (a major bilateral donor), private companies, African states and communities, and NGOs. Drawing on an innovative process developed by a Japanese company to make cheap and effective insecticide-treated nets, various actors funded the purchase of these life-saving nets; states and groups promoted their use; and the technology was transferred to an African company for domestic production. ExxonMobil has donated chemical components, and nets are distributed through gas stations in areas where malaria is endemic. These nets have also been promoted by NGOs like Doctors Without Borders, among others. The Roll Back Malaria Partnership is an excellent example of a partnership among a variety of actors participating in global governance activities.

Such partnerships between the UN and businesses now constitute a "vast and expanding" universe, including "virtually every global development issue" (Gregoratti 2014: 310). Some 1,500 partnerships were listed on the business.un.org database in 2012, with more than 300 others listed by the UN Commission on Sustainable Development. As noted in Chapter 1, they have had a major impact on thinking about development and how to deliver it. Partnerships include financial and in-kind donations as well as mobilization of market expertise, marketing developing-country handicrafts, conducting workshops, and convincing corporations to sign to principles of conduct.

### Social Movements

Social movements represent a looser mass-based association of individuals and groups dedicated to changing the status quo. Such movements may form around major social cleavages such as class, gender, religion, region, language, or ethnicity, or around progressive goals such as the environment, human rights, and development, or around conservative goals such as opposition to abortion, family planning, and immigration. Although NGOs often play key roles in social movements, helping to frame issues to make them resonate with the public and helping to mobilize the necessary structures and resources, social movements usually involve sustained public activities such as mass meetings, rallies and demonstrations, as well as use of the public media to engage individuals. Movements may even help to forge new identities—as constructivists assert—among women, indigenous peoples, victims of human rights violations, and the poor. Social movements vary enormously in the types of formal or informal structures they use to mobilize support—from activist networks to national and transnational social actions; they also vary in their repertoires, staying power, and effectiveness (Tilly 2004). The women's movement is discussed in Chapters 9 and 10, the human rights movement in Chapter 10, and the antiglobalization movement in Chapter 8.

The world witnessed the power of social movements beginning in December 2010 when a Tunisian produce vendor named Mohammed Bouazizi burned himself to death in protest of the harassment he was subjected to by the authorities. His death was communicated around the country and the region and quickly became a rallying point for disgruntled young people across the Arab world. Massive rallies were organized, mostly through social media, in capitals and other cities in Tunisia, Libya, Bahrain, Egypt, Syria, and Yemen that led to the downfall of several regimes. The movement has been described as "leaderless," with many groups taking it upon themselves to announce events, encourage participation, and even provide training on how to thwart efforts by the police to repress the protesters, sometimes with help from foreign civil rights activists and Western governments.

Sometimes the UN has been accused of co-opting or "taming" social movements by bringing them into a state-dominated, mainstream institution, and while this may happen sometimes, IGOs also provide important resources for social movements. They help them gain access to state actors, NGOs, and IGO staff members, thereby increasing their chances of influencing policy debates (Smith and Wiest 2012: chap. 5). For example, as described in Chapter 10, the lesbian, gay, bisexual, and transgender (LGBT) community has reframed the debate over gay rights in terms of international human rights.

### A Global Civil Society?

There is a common tendency to equate NGOs with civil society, but the latter is really a broader concept, encompassing all organizations and associations that exist outside of the state and the market (i.e., government and business). It includes not just the kinds of advocacy groups discussed here, but also associations of professionals (doctors, lawyers, scientists, journalists), labor unions, chambers of commerce, religious groups, ethnic associations, sporting associations, and political parties. Most critically, civil society links individual citizens. In Paul Wapner's words (1996: 5), it is an arena in which "people engage in spontaneous, customary and nonlegalistic forms of association" to pursue common goals. As a result, individuals establish relationships and shared frames or understandings that govern future behavior.

Have individuals and groups connected across nations to a sufficient extent to suggest that we now have a global civil society? Do individuals have an associational life beyond the state? Are the norms and values that individuals hold shared transnationally? Is there a nascent global civil society that is democratizing global governance? Many are enthusiasts. They see the growing universalization of democratic values, better accountability, and more inclusiveness with an expanding civil sphere that is separate from the Westphalian state system. Still others are critics. To them, the so-called global civil society is unrepresentative; rather than challenging the power of states, it is joining them (Dryzek 2012). Marxists and neo-Marxists, for example, are particularly critical, viewing NGOs and other NSAs as actual instruments of hegemonic states. They do not see democratization of governance, but rather continued concentration of power in hegemonic states (Heins 2008: 101–102). Yet all agree that nonstate actors have grown in both numbers and importance.

## The Growth of Nonstate Actors

There is no disputing that the number of NGOs has increased exponentially since the mid-1970s, as Figure 3.1 illustrates; currently there are over 8,500 international NGOs and several million national and indigenous NGOs. The growth has been exponential particularly since World War II and in certain issue areas such as human rights and the environment. One explanation focuses on bottom-up societal changes—advances in communication and transportation and growing secular trends to address the needs of "the other" (Heins 2008: 44–45). Another sees proliferation of NGOs as a top-down phenomenon. As Kim Reimann (2006: 48) explains, "Just as the emergence of the nation-state and periods of state-building at the national level stimulated the growth of new forms of citizen activism and organization in the industrialized West, the creation of new international institutions and their rapid growth in the postwar period have stimulated NGO growth worldwide by providing new political opportunities and incentives to organize." Yet NGOs are not just a late-twentieth-century phenomenon; they have also played roles in developing international law and organization for more than two centuries.

## A Historical Perspective on the Growth of NGO Influence

The anti-slavery campaign was the earliest NGO-initiated effort to organize transnationally to ban a morally unacceptable social and economic practice. Its genesis lay in the establishment in 1787 and 1788 of societies dedicated to the abolition of slavery in Pennsylvania, England, and France. The history of this campaign, spanning much of the nineteenth century, is examined in Chapter 10.

In Europe and in the United States, peace societies also began appearing during the nineteenth century. A group of peace societies convened their first congress in 1849, developing the first plan for what later became the Permanent Court of Arbitration. Peace societies joined in supporting many of the ideas emerging from the Hague Conferences at the end of the century, including the commitment to finding noncoercive means for dispute resolution. By 1900, there were 425 peace societies throughout the world (Charnovitz 1997).

The nineteenth century also saw the establishment of transnational labor unions, NGOs promoting free trade, and groups dedicated to the strengthening of international law. In 1910, NGOs convened the World Congress of International Associations, with 132 groups participating, and from this emerged the Union of International Associations, which still today serves as the international organization documenting the landscape of international organizations. NGOs were heavily involved in promoting intergovernmental cooperation and regime creation during the nineteenth century in functional areas such as transportation, workers' rights, conservation of species, and sanitation.

Among the NGOs founded in the nineteenth century was the highly influential International Committee of the Red Cross. Founded during the 1860s by Swiss national Henry Dunant and other individuals concerned with protecting those wounded during war, several conferences were organized to elucidate principles governing care of wounded individuals, rights of prisoners of war, and neutrality of medical personnel. The ICRC and its national affiliates became the neutral intermediaries for protecting wounded individuals during war, and the 1864 Geneva Convention for the Amelioration of the Condition of the Wounded in Armies in the Field laid the foundation for international humanitarian law. The unique role and special responsibilities of the ICRC are examined later.

In the twentieth century, peace groups such as the League to Enforce Peace and the League of Nations Society of London developed the ideas that shaped the League of Nations and later the United Nations. The League of Nations Covenant contained one provision dealing with NGOs, calling upon members "to encourage and promote the establishment and cooperation of duly authorized voluntary national Red Cross organizations having as purposes the improvement of health, the prevention of disease, and the mitigation of suffering throughout the world" (Article 25). The League of Nations also invited NGOs to participate in other meetings, such as the 1920 Financial Conference in Brussels, the League's Maritime Committee, the 1927 World Economic Conference, and the 1932 Disarmament Conference. Many specific NGO proposals were incorporated into draft treaties. NGOs were actively involved in the League's work on minority rights, particularly in submitting petitions. In 1920, Jeglantyne Jebb, founder of Save the Children International Union, drafted the Declaration of the Rights of the Child, which was approved by the League Assembly in 1924. Save the Children and other NGOs were represented on the League's Child Welfare Committee, and women's groups were represented on the League's Committee on Traffic in Women and Children. In both cases, NGO representatives were considered full members of the committees, except that they lacked the right to vote. Many NGOs established offices in Geneva to facilitate contacts with the League (and have remained there, since Geneva is the European headquarters of the UN).

Between 1930 and 1945, NGOs' influence diminished, in large part because governments were preoccupied with rising security threats and economic crisis, and the League's role declined. As planning for the postwar order proceeded after 1943, NGOs again became important sources of ideas in shaping the UN Charter and other post–World War II steps. Indeed, there were representatives of 1,200 voluntary organizations at the San Francisco founding conference of the UN. They were largely responsible for both the wording "We the peoples of the United Nations" and the specific provisions for NGO consultative status with ECOSOC, as discussed later. In 1948 there were 41 formally accredited groups; in 2014 there were 3,900. Since our purpose here is not to provide a systematic history of NGO development, we shall leap ahead to analyze the proliferation of NGOs that began in the 1970s and the intensification of their involvement in global governance.

## Explaining the Accelerated Growth of Nonstate Actors' Participation

What has spurred the accelerating growth of NGOs, networks and coalitions, and social movements and their influence on global governance since the 1970s? With globalization, an increasing number of interdependence issues have required transnational and intergovernmental cooperation. NGOs, with their ability to collect and disseminate information, mobilize key constituencies, and target resources on particular goals, have developed to fulfill these needs. The Cold War's end and the spread of democratic political systems and norms in the 1980s and 1990s also explain the growth of NSAs' participation. As social, economic, and cultural issues attract more attention, more NGOs and civil society groups are formed, empowering individuals to become more active politically. In addition to these two broad trends, discussed in Chapter 1, two other developments have played a role in the growth of NGOs: UN-sponsored global conferences and the communications revolution.

*UN-sponsored global conferences.* UN-sponsored ad hoc and global conferences in the 1970s, 1980s, and 1990s, as discussed in Chapter 4, involved increasing participation by NGOs, as shown in Table 6.1. Since the early 1970s, NGOs, networks, and coalitions have sought opportunities to participate in agenda-setting and negotiations. What is somewhat less clear, however, is the degree to which participation in these conferences actually increased NGO access to various parts of the UN system and their influence.

Beginning with the 1972 UN Conference on the Human Environment, in Stockholm, NGOs organized a parallel forum, with almost 250 NGOs participating, a pattern that was repeated at each subsequent conference, with steadily growing numbers. At the 1992 UN Conference on the Environment and Development in Rio de Janeiro, some 1,400 NGOs were represented in the NGO forum. First, the conferences were intended to draw attention to select global issues and to mobilize the international community to take steps to address the issues. Hence, they put issues on the map that NGOs were often far better equipped to address than were many governments. Second, they created opportunities for NGO influence throughout the conference preparatory processes and follow-up. The final document of the Rio Conference, Agenda 21, assigned a key role to NGOs in implementation of conference outcomes, calling for IGOs to utilize the expertise and views of NGOs in all phases of the policy process. Third, the parallel NGO

**Table 6.1   Participation at Selected UN-Sponsored Global Conferences and Summits**

| Conference/Summit Focus | Number of States | Number of NGOs[a] |
|---|---|---|
| Environment (1972) | 114 | 250 |
| Children (1990) | 159 | 45 |
| Environment and development (1992) | 172 | 1,400 |
| Human rights (1993) | 171 | 800 |
| Population and development (1994) | 179 | 1,500 |
| Social development (1995) | 186 | 811 |
| Women (1995) | 189 | 2,100 |
| Human settlements (1996) | 171 | 2,400 |
| Sustainable development (2002) | 191 | 3,200 |
| Sustainable development (2012) | 192 | 737 |

*Note:* a. Figures vary considerably among different sources.

forums spurred networking among participating groups by bringing them together from around the world for several days of intensive interactions. Those links have enabled NGOs to play an important role in monitoring follow-up activities.

Each conference has been free to adopt its own rules for NGO participation. For example, the NGOs present in Stockholm were permitted to make formal statements to the conference with no limits. At the 1980 Second World Conference on Women in Copenhagen, NGO representatives were granted only fifteen minutes of total speaking time. At the 1985 conclusion of the Vienna Convention on Ozone Depleting Substances, no NGOs were present; in 1987, NGOs were permitted to speak at the Montreal conference, where the follow-up protocol to the Vienna Convention was drafted; and in 1989, there were ninety NGOs in active attendance at the London Conference on Saving the Ozone Layer. Thereafter, environmental NGOs were intimately involved in the preparations for the 1992 Rio Conference on the Environment and Development and in the negotiations on conventions for biodiversity and climate change. At the Habitat II conference in 1996, NGO representatives were allowed to sit with governments and to introduce amendments to texts. In contrast, the 1993 human rights conference excluded NGOs from the official process, in large part because many Asian and Arab states lobbied to restrict NGO access. Not all issue areas are equally populated with NGOs, and in any case the nature of NGO participation varies widely. Yet according to a recent study of NGOs' interactions with UN agencies, neither the explosion of NGOs nor their participation in the large UN global conferences have contributed to their increased access to IGOs, including the UN, or to the "emergence, spread, and consolidation" of the norm of NGO participation (Tallberg et al. 2013: 241).

Since 2000 and because of the limitations on conferences discussed in Chapter 4, there have been fewer gatherings, and the rules for access have become more restricted. Yet the global conferences have provided a critical symbolic and practical opportunity for NGOs to flourish and forge valuable networks for advancing their causes in states and international bodies.

*The communications revolution.* Although NGOs have benefited enormously from the face-to-face gatherings at global conferences, the communications revolution has made it possible to link individuals and groups without such contacts. The fax and, most important, the Internet and e-mail have made cohesion not tied to location possible.

Craig Warkentin (2001) identifies six ways in which NGOs have used the Internet: to facilitate internal communication and communications with partner organizations, to shape public perception, to enhance member services, to disseminate information, to encourage political participation, and to realize innovative ideas. E-mail and fax also greatly increased the volume and speed of interactions in the 1990s. Websites enable NGOs to widely disseminate a particular picture of themselves and their work, recruit new members, communicate with existing members, make a large amount of information publicly available, solicit contributions, and encourage people to participate politically in specific and often electronic ways. Thus the number of actors who matter increases, and the number who have authority is reduced (Mathews 1997: 50–51).

The Arab Spring has often been mentioned as a model of how social media can translate general discontent into revolution. Soon-to-be-deposed governments across North Africa felt that Twitter and Facebook were enough of a threat that they actively interfered with their operation or shut off access to the Internet in the case of Egypt. Major anti-regime demonstrations were often preceded by very high activity on Twitter and Facebook (Howard et al. 2011; Simmons 2011). Many political parties dramatically increased their website content to take advantage of increased traffic. Likewise, virtual communities sometimes became face-to-face associations as relationships moved from Facebook to Tahrir Square and international media outlets broadcast videos filmed by people in the streets and relied on bloggers for updates. These messages were heard in Tunisia, Egypt, Bahrain, Libya, Syria, Morocco, Jordan, and beyond. Of course, none of this would have happened without the very high levels of Internet and social media access among young, educated people who were already exasperated by authoritarian governments and poor government policies that produced high food prices and high unemployment.

NGOs that care deeply about specific issues link with each other in order to achieve their goals. Global conferences and the communications revolution have facilitated the growth and the networking process. What is inescapable now are the density, size, and professionalism of these networks that have emerged as prime movers, framing issues and agendas, mobilizing constituencies in targeted campaigns, and monitoring compliance. As Margaret Keck and Kathryn Sikkink (1998: x) point out: "Transnational networks multiply the voices that are heard in international and domestic politics. These voices argue, persuade, strategize, document, lobby, pressure, and complain. The multiplication of voices is imperfect and selective—for every voice that is amplified, many others are ignored—but in a world where the voices of states have predominated, networks open channels for bringing alternative visions and information into international debate."

## NGO Roles
The various general roles that nonstate actors, and particularly NGOs, play in global governance are summarized in Figure 6.2. NGOs can seek the best

---

**Figure 6.2    NGO Governance Functions**

- Gather and publicize information
- Frame issues for public consumption
- Create and mobilize networks
- Enhance public participation
- Advocate changes in policies and governance
- Promote new norms
- Monitor human rights and environmental norms
- Participate in global conferences:
    Raise issues
    Submit position papers
    Lobby for viewpoint
- Perform functions of governance in the absence of state authority

---

venues to present issues and to apply pressure. They can provide new ideas and draft texts for multilateral treaties; they can help government negotiators understand the science behind environmental issues they are trying to address. Development and relief groups often have the advantage of being "on the ground," neutral, and able to "make the impossible possible by doing what governments [and sometimes IGOs] cannot or will not" (Simmons 1998: 87).

Since the end of the Cold War, NGOs have played a particularly critical role in what Michael Barnett (2011) has called the age of "liberal humanitarianism." States, IGOs, and especially NGOs are heavily engaged in emergency relief work and nation-building activities with the aim of consolidating democracy and economic openness. Tens of thousands of NGO workers have fanned out across the globe, perhaps as many as 200,000 individuals working to provide basic services with governments, private donors, as well as international agencies contracting with NGOs to carry out this work. For example, International Relief and Development received $2.4 billion from the US Agency for International Development between 2007 and 2013 for its work in Afghanistan, Iraq, and elsewhere. Following the devastating earthquake in Haiti in 2010, donors pledged $10 billion in aid, nearly all of which was to go to the local and international NGOs tasked with carrying out relief and reconstruction.

Many of these NGO workers are driven not only by altruism but also by a sense of purpose guided by their professional training. Nurses, accountants, lawyers, engineers, and others answer not just to their respective agencies and clients but also to professional organizations with standards of training and conduct, knowing they will be held accountable for their performance long after the assignment is over. As more and more such professionals join agencies engaged in humanitarian work, for example, other NGOs must compete to recruit them and professionalize existing staff in order to be taken seriously by donors. Some NGOs such as Bioforce train would-be humanitarian workers with specialized courses culminating in certificates and licenses. Humanitarian workers have also organized professional associations. The World Association for Disaster and Emergency Medicine, for example, tends to multiple NGO tasks, applying knowledge learned from data collected through qualitative and quantitative research and developing strategies aimed at achieving specific objectives within their area of expertise, in this case human health.

## NGOs' Relationships to IGOs

In order for nonstate actors to play roles in global governance, they need access to the places where decisions are made, where states endeavor to achieve consensus on norms and principles, hammer out the texts of the treaties and conventions that codify rules, coordinate their policies, resolve their disputes, and allocate resources to implement programs and activities, and where international bureaucrats do their work. To exercise influence over governments' positions and IGO policies and programs, NGOs need access and recognition of their right to be consulted, lobby, participate, provide data, and even vote.

Some IGOs have provisions in their charters for participation of nonstate actors; others have gradually established informal procedures for consultation or participation; some organizations have done little or nothing to accommodate demands from NGOs for greater voice. Although the early history of NGO and governmental interactions showed that established procedures were not essential, recent efforts by states to exclude NGO participation in global conferences shows the benefits of constitutional provisions. We see five types of NGO activities in IGOs: (1) consultation in regime creation and implementation, (2) lobbying, (3) surveillance of governmental activities, (4) involvement in international program implementation, and (5) participation in decisionmaking. The pressures on the UN and other IGOs to accommodate and collaborate with NGOs come from NGOs themselves, as well as from donor governments that favor grassroots participation; these pressures have increased dramatically since the mid-1980s.

Jonas Tallberg and colleagues (2013) have conducted the first empirical study of participation of transnational nonstate actors in IGOs. It includes access not only for NGOs, but also for foundations, religious organizations, labor unions, for-profit MNCs, and business associations. The dataset includes fifty IGOs, a stratified random sample from 182 IGOs, and almost 300 suborganizational bodies between 1950 and 2010. Some of the empirical findings are consistent with anecdotal generalizations. The study found, for example, that IGOs have opened up with "deeper, broader, more permanent, and more codified access rules, but also an increase in the number of access arrangements per body" (70). Although access is being granted for monitoring and enforcement functions, there is less access in decisionmaking bodies. Access is most favorable for human rights, trade, environment, and development NSAs, while finance and security groups have the least-favorable arrangements. Only the larger economic IGOs such as the IMF and World Bank have opened up to maintain their own legitimacy in the face of strategic pressures. Indeed, most IGOs operate well out of the public eye, which makes the trend of increasing access over the last twenty years surprising.

Why do IGOs grant access to NGOs? Based on their empirical data, Tallberg and colleagues. (2013: 22) draw on institutional design theories to suggest three theoretical logics. First, IGOs may permit access for functions that they themselves are less able to perform. Second, IGOs may open up to transnational activities and NGOs in order to quell public opposition, opposition that endangers the IGOs' own legitimacy and authority. Finally, IGOs may grant access as a way to promote the norm of participatory democracy. Not only may different IGOs have different motivations, but different subbodies within an IGO may have their own reasons. Tallberg and colleagues (2013: 139) did find that diffusion of IGO access has contributed to the spread of access, as decisionmakers are influenced by the adoption of access rules in other bodies. We look here in more detail at NGO access in the UN system.

## The United Nations

Although the UN's members are states, the organization has long recognized the importance of nongovernmental organizations. Article 71 of the Charter authorized ECOSOC (but not the General Assembly) to grant consultative status to NGOs. Resolution 1296, adopted in 1968, formalized the arrangements for NGO accreditation. Their influence occurred primarily within ECOSOC's subsidiary bodies, and most especially within the Commissions on Human Rights, Status of Women, and Population.

To accommodate growing NGO activism, ECOSOC Resolution 31, in 1996, granted access to national-level NGOs and amended the existing roster system. As noted earlier, 3,900 NGOs enjoyed consultative status in 2014. NGOs having general status have the broadest access to UN bodies: they may consult with officials from the Secretariat, place items on agendas in ECOSOC and functional commissions and other subsidiary bodies, attend meetings, submit statements, and make oral presentations with permission. NGOs having special status enjoy many of the same privileges, but they may not suggest items for ECOSOC's agenda. Roster organizations' access is more limited; they can attend meetings within their field of expertise and submit statements, but only at the invitation of the Secretary-General or ECOSOC.

There are UN NGO liaison offices in Geneva and New York and dozens of other specific offices for NGO activities are tied to various UN specialized agencies. The UN buildings, despite their tighter security regulations since 9/11, have become places for informal interactions among NGOs, state representatives, and Secretariat personnel. Information and expertise are shared, activities and issues promoted, and UN programs monitored.

Since the late 1980s, NGOs have not only had access to ECOSOC and the Secretariat, but also gained access to several committees of the General Assembly, including the Third Committee (Humanitarian and Cultural) and the Second Committee (Economic and Financial). Four NGOs—the International Federation of the Red Cross and Red Crescent Societies, the ICRC, the Interparliamentary Union, and the Sovereign Military Order of Malta— have special privileges and participate as observers in General Assembly sessions.

The Security Council has also initiated selective consultations with NGOs, particularly in relationship to humanitarian crises. In 1997, for the first time, the Security Council permitted representatives from Oxfam, CARE, and Doctors Without Borders to speak on the crisis in the Great Lakes region of Africa. Since then, key humanitarian NGOs have participated in Security Council discussions on a number of issues, including HIV/AIDS as a security issue (2000) and the 2014 Ebola outbreak. In 1995, the NGO Working Group on the Security Council was formed, organized by Amnesty International, the Global Policy Forum, EarthAction, and the World Council of Churches, among others. It now numbers some thirty NGOs with strong interest in the work of the Security Council. The Security Council president and UN officials meet with them periodically, as do various permanent representatives from the Security Council. These meetings are off-the-record and in private, with the expectation that such informal consultation can help maintain strong ties, be an avenue of policy input, and provide another way to enhance the transparency of the Security Council (Alger 2002: 100–103).

NGOs continue to lobby for greater participation rights through the Conference of Non-Governmental Organisations in Consultative Status with the United Nations Economic and Social Council (CoNGO). In particular, CoNGO has lobbied for standardized procedures for determining access to conferences. The 2003 Cardoso Report called for enhanced relationships between the UN and all relevant partners in civil society, with the UN serving as a convener of multiple constituencies, facilitating rather than undertaking operations. Although NGOs became core participants, both formally and informally, the report itself did not acknowledge the multiple ways NGOs already took part in UN activities, nor did it differentiate among various sectors of civil society (Willetts 2006).

There are deep divisions among member states, NGOs themselves, and the UN Secretariat itself over NGO participation. Many governments have mixed or even negative feelings about NGOs. For example, governments in Africa, Asia, and Latin America often feel threatened by the pressures of human rights NGOs; G-7 governments do not always welcome NGO pressure for economic justice; and the Non-Aligned Movement opposes expanded NGO access to the General Assembly. "Delegations feared changes that might weaken or even eventually sweep away nation-states' monopoly of global decision-making" (Paul 1999: 2). NGOs, too, are divided. Some major international groups worry about their influence being diluted by an influx of new, smaller NGOs. The latter tend to view the older NGOs as a privileged elite, while the UN Secretariat is cognizant of the need to control finances and streamline procedures (Alger 2002).

### UN Agencies

The UN's nineteen specialized agencies, each with its own member states, secretariat, headquarters, and budget, provide additional access points for NGOs. In some cases, they have a longer history of involving NGOs. In the ILO, for example, representation of labor groups was institutionalized in the unique tripartite system from the very beginning, as discussed in Chapter 3. UNESCO's constitution calls for "consultation and cooperation with NGOs," and its scientific, educational, and cultural interchanges involve over 300 international NGOs. In general, NGO participation depends on the aims of the agency. The broader its functions in the social areas, the broader and deeper the NGO participation; the narrower and more technical its tasks, the fewer the number of NGOs involved.

Most UN agencies with field programs and offices, particularly in the areas of humanitarian relief and economic development, now contract with NGOs to provide services and frequently involve NGOs in decisionmaking. Their involvement has been particularly apparent in the activities of the UN High Commissioner for Refugees since the early 1990s in the many complex emergencies from Somalia and Rwanda to the Democratic Republic of Congo, Syria, and South Sudan. Services, including food and medicine, are purchased by the UNHCR and the World Food Programme and delivered to the local population by CARE, Doctors Without Borders, and Oxfam, among others. The WFP, for example, maintains a working relationship with over 2,800 NGOs.

The main coalitions of humanitarian NGOs—InterAction, the International Council of Voluntary Agencies, and the Steering Committee for Humanitarian Response, along with the ICRC and International Federation of the Red Cross and Red Crescent Societies—serve with the Inter-Agency Standing Committee. This committee is chaired by the Undersecretary-General for Humanitarian Affairs and Emergency Relief Coordination, who, together with the UN High Commissioner for Refugees, also meets regularly in New York and Geneva with the main operational NGOs in the field (CARE, the International Rescue Committee, World Vision, Doctors Without Borders, Oxfam, etc.), because they depend on the talent, resources, and flexibility of the major NGOs to address crises. These same organizations have become sufficiently important that they command ready access to the UN Secretary-General as well.

In the area of humanitarian assistance the ICRC plays a unique role due to its responsibilities as guarantor of international humanitarian principles. Most critical to understanding this culture is the commitment to neutrality, impartiality, and independence. The organization takes no position on conflicts in which help is given. Because the ICRC maintains neutrality, aid can be delivered in an impartial and independent way. Thus the duty of the ICRC is to act and aid all parties, protecting those injured in war and prisoners of war and providing emergency aid to civilian victims of war. Generally, the ICRC, unlike other NGOs, works quietly, refusing to publicly condemn or call attention to violations of humanitarian law. Occasionally, however, individuals in the ICRC have exposed abuses, such as in Bosnia and Iraq, through leaks to other NGOs or to the press. In the 2009 conflict in Gaza, however, the ICRC took the unusual step of publicly criticizing the Israeli military for failing to meet its obligations to wounded civilians. In 2010 it called the Israeli blockade of Gaza a violation of the Geneva Conventions, and in 2014 it denounced the killing of civilians, including two Red Cross workers, and the Israeli bombing of a hospital. Even though the largest proportion of ICRC funding (80–90 percent) comes directly from a few key states, all contributing states agree not to attach conditions to these funds, and no funds are earmarked for specific causes (Forsythe 2005).

There are often major tensions, however, in UN-NGO efforts to deal with the chaos of complex humanitarian emergencies. They bring different mandates and competencies to the relief efforts; they compete with each other for scarce donor government resources; they serve different constituencies; and they measure success in different ways. NGOs work with fewer inhibitions about state sovereignty, governmental approval, and strategic coherence than do UN agencies that depend on governmental support. UN agencies, however, lack grassroots links and sufficient staff to carry out operations in remote areas, hence the recent efforts to enhance operational coordination.

Similar involvement with NGOs occurs in development. Since the UN Development Programme adopted a focus on sustainable development in 1989, participatory community development, an essential part of that agenda, has utilized NGOs as conduits to local communities, drawing on them for assessments of local needs and subcontracting with them to deliver services. Actual results, measured by contacts with community associations and indigenous NGOs, have varied from country to country and program to program.

One extensive study of NGOs in the FAO (McKeon 2009) reminds us that NGOs do not speak as a united group. There are conflicts between NGOs and not-for-profit groups like agribusiness associations, between larger and local NGOs, and between traditional NGOs and growing social movements. The study also finds that while NGOs have played a key role in helping to frame food as a basic human right, their presence in technical committees and commissions, where the bulk of decisionmaking takes place, is "scanty and discontinuous" (McKeon 2009: 30). This has led one civil society participant to question: "We are being listened to but are we being heard?" (quoted in McKeon 2009: 132).

### The Major Economic Institutions
The explosion of NGO activity and the pressure for access are particularly well publicized in the major international economic organizations within the UN system. None of the Bretton Woods institutions, when established, included any provisions for NGO participation, not even for any advisory role. Over time, however, changes in rules and practices pushed by the NGOs themselves have contributed to greater involvement of NGOs, networks, and actors in partnerships.

Some economic organizations have been more open than others, especially in particular policy fields. In the late 1970s, women's and environmental NGOs began to lobby the World Bank, pushing for a women-in-development agenda and a procedure to conduct environmental impact assessments on prospective projects. The Bank responded by establishing the post of adviser on women in 1977 and an environment department in 1987. Environmental groups have targeted campaigns against specific Bank projects such as big dams; they have cultivated formal and informal contacts with Bank staff; they have honed their research and hence the expertise they bring to discussions of environmental issues; and they have utilized national and international networks in their efforts to achieve Bank reform (O'Brien et al. 2000: 128–130). The NGO task became easier when the Bank itself increased public access to its documents through the NGO-created Bank Information Center and a joint NGO-Bank committee that facilitates access to senior Bank staff.

Since 1994, when the World Bank shifted emphasis to participatory development approaches, it has provided legitimacy to NGO involvement, seeing collaboration with NGOs as a way to improve its efficiency as a development agency, as described in Chapter 9. The shift in the Bank's approach was part of a broader shift toward civil society empowerment among multilateral development agencies in the 1980s that NGOs helped bring about. The reason, as one observer noted, is that NGOs "are perceived to be able to do something that national governments cannot or will not do" (quoted in Stiles 1998: 201). The regional development banks, also described in Chapter 9, have tended to follow the World Bank's lead with respect to NGO links. One result of the banks' opening to NGO participation, however, is that they now face escalating demands for more NGO participation in policymaking, since NGOs claim they better represent grassroots movements and organizations, even in countries with elected governments (Casaburi et al. 2000).

In contrast, the IMF has been very slow to provide formal access for NGOs, since its specialized focus on monetary policy does not lend itself easily to NGO input and finance is generally considered to be a more sovereignty-sensitive area. Yet during the 1990s, under intense pressure resulting from the debt crisis, the IMF expanded relations with civil society groups, including business associations, academic institutes, trade unions, NGOs, and religious groups. The success of Jubilee 2000, a popular movement in the 1990s that advocated debt cancellation, in getting the IMF and other lenders to support debt reduction for the most heavily indebted developing countries, was illustrative of the shift

Outside the UN system at present, but crucial to international economic governance and of intense concern to many environmental NGOs, labor unions, NGOs concerned with economic justice, and activists involved in the backlash against globalization, is the World Trade Organization. GATT, the WTO's predecessor, did not establish any formal links with NGOs, and a "culture of secrecy" dominated multilateral trade negotiations. The 1995 agreement establishing the WTO, however, did empower the General Council to "make appropriate arrangements for consultation and cooperation with nongovernmental organisations concerned with matters related to those of the WTO" (Article v.2). Likewise, Article 13.2 permitted dispute settlement panels to seek information from "any relevant source" and to consult experts.

As a result of these constitutional provisions and a 1996 decision, the WTO Secretariat has primary responsibility for relations with NGOs. This has been pursued thus far in two ways: through regular secretariat briefings for NGOs and through symposia with NGO representatives. In addition, the WTO's General Council agreed to provide information on WTO policymaking and to circulate most documents as unrestricted. What the WTO has not done, however, is to grant NGOs any form of consultative status, and this has been one reason for the confrontational relationship with NGOs described in Chapter 8. The WTO's ambivalence regarding NGO participation was exacerbated by what officials perceived as the lawlessness surrounding the Seattle trade meetings in 1999, when thousands of protesters were able to directly confront delegates. The next ministerial meeting was held in Qatar, an autocratic state located on the Arabian peninsula where protests could be contained. Another explanation is that the most vocal NGOs espouse ideas that challenge liberal economic theory. Hence, what they seek is not just participation in the WTO (and other major economic organizations) or greater accountability procedures, but sometimes radical changes in institutional structures, policies, and programs. Because of the resurgence of economic liberalism in the 1990s, the WTO and other economic institutions have resisted major changes in approach, fueling antiglobalization sentiments. Chapter 8 describes in detail the accommodations that have been made. Despite this ambivalence regarding NGO participation, many have contributed to setting the WTO's agenda, especially with respect to topics of importance to developing counties that receive relatively little attention (Murphy 2010).

### NGO Participation in UN-Sponsored Global Conferences

How NGOs participate in global conferences has expanded over time, with a general pattern emerging. Before most conferences begin, NGOs undertake considerable publicity and agenda-setting activities. For example, prior to the first UN Special Session on Disarmament in 1978, NGOs organized meetings and activities, especially through churches, to engage the public in debate; they published materials to increase public awareness of disarmament issues; some groups initiated protest activities in the United States, Canada, Western Europe, and Japan to pressure governments; and a Washington, DC–based network of forty US groups tried to influence US policy by meeting with government officials and members of Congress, knowing how important US leadership would be. NGOs promoted transnational networking by convening the International NGO Conference on Disarmament in the spring of 1978, prior to the intergovernmental conference itself, with 500 representatives of eighty-five different international NGOs and over 200 national NGOs from forty-six different countries (Atwood 1997). Women's NGOs followed a similar strategy leading up to each of the four global women's conferences (1975, 1980, 1985, 1995). NGOs convened local, subregional, national, regional, and international meetings to discuss the issues, using the occasions to pressure national delegations and develop a global strategy. Such meetings formed a critical link with grassroots constituencies.

A variety of NGO activities have also taken place during the actual global conferences. For example, during the disarmament conferences, representatives from the NGO community organized sessions with official delegates; provided information in informal briefings to those who were not acquainted with the issues, particularly delegates from small and poor countries; and organized joint activities at the conferences. NGOs lobbied governments and also provided a variety of parallel activities for NGOs themselves, aimed at mobilizing public awareness about disarmament, establishing and strengthening NGO networks, and providing information and services to NGO participants. Although there was no parallel NGO forum during the 1978 disarmament conference, parallel conferences became the norm for conferences during the 1990s.

The activity of NGOs in the disarmament discussions established precedents that were followed in the subsequent women's conferences and those on human rights and the environment. NGO activity proved particularly significant in connection with the 1992 UN Conference on the Environment and Development, held in Rio de Janeiro; the 1994 International Conference on Population and Development, held in Cairo; and the 1995 Fourth World Conference on Women, held in Beijing. Sometimes, individuals from NGOs have been included on government delegations to a conference. In some cases, this was done with the understanding that the individual's role was to advise the government, but not to conduct negotiations without government instruction; in other cases, individuals were free to represent their NGO and to conduct negotiations. For the 1994 Cairo Conference, for example, governments were urged to include NGOs on their delegations. Many would argue that this NGO activity represents the "democratization" of international relations by promoting the involvement of ordinary people in addressing global issues and the nascence of a global civil society.

The impact of NGOs on the substantive outcomes of global conferences is difficult to measure. One comparative study of six global conferences during the 1990s found that the relative impact of the NGOs depended on whether the conference agenda was linked to sovereignty issues, noting that "the more states link conference topics to sovereignty issues, the less ready states were to permit the open contestation and mutual accountability at the UN conferences" (Friedman, Hochstetler, and Clark 2005: 130). At three of the conferences (1992, Environment and Development; 1993, Human Rights; 1995, Women), states were less willing to relinquish autonomy and sovereign control to societal actors like NGOs. At three other conferences (1994, Population and Development; 1995, Social Development; 1996, Human Settlements), NGO participation did not threaten state sovereignty and hence states permitted a greater role for NGOs. In general, the research found that "states only provisionally accepted NGOs' contributions to UN conference processes. They stood firm on their claims to ultimate sovereignty over the issues that most affect their ability to control the distribution of power and resources, whether at home or abroad. When NGOs sought to engage states, many states seemed to respond by calculating their interests rather than by cultivating an intimate and ongoing relationship with NGOs" (Friedman, Hochstetler, and Clark 2005: 162).

Analyzing formal nonstate access to IGOs does not answer some critical questions. Do these actors actually participate? Which actors are most effective in influencing policy and in their other roles? Why? Not all NGOs are created equal; they vary as widely as states in their size, capabilities, experience, and interests. And, as with world politics itself, NGOs based in the global North tend to be more active and potentially influential than those from the global South.

## NGO Influence and Effectiveness

Social scientists face a major challenge in tracing, substantiating, and measuring the influence and effectiveness of NGOs and other nonstate actors. The sheer numbers and diversity of groups pose challenges for systematic data-gathering and for evaluating influence and effectiveness. There is also the normative challenge of maintaining distance from the views of NGOs themselves, which often claim greater influence than may in fact be the case.

### NGO Influence

Nonstate actors lack the types of power traditionally associated with influence in international politics. They do not have military or police forces, like governments, and they tend to have only limited economic resources, unlike governments and MNCs. Instead, they must rely on soft power and the willingness of states and international bureaucrats to grant them access. For advocacy groups, key resources are credible information, expertise, and moral authority that enable them to get governments, business leaders, and publics to listen, recalculate their interests, and act. For operational or service groups, this means having organizational resources such as flexibility to move staff rapidly to crisis areas and strong donor bases, or links with grassroots groups that enable them to operate effectively in often remote regions of developing countries. For all types of NGOs, influence depends a great deal on their flexibility in employing a variety of tactics and strategies. In short, to be influential, NGOs must think strategically about how they operate, their choice of venue and strategy, the coalitions they form, the networks to which they are attached, the issues they pursue, and their use of resources. Figure 6.3 illustrates the multiple routes for NGO influence. Yet measuring influence is always problematic. NGO influence can be systematically traced in particular organizational settings. Michele Betsill and Elisabeth Corell (2008), for example, present an analytical framework for assessing the influence of NGO diplomats in international environmental organizations. Did NGOs influence the negotiation of a text? Were they able to change agendas? What did NGOs do to influence the position of key actors? What role did they play in influencing the negotiating outcome in terms of procedures or substance? Focusing on NGO roles in negotiations, however, does not answer other key questions. Did NGOs' actions result in a change in governmental policy? A change in IGO programs? A change in the actual behavior of states, international institutions, and corporations? Since NGOs are active in many different arenas, this makes measuring their influence all the more difficult to chart. There may be many explanations for changes in policy and behavior besides the influence of nonstate actors.

NGOs' influence can be measured in part by the expansion of the scope of activities and by the increase in numbers of NGOs. These trends vastly expand the potential reach of transnational networks, the mobilization potential of advocacy campaigns, and the monitoring and implementation capabilities of NGOs. Another measure of certain NGO and other NSA influence is their increasing international recognition, as exemplified by the Nobel Peace Prize. Over the past century, the Nobel Peace Prize has been awarded to nonstate actors on eleven occasions: the Institut de Droit International (1904), the Red Cross (1917, 1944, 1963), Amnesty International (1977), International Physicians for the Prevention of Nuclear War (1985), the International Campaign to Ban Landmines (1997), Doctors Without Borders (1999), Wangari Maathai for the Green Belt Movement (2004),

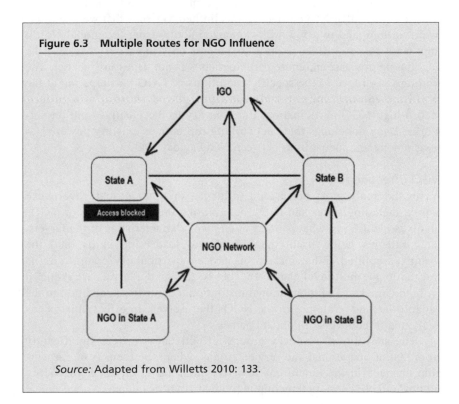

**Figure 6.3   Multiple Routes for NGO Influence**

*Source:* Adapted from Willetts 2010: 133.

Muhammad Yunus and the Grameen Bank (2006), and the Intergovernmental Panel on Climate Change (2007). The prize brings critical attention to the organization and its cause more generally.

There is also the possibility that NGO influence may be cyclical and time-dependent. During the period between 1850 and 1914, NGO roles in global governance continuously increased, then fell during World War I, only to rise significantly during the 1920s, and decline again in the 1930s and early 1940s. Their influence in global governance rose again after World War II, leveled off in the 1950s, began to rise in the 1960s, and surged in the 1990s. There is no assurance, however, that this influence will continue this upward trajectory. One study suggests that there are two key variables influencing the cycle: the needs of governments and the capabilities of NGOs (Charnovitz 1997: 268–270).

Finally, in analyzing NGO influence, it may be important to consider the questions of whose influence is at play, what is influenced, and whether NGO participation is inherently good. Charlotte Dany (2014: 425) charts what she terms the "Janus-faced" nature of NGO participation—that is, its good and bad effects. Focusing on the World Summit on the Information Society (WSIS), which took place in two phases, in 2003 and 2005, her research shows that NGO influence was limited to issues that were less relevant to them and to a few well-organized actors from the global North; they were able to influence draft documents only in earlier phases of the negotiating process; and more participation was not necessarily better. The findings are traced to the specific conditions of NGO participation at the WSIS and internal and external constraints placed on what was, in fact, record-high NGO participation. But contrary to the positive spin on networks, Dany concludes that "networking reproduces existing power relations among and inequalities between NGO actors" (433).

## NGO Effectiveness

As in the analysis of power and influence of other global governance actors, including states and IGOs, determining the effectiveness of NGOs involves identifying what is being attempted, characteristics of the targets, the strategies being used, managerial and leadership skills, and the resources applied. What makes this process particularly complex is its transnational, multilevel character. That is, data and analysis are required on both domestic and international institutional contexts, in addition to the capabilities and strategies of the NGOs themselves. In effect, this means analyzing three levels of political games.

The analysis of advocacy groups' effectiveness differs significantly from that of operational and service groups, where the focus is on measurable changes in the conditions toward which aid is directed. Advocacy groups' effectiveness in targeting individual countries depends a great deal on the "characteristics of the targets and especially their vulnerability to both material and moral leverage" (Keck and Sikkink 1998: 207). If a country cares a great deal about its international image, it may be sensitive to external or transnational pressure. The openness of domestic institutions in countries targeted by advocacy campaigns will affect NGOs' leverage, channels for exercising influence, and potential effectiveness, as will the strength of domestic civil society. It was harder, for example, for NGOs to halt construction of the Three Gorges Dam in China, where civil society is weak, than the Narmada Dam in India, where civil society is strong. Likewise, as we have seen earlier, the openness of IGOs to NGO access and participation will be a significant variable in their ability to exercise influence.

Most critically, NGOs' effectiveness must be measured by their impact on people and problems over the long term. It is not enough to get declarations approved, plans adopted, organizations formed, or treaties signed, although those can be major accomplishments. The ultimate measures of NGOs' effectiveness and influence lie in the difference they have been shown to make in the problems they claim to address. Was a humanitarian crisis alleviated? Did development aid channeled through NGOs improve the well-being of individuals? Have the efforts of climate change proponents been successful in reducing greenhouse-gas emissions? These are some of the questions addressed in subsequent chapters, where both the influence and the effectiveness of IGOs and NGOs are examined.

### Limits on NGO Influence and Effectiveness

In terms of size, resources, power, and legitimacy, NGOs clearly cannot and should not replace states and IGOs. There are at least four significant limits on NGOs' influence and effectiveness. The first set of limits arises from the size and diversity of the NGO community. NGOs have no single agenda; those working within the same issue may have divergent, even competing agendas. During the 1980s, for example, the nuclear freeze movement was quite splintered. The US-based Nuclear Weapon Freeze Campaign focused on stopping the US-Soviet nuclear arms race, emphasizing that both sides should take action. In contrast, the European counterparts were most concerned with the planned deployment of weapons in Europe. They advocated unilateral action to prevent deployment. The failure of these groups to unite is one explanation for their limited impact during the 1980s (Cortright and Pagnucco 1997). During the women's conferences of the 1990s, NGOs pushing for women's rights faced pressures from religious groups or other NGOs supporting traditional family values and opposing birth control. Such pressures can, under certain circumstances, cancel each other out. Groups concerned with human trafficking have not succeeded in forming an effective network, unlike those groups focusing on violence against women. The fact is that groups can be found on almost any side of every issue, resulting in countervailing pressures, competition for influence, and decreased effectiveness.

The second set of limits arises out of the multilevel games in which NGOs must be effective to be successful. Whether they are working from the bottom up, from the grassroots level to the national, transnational, and global levels, or top down from lobbying IGOs to national and local constituencies, NGOs may fail to persuade key people at any one of these levels and find their influence limited. NGOs are especially restricted by governments that can impose unreasonable registration and reporting requirements. For NGOs operating in zones of conflict, the problems may be particularly acute. In the Syrian civil war, for example, both the government and the rebel groups have significantly hampered the delivery of humanitarian relief by the UNHCR, other international agencies, and NGOs. Failure to provide security and restrictions on NGO movement are both major impediments to NGO influence and effectiveness, with numerous NGO workers killed or abducted in the course of their duties.

Lack of funding is a third and significant limit on NGO influence and effectiveness. NGOs do not have the option of collecting taxes like states. If they take money from corporations or governments, they risk compromising their independence, their very identity as an organization, and their ability to "bite the hands that feed them" (Spiro 1996: 966). When 80 percent of CARE's funding comes from the US government, there are clear incentives for following government mandates. As the US government and other governments and IGOs have channeled more development and humanitarian assistance to NGOs, the latter have become much more dependent on this funding. Not only can public funding weaken NGO independence, but so also can private funding when external restrictions and conditions are imposed.

A fourth danger limiting NGOs is that they may become overly bureaucratized. While many NGOs began as loosely organized structures run by volunteer staff, they often now have professional staff. Both public and private donors increasingly want standardized procedures and templates to account for resources and to evaluate how efficiently projects have been carried out. Yet the very professionalization and standardization of NGO management may have unintended consequences, undermining flexibility, innovation, and responsiveness to the conditions on the ground, or causing NGOs to conceal information and engage in rent-seeking, to the exclusion of humanitarian principles or other normative concerns (Goodhand 2006: 144).

In short, for NGOs to have influence and be effective, they must be credible; they must take steps to ensure that they are believed. Failure to achieve credibility will diminish NGOs' influence and effectiveness. Peter

Gourevitch and David Lake (2012) propose a number of strategies for increasing credibility. These include promoting shared values, adopting autonomous governance structures, increasing transparency, and becoming more professional. They recommend that NGOs whose purpose is fact-checking and monitoring can actually enhance their credibility over time as NGO officials learn to work with multiple audiences.

## NGOs: A Love Affair Cooling?

The explosion in the number, activities, and success of nonstate actors, particularly NGOs, has led scholars to assert that the trend is "one of the most profound changes in global governance over recent decades" (Tallberg et al. 2013: 235). But Paul Wapner (2007: 85–86) and others question whether this love affair has started to wane.

The answer is yes. Volker Heins (2008: 41) describes NSAs as "benign parasites" that are "much like other political actors. They are self-interested entities engaged in advancing their own agendas. They are often nondemocratic, hierarchical groups concerned with their financial and publicly perceived longevity. Most are self-appointed, rather than representative, political agents."

With so many NGOs seeking subcontracts for humanitarian and development projects, each is forced to compete vigorously against others for funding. In their scramble to win short-term projects, they cut corners to maximize efficiency, jeopardizing both long-term project viability and normative goals (Cooley and Ron 2002). NGOs may also "aggressively market" themselves to be attractive to rich clients and patrons (Bob 2005). Worse yet, NGO field personnel have been accused of egregious misconduct. For example, over sixty-seven individuals from forty aid agencies were cited for distributing food in return for sexual favors in refugee camps during the civil war in Sierra Leone. The UNHCR and Save the Children, in turn, were accused of hiding the scope of the scandal (Smillie and Minear 2004: 38–41). In Haiti, an NGO was accused of kidnapping children and sending them out of the country for adoption, although it was later learned that many of the children were not orphaned. In short, NGOs sometimes behave (and misbehave) just like MNCs, IGOs, and states.

The activities of NSAs may lead to unintended results or even harmful outcomes (DeMars 2005). Peter Uvin (1998) makes the case that the development enterprise in Rwanda in the early 1990s, largely implemented by NGOs, had the unintended effect of establishing the structural conditions upon which the 1994 genocide was built. By ignoring the politics of the regime, NGOs were co-opted by the government, leading to devastating consequences. Following the genocide, the actions of the UNHCR and NGOs also had unintended and detrimental consequences. Fiona Terry

(2002: 2) reveals how the UN refugee camps run by NGOs, including Doctors Without Borders, actually protected many of the leaders and perpetrators of the genocide. Camp leaders were able to divert resources to finance further bloodshed. "In short, humanitarian aid, intended for the victims, strengthened the power of the very people who had caused the tragedy." Some NGOs, like the French chapter of Doctors Without Borders and the International Rescue Committee, withdrew their aid, contending that assistance could not be provided in such militarized conditions, while other NGOs, including other branches of Doctors Without Borders, decided to continue working in the camps to provide relief. The question is about what enhances long-term NGO viability—staying the course or withdrawing when humanitarian objectives are jeopardized.

The activities of NGOs may also lead to backlash in the policymaking community. The limits imposed on NGOs at the UN since 1998, the US-backed decision not to hold further global conferences, the opposition of many developing countries to hearing NGO representatives in UN human rights bodies, and the decision to hold the WTO 2001 ministerial meeting in Qatar, where NGO presence could be sharply limited, demonstrate that governments are skeptical about the motives and power of NGOs and that states retain the power to shut them out of international institutional decisionmaking forums, even if they have agreed to provide other types of access.

Still worse, backlash has arisen over NGOs taking over the role of states. In Haiti, for example, the government was pressured by donors to privatize many public activities following the 2010 earthquake, and NGOs moved in to provide such basic services as elementary education, emergency health services, and sanitation. As reported by analysts at the United States Institute of Peace, "the Haitian people have learned to look to NGOs, rather than the government, for provision of essential services. Funneling aid through NGOs perpetuated a cycle of low capacity, corruption and accountability among Haitian government institutions" (Kristoff and Panarelli 2010). The same concerns have been voiced about NGOs in Afghanistan.

NGOs increasingly work in conflict conditions, leading to the "NGO-ization of war" (DeMars 2005: 138). Warring states and parties such as militias and paramilitary groups include the operations of NGOs in their strategy. Thus, NGOs may be used as or have the unintended consequence of being "force multipliers" (Lischer 2007). Humanitarian NGOs are used to fulfill military and political goals by state funders, working in some cases along with soldiers, providing intelligence (such as in Afghanistan), or augmenting undermanned peacekeeping forces (such as in Darfur). The result, intended or not, is that humanitarian workers become military targets in need of security and, by being closely identified as surrogates, lose any semblance of neutrality or independence. NGOs, then, not only are dependent on the funds provided by governments, but also become identified with state policies.

## Representation, Transparency, and Accountability

The love affair with NGOs is being replaced by key questions. Whom do NGOs represent? Frequently, they claim to represent the "true" voice of broad groups of people—the poor, women, the elderly, children, unemployed persons, peasants, immigrant workers, the oppressed. Representativeness is something that elected governments claim as the basis of their legitimacy. Yet how can we be sure these groups are indeed NGOs' constituents? Often in the case of transnational networks or large international NGOs, it is an elite group based in a large Northern city that claims to speak on behalf of poor, disadvantaged people in another part of the world. This criticism is less valid than in the past, as NGOs and grassroots groups have proliferated in developing countries and Northern NGOs have learned to treat the latter more as partners, but it is still relevant, as many NGOs in developing countries depend on their Northern partners for funding and other organizational resources, and Northern NGOs still tend to have more organizational resources and capabilities than those in the South. The key question is whether those claiming to be represented actually have a voice and how they participate.

A further aspect of the representativeness issue is the reality that a handful of large international (Northern-based) NGOs dominate most issue areas. Eight major NGO federations, including CARE, Oxfam, World Vision, Doctors Without Borders, and Save the Children, control the majority of humanitarian relief funds. Since IGOs cannot be expected to grant consultative or participatory rights to all NGOs, how can the worth of a given NGO be determined? Should only the largest, most international, best-funded NGOs be chosen? What criteria, if any, should be used for selection on the basis of orientation or agenda? The UN's revised criteria permitting accreditation of local indigenous NGOs endeavor to respond to these questions and expand representativeness within the UN system.

Representativeness is one dimension of relative democratization; transparency is another. Openness of communication and information are key attributes of democratic institutions. Yet very few NGOs provide information about their personnel, operations, funding sources, and expenditures.

Should NGOs, then, be subject to the types of pressures that have been placed on governments by the World Bank and IMF to make their economic and fiscal policies more transparent, for example, or on corporations by governments and IGOs to be more open about their operations? Governments can, of course, require NGOs to report on funding and expenditures as part of their licensing requirements and as conditions for contracts.

NGOs can also regulate themselves and become more transparent to increase their credibility as contributors to global governance.

Both representativeness and transparency link to the question of NGOs' general accountability. NGOs and their networks tend to serve narrow mandates. They do not usually face trade-offs among issues in the same ways that governments do. This is what gives them freedom to pursue a campaign against landmines or human rights violations or whaling. Their leaderships generally enjoy a great deal of discretion in deciding what policies to pursue and in what way. Yet what are the safeguards besides their own moral integrity and the knowledge that if they get it wrong they lose some of their credibility? Are NGOs truly accountable to their constituencies and the people they claim to represent? Only if nonstate actors can be made accountable can they be perceived as legitimate and thus help to narrow the democratic deficit of global governance.

For several years in the mid-2000s, the nongovernmental organization One World Trust published annual reports comparing accountability of IGOs, NGOs, and MNCs. In general, these reports showed that IGOs are more accountable and more transparent than NGOs, while NGOs are more representative than either IGOs or MNCs. In each category, specific IGOs, NGOs, and MNCs bucked the dominant trends. One World Trust in 2011 published *Pathways to Accountability II*, its sixth major revision of the Global Accountability Framework, a more nuanced template for evaluation. Unfortunately, no empirical studies using this revised framework had been published as of 2014.

### Serving the Public Good?

Many NGOs do contribute positively to the global public good. The evidence lies in the success NGOs can claim in institutionalizing human rights norms, providing humanitarian relief, and promoting environmental protection and corporate good practices, as well as in alleviating poverty, disease, and malnutrition. Especially when compared to other types of service providers—firms, governments, and IGOs—NGOs and other private actors measure up fairly well. Most of the best-known NGOs do not expect payment from recipients (unlike firms); they do not allow ethnic/racial or gender bias to color their decisions (unlike many governments); and they are willing to work in almost any country under almost any conditions (unlike some IGOs that must abide by sanctions regimes). Not all are like Doctors Without Borders, whose volunteers are paid well below market rates, serve people suffering the most contagious diseases, and work in some of the most difficult conditions in the world. Yet we must be mindful of the dangers of broad generalization, both about the character of NGOs (not all "wear white hats") and about the scope of the problems they seek to alleviate. There are clear limits to their influence and effectiveness.

## State Sovereignty and Nonstate Actors' Influence

The proliferation of nonstate actors and their expanding influence across issue areas potentially affects state sovereignty, although IR theorists disagree on the extent. Many liberals argue that nonstate actors have become increasingly important. Although NGOs may represent a variety of contending interests, some liberals conclude that state sovereignty is being compromised, challenged, or even usurped by a nascent global civil society. Constructivists, too, recognize the key role of ideas and norms for which NGOs and other nonstate actors may be important sources and transmitters. And since they believe that states' interests are not fixed, constructivists consider that states may be influenced by actions of nonstate actors. The frontier between what is domestic and what is international has become increasingly blurred. As a result, Keck and Sikkink (1998: 212) note: "Sovereignty is eroded only in clearly delimited circumstances"—in particular issue areas—and states retain the ability to reassert control, albeit at a high price in some circumstances.

Other scholars do not see the proliferation and increasing power of NGOs as undermining state sovereignty. To some political realists, since NGOs hardly appear as viable international actors, they pose no threat to state sovereignty. Heins (2008: 102–104) even makes the argument that NGOs not only do not undermine state sovereignty, but also contribute to its resilience. Barnett (2011) notes that humanitarian agencies can often be paternalistic, offering their own version of right and wrong without regard to local culture and public opinion and creating dependency on their services rather than promoting self-reliance.

Yet while state and nonstate actors may have differentiated responsibilities, ultimately authority rests with states, as discussed in Chapter 1, and this is the essence of sovereignty. States remain central to global governance, no matter how much political authority is decentralized and power diffused among nonstate actors. We now turn to issues of peace and security, an exploration of which makes clear that states working through IGOs retain authority, although nonstate actors both on the dark side and as initiators of policy change have become increasingly important to global governance.

## Suggested Further Reading

Gourevitch, Peter A., and David A. Lake, eds. (2012) *The Credibility of Transnational NGOs: When Virtue Is Not Enough.* New York: Cambridge University Press.

Joachim, Jutta, and Birgit Locher, eds. (2008) *Transnational Activism in the UN and EU: A Comparative Study.* London: Routledge.

Keck, Margaret E., and Kathryn Sikkink. (1998) *Activists Beyond Borders: Advocacy Networks in International Politics.* Ithaca: Cornell University Press.

Reinalda, Bob, ed. (2011) *The Ashgate Research Companion to Non-State Actors.* Surrey: Ashgate.

Tallberg, Jonas, Thomas Sommerer, Theresa Squatrito, and Christer Jönsson. (2013) *The Opening Up of International Organizations: Transnational Access in Global Governance.* London: Cambridge University Press.

Willetts, Peter. (2010) *Non-Governmental Organizations in World Politics: The Construction of Global Governance.* London: Routledge.

Wong, Wendy. (2014) *Internal Affairs: How the Structure of NGOs Transforms Human Rights.* Ithaca: Cornell University Press.

## Internet Resources

Amnesty International: www.amnesty.org

CARE: www.care.org

Catholic Relief Services: www.crs.org

Conference of Non-Governmental Organizations in Consultative Status with the United Nations (CoNGO): www.ngocongo.org

Consultative Group on International Agricultural Research: www.cgiar.org

Doctors Without Borders: www.doctorswithoutborders.org

EarthAction: www.earthaction.org

Friends of the Animals: http://friendsofanimals.org

Greenpeace: www.greenpeace.org

International Campaign to Ban Landmines: www.icbl.org

International Chamber of Commerce: www.iccwbo.org

International Committee of the Red Cross: www.icrc.org

International Federation of Red Cross and Red Crescent Societies: www.ifrc.org

International Rescue Committee: www.rescue.org

International Save the Children Alliance: www.savethechildren.net

Interpol: www.interpol.com

IUCN–World Conservation Union: www.iucn.org

One World Trust: www.oneworldtrust.org

Oxfam: www.oxfaminternational.org

Roll Back Malaria Initiative (WHO): www.rbm.who.int

Save the Children Federation: www.savethechildren.org

Transparency International: www.transparency.org

Union of International Associations: www.uia.org

World Association for Disaster and Emergency Medicine: www.wadem.org

World Vision: www.worldvision.org

World Wide Fund for Nature: wwf.panda.org

# 7

# The Search for
# Peace and Security

## Case Study: Somalia as a Watershed

In 1991 and 1992, civil order in Somalia totally collapsed as warring clans seized control of different parts of the country. Widespread famine and chaos accompanied the fighting, forcing hundreds of thousands of civilians to the brink of starvation. Food was a vital political resource for the Somali warlords and a currency to pay the mercenary gangs who formed their militias. In November 1992, with as many as a thousand Somalis dying every day and three-fourths of Somalia's children under the age of five already dead, UN Secretary-General Boutros Boutros-Ghali informed the Security Council that the situation "had deteriorated beyond the point at which it is susceptible to the peacekeeping treatment. . . . The Security Council now has no alternative but to decide to adopt more forceful measures" (UN 1992: 2).

More than twenty years later, although Somalia has finally made some gains in establishing a national government and functioning economy, an African Union peacekeeping force of over 21,000 personnel from six African countries is still deployed in the country; conflict and drought-induced famine remain a threat, taking more than 200,000 lives in 2011–2012; more than 1 million Somalis are displaced within the country and almost 1 million are refugees in neighboring Uganda and Kenya. In addition, the al-Qaeda–linked terrorist group al-Shabab is still active in the country, has carried out bombings and raids in neighboring Uganda and Kenya, and is considered a threat to the United States because of its success in recruiting Somali Americans. Somalia, therefore, offers an excellent case study of contemporary threats to international peace and security and the governance dilemmas posed by the changing nature of armed conflicts, state failure, complex humanitarian crises, internationally linked terrorist groups, and the links between nonstate actors and criminal activities.

The UN was initially slow to react in 1992 because the Security Council assumed that it needed the consent of the Somali warlords to provide humanitarian assistance, as in traditional peacekeeping operations. A contingent of 500 lightly armed Pakistani peacekeeping troops, deployed in August 1992 as the UN Operation in Somalia (UNOSOM I) with a mandate to protect relief workers, proved totally inadequate for the task at hand.

On December 3, 1992, under Resolution 794, the Security Council authorized a large US-led military and humanitarian intervention that included 26,000 US troops—the Unified Task Force on Somalia (UNITAF), known to the American public as Operation Restore Hope. Its goal was to secure ports and airfields, protect relief shipments and workers, and assist humanitarian relief efforts. At this point, there were forty INGOs operating in Somalia, including the major relief groups. The UN Secretary-General also wanted UNITAF to impose a cease-fire and disarm the factions, but the outgoing George H. W. Bush and incoming Bill Clinton administrations would agree to commit US forces only to limited humanitarian tasks. US officials thought the Somali operation would be "an easy victory," but this misjudgment proved fatal. Their disagreement with UN officials over objectives complicated relations between the various UN contingents in Somalia.

Still, the US-led effort largely achieved its humanitarian objectives, supplying food to those in need and imposing a de facto cease-fire in areas of its deployment. Yet the larger tasks of peacemaking in Somalia remained unfulfilled. In 1993, as UNITAF was replaced by UNOSOM II—a smaller force lacking much of the heavy equipment and airpower the US had brought to Somalia—it was authorized to use force when disarming the warring factions, but that exposed the peacekeepers to increased risk as some of the militias—especially those led by General Mohamed Farah Aidid—resisted such efforts. After twenty-three Pakistani soldiers were killed in June 1993, UNOSOM II gave up any pretense of impartiality and targeted General Aidid for elimination. This converted the UN's role from neutral peacekeeper to active belligerent, putting UNOSOM "in the worst of all possible worlds . . . [and] made it one of the players in the conflict" (Conroy 1994: 12).

In October 1993, eighteen US soldiers were killed by Aidid's soldiers and the body of one was dragged through the streets of Mogadishu, leading to a public outcry in the United States that echoed unease in other countries over the UN's role in Somalia. This event inspired the book and movie *Blackhawk Down*. Nowhere else was the reaction as far-reaching, however, and little note was taken of the hundreds of dead Somalis. President Clinton announced that the US contingent would be strengthened temporarily, then withdrawn by March 1994. Peacekeeping operations in Haiti and Bosnia were also affected as the administration rethought its commitment to the UN, especially to operations that entailed risk of casualties. Six months later, in April 1994, the United States blocked any meaningful response by the Security Council to the unfolding genocide in Rwanda, unwilling even to contemplate another international intervention in a messy African civil conflict. In June 1994, President Clinton released Presidential Decision Directive 25, which sharply restricted the circumstances under which the United States would support UN peacekeeping operations.

UNOSOM generated considerable controversy (see Clarke and Herbst 1996). It began at the height of post–Cold War enthusiasm for UN peacekeeping, but because the United States wanted to keep the operation short, and was afraid to risk the lives of its soldiers, the Somali warlords gained leverage by targeting US and other UN forces. After the United States withdrew its troops in March 1994, it was only a matter of time before all UN forces were withdrawn. UN operations in Somalia ceased in March 1995, having succeeded in ending the famine but not in helping the Somalis to reestablish a national government or to end their internal strife.

In the late 1990s, there were several regional efforts to help the Somali warlords and clans negotiate an end to fighting and several attempts to set up a transitional government. Within Somalia, northern clans declared independence as the Republic of Somaliland and leaders in the northeast formed the self-governing Puntland State (neither was internationally recognized). Islamic courts and charities became increasingly active, seeking to establish an Islamic state in Somalia and, in the wake of the 9/11 attacks on the United States, drew US attention to Somalia as a possible haven for international terrorists. In 2006, heavy fighting between the Union of Islamic Courts (UIC) and clan militias supporting the transitional government then in place broke out. A mediation effort by the Arab League failed to achieve any agreement. Concerned about the UIC's alleged links to international terrorist groups, Ethiopia sent troops (with US backing, including air attacks) to force out the UIC and install a new transitional government, provoking violent resistance and rising militancy. The fighting also triggered major humanitarian and security crises, resulting in large-scale famine in 2008 and over a million displaced persons. And a branch of the UIC, al-Shabab, emerged to continue the fight against the transitional government and foreign forces, gaining control of much of southern Somalia by late 2008.

In 2007, the UN Security Council authorized an African Union peacekeeping operation (AMISOM) to protect the transitional government. The force was initially small (1,500) in anticipation that it would be replaced by a larger UN mission, but expanded significantly when that did not materialize. Its enlarged mandate included pushing al-Shabab out of southern Somalia, facilitating the peace process, helping local institutions take root, and offering free social services. The Security Council also authorized logistical support, including a UN support office and EU training mission to strengthen the Somali security forces. In late 2008, after pirates based in the Puntland region of Somalia became a major threat to shipping in the Gulf of Aden—a manifestation of continuing weak government—the UN Security Council authorized a multinational anti-piracy effort, as discussed later in the chapter.

The strengthened AMISOM forces along with newly trained Somali forces were able to greatly expand control of much of the country by 2012; a new federal parliament was established and elections for a new president were held in 2012 as well. In early 2013, the UN political mission for Somalia relocated to Mogadishu after seventeen years in Nairobi—a measure of the improved security. Although the piracy problem had diminished by 2013, al-Shabab attacked non-Muslims in neighboring Kenya and Ethiopia in 2014. Thus, Somalia's problems continue to threaten international peace and security and multifaceted efforts to address those problems and to consolidate peace within Somalia continue.

Somalia remains a symbol of a failed UN post–Cold War peacekeeping effort and offers a set of lessons, rightly or wrongly, for peacekeeping in situations of state failure, civil war, and complex humanitarian disaster. It is a critical case for understanding the dilemmas posed by the changing nature of armed conflicts after the Cold War's end; by complex humanitarian crises, state failure, and internationally linked terrorist groups in an era when human security is often seen as more important than state security; and by the international community's efforts to use a variety of governance approaches to address threats to peace and security.

## Wars as the Genesis for Security Governance

War historically has been *the* fundamental problem in international politics; it has also been a primary factor motivating the creation of IGOs, from the Concert of Europe in the nineteenth century to the League of Nations and the UN in the twentieth century. Underlying functionalist theory is the premise that getting states to work together in solving practical problems of international relations will build the conditions for enduring peace. International law was traditionally seen as providing the rules that would help create order in the relations among states, and international courts or arbitration procedures would provide the means to settle legal disputes peacefully. Hence, despite being the most destructive century in human history, the twentieth was also the century of developing various governance approaches for preventing war.

Yet the nature of wars and conflicts has changed in significant ways in the past seven decades, and concepts of security have also evolved. Studies of war have shown a sharp decrease in the incidence of interstate war (wars between two or more states) and none between major powers or advanced industrial countries since 1945. The primary ones since 1980 have been the Iran-Iraq War (1980–1988), the Ethiopia-Eritrea War (1999–2000), and the Russo-Georgia War (2008). In contrast, the number of intrastate (internal) armed conflicts rose dramatically from the mid-1950s to the mid-1990s, and declined thereafter (see Figure 7.1). This trend has resulted from struggles for self-determination, such as those of the Tamils in Sri Lanka and the Muslims in Indian-administered Kashmir; the collapse of weak states, as in Somalia; ethnic conflicts, as in the former Yugoslavia and Rwanda; and civil wars between governments and opposition groups, such as the north-south civil war in Sudan (1983–2005) and between Nigeria and Boko Haram (since 2009). Some civil wars, such as in the Democratic Republic of Congo (1996–2001) and Libya (since 2011), have been internationalized with intervention by other states in support of either the government or opposition groups. Although several major studies show a decline in the numbers of active conflicts of all types since the mid-1990s, armed conflicts remain a major problem (Backer and Huth 2014; Goldstein 2011; Human Security Report Project 2013).

A major question for researchers has been whether the downward trend in active conflicts indicates fewer new conflicts or greater effectiveness in

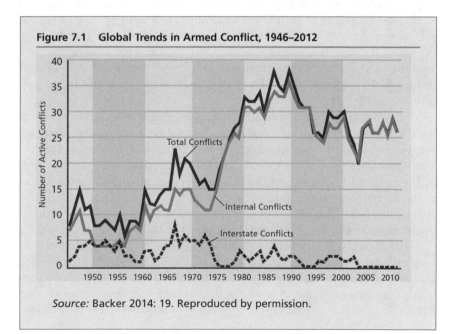

**Figure 7.1    Global Trends in Armed Conflict, 1946–2012**

*Source:* Backer 2014: 19. Reproduced by permission.

resolving old ones. In the 1990s and early 2000s, there was a surge in terminations, which led researchers to conclude that conflict resolution efforts had become more effective (Hewitt 2008: 24). Particularly troublesome now is the evidence of recurrences—that is, conflicts that are terminated or become inactive for a period of time, only to reignite—a problem that David Backer and Paul Huth (2014: 22) find greater than in the past, preventing a sustained downward trend. Still, research also shows a decline in the onset of new conflicts, which is encouraging, and a dramatic decline in deaths from war. A number of observers now note, however, the persistence of smaller-scale rebellions and insurgencies and the transformation of organized violence through links to transnational criminal networks, looting of resources as in Eastern Congo, and drug trafficking in many conflict areas. Thus, the World Bank's 2011 report noted the remaining forms of conflict and violence do not "fit neatly either into 'war,' or 'peace,' or into 'criminal violence,' or 'political violence'" (World Bank 2011b: 2).

Many post–Cold War intrastate conflicts have been accompanied by humanitarian disasters resulting from the fighting, from ethnic cleansing or genocide, from the collapse of governmental authority, and from famine and disease. Traditionally, security in the Westphalian system meant *state* security—the security of borders, control over population, and freedom from interference in the government's sovereignty over its internal affairs. With the body of internationally recognized human rights norms steadily expanding after World War II, the balance between the rights of sovereign states and the rights of people began to shift. Increasingly, it was argued that *human* security should take precedence over security of governments or states. This shift has provided support for the emerging norm of a responsibility to protect and legitimacy for armed intervention to protect human beings against the violence of governments, paramilitary forces, militias, and police.

The changing nature of conflicts and complex humanitarian disasters are two major challenges to peace in the twenty-first century. The others are weapons of mass destruction (chemical, biological, and nuclear) and terrorism. None are new. Efforts to deal with the former date to the earliest days of the League of Nations and the UN; efforts to deal with the latter began with the rise of international terrorism in the 1970s. Both gained new momentum with Iraq, North Korea, and Iran's defiance of international nuclear controls in the 1990s and the September 11, 2001, attacks.

The security governance approaches include many core elements of international law and organizations (see Figure 7.2). The UN provides the global structures for dealing with security issues, and the five major geographic regions each have at least one IGO dealing with security issues (see Figure 7.3). As Inis Claude (1964: 198) noted in his classic text *Swords Into*

*Plowshares:* "Collective approaches to peace must rest upon assumptions concerning the nature and causes of war. . . . [V]arious approaches to peace through international organization have been advocated, formulated, and attempted, each of them resting upon a distinctive conception of the nature of war and therefore emphasizing a correspondingly distinctive solution for the problem of war." In addition, many INGOs have long been active in trying to promote peaceful settlement of conflicts, disarmament, and humanitarian relief (see Figure 7.4).

---

**Figure 7.2   Security Governance Approaches**

- Global IGOs
- Norms on the use of force
- International conventions
- Regional security organizations
- Enforcement mechanisms
- Peaceful settlement mechanisms
- Peacekeeping
- Humanitarian intervention
- Peacebuilding

---

**Figure 7.3   Global and Regional Security IGOs and Related Entities**

*United Nations*

Security Council
General Assembly
Office of the Secretary-General
International Court of Justice
Comprehensive Test Ban Treaty Organization
High Commissioner for Refugees
International Atomic Energy Agency
Office for Coordination of Humanitarian Affairs
Organization for the Prohibition of Chemical Weapons
Department of Peacekeeping Operations
Peacebuilding Commission

*Regional IGO Venues for Security*

Africa: AU, ECOWAS, IGAD, SADC
Asia: ARF, ASEAN, SCO
Europe: EU, NATO, OSCE
Latin America: OAS
Middle East: Arab League, GCC

---

**Figure 7.4    Security-Related INGOs**

Peace Groups

---

Global Centre for the Responsibility to Protect
International Crisis Group
International Peace Institute
Stockholm International Peace Research Institute
Women's International League for Peace and Freedom

Disarmament Groups

---

Cluster Munition Coalition
Greenpeace
International Campaign to Ban Landmines
International Physicians for the Prevention of Nuclear War

Humanitarian Relief Groups

---

CARE
Catholic Relief Services
Doctors Without Borders
International Committee of the Red Cross
Lutheran World Federation
Oxfam
Save the Children Federation
World Vision

---

## IGOs and Security

The idea of a global organization to promote security among states was born in the early years of the twentieth century and promoted by prominent statesmen and peace groups during World Wars I and II. The history of these efforts is covered in Chapter 3. Particularly after World War I, large numbers of statesmen and citizens repudiated the conventional balance-of-power approach to dealing with international conflict—a sentiment that was reinforced by the outbreak of World War II.

Both the League of Nations and the UN reflected convictions that a permanent international organization made up of all peace-loving states could prevent future wars. The League of Nations Covenant and the UN Charter focused extensively on basic principles for preventing war, on mechanisms for peaceful settlement of disputes, and on provisions for enforcement actions. Both recognized the special prerogatives of major powers with respect to peace and security and the necessity of a small decisionmaking body with authority to take action on behalf of all members. A key difference was the League's requirement for unanimity among Council members, in contrast to the UN Security Council's requirement for a majority of the nonpermanent members, coupled with no opposition from any permanent member (the veto power).

Both the UN and the League of Nations were also based on the concept of collective security, articulated by US president Woodrow Wilson, as an alternative to the traditional balance-of-power politics that had frequently led to wars. Regional security arrangements established during the Cold War were either traditional alliances—formal or informal commitments for mutual aid in case of attack—or collective defense organizations, such as NATO, that involved more institutional development and commitments on the part of members. The ASEAN Regional Forum, established in the mid-1990s, represents a very different approach in its focus on confidence building and conflict prevention through increased communication, as discussed in Chapter 5. The EU's rapid reaction force has been deployed in several conflict areas since 2003. Both the Economic Community of West African States and the Southern African Development Community have taken on security obligations when the UN and OAU or AU have been unable to act. The Shanghai Cooperation Organization was established in part to address the growing threat of terrorism in Central Asia since 2000.

The UN Charter is clear that the Security Council has sole authority to authorize the use of force and to obligate member states to undertake sanctions, except in situations where states may exercise their right of individual or collective self-defense (Article 51). Although this opens the door for regional organizations to use force for collective defense and for the UN to utilize regional security agencies for enforcement action, Article 53 clearly states that "no enforcement action shall be taken under regional arrangements or by regional agencies without the authorization of the Security Council." Regional organizations are to inform the Security Council of any activities, planned or undertaken, to maintain international peace and security (Article 54). The NATO bombing of the former Yugoslavia and Kosovo in 1999 was not authorized by the Security Council, which contributed to the intense controversy over the legitimacy of those actions. Its 2011 involvement in Libya, discussed later, was indirectly authorized by the Security Council, although it too became controversial.

Although the UN Charter's provisions implied a sharing of responsibility between the UN and regional organizations, there was no clear division of labor. This only became important after the Cold War's end, when the UN undertook more peace operations than at any previous time and regional organizations took a number of initiatives to address the upsurge in violent conflicts. In 1992, Secretary-General Boutros Boutros-Ghali's *An Agenda for Peace* called for more regional action and cooperation with the UN to share the burden. Since then, there have been numerous cases of peacekeeping and enforcement activity by regional and subregional organizations, sometimes delegated under Security Council authorization, sometimes with retroactive approval, sometimes in collaboration or partnership, and sometimes transitioning to a UN operation. These are further discussed below.

The UN and regional IGOs utilize various governance approaches to peace and security problems. UN efforts have included different types of peaceful settlement approaches such as mediation and good offices; until after the Cold War, peacekeeping operations were largely used in lieu of enforcement; since 1990 the UN has undertaken many new peace operations with mandates ranging from enforcement to postconflict peacebuilding along with sanctions and other measures. The UN also has a long record in the field of disarmament and has been involved in efforts to address terrorism, primarily through establishing international law. ASEAN, the OAU/AU, and the OAS have frequently used preventive diplomacy and mediation. The Arab League, ECOWAS, the OAS, and the EU have all employed sanctions, while NATO, the AU, ECOWAS, SADC, and the EU have all undertaken peace operations. The ASEAN Regional Forum illustrates informal dialogue as an approach to security cooperation. The Shanghai Cooperation Organization has particularly focused on developing antiterrorism capabilities.

## NGOs and Security

Security-related INGOs vary considerably. Some are think tanks whose research aids other groups. For example, the Stockholm International Peace Research Institute (SIPRI) conducts research on conflict, arms transfers, and military budgets to inform understanding about conditions for a stable peace, while the International Peace Institute (IPI), in New York, specifically seeks to channel policy research and expert advice into the UN. The International Crisis Group (ICG), founded in 1995, has become a leading independent source of analysis and advice on conflict prevention and solution to governments and IGOs, including the UN and EU. Unlike SIPRI and the IPI, however, the ICG also seeks to mobilize effective international action. What distinguishes it from most advocacy organizations is its advocacy at the highest levels of government and IGOs, with key roles being played by prominent former government officials such as US senator George Mitchell, the ICG's first chair, who mediated the Northern Ireland settlement in the late 1990s; Gareth Evans, former foreign minister of Australia; and Louise Arbour, former UN High Commissioner for Human Rights. The ICG is based in Brussels, but has offices on five continents and its field staff cover situations of potential or actual conflict around the world. The group is particularly noted for its "crisis alerts," for advising peace negotiations, for its detailed analysis, and for its high-level advocacy with policymakers on preventing, managing, and resolving conflicts.

Some INGOs focus primarily on arms control and disarmament issues. Greenpeace, for example, has long been active in efforts to block nuclear testing and advocating the elimination of all nuclear weapons. The International Campaign to Ban Landmines and the Cluster Munition Coalition illustrate NGO advocacy coalitions that secured international arms control treaties. These efforts are discussed later in the chapter.

Other security-related INGOs are involved in humanitarian relief operations. The relief organizations listed in Figure 7.4 represent but a small proportion of the total number of relief-oriented NGOs. Among them, the ICRC has a unique status because of its special responsibilities under the Geneva Conventions for holding states accountable for violations of humanitarian law and for protecting and assisting military and civilian victims of conflict. It also has observer status in the UN General Assembly because of this unique role.

As Thomas Weiss and Ramesh Thakur (2010: 85) have noted: "Partnerships between state, intergovernmental, and nongovernmental actors have become the norm rather than the exception in preventing, managing, and resolving conflict. . . . '[G]ood' global governance does not imply exclusive policy jurisdiction by any one actor but rather a partnership among a variety of actors." This has become increasingly true across a range of governance issues, including threats to security.

## Norms Related to the Use of Force

From the dawn of history, leaders of tribes and nations have claimed the right and even duty to engage in large-scale organized violence as a last resort. Although during the Middle Ages some theologians sought to limit this resort to violence to specific situations and to restrain the levels and targets of violence, warfare was still considered acceptable and even noble. This all began to change in the early twentieth century.

*Outlawing war.* The Covenant of the League of Nations required member states to respect and preserve the territorial integrity and political independence of states and to try different methods of dispute settlement, but it contained no explicit prohibition on the use of force to settle disputes. In 1928, most states signed the Pact of Paris, also known as the Kellogg-Briand Pact, "to condemn recourse to war for the solution of international controversies, and renounce it as an instrument of national policy." This was the basis for Article 2 (sections 3 and 4) of the UN Charter, which obliged all members to settle disputes by peaceful means and "to refrain in their international relations from the threat or use of force against the territorial integrity or political independence of any state."

The reality is more complicated. The use of force for territorial annexation is now widely accepted as illegitimate: witness the broad condemnation of Iraq's invasion of Kuwait in 1990 and the large number of states that contributed to the US-led multilateral effort to reverse that occupation as well as the international condemnation of Russia's annexation of Crimea in 2014. The use of force in self-defense against armed attack is accepted and was the basis for the Security Council's authorization of US military action in Afghanistan after the September 2001 attacks. International norms prescribe, however, that the response must be proportional to the provocation—the basis for widespread condemnation of Israel's large-scale military responses in 2006, 2009, and 2014 to rockets fired by Hezbollah and Hamas from Lebanon and Gaza respectively. A large majority of states accept the legitimacy of using force to promote self-determination, to replace illegitimate regimes, and to correct past injustices. The UN Security Council refused in 2003 to authorize use of force against Iraq, leading the United States to form an ad hoc coalition for a preventive war to remove Saddam Hussein from power and to destroy the weapons of mass destruction that the US claimed Iraq still possessed. As discussed later in the chapter, the lack of agreement on a definition of terrorism complicates international efforts to create a norm outlawing terrorism.

*Promoting human security and humanitarianism.* There are a number of other important norms relating to the use of force that have emerged out of a century and a half of concern for the effects of war on people, particularly civilians, wounded soldiers, prisoners of war, and refugees. These include the humanitarian norms contained in the four 1949 Geneva Conventions, which have been ratified by 196 states, and their three additional protocols; international refugee law, particularly the 1951 UN Convention Relating to the Status of Refugees and its 1967 protocol; the taboos on the use of chemical and nuclear weapons; and certain other arms control treaties.

The Geneva Conventions form the core of international humanitarian law—designed to protect civilians, prisoners of war, and wounded soldiers as well as to ban particular methods of war (e.g., bombing hospitals). They also form the legal basis for war crimes. International refugee law, as discussed in Chapters 3 and 10, provides legal protection for those displaced across international frontiers. International human rights law, including the Universal Declaration of Human Rights, the International Covenant on Political and Civil Rights, and the conventions on torture, genocide, refugees, and children, together with the fundamental principle of nondiscrimination between peoples enshrined in Article 1 of the UN Charter, is the basis for crimes against humanity (see Figure 7.5). Both war crimes and crimes against humanity are also now spelled out in Articles 7 and 8 of the International Criminal Court's Rome Statute, along with genocide. Most of the norms regarding armed conflict apply only to interstate wars and to states, however, not to nonstate actors; only the second protocol to the Geneva Conventions applies to noninternational conflicts.

What constitutes war crimes, crimes against humanity, or acts of genocide has gradually expanded to include sexual violence and rape and targeting civilians more generally as tactics of war. In milestone actions in 2000

---

**Figure 7.5     Crimes Against Humanity (Rome Statute, Article 7)**

"Crime against humanity" means any of the following acts when committed as part of a widespread or systematic attack directed against any civilian population, with knowledge of the attack.

- Murder
- Extermination
- Enslavement
- Deportation or forcible transfer of population
- Imprisonment or other severe deprivation of physical liberty
- Torture
- Rape, sexual slavery, and forced prostitution, pregnancy, or sterilization
- Persecution of any group or collectivity based upon political, racial, national, ethnic, cultural, religious, or gender grounds
- Enforced disappearance of persons

---

and 2008, the Security Council mandated gender training in peacekeeping operations, protection of women and girls, and gender mainstreaming in the UN reporting and implementation systems relating to peace and security (Resolution 1325), and condemned sexual violence when used to deliberately target civilians in wartime (Resolution 1820). To promote the new norm, most peacekeeping operations now routinely include language on protection of civilians (POC) and on women and gender, designating gender advisers and gender-sensitive training programs (Hudson 2009).

The expansion of human rights and humanitarian norms has placed new demands on the UN, other IGOs, and international actors to curb abuses in the face of publicity by the media and global networks of NGOs of situations involving mass starvation, ethnic cleansing, genocide, gender-based violence, use of chemical weapons, and other atrocities. This has led to debate over humanitarian intervention, invoking differing views of state sovereignty and concerns about just cause and authority derived from the "just war" tradition. The Genocide Convention (1948) provides for the possibility of UN action under the Charter to prevent or suppress crimes against humanity. The International Criminal Court provides the means to prosecute those accused of crimes, as discussed in Chapter 10.

Military intervention to enforce compliance, however, is a different story. Although the Universal Declaration of Human Rights warns that people whose rights are violated may "be compelled to have recourse, as a last resort, to rebellion against tyranny and oppression," does large-scale human suffering justify the use of armed force to rescue others even in situations where governments may be the primary perpetrators?

Since the late 1990s, NGOs, civil society activists, prominent individuals, and an independent international commission have pushed for acceptance of national and international accountability, for using human rights norms to judge state conduct, and for new interpretations of sovereignty. With the failure of the UN and international community to halt the 1994 genocide in Rwanda and the controversy over NATO's 1999 intervention in Kosovo to halt large-scale ethnic cleansing by Serbian forces, UN Secretary-General Kofi Annan articulated his own views on how state sovereignty was being redefined in his 1999 address to the General Assembly. These developments, he said, "demand of us a willingness to think anew—about how the United Nations responds to the political, human rights and humanitarian crises affecting so much of the world" (Annan 1999). In 2000, Annan called for an effort to forge consensus on when intervention should occur, under whose authority, and how.

In response, the Canadian government established the independent International Commission on Intervention and State Sovereignty (ICISS). Led by former Australian foreign minister Gareth Evans and Mohamed Sahnoun of Algeria, the ICISS proposed six criteria for military intervention for human protection: right authority, just cause, right intention, last resort, proportional means, and reasonable prospects. The "threshold" criteria include "large scale loss of life, actual or apprehended, with genocidal intent or not, which is the product either of deliberate state action, or state neglect or inability to act, or a failed state situation; or large scale 'ethnic cleansing,' actual or apprehended, whether carried out by killing, forced expulsion, acts of terror or rape" (ICISS 2001: 32). The commission's report articulated the responsibility to protect (R2P) as an obligation of states and the international community and endorsed the Security Council as the only body with the authority to deal with intervention issues.

International law requires multiple cases to demonstrate the existence of a new customary practice. When new norms are emerging, there is often a period of conflict between advocates of the new and supporters of the old (Finnemore and Sikkink 1998; Sandholtz and Stiles 2009). If a large enough group of states is prepared to adopt the new, it will replace the old. Those violating the old norm can set in motion "norm cascades" that result in new norms replacing the old. But new norms usually do not replace the old without considerable debate. The debate over whether there is a norm of humanitarian intervention, therefore, is likely to persist for some time. Although the 2005 UN World Summit endorsed R2P, Security Council members never translated that into authorization for sufficient force to halt the genocide in Darfur (see Chapter 10) or ethnic cleansing bordering on genocide in South Sudan, for example. They did authorize action in Libya in 2011, but not in Syria, as discussed later. Some analysts are skeptical that the UN Security Council will authorize any humanitarian interventions in the future.

The debate over R2P has raised the issue of who can legitimately authorize humanitarian intervention, especially involving armed force, and has reinforced the view that only the UN Security Council has this authority. Given their colonial experiences, many Asian and African countries are skeptical about altruistic claims by Western countries. Along with Russia and China, they have insisted on Security Council authorization as a prerequisite to protect them against new forms of imperialism on the one hand and to preserve the principle of nonintervention on the other. As controversial as the norm of R2P may be, norms matter, as Ramesh Thakur (2006: 162) reminds us: "norms, not deterrence, have anathematized the use of nuclear weapons as unacceptable, immoral and possibly illegal under any circumstance—even for states that have assimilated them into military arsenals and integrated them into military commands and doctrines." The taboo on the use of nuclear weapons arose from nuclear weapons being defined as "disproportionately lethal" (Price and Tannenwald 1996: 138). It is matched by a similar norm and a ban on chemical weapons that evolved out of the Hague Declaration of 1899, which symbolically linked these weapons with "standards of civilized conduct" (Price and Tannenwald 1996: 131). More recently, norms have also been established to ban the manufacture, stockpiling, and use of other weapons that cause unnecessary human suffering, specifically biological weapons, antipersonnel landmines, and cluster munitions.

The norms on the use of force, humanitarian intervention, human security, and certain weapons are strongly influenced by different international relations theories.

## Linking International Relations Theories and Security Governance

International relations theorists differ sharply in their views of appropriate strategies for responding to the use of armed force and conflicts. Realists come in "hard" and "soft" varieties when dealing with threats of force, breaches of the peace, and conflict resolution. The "hard" variety hold firm to traditional realist views about states' likely use of force. They don't see many differences between the dynamics that give rise to interstate and intrastate conflicts. Security dilemmas affect parties to both. In realists' eyes, balance of power and force itself are key means of resolving conflicts. Hence, other states might deny arms to the stronger side of a conflict or provide them to the weaker side in an effort to create a balance of power. For realists, it is the great powers that dominate and govern the international system, and they reserve the right to decide if and when intervention should occur and by whom.

The "soft" variety of realists come closer to liberals in some respects, as they envisage a broader range of options and actors. Diplomacy and mediation are among the options that "soft" realists consider valuable for dealing with conflicts and use of force, in order to change parties' cost-benefit analyses in favor of peaceful settlement versus war. They also recognize the role of international organizations and states other than great powers as interveners.

Liberals have traditionally supported international law and organization as approaches to peace, and most kinds of security governance are based on liberal theory. Liberalism sees NGOs and IGOs, as well as individuals, states, and ad hoc groups, among the actors that may play roles as third parties in peaceful efforts to settle disputes, avert war, stop fighting once it has started, secure a negotiated settlement, and build conditions for lasting peace. Liberal democratic peace theory, discussed in Chapter 2, is a foundation for contemporary postconflict peacebuilding activities. Roland Paris (2004), for example, examines the theory's validity for peacebuilding in countries emerging from civil conflicts since 1990. Virginia Page Fortna (2004b) uses liberal cooperation theory to explain how the content of agreements shapes the durability of peace in the aftermath of war.

Since the mid-1990s, constructivism has contributed substantially to understanding the evolution and role of norms as well as to reconceptualizing security. Constructivists have examined how the norms on the use of force have changed and what groups should be protected (Finnemore 2003). They have showed how norms against specific weapons, most notably the taboos on the use of chemical and nuclear weapons, have evolved over time. Along similar lines, feminist theorists have called for rethinking traditional notions of security to include individuals and other sources of insecurity (Enloe 2004; Tickner 2001).

Contemporary radical thinkers also challenge the conceptualization of security by arguing that states and power elites often manipulate the concept in order to establish greater control over society and persuade citizens to make sacrifices. During the Cold War, the US and Soviet Union attempted to paint their ideological struggle as a fight for the soul of humankind, while the contemporary war on terror revives old notions of an existential fight between civilized nations and mysterious barbarians (Buzan and Waever 2009). On the other hand, NGOs and IGOs are attempting to redefine security in terms of human security, with important implications for the role of nonstate actors in advancing welfare and considerations of personal safety.

The rich literatures on interstate and civil wars as well as on conflict resolution, in sum, draw on multiple schools of thought, so there is no definitive theory setting forth clear conditions under which wars will occur or peace will be secured. Michael Doyle and Nicholas Sambanis (2006), for example, draw upon the extensive literature on civil wars and the political, economic, psychological, rational choice, and constructivist theories that explain their onset, duration, termination, and magnitude, as well as data on all civil wars since 1945, to examine the implications of the theories for UN intervention. The contextual factors shaping human choices—the choice for war and the choice to settle a dispute peacefully—defy tidy theorizing. In short, we know a lot about both, but not enough to lay out a formula for governance.

## Mechanisms for the Peaceful Settlement of Disputes

The broadest category of security governance approaches is also the oldest. As early as the Greek city-states, there was agreement about the desirability of settling disputes peacefully. The 1899 and 1908 Hague Conferences produced the Conventions for the Pacific Settlement of International Disputes, laying the foundations for mechanisms still in use today. These assume that war is a deliberate choice for settling a dispute and that it is possible to create mechanisms to influence actors' choices. For example, one assumption is that war can result from ignorance and that providing information through an independent commission of inquiry can change the choice. Another assumption is that states often get themselves into "dead-end streets" from which a third party mediator can help them escape. The Hague Conventions established the international community's stake in preventing war. They created mechanisms for third-party roles, variously labeled good offices, inquiry, mediation, conciliation, adjudication, and arbitration, which were incorporated into the League of Nations Covenant and Chapter VI of the UN Charter. The latter specifies a sequence of ways the Security Council can promote peaceful settlement of disputes, from inquiry to mediation.

The involvement of the UN, regional IGOs, NGOs, individuals, states or coalitions of states, or ad hoc groups in efforts to find a peaceful settlement of a conflict is a third-party intervention. UN Secretaries-General have often offered their "good offices" for peacemaking initiatives, with or without a Security Council mandate. Such efforts can range from simply getting the parties together, to actual mediation by either the Secretary-General or a designated special representative. Similar roles have been undertaken on occasion by officials of the EU, OAS, and OAU/AU. Some high-profile, long-running situations such as the Arab-Israeli-Palestinian conflict generate multiple third-party efforts over time. Sometimes those efforts occur sequentially; sometimes they are simultaneous; but they are often messy and rife with questions of who does what, when, and where.

The use of peaceful settlement mechanisms, however, does not necessarily mean no use of armed force. Force can be critical to securing a peaceful outcome in some situations, helping to change the perceptions of the parties regarding the costs and benefits of continued fighting. Cutting off the supply of money and arms, or engineering a change of leadership particularly in a civil war, may also lead to a peaceful settlement as the costs and benefits are recalculated. Every situation is unique.

Determining who can most effectively intervene, what means are required, and what political goals should be set are key issues. And what constitutes success? Is it a permanent end to a conflict (Liberia's civil war); a freeze on active fighting (stalemate in Cyprus); a short- to medium-term end to violence (independence for South Sudan); getting parties who previously would not speak to each other to meet face-to-face (Israeli-Palestinian Oslo peace process); or building the foundations for long-term peace (Kosovo, East Timor, and Burundi)? Many answers to the who, what, and when questions depend upon the stage of the conflict at which intervention occurs. Trying to deal with a conflict situation before the level of armed violence escalates rapidly can be very different from trying to find a peaceful solution to a conflict with high levels of violence that has been ongoing. Long-standing, intractable conflicts (Kashmir, Northern Ireland, Cyprus) seem to defy many efforts at peaceful settlement; some conflicts, such as Somalia in the late 1990s, become orphans when outsiders lose interest; others, such as that between the Tamil Tigers and the government of Sri Lanka, get neglected or forgotten by the international community (Crocker, Hampson, and Aall 2004).

Since the explosion of conflicts and peacemaking initiatives following the Cold War's end, there have been a number of systematic efforts by scholars and practitioners to study and draw lessons (Crocker, Hampson, and Aall 1999, 2004, 2011; Stedman, Rothchild, and Cousens 2002). The result is more consensus among scholars and practitioners about the requirements for successful third-party intervention, preventing or ending war, and getting parties to conflicts to implement peace agreements, although there are many conclusions about conditions that may contribute to success or failure.

## Mediation

Mediation is a key tool for peaceful settlement of disputes—"a mode of negotiation in which a third party helps the parties find a solution which they cannot find by themselves" (Zartman and Touval 1996: 446). It may involve persuading the parties to accept mediation in the first place or include multiple mediators over time, for different phases of a conflict, and a search for settlement. For mediation to have a chance, a conflict must be at what is called a "hurting stalemate" or "ripeness" stage, when parties see the costs of continuing the conflict as greater than the benefits of doing so and hence are more willing to consider some form of settlement.

Mediators can come from a single powerful state such as the United States, a middle power such as Norway or Canada, an ad hoc group of states, an IGO, or an NGO; occasionally, they may be prominent individuals acting on their own, such as former US president Jimmy Carter. "Multiparty mediations" involve multiple mediators simultaneously or sequentially, such as in Middle East peace efforts over the years by the UN, EU, United States, Egypt, the Quartet, and nongovernmental groups. To be effective, the mediator has to make a coherent whole out of multiple initiatives of individuals, states, and organizations, build on earlier efforts, and move the process forward.

A mediator may play a variety of roles: organizer, educator, visionary, interpreter, conciliator, provocateur, risk-taker, catalyst for change, and policymaker (Crocker, Hampson, and Aall 1999: 686). Even without political power or economic resources, a nonofficial mediator such as former president Carter or the nongovernmental Centre for Humanitarian Dialogue in Geneva can be helpful in the early pre-negotiation phase of a peace process in bringing parties together, especially if there is a nonstate armed actor involved (Whitfield 2007: 42). Some situations, however, call for "mediation with muscle," such as only the United States can provide for settling the Israeli-Palestinian conflict (Hampson 2001: 400), by providing both incentives and assurances for formal settlements.

Relationships matter, including relationships of trust with the parties to the conflict, with a sponsoring institution such as the UN, with a mediator's own government, and with other third parties (Kydd 2005). George Mitchell's 2009 appointment by US president Barack Obama as special envoy for the Middle East was initially welcomed by all parties because of the evenhandedness Mitchell had shown when he headed a fact-finding commission in the region in 2000–2001, his Lebanese ancestry, and his success in mediating the 1998 Northern Ireland Good Friday Agreement. Staying power also matters—that is, the ability and willingness to stick with the mediation process as long as necessary. Speaking of Mitchell's success in Ireland, for example, a former aide commented: "He's got this incredible patience to sit there until the deal is done. He deserves the iron trousers award" (quoted in Richter and Chu 2009).

Since 1988, a large number of conflicts have been ended at least temporarily through negotiation, many of them through mediation. This trend has encouraged still more efforts at mediation, even of intractable conflicts, by the UN and a host of other actors. Regional IGOs such as the OSCE, the OAS, ECOWAS, SADC, and the AU have developed their capacities to deal with internal conflicts in particular; Norway became involved in peacemaking in the Middle East, Sri Lanka, the Philippines, Guatemala, and Sudan; the Sant'Egidio Community, an Italian Catholic NGO, played an active role in the peacemaking and peacebuilding process in Mozambique, illustrating the mediating roles NGOs have played; Pope Francis was instrumental in negotiations between the United States and Cuba in 2014; and a number of ad hoc groups have formed to aid peacemaking efforts.

The first such ad hoc group was the Contact Group for Namibia, formed in 1978 by the United States, Canada, the United Kingdom, France, and Germany. It was able to negotiate an agreement for Namibia's independence from South Africa in part because of the relationships the countries had with the different parties, including the South West Africa People's Organization (SWAPO). The group was unable, however, to persuade South Africa to implement the agreement until more than a decade later (Karns 1987). The contact group idea was later adopted by two groups of Latin American countries to mediate in the Central American conflicts of the 1980s; it has been employed in a number of other situations since, including to address the problem of piracy off the coast of Somalia and the violence between pro-Russian separatists and the government in eastern Ukraine. In addition, numerous "friends" groups have formed to aid the UN Secretary-General in addressing conflicts in Haiti, Angola, Iraq, and elsewhere (Whitfield 2007). Since 2002, the Middle East Quartet, made up of senior UN, EU, US, and Russian officials, has endeavored to support the Israeli-Palestinian peace process.

Mediation does not work in all situations, even if the mediator is a good fit and skillful and even if the situation is thought to be "ripe." The global landscape is littered with failed attempts. But it has been one of a number of tools employed in recent years in efforts to prevent violent conflicts.

### Preventive Diplomacy

Preventive diplomacy has received significant attention since the publication in 1992 of *An Agenda for Peace,* in which then–UN Secretary-General Boutros Boutros-Ghali (1992: 45) defined preventive diplomacy as "action to prevent disputes from arising between parties, to prevent existing disputes from escalating into conflicts and to limit the spread of the latter when they occur." Most often, this takes the form of diplomatic efforts, sometimes coupled with sanctions of some sort. From late 1992 until 2001, however, the UN deployed a thousand peacekeeping troops to prevent the spread of violence from other regions of the former Yugoslavia into Macedonia—an important innovation.

The actors involved in preventive activities have proliferated greatly in recent years. The OSCE, OAS, ASEAN, AU, ECOWAS, GCC, and other regional organizations have all established regional prevention initiatives, with the AU's being particularly active. The UN itself has created three regional offices for preventive diplomacy, in Central Asia, West Africa, and Central Africa. NGOs have created the Global Partnership for the Prevention of Armed Conflict, for example, and a variety of other nongovernmental, private actors including local civil society groups are active in preventive activities. Also, as discussed earlier, the International Crisis Group has emerged as a key actor.

The tools for preventive activities include early warning, fact-finding missions, political missions, special envoys, early response systems, good offices, mediation, conciliation, and locally based "infrastructures for peace." Multilateral political missions are at the heart of the UN's preventive activities. In 2013, there were thirty-seven such missions, ranging from large ones in Iraq and Afghanistan to small ones in Nepal and Sierra Leone. The EU, AU, ECOWAS, OSCE, and OAS also have political missions in the field—all of them characterized by being largely civilian international officials and experts with a mandate to "foster sustainable political settlements." Some staff may focus on human rights or legal issues; others may be constitutional experts, while still others provide technical support for managing elections. These political missions have "a track record in helping fragile states avoid full-scale conflict—but they are typically support actors rather than the stars of conflict prevention. At all phases of the conflict cycle, missions can facilitate political processes, but they cannot do so if the potential parties to a conflict do not want their assistance" (Gowan 2011). In addition to political missions, the UN established the Standby Team of Mediation Experts in 2008, consisting of eight individuals experienced in mediation and peacebuilding who bring specialized skills such as expertise in natural resources, property rights, and constitution-making. The team is operated by the Norwegian Refugee Council and was deployed more than seventy times in 2012 to over thirty countries.

The nature of preventive diplomacy tends to vary with phases of the conflict cycle. In situations of latent tension such as in Eastern Europe and Central Asia following the Cold War's end, the OSCE has been active in helping to address issues of minority rights, particularly among ethnic Russians in newly independent former Soviet republics. Other actions may involve providing early warning of looming escalations in conflict as the OSCE did in Kyrgyzstan in 2010. The OSCE has played an active role in eastern Ukraine in monitoring violence between pro-Russian separatists and the government that began in 2014 and in efforts to secure a cease-fire. ECOWAS maintains offices in Burkina Faso, Gambia, Liberia, and Togo precisely for this same purpose (Gowan 2011). In situations of rising tension, active diplomacy such as that by the head of the UN's Regional Centre in Central Asia in cooperation with counterparts from the OSCE and EU helped the Kyrgyz government move beyond the 2010 interethnic violence thanks in part to their relationships with national and regional leaders that had been developed previously. When all-out conflict threatens, as it did in Kenya following presidential elections in 2007, intense, well-coordinated, and well-supported diplomatic efforts can still "save the day" as happened under the AU-mandated leadership of former UN Secretary-General Kofi Annan, whose mediation was supported by UN staff and advisers from the NGO Center for Humanitarian Dialogue (Gowan 2011).

Since preventive diplomacy is intended to change the calculus of parties regarding the purposes to be served by political violence and to deter them from choosing to escalate the level of conflict, it may be far easier to do early in a conflict, when the level of violence is low. It becomes increasingly difficult as violence grows. Studies have shown opportunities missed, for example, in Somalia, Bosnia, Rwanda, Kosovo, and Zaire in the 1990s (Sahnoun 1994; Jentleson 1999) as well as Syria, Sri Lanka, Darfur, and Côte d'Ivoire more recently (Hara 2011). The costs of failing, in terms of both lives and treasure, are high. One study estimated that had the United States and Europeans succeeded in preventing the Bosnian war, their costs would have been $33.3 billion, as opposed to the estimated $53.7 billion they spent on intervention (up to the Dayton Accords in 1995). The UN's preventive deployment in Macedonia cost $0.3 billion, compared with an estimated $15 billion had that conflict escalated to intermediate levels (Brown and Rosecrance 1999: 225). The World Bank (2011b: 5–6) calculated the costs of failing to prevent conflicts in economic and human terms. In countries with major violence between 1981 and 2005, the poverty rate was 21 percent higher than in countries without violence, and the average cost of civil war was thirty years of GDP growth for a midsize developing country, while trade levels have taken twenty years to recover after major episodes of violence. While males suffer a disproportionate number of casualties, the Bank reported, women and children make up 80 percent of refugees and internally displaced persons.

The UN has sought to increase its own capacity in early warning and preventive diplomacy since the mid-1990s. Both member states and UN officials have long been reluctant to provide the UN with intelligence-gathering capability, fearing that the UN's impartiality would be impaired. But in 2000, the high-level panel chaired by Lakhdar Brahimi recommended the enhancement of UN intelligence capabilities (UN 2000). In 2005, the Joint Mission Analysis Centre was created within the Department of Peacekeeping Operations (DPKO) and in 2007 and 2010 additional intelligence-gathering apparatus was established to provide more strategic-level analysis. Efforts continue to improve the UN's tools for preventive diplomacy and coordination with other actors. Ban Ki-moon noted, however, that "no matter how accurate the early warning, the real test is whether it leads to early action . . . the challenge the international community can find hardest to meet" (UN Secretary-General 2011).

### Adjudication and Arbitration

Two other tools for peaceful settlement—adjudication and arbitration—are legal in character and involve referring a dispute to an impartial third-party tribunal for a binding decision. These methods emphasize finding a basis for settlement in international law rather than in a political or diplomatic process or formula, but can be used only when states give their consent to submit a dispute and be bound by the outcome. The two differ in the permanence of the tribunals, the scope of their jurisdiction, and the extent to which parties can control the selection of arbitrators or judges.

Arbitration involves the settlement of disputes on the basis of certain legal criteria by individuals who are assigned to the task on an ad hoc basis, usually by the disputants themselves. Once the problem is resolved, the arbitrators are relieved of their duties. Arbitration dates back at least to the early Greek city-states. It was incorporated into the 1814 Treaty of Ghent between the United States and Great Britain and it was employed for settling the *Alabama* claims between the United States and Great Britain arising out of the US Civil War. The Hague Peace Conference of 1899 established the Permanent Court of Arbitration at The Hague, which is a list of potential international arbitrators—lawyers, judges, diplomats, academics, and former government officials. Arbitration panels can be composed of a single neutral individual such as the UNSG or a panel of three individuals (two of whom have been chosen by the parties, plus a neutral third member selected by agreement, or an impartial third party such as the president of the ICJ). Tribunals can have up to nine members, as in the case of the Iran-US Claims Tribunal, which has been working since 1981 to arbitrate several thousand claims arising out of the seizure of US hostages by Iran in 1979. The agreement between parties to resort to arbitration defines the issues to be decided, the method for selecting arbitrators, the machinery and procedures to be used, and how the expenses will be paid.

About 450 international arbitrations were conducted between 1800 and 1990 (Bilder 1997: 160). Somewhat surprisingly, the Permanent Court of Arbitration has handled a large number of cases in recent years, including both interstate cases and ones involving a state party and a private corporation. Among them are the border dispute between Ethiopia and Eritrea (2009), the Abyei disputed border region between Northern and Southern Sudan (2009), Chevron and Texaco versus Ecuador (2011), and the Bay of Bengal Maritime Boundary between India and Bangladesh (2014). The court is more active now than at any time in the past.

The ICJ and other international courts have one primary advantage over arbitral tribunals: they are already in existence and the international community pays the expenses of the proceedings. Distinguishing between legal or justiciable disputes and political or nonjusticiable disputes is a difficult task, however, and countries that wish to avoid adjudication will frequently protest that certain disputes are inherently inappropriate for adjudication. Iran made this argument in the case concerning US diplomatic and consular staff in the Tehran hostages case (ICJ Contentious Case 1980), as did the United States in the Nicaragua case (ICJ Contentious Cases 1984b, 1986), although neither claim was persuasive and the cases moved forward, as discussed later. There can also be significant questions regarding the ICJ's jurisdiction to hear a case. The court routinely holds initial hearings to determine whether both states have in fact consented, and whether it does in fact have jurisdiction. Sometimes, unwilling respondent states will refuse to appear before the court at all—as did France in a case brought against its nuclear testing by Australia and New Zealand (ICJ Contentious Case 1974), Iran in the Tehran hostages case, and the United States in the Nicaragua case.

The Nicaragua case illuminates the limitations on adjudication for dealing with peace and security issues. It arose out of the 1979 victory of the left-wing Sandinistas over longtime Nicaraguan dictator General Somosa, and US concerns about their ties to Cuba and the Soviet Union. In 1984, Nicaragua brought suit in the ICJ, charging that the United States was illegally using military force against it and intervening in its internal affairs. Because it involved one of the two superpowers, the case was closely watched by many less developed countries. The United States argued that the ICJ had no jurisdiction over the case. When the court determined that it did have jurisdiction, the United States announced it would not participate in the proceedings, withdrew its acceptance of the court's jurisdiction for any Central American case, and terminated its acceptance of the court's compulsory jurisdiction whereby states commit to participating in ICJ cases in advance.

The ICJ's 1986 ruling represented a stunning defeat for the United States and a moral victory for Nicaragua. The court found that the mining of Nicaragua's harbors, attacks on port installations, and support for the Contras infringed upon the prohibition against use of force. The justices rejected the US claim of collective self-defense on behalf of El Salvador. The court also found no basis in international law for a general right of intervention in support of an opposition to the government of another state, however just its cause might appear.

The case had little impact on the conflicts in Central America, but did lead to a significant increase in the ICJ's stock among developing countries. Thereafter, many accepted the ICJ's jurisdiction, withdrew previous reservations to ICJ jurisdiction, and brought cases before the court. The case reinforced suspicions in the United States about international institutions, yet the United States brought new cases to the court thereafter and participated in others, such as one brought by Libya after the United States tried to extradite two Libyan intelligence agents who were suspects in the bombing of Pan American Flight 103 over Lockerbie, Scotland.

States have used both adjudication and arbitration to resolve territorial and maritime boundary disputes, questions of river usage, and fishing zones. In fact, the numbers of territorial disputes submitted for both has increased greatly since the late 1990s. In 2014, six of the fourteen pending contentious cases on the ICJ's docket involved territorial disputes, including Costa Rica–Nicaragua (three cases), Bolivia-Chile, and Somalia-Kenya. What leads states to use arbitration or adjudication? Beth Simmons (2002) explored the answer to this question in relation to territorial disputes, noting that realist theory sees territory as a zero-sum issue. Yet, she argues, there are joint gains to be reaped from settling territorial disputes, such as greater stability for private investment and greater opportunities for trade as well as reduced need for military expenditures. For example, the United States and Canada accepted a maritime boundary delimitation by the ICJ despite the fact that both objected to the court's reasoning. Resolving the dispute took precedence over winning or losing. In addition, domestic groups may more readily accept an arbitration or ICJ judgment than a negotiated one. In some cases, bilateral treaties specify arbitration or adjudication to resolve disputes. For example, because bilateral treaties between the United States and Iran stipulated submitting disputes to the ICJ, the United States based its Tehran hostages appeal on those treaties, as well as on the Vienna Conventions on Diplomatic Relations. Despite agreeing to be bound by the outcome, however, one or another party to arbitration or adjudication may decide not to implement a settlement, giving rise to compliance and enforcement issues. They may seek Security Council help in enforcing a judgment, as Nicaragua did, or enlist a UN-appointed Mixed Commission to implement a ruling, as Cameroon and Nigeria did following the ICJ's 2002 decision on their border, or use other "self-help" measures to secure compliance of the recalcitrant party. In other situations, such as the Permanent Court of Arbitration's ruling on the Ethiopia-Eritrea border, one party may reject the decision and war may ensue, giving rise to yet other types of actions to end the conflict.

## Collective Security, Enforcement, and Sanctions

Collective security is based on the conviction that peace is indivisible and that all states have a collective interest in countering aggression whenever and wherever it may appear. States commit to defending any member of the collective security arrangement against attack by any other state, including other members of the arrangement. It assumes that potential aggressors will be deterred by the united threat of counterforce mobilized through an international organization like the League of Nations or the UN. If enforcement is required, however, then a wide range of economic and diplomatic sanctions as well as armed force may be utilized.

The League of Nations, as noted in Chapter 3, failed to respond to the Japanese invasion of Manchuria in 1931, and responded belatedly with voluntary sanctions in the case of the Italian invasion of Ethiopia in 1935. Chapter VII of the UN Charter (see Figure 4.1) provides the legal foundation for the UN's collective security role and for enforcement decisions that bind all UN members, specifying actions the UN can take with respect to threats to the peace, breaches of the peace, and acts of aggression. Because of the P-5's veto power in the Security Council, the UN is a limited collective security organization. The Cold War made concurrence among the Security Council's members almost impossible to achieve, and Chapter VII was invoked on only two occasions. As a result, the UN dealt primarily with regional conflicts, utilizing various forms of peacekeeping and mechanisms for peaceful settlement of disputes. The situation changed dramatically in the late 1980s with the Cold War's end, unprecedented cooperation among the P-5, and the success of the Gulf War. Since 1989, the Security Council has invoked Chapter VII on many occasions to authorize the use of force and various types of sanctions by the UN alone, by a regional organization such as NATO (Bosnia and Afghanistan), or by a "coalition of the willing" led by a country willing to commit military forces to the effort, such as the United States (Haiti), Australia (East Timor), France (Rwanda, Côte d'Ivoire, Mali), and Great Britain (Sierra Leone). It has become common for most peacekeeping operations, in fact, to have a mandate under Chapter VII. As discussed later, this has blurred the line between enforcement and peacekeeping.

As interstate conflicts have become only one source of international danger, and as threats from intrastate conflicts, nonstate actors, terrorism, large-scale humanitarian crises, WMD proliferation, and climate change have grown, the concept of collective security has also undergone change. Increasingly, the UN and international community are engaged in managing a wide array of threats to human security. Hence the bases for collective security and Chapter VII enforcement have expanded. The 2004 report of the UN-appointed High-Level Panel on Threats, Challenges, and Change captured this emerging reconceptualization of shared vulnerability to a wide variety of threats as the new basis for UN-led collective security (UN 2004). The 2005 World Summit partially embraced the panel's ideas and advocated stronger relations between the UN and regional and subregional organizations.

## Collective Security Efforts Involving Armed Force

*Korea.* The UN's response to North Korea's invasion of South Korea in June 1950 still stands as the closest the organization has ever come to collective enforcement action. The sanctioning of US-led UN forces to counter the invasion was made possible by the temporary absence of the Soviet Union from the Security Council in protest against the UN's refusal to seat the newly established communist government of the People's Republic of China. The "Uniting for Peace" resolution was used by the General Assembly to authorize continuance of those forces once the Soviet Union returned to the Security Council and exercised its veto. The UN provided the framework for legitimizing US efforts to defend the Republic of Korea and mobilizing other states' assistance. A US general was designated as the UN commander, but took orders directly from Washington. Some fifteen states contributed troops during the three-year war. Since the 1953 cease-fire, the United States has maintained a strong military presence in South Korea; the UN has maintained a token presence.

*The Gulf War.* Iraq's invasion of Kuwait in the summer of 1990 triggered unprecedented actions by the UN Security Council in response to this act of aggression against a UN member state. Unity among the P-5 (including the Soviet Union despite its long-standing relationship with Iraq) facilitated the passage of twelve successive resolutions over a four-month period, activating Chapter VII of the Charter. These included, most importantly, Resolution 678 of November 29, 1990, which authorized member states "to use all necessary means" to reverse the occupation of Kuwait and "restore peace and security in the region."

The military operation launched under the umbrella of Resolution 678 and Article 42 of the Charter was a US-led multinational effort resembling a subcontract on behalf of the UN. US commanders did not regularly report to the UN Secretary-General, nor did senior UN personnel participate in military decisionmaking. UN flags and symbols were not used by coalition forces. After the fighting ceased in late February 1991, a traditional, lightly armed peacekeeping force (the UN Iraq-Kuwait Observer Mission [UNIKOM]) was organized to monitor the demilitarized zone between Iraq and Kuwait.

The US-led military action in the Gulf was widely regarded as exemplifying a stronger post–Cold War UN. Because Germany and Japan contributed substantial monetary resources but were excluded from key decisions, since they were not Security Council members, this spurred their interest in securing permanent seats. Many developing countries, while supporting the action, were also troubled by the autonomy of the US-led operation. The Gulf War marked only the beginning, however, of efforts to deal with Iraq's threats to regional peace.

*Bosnia and Kosovo.* In 1992, after the failure of various peacemaking efforts following the breakup of Yugoslavia and of the UN peacekeeping force (the UN Protection Force for Yugoslavia [UNPROFOR]) to stop the escalating fighting in Bosnia-Herzegovina, the UN Security Council invoked Chapter VII, calling on member states to "take all necessary measures," nationally or through regional organizations, to facilitate delivery of humanitarian aid (Resolution 770). It authorized the creation of UN safe areas in six Bosnian cities and enforcement of a no-fly zone, removal of heavy weapons from urban centers, economic sanctions on Serbia and Montenegro, and air strikes against Bosnian Serb forces that were attacking the safe areas. In the first instance of cooperation between UN peacekeepers and a regional military alliance, US and European forces under NATO auspices monitored compliance with the economic sanctions, implemented the no-fly zone over Bosnia, and eventually, in August 1995, conducted air strikes against Bosnian Serb positions that helped create conditions for negotiating a peace agreement. Not only was this a first for the UN, but it was NATO's first-ever enforcement action. In the context of the debate over NATO's post–Cold War role, discussed in Chapter 5, its actions in Bosnia set precedents for a much more active role in the Balkans and beyond Europe.

NATO's second enforcement action occurred in another part of the former Yugoslavia, namely the province of Kosovo. It was extremely controversial because it occurred without prior authorization from the UN Security Council due to opposition from Russia and China. In March 1999, NATO began more than two months of aerial bombing in Kosovo and parts of the former Yugoslavia itself after Yugoslav (Serbian) rejection of a negotiated settlement for Kosovo and growing evidence of ethnic cleansing. Kofi Annan captured the dilemma Kosovo posed when he stated: "It is indeed tragic that diplomacy has failed, but there are times when the use of force may be legitimate in the pursuit of peace. . . . [But] the Council should be involved in any decision to resort to the use of force" (UN 1999c). Russia, China, and other countries loudly protested the illegality of NATO intervention, but the UK argued that "force can also be justified on the grounds of overwhelming humanitarian necessity without a [Security Council resolution]" (Roberts 1999: 106). The rejection of Russia's draft Security Council resolution condemning the NATO action by a vote of twelve to three is cited by proponents of legality as evidence of emerging customary law. Yet the debate over NATO's military action reflected concerns that it worsened the humanitarian crisis by contributing to the huge refugee outflow, civilian casualties of bombing, and destruction of infrastructure such as power plants and bridges on the Danube River. In both Bosnia and Kosovo, NATO also provided postconflict stabilization forces with peacekeeping mandates, as discussed later.

*Afghanistan.* Within twenty-four hours of the September 11, 2001, terrorist attacks on the United States, the UN Security Council approved Resolution 1368, which, among other things, recognized the US right to self-defense under Article 51 of the UN Charter. The United States interpreted the resolution as providing an international legal basis for its military action against the Taliban regime and al-Qaeda camps in Afghanistan one month later, with the private approval of the Security Council. Following the December 2001 Bonn Conference, which established the Afghan Interim Authority, Security Council Resolution 1386 authorized the British-led International Security Assistance Force (ISAF) with enforcement power under Chapter VII, to help the Afghan transitional authority maintain security.

In 2003, NATO took control of ISAF, with the United States continuing combat operations against al-Qaeda and the Taliban under Operation Enduring Freedom. NATO's ISAF mandate envisioned the operation as limited to peacekeeping and peacebuilding, but the weakness of the Afghan government and the resurgence of the Taliban turned it into something more. Security Council Resolution 1776 (2007) mandated ISAF to disarm militias, reform the justice system, train a national police force and army, provide security for elections, and combat the narcotics industry. From 2006 onward, the distinction between US-led combat operations and NATO/ISAF actions blurred as the latter took on more offensive operations. At its height in 2008, ISAF had over 50,000 troops from forty countries, but NATO commanders faced significant difficulties persuading European members to contribute troops and not to impose restrictions on how those forces could be used.

NATO's enforcement action in Afghanistan was seen as a major test of its ability to operate outside Europe—a test of both military capabilities and political will. Like the United Nations, NATO was established to deal with traditional interstate security threats. Afghanistan, however, exemplifies the complexity of security governance challenges in the twenty-first century, when "extreme belief systems . . . unstable and intolerant societies, strategic crime and the globalization of commodities and communications combine to create a multidimensional threat transcending geography, function, and capability" (Morelli and Gallis 2008: 31).

*Libya and humanitarian intervention.* In Libya, the mass demonstrations that marked the 2011 Arab Spring turned into civil war, as the eastern half of the state declared autonomy and factions in the military and government defected from the government ruled by Colonel Muammar Qaddafi for over forty years. Qaddafi publicly predicted "rivers of blood" and "hundreds of thousands of dead"; he threatened to use all weapons available "to cleanse Libya house by house"; and he referred to the protesters as "cockroaches," the same term used by Hutus to dehumanize the Tutsis during the 1994 Rwandan genocide. The international community feared a humanitarian crisis and the threat this posed to both Libya's people and the large number of foreign nationals in Libya.

The UN Security Council initially imposed targeted sanctions on Libya, freezing assets, imposing an arms embargo, and referring the matter to the International Criminal Court (Resolution 1970). Citing "widespread and systematic attacks," the Council stated that government actions "may amount to crimes against humanity" and that Libyan authorities had a responsibility to protect the population. With violence mounting, this was followed three weeks later by Resolution 1973, authorizing UN members to "to take all necessary measures" to protect civilians, establish a no-fly zone, enforce the arms embargo, and undertake air strikes and military action short of landing troops. It was the Council's first approval of enforcement of R2P. The resolution received ten affirmative votes and five abstentions (Russia, China, India, Germany, and Brazil), thanks in no small part to the support of the Organisation of Islamic Cooperation, the Gulf Cooperation Council, and the Arab League and the fact that Qaddafi had few friends.

Like other UN-authorized operations requiring strong military assets, enforcement began with air strikes by the United States, France, Italy, Canada, and Britain designed to protect civilian supporters of the secessionists and establish a no-fly zone. NATO subsequently took over the bulk of military operations, aided by the US military, Qatar, Jordan, the United Arab Emirates, and Sweden. Yet as the intervention dragged on in 2011, concerns even among R2P advocates grew that it had become a justification for war. And, as discussed further later, Libya did not set a precedent for UN-authorized enforcement in the subsequent humanitarian crisis in Syria.

*Anti-piracy enforcement.* In a further illustration of the changing nature of security threats, maritime piracy—an ancient problem—became a new problem. Although piracy had long been a problem in Southeast Asia, particularly in waters of the Indonesian archipelago, these had been brought under reasonable control as Malaysia and Indonesia set aside their fears of encroachment and allowed each other's navies to pursue pirates after 2000. More than a hundred pirate attacks were launched on ships in the Gulf of Aden and off the coast of Somalia in 2008, however, significantly disrupting major shipping routes. For the first time, in December 2008, the UN Security Council unanimously authorized the use under Chapter VII of "all necessary means" against piracy and armed robbery at sea by states as well as regional and international organizations (Resolutions 1846 and 1851). NATO and the EU sent ships for a multinational naval task force, as did a number of countries including India, Russia, Japan, South Korea, and China. The Council was careful to make clear, however, that its authorization applied only to the situation in Somalia and "shall not affect the rights or obligations or responsibilities of Member States under international law . . . [nor] be considered as establishing customary international law" (Resolution 1851). Between 2008 and 2011, more than four hundred ships were hijacked, boarded, or fired upon by pirates operating from Somalia. As a result of the naval enforcement on the one hand and the efforts to address Somalia's own problems on the other, piracy off the Somali coast diminished by 2012.

## Enforcement and Sanctions

International efforts to meet the challenges of extremism, piracy, terrorism, cross-border insurgencies, and other twenty-first-century threats to peace illustrate the blurring of lines between different governance approaches. Sanctions have long been a favorite tool in states' efforts to get others to do what they want them to do. Since 1990, these have become an integral part of many enforcement efforts.

Unilaterally imposed sanctions, however, have always been problematic, because they do not close off alternative markets and sources of supply for the targeted states. Yet organizing multilateral sanctions without a multilateral forum or organization through which to reduce the diplomatic transaction costs of securing other states' cooperation is a difficult undertaking. Hence, beginning with the League of Nations, the potential for using sanctions as an instrument of security governance was significantly enhanced. Multilateral sanctions were rarely used, however, until the 1990s. The League applied voluntary sanctions once (Italy). The UN imposed mandatory sanctions under Chapter VII only twice (Southern Rhodesia and South Africa) before 1990. The Arab League imposed sanctions on Israel in 1948, and the OAS imposed them on Cuba between 1964 and 1975. The United States organized multilateral sanctions involving sensitive technologies against the Soviet Union and other communist countries through an ad hoc group known as CoCom (Coordinating Committee for Multilateral Export Controls). The Commonwealth imposed a sports ban and other sanctions on South Africa in the 1970s and 1980s. As discussed in Chapter 5, the OAS and AU have both used suspensions of membership to promote the norm of democratic rule and punish illegitimate changes in government such as military coups.

Sanctions have now become a key enforcement instrument, particularly for the UN, serving one or more purposes: to coerce a change of behavior, to constrain access to critical goods and funds and thereby raise costs and force changes in a target's behavior, or to signal and stigmatize targets in support of international norms (Biersteker et al. 2013). Beginning with the sanctions imposed on Iraq in 1990, the Security Council utilized different forms of sanctions in fourteen situations over the next eleven years, leading one study to dub the 1990s the "sanctions decade" (Cortright and Lopez 2000). Over the twenty-year period from 1992 to 2012, the Council imposed sanctions in twenty-two situations. Fourteen of the cases involved peace enforcement, all but one in intrastate conflicts; four related to terrorism; three related to proliferation of WMD, specifically nuclear weapons;

four related to upholding democratically elected governments; and one related to R2P.

Regional organizations have also applied sanctions in many of the same situations, and very often the sanctions are combined with negotiations, a peacekeeping operation, military force, or legal action such as through the ICC. Some of the sanctions regimes have now been in place for twenty or more years, but have changed over time with different goals and targets. In addition, states (especially the United States) have imposed unilateral arms embargoes, as well as trade restrictions and other measures. In 2014, the United States, EU, and a number of other countries imposed a series of sanctions on Russia following its annexation of Crimea and support for separatists in Ukraine.

As Thomas Biersteker and colleagues (2013: 15) note, "Because the affirmation of an international norm is embedded in the *signaling* aspect of every episode, sanctions function as a central mechanism for the strengthening and/or negotiation of international norms." Their study of UN sanctions found that the primary norms include the prohibition of war and armed conflict (Angola, Sierra Leone, Ethiopia, Eritrea, DRC); human rights (Yugoslavia, Rwanda, Afghanistan, Sudan); counterterrorism (Libya, Sudan, the Taliban/al-Qaeda); nonconstitutional changes in government (Haiti, Guinea-Bissau, Côte d'Ivoire); nuclear nonproliferation (Iran and North Korea); the authority of the Security Council; and protecting civilian populations under the R2P norm (Libya). In addition, secondary norms such as the prohibition on the use of child soldiers and sexual and gender-based violence may be involved. As this list indicates, the purposes for which sanctions have been employed since the early 1990s have broadened, although 60 percent are still related to armed conflicts (Biersteker et al. 2013).

Sanctions are typically viewed as a cheaper and easier tool for coercion and punishment than the use of armed force. Comprehensive trade sanctions are expected to have a political effect by imposing the costs of economic and other forms of deprivation on the offending state's government and people. By implication, the pain of sanctions will be lifted once there is a change of behavior, which may also mean a change of government. An alternative approach to sanctions is a bargaining model (carrot-and-stick approach) in which specific types of sanctions are integrated with inducements to effect a step-by-step change process. The target state is offered rewards for taking successive steps in the desired direction, rather than having to do everything that was expected in order to see any lifting of sanctions. The range of sanctions has included not only comprehensive economic and trade restrictions, but also more targeted measures. We use three case studies here to illustrate the experience with and lessons from the UN's use of both comprehensive and targeted sanctions.

*Iraq and the problems with comprehensive sanctions.* When Iraq invaded Kuwait in August 1990, the Security Council immediately invoked Chapter VII to condemn the invasion and demand withdrawal. Subsequent resolutions imposed mandatory economic and transport sanctions against Iraq and established a sanctions committee to monitor implementation. Following the Gulf War's end, in April 1991, Resolution 687 enumerated terms of the cease-fire agreement and a far-reaching plan for the destruction, under international supervision, of Iraq's chemical and biological weapons and ballistic missiles, the renunciation of nuclear weapons, and the placement of all nuclear-usable material (such as for power plants) under international control. The comprehensive sanctions were to continue until all the provisions were carried out to the Security Council's satisfaction, with the exception of oil sales authorized under the 1995 Oil-for-Food Programme, which allowed the Iraqi regime to sell a limited amount of oil on international markets to pay for food and medical supplies, as discussed in Chapter 4.

By the late 1990s, the Iraq sanctions had become controversial and malnutrition, contaminated water supplies, increased infectious disease, and higher infant and child mortality rates had produced a humanitarian crisis that generated widespread sympathy and calls for ending sanctions (Garfield 1999). The suffering was not entirely attributable to sanctions, as the Iraqi government exacerbated the crisis for political purposes. Sanctions fatigue among neighboring and other nations that relied on trade with Iraq grew, and compliance eroded as unauthorized trade and transport links multiplied (Cortright and Lopez 2002: 1). The United States and United Kingdom, however, insisted on complete compliance before the sanctions could be lifted and rejected proposals to reward Iraq's cooperation and encourage further progress by partially lifting sanctions. The result was a stalemate, since Saddam Hussein was widely thought to believe that the United States and United Kingdom would only be satisfied with his ouster (Thakur 2006: 145).

In 2001 and 2002, NGOs, human rights groups, and independent research centers initiated proposals for "smart sanctions" intended to keep the pressure on Iraq to comply with the disarmament provisions by hitting the government's leaders where it would hurt, but to lift most restrictions on civilian imports.

In retrospect, former Canadian UN ambassador David Malone (2006: 135) concluded: "On many levels, the Program [i.e. sanctions] worked: it saved many lives, it drove the disarmament process, and it prevented rearmament by keeping the lion's share of Iraq's oil wealth and imports—which could be used to produce WMD—out of the hands of Saddam Hussein. . . . [T]he Iraqi military and weapon programs had, in fact, steadily eroded under the weight of sanctions." Still, there was significant corruption through the Oil-for-Food Programme and the sanctions created broad resentment of the United States and its allies, which were seen as the key supporters of sanctions. Thus the sanctions may have had the unintended consequence of fueling militant Islam and anti-Westernism.

The Iraq experience demonstrated three problems with comprehensive sanctions. The first involved the large-scale negative humanitarian effects especially of general trade sanctions. This changed many people's perception of the pain/gain trade-offs in sanctions. The second problem was that strangling a target state's economy did not necessarily impose any economic pain on government leaders, in terms of their personal wealth and resources, and prospects for compliance were low unless sanctions affected them specifically. Third, in intrastate conflicts and failed states, generalized sanctions were largely ineffective in an environment absent normal governmental controls over taxation, documentation of imports and exports, or borders.

In short, a major lesson was that sanctions must be tailored to the specific situation if they are to be effective. Since 1994, no new comprehensive sanctions have been initiated by either the Security Council or regional organizations. Instead, targeted sanctions have been used, including arms embargoes (the most common); diplomatic sanctions (suspensions from IGO membership, limiting diplomats' travel); financial sanctions (notably freezing assets of governments and individuals, investment bans, limits on banking services); travel bans and aviation sanctions (prohibiting international transit by air and naval carriers); and commodity sanctions (e.g., trade in oil, timber, and diamonds) (see Table 7.1). Targeting has involved not just "what" but also "who." Targets have included entire governments, government leaders, rebel factions, terrorist groups, leaders' family members, and specific individuals. Humanitarian impact assessments are standard practice now, though they are often difficult to conduct.

In the late 1990s, the Security Council also recognized that monitoring was crucial to getting states and other actors to comply with sanctions. Since then, each sanctions regime has had an independent expert panel to gather data on sanctions violators, supply routes, networks, and transactions. The Council has named and shamed violators by publicly identifying them and, in 2001, imposed sanctions on Liberia for violating sanctions imposed on Sierra Leone and the Revolutionary United Front (RUF), the rebel group whose actions contributed to prolonging the terrible violence in Sierra Leone. The Council also strengthened the UN's own capacity to administer various types of sanctions. In addition, in 2000 the Council began to set time limits (generally twelve months) for sanctions, thereby forcing itself to review the sanctions and decide whether they should be renewed or changed.

Many actors are involved in monitoring and enforcing sanctions, including government finance and trade ministries, border control agencies,

**Table 7.1   Selected UN Sanctions by Type, 1990–2014**

| Type of Sanction | Target Country or Entity[a] | Duration |
|---|---|---|
| Comprehensive sanctions | Iraq | 1990–2003 |
| | Yugoslavia | 1992–1995 |
| | Haiti | 1993–1994 |
| Arms embargo | Iraq | 1990 |
| | Afghanistan | 1990–2000 |
| | Yugoslavia | 1991–1996, 1998–2001 |
| | Libya | 1992–2003 |
| | Somalia | 1992– |
| | Angola and UNITA | 1993–2002 |
| | Sierra Leone (RUF only) | 1998– |
| | al-Qaeda and Taliban | 1999 |
| | DRC | 2003–2008 |
| | Liberia (militias) | 2003– |
| | Côte d'Ivoire | 2004– |
| | Sudan (militias) | 2004– |
| | Iran | 2006– |
| | North Korea | 2006– |
| | DRC (militias) | 2008– |
| | Libya | 2011– |
| | Taliban (targeted) | 2011– |
| | ISIL and al-Nusra Front | 2014– |
| Export or import limits (ban exports of selected technologies, diamonds, timber etc., or place embargo on imports of oil, etc.) | Cambodia (logs, oil) | 1992–1994 |
| | Angola (diamonds) | 1993, 1998–2002 |
| | Sierra Leone (oil, diamonds) | 1997–1998, 2000–2003 |
| | Liberia (diamonds) | 2001–2007 |
| | Liberia (timber) | 2003–2006 |
| | Côte d'Ivoire (diamonds) | 2004–2014 |
| | Somalia (charcoal) | 2012– |
| Asset freeze | Yugoslavia | 1992–1995, 1998–2000 |
| | Libya | 1993–1999 |
| | Angola (UNITA only) | 1998–2002 |
| | al-Qaeda and Taliban (targeted) | 2000– |
| | DRC (militias) | 2003– |
| | Côte d'Ivoire (targeted) | 2004– |
| | Sudan (targeted) | 2004– |
| | Lebanon (targeted) | 2005– |
| | Iran (targeted) | 2006– |
| | North Korea (targeted) | 2006– |
| | DRC (targeted) | 2008– |
| | Libya (targeted) | 2011– |
| | ISIL and al-Nusra Front | 2014– |

*(continues)*

the US Treasury Department, and nuclear regulatory agencies. The Financial Action Task Force (FATF), created by the G-7 in 1989, enforces anti-money-laundering measures, and the Offshore Group of Banking Supervisors monitors offshore banking. NGOs now play significant roles also in the implementation, monitoring, and evaluation of sanctions, such as in monitoring and documenting illegal trade in conflict diamonds.

**Table 7.1    continued**

| Type of Sanction | Target Country or Entity[a] | Duration |
|---|---|---|
| Denial of visas (travel bans) | Libya | 1992–1999 |
| | Angola (UNITA only) | 1997–2002 |
| | Sudan | 1998– |
| | al-Qaeda and Taliban | 1999–2001 |
| | Afghanistan | 2001–2003 |
| | al-Qaeda (targeted) | 2002– |
| | Liberia (targeted) | 2003– |
| | Côte d'Ivoire (targeted) | 2004– |
| | DRC (militias) | 2004– |
| | Sudan (targeted) | 2004– |
| | Iran (targeted) | 2006– |
| | North Korea (targeted) | 2006– |
| | DRC (targeted) | 2008– |
| | Libya (targeted) | 2011– |
| | Taliban (targeted) | 2011– |
| | Guinea-Bissau (targeted) | 2012– |
| | ISIL and al-Nusra Front | 2014– |
| Cancellation of air links | Libya | 1992–1999 |
| | Afghanistan | 1999–2001 |

*Note:* a. The term *targeted* in this column indicates that the relevant UN sanctions committee maintains a list of specific individuals and entities that are targeted by the sanction.

The impact of lessons learned in the 1990s about how to target and monitor sanctions to strengthen their impact and respond more effectively to various threats to international peace and security can be seen in the cases of counterterrorism and Iran.

*Countering international terrorism.* Beginning in the early 1990s, the UN and EU imposed various types of sanctions, including diplomatic and aviation bans, on Libya and Sudan, as well as on Afghanistan's Taliban regime, for their roles in supporting terrorism. Also, the United States has used the State Department's "List of States Sponsoring Terrorism" as a basis for unilateral sanctions ranging from a ban on economic aid and dual-use technologies to voting against World Bank loans for these same countries as well as Cuba, Syria, and North Korea.

Sanctions intended to disrupt or cut off sources of funds for terrorists are crucial and depend particularly on the US Treasury for implementation as well as the cooperation of offshore financial havens in Caribbean and Pacific island nations such as Barbados, Antigua, Nauru, and Vanuatu. They require countries to develop the legal and technical capabilities (and be willing) to monitor financial transactions, interdict accounts of particular individuals, and act quickly in order to deny terrorists time to move funds. UN sanctions imposed in 1999 on Taliban-controlled Afghanistan for its support of al-Qaeda (Resolution 1267) included a freeze of all financial assets along with an arms embargo and travel ban. These were extended and strengthened in subsequent resolutions to target more than 500 individuals and groups associated with the Taliban and al-Qaeda (but not Afghanistan itself after 2001), and the Security Council's 1267 Committee, assisted by experts in international financial transactions, border enforcement, drug trafficking, arms embargoes, and counterterrorism legislation, monitors compliance. One success in these efforts came with Libya between 1999, when sanctions were temporarily suspended after the suspects in the Pan Am Flight 103 bombing were turned over for trial, and 2003, when the trials were concluded, compensation to victims' families was provided, and Libya renounced terrorism (Biersteker et al. 2013: 25).

The most extensive set of measures was taken following the September 2001 attacks when the Security Council adopted Resolution 1373, requiring all states to block funding and recruitment for terrorist groups, freeze their assets, and deny them safe haven. It also established the Counter-Terrorism Committee (CTC) to monitor states' actions, as well as a group of independent experts to assist the committee with implementation, as discussed in Chapter 4 and later in this chapter. As we will see, the type and scope of sanctions depended heavily on the type of problem being addressed.

*Using sanctions to halt Iran's nuclear weapons program.* Since 2006, UN and EU sanctions have been used to try to prevent Iran from developing nuclear weapons. The Security Council's first sanctions resolution (1737), in 2006, called for Iran to cooperate fully with the IAEA and to suspend all enrichment and reprocessing activities and for states to block the direct or indirect supply, sale, or transfer of any items, materials, goods and technology that could contribute to Iran's enrichment-related and reprocessing activities and ballistic missile programs "from their territories, or by their nationals or using their flag vessels or aircraft." It also imposed financial sanctions and created a monitoring body, the 1737 Committee. The Council clearly spelled out humanitarian exemptions as well as the actions Iran must take for the sanctions to be suspended or terminated. A second resolution (1747), in 2007, authorized inspections of sea and air cargo to and from Iran, tightened monitoring of Iranian financial institutions, extended travel bans and asset freezes, and enlarged the list of targeted individuals and companies.

Resolutions in 2008 (1803) and 2010 (1929) further extended the sanctions, targeting Revolutionary Guard–owned businesses, the shipping industry, and the commercial and financial sector. The EU added a ban on oil purchases from Iran in 2012. Altogether, the UN, EU, and extensive US sanctions have isolated Iran from the international banking system, banned investment and aid to Iran's energy sector, blocked US and European firms from doing business in the country, and progressively added to the list of individuals, companies, banks, and organizations targeted for asset freezes. Sanctions are estimated to have led to a 25 percent reduction of Iran's GDP between mid-2012 and 2014, and do appear to have had some effect, as we will see in the later discussion of current Iranian policy shifts. The 2012 election brought President Hassan Rouhani to office vowing to try to lift the sanctions and improve the devastated economy. Much hinges on the outcome of the P-5+1 talks (the P-5 plus Germany) under way since 2012 and anticipated to conclude in mid-2016.

* * *

The UN's extensive use of sanctions since 1990 has highlighted the challenges of making sanctions work. Effective implementation of sanctions requires a great deal of specific knowledge about the country, individuals, and groups being targeted; it requires identifying funds belonging to those who are targeted, such as specific government agencies, companies, and individuals, and acting quickly to block access. Yet studies of targeted sanctions have highlighted both operational and political difficulties in achieving their objectives. Operational effectiveness is impeded by legal loopholes and lack of trained staff and adequate budgets in both the UN Secretariat and member governments, and exacerbated by weak border control systems and corruption in many countries. Political impediments include the reality that "implementation of sanctions of whatever kind by all UN members cannot be taken for granted. . . . Vigorous follow-up of sanctions violations, if and when detected, is a largely unsolved problem" (Doxey 2007: 58). Despite these difficulties, targeted sanctions with more careful monitoring of compliance have become the norm, even though their effectiveness as a global governance tool remains at issue. One difficulty in establishing their effectiveness is determining that it was sanctions and not something else that induced compliance. Another is that each sanctions case is unique and "previous experiences are not necessarily predictive of future outcomes" (Biersteker et al. 2013: 1). One comprehensive study of economic sanctions showed them to be successful (itself difficult to define) in only 34 percent of the 204 cases examined (Hufbauer et al. 2007: 158–159), but noted that the success rate is much higher for "modest policy changes" versus regime change or efforts to compel a target country to take actions it resists. The UN Targeted Sanctions Project has found that arms embargoes are among the least-effective sanctions if not complemented by measures targeting individuals or commodities, while commodity sanctions, particularly those targeting the diamond trade, are "highly effective." In relationship to coercing, constraining, or signaling goals, the study found that on average sanctions were effective in doing one of these 22 percent of the time. Efforts to coerce were the least successful; those aiming to constrain or signal were much more successful (Biersteker et al. 2013: 1).

Sanctions can have unintended consequences as well. They create incentives for evasion (diversion of trade, black markets, safe havens, reflagging vessels, diversification of funds), which the UN Targeted Sanctions Project found in 90 percent of cases. They thereby contribute to corruption and criminality (69 percent of cases); create burdens on neighboring states; strengthen authoritarian rule (54 percent of cases); and divert resources (44 percent of cases). Ineffective sanctions have also been shown to harm the legitimacy and authority of the Security Council itself (Biersteker et al. 2013). Thus, although "smart sanctions may satisfy the need . . . to 'do something,' . . . and they may serve to unify fraying coalitions and isolate a rogue regime . . . they are not a magic bullet for achieving foreign policy goals" (Hufbauer et al. 2007: 141).

## Peace Operations

Peacekeeping as a security governance approach was initiated during the Cold War, when neither sanctions nor other enforcement tools were easily used, at least by the UN. Since the Cold War's end, peacekeeping's use has broadened to include a variety of tasks, and the line between peacekeeping and enforcement has been blurred in a number of situations requiring greater use of force.

The UN and regional IGOs more recently have deployed various types of peace operations to help maintain cease-fire agreements, to stabilize conflict situations, to create an environment conducive to peaceful settlement, to help implement peace agreements, to protect civilian populations at risk in humanitarian crises, and to assist in laying the foundations for durable peace. With more than sixty-five operations since 1948, the majority of them initiated since 1990, sixteen operations in the field at the end of 2014 with more than 112,000 personnel (military and civilian), and a 2015 budget of more than $7 billion, peacekeeping in various forms has become "one of the most visible symbols of the UN role in international peace and security" (Thakur 2006: 37). It has also become a major activity for several regional organizations, most notably the AU and the EU. The vast majority of all contemporary peace operations are in Africa, and many of these involve multiple organizations (e.g., the UN and the EU together with ECOWAS or the AU) carrying out different parts of mandates from the UN Security Council. This has made Africa a "giant laboratory for global peacekeeping" (Adebajo 2014: 183). Yet as Paul Williams (2011: 192) notes, "No two peace operations are the same, and hence they all face a unique set of challenges."

## Distinguishing Between Enforcement and Peacekeeping

The UN invented peacekeeping during the Cold War to enable it to play a positive role in dealing with regional conflicts at a time when hostility between East and West prevented the use of the Charter provisions for collective security and enforcement. It has long defined peacekeeping as "an operation involving military personnel, but without enforcement powers, undertaken by the United Nations to help maintain or restore international peace and security in areas of conflict" (UN 1996: 4). Absent a Charter provision, peacekeeping lies in a "grey zone" between the peaceful settlement provisions of Chapter VI and the military enforcement provisions of Chapter VII, and is sometimes referred to as "Chapter VI and a half." Some operations in the 1990s crossed that grey zone and more closely resembled enforcement, creating controversy and operational problems, which we address later.

Since the Cold War's end, "peacekeeping has evolved from a primarily military model of observing cease-fires and the separation of forces after inter-state wars, to incorporate a complex model of many elements—military, police and civilian—working together to help lay the foundations for sustainable peace" (UN 2008: 18). It has become common, therefore, to distinguish between traditional peacekeeping and complex, multidimensional peacekeeping and peacebuilding operations. Thus, peacekeepers' tasks have varied significantly over time and with Security Council mandates for different types of peace operations, as outlined in Figure 7.6.

The key distinction between enforcement and peacekeeping lies in three principles that have guided traditional UN peacekeepers: consent of the parties, impartiality, and use of military force only as a last resort and in self-defense.

## Traditional Peacekeeping

Peacekeeping was first used in the Middle East and Asia in 1949, when small numbers of military observers were deployed to monitor armistice agreements that halted fighting between Israel and the Arab states, and India and Pakistan. Beginning in 1956, it became a valuable tool for the UN in dealing with conflicts in the Middle East (four traditional peacekeeping operations in the Arab-Israeli conflict alone) and other areas where the interests of the United States and the Soviet Union were not directly at stake at a time when Cold War tensions made it impossible to employ collective security or enforcement measures.

As Table 7.2 illustrates, traditional peacekeeping is still important in the Middle East. In the late 1980s, it was also used to facilitate the withdrawal of Soviet troops from Afghanistan and supervise the cease-fire between Iran and Iraq. It was used to monitor the cease-fires along the Iraq-Kuwait border after the Gulf War in 1991 and between Ethiopia and Eritrea

---

**Figure 7.6　Peace Operations Tasks**

---

- *Traditional Operations*
  Observation, monitoring, and reporting
  Cease-fires and withdrawal of forces
  Investigate complaints of violations
  Separation of combatant forces
  Establish buffer zones
  Use of force only for self-defense

- *Complex, Multidimensional Operations*
  Observation and monitoring
  Cease-fires and withdrawal of forces
  Democratic elections
  Human rights
  Arms control

- *Separation of Combatant Forces*
  Establish buffer zones
  Deter onset or spread of war

- *Limited Use of Force*
  Maintain or restore civil law and order
  Restore peace
  Deliver aid

- *Humanitarian Assistance/Intervention*
  Open food and medical supply lines; guard supplies
  Protect aid workers
  Protect civilians, displaced persons, and refugees
  Create safe havens

- *Peacebuilding (Nation-/Statebuilding)*
  Rebuild and train police
  Repatriate refugees
  Provide interim civil administration
  Oversee transition to indigenous authority

---

in 2001. All of these conflicts were interstate conflicts. The peacekeepers' purpose was to contain fighting or stabilize a cease-fire until negotiations produced a lasting peace agreement. The peacekeepers were either unarmed or lightly armed, often stationed between hostile forces to monitor truces and troop withdrawals, provide a buffer zone, and report violations, and authorized to use force only in self-defense. The size and limited capacity of a traditional peacekeeping force mean that it cannot stop a party that is determined to mount an offensive, as Israel has repeatedly shown in attacking Lebanon despite the presence of the UN Interim Force in Lebanon (UNIFIL). Host-state consent for a peacekeeping force can be withdrawn, however, forcing the withdrawal of troops, as happened in the Sinai when Egypt withdrew its permission for the UN Emergency Force (UNEF I)

**Table 7.2    Traditional UN Peacekeeping Operations (representative cases)**

| Operation | Title | Location | Duration | Maximum Strength |
|---|---|---|---|---|
| UNEF I | First UN Emergency Force | Suez Canal, Sinai peninsula | November 1956–June 1967 | 3,378 troops |
| UNFICYP | UN Peacekeeping Force in Cyprus | Cyprus | March 1964– present | 6,411 military observers |
| UNEF II | Second UN Emergency Force | Suez Canal, Sinai peninsula | October 1973– July 1979 | 6,973 troops |
| UNDOF | UN Disengage-ment Observer Force | Syrian Golan Heights | June 1974– present | 1,250 military observers |
| UNIFIL | UN Interim Force in Lebanon | Southern Lebanon | March 1978– present | 11,790 troops, 1,004 civilians |
| UNIIMOG | UN Iran-Iraq Military Observer Group | Iran-Iraq border | August 1988– February 1991 | 400 military observers |
| UNMEE | UN Mission in Ethiopia and Eritrea | Ethiopia-Eritrea border | September 2000–July 2008 | 3,940 troops, 214 police |

immediately before the onset of the 1967 Arab-Israeli War. Negotiations with the DRC averted the forced withdrawal of the UN force there in 2011.

During the Cold War many important issues of peace and security, including the Vietnam conflict, never made it onto the UN agenda. Yet the innovation of UN peacekeeping provided a valuable way of limiting super-power involvement in regional conflicts and coping with threats to peace posed by the emergence of new states, border conflicts among those states, and intractable conflicts in Kashmir, the Middle East, and Cyprus. In the process, the UN and international community developed a body of experi-ence and practice in peacekeeping that proved even more valuable in the late 1980s and the 1990s, when the Cold War's end created political condi-tions conducive to expanding the tasks given to peacekeepers (and new types of threats demanding creative responses). The success of its peace-keeping activities in the late 1980s earned the UN the Nobel Peace Prize in 1988, and led to many new missions.

The principles that guided traditional peacekeeping have become more problematic with different types of operations since 1990, particularly those in intrastate conflicts that have required a more "muscular" and multidi-mensional approach.

## Complex, Multidimensional Peacekeeping

Complex peacekeeping has involved more troops, often more heavily equipped than traditional peacekeepers, and with mandates that permit the use of force other than in self-defense. The line between peacekeeping and enforcement has clearly been blurred in such cases, with no peace to keep, no cease-fire to monitor, and no consent for the mission from local parties that are not states or perhaps failed states, such as in Somalia and the Democratic Republic of Congo. The resolutions for most peace operations now invoke Chapter VII not only to provide the legal basis for a range of actions, but also to show the Security Council's political resolve and remind member states' of their obligations to give effect to Council decisions, further blurring the distinction between peacekeeping and enforcement. Most operations since 1990 have also included police and civilian personnel to carry out various parts of complex mandates. The line has also been blurred in peace operations undertaken by regional IGOs such as ECOWAS, NATO, the AU, and the EU.

Even before 1990, shifts in US and Soviet foreign policy, the quiet diplomacy of UN Secretary-General Javier Pérez de Cuéllar, and the ripeness of long-standing conflicts in Central America (Nicaragua and El Salvador), Southern Africa (Namibia), and Southeast Asia (Cambodia) led to new types of UN missions as part of peace agreements. The governance challenge was not only how to end the conflicts, but also how to prevent renewed hostilities and build stable, democratic polities. Beginning with Somalia in 1992, subsequent missions further transformed the practice of peacekeeping as the UN and its members confronted the need to do something about the rise in intrastate conflicts, which was often accompanied by humanitarian crises and, in cases such as Somalia and the DRC, the collapse of state structures. The Security Council responded incrementally to the different situations, with the net result being mandates for peace operations stretching the traditional principles of consent, impartiality, and limited use of force. UN Secretaries-General since 1990 have all contributed ideas and initiatives to this new approach to peacekeeping, as did the 2000 report on UN peacekeeping reform by the Panel on United Nations Peace Operations, known as the Brahimi Report, and a number of subsequent reports within and outside the UN.

The UN defines multidimensional peacekeeping operations as "operations comprising a mix of military, police and civilian components working together to lay the foundations of a sustainable peace" (UN 2008: 97). While troop contingents in such operations may engage in observer activities characteristic of traditional operations, they are more likely to be monitoring the cantonment, disarmament, and demobilization of military forces and clearing landmines. Other military personnel, civilians, and police, along with NGOs and UN agencies such as the UNHCR, UNICEF, and the

UNDP, are involved in restoring law and order; repatriating and resettling refugees; organizing and supervising democratic elections; human rights monitoring and promotion; and rebuilding the police and judiciary—tasks that are variously characterized as peacebuilding or statebuilding. In four post–Cold War situations (Namibia, Cambodia, Kosovo, and East Timor), the UN also provided interim or transitional civil administration.

Most of these tasks are also associated with the concept of postconflict peacebuilding. Of the fifty-six peacekeeping operations the UN has undertaken between 1988 and 2014, twenty-nine have involved peacebuilding tasks, some of which the UN and other actors may initiate even before a conflict is fully ended. The specific contours of a peace operation whose mandate includes peacebuilding depend on the nature of the conflict situation as well as the political will in the Security Council. Because such operations typically include various UN agencies, regional IGOs, and NGOs, coordinating the military and civilian components is a significant challenge, as explored later. Table 7.3 shows selected complex UN peacekeeping operations, including the variety of tasks undertaken. Case studies of the former Yugoslavia and Democratic Republic of Congo, where there were large humanitarian crises but there was no peace to be kept, illustrate the challenges faced by and the evolution of missions over time.

*Former Yugoslavia and Bosnia-Herzegovina.* Yugoslavia's disintegration into five separate states in the early 1990s unleashed the fiercest fighting in Bosnia-Herzegovina where Croats, Serbs, and Bosnian Muslims were intermingled. Nationalist leaders of each group fueled ancient suspicions and hostilities; each group's military and paramilitary forces attempted to enlarge and ethnically cleanse its territorial holdings. The resulting war killed more than 200,000 people, produced millions of refugees, and subjected thousands to concentration camps, rape, torture, and ethnic cleansing. The ferocity of the conflict shocked those who thought that Europe in the 1990s was immune from such horrors. It also raised issues central to international order and international law, such as self-determination, individual and group rights, and the use of force to serve humanitarian ends.

Between 1991 and 1996, the Security Council devoted a record number of meetings to debate whether to intervene, to what end, and with what means. UN peacekeepers, when finally sent to the region in 1992, encountered massive violations of human rights, a situation demanding more vigorous military action, and very little interest by the parties in making peace. Yugoslavia came to represent a microcosm of problems with what were then new types of peacekeeping, Chapter VII enforcement actions, efforts to address human rights abuses, and UN member states' failure to provide adequate resources to carry out the Security Council's mandates.

Initially, the United Nations largely deferred to EU diplomatic efforts, consistent with Chapter VIII of the Charter, first to find a peaceful settle-

**Table 7.3  Selected Complex UN Peacekeeping Operations**

| | Somalia | Cambodia | East Timor | East Timor | Bosnia/Croatia | DRC | Sudan/Darfur | DRC | Côte d'Ivoire |
|---|---|---|---|---|---|---|---|---|---|
| Mission | UNOSOM II | UNTAC | UNTAET | UNMIT | UNPROFOR | MONUC | UNAMID | MONUSCO | UNOCI |
| Duration | May 1993–May 1995 | July 1991–April 1995 | October 1999–May 2002 | August 2006–December 2012 | February 1992–December 1995 | November 1999–July 2010 | July 2007–present | May 2010–present | February 2004–present |
| **Maximum strength** | | | | | | | | | |
| Civilians | 2,800 | 1,500 | 2,482 | 1,266 | 4,532 | 3,756 | 3,432 | 3,769 | 1,126 |
| Military liaisons | | | | 34 | | | | | |
| Observers | | | 118 | 19 | 684 | 760 | 242 | 760 | 200 |
| Police | | 3,359 | 1,288 | 1,608 | 803 | 1,229 | 4,618 | 1,270 | 1,000 |
| Troops | 28,000 | 15,900 | 6,281 | | 38,599 | 19,815 | 16,919 | 19,815 | 7,500 |
| Chapter VII authority | ✓ | | ✓ | | ✓ | ✓ | ✓ | ✓ | ✓ |
| **Military tasks** | | | | | | | | | |
| De-mining | ✓ | ✓ | | | | ✓ | | | ✓ |
| Disarmament | ✓ | ✓ | ✓ | | ✓ | ✓ | | | ✓ |
| Monitor cease-fire | ✓ | ✓ | ✓ | | ✓ | ✓ | ✓ | | ✓ |
| Peace enforcement | ✓ | ✓ | ✓ | | ✓ | ✓ | ✓ | | ✓ |
| **Refugee and humanitarian aid** | | | | | | | | | |
| Assist civilians | ✓ | ✓ | ✓ | | ✓ | ✓ | ✓ | | ✓ |
| Refugee return | ✓ | ✓ | ✓ | | ✓ | ✓ | | | ✓ |
| Protect international workers | | | | | | ✓ | ✓ | | ✓ |
| **Civil policing** | | | | | | | | | |
| Police retraining | | | ✓ | ✓ | | ✓ | | ✓ | ✓ |
| **Electoral assistance** | | | | | | | | | |
| Monitor elections | | ✓ | ✓ | ✓ | | ✓ | | | ✓ |
| **Legal affairs** | | | | | | | | | |
| Constitution/judicial reform | ✓ | ✓ | ✓ | ✓ | | ✓ | | ✓ | |
| Human rights oversight | | ✓ | ✓ | ✓ | | ✓ | ✓ | ✓ | ✓ |
| Administrative authority | | ✓ | ✓ | | | | | | ✓ |

ment and then to negotiate repeated cease-fire agreements. The UN Protection Force for Yugoslavia (UNPROFOR) was authorized in February 1992 and its mandate gradually broadened from maintaining a cease-fire in the heavily Serbian areas of Croatia, disbanding and demilitarizing regular and paramilitary forces, and delivering humanitarian assistance, to creating safe areas for refugees in Bosnia, relieving the besieged city of Sarajevo, protecting basic human rights, and using NATO to enforce sanctions, a no-fly zone, and safe areas, as well as conduct air strikes on Serbian forces.

By late 1992, with no cease-fire in place, the Security Council invoked Chapter VII for the first time in conjunction with the peacekeeping mission and called for member states to "take all necessary measures" (Resolution 770). As discussed earlier, this turned UNPROFOR into more of an enforcement operation and the first experiment in cooperation between UN peacekeepers and NATO forces. At its height, as shown in Table 7.3, UNPROFOR had over 38,000 troops, including British and French contingents. Yet they were far fewer and less heavily equipped than its military commanders deemed necessary for the tasks they had been given, particularly the task of protecting the six safe areas, for which they had requested 30,000 troops. Under constant pressure for further action, the Security Council met almost continuously and passed resolution after resolution, progressively enlarging UNPROFOR's mandate, but resolutions did not produce the manpower or the logistical, financial, and military resources needed to fulfill the enlarged mandate. All sides interfered with relief efforts and targeted UN peacekeepers and international aid personnel. The UN-declared safe areas were anything but safe for the civilians who had taken refuge in them. Srebrenica, in particular, became a humiliating defeat when UN peacekeepers failed to prevent the massacre of more than 7,000 Bosnian Muslim men and boys by Bosnian Serbs in July 1995 (UN 1999a).

The UN's peacekeeping role in Bosnia ended with the US-brokered Dayton Peace Accords of November 1995. UNPROFOR was replaced by NATO's Implementation Force (IFOR), which comprised 60,000 combat-ready troops, including 20,000 Americans and units from almost twenty non-NATO countries (including Russia). This was NATO's first effort at traditional peacekeeping: separating forces, supervising withdrawals, interposing themselves between parties, and providing a safe environment for peace to take root. NATO commanders refused to arrest prominent war criminals and deliver them to the International Criminal Tribunal for the Former Yugoslavia (ICTY), however, which was established in 1993.

In late 1996, IFOR was replaced by the smaller Stabilization Force (SFOR); the EU took over from NATO in 2004 and continues to operate the small EUFOR Althea under Security Council authorization, with troops from twenty-four countries as of late 2014. The primary purpose is to maintain a safe and secure environment, to ensure compliance with the 1995 Dayton agreement, and to provide capacity building for Bosnian forces.

Since 1995, many other organizations have been involved in implementing different parts of the Dayton Peace Agreement and dealing with Bosnia's extensive postconflict peacebuilding needs. For example, the UN was charged with monitoring and reforming Bosnia's police forces, a mission that ended in 2002; the OSCE has been responsible for overseeing elections and, along with NGOs, promoting human rights and civil society groups; the UNHCR has overseen the return, resettlement, and rehabilitation of refugees and internally displaced persons; the World Bank, European Bank for Reconstruction and Development, and NGOs have promoted economic development. Overseeing the civilian side of implementation, with legal authority over Bosnia's institutions but without authority over the various international agencies, has been the so-called high representative appointed by the ad hoc International Conference on the Former Yugoslavia, composed of the United States, European Union, and other major parties. The large number of NGOs and IGOs active in Bosnia has presented a host of coordination problems. Almost twenty years after the Dayton agreement, Bosnia remains a kind of international protectorate under the quasi-colonial authority of the high representative. The country is still dependent on aid; its economy remains highly criminalized and lags behind comparable economies in Eastern Europe, with high unemployment and poverty rates. With the persistence of the Serb Republika Srpska, the country remains effectively partitioned and nationalist parties still dominate the government.

The international community's experience in Bosnia demonstrates the difficulties of complex, multidimensional peace operations. The peacebuilding components signify the recognition that in societies rent by civil strife, failure to address root causes of conflict may lead to a new cycle of violence. The resources expended—60,000 troops and more than $5 billion in aid for a country of 4 million people—have yielded what one study published a decade after the Dayton agreement called "a vastly improved but still frankly disappointing outcome" (Cousens and Harland 2006: 121). This level of international engagement, the study's authors added, was "unlikely to be replicated in many other contexts, particularly where the strategic interests of key states and organizations are not seen to be heavily at stake." Such has been the situation in the Democratic Republic of Congo, which we examine next. It has ten times more people and fifty times more territory than Bosnia, and a conflict far more violent and complex, but only after more than five years of fighting (and a peace agreement) did the peacekeeping force reach one-sixth the size of NATO's IFOR and receive Chapter VII authority. Fifteen years later, the DRC case exemplifies most clearly a multidimensional peace mission operating in a situation of internationalized civil war with multiple belligerents, large-scale humanitarian crisis, lootable resources, and a failing state.

*Democratic Republic of Congo: The "infinite crisis."* Crises in the Congo have threatened international peace and security in three different periods. The first occurred when the Congo gained independence from Belgium in 1960 and civil order collapsed, leading to a four-year UN peace operation that presaged many post–Cold War complex operations but failed to create much stability. The second followed the genocide in Rwanda in 1994, when Hutu extremists responsible for the genocide fled to UN-operated refugee camps in Eastern Zaire, as it was then called, and no peacekeeping force was established to disarm or prevent them from regrouping and carrying out attacks inside Rwanda. The third began with a 1996 rebellion against longtime Zairean dictator Colonel Joseph Mobutu, backed by Uganda and Rwanda. Rwanda's interest had much to do with the continuing problem of the Hutu militias based inside the Congo. Uganda supported Rwanda's postgenocide Tutsi government and opposed Congo's dictator, who had allowed Ugandan opposition groups to launch attacks from its territory. Following Mobutu's ouster, a wider war erupted in 1998. Laurent Kabila, the new leader of the renamed Democratic Republic of Congo, antagonized Rwanda and Uganda as well as powerful Congolese figures and ethnic groups, leading the two countries to intervene on behalf of antigovernment groups. Angolan and Zimbabwean forces intervened on the side of the DRC government along with troops from Namibia, Chad, Eritrea, and Sudan, the Rwandan Hutu militia, and other militias that supported government forces as well as their own agendas.

Since 1998, the "infinite crisis" in the DRC has been through several phases and shows little sign in late 2014 of ending. Each phase has been marked by changes in who is involved in peace operations in the country and the nature of mandates.

Dubbed "Africa's First World War," the 1998–2002 war was incredibly complex, with the various rebel and militia groups and troops from the other African countries competing for political power and access to the Congo's vast mineral deposits. It was also disastrous for civilians, millions of whom were displaced and died of war-related diseases and starvation. Despite the signing of a peace agreement in late 2002, smaller-scale violence persisted, as has the massive humanitarian crisis, with large population displacements, extremely violent systematic rapes, and collapse of the health and food systems. The death toll between 1998 and 2009 is estimated at 5.4 million people, making this the world's deadliest conflict since World War II. The economic interests of neighboring states and various militias have been central to the conflict's persistence and a major impediment to peacemaking efforts. The inability or unwillingness of the Congolese government to control its own troops has contributed to the human-

**Map 7.1   The Democratic Republic of Congo**

itarian crisis. The UN force has been tarnished by failure to protect civilians adequately and by widespread sexual exploitation and abuse by peacekeepers that led to organizational changes, new policies, and training procedures for all peacekeeping personnel.

Initial efforts to halt fighting in the DRC were led by African countries in SADC as well as the OAU and the Francophonie (the organization of former French-speaking colonies). The 1999 Lusaka Agreement, mediated by SADC, was the basis for the UN's initial action. But given the enormity of the tasks and recent UN failures in Somalia, Bosnia, and Rwanda, as well as demands for new operations at that time in Kosovo, Sierra Leone, and East Timor, both member states and the UN Secretariat were reluctant to take on another major operation. Secretary-General Kofi Annan, in fact, warned: "In order to be effective, any United Nations peacekeeping mission in the Democratic Republic of the Congo, whatever its mandate, will have to be large and expensive. It would require the deployment of thousands of international troops and civilian personnel. It will face tremendous difficulties, and will be beset by risks. Deployment will be slow" (UN 1999d).

The UN Organization Mission in the Democratic Republic of Congo (MONUC) was authorized by the Security Council in November 1999 (Resolution 1279) as a small observer force of 4,900 personnel. It took three years, however, to reach that strength, as member states were reluctant to contribute troops. In addition, the DRC government initially refused to let MONUC deploy outside the capital and there were numerous ceasefire violations. The situation began to improve in 2001 when the Security Council condemned Rwanda's and Uganda's continuing presence and demanded their withdrawal, while approving changes in MONUC's operation (Resolution 1341). With SADC and OAU mediation, the DRC government and various rebel groups reached agreement in 2002 to form a transitional government, with MONUC tasked to help disarm the militias, albeit still without enforcement power.

In 2003, an upsurge of ethnic violence in Ituri province in the east led the Security Council to authorize deployment under Chapter VII of an interim emergency multinational force (Resolution 1484). The French-led EU operation, Operation Artemis, was the EU's first military operation. Mandated to reinforce MONUC and halt the rapidly deteriorating humanitarian situation in the city of Bunia, troops from five EU countries were on the ground within a week, but the operation was limited in duration (three months) and scope (securing the situation only in Bunia itself, not the Ituri region). In 2004, the Security Council strengthened MONUC's mandate, authorizing use of force to protect civilians, assist the transitional government, fill the security vacuum, and disarm and repatriate former armed militias, including the Rwandan Hutu *genocidaires*. It also authorized an increase in the number of troops to 16,700—fewer than requested. In short, it took four years for MONUC's mandate to evolve from traditional peacekeeping as an observer force into a complex, multidimensional operation involving peace enforcement and protection of civilians. Not only was MONUC understaffed for its mission, but with its more aggressive tactics the UN peacekeepers also became targets themselves—just as in Somalia.

Following the 2002 peace agreement, some peacebuilding activities were begun. In 2006, with support of an EU rapid reaction force and EU funding, the DRC held its first multiparty presidential and parliamentary elections in forty years—a sign that despite continuing problems, the transitional government was making progress with MONUC's help. MONUC itself was deployed throughout the country during the election period. Remarkably, the elections were considered reasonably free and fair.

Despite these signs of progress, violence persisted and, after 2008, worsened in the DRC's eastern provinces, particularly North and South Kivu, and the DRC remained highly unstable. The Hutu militias were still active, along with various Congolese militias, the Rwandan and Ugandan government troops, and the Ugandan-based Lord's Resistance Army. Illegal exploitation and looting of the DRC's rich natural resources continued to support the various armed groups. The humanitarian crises also continued, with ethnic cleansing, communal violence, and the worst instances of sexual violence in the world committed by militias and Congolese government troops alike engaging in widespread rape.

Although most UN member states had hoped that MONUC would be withdrawn after the 2006 elections, the Security Council successively increased the size and mandate of the force over the next three years in an effort to address the persistent violence and continue various peacebuilding activities. At its peak size of over 19,000 uniformed military and police, it was the largest UN peacekeeping mission (see Table 7.3). In 2009, MONUC undertook more robust efforts to stabilize eastern DRC in conjunction with Congolese national troops. These operations, however, proved controversial because of the army's record of human rights abuses and the UN peacekeepers' failure to protect civilians. They also led to tensions with the government and, finally, to a request that the UN withdraw all peacekeeping forces by mid 2011.

Under diplomatic pressure, the DRC government softened its position, and an agreement was reached in 2010 on reconfiguring the UN operation as a stabilization mission (the UN Organization Stabilization Mission in the Democratic Republic of Congo, or MONUSCO after its French name). The mandate concentrated on civilian protection and military operations in eastern DRC, plus establishing a reserve force to react to incidents throughout the country.

Violence and political instability persisted in the Congo, and in 2012 a new rebel group, M23, backed by Rwanda and Uganda, emerged to pose serious security problems, leading to the fall of the city of Goma to M23 forces as Congolese troops fled and MONUSCO forces provided little resistance (or protection for civilians). This galvanized several important steps. They included a Security Council–imposed arms embargo on M23 as well as targeted sanctions on its leadership, and a framework agreement signed by the UN, the AU, SADC, the International Conference on the Great Lakes Region, and eleven neighboring countries, with Rwanda and Uganda pledging not to interfere in the Congo's internal affairs. The Security Council also authorized an intervention force and use of surveillance drones to monitor the DRC's borders.The latter two steps proved to be the most significant in the short run at least, but raised serious questions about the nature of UN peacekeeping in the longer run.

The Force Intervention Brigade, composed of 3,000 South African, Tanzanian, and Malawian crack troops with tanks and helicopter gunships, was initially deployed in mid-2013 under MONUSCO and alongside the Congolese army to "prevent the expansion of all armed groups, neutralize these groups and disarm them" (Resolution 2098). By late October 2013, the brigade and the Congolese army had captured M23 strongholds and peace talks were under way. Jean-Marie Guéhenno, former head of the UN's DPKO, noted, however, that "it's not a SWAT team that's going to clean up a bad neighborhood. That requires politics" (Kulish and Sengupta 2013: A10). And, indeed, the DRC government walked out of the peace talks.

The use of the intervention brigade, which was authorized to continue into 2015, has raised concerns among aid organizations about the risks to the officials on the ground, as well as for future peacekeeping operations and the willingness of troop-contributing countries to put their soldiers at greater risk. While the Security Council was careful to make clear that the force set no precedents for "the agreed principles of peacekeeping," others see it as a "stronger approach that can give peacekeeping operations more strength in the future and help resolve knotty problems" (Kulish and Sengupta 2013: A10). An International Peace Institute assessment in late 2014 of the legal issues raised by the intervention brigade's mandate notes that these were "not fully considered or understood in March 2013, and that they have political and practical consequences" (Sheeran and Case 2014: 1). That mandate allows the force to move toward a more traditional warfighting mode and makes MONUSCO as a whole a party to the armed conflict. As a result, military members of MONUSCO lose legal protections afforded to them under international law. The report notes that the legal issues will affect other UN operations, especially those in "high-threat environments" where their mandates make it likely they, too, may become parties to the conflict and be seen as "taking sides." It quotes Russian ambassador Vitaly Churkin suggesting that "what was once the exception now threatens to become unacknowledged standard practice, with unpredictable and unclear consequences" (Sheeran and Case 2014: 19).

The problems in the DRC defy categorization or comprehension. Bearing some resemblance to Somalia, the DRC is a weak state teetering on the brink of failure, whose conflict includes various warlords and their militias. As in Bosnia, however, massive human rights violations and displacements have marked the conflict. Yet the DRC conflict is far more complex than those in either Somalia or Yugoslavia. The Congo's huge size has presented enormous logistical and operational difficulties that have magnified the cost of peace operations since roads and railroads are virtually unusable, requiring the use of more expensive air transport. Neither SADC nor the AU had the resources for significant enforcement action (and some of the parties involved in the conflict were SADC members). Hence, the challenges it poses to international peace and security governance are enormous.

Because the DRC lies in the heart of Africa, it has implications for much of the continent, but this also means that it has been of limited importance to the major powers. And, while the UN and other international actors have largely focused on national and regional causes of the violence, there are long-standing local conflicts over land, the DRC's rich resources, and political power that need to be addressed. One scholar who has worked in the DRC since 2001 found that the international actors have viewed the extensive grassroots violence as "a normal feature of life" and not as a problem that they could or should address. She faults the dominant peace-building culture in the UN as well as virtually all the other state and non-state actors for the failure of peace processes (Autesserre 2010). Indeed, the efforts by the international community have been largely top-down efforts aimed at statebuilding and military action against armed groups where local resolution strategies are called for (International Crisis Group 2013).

*Emergent issues in complex peacekeeping.* The case of the DRC, as well as two cases in 2013 and 2014, Mali and the Central African Republic (CAR), are raising significant concerns about that line between peacekeeping and peace enforcement, leading one researcher to question what happens with "the UN at war" (Karlsrud 2015). Specifically, the concerns arise from the authorization of the Force Intervention Brigade of troops from SADC countries to "neutralize and disarm" a particular militia (M23) in the DRC (Resolution 2098); the mandate for a UN mission combining AU, ECOWAS, Malian, and French special forces to effectively conduct war against al-Qaeda in the Islamic Maghreb (AQIM), liberation movements, and organized crime in Mali (Resolution 2100); the use of drones for reconnaissance on militia activity in the DRC and creation of a multinational intelligence unit in Mali; and, in the CAR, authorization to take over responsibility from the AU, ECOWAS, France, and the EU for stabilizing the country and stopping the ethnic cleansing (some would say genocide) of Christian groups (anti-Balaka) against Muslims (Resolution 2149). These mandates amount to a "doctrinal change in UN peacekeeping, towards stabilization and peace enforcement missions," with potentially serious ramifications for the operations and how they are perceived, and for troop-contributing countries (Karlsrud 2015: 41).

As the UN's experience in Somalia in 1993 demonstrated, the targeting of "an enemy" is particularly problematic if the UN wishes to maintain its impartiality. The authorization to use force other than to protect civilians for a limited period of time looks more like war than keeping peace and jeopardizes the safety of peacekeepers themselves as well as civilian and humanitarian UN workers. There are, indeed, concerns within the UN Secretariat and in the field about the implications of these developments, no consensus among member states about their desirability, and wariness among troop-contributing countries about the risks to troops themselves. John Karlsrud (2015: 50) asks whether this signifies "a need to update principles, or whether this is a function of practice leaving still valid principles behind."

### Postconflict Peacebuilding and Statebuilding

In various forms and degrees, postconflict peacebuilding activities are an integral part of most complex, multidimensional UN peace operations today, involving a variety of UN agencies and other IGOs and NGOs. The concept itself was first put forward by former Secretary-General Boutros Boutros-Ghali in *An Agenda for Peace* (1992), but the roots lie in the history of the UN's role in the process of decolonization and in its responses to the Namibia, Cambodia, and Central America conflicts in the early 1990s. Boutros-Ghali and other entrepreneurial UN officials contributed, as did the changes in the international system that marked the Cold War's end (Karns 2012).

The core ideas involve preventing renewed hostilities and aiding countries in building the foundations for long-term stability, including democratic polities. When the UN first undertook some of these tasks, however, there were serious questions regarding its authority for doing so, given Article 2(7) of the UN Charter—long seen as marking the line between states' sovereignty and UN authority. In a short period at the beginning of the 1990s, the Security Council authorized a series of missions that crossed the line and the Security Council's endorsement of *An Agenda for Peace* marked their acceptance.

At the heart of peacebuilding is the recognition that "prevention and rebuilding are inextricably linked . . . [and] a formal agreement ending a civil [war] is meaningless unless coupled with long-term programs to heal the wounded society" (Weinberger 2002: 248). Peacebuilding operations themselves, therefore, are complex and multifaceted, often including long lists of military and civilian tasks associated with such operations (see Figure 7.6). Barnett and colleagues (2007: 44) found significant agreement "that peacebuilding is more than stability promotion; it is designed to create a positive peace, to eliminate root causes of conflict, to allow states and societies to develop stable expectations of peaceful change." Some analysts suggest that the very breadth of the concept is problematic, given the lack of an agreed definition, and since often there is no clear end to violence and beginning to postconflict activities, many peacebuilding activities take place simultaneously with efforts to end violence, as the DRC case illustrates. In some cases, such as Kosovo and East Timor, the UN has gone beyond peacebuilding to activities associated with actual statebuilding—that is, working with local actors to create the foundations and institutions of a government. To examine the evolution of postconflict peacebuilding and statebuilding operations, we look at the first two such missions in Namibia and Cambodia, then at the later operations in Kosovo and East Timor.

*Namibia: The first experiment in peace- and statebuilding.* A former German colony (South West Africa) that was administered by South Africa as a
League of Nations mandate after World War I, Namibia became the object
of intense international efforts through the UN over many years to secure
its independence. In the late 1970s, the Security Council approved a plan
setting the terms for this with the approval of South Africa and the main
Namibian liberation group (Karns 1987). Implementation stalled, however,
for a decade, until there was agreement on the withdrawal of both Cuban
and South African troops from neighboring Angola.

The UN Transition Assistance Group in Namibia (UNTAG), deployed
in April 1989, had the most ambitious and diverse mandate of any UN mission to that time. It included supervision of the cease-fire between South
African and South West Africa People's Organization (SWAPO) forces,
monitoring the withdrawal of South African forces and the confinement of
SWAPO forces to bases, supervising the civil police force, securing repeal
of discriminatory legislation, arranging for the release of political prisoners
and return of exiles, assisting in drafting a new constitution, and creating
conditions for free and fair elections. With military and civilian personnel
from 109 countries, UNTAG managed the process by which Namibia
moved step-by-step from South African rule to a cease-fire, full independence, and political stability (Howard 2008). UNTAG is widely regarded as
one of the UN's greatest peacekeeping success stories. That success, however, owed much to factors that have not been present in other situations,
including the presence of South Africa's competent administration and
security forces, agreement on how to reach the goal of Namibian independence, and a strong sense of responsibility for providing the necessary
resources (Dobbins et al. 2005: 42). The experience in Namibia led the UN
to undertake other complex missions, not all of which enjoyed the same
success. One of those was the Cambodian peace operation.

*Cambodia: Experimenting with interim administration.* In 1991, following the twenty-year civil war in Cambodia, the Agreements on a Comprehensive Political Settlement of the Cambodia Conflict were signed in Paris
with US, Soviet, Chinese, and Vietnamese support. ASEAN also played a
key role in the search for a diplomatic settlement. The agreements "charged
the UN—for the first time in its history—with the political and economic
restructuring of a member state as part of the building of peace under which
the parties were to institutionalize their reconciliation" (Doyle 1995: 26).

A small advance mission helped the four Cambodian parties implement
the cease-fire. In 1992, the UN Transitional Authority in Cambodia
(UNTAC) was deployed under a mandate that called for up to 22,000 military and civilian personnel. UNTAC's military component was charged
with supervising the cease-fire and disarming and demobilizing forces; the

civilian personnel had responsibility for Cambodia's foreign affairs, defense, finance, and public security. UN personnel also monitored the police, promoted respect for human rights, assisted in the return of 370,000 Cambodian refugees from camps in Thailand, organized the 1993 elections that returned civil authority to Cambodians, and rehabilitated basic infrastructure and public utilities. As then–Secretary-General Boutros Boutros-Ghali observed, "Nothing the UN has ever done can match this operation" (UN 1993: 26).

UNTAC's presence helped end Cambodia's civil war and bring a peace of sorts to most of the country. UNTAC was unable, however, to achieve a full cease-fire and demobilization of forces, or complete its civil mission. General John Sanderson (2001: 159), the Australian commander of UNTAC from 1992 to 1993, has observed: "UNTAC was a peacekeeping mission which achieved its objectives but failed to leave the country in the progressive democratic state intended by those who set up the peace process." He cited insufficient attention to building an effective rule-of-law and justice system and the UN's limited role in the constitutional process. In this respect, the UN's mandate was not ambitious enough if long-term stability was the goal. UNTAC was abruptly terminated in 1993 after Cambodia's successful elections that year, following which a military coup in 1997 erased many of its gains. Cambodia, therefore, illustrates the difficulty of carrying out all aspects of a complex peacekeeping and peacebuilding mission.

*Kosovo and East Timor: The challenges of state-making.* The UN built on its experience in Namibia and Cambodia to address the situations in both Kosovo and East Timor in the late 1990s, undertaking multidimensional operations with even more extensive peace and statebuilding responsibilities. In neither case, however, was there a prior peace agreement or an existing state; both were provinces of other countries (Yugoslavia/Serbia and Indonesia); both cases involved the initial use of force by a coalition of the willing—the United States and NATO in the case of Kosovo, and a UN-authorized Australian-led force in the case of East Timor. In the case of Kosovo, international legal status was among the questions to be determined; in East Timor, as in Namibia, the outcome was to be independent statehood.

Following NATO bombing of Serbia and intervention to protect Kosovar Albanians in 1999 from ethnic cleansing by Serbian/Yugoslav military forces that displaced more than a million people, Security Council Resolution 1244 (1999) authorized the UN Mission in Kosovo (UNMIK) to undertake wide-ranging civilian administrative functions, in conjunction with a NATO peacekeeping force (KFOR). These duties included maintaining civil law and order, aiding in return of refugees, coordinating humanitarian relief, supporting reconstruction of key infrastructure, promoting Kosovo's autonomy and self-government, and helping to determine Kosovo's future legal status. The head of UNMIK, a Special Representative of the Secretary-General (SRSG), was expected to coordinate the work of several non-UN organizations, among which various functions were divided, but over which he had little power. The Kosovo mission was the first UN mission designed with other IGOs as full partners. The UN had chief responsibility for civil administration, police, and justice; the OSCE handled democratization and institution building; the EU was responsible for reconstruction and development; and the UNHCR was responsible for all humanitarian matters. A contact group (United States, United Kingdom, France, Germany, Italy, and Russia) originally formed in the early 1990s to address Yugoslavia's breakup provided a political mechanism to ensure the support of key powers for UNMIK.

There have, however, been a number of problems with the Kosovo mission. First, the Albanian Kosovars clearly sought independence, but the mandate called for respecting Yugoslavia's sovereignty and the protection of Serbs living in Kosovo who wanted to be part of Yugoslavia (now Serbia). Thus, it was unclear when and how independence could be achieved given Serbia's strong opposition, supported by Russia and others, and the absence of any international agreement. Second, it proved particularly difficult to recruit adequate numbers of police for UNMIK. Third, coordination among the partner organizations has been hampered by different organizational objectives and cultures, and the UN has no authority to impose coordination. Fourth, Kosovo's economy has become extensively criminalized, with little done by UNMIK to curb transnational drug, organ, and human trafficking. Despite the difficulties, the international statebuilding efforts supported by various actors did succeed in collaboration with local actors in building two effective state bureaucracies—the police and customs services. The key, Elton Skendaj (2014: 460) argues, was "insulating public administrators from public influence, and thereby recruiting and promoting officials according to merit."

In 2006, the UN's Special Envoy for Kosovo, Martti Ahtisaari, initiated a diplomatic process to determine Kosovo's final status, which led to a proposal for self-government under EU supervision—thus continuing indefinite international supervision and leaving Kosovo's legal status undetermined. In 2008, Kosovo's Provisional Self-Government Assembly declared the country's independence and received recognition from sixty-nine UN members, including the United States and many European countries, but strong opposition from Russia and Serbia. Responsibility for policing and rule of law were transferred from UNMIK to the EU in 2008, with the EU Rule of Law Mission in Kosovo (EULEX) becoming the EU's largest civilian mission; UNMIK retains responsibility for promoting security, stability, and respect for human rights; there is an EU-appointed special representative in Kosovo; and 5,000 NATO KFOR troops remain in place. In 2010, the ICJ issued a ruling that Kosovo's declaration of independence did not violate international law. Kosovo itself declared the end of "supervised independence" in 2012, but that did not change the basically frozen situation.

The difficulties of statebuilding in Kosovo have been reinforced by the experience in East Timor (now Timor-Leste), where the transition to independence under UN auspices initially seemed successful, but the newly independent government proved to have little capacity beyond its capital and the UN was forced to return in 2006 when riots and political instability suggested that it left too soon. This mission was undertaken in 1999 after almost fifteen years of UN-mediated efforts to resolve the status of East Timor—a former Portuguese colony seized by Indonesia in the mid-1970s—when, after a UN-organized vote endorsed independence, violence broke out, Indonesian troops failed to restore order, and almost half a million East Timorese were displaced from their homes. The Security Council initially authorized the Australian-led multinational force to restore order and then created the UN Transitional Administration in East Timor (UNTAET) with an ambitious and wide-ranging mission ranging from exercising all judicial, legislative, and executive powers to assisting in development of state services and humanitarian aid, promoting sustainable development, and building the foundation for stable liberal democracy.

As in Kosovo, the UN's role in East Timor involved collaboration with other international organizations—both IGOs and NGOs—and a very ambitious mandate with a short timeline. But East Timor faced a far greater problem—total destruction wrought by the Indonesia-backed militias and the departure of all civilian administrators. Unlike in Kosovo, however, the UN's charge was unequivocal: UNTAET was to lead the territory to statehood. Still, there was no roadmap to follow and little knowledge of the situation (nor regard for local expertise, according to various sources; for example, see Butler 2012). Sergio Vieira de Mello, the SRSG in charge, admitted, "We had to feel our way, somewhat blindly, towards [the two-phased strategy of devolving executive power] wasting several months in doing [so]" (Vieira de Mello 2001).

Despite Timorese complaints of delay and insufficient empowerment, in 2002, after just three years, elections were held and an independent Timor-Leste was recognized. A small UN operation continued to provide support for stability, democracy, justice, law enforcement, and external security until 2005, when it was terminated despite Timor's lack of economic development and still shaky political institutions. Grievances within the armed forces led to intercommunal violence and political tensions, producing a crisis in 2006. The Security Council authorized the new UN Integrated Mission in Timor (UNMIT) with a mandate very similar to that of

UNTAET to support the government and relevant institutions to consolidate political stability and ensure security (Resolution 1704), but with fewer personnel and resources. The 2006 crisis, however, had revealed the weakness of government institutions, the police, and the military, as well as rivalries among leaders, regional differences, and a culture of violence. In the view of the International Crisis Group (2008: 1), Timor-Leste was a "failed state in the making." One of the major problems with the UN administration had been its failure to "share power sufficiently with Timorese counterparts early on and failing to shift power more fully to them early enough" (Braithwaite 2013: 103). There was also a presumption that Timor lacked institutions and, therefore, UN staff sought to create them rather than working with indigenous justice institutions, a critique similar to those made about the DRC—in other words, a failure to understand local conditions. Whether the earlier UN mission had failed in its mandate, or underlying local factors were responsible for the 2006 crisis, continues to be a matter of debate (Tansey 2014). In any case, "from the UN perspective, the possibility of state failure in Timor-Leste was untenable . . . a major failure of the UN itself . . . due to the sunk costs involved" (Butler 2012: 96).

UNMIT terminated its mission in December 2012, following a two-year transition process that included national elections that met international standards, the formation of a new government, and working with the parliament, civil society, and media to create a resilient state. The transition plan also included the creation of a follow-on UN political mission that is focusing on development of the police force with the financial support of Australia and New Zealand. Timor-Leste is endowed with major oil and gas reserves, which have helped to support the new country's stability but are not a panacea for its continuing weaknesses.

\* \* \*

In short, peacebuilding as statebuilding entails major challenges for the international community. The interim administrations in Kosovo and Bosnia, where internationally appointed representatives retain authority, have been described as forms of international trusteeship, protectorates, and even neoimperialism, given that the circumstances under which international oversight will be terminated are unclear. And, as the case of East Timor shows, if a statebuilding process is flawed or ends too quickly or lacks sufficient resources, further international involvement may well be required.

Nowhere today are these challenges perhaps more evident than in the Republic of South Sudan—the world's newest state—which gained independence following the 2005 Comprehensive Peace Agreement ending the Sudan's long-running civil war between north and south and the resulting

2011 referendum in the south. South Sudan, however, came into existence with unresolved disputes with Sudan over borders and division of oil revenues and little infrastructure or government institutions.

The UN Mission in South Sudan (UNMISS), authorized by the Security Council in July 2011 (Resolution 1996), is tasked with supporting the development of state institutions and has a Chapter VII mandate to use force to protect civilians. The DPKO, however, had great difficulty securing commitments for troops and equipment, especially much needed helicopters, for UNMISS. Other key actors are the EU, the AU, the Intergovernmental Authority for Development (IGAD), the United States, which played a major role in the peace negotiations, and China, which has a strong interest in South Sudan's large oil reserves. A separate UN Interim Security Force was authorized in Abyei—a territory claimed by both Sudan and South Sudan.

Little more than two years after independence, the new country had descended into open civil war as a result of splits between the former guerrilla leader turned president, Salva Kiir, and his vice president, Riek Machar. By early 2014, more than a million people had been displaced and over 10,000 killed; ethnic cleansing bordering on genocide between Dinka and Nuer elements accompanied great brutality in killing; tens of thousands of people took refuge within UN bases, yet the bases and UN peacekeepers were also attacked by heavily armed militias. The enormous humanitarian crisis includes threat of widespread famine. By the end of August 2014, the UN DPKO's head called the humanitarian operations in South Sudan the largest in the world. IGAD has had the lead role in trying to obtain a cease-fire, but calls for IGAD to impose more punitive measures or for the Security Council to impose an arms embargo or targeted sanctions against senior South Sudanese officials had not been met by early 2015. Rather, the UN special envoy reported that hardliners on both sides seemed bent on a military solution (Security Council Report 2015).

In many respects, the situation in South Sudan resembles the DRC far more than the situations in Namibia, Cambodia, Kosovo, or East Timor. And it is perhaps instructive that there was no desire to create a transitional administration or international authority in South Sudan. If or when the fighting ends, as the International Crisis Group report of April 2014 noted, "the country needs fundamental reworking of the governance agreement between and within elites and communities if a negotiated settlement is to lead to a sustainable peace" (ICG 2014).

### The Challenges of Organizing for Peace Operations

Given the evolution from traditional peacekeeping to complex "muscular" peacekeeping to peacebuilding and statebuilding, organizing these various peace operations has become more complex. When a new UN mission is approved or a mission mandate expanded by the Security Council, the UN's Department of Peacekeeping Operations and Department of Field Support are responsible for determining the exact requirements, seeking the necessary military and civilian contingents and logistical support, and servicing the operation. The UNSG appoints a force commander from the top officer corps of a member country and, for major operations, also appoints a special representative to oversee the entire mission. Most likely, there is already a UN political mission on the ground. When a peace operation includes the organization and supervision of elections, the UN's Electoral Assistance Division, established in 1992, is also involved.

The size of peace operations—whether UN, regional, hybrid, or partnering—has varied widely, from small monitoring missions numbering less than a hundred, to major operations in the Congo in the 1960s; Cambodia, Somalia, and Bosnia in the early 1990s; and the DRC, Somalia, and Darfur today requiring over 15,000 troops. Table 7.3 shows the mix of troops, local and international civilians, and police that make up multidimensional operations. It is not uncommon for the number of troops and police, however, to be significantly smaller than the number authorized by the Security Council. For example, the joint UN-AU mission in Darfur, authorized in 2007, was at barely 75 percent of strength at the beginning of 2009. In 2012, it still had fewer troops and police than authorized. The larger and more complex the operations, the greater the organizational challenges for the UN (and other IGOs).

Since the permanent UN military forces envisioned by the Charter (Articles 43–45) were never created, the UN has relied on ad hoc military, civilian, or police units volunteered by member states to create multinational operations. During the Cold War, these were drawn almost exclusively from the armed forces of states other than the P-5 (often middle powers and nonaligned members such as Canada, India, Sweden, Ghana, and Nepal) to keep the two superpowers out of regional conflicts or, in the case of postcolonial problems, to keep former colonial powers from returning.

Major powers, including the United States, Great Britain, France, and Russia, have also contributed forces since the end of the Cold War and especially with much larger peace operations. Top troop contributors to UN missions in 2014 were Pakistan, Bangladesh, India, Ethiopia, and Nigeria; top police contributors were Bangladesh, Jordan, and India. China first made personnel (civilian police) available for the UN mission in Haiti in 2004; in 2014, it had about 2,200 military and police deployed in nine UN operations. Overall, in 2014, the UN had more than 104,000 troops, police, and military observers deployed in sixteen missions, with 128 member states making contributions ranging from 3 to 10,000 persons.

An important innovation in personnel followed Security Council Resolution 1325 (2000), which called for greater participation of women in peacekeeping and protection activities. As of early 2015, there were more than 500 women in four all-female police units and over 4,000 women in UN peace operations overall. That represents a quadrupling of female military and police personnel since the first statistics were published in 2005, but still represents barely 3 percent of personnel. India deployed the first female police unit, to Liberia in 2007; three others have since been deployed: two from Bangladesh to Haiti and the DRC; one from Samoa to Timor Leste; and another from Peru to Haiti. The impetus for adding women came both from the advocacy of women's NGOs prompted by sexual violence in conflicts, and from gender-based violence committed by peacekeepers themselves. Female peacekeepers may also serve as role models to local women, address needs of female ex-combatants, and help make the peacekeeping force more approachable to local women (Dharmapuri 2013).

It has become increasingly difficult to get states to contribute military forces (or other types of personnel) for peace operations. Under complex peacekeeping, with the higher likelihood of casualties, many member states have been less willing to allow their troops to participate. Furthermore, some countries' units have proven more effective than others, making them more desirable. Sexual misconduct by some peacekeepers has created thorny issues for both the DPKO and contributing states. Civilian police units have proven even harder than military units to recruit for peace operations, as few states have police officers readily available or trained for international duties and situations that are likely to be very different from what they are accustomed to (Diehl 2008: 86). And few states have women military or police to offer.

For many countries, however, there are important goals to be served by peacekeeping participation. The difference between poorer countries' military salary levels and those paid by the UN makes troop contributions economically attractive. Small states such as Fiji and Nepal gain prestige, valuable training, and field experience by participating in UN peacekeeping. Canada and the Nordic countries long saw peacekeeping contributions as a way to underscore their commitment to multilateralism in addressing world problems. Brazil, Japan, and Germany's contributions, by contrast, reflected their desire to secure permanent seats on the Security Council. China's participation reflects its shifting interests and growing role in global governance. There has been a steady decline, however, in peacekeepers from Western developed countries; hence the heavy UN reliance on personnel from African and South Asian countries. There are fears that this could undermine future UN peacekeeping if developing countries perceive that they bear an unfair and disproportionate burden.

Regional and subregional organizations have also become part of the mix of complex peacekeeping and peacebuilding operations. The sheer number of new operations (fifteen) that the UN undertook between 1989 and 1993 taxed its capacity to organize and supervise missions. And the failure of the Security Council to act in a timely fashion regarding conflicts in several African countries, including Liberia, Sierra Leone, and Sudan, led Secretary-General Boutros-Ghali (1992: 64) to call for greater participation by regional organizations to share the burden and "contribute to a deeper sense of participation, consensus and democratization in international affairs." By the late 1990s, there were more regional IGO peace operations than UN operations, a trend that has shifted since 2003 with more efforts involving both the UN and regional IGOs in addressing threats to peace and security, particularly in Africa.

Between 1990 and 2003, African subregional organizations, particularly ECOWAS and SADC, took up the challenge, in part because the OAU lacked peace operation capabilities. ECOWAS undertook peace operations in Liberia and Sierra Leone and later in Guinea-Bissau, Côte d'Ivoire, and Mali; SADC sent peacekeeping troops into the DRC and Lesotho in 1998. Between 2003 and 2009, the newly created AU undertook nine operations. Overall, between 1990 and 2009, there were twenty-four UN peacekeeping operations in Africa and eleven non-UN, non-African operations mounted mostly by the EU (Williams 2011).

Other regional organizations have also undertaken peacekeeping activities. The OAS was part of a joint UN operation in Haiti in 1993; NATO sent peacekeepers (as well as combat troops) to Bosnia, Kosovo, and Afghanistan, then handed over responsibility in the first two to the EU in 2004 and 2008 respectively; Russia and the Commonwealth of Independent States took on peacekeeping roles in three civil conflicts arising from the collapse of the Soviet Union (Moldova, Georgia, and Tajikistan) with UN observers to ensure international oversight; the OSCE has monitored many situations in Central and Eastern Europe and Central Asia, including the conflict and cease-fire in Ukraine in 2014.

Since 2003, the AU, the EU, ECOWAS, and NATO have emerged as the primary regional organizations involved in peace operations, often in partnerships with the UN (and each other) ranging from sequential deployments (for example, a transition from ECOWAS to the UN in Liberia and Sierra Leone) to integrated "hybrid" missions (for example, the AU and UN in UNAMID in Darfur). Despite the greater involvement of regional and subregional organizations, the UN still has the largest number of military personnel in peace operations (Center on International Cooperation 2013: 8). Particularly in Africa, however, the UN-AU relationship offers ways of delivering more effective peace operations in the future if decisionmaking is harmonized and institutionalized and a new financing mechanism and coordinated reassessments instituted (Williams and Dersso 2015).

The increased involvement of regional IGOs in peace operations has raised issues of authority and legitimacy. In some cases, the UN Security Council has delegated responsibility to a regional IGO or given its approval retroactively; in other cases, regional operations have been undertaken in collaboration or partnership with the UN and, in a few cases, have subsequently transitioned to a UN operation (see Table 7.4). Often when there is a transition from a regional to a UN peacekeeping force, soldiers from NATO or the AU have simply changed their hats to don the UN's blue berets and the UNSG has named a new commander. Although none of the regional organizations were designed specifically to complement the UN's role, as discussed earlier, Chapter VIII of the UN Charter clearly envisioned the possibility of such entities and Article 52 encourages regional efforts to settle disputes peacefully.

**Table 7.4    Regional Organizations and Peace Operations (selected cases)**

| Conflict | Regional IGOs | Transition to UN Operation? | Partnership with UN? | Duration |
|---|---|---|---|---|
| Liberia | ECOWAS | Yes | No | 1990–1997 |
| | ECOWAS | Yes | No | 2003–2004 |
| Bosnia | NATO | No | Yes | 1995–2003 |
| | OSCE | No | Yes | 1995– |
| | EU | No | Yes | 2003– |
| Guinea-Bissau | ECOWAS | Yes | No | 1998–1999 |
| | ECOWAS | No | Yes | 2012– |
| Sierra Leone | ECOWAS | Yes | No | 1998–1999 |
| DRC | SADC | Yes | Yes | 1998–2002 |
| | AU | No | Yes | 1999– |
| | EU | No | Yes | 2003, 2006, 2007– |
| Kosovo | NATO | No | Yes | 1999–2008 |
| | OSCE | No | Yes | 1999– |
| | EU | No | Yes | 2008– |
| Burundi | AU | Yes | No | 2001–2004, 2006–2009 |
| Côte d'Ivoire | ECOWAS | Yes | No | 2003–2004 |
| Sudan/Darfur | IGAD | No | No | 2003–2005 |
| | AU | Yes | Yes | 2004–2007 |
| Indonesia/Aceh | ASEAN, EU | No | No | 2005–2006 |
| South Sudan | AU, IGAD | Yes | Yes | 2005–2011 |
| | EU | | | 2012– |
| Central African Republic | CEMAC | Yes | No | 2006–2007 |
| | EU, AU | Yes | No | 2014– |
| Somalia | AU | No | No | 2008– |
| Mali | ECOWAS, AU | Yes | Yes | 2012– |
| | EU | | | 2013– |

Regional and subregional IGOs vary widely in their organizational capacities. Resource constraints particularly afflict all of the African organizations. As a result, capacity-building efforts have been under way since the mid-2000s, supported by the G-8's Global Peace Operations Initiative and the EU's African Peace Facility. NATO is the exception to the general rule that IGOs do not have any military capabilities except those that their members commit for action on an ad hoc basis, but the earlier discussion of its role in Afghanistan showed the difficulties even it has encountered in getting members to commit troops and not limit their use. As discussed in Chapter 5, the EU's rapid reaction force is relatively recent. That capability proved vital on three occasions in the DRC and has been utilized more recently in a number of situations.

The problem of recruiting forces has led to periodic proposals for a permanent or standby peacekeeping force under the UN or a regional organization. The EU's rapid reaction force is one example. The AU also has plans for such a force. Absent a multilateral force, a few countries, notably Canada and the Scandinavian countries, have earmarked portions of their military forces specifically for peacekeeping assignments and trained them accordingly. International peacekeeping centers have now been established in many countries and on all continents to train military, police, and civilians.

With peacebuilding activities an integral part of virtually all complex, multidimensional UN peace operations now, they have also become part of the activities of many UN agencies and other organizations. Given the number of non-UN actors involved, there has been a continuing call for better coordination and sustained international efforts. The establishment of the UN Peacebuilding Commission (PBC) in 2006, bringing together all the relevant actors to develop integrated strategies and sustained attention for postconflict peacebuilding and recovery, was designed to meet that call.

The PBC is composed of thirty-one UN member states, including the P-5. It forms what are known as "country-specific configurations" for each of the countries in which it is involved; these include the thirty-one PBC members; the World Bank, IMF, and regional banks; top providers of financial aid, military personnel, and civilian police in the country; relevant regional and subregional organizations; the senior UN representative in the field; and other relevant UN staff. In short, the PBC itself, and particularly the country configurations, are expected to serve as an intergovernmental advisory body to bring together all relevant actors, marshal resources, and advise on strategies, with a permanent representative of a member state serving as an advocate for the country. The UN General Assembly created the Peacebuilding Fund for postconflict reconstruction, to be financed by voluntary contributions, and the Peacebuilding Support Office within the

Secretariat. The three institutions together constitute what is now called the UN's "peacebuilding architecture."

The first two countries referred to the PBC by the Security Council were Burundi and Sierra Leone; subsequently the Central African Republic, Guinea, Liberia, and Guinea-Bissau have been added. In each of the countries on its agenda, consultations between the PBC and government identify critical areas for consolidating peace, such as strengthening the rule of law, security sector reform, promoting good governance, and youth employment and specific peacebuilding projects for funding by the UN and international and national donors. The fund also supports projects in non-PBC countries to avert the risk of relapse into conflict, help implement peace agreements, or strengthen peacebuilding efforts. In the later section on evaluating peace operations, we look further at the PBC's track record to date.

A significant aspect of many complex peace operations has been the intermingling of armed conflict and large-scale humanitarian crises. These have given rise to debate over the international community's responsibility to protect civilians.

### Humanitarian Intervention: The Debate over R2P and Protection of Civilians

Horrific as earlier twentieth-century conflicts were, many post-1990 conflicts have been marked by major humanitarian crises, genocide, crimes against humanity, widespread human rights abuses, huge numbers of refugees and IDPs, and deliberate targeting of civilians (see Table 7.5). UN peace operations and the UNHCR, the UN Office for the Coordination of Humanitarian Affairs (UNOCHA), and humanitarian NGOs have been challenged as never before. The very fact that the Security Council during the 1990s repeatedly referred to humanitarian crises as threats to international peace and security under Chapter VII marked a change.

The responses by the international community to these humanitarian crises have been inconsistent and selective, however. The creation of safe havens and no-fly zones in northern and southern Iraq in April 1991 protected Iraqi Kurds and Shiites, without the consent of state authorities. The UN intervened in Somalia and NATO in Kosovo, but responded only partially to the genocide in Rwanda and belatedly to that in Darfur, as examined in Chapter 10. Varying great-power interests and political will in the Security Council, as well as selective media and NGO attention, all play a role in determining which situations get attention.

Two major consequences of the change in the 1990s have been the debate over the responsibility to protect (R2P) norm and the protection of civilians (POC) mandate now included in many peace operations. While R2P and POC are related—"sisters but not twins" as one scholar puts it (Popovski 2011), they differ, he argues, in that R2P applies to situations of

**Table 7.5   Selected Post–Cold War Humanitarian Crises**

| Crisis Period | Country | People at Risk |
|---|---|---|
| 1991 | Iraq (northern) | 2.5 million refugees |
| 1991–1995 | Bosnia | 250,000 deaths<br>1.4 million refugees<br>2.7 million displaced |
| 1992–1993 | Somalia | 300,000 deaths<br>1 million refugees<br>95 percent of population malnourished |
| 1994 | Rwanda | 850,000 deaths<br>1.1 million refugees |
| 1995–1996 | Burundi | 150,000 deaths<br>1 million displaced |
| 1998– | Democratic Republic of Congo | 5.4 million deaths (est. as of 2008)<br>493,000 refugees (July 2014)<br>2.6 million displaced (July 2014) |
| 1999 | Kosovo | 800,000 refugees |
| 2003– | Sudan/Darfur | 300,000 deaths (est. July 2014)<br>670,000 refugees (est. July 2014)<br>2.3 million displaced (est. July 2014) |
| 2011– | Syria | 220,000 deaths (est. Jan. 2015)<br>3.9 million refugees (est. Mar. 2015)<br>7.6 million displaced (est. Dec. 2014) |

mass atrocities and involves all types of war crimes—a narrower scope than POC, which applies to the effects of armed conflicts on civilians and only those war crimes that involve civilians. Where POC applies to all parties in a conflict (states and nonstate actors), R2P applies only to states. Altogether, between 2006 and late 2014, the Security Council approved twenty-six resolutions referring to R2P and/or POC.

What has particularly been missed in debates over R2P, however, is that this norm is not just or primarily about military intervention. "R2P is about a whole continuum of reaction from diplomatic persuasion, to pressure, to non-military measures like sanctions and International Criminal Court process, and only in extreme, exceptional and last resort cases military action" (Evans 2012). Primary responsibility lies with sovereign states to protect their own people, secondarily with the international community; when prevention fails and a state is not protecting its own people, then the UN has responsibility for acting under the Charter.

Since the 2011 intervention in Libya, there has been vigorous debate in scholarly and policy circles about "why Libya and not Syria" and whether the UN and international community's failure to intervene in Syria marks the death of R2P. There is consensus that the situations were not directly comparable. The UN-sanctioned intervention in Libya had strong endorsements from four regional organizations—the Arab League, GCC, OIC, and AU—and Qaddafi had few friends. Plus the United States, Britain, and France were willing to act and believed that they could foil Qaddafi's threat of mass atrocities relatively quickly and easily. Although there were no explicit references to R2P in Security Council debates, analysts have concluded that "states were surely moved to intervene, or not to block intervention [in Libya], in large part because of the power of ideas and norms of human protection related to R2P" (Glanville 2014). Others argue that the intervention in Libya marks the "furthest point in the swing of the R2P pendulum" (Morris 2013: 1265).

But because the NATO intervention evolved to include regime change, however, the doubts that Russia, China, Brazil, India, and others had quickly turned to opposition, creating a "shadow of Libya" effect over Security Council discussions of possible action in Syria. To be sure, the humanitarian crisis in Syria has been far greater than any imagined in Libya, but the problems are attributable not only to the Assad government, but also to various rebel groups and militias. There has been no call from the Arab League, GCC, or OIC for intervention; the Arab states are divided. Perhaps most important, Assad has two powerful friends—Russia and China—exercising their veto power in the Security Council, and the United States has been unwilling to act.

Why has there been no invocation to protect civilians in the Syria case? After all, as of 2014, there have been ten UN operations with POC mandates. The Security Council has held regular meetings on the subject since 1999 and along with the Secretary-General has issued both country-specific and thematic resolutions on both genocide and protection of civilians in armed conflict. Also, there are now senior advisers to the UNSG on both genocide and protection of civilians in armed conflict; the UN's High Commissioners for Human Rights and Humanitarian Affairs have regularly pleaded for action.

There is little doubt that the Security Council's inability to act in the Syrian crisis—even to condemn the use of force against civilians by the Syrian government and the humanitarian crisis—has been shameful. In fact, in August 2012 the General Assembly, by a vote of 133 in favor with 12 opposed and 31 abstentions, deplored the Council's failure to respond to the crisis and condemned the "widespread and systematic gross violations of human rights" by the Syrian government and pro-government militias (Resolution 66/253B). In March 2015, twenty-one aid agencies criticized the Council for not enforcing its own measures and called the failure to act "a stain on the conscience of the international community." Secretary-General Ban Ki-moon called the P-5 "incapable of taking collective action" and spoke of an "exponential rise in war crimes" as a result (Sengupta 2015a: A4). Yet it is important to note that international military intervention has not generally been considered the appropriate, just, or prudent response, particularly prior to the Syrian government's chemical weapons attack that killed 1,400 civilians in August 2013. It was, in short, "very difficult to see how an external military intervention could do more good than harm" (Glanville 2014). Clearly, an important lesson is that many states remain wary of approving an outside intervention in an intrastate conflict without that state's consent and when the interests of several great powers oppose intervention. Some have also argued that the UN's inability to act demonstrates how power is "moving away from the West" and a "new era of multi-polarity has begun" (Hehir 2014).

The debate about the future of R2P and humanitarian intervention is likely to persist. Almost simultaneously with the intervention in Libya and the beginning of Syria's civil war, the Security Council authorized the UN Operation in Côte d'Ivoire (UNOCI) to use "all necessary means" to protect civilians (Resolution 1975) and, in effect, help oust Laurent Gbagbo, who had refused to leave office after losing the presidential election in 2010. Both the AU and ECOWAS had recognized his opponent, Alassane Ouattara, as president-elect, there were warnings from the special advisers to the UNSG on genocide and R2P of the possibility of mass atrocities; UN and French forces turned the tide, blurring the line between POC and regime change and raising concerns about compromising the UN's impartiality in the situation. As in the Libyan case, however, in Syria regional IGOs played a major "gatekeeping" role in justifications of UN intervention (Bellamy and Williams 2011). This raises the question of which regional organizations can legitimately claim that role, however, and opens the possibility of forum-shopping—that is, using a variety of institutions in search of the most favorable outcome.

The bigger debate concerns whether R2P has a future and to what degree it has been internalized. No diplomat wants to appear to block action when many are dying, thus "diplomatic acuity may yet serve to ensure that R2P does not lose all of the ground gained so far" (Morris 2013: 1278). But as one of R2P's ardent proponents suggests, "Syria demonstrates, if there was any doubt, that a robust R2P response is never automatic . . . and [Syria] was distinctly more complicated, chancy, and confused than Libya" (Weiss 2014a).

If a norm of humanitarian intervention is ultimately confirmed, then there is all the more need for early warning, for preventive actions, and for peacebuilding once interventions have taken place, as the chaos that has engulfed Libya since the fall of Qaddafi demonstrates. In the future, however, partnerships involving the UN and regional IGOs, bolstered perhaps by a coalition of powerful states, are likely to mark international humanitarian interventions. The UN-AU Hybrid Mission in Darfur (UNAMID) demonstrates the problems a humanitarian intervention mission inadequately equipped even for peacekeeping can encounter, however, when it does not have sufficient support from major powers, is faced with opposition from both government and rebel forces, and lacks good leadership. A scathing three-part report published in 2014 recounts the failure of the peacekeepers to prevent the abduction of civilians and to confront the Sudanese government over its deliberate targeting of civilians and peacekeepers alike (Lynch 2014a). It also notes the failure of DPKO, the AU, and the Security Council to respond effectively and quotes an unnamed UN official saying, "We would love to declare defeat but we can't. We have to accept this as a quagmire." There is a clear sense that the mission was set up to fail (Lynch 2014b). Given the problems in Darfur, Syria, and elsewhere, the future of R2P and humanitarian interventions is likely to continue to be marked by selectivity and inconsistency in practice as Aidan Hehir (2013) and others have noted.

### Evaluating Success and Failure in Peace Operations

What defines success in peace operations? The absence of armed conflict? The end of a humanitarian crisis? A political solution in the form of a peace agreement? A "positive peace" that addresses the root causes of a conflict? Establishment of a stable, liberal, democratic state? A period of years (two, five, ten) without renewed fighting? The successful holding of free elections? The completion of a mandate? Success in protecting civilians?

Because the mandates of different types of peace operations differ significantly, the answer to this question of success must be linked to those different missions—unarmed observer missions, traditional peacekeeping missions with the consent of the parties, multidimensional complex peacekeeping, peacebuilding operations, and enforcement missions. Also, the various stakeholders in peace operations may well have different standards for judging success (Diehl 2008: 119; Autesserre 2014: chap. 1). In complex missions, there may be instances of both success and failure. The local population may define success in terms of returning to their homes or a perceived reduction in the possibility of renewed violence. Success for a belligerent may be negotiating a cease-fire and gaining time to rearm. To a troop-contributing country, having the troops return home marks success. For the UN Secretariat, it may simply be completion of the mandate or the successful holding of UN-organized elections. For the international community, establishing long-term stability may define success.

Since the late 1990s, there have been a number of empirical studies of peace operations using different categories of operations, types of conflicts, and time periods. There are significant methodological issues and variations in datasets that make comparability difficult, however (Diehl and Druckman 2010; Tansey 2014: 174). Yet there is considerable consensus emerging from these studies as well as some important divergence. There are also important insights into various factors that relate to success and failure and lessons for the UN and other IGOs as well as for policymakers.

The studies of various types of peace operations have shown the importance of situational factors that can affect success and failure, particularly in cases of civil war. With respect to interstate wars, however, there is strong evidence that observer or traditional peacekeeping missions reduce the risk of resumed fighting (Diehl 2000). In civil wars, the number and coherence of belligerents, the deadliness of the conflict, the roles of neighboring states, the presence of spoilers, a coerced peace, and the availability of lootable natural resources can all affect the outcomes of peace operations (Stedman, Rothchild, and Cousens 2002). As Virginia Fortna (2004a: 283) observes, "If peacekeepers tend to deploy only to relatively easy cases . . . [s]uch a policy would help the UN and the international community to avoid embarrassing failures, but . . . it will also ensure the irrelevance of peacekeeping." Yet research shows that peacekeepers have actually deployed to the "hard cases," after long wars that end (or persist) in a stalemate, and where there are three or more parties.

In addition to particularities of the conflict environment, there are a number of factors that correlate with success (or failure). Some, such as the desire of combatants for peace, a negotiated peace settlement, and the consent and cooperation of the parties, may seem obvious. The difficulty of a peace operation's mission and its mandate are important variables, as are the degree of international support, the resources made available, and the leadership, command structure, and quality of mission personnel, who must turn vague Security Council mandates into concrete tasks for implementation in various parts of a country. Studies have also shown that learning and adaptation by UN personnel both in the field and at UN headquarters in New York make a major difference (Dobbins et al. 2005; Howard 2008).

The timing of both deployment and withdrawal is also critical. Many critics have noted the long delay in deployment of UNTAC (eight months), compared to the UN's average deployment time in the 1990s of four to six months. The Brahimi Report (UN 2000) on UN peace operations, concluded that the first twelve weeks after a cease-fire or agreement were key. After that, peace may begin to unravel and the parties lose confidence in the process. Improved military planning enabled the UN to deploy approximately 6,000 troops each to four operations—in Burundi, Haiti, eastern DRC, and Côte d'Ivoire—within a few weeks in 2004. A recent study of four regional organizations involved in peace operations shows that the EU's response time has been the longest (six months), with the OSCE, OAS, and AU averaging just over or under four months. The variations are explained by differences in organizational decisionmaking processes and by levels of informal interaction (Hardt 2013: 379).

In multidimensional operations, other factors that may contribute to success include the demobilization and demilitarization of soldiers; the widespread deployment of police monitors along with police and judicial reform; the extensive training of election monitors; appointment of women protection advisers in missions where sexual violence has been a feature of the conflict; and most critical, continuous political support, patience, and adequate resources.

Multidimensional operations involving arms control verification, human rights monitoring, and election supervision tend to be successful, because they are most similar to traditional peacekeeping. They are generally linked to a peace agreement and hence involve consent of the parties. Thus, UN peacekeepers have compiled an excellent record, for example, in facilitating elections in Namibia, Cambodia, Mozambique, Eastern Slavonia, East Timor, and even the DRC. More generally, multidimensional operations have reduced the risk of war by half, but enforcement missions have been more associated with unstable peace (Fortna 2004a: 283–285). Yet there is a disturbing rate of conflict recurrence, estimated at between 20 percent and 56 percent for all civil conflicts (Fortna 2008: 104–116). Thus, "peacekeeping is clearly not a magic bullet" for containing conflicts, preventing their recurrence, or creating conditions for durable peace (Fortna 2004b: 193). In her own later work, however, Fortna concluded that peace is more durable when peace operations have been deployed, and that such operations lengthen the time for war recurrence. Among the reasons are that peacekeepers make attacks more difficult and lessen the possibility of accidents or minor incidents escalating into wider conflict (Fortna 2008: 155).

Research on peace operations in difficult civil wars and peacemaking efforts has shown that peacekeeping has little or no significant effect on mediation or negotiation success, while failed peacekeeping efforts have a negative effect on diplomatic initiatives in both interstate and civil wars (Greig and Diehl 2005). For example, in the DRC case, the Security Council delayed establishment of MONUC until after the Lusaka Agreement was in place, with consequent large loss of civilian lives in the interim. Yet MONUC did not facilitate conclusion of a comprehensive agreement that would hold, nor was it able to stop the fighting entirely and the horrific violence against civilians. Therefore, as Paul Diehl and Alexandru Balas (2014: 154) conclude, "it might be too much to expect those [missions in the most difficult conflicts] to make a significant difference in the behavior of implacable enemies." With regard to operations involving peacebuilding efforts, judging relative success depends on the standard applied (legitimate political institutions meeting minimal societal needs, redressing root causes, or no renewed large-scale violence plus improved governance) as well as on the time frame. Currently, there is "insufficient consensus on concepts, tools, and processes to measure peacebuilding and statebuilding"

(McCandless 2013: 228). Yet, others have tried just that and the results show the rate of success for peacebuilding varies from 31 percent to 85 percent, with divergent views making clear conclusions difficult (cited in Autesserre 2014: 22). Success on one dimension is not necessarily followed by success in another. Alex Bellamy and Paul Williams (2011), for example, found that the UN operation in Côte d'Ivoire had qualified success in limiting and containing violence and some success with regard to democratization, but failed to promote disarmament, demobilization, and reintegration. Using the ambitious standard of redressing root causes of conflict, Roland Paris (2004) categorized only Namibia and Eastern Slavonia as successful among eleven UN postconflict peacebuilding operations. Michael Doyle and Nicholas Sambanis (2006) found that peacebuilding efforts in over half of the civil wars ending between 1945 and 1999 failed by either the standard of merely keeping the peace or that of no renewed fighting and improved governance when assessed two or five years after the end of a peacebuilding operation. They further found, however, that UN multidimensional missions significantly increased the chances for success, especially in civil wars—a finding corroborated by James Dobbins and colleagues (2005). Charles Coll (2008) found that 60 percent of UN peacebuilding missions between 1987 and 2007 experienced no renewed conflict within five years.

Given concerns about weak and failed states as sources of security threats, successful peacebuilding has increasingly been linked to various statebuilding efforts such as security sector reform and judicial reform. Yet studies have also shown the tensions between these two processes. On the one hand, keeping an international military presence to ensure security may reduce the sense of urgency to build national capacity to control violence (Call and Cousens 2008: 10). On the other, there is the uncertainty of when to end international transitional authority, such as in Bosnia, Kosovo, and East Timor—uncertainty that may actually prolong the peacebuilding process and highlight the puzzle about what constitutes successful peacebuilding.

Should peacebuilding and statebuilding—and the broad range of activities included—be assessed against the Western blueprint for a liberal peace and a liberal concept of governance involving representative democracy, the rule of law, and a market economy? That has certainly been a widely shared assumption, and blueprints and checklists marked many of the early peacebuilding efforts. Yet Barnett and colleagues (2014: 608) note that "the weight of the evidence is increasingly pointing to the conclusion that, if democracy is the measure of a successful outcome, peacebuilding has a poor track record." Their conclusions show that local conditions determine whether peacebuilding is likely to make an impact on the prospect of a liberal peace, some being unfavorable (Cambodia), some being favorable (Namibia). In still other cases that they label "compromised peacebuilding," there may be a mixture of liberal and illiberal outcomes, including the symbols of liberal democracy ("ceremonial democracy") that may improve the chances of a liberal peace in the long term (617).

With regard to statebuilding, the dominant assumption has been that nation-states can be rebuilt in a relatively short time span despite the fact that nation-building historically has been a bloody and rarely, if ever, democratic process (Schulenburg 2014: 7). Yet the various international agencies involved in supporting statebuilding efforts, such as the OECD, World Bank, and UNDP, all have different approaches, assumptions, and definitions "driven as much by ideology and institutional mandates [as by] evidence" (McCandless 2013: 235). The reality is that peacebuilding and statebuilding are expensive and long-term, and involve many actors, making it difficult to establish metrics to assess success and failure.

In evaluating peacebuilding, it is important to ask what the decade-long experience of the Peacebuilding Commission shows. Of the first six countries on the PBC's agenda, only Liberia has remained free of political violence following the end of its civil war in 2003 and, unlike the others (Sierra Leone, Burundi, Guinea-Bissau, the CAR, and Guinea), had a UN peacekeeping mission with military observers and police deployed across the country at the time it was placed on the PBC's agenda. For each country, consultations between the PBC and government identify critical areas for consolidating peace, such as strengthening the rule of law, security sector reform, promoting good governance, and specific peacebuilding projects to be funded by the UN and other international and national donors. There has been considerable disappointment, however, on the resource-mobilization side, as increased fundraising capacity has been a major reason for countries to seek to be on the PBC's agenda. Sierra Leone, for example, has benefited from major World Bank and EU investments in youth unemployment and energy in addition to African Development Bank, UN, and UK funding, and Liberia has had the benefit of significant Swedish presence in the field along with heavy investment in priority PBC areas. In contrast, PBC work in Guinea-Bissau was halted after the 2012 coup, and fundraising for the CAR failed to obtain pledges in 2009 and was halted in 2012 (*Security Council Report* 2013a).

Whether the PBC can truly improve the international community's ability to build on the lessons of earlier missions is questionable. The political instability in four of the six countries on the PBC's agenda makes this even more uncertain. Relationships between PBC missions, governments, and other UN missions and personnel in the field are neither well defined or well coordinated, and largely depend on personalities. The result is many different programs, agencies, and funds operating in the same country with different cultures, administrative processes, communication systems, and policy guidance (*Security Council Report* 2013a).

In short, there is no formula for peacebuilding and statebuilding. Each situation is unique and requires getting the implementation environment right. While Kosovo and Bosnia show that lengthy stays do not guarantee success, East Timor shows that early departure can link to failure (or the need to return). Sustained attention, political will, and resources are clearly crucial, including the support of neighboring states, donor agencies, major powers, and most importantly local citizens and elites. As discussed earlier, peace and peacebuilding mean different things to different people. Séverine Autesserre (2010, 2014) has been particularly critical of the neglect of on-the-ground dynamics. Drawing on extensive interviews in the DRC and Timor-Leste, she has shown how divergent understandings can be. For her, a peacebuilding mission is only effective "when a large majority of the people involved in it view it as such" (2014: 23)—an approach that takes into account the assessments of both external and local stakeholders. Erin McCandless (2013: 240–241), too, has found that local aid recipients want more ownership of the peacebuilding process. "We do not wish to be measured and held accountable to externally developed criteria," she quotes some aid recipients as saying. "We need tools we can understand and use in our own contexts . . . we want a bottom up process; we are our own experts." The UN, in McCandless's view, generally "appears to learn lessons rather slowly in this regard," even with more than half a century of experience (242). The challenge of moving away from templates and getting agreement on basic measures for peacebuilding and statebuilding is both technical and political, McCandless concludes—further testimony to the difficulty of evaluating success and failure in peace operations.

## Arms Control and Disarmament

The concept of disarmament, which includes limiting, controlling, and reducing the weapons for waging war, has long had a prominent place in proposals to promote peace. Thucydides reported that Sparta sought to get Athens to abstain from building fortifications. Immanuel Kant called for eliminating standing armies in his "Preliminary Articles of Perpetual Peace Between States," and Jeremy Bentham published a set of arms control proposals as a prelude to peace. Numerous proposals were put forward in the nineteenth century by heads of state and newly formed peace groups, but only in the twentieth century would they begin to bear fruit.

Disarmament and arms control are believed by their advocates to reduce the levels of violence in war, diminish the urge to engage in an arms race, redirect funds to more socially beneficial activities, and reduce the chances of accidental war. They may also lead to habits of cooperation and trust that will defuse conflict and promote peace.

The history of disarmament and arms control efforts, in fact, is a mixed one. The movement has been highly successful in getting the subject established permanently on IGO agendas. Yet as Inis Claude (1964: 267) notes, "it is important to avoid confusing long hours of international debate, vast piles of printed documents, and elaborate charts of institutional structure with meaningful accomplishment." Still, there have been some notable achievements since the early 1960s, particularly with regard to controlling chemical, biological, and nuclear weapons of mass destruction as well as landmines, cluster munitions, and small arms.

## Putting Arms Control on the Agenda

The effort to create international rules and agreements limiting armaments began with the first Hague Conference in 1899 with a resolution urging states to reduce their military budgets and a declaration banning the use of asphyxiating artillery shells. The latter was the first key step in creating the taboo on chemical weapons. Peace groups pushing for more pioneered a number of strategies used by NGOs much later in the twentieth century, such as petitions, lobbying of delegates, and publication of a daily chronicle. At the Paris Peace Conference in 1919, groups such as the Women's International League for Peace and Freedom pushed for arms control. Article 8 of the League of Nations Covenant charged the League Council with responsibility for drafting disarmament agreements. The League confronted sharp national differences, however, over the relationship of disarmament to security guarantees and relative power positions. The major arms control agreements of the interwar period were largely negotiated outside the League. These included the 1922 Washington Naval Conference, in which the United States, Great Britain, Japan, France, and Italy agreed to limit the number of battleships and not to build any new ones for ten years. The London Naval Treaty of 1930 extended the moratorium and set limits on the size of destroyers and submarines. The most enduring arms control agreement is the 1925 Geneva Protocol for the Prohibition of the Use in War of Asphyxiating, Poisonous, or Other Gases, and of Bacteriological Methods of Warfare, which entered into force in 1928 and remains in effect today.

Those negotiating the UN Charter did not envision a major role for the UN with respect to arms control and disarmament, although Article 26 did give the Security Council responsibility for formulating plans for regulation of armaments. Disarmament as an approach to peace had been discredited during the interwar era because it had failed to avert the outbreak of World War II. The use of two atomic bombs on Japan on August 6 and 10, 1945, initiated a scientific and technological revolution in warfare, however, and immediately put disarmament and arms control on the new body's agenda, with the General Assembly's very first resolution calling for the creation of the Atomic Energy Commission to propose how to ensure that atomic energy was only used for peaceful purposes. Hence the nuclear threat transformed world politics itself and also made the UN a key place for pursuing disarmament and arms control agreements. As with all international treaties, the UN is the depository for such agreements.

Arms control and disarmament efforts have also been directed at concluding international conventions limiting or banning various categories of weapons, reducing arms expenditures, transfers, and sales, and establishing mechanisms for monitoring and enforcing states' compliance. Such negotiations are difficult, because they involve both technical and political decisions. Since the 1990s, an added challenge has been limiting nonstate actors' access to arms and, in particular, preventing terrorist groups from gaining access to WMD.

Over time, the UN General Assembly has played a key role in developing arms control and disarmament norms and international law, including the 1967 Treaty on Nuclear Non-Proliferation, the 1996 Comprehensive Test Ban Treaty, and the 2014 Arms Trade Treaty. The Assembly also created the Disarmament Commission in 1952, replacing the Atomic Energy Commission and the Commission for Conventional Armaments, and established the Conference on Disarmament in 1979 as the primary negotiating forum following the Assembly's Special Session on Disarmament in 1978. Over time, there have been reorganizations with accompanying name changes, much of this reflecting a debate about which countries should participate in disarmament negotiations. In reality, the most fruitful negotiations on most issues have often taken place outside the UN among the relevant major powers, producing the Strategic Arms Limitation Talks agreements (SALT I and II) in the 1970s and the Strategic Arms Reduction Treaty (START) in the 1990s, among other agreements. The cases of landmines and cluster munitions have demonstrated the ability of middle powers and coalitions of NGOs to provide leadership for arms control initiatives without major-power participation, in view of "a widespread sense that the UN [particularly the Conference on Disarmament] has become dysfunctional and moribund as a forum for negotiating arms control and disarmament treaties" (Thakur 2006: 165). Regional IGOs have addressed arms control issues largely through efforts to create regional nuclear weapon–free zones.

### Limiting Proliferation of Nuclear Weapon Capability

Efforts to contain the spread of nuclear weapons have rested on three pillars: norms, treaties, and coercion (Thakur 2006: 161). Preliminary agreements between the United States and Soviet Union were crucial in creating an international regime for nuclear nonproliferation. Following President Dwight Eisenhower's "Atoms for Peace" proposal in 1954, the two superpowers had (surprisingly) collaborated in creating the International Atomic

Energy Agency in 1957 to spread information about peaceful uses of atomic energy and provide a system of safeguards to prevent diversion of fissionable material. General Assembly resolutions from 1959 on called for a nonproliferation treaty and, in 1965, outlined five principles of nonproliferation submitted by nonaligned countries. In 1967, the Soviet Union, United States, and United Kingdom signed the Treaty on the Non-Proliferation of Nuclear Weapons (NPT), which was then opened to other nations to sign and entered into force in 1970. One hundred ninety states are now parties to the NPT.

The NPT is a bargain between the declared nuclear weapon states and the non–nuclear weapon states, with the latter pledging not to develop nuclear weapons, and the former promising to give up their own nuclear weapons at some future time and to aid the latter in gaining access to peaceful nuclear technologies. It effectively creates a two-class system, with five declared nuclear weapon states (the United States, the Soviet Union/Russia, the United Kingdom, France, and China) and all others being non–nuclear weapon states. This two-class system has always been offensive to some states, most notably India, which conducted a peaceful nuclear test in 1974 and five weapon tests in 1998. India, Pakistan, Cuba, North Korea, and Israel are the only states that are not parties to the NPT, and all but Cuba have nuclear weapons. Three states that previously had nuclear weapon programs—South Africa, Brazil, and Argentina—but abandoned them, became parties to the treaty in the 1990s, along with three new states—Belarus, Kazakhstan, and Ukraine—that gave up nuclear weapons left on their territory after the dissolution of the Soviet Union.

The 1995 UN-sponsored NPT review conference agreed to an indefinite extension of the treaty, conditioned on renewed efforts toward disarmament, a pledge by the nuclear weapon states to conclude the Comprehensive Test Ban Treaty, and five-year reviews. The 2010 review conference concluded with an affirmation of parties' commitment to nuclear disarmament. Although the global nuclear stockpile has fallen dramatically from its Cold War peak, none of the five declared nuclear weapon states has a serious plan for disarmament and most are engaged in modernizing their weapon systems.

The IAEA is a critical part of the nuclear nonproliferation regime, especially its safeguard system of inspections, which provides transparency about the security of non–nuclear weapon states' nuclear power plants— that nuclear fuel is not being diverted from peaceful to weapon purposes. The IAEA system is supplemented by the export control agreements of the forty-four-member Nuclear Suppliers Group.

Although the IAEA system appeared operational and reliable for many years, the discovery of a secret Iraqi nuclear weapons program in 1991— in direct violation of Iraq's IAEA safeguard agreements and its obligations under the NPT—brought the entire system under scrutiny. It also drew the UN Security Council into discussion of arms control issues for the first time. The Gulf War cease-fire resolution (Security Council Resolution 687) created the Iraq disarmament regime, the most intrusive international inspections regime ever established. To oversee the destruction of Iraq's chemical and biological weapons and missiles as well as production and storage facilities, and to monitor its long-term compliance, the Security Council created the UN Special Commission for the Disarmament of Iraq (UNSCOM) (Resolution 699). The IAEA was responsible for inspecting and destroying Iraq's nuclear weapons. The focus on WMD and ballistic missiles was the result of Iraq's use of chemical weapons against Iran and its Kurdish population, and ballistic missiles against Iran, the United States, and Israel, as well as the potential threat posed to neighboring countries (including Israel), and concerns about proliferation.

Between 1991 and 1998, inspectors moved throughout Iraq, carrying out surprise inspections of suspected storage and production facilities, destroying stocks of materials, and checking documents. Iraq continually thwarted UNSCOM and IAEA inspectors, removing equipment, claiming to have destroyed material without adequate verification, and arguing that some sites were off-limits. It severed all cooperation in 1998 and inspectors were withdrawn. UNSCOM's successor, the UN Monitoring, Verification, and Inspection Commission (UNMOVIC), began inspections anew in 2002. Along with the IAEA, it verified that Iraq had not rebuilt its program and rebuffed various allegations until its work was cut short by the US invasion in 2003.

The problems that the IAEA and UNSCOM encountered in Iraq mirror the broader problems with international enforcement and with the two other states with nuclear programs—North Korea and Iran. After the revelations about Iraq's nuclear program in 1991, the IAEA Board of Governors strengthened nuclear safeguards through increased access to information, facilities, and sites. The IAEA and the Security Council have both been involved in efforts to enforce North Korea and Iran's compliance with the NPT, while ad hoc groups of states have managed diplomatic initiatives in both cases.

*North Korea and Iran.* In 1993, North Korea refused to admit IAEA inspectors to suspected sites and threatened to withdraw from the NPT. A 1994 agreement brokered by the United States froze North Korea's nuclear program in return for two proliferation-resistant nuclear reactors and fuel oil, but in 2002 it abrogated the agreement and expelled the IAEA's inspectors. The United States initially refused to resume negotiations, then acceded to Six-Party Talks (the United States, China, South Korea, North Korea, Russia, and Japan) that began in 2006. During the interim, North

Korea withdrew from the NPT, produced additional plutonium for bombs, tested its first device, declared itself a nuclear weapon state, and refined its missile technology. In response, the Security Council approved targeted sanctions on North Korea (see Table 7.1). After North Korea detonated a second nuclear device in 2009, the Council enhanced the sanctions to allow UN members to inspect cargo vessels and planes suspected of carrying military material in or out of the country. The sanctions were further tightened in 2012 and 2013 in response to additional nuclear tests, a long-range missile launch, and North Korean threat of a preemptive nuclear strike on the United States and South Korea. The Six-Party Talks have been suspended since 2009 and, while China has made efforts to restart them, North Korea has insisted talks resume "without conditions"—a nonstarter for the United States and others.

Iran remains a major concern despite its announced intention to develop nuclear capacity only for peaceful purposes. The extent of its nuclear program had eluded IAEA inspectors until 2003. Many of its activities are permissible under the NPT, but because they have been carried out surreptitiously, there is concern that Iran actually seeks to develop the capacity to build and deliver nuclear weapons. Initially, the EU, and particularly Germany, Britain, and France, took the lead in 2004–2005 to get Iran to stop its nuclear enrichment program in return for aid in building a light water nuclear reactor and guaranteed supplies of enriched fuel. In 2005, however, the IAEA's board voted twenty-two to one, with twelve abstentions, to report Iran's failures and breaches of its NPT obligations to the Security Council. Despite Iran's threat to withdraw from the NPT if sanctions were imposed, the Council proceeded in 2006 to approve and periodically thereafter extend sanctions (see Table 7.1). The 2008 resolution (1747), for example, authorized inspections of sea and air cargo to and from Iran, tightened monitoring of Iranian financial institutions, extended travel bans and asset freezes, and enlarged the list of targeted individuals and companies. It also welcomed a proposal of the P-5 plus Germany (P-5+1) to offer economic incentives and technology transfer in the civilian nuclear field if Iran permanently gave up its uranium enrichment program.

In contrast to the North Korean case, there have been active and potentially productive negotiations between Iran and the P-5+1 under way since 2012. Iran has not yet tested a nuclear weapon; it remains a party to the NPT and has permitted IAEA inspections, albeit keeping some suspected sites "off limits." It has also indicated interest in a deal that would secure the ending of sanctions. Intense negotiations in 2014 and 2015 sought to resolve what capabilities Iran would be allowed to keep, the length of time an agreement would be in effect, and the speed with which UN sanctions might be lifted.

The danger to the international community if it fails to halt North Korea's and Iran's nuclear programs is threefold: first, the greater risk of weapons being used; second, the risk that other countries in both regions will feel pressured to reconsider their non-nuclear status; and third, the risk that one or both will supply nuclear weapons to al-Qaeda or some other nonstate group. These risks clearly threaten the entire NPT regime.

There are other nuclear proliferation concerns, however. These include the security of controls on nuclear materials and scientists in Russia and other areas of the former Soviet Union. The US-funded Cooperative Threat Reduction Program was created in the 1990s to secure loose nukes in the former Soviet Union, but the agreement with Russia was not renewed in 2013.

After the discovery in 2004 that Pakistan's chief nuclear scientist, A. Q. Khan, had orchestrated a secret global network of nuclear suppliers, it became clear that new safeguard strategies were needed to prevent proliferation. In response, in 2004 the Security Council approved Resolution 1540, which affirmed WMD proliferation as a threat to international peace and directed states to enact and enforce domestic legislation to protect and block illicit trafficking in WMD materials. As discussed in Chapter 4, this is one of the legislative-type actions by the Security Council that imposes reporting obligations on UN members.

An additional effort to address the threat of nuclear terrorism began when US president Barack Obama convened the first Nuclear Security Summit in 2010 with the aim of establishing clear controls over nuclear materials. Two subsequent summits have involved reviews of countries' work to improve their nuclear security. The fourth summit is scheduled for 2016, but with the crisis over Ukraine in 2014, Russia announced that it would not attend, preferring to work with the IAEA.

The NPT regime also includes a ban on testing. After the Cuban missile crisis in 1962, the United States, the Soviet Union, and Great Britain took the first step with the Partial Test Ban Treaty. In the 1990s, France and China, under pressure from Asia-Pacific countries and a legal challenge from New Zealand in the ICJ, agreed to stop testing, and in 1996 the Comprehensive Test Ban Treaty (CTBT) was concluded under UN auspices. India's and Pakistan's 1998 tests set back efforts to bring the CTBT into force, but the most important blow was the US Senate's failure to ratify the treaty in 1999.

The CTBT is intended to serve two key roles: to prevent the declared nuclear weapon states and other parties to the treaty from developing new weapon designs, and to reconfirm the norm against nuclear proliferation. It strengthens the NPT regime with an international monitoring system, authority to conduct challenge inspections in cases of suspected cheating, and establishment of the Comprehensive Test Ban Treaty Organization to implement the verification procedures. Although ratified by 163 states at the end of 2014, the CTBT can only enter into force after ratification by the group of forty-four nations that as of 1996 had nuclear research or nuclear power reactors. This group includes all the states known or suspected to have nuclear weapons, as well as Iran. In addition to the United States, both China and Israel have yet to ratify the treaty; three states in the group—India, Pakistan, and North Korea—have yet to sign the treaty. A global moratorium on testing, however, has been in effect since 1998. The treaty's verification system consists of a global monitoring system with seismic and other sensors in 337 locations around the world to detect signs of nuclear explosions.

The final piece of the nonproliferation regime comprises the treaty-based regional nuclear weapon–free zones. Five zones now exist, in Latin America, Southeast Asia, the South Pacific, Africa, and Central Asia (see Figure 7.7). They preclude nuclear weapon states from placing nuclear

---

**Figure 7.7   Major Governance Approaches for Weapons of Mass Destruction**

| | |
|---|---|
| 1925 | Geneva Protocol on Chemical and Biological Weapons (1928) |
| 1957 | International Atomic Energy Agency |
| 1963 | Partial Test Ban Treaty |
| 1967 | Outer Space Treaty (1967) |
| 1967 | Treaty of Tlatelolco (Latin American Treaty for the Prohibition of Nuclear Weapons) (1968) |
| 1968 | Nuclear Non-Proliferation Treaty (1970) |
| 1971 | Seabed Treaty (1972) |
| 1972 | Biological Weapons Convention (1974) |
| 1979 | SALT Treaty (United States, Soviet Union) |
| 1980 | Convention on the Physical Protection of Nuclear Materials (1987) |
| 1985 | Treaty of Rarotonga (nuclear-free zone in South Pacific) (1986) |
| 1991 | START I Treaty (United States, Russia) |
| 1993 | Chemical Weapons Convention (1997) |
| 1993 | START II Treaty (United States, Russia, three former Soviet republics) (2000) |
| 1995 | Bangkok Treaty (nuclear weapon–free zone in Southeast Asia) (2002) |
| 1996 | Comprehensive Test Ban Treaty; Preparatory Commission for the Comprehensive Test Ban Treaty Organization |
| 1996 | Indefinite Extension of Nuclear Non-Proliferation Treaty |
| 1996 | Pelindaba Treaty (nuclear weapon–free zone in Africa) (2009) |
| 2006 | Treaty on a Nuclear Weapon–Free Zone in Central Asia (2009) |

*Note:* Parenthetical dates indicate years of entry into force as determined by the minimum number of ratifications needed.

weapons on the territory of states within the zone, and prohibit the acquisition, testing, manufacture, or use of such weapons. Protocols attached to each of the treaties and signed by the nuclear weapon states bind the latter to respect de-nuclearization and not to use or threaten to use nuclear force against any of the parties. These zones indicate the widespread support for nuclear disarmament outside the relatively small group of states that already have or seek to acquire nuclear weapons.

Nuclear proliferation will remain a high-priority issue for the foreseeable future, given the lack of evidence that the nuclear weapon states take seriously the NPT pledge to disarm themselves, the threat that Iran and North Korea pose to the regime, and concerns about terrorist groups obtaining nuclear weapons. Yet targeting only "rogue" states and allowing others such as India, Pakistan, and Israel to be accepted as de facto nuclear weapon states, in one analyst's view (Thakur 2006: 175), "hardens the determination of the 'rogues' to acquire the most lethal weapons precisely in order to check armed attacks they fear will be launched by the USA." There is also concern that even if agreement with Iran is achieved, regional rivalries and instability in the Middle East may lead Saudi Arabia and possibly Egypt to seek nuclear weapons. There is wide agreement that nuclear nonproliferation ultimately depends on the nuclear weapon states taking further steps toward disarmament, and that the dangers posed by a world with more countries (let alone nonstate actors) having nuclear weapons is growing not shrinking. Concerns about two other types of WMD—chemical and biological weapons—also persist.

### Chemical and Biological Weapon Prohibition

The taboo on chemical weapons has existed for more than a century. The issue is especially troublesome because many of the ingredients in chemical weapons, unlike nuclear weapons, are used in ordinary industrial and agricultural production. It is therefore impractical to eliminate their manufacture entirely. Instead the focus must be on their use.

When the Hague Conference of 1899 issued its declaration banning asphyxiating shells, such weapons did not exist. Later prohibitions on chemical weapons, including the 1925 Geneva Protocol that banned both chemical and bacteriological weapons, reaffirmed the Hague norm based on reactions to the use of chemical weapons in World War I. A campaign against gas warfare and the chemical industry successfully defined use of chemical weapons as "a practice beyond the pale of civilized nations" on the grounds that these were "an especially inhumane method of warfare" (Price and Tannenwald 1996: 129). There is also a rather remarkable history of nonuse of chemical weapons since the 1920s, with only a few exceptions, including notable ones by Iraq in the 1980s, Aum Shinrikyo in the Tokyo subway in 1995, and Syria in 2013.

Beginning in 1969, the issue of both chemical and biological weapons appeared regularly on the agenda of the UN General Assembly, but Cold War politics—notably US opposition—blocked action. Pressures for controls on these weapons stemmed from the fact that large stockpiles of various chemical and biological weapons were known to exist in a number of countries. Although the destructive power of nuclear weapons is well known, that of chemical and biological weapons is less so. Chemical weapons, if effectively used, have the potential to kill tens of thousands of people; the potential toll from biological weapons could number in the hundreds of thousands. Thus it is hardly surprising that major efforts for more than a century have been directed at suppressing chemical and biological weapons as instruments of warfare. These efforts have been given added impetus with the threat that terrorist groups, who cannot be bound by international treaties, could acquire and use such weapons.

Following unilateral renunciation by the United States of the use or production of biological weapons in 1969, the Convention on the Prohibition of the Development, Production, and Stockpiling of Bacteriological (Biological) and Toxin Weapons and on Their Destruction (the Biological Weapons Convention [BWC]) was concluded in 1972. It came into force in 1975 and now has 170 parties. The BWC is a true disarmament treaty that calls for destruction of existing stocks and restriction of materials to research purposes. Its major weakness is the absence of any verification or inspection mechanism. Several states, most notably Iran, North Korea, Syria, and Russia, are still thought to possess such weapons. In 1994, a group of experts was authorized to draft proposals for a protocol to strengthen the BWC, but the United States rejected the draft text in 2001, insisting that a traditional arms control approach would not work and that the draft protocol would compromise US national security and confidential business information of the biotech industry. This effectively ended negotiations on a BWC protocol. The ongoing biotechnology revolution creates a future proliferation risk.

The September 2001 terrorist attacks on the United States and the subsequent anthrax scare led the United States to push a different approach, involving an initiative by the G-8 in 2002 to create a Global Partnership Against the Spread of Weapons and Materials of Mass Destruction, to which the George W. Bush administration pledged $10 billion. In addition, the WHO strengthened its surveillance system in the event of biological weapon attacks; the Australia Group, established in 1985 by thirty-three states to coordinate national controls on chemical and biological weapons technology and exports, together with the EU Commission, tightened export control measures in 2002 to keep chemical and biological weapons out of the hands of terrorist groups; and NATO also took initiatives to deal with biological weapon attacks. Still, many European and developing countries were deeply troubled by the US rejection of the BWC revision process, and it will likely be many years before tighter controls on biological weapons are negotiated.

Although stalled during the Cold War, the Chemical Weapons Convention (CWC) was finally signed in 1993, banning the production, acquisition, stockpiling, retention, or usage of such weapons. Like the BWC, it calls for the complete destruction of all weapons and production facilities in a phased process that was originally to terminate in 2012, but will take up to 2023 for the United States, Libya, and Russia. Unlike the BWC, the CWC includes on-site verification provisions and the threat of sanctions against violators, including those that have not signed the treaty. It came into effect in 1997 and now has 190 parties. The Organization for the Prohibition of Chemical Weapons (OPCW) began operations in early 1997 and has since conducted hundreds of inspections at military and industrial facilities. In 2014, five countries still had stockpiles (the United States, Russia, Iran, North Korea, and South Korea), and the thirteen countries with production facilities had all deactivated them, with more than 90 percent of those facilities having been destroyed or converted to civilian use. As of 2013, global stockpiles of chemical weapons had verifiably been reduced by more than 80 percent since 1997—no small accomplishment for disarmament.

The key difference between the chemical and biological weapons conventions and the NPT is the acceptance by all parties of a total ban on possession, development, and use of these weapons of mass destruction. There is no two-class system; total disarmament is the core regime norm. The chemical and biological weapons treaties require parties to enact domestic legislation to permit criminal prosecution of individuals and companies that violate treaty provisions. All three treaties have in common an initial agreement between the United States and the Soviet Union/Russia. For the CTBT, commitments from France and China were key. Only by having these major powers "on board" could the UN proceed with drafting the treaties. The experiences of the CTBT and BWC also demonstrate the damage done when US support for multilateral arms control treaties is lost. The experience with the intrusive WMD disarmament program in Iraq, however, demonstrated both the possibilities of international monitoring as a tool of disarmament and the particular difficulties of enforcing compliance with international norms on chemical and biological weapons. Although the IAEA succeeded in destroying Iraq's existing nuclear weapon materials and production facilities, UNSCOM was unable to certify that it knew the full extent of Iraq's chemical and biological weapon–production facilities, since materials are easily concealed. That process, however, was completed in 2007.

The case of Syria and chemical weapons in 2013–2014 is also instructive and has clearly reinforced both the taboo on the use of such weapons and the chemical weapons regime. In July 2012, Syria confirmed that it had chemical weapons but stated that they would only be used against an outside aggressor. Yet in a six-month period, there were at least six reports that Syrian government forces had used various types of chemical weapons, leading UNSG Ban Ki-moon to announce that the UN, together with the WHO and OPCW, would conduct an investigation.

In mid-August 2013, the Syrian government agreed to allow a UN inspection team into Syria to investigate three possible uses, but not to establish who used the weapons. Days later, there were reports of a large-scale chemical weapons attack in the Damascus suburbs with thousands of noncombatant victims. This triggered emergency meetings of the Security Council and the threat of US military strikes. A French government report found that the Assad regime had used Sarin gas in those attacks, hence violating the 1925 Geneva Protocol. Instead of military intervention, however, there was a remarkable diplomatic initiative that led to an agreement negotiated by the United States and Russia with Syria acceding to the CWC and to a plan to account for, inspect, control, and destroy its chemical weapons stockpile and production facilities within a year. In short order, Syria had submitted a declaration of its stockpiles, the OPCW and UN began destruction, and by the end of October the OPCW had inspected twenty-one of twenty-three production facilities. In January 2014, the first shipment of weapons was loaded on a Danish ship and six months later the last 8 percent were shipped out. Destruction of the weapons themselves was carried out at sites in several countries, and Syria's facilities were to be destroyed or permanently sealed. For its work, the OPCW received the 2013 Nobel Peace Prize.

### Banning Landmines and Cluster Munitions: The Role of NGOs

A very different path to arms control, however, was followed in an initiative involving a very conventional but widely used and deadly weapon—landmines, together with cluster munitions. Both, however, reflect humanitarian concerns far more than the security threats posed by WMD. Just as nuclear arms were a symbol of the Cold War, antipersonnel landmines are a symbol of conflicts in the post–Cold War era. These weapons have been widely used by regular and irregular military forces in conflicts from Angola, Afghanistan, Cambodia, and Bosnia to Sri Lanka, the DRC, and Kashmir. They are indiscriminate and long-lasting, however, and cause extensive civilian casualties as unsuspecting people go into mined areas. Although landmines cost as little as $3 each, de-mining can cost $300 to $500 per mine. They captured the attention of NGOs in a way not seen in other arms control issues, in part because they are a human security issue.

The International Campaign to Ban Landmines (ICBL), a network of more than a thousand organizations in sixty countries, including the Vietnam Veterans of America Foundation, Human Rights Watch, and the ICRC, was formed in 1993 to campaign for a ban on the use, production, stockpiling, and sale, transfer, or export of antipersonnel landmines. Its primary goal was to conclude, implement, and monitor a landmine treaty and to provide resources for de-mining, mine awareness programs, and victim rehabilitation and assistance. In a record time of fourteen months between October 1996 and December 1997, under the leadership of Canadian foreign minister Lloyd Axworthy, countries that supported a treaty banning landmines participated in the ad hoc Ottawa negotiating process, bypassing the UN Conference on Disarmament. Over a hundred countries signed the Convention on the Prohibition of the Use, Stockpiling, Production, and Transfer of Anti-Personnel Mines and on Their Destruction, and in 1999 the treaty came into force. In acknowledgment of the ICBL's success, the organization and its coordinator, Jody Williams, were awarded the Nobel Peace Prize in 1997.

Among the convention's unusual features is the detailed role outlined for NGOs, particularly the ICRC, in assessing the scope of the problem and providing financial and technical resources for implementation. NGO monitors report through the UN Secretary-General to meetings of state parties that are attended by relevant governmental and nongovernmental organizations. The UN had "mine action" programs in thirty countries and territories in 2014, with NGOs doing much of the de-mining and mine-risk education. Local UN support groups, such as the United Nations Association of the United States of America (UNA-USA), ran "adopt a minefield" programs for a number of years to pay for de-mining activities.

The ICBL continues its work to universalize the treaty and promote mine clearance, survivor assistance, and stockpile destruction. As of 2014, 162 countries had ratified the treaty; mine use has ceased in several countries where it was prevalent; there have been large reductions in mine stockpiles; casualties from landmines have declined significantly; and production and trade have ended in thirty-eight countries. Myanmar, China, India, North and South Korea, Pakistan, Russia, Iran, and the United States are among the thirteen countries still producing mines. The United States announced in 2014 that it would abide by the treaty except for landmines used in Korea.

The effort to ban landmines is unique in the annals of arms control because of NGOs' key roles in pushing the issue and in the treaty's implementation. With support from the ICBL, the same approach was taken by another coalition—the Cluster Munitions Coalition, formed in 2003 to address the problem of cluster bombs and comprising some 300 NGOs in over eighty countries. In this case, Norway took the lead for the Oslo

Process, through which a core group of states, together with the Cluster Munition Coalition, the ICRC, and the UN, pushed the negotiation of a treaty banning these weapons. The Convention on Cluster Munitions, signed by ninety-four states in December 2008, like the landmine treaty, was concluded in a short period, in this case eighteen months. As of 2014, it had been ratified by eighty-eight states. This arms control effort was successful in large part because of the NGO campaign's emphasis on the humanitarian problem these weapons pose, since the majority of victims are civilians. Hence the treaty also calls not only for a ban on cluster munitions, but also for clearance efforts, stockpile destruction, and victim assistance, with extensive global civil society involvement. In 2011, the ICBL and Cluster Munition Coalition merged into one structure to realize organizational efficiencies while still continuing their separate campaigns.

## Dealing with Terrorism as a Threat to Global Peace and Security

Terrorism is an old threat to individual, state, and regional security that is now universally recognized as a threat also to global peace and security and "both a challenge to and a challenge for multilateral institutions" (Luck 2006: 336). Historically, terrorist acts were often individual acts of violence against a ruler or tools of separatist and other groups seeking a homeland or regime change. Organized state terrorism reached its zenith in Nazi Germany and in the Soviet Union under Joseph Stalin. Since the 1970s, much of the terrorist activity has originated in the Middle East, from the Palestinians' quest for self-determination, their own internal conflicts over strategy, rivalries among various Islamic groups, and the rise of Islamic fundamentalism. Since 1980, religious-based groups (Islamic and others such as Hindu nationalists) have increased significantly. Many were trained in Afghanistan during the mujahidin's war against the Soviet Union in the 1980s and went on to commit many terrorist acts in the 1990s. Of particular importance was the development of al-Qaeda—the shadowy network of Islamic fundamentalist groups in many countries discussed in Chapter 6. In Latin America, the most pressing problem is terrorism perpetrated by large, illegal drug syndicates aimed at controlling local governments and police forces. Data on terrorist attacks show that Latin America (particularly Colombia, Peru, and El Salvador) had the highest share of attacks between 1970 and 2008, with the Middle East second and South Asia third. The latter two regions have had the highest numbers of attacks since 2009 (LaFree and Dugan 2014: 36–37).

The tactics of terrorists and whether the actions were local or global have tended to drive international responses. From the late 1960s through the 1970s, airline hijackings were a popular terrorist method for projecting a message. Among numerous cases, members of the Lebanese Party of God seized a TWA flight to Beirut in 1985, and Abu Nidal's Arab Revolutionary Command hijacked an Egypt Air flight to Malta, also in 1985. Hostage-taking has been another tactic used by terrorist groups. Two notable incidents include the 1979 hostage-taking of fifty-two American diplomats at the US embassy in Iran, and the 1985 seizure of the Italian cruise ship *Achille Lauro*. The most common terrorist incidents involve the use of bombs on airplanes, trucks, cars, and ships, or in suicide attacks. Prominent examples include Pan American Flight 103, which blew up over Lockerbee, Scotland, in 1988; the 1983 bombing of the US Marine barracks in Lebanon, which killed 241 marines; the 1995 and 1996 bombings in Saudi Arabia against US military installations; and the boat-delivered bombing of the USS *Cole* in 2000 in Yemen. In addition, although the four planes involved in the 9/11 attacks were initially hijacked, they were turned into lethal weapons of mass destruction in a new twist on the old car-bomb strategy. Suicide bombings were pioneered by young members of the Tamil Tigers in Sri Lanka, and then adopted by young Palestinians during the second intifada, the 9/11 hijackers, Sunni insurgents and al-Qaeda in Iraq, and Islamic militants in Afghanistan, Pakistan, and elsewhere. Concerns about terrorist groups gaining control of WMD or the materials to produce them magnify the importance of controlling these weapons, particularly nuclear materials, as previously discussed.

Speaking at a special Security Council session in 2014, UN Secretary-General Ban Ki-moon said that "the world is witnessing a dramatic evolution in the nature of the terrorist threat" (UN 2014b). There has been a dramatic upsurge in the number of terrorist attacks and the number of people killed since 2011, as well as a significant shift in where terrorist attacks are taking place. The 2014 Global Terrorism Index reported 9,814 attacks in eighty-seven countries in 2013, a 60 percent increase in the number of countries that experienced fifty or more deaths since the previous year, and a 61 percent increase in fatalities from the previous year to 17,958 worldwide—the highest ever to date. Just four groups were responsible for the majority of fatalities between 2000 and 2013: al-Qaeda, the Taliban (in both Afghanistan and Pakistan), Boko Haram in Nigeria, and Islamic State of Iraq and Syria (ISIS). These groups are no longer dependent upon state sponsorship, but draw their funding from a variety of nonstate sources, including criminal activities, foreign charities, ransom from kidnappings, and private donations from citizens of the Gulf states. Whereas nationalist and separatist groups were predominant in 2000, religion and sectarianism have now become the driving forces behind terrorism (Institute for Economics and Peace 2014). A Rand Corporation report notes that "since 2010, there has been a 58 percent increase in the number of jihadist groups, a doubling of jihadist fighters and a tripling of attacks by Al Qaeda affiliates" (cited in Rothkopf 2014). There has also been a sharp increase in the numbers of young men and women from Europe and elsewhere traveling to Syria to join extremist groups.

The rapid advance of ISIS in 2014 introduced a new and dangerous dimension to terrorism: the seizure of territory and declaration of a caliphate—a single, transnational Islamic state based on sharia law. Its brutality toward non-Muslim and non-Arab minorities, Shiites, and all who opposed it included beheadings and mass slaughter even of women and children. With its control and administration of territory and cities in Iraq and Syria, the declarations of allegiance from other jihadist groups in Afghanistan, Egypt, Libya, Nigeria, and Yemen, plus its ambition to create an Islamic state throughout the Middle East and Africa, ISIS in 2015 posed a major threat. It also posed a threat to Europe, the United States, and other areas because of concerns about foreign fighters returning home.

In short, as David Rothkopf (2014) has noted, "terrorism is spreading worldwide . . . [and] global terror trends are heading in an ever more dangerous direction." This poses major challenges for global governance, particularly for developing governance responses at national, regional, and international levels. The challenges are magnified by the fact that perceptions of the threat continue to vary and there is still no agreement over what constitutes terrorism. As with many other areas of governance, compliance and enforcement are major issues, as is the need for capacity building in various approaches to counterterrorism.

### International Responses to Terrorism

Although there had been a growing effort to address terrorism beginning in the 1970s, it was the 9/11 attacks in the United States, followed by a series of other attacks including the Madrid train bombings (2004) and London transport attacks (2005), that truly galvanized IO activity. As a result, the UN system has become the hub for the global regime for terrorism because of its global reach, legitimacy, and legal authority, although limited resources and operational capacity except within relevant special agencies mean that a number of counterterrorism activities take place elsewhere. Currently, thirty bodies within the UN system are engaged in counterterrorism efforts, along with the international police agency Interpol, several bodies within the EU, counterterrorism entities within the G-8, APEC, OAS, ECOWAS, AU, and SCO, and a number of functional IGOs outside the UN system. States, too, play an active role, though they differ in their approaches to dealing with terrorism. Whereas the United States, for example, has often taken a military approach first (e.g., using drones against al-Qaeda in Yemen and al-Shabab in Somalia, and air strikes against ISIS in Syria and Iraq) and a law enforcement and transnational cooperation approach second, a number of regions, including Europe, have emphasized law enforcement, regional cooperation, and crime-fighting measures. Weak or failed states such as Somalia, Afghanistan, and Pakistan are important because they create gaps in international efforts to control borders and the flow of people, money, and arms as well as to deny terrorists sanctuaries for training camps and operations. The 2011 ousting of Qaddafi in Libya created a significant flow of weapons and fighters southward into Mali, strengthening al-Qaeda in the Islamic Maghreb (AQIM) there. And, as previously noted, Syria's civil war has strengthened a number of radical Islamist groups fighting against the Assad government, including ISIS.

The international governance responses to terrorism by IGOs and states have included developing a global legal regime to outlaw various types of terrorist actions; applying sanctions and using military force against state sponsors of terrorism and against the Taliban in Afghanistan and Pakistan, against AQIM in Mali, Boko Haram in Nigeria, and against ISIS in Syria and Iraq; and enhancing the capacities of states and international police agencies to track, gather intelligence on, and arrest suspected terrorists and to enhance border controls. In addition, the responses include controls on WMD to prevent terrorists from gaining possession of weapons or their materials, regulating the flow of money that finances terrorism, and coordinating interstate activities.

*Developing the global legal regime.* Between 1963 and 2014, the UN General Assembly and the International Civil Aviation Organization fostered the conclusion of fourteen international conventions and four supplementary protocols that form the heart of the global legal regime against terrorism, all but four of which have entered into force as of the end of 2014. They create norms outlawing terrorist acts against civil aviation, airports, shipping, diplomats, and nuclear materials (see Figure 7.8). They also address the problems of bombings, terrorist financing, and nuclear terrorism. Since the 9/11 attacks, there has been a concerted effort to secure universal ratification, with technical assistance provided to countries whose legal systems are weak.

There is as yet no comprehensive convention against terrorism because of the long-standing difficulty in getting agreement on a definition. Since terrorism is inherently political, it triggers different reactions depending on perceptions about the aims of the terrorists and whether they are justified. Two issues have dominated the discussion: whether official acts of a state's armed forces should or should not be included in the definition of terrorism, and whether violent acts conducted in a struggle against foreign occupation should be considered terrorism. In the first case, the United States and its allies have sought to exclude acts of official armed forces from any definition. In the second case, the OIC and AU distinguish between "acts of ter-

---

**Figure 7.8     The Global Counterterrorism Legal Regime (selected conventions and protocols)**

---

*Conventions Relating to Terrorism in Transportation*
1969     Convention on Offences and Certain Acts Committed on Board
         Aircraft
1971     Convention for the Suppression of Unlawful Seizure of Aircraft
1989     Protocol on the Suppression of Unlawful Acts of Violence at Airports
         Serving International Civil Aviation
1992     Convention for the Suppression of Unlawful Acts Against the Safety
         of Maritime Navigation

*Conventions Relating to Weapon Controls*
1987     Convention on the Physical Protection of Nuclear Material
1998     Convention on the Marking of Plastic Explosives for the Purposes of
         Detection
2007     International Convention for the Suppression of Acts of Nuclear
         Terror

*General Conventions*
1977     Convention on the Prevention and Punishment of Crimes Against
         Internationally Protected Persons, Including Diplomatic Agents
1983     International Convention Against the Taking of Hostages
2001     International Convention for the Suppression of Terrorist Bombings
2002     International Convention for the Suppression of the Financing of
         Terrorism

*Note:* Dates indicate years of entry into force as determined by the minimum number of ratifications needed.

---

rorism and acts committed in the fight for self-determination or against occupation" (Rosand and Millar 2007: 53). Both the OIC and the AU have made this distinction in their terrorism conventions, something Western states generally reject. A major step toward a consensus definition of terrorism and a comprehensive convention, however, occurred with the 2005 UN World Summit Outcome, which condemned terrorism "in all its forms and manifestations, committed by whomever, wherever and for whatever purposes, as it constitutes one of the most serious threats to international peace and security" (UN 2005). In practice, however, states continue to act on the basis of competing definitions.

The global legal regime to counter terrorism also includes several UN Security Council resolutions adopted under Chapter VII authority, which therefore impose legal obligations on member states. The first and most important is Resolution 1373 (2001), adopted following the 9/11 attacks. It was unprecedented in obliging all states to block the financing and weapons supply of terrorist groups, freeze their assets, prevent recruitment, deny them safe haven, and cooperate in information-sharing and criminal prosecution. In addition, Resolution 1373 established the Counter-Terrorism Committee (CTC), a committee of the whole Security Council, as discussed in Chapter 4, that monitors states' capability to deny funding and haven to terrorists under threat of sanctions for noncompliance. In 2004, the Security Council established the Counter-Terrorism Executive Directorate (CTED) to provide it with more permanent staff.

A key aspect of Resolution 1373 is its reporting requirements. The CTED assists committee members in reviewing and analyzing reports from member states concerning their counterterrorism actions. In an extraordinary show of compliance, every UN member state submitted a report for the first round; response has been more variable since then, suggestive of reporting fatigue. The threat of sanctions has also been dropped in favor of a more facilitative role for the CTED. The reports, however, provide a large body of information on the counterterrorism capabilities of most UN members, but a significant burden for processing and are no longer publicly available.

Significant questions have been raised about whether the Security Council exceeded its Charter mandate with Resolution 1373. As noted in Chapter 4, former Canadian UN ambassador David Malone (2006: 265) has argued that Resolution 1373, along with other actions such as those against Iraq's WMD programs, have shifted the Council "to a mode in which it sits at the apex of a global legal-regulatory architecture . . . and controversially legislates for all states on critical new security threats such as terrorism and WMD." There has also been concern about the absence of human rights protections in the resolution.

In 2004, the Security Council approved Resolution 1540, affirming that WMD proliferation is a threat to international peace and security, and requiring states to take legislative and other steps to prevent nonstate actors (including terrorist groups) from gaining access to weapons of mass destruction and WMD materials and to report on their efforts. The Council created the 1540 Committee to monitor states' compliance and a group of eight experts to support the committee's work and assist states in devising measures to keep WMD out of the hands of terrorists. That 129 states submitted reports by April 2006 was seen by experts as one measure of initial success (Bosch and van Ham 2007: 212).

In 2014, in response to growing concerns about foreign fighters returning home, the Security Council acting under Chapter VII unanimously passed Resolution 2178, defining the term "foreign terrorist fighter," condemning violent extremism, expressing concern about the use of the Internet to incite others to commit terrorist acts, and requiring countries to prevent the entry or transit of individuals believed to be traveling for terrorism-related purposes. It also requires countries to prevent and suppress recruiting and financing of foreign fighters and requires them to have laws that permit prosecution of their nationals and others who attempt to travel for such purposes, all indicative of a multifaceted approach. As UN Secretary-General Ban Ki-moon said, "we must also tackle the underlying conditions that provide violent extremist groups the opportunity to take root" (UN 2014b).

The global legal regime is complemented by conventions concluded by eight regional or multiregional organizations, including the Arab League, OIC, Council of Europe, OAS, South Asian Association of Regional Cooperation (SAARC), Commonwealth, OAU/AU, and SCO.

*Enforcement.* The use of sanctions to deal with state sponsors of terrorism and al-Qaeda was discussed earlier in the chapter, as was the US military action against Afghanistan's Taliban regime and al-Qaeda following the 9/11 attacks. In 2011, the Security Council split the sanctions regime targeting al-Qaeda and the Taliban, creating a separate sanctions list of individuals, groups, and undertakings associated with al-Qaeda. Then, in response to the changing nature of the al-Qaeda threat, the Council further strengthened the sanctions regime in 2014 (Resolution 2161)—the eleventh resolution dealing specifically with al-Qaeda since 1999. Given the latter's evolution and diffusion, however, some critics complain that the targeting lists have not been updated or expanded regularly enough (Council on Foreign Relations 2013).

To date, the UN sanctions on state sponsors of terrorism have been more effective than those on al-Qaeda and associated nonstate groups. In this regard, the Libyan case is particularly instructive because of the success in getting that country to end its sponsorship and support of terrorist groups as well as its nuclear program. The effort, however, took almost thirty years and a combination of multilateral and unilateral sanctions, beginning with a US ban on military equipment sales to Libya in 1978; listing Libya on the US State Department's list of state sponsors of terrorism in 1979; diplomatic and economic sanctions against Libya for its support of international terrorism in 1981; and freezing Libya's assets and imposing comprehensive trade and financial sanctions in 1986. Only after conclusive evidence linked Libya to the bombings of Pan Am Flight 103 and UTA Flight 772 did the United States, France, and Britain initiate multilateral efforts by taking the issue to the Security Council. Resolution 731 (1992) was the first Chapter VII resolution to condemn terrorist acts and Libya's role in the airline bombings. Subsequent resolutions imposed the first targeted sanctions on civil aviation, arms sales, and diplomatic links, leading to Libya's isolation from the rest of the world. Support for the UN sanctions, however, was slipping; diplomatic initiatives and a 1998 ICJ ruling opened the way to an agreement to turn over the suspects in the bombings for trial in the Netherlands and for Libya to pay compensation to the families of those killed on both flights. The UN sanctions were lifted in 2003; it took until 2006 for the United States to lift its sanctions and to remove Libya from the list of states sponsoring terrorism.

As discussed in Chapter 5, the Shanghai Cooperation Organization is unique among regional organizations in having prepared itself for military enforcement action against terrorism through joint military exercises conducted in 2003, 2007, and 2012. NATO's operation in Afghanistan has clearly been directed against Islamic militants and the Taliban, in addition to its efforts to strengthen Afghanistan's own government. Further examples of regional organization enforcement efforts relating to terrorism include the AU's work in combating al-Shabab in Somalia and, together with ECOWAS and French forces, against AQIM and other extremist groups in Mali in 2012–2013. The latter mission transitioned to a UN mission in 2013—the Multidimensional Integrated Stabilization Mission in Mali (MINUSMA). In 2014, the United States put together an ad hoc coalition of Arab and other countries to deal with the threat ISIS posed to Syria, Iraq, and regional stability in the Middle East. In 2015, the AU and ECOWAS authorized Cameroon, Chad, and Niger to aid Nigerian forces in combating Boko Haram.

*Building state capacities to combat terrorism.* Building the capacity of states to control their borders, improve their laws and banking systems, and enhance their ability to take other steps to combat terrorism is critical to global governance efforts. Technical assistance is provided by a variety of international actors, with the UN's CTED playing a key role in strengthening the counterterrorism capabilities of member states. The directorate has assisted states in drafting legislation and adapting money-laundering laws and controls on informal banking systems, and provided training in counterterrorism standards. The need, however, has been greater than the supply of its services. The UNODC's Terrorism Prevention Branch assists states in ratifying and implementing the conventions, strengthening national criminal justice systems, and drafting legislation. The Commonwealth Secretariat provides model laws on money laundering for common-law countries. G-8 members have provided bilateral aid for drafting legislation on money laundering as well. The IMF provides technical assistance with legislation to counter financing for terrorism more generally. In the 2000s, the EU used a unique "twinning program" that paired older EU members with candidate countries to share counterterrorism expertise and provide assistance in conforming to EU standards on border controls and legislative, judicial, and administrative procedures.

*Cutting off terrorists' financing.* Key to counterterrorism efforts is cutting off the sources of funds for terrorist activities and related money-laundering and financial crimes. Most states have inadequate money-laundering legislation and ability to monitor financial transactions or the informal banking networks that are widely used by many terrorist organizations. Al-Qaeda raises money from a variety of sources and moves in many different ways. ISIS has garnered funds by selling oil from wells it controls as well as looting bank vaults in cities it has seized; the Taliban relies on heroin sales; and al-Shabab benefits from the sale of charcoal.

Targeted sanctions provide one means for addressing the problem of terrorist financing, but there are also some significant governance challenges to surmount in order to make such sanctions effective, such as ending bank secrecy (including for Swiss banks) and regulating offshore financial havens in Caribbean and Pacific island nations. Countries have to develop the legal and technical capabilities to monitor financial transactions, interdict accounts of particular individuals, and act quickly in order to deny terrorists time to move funds. The US government and other major financial powers (mostly OECD countries) are central actors. With ransom from kidnapping emerging as a major source of funding for terrorists, however, the only way to thwart this development is to get states and private entities to refuse to pay them.

The Convention for the Suppression of Financing for Terrorism, which came into force in 2002, provides the normative and legal basis for these activities. Key actors include the US Treasury Department, finance ministries, major banks, the IMF, the Financial Action Task Force (FATF), the Asia-Pacific Group on Money Laundering, the Middle East and North Africa Task Force on Financial Action, and the Caribbean Financial Action Task Force. There is no central international organization, however, with the mandate and expertise to coordinate global efforts to deal with the problem of terrorist financing.

Absent such an organization, the FATF, for example, develops and promotes policies at the state and international levels to combat money laundering and terrorist financing. As noted earlier, it is crucial to the enforcement of financial sanctions because of its role in combating money laundering for drug trafficking and other transnational crimes, and in 2012 the FATF created a stronger framework linking counterterrorist financing measures with anti-money-laundering controls that will better enable it to address the link between terrorist financing, corruption, and transnational crime (Council on Foreign Relations 2013). It sets global standards and monitors members' progress and trends. As of 2014, thirty-four states are members, along with two international bodies—the European Commission and the Gulf Cooperation Council. Membership requires adoption of money-laundering legislation and an FATF evaluation. The FATF also works with nine regional bodies in Asia, Africa, Europe, and Latin America and thereby covers a network of 182 jurisdictions. Its forty recommendations form the core of the money-laundering regime; after 9/11, when it began focusing on terrorist financing, it added nine special recommendations on terrorist financing. Most states have accepted both sets of recommendations.

One of the FATF's major challenges is that terrorist financing is a moving target, given the continual evolution of money laundering and the use of noncash types of transactions through charities, informal banking systems, and commodities such as diamonds, heroin, charcoal, and metals, which are hard to track. Furthermore, the amounts of money required for most terrorist activities are small in comparison to those for other criminal activities. The FATF uses a peer review process of monitoring and assessment along with self-reporting to identify areas in which technical assistance and aid should be targeted (Gardner 2007).

*Criminal justice approaches.* Beyond creating a framework of international rules dealing with terrorism, interrupting the flow of money to terrorist groups and enhancing state capacities are state and multilateral efforts to increase security, tighten border controls, step up counterintelligence activities, and improve cooperation among law enforcement agencies. The two international police agencies—Interpol and Europol are particularly important in tracking and apprehending terrorists.

The EU has been especially active with respect to criminal justice approaches. Among the key developments have been a European arrest warrant, enhanced enforcement and intelligence cooperation through Europol, judicial cooperation through the European Judicial Cooperation Unit (Eurojust), and identification of presumed terrorist groups. As discussed in Chapter 5, justice and home affairs were added as a third pillar of the EU by the Treaty of Amsterdam. Still, cooperation was slow to develop in these areas prior to 2004, when the Madrid train bombings provided "a grim reminder to EU member states of the costs of moving too slowly to implement counter-terrorism measures" (Bures and Ahern 2007: 216). Beginning in 2014, the concerns about returning foreign fighters prompted a new look at border security, specifically in regard to monitoring those who have traveled to certain areas such as Iraq, Somalia, Syria, and Yemen where Islamic extremist groups were active.

*Coordinating strategy and action.* In 2006 the General Assembly adopted the United Nations Global Counter-Terrorism Strategy (A/RES/60/288)—the first attempt to provide a comprehensive global framework for addressing the problem of terrorism. That strategy is built around four pillars—addressing conditions conducive to the spread of terrorism, preventing and combating terrorism, building state capacity, and defending human rights while combating terrorism. A Counterterrorism Implementation Task Force, composed of representatives from various specialized agencies, the DPKO, the CTED, the 1540 Committee, many other UN offices, and Interpol, works to ensure overall coordination of activities throughout the UN system. It has faced the same types of problems as have ECOSOC and other UN coordination initiatives, namely the absence of a central UN system budget and the variations in agency budgets, priorities, and cultures.

Several other IGOs have taken their own initiatives to coordinate counterterrorism efforts. The EU, in addition to its action plan, has created the position of a counterterrorism coordinator. APEC, ECOWAS, and ASEAN all have created counterterrorism task forces. The OAS not only created the Inter-American Committee Against Terrorism but also established a separate secretariat to support its work. Since terrorism has been a central issue on the Shanghai Cooperation Organization's agenda, its Regional Anti-Terrorism Structure, established in 2002 and discussed in Chapter 5, represents a significant part of that organization's activities. Still, other than the EU, most of these institutions lack capacity, funding, and political will to pursue counterterrorism effectively, let alone in coordination with UN and other regional programs (Council on Foreign Relations 2013).

Many security governance approaches—such as preventive diplomacy, adjudication, mediation, peacekeeping, and arms control—are irrelevant when dealing with terrorism. Meanwhile, the rapid evolution of the threat is posing serious challenges to peace and security in a growing number of countries and regions. This makes all the more urgent the search for effective means of addressing the threat and its root causes. It requires delegitimizing the appeal of suicide bombings among young people in groups such as Hamas, Islamic Jihad, and Boko Haram. In cases where grievances are known, such as the Palestinian cause, renewed efforts to find peaceful and just solutions are needed. In cases such as al-Qaeda, where there are no specific political objectives but rather broad anti-American and anti-Western sentiments, fundamentalist Islamic or other religious concerns, or deep alienation from static societies such as Saudi Arabia and Egypt, identifying appropriate governance responses is a far more elusive task.

## The Challenges of Human Security

We began this chapter with a case study of the conflict in Somalia, which is emblematic of the post–Cold War security problems of the 1990s and the contemporary problems of weak states and terrorism. We end with the growing security threats that terrorism poses to people, states, and regions. In the intervening years, an extraordinary variety of threats to international peace and security arose and a corresponding variety of new governance approaches were introduced while not negating the continuing value of older governance approaches.

Traditionally, international peace and security have meant states' security and the defense of states' territorial integrity from external threats or attack. But as the R2P and POC norms suggest, the concept of human security—the security of human beings in the face of many different kinds of threats—has gained increasing attention. The growing concerns for human security are reflected in discussions in successive chapters about the need to eradicate poverty and reduce the inequalities exacerbated by globalization, to promote environmentally sustainable development and greater respect for human rights, particularly the rights of women and children, to prosecute war crimes and crimes against humanity more aggressively, and to address the security threats posed by climate change. The concept of human security has arisen from greater understanding of how socioeconomic deprivation and exclusion, human rights abuses, and environmental and epidemiological threats have "a direct impact on peace and stability within and between states" (Newman 2001: 241). It has been fostered by interested states such as Canada, civil society networks, and UN agencies such as the UNHCR, UNICEF, and UNIFEM. In short, threats to peace and security are defined not only in terms of state security but also in terms of human security. Yet existing security governance structures are ill equipped to deal with many new issues. Hence the challenge is to enhance the effectiveness of existing governance for dealing with ongoing problems and to find innovative approaches for emerging ones.

## Suggested Further Reading

Biersteker, Thomas, Sue Eckert, and Marcos Tourinho, eds. (2015) *Targeting Sanctions: The Impacts and Effectiveness of UN Action*. New York: Cambridge University Press.

Center on International Cooperation at New York University. (2013) *Annual Review of Global Peace Operations*. Boulder: Lynne Rienner.

Cortright, David, and George A. Lopez, eds. (2007) *Uniting Against Terror: Cooperative Nonmilitary Responses to the Global Terrorist Threat*. Cambridge: MIT Press.

Diehl, Paul F., and Alexandru Balas. (2014) *Peace Operations*. 2nd ed. Malden, MA: Polity.

Jenkins, Rob. (2013) *Peacebuilding: From Concept to Commission*. New York: Routledge.

MacFarlane, S. Neil, and Yuen Foong Khong. (2006) *Human Security and the UN: A Critical History*. Bloomington: Indiana University Press.

Paris, Roland, and Timothy D. Sisk, eds. (2009) *The Dilemmas of Statebuilding: Confronting the Contradictions of Postwar Peace Operations*. New York: Routledge.

Ramcharan, Bertrand G. (2008) *Preventive Diplomacy at the UN*. Bloomington: Indiana University Press.

## Important Databases

Global Terrorism Index: http://economicsandpeace.org/research/iep-indices-data/global-terrorism-index

University of Maryland Center for International Development and Conflict Management, International Crisis Behavior Project and Minorities at Risk Project: www.cidcm.umd.edu/mar/
Uppsala Conflict Data Program: www.pcr.uu.se/research/ucdp


## Internet Resources

Center for Nonproliferation Studies: www.cns.miis.edu
Cluster Munition Coalition: www.stopclustermunitions.org
European Union external relations: www.ec.europa.eu/politics/external_relations/-foreign_affairs
Global Centre for the Responsibility to Protect: www.globalr2p.org
Human Security Report Project: www.hsrgroup.org
International Atomic Energy Agency: www.iaea.org
International Campaign to Ban Landmines: www.icbl.org
International Crisis Group: www.crisisgroup.org
Organization for the Prohibition of Chemical Weapons: www.opcw.org
Preparatory Commission for the Comprehensive Test Ban Treaty Organization: www.ctbto.org
Stockholm International Peace Research Institute: www.sipri.org
UN Department of Peacekeeping Operations: www.un.org/en/peacekeeping
UN Office of Disarmament Affairs: www.un.org/disarmament
UN Peacebuilding Commission: www.un.org/peace/peacebuilding
UN Security Council Counter-Terrorism Committee: www.un.org/en/sc/ctc
UN Targeted Sanctions Consortium: http://graduateinstitute.ch/un-sanctions

# 8

# Global Economic Governance

## Case Study:
## The Global Financial Crisis of 2008

In the fall of 2008, the global financial system came close to collapse, resulting in the greatest challenge to the global economy since the Great Depression of the 1930s. Global stock markets plummeted; one of the world's largest banks collapsed; both industrial output and world trade levels dropped far more than they had in 1929; global foreign direct investment and flows of remittances from migrant workers plunged; and global unemployment increased by an estimated 14 million people just in 2008. In the United States, unemployment more than doubled. Consumer demand plummeted and credit became almost impossible to obtain. In 2014, the effects of the crisis continued to ripple through the global economy.

What can be learned about global economic governance from how various actors responded and the policies that have been put in place? Daniel Drezner (2012: 1) argues that "the system worked," writing: "A review of economic outcomes, policy outputs, and institutional resilience reveals that these regimes performed well during the acute phase of the crisis, ensuring the continuation of an open global economy." While others disagree with this assessment, the global economy has rebounded relatively well—far better than was the case in the aftermath of the Great Depression.

The way the 2008 crisis rippled around the world was indicative of global economic interdependence, although the effects of the crisis were not felt equally in all parts of the world. The United States and Europe were most severely affected; many developing countries much less so. States such as China, South Korea, and Japan, dependent on exports to the United States and Europe, saw their markets shrink and export earnings fall. Oil prices dropped by 69 percent between July and December 2008, severely affecting oil-exporting countries such as Saudi Arabia, Russia, Angola, and Venezuela. In emerging markets of Eastern Europe, the Baltic

379

states, and other former Soviet Union states, private foreign investment plummeted in 2008 to less than half that of a year earlier. In late 2008, Iceland became the first state victim when its banking system collapsed. The speed and depth of the collapse of global financial markets and international trade were breathtaking. Over $10 trillion in wealth was lost to households worldwide.

The crisis had many causes: irresponsible lending in the United States and Europe; central bankers and other regulators who tolerated risky practices; a glut of savings in Asia that reduced global interest rates; years of low inflation and stable growth that made people overconfident. It "highlighted the fragility, volatility, and occasional catastrophe that come with globalized capital markets" (Drezner and McNamara 2013: 155). Initial responses to the financial crisis were mostly unilateral. Both the United States and various EU member governments took unprecedented steps to bail out banks and insurance companies to get credit markets functioning and stimulate investor confidence. Fairly quickly, however, central banks such as the US Federal Reserve, the Bank of England, and the European Central Bank, undertook coordinated action, cutting interest rates and expanding credit facilities to avert a currency crisis. Those actions were critical to preventing a deeper depression. In 2008 and 2009, all the major economies implemented major stimulus packages to address the unemployment, drop in investment, and tight credit effects of the crisis.

The IMF initially responded to the crisis by making available almost $250 billion for credit lines, then tripled that to $750 billion in 2009. Iceland became the first Western country to borrow from the IMF since 1976. Substantial emergency loans were also made to Ukraine, Hungary, and Pakistan. In addition, the IMF created the Short-Term Liquidity Facility for emerging-market countries. It reorganized the Exogenous Shocks Facility, designed to help low-income states, to provide more rapid assistance. Subsequently, the International Development Association (IDA) of the World Bank Group increased its resources for lending to some of the poorest developing countries, and ASEAN broadened its Chiang Mai Initiative to create an arrangement for currency liquidity.

Yet none of the existing institutions were up to the task of coordinating responses. Both short-term emergency responses were needed as well as better long-term cross-border supervision of financial institutions, global standards for accounting and banking regulation, and an early warning system for the world economy (Cooper and Thakur 2013: 13). US president George W. Bush's decision to convene the G-20 at the leaders level for the first time in the Summit on Financial Stability and the World Economy in November 2008 marked a recognition of those shortcomings and the need for a new approach, one that recognized that any solution to the crisis needed to include developing countries such as China, India, Brazil, and Mexico.

Thus the crisis also brought a major geopolitical shift, with the G-7, dominated by major developed countries, supplanted as the principal global economic forum by the G-20 (see Figure 8.1). Over the course of ten months, the G-20 leaders met an unprecedented three times, establishing the group's reputation as a crisis first-responder. They produced a number of major initiatives, including support for large domestic stimulus packages and new resources for the IMF, World Bank, and IDA; they took steps to prevent a rise in trade protectionism and reconfigured the Financial Stability Forum into the Financial Stability Board. Indeed, one of the G-20's accomplishments and an unexpected outcome of the crisis was the revitalization of the IMF, making it the site of an early warning system for future crises (Cooper and Thakur 2013: 78).

A key to the G-20's ability to orchestrate rapid responses to the crisis was the experience of members' finance ministers in meeting with one another regularly and engaging in frank, unscripted exchanges with all members. The difference in moving to the summit level was that leaders had the ability to make commitments, deals, and concessions to solve problems.

In this chapter, we address the global and regional governance structures for finance, trade, and macroeconomic policy coordination that long revolved around developed states, and then in Chapter 9 turn to governance for economic and human development in the developing world.

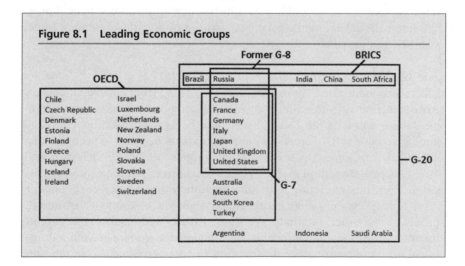

Figure 8.1   Leading Economic Groups

## An Evolving Global Economy

The visibility of economic issues today makes it hard to remember that international economic relations are now vastly different than they were at the end of World War II in 1945, let alone in 1900. In 1945, there were roughly fifty sovereign states; economies were largely national; there was limited interdependence; policies were elite-led. There were also four competing sets of ideas and economic systems in the world. The Soviet Union had established a model of socialist, command economies, dominated by central planning and state ownership. There were a handful of liberal market systems, led by the United States. The imperial preference systems of the major European colonial powers maintained privileged relationships between their economies and colonies. Finally, a majority of countries pursued mercantilist, statist economic policies. Tariff and other barriers impeded the growth of trade, movement of capital, and convertibility of currencies. There were no precedents and no international institutions for providing assistance to countries experiencing economic difficulties, or for development.

Today, there are 193 sovereign states; almost all national economies are open to some degree and linked in patterns of complex interdependence that include globalized production in some industries, global financial markets, and vastly expanded world trade—elements of a single global economy. Multinational corporations, international banks, and markets are important actors alongside states, and NGOs have become increasingly vocal. Liberal (or neoliberal) market capitalism is the dominant economic approach, with various adaptations. Recognizing the need for expanded global economic governance, states and nonstate actors have established a large number of formal and informal international institutions to help manage international economic relations, and to promote development, trade, stability, and growth.

### The Globalization of Liberal Economic Norms

Liberal economic norms have a long genesis, dating from eighteenth-century British economist Adam Smith down to contemporary thinkers. Underpinning these norms is the belief that human beings act in rational ways to maximize their self-interest. As a result, markets develop to produce, distribute, and consume goods, enabling individuals to improve their own welfare. Competition within markets ensures that prices will be as low as possible. Thus, in stimulating individual (and therefore collective) economic growth, markets epitomize economic efficiency. Government institutions provide basic order, facilitate free flow of trade, and maximize economic intercourse. At the international level, if national governments and international institutions encourage the free flow of commerce and do not interfere in the efficient allocation of resources provided by markets, then increasing interdependence among economies will lead to greater economic development for all states.

Yet not all states face the same problems, nor have all adopted liberal economic norms to the same degree and in the same way. Indeed, some states reject them. Some states have prospered; many, including a large number of developing countries, are still struggling. A group of emerging economies, including the BRICS, ASEAN states, and Mexico, have made significant economic gains, though not all people within each country have benefited from the gains. While Russia moved initially toward a more market-oriented system in the 1990s, the government's role in the economy has again been strengthened and the economy has become highly dependent on oil and gas exports. China, too, has shifted from a communist system to a more market-oriented one, but state-owned firms and banks still control a significant portion of its economy. The liberal economic system established at the end of World War II under US leadership looks quite different today.

One major challenge to economic liberalism came from statist mercantilism, which emphasizes the role of the state and the subordination of all economic activities to the goal of statebuilding. Where liberals see the mutual benefits of international trade, mercantilists see states as competing with each other to improve their own economic potential. Statist policies stress national self-sufficiency rather than interdependence, limited imports of foreign goods through substitution of domestic products and high tariffs, and restricted foreign direct investment. The "tigers" of East Asia, including South Korea, Singapore, and Taiwan, successfully used this approach to economic development during the 1980s and early 1990s, as discussed in Chapter 9. Yet many states that pursued statist approaches during earlier stages of their development have since opened their economies and accepted the central roles of the Bretton Woods institutions in global economic governance.

### The Bretton Woods Institutions:
### The Core of the Liberal Economic Order

The Bretton Woods institutions have been integral to the growth of a liberal economic order. As discussed in Chapter 3, the World Bank was to rehabilitate war-damaged economies and provide needed development capital. The IMF was to provide short-term aid to compensate for balance-of-payments shortfalls and ensure a stable monetary system. Together, the IMF and World Bank were to be the lubricant needed to allow all states to slide into a more globalized world economy. The General Agreement on Tariffs and Trade was to facilitate economic growth through reduced barriers to international trade. Later, when GATT was transformed into the World Trade Organization, it provided a dispute settlement body for trade grievances to be heard and enforced. In this sense, the GATT/WTO helped reassure states that lowering barriers to foreign products did not mean they would be exploited.

In their original incarnations, the institutions adopted a type of Keynesian approach that saw a strong role for governments in promoting both liberal trade and investment policies as well as stimulating growth during periods of economic contraction. This mix of policies was intended to result in an ever-expanding global market while reassuring those who might be overwhelmed by international forces that the state would help them transition to the new environment (Ruggie 1982). Full employment, equalization of incomes, and a strong social safety net were key parts of this social contract.

During the 1990s, however, there emerged a version of liberal economic ideology called the Washington Consensus. This held that only by following the "correct" economic policies, as espoused by the Bretton Woods institutions and the US government, could states achieve economic development. Ingredients of the consensus included fiscal discipline; privatization of industry; liberalization of trade and foreign direct investment; government deregulation in favor of open competition; and tax reform. The Washington Consensus became the dominant approach undergirding almost all international development lending and IMF aid to countries experiencing financial and debt crises.

In particular, the IMF (along with the World Bank) used its resources as leverage to persuade states to adopt these liberal measures—often in the face of strong local opposition. This "conditionality" stipulated that funds would only be available to states that committed to these measures, even if the result was a reduction in social spending, increased income inequality, and even increased poverty. This was applied to developing countries during the debt crises of the 1980s and 1990s as well as the Asian financial crisis of 1998, with mixed results. Today, "austerity" is a familiar term around the world. In Europe, the European Commission and European Central Bank have teamed with the IMF to impose harsh medicine like that of the Washington Consensus on such countries as Greece and Spain to resolve what they view as profligate spending and economic mismanagement.

The Washington Consensus (and its particulars) unraveled as the Bretton Woods institutions and major donor states recognized the limits of such a cookie-cutter approach to countries' debt and financial crises and the need for local solutions to closing the finance gap and finding the appropriate mix of economic and governance policies. As discussed earlier, the 2008 global crisis led to some reforms in the Bretton Woods institutions. Since 2010, the G-20 have consistently advocated a pro-growth strategy supporting state investment to stimulate economic activity.

### The Role of Multinational Corporations

MNCs are the vanguard of the liberal order. They are "the embodiment par excellence of the liberal ideal of an independent world economy. [They have] taken the integration of national economies beyond trade and money to the internationalization of production. For the first time in history, production, marketing, and investment are being organized on a global scale rather than in terms of isolated national economies" (Gilpin 1975: 39). For liberals, MNCs represent the most efficient mechanism for economic development and improved well-being. They invest capital worldwide, open new markets, introduce new technologies, provide jobs, and finance projects that industrialize and improve agricultural output. They are the transmission belt for capital, ideas, and economic growth, and are important parts of global economic governance.

Early forerunners of today's MNCs included the Greek, Phoenician, and Mesopotamian traders, and the British East India, Hudson Bay, Levant, and Dutch East India companies in the seventeenth and eighteenth centuries. The prominence of MNCs has increased dramatically, however, since the 1960s, facilitated in part by the formation of the European Common Market and by liberalization of trade generally.

The significance of multinational corporations cannot be overstated. In 2007, before the global financial crisis, more than $2 trillion was invested overseas by private firms seeking long-term control of foreign operations. Although the pace slipped in subsequent years, in 2011 it was up to $1.5 trillion and rising. While roughly 80 percent of foreign direct investment comes from developed countries, more and more comes from firms based in developing countries. Chinese companies, many of them private, are a significant source of new investment, with almost half of that investment going to developing countries.

### Private International Finance

It is also difficult to overstate the importance of private international finance in the contemporary world economy. It includes pure banking transactions such as deposits and loans involving private individuals, firms, governments, brokerage houses, and hedge funds, as well as the gamut of transactions involved in the stock market. One could add the roles of insurance companies, mortgage companies, bond-rating agencies, financial advisers, and currency-exchange companies in moving funds around the world.

The scale of activity in international private finance is massive. Each day roughly $4.5 trillion crosses international borders, including $110 billion in the form of loans and $150 billion in the form of portfolio investment (stocks and bonds) and between $50 and $100 billion in purely speculative currency exchanges. This implies that much of the world's assets and goods, constituting an annual global product of roughly $45 trillion (2012), change hands many times over each year. Tens of thousands of financial institutions are involved in these transactions. When the United States negotiated for access to information about bank accounts held by Americans overseas, it secured agreement from a staggering 77,000 different financial institutions! And this covered only seventy countries. The total number of institutions that engage in international transactions could be several times that figure.

Among the new financial actors are sovereign wealth funds. While these are state-owned, the managers use market financial instruments, including stocks, bonds, precious metals, and property. Formed in capital-surplus countries such as China and in the major petroleum exporters such as Kuwait, the United Arab Emirates, Norway, Russia, and Canada, these wealth funds move capital quickly across national boundaries, taking advantage of currency differentials and trading in new financial instruments to maximize their long-term economic returns, while serving as a source of capital for other states.

Although most of these entities operate in the developed world, an ever-increasing proportion of transactions take place in the global South— particularly among the BRICS. The world's three largest corporations are now Chinese banks, with combined assets of $7 trillion in mid-2014.

### Shifting Global Economic and Political Power

The rise of China as a global economic power, the rise of the BRICS, and the relative decline of the United States are changing how rules are shaped and enforced. China's gross domestic product in 2004 ranked fifth in the world, but by 2010 was the second largest, and by late 2014 the IMF ranked it number one, although others project it will be 2018 or later before China surpasses the United States. China's growth still far outpaces the much slower rates of leading developed countries, although its per capita income lags far behind. China's economic strategy, with its emphasis on state-guided exports, presents a direct challenge to Bretton Woods models. China has developed a massive trade surplus, exporting roughly $30 billion more than it imports. With large financial surpluses, it can provide credit to the rest of the world—including the United States, where China owns $1.3 trillion in federal bonds (funds without which the United States would be forced to dramatically increase taxes and reduce spending). Since mid-2013, China has also pursued a much more assertive foreign policy under President Xi Jinping, raising tensions over political and security issues. As discussed earlier, this could portend future clashes and even system change.

These developments have resulted in pressures to change voting structures of the Bretton Woods institutions, or, failing that, replacing them with organizations that reflect changing power relations. In fact, the BRICS created two new financial institutions in 2014: the New Development Bank, to finance infrastructure and sustainable development projects, and a foreign currency reserve pool that will be rivals to the World Bank and IMF. While China is the main contributor in both cases, the membership is broad and each state has a vote, with no veto power. Yet although the BRICS countries differ with the West over many issues such as market access, investment regulation, and intellectual property rules, they share little in common, making it unclear how soon and how well the new institutions begin functioning.

Because international finance and trade have been dominated by developed countries since World War II, governance too has primarily involved the major Western economic powers. Only now, with China's rise and that of other emerging economies, are the politics of global economic governance shifting significantly.

## Governance of Global Finance

### Global Currency Governance: From the Gold Standard to the Float, BIS, and IMF

States, markets, firms, banks, and international institutions are all actors in the governance of international finance today. They have generally preferred stable currencies and readily available credit with sufficient capital for long-term investment and trade. They have also often sought to control the movement of capital, but it is not possible to do all at the same time. Currency values generally respond to market forces. Traders are willing to pay more for the currency of a country with a large, well-managed economy rather than its opposite, and as a country's economy moves in one direction or the other, the value of its currency will generally rise or fall. If states seek to control the value of their currencies, they must also take steps to control how attractive their overall economies will be relative to the economies of other states. Countries may resist allowing their currencies to rise, since this makes exports more expensive for foreign customers. Conversely, states may resist acknowledging that their currency has lost its value, since this makes imports more expensive, which can lead to rising prices overall. More prestige is attached to a strong currency as well, but artificially high or low currencies usually produce profound imbalances around the world.

At different times throughout history, gold was the linchpin of the world currency system. Most recently this occurred during the 1920s, when the value of the US dollar was linked to gold. A few other currencies were also linked to gold, but the Great Depression made this arrangement unsustainable. After World War II, the US dollar returned to the gold standard, although since it was the only currency to do so, and other currencies attempted to "peg" (or establish their value in relation) to that of the US dollar. This "dollar-gold" standard helped consolidate the role of the United States as the world's creditor and manager of the international financial system. For twenty-five years, the world went through a period of relatively stable exchange rates and high confidence in the dollar, which in turn stimulated long-term international investment and the postwar recovery of Europe and Japan.

The US dollar was taken off the gold standard in 1971 due to pressures on the US economy from increasing trade deficits. Instead, to restore trade balance and address other cash-flow issues, the United States allowed the free market to establish the exchange rate for the dollar. This produced a crisis in international finance, as some feared a return to the financial instability of the 1920s. Instead, currency values stabilized with the help of periodic coordinated actions by the world's central bankers and the IMF. The floating currency system has actually provided more flexibility than the system of fixed exchange rates and the gold standard, as it allows currencies to rise and fall with fluctuations in the major economies. Two international institutions have been important: the Bank for International Settlements (BIS) and the IMF.

*The Bank for International Settlements.* The BIS was the first public international financial institution, established in 1930 by the central bankers of the United States, Japan, and several European states as a means of coordination. It was soon asked to intervene to bail out an increasing number of collapsing currencies. Although it was unable to prevent the unfolding Great Depression, it has remained in existence and was put to work after World War II to facilitate exchanges between various European central banks until the IMF was able to begin making loans in the early 1950s. While it played a secondary role thereafter, the BIS is still an important source of banking advice, particularly regarding banking reserves designed to ensure solvency.

The Basel Committee on Banking Supervision was created within the BIS in 1974 to facilitate cooperation between government agencies that supervise and regulate banks. It has established standards by which banks are to be regulated and, in that role, is central to how global financial governance works. Despite its global reach, however, the committee has a small secretariat and is made up of representatives from the central banks and bank regulatory agencies in only twenty-two countries. Because of the importance of these countries and their central banks, there are "strong incentives" for other states to follow the same standards. The IMF, other financial institutions, and international capital markets also use the standards to evaluate the soundness of banks (Young 2011: 39).

*The International Monetary Fund.* Originally, the IMF's purpose was to lend money to countries to meet short-term fluctuations in currency exchange rates, thus enabling member states to establish free convertibility among their currencies and maintain stable exchange rates. Funds to meet "temporary" balance-of-payments difficulties were allocated by quotas. Members contributed to the Fund according to quotas negotiated every five years. These were paid both in gold and in local currency (later, so-called special drawing rights provided added liquidity). Members could withdraw funds according to the amount contributed, with a onetime service charge of three-quarters of a percent on each transaction plus a charge based on length of time the money was borrowed. These arrangements were typically for twelve to eighteen months. While quota restrictions have been relaxed, the IMF still meets this need through "standby" arrangements.

The IMF is rather unusual in that its structure more resembles that of a corporation than that of a traditional international organization (see Figure 8.2). Like many corporations, it has a strong and highly expert staff, of 2,600, headed by a managing director (a European by tradition), most of whom have PhDs in economics from prestigious universities. Their expertise gives their opinions and analysis special weight, particularly when they advise leaders of developing countries. The IMF managing director or one of the deputies chairs the Executive Board of twenty-four members, conducts its business, proposes all actions, and generally has "the last word." Each member of the Executive Board represents one country or group of countries and exercises voting power commensurate with the quota (equivalent to the amount of contributions) it holds. Despite this formal voting structure, the Executive Board is more active with regard to general policy issues, while the decisions about loan programs for individual countries are worked out in confidential negotiations between IMF personnel and the governments concerned (Stone 2011: 60, 77).

From the beginning, the IMF's Executive Board allowed countries with greater involvement in international finance and larger quota shares to also wield more votes. The result is that the five largest vote-holders can shape IMF policy, not only in terms of overall policy direction but also with respect to particular loans. Mark Copelovitch (2010) found, for example, that where a country's financial troubles are likely to cause harm to one of the top five Executive Board members, funds are dispersed more quickly, in larger amounts, and with fewer conditions or stipulations. The United States, as the dominant economic power, has the most influence, and the formal weighted voting arrangements give it a veto over certain key decisions. Informally, and especially in a crisis, US influence is even more pronounced due in part to the IMF's location in Washington, DC, and its close relationships with US Department of Treasury officials (Stone 2011).

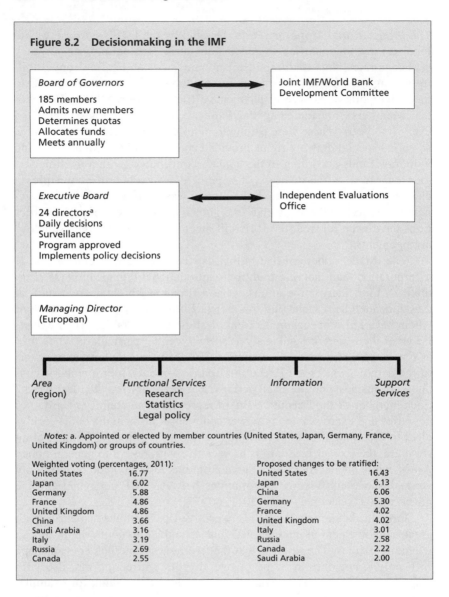

**Figure 8.2    Decisionmaking in the IMF**

*Board of Governors*

185 members
Admits new members
Determines quotas
Allocates funds
Meets annually

Joint IMF/World Bank
Development Committee

*Executive Board*

24 directors[a]
Daily decisions
Surveillance
Program approved
Implements policy decisions

Independent Evaluations
Office

*Managing Director*
(European)

*Area*
(region)

*Functional Services*
Research
Statistics
Legal policy

*Information*

*Support
Services*

*Notes:* a. Appointed or elected by member countries (United States, Japan, Germany, France, United Kingdom) or groups of countries.

| Weighted voting (percentages, 2011): | | Proposed changes to be ratified: | |
| --- | --- | --- | --- |
| United States | 16.77 | United States | 16.43 |
| Japan | 6.02 | Japan | 6.13 |
| Germany | 5.88 | China | 6.06 |
| France | 4.86 | Germany | 5.30 |
| United Kingdom | 4.86 | France | 4.02 |
| China | 3.66 | United Kingdom | 4.02 |
| Saudi Arabia | 3.16 | Italy | 3.01 |
| Italy | 3.19 | Russia | 2.58 |
| Russia | 2.69 | Canada | 2.22 |
| Canada | 2.55 | Saudi Arabia | 2.00 |

*The IMF as global financial crisis responder.* Beginning with the 1982 Mexican debt crisis, the IMF took on the role of intermediary in negotiations between creditor and debtor countries, then became involved in bailouts and structural adjustment lending. It took the 1998 Asian financial crisis to demonstrate that all crises are not alike and that the IMF's prescriptions were not always correct. Still, through the 1980s and 1990s, the

IMF requirements for structural adjustment lending required recipients to institute economic policy reforms or achieve certain conditions (referred to as conditionality) in return for financial assistance. The conditions are aimed at overcoming structural bottlenecks in countries' domestic economies and governmental policies, as well as stimulating trade liberalization and private sector involvement. Figure 8.3 shows the diverse range of suggested policies, all of which are compatible with liberal economic norms. The IMF's role in dealing with developing countries' debt is discussed further in Chapter 9.

The IMF's response to the 1997–1998 Asian financial crisis had mixed results. Beginning in Thailand in 1997, the crisis spread to other countries in Asia, including Indonesia and South Korea in early 1998; exchange rates plummeted, stock markets fell, and real GDP dropped. Millions of people were forced back into poverty. The huge inflows of private investment capital that had fueled rapid development stopped, creating a crisis of confidence in the Asian economies. The crisis revealed the weakness of many Asian countries' banking systems, their heavy levels of short-term debt and current-account deficits, along with the corruption of "crony capitalism" that closely tied business and government.

The IMF responded to the 1998 crisis with large, controversial bailout packages to three of the affected countries (Thailand, $17 billion; Indonesia, $36 billion; and South Korea, $58 billion), in addition to lengthy sets of conditions that each country was supposed to follow and monitoring devices to ensure compliance. Governments had to agree to carry out extensive structural reforms that would transform their economies from semi-mercantilist to more market-oriented. In South Korea, the government lifted restrictions on capital movements and foreign ownership and permitted companies to lay off workers, for example. The reforms were largely successful from an economic perspective, but they also led to a public backlash, a boycott of foreign products, and exposés of how foreigners benefited at the expense of Koreans (Moon and Mo 2000).

The IMF approach was similar to that in previous crises in Latin America in the 1990s (particularly in Argentina), calling for higher interest rates and taxes, reduced public spending, breaking up of monopolies, restructuring of banking systems, and greater financial transparency. Yet the IMF misdiagnosed the problem and its prescription proved inappropriate, especially in the Indonesian case. The Asian crisis was not the same as Latin American crises. High interest rates pushed more indebted companies into bankruptcy; budget cuts eliminated social services and pushed more families below the poverty line, leading to backlash against governments and the IMF.

The IMF also played a key role in the transitions of Russia and other former communist countries to market economies during the 1990s. It pro-

---

**Figure 8.3    IMF Structural Adjustment Programs**

---

*Profile of a Country in Need of Structural Adjustment*
- Large balance-of-payments deficit
- Large external debt
- Overvalued currency
- Large public spending and fiscal deficit

*Typical Goals of Structural Adjustment Programs*
- Restructure and diversify productive base of economy
- Achieve balance-of-payments and fiscal equilibrium
- Create a basis for noninflationary growth
- Improve public sector efficiency
- Stimulate growth potential of the private sector

*Typical Structural Adjustment Policies*
Economic Reforms
- Limit money and credit growth
- Devalue the currency
- Reform the financial sector
- Introduce revenue-generating measures
- Introduce user fees
- Introduce tax code reforms
- Eliminate subsidies, especially for food
- Introduce compensatory employment programs
- Create affordable services for the poor

Trade Liberalization Reforms
- Remove high tariffs and import quotas
- Rehabilitate export infrastructure
- Increase producers' prices

Government Reforms
- Cut bloated government payroll
- Eliminate redundant and inefficient agencies
- Privatize public enterprises
- Reform public administration and institutions

Private Sector Policies
- Liberalize price controls
- End government monopolies

---

vided financial resources to make external adjustment more orderly, including credits of $27 billion to enable states to avoid external arrears and ease debt servicing. Russia alone received $11.2 billion during its 1998 financial crisis. The most advanced economies in Central Europe and the Baltic states achieved rapid success, using the funds to liberalize foreign trade and reduce inflation. Although economic liberalization supported by the IMF paved the way to a resumption of growth in Russia after its 1998 crisis, Russia's subsequent economic boom owed much to the skyrocketing price of petroleum and new governmental controls. Yet those same petroleum markets are also highly volatile, and declines in oil prices in late 2014, combined with the effects of Western sanctions following Russia's takeover of Crimea, have had a negative effect on the Russian economy, which now rises and falls with the globalized economic system.

The negative outcomes to some of these crises shook faith in the IMF and liberal economic solutions, and help explain why the Fund's response to the 2008–2009 global financial crisis was initially muted. Yet not only was the IMF revitalized as a result of that crisis, but it also took an active role in the euro crisis that followed (discussed later). In 2014 the IMF intervened with $17 billion in funding to help the embattled pro-Western regime in Ukraine following the ouster of pro-Russian president Viktor Yanukovych, albeit with a package of stringent austerity measures similar to those imposed in earlier crises. The Fund was criticized by some for taking sides in the country's political crisis, but its Western supporters viewed the measures as essential to keeping Ukraine's sovereignty and economy intact.

Critics of IMF responses have focused on the so-called moral hazard problem of IMF rescue packages that encouraged international investors and states to engage in still more reckless behavior because they counted on the Fund's safety net. Whose interests was the Fund serving? Others think that more money and fewer conditions would help pull countries out of crisis faster. Still others advocated limiting the Fund's attention to balance-of-payments issues and crisis management, not development or economies in transition. And some critics focused on the secrecy of negotiations between the Fund and member countries, arguing for greater transparency in IMF decisionmaking. Even the IMF itself has been retreating from its earlier commitment to fiscal discipline and free markets. Not only has it encouraged governments to continue spending to stimulate growth, but in 2014 the IMF's managing director, Christine Lagarde, endorsed internal IMF studies that showed the need to reduce income inequality to achieve sustainable growth and social stability.

*IMF surveillance.* In addition to the structural adjustment requirements, the IMF introduced a surveillance process in the late 1970s, involving annual consultations with member governments to appraise exchange-rate policies within the framework of general economic and policy strategies. The purpose is to anticipate risks to stability and advise on policy adjustments before crises break out. The IMF offers technical assistance to members whereby state officials are trained at the IMF Institute and in regional training centers in data collection, bank management, and fiscal and monetary policy. Three regular publications are an important part of the surveillance process: *World Economic Outlook,* the *Global Financial Stability Report,* and the *Fiscal Monitor.*

Since 2000, the IMF's surveillance functions have grown in importance and expanded, even as structural adjustment lending has declined. In 2011, the IMF added regular "spillover reports" on the impact of the five largest economies (China, the eurozone, Japan, the United States, and the United Kingdom) on their partner countries. Thus, while it may appear that the IMF often targets developing more than developed countries, it has, in fact, issued critical reports on US and European policies.

*IMF reform.* In the wake of the 1997 crisis, the IMF set up systems to improve monitoring of the international financial system, so-called fire alarms, to better anticipate financial meltdowns. It also set up a credit line to provide another account from which countries in trouble could draw, despite some opposition by Germany and other "tight money" European countries (de Beaufort Wijnholds 2011: 125). As part of the negotiation on the credit line, the IMF put in place a system whereby governments would be expected to divulge details of their national accounts that had previously been confidential. For those more eager to trade on global capital markets, even more information was expected. However, the IMF has resisted providing specific credit scores on countries, although enough information is now available to draw fairly specific inferences.

Following the 2008 financial crisis and the elevation of the G-20 as a key part of global economic governance, proposals were put forward to significantly increase the quotas, and hence the votes, of G-20 members that were considered underrepresented on the IMF Executive Board. Specifically, reforms agreed to in 2010 will double the quotas, while shifting about 6 percent of quota shares from overrepresented to underrepresented member countries and still another 6 percent to dynamic emerging-market and developing countries. With that realignment, China would become the third largest member country in the IMF, and Brazil, China, India, and Russia would be among the ten largest shareholders in the Fund. At the same time, the quotas and voting share of the poorest member countries would be preserved. Despite acceptance in March 2015 by 147 IMF member states, representing 77 percent of voting shares, however, the reforms had yet to be approved by the US Congress, leaving in doubt whether the quotas will be realigned in the near future.

*The Financial Action Task Force.* As discussed in Chapter 7 with regard to cutting off terrorist financing, the FATF, established in 1989, plays a major role in global efforts to address the problems of money laundering and terrorist financing. It operates as an independent entity based at the Organization for Economic Cooperation and Development in Paris. The 2009 G-20 summit in Pittsburgh added corruption to the agenda of the FATF, whose primary outputs are sets of recommendations for actions by states and monitoring compliance. The FATF currently has thirty-six members, including two regional IGOs (the EU Commission and GCC) and Hong Kong as a separate jurisdiction. As Ian Roberge (2011) notes, the FATF has placed the issue of illicit financial activities on the international agenda, and provided a forum for discussion that facilitates policy innovation and diffusion, and is small enough and flexible enough to act quickly. The standards are well known in the financial sector, although compliance is lowest, surprisingly, with firms in industrialized countries. That said, firms are less likely to break the rules if terrorist financing is involved (Findley, Nielson, and Sharman 2014).

*From interstate to private governance in finance.* Since the mid-1980s, when many countries in the West began to privatize and deregulate various industries, including insurance and securities, private governance in the field of finance and self-regulating mechanisms has become more common. Associations of different businesses have taken the initiative to establish industry-wide standards or norms of appropriate behavior and to cooperate in order to manage markets. The International Organization of Securities Commissioners, established in 1983; the International Accounting Standards Board, created in 2001; and the International Association of Insurance Supervisors, founded in 1994, for example, have all developed rules and standards for their members to make their markets more secure and orderly. In many cases, these rules and guidelines are subsequently adopted by states themselves.

Bond-rating agencies such as Moody's Investors Service and Standard & Poor's illustrate a type of private governance developed by interfirm cooperation. They operate by selling their expertise at assessing the creditworthiness of various institutions to private firms and investors. One scholar labels such institutions "embedded knowledge networks" and characterizes them as often acting as "disinterested experts in assessing high-value transactions and in validating institutional norms and practices" (Sinclair 2001: 441). Such networks ensure investors' transparency, provide information to the markets, and establish rules for reporting, all of which are essential governance functions. Their ratings (AAA, AA, B) constitute a transnational surveillance system for private market investors as well as state authorities.

The ratings cannot always be trusted, however. Many of the large financial institutions that were given triple-A ratings in 2007 went bankrupt in 2008, leading states to more tightly regulate bond-rating agencies. For example, in the United States, the Dodd-Frank Act of 2010 requires more transparency with respect to rating methodology and accuracy over time as well as to limit conflicts of interest such as when ratings agencies must rate their own customers. European regulators have been concerned about the opposite problem, namely ratings agencies that are too quick to declare a country as being in trouble. The EU has threatened legal action against major bond-rating agencies for violating EU regulations in downgrading various countries' sovereign debt.

## Governance of Trade: From GATT to the WTO

In liberal economic theory, trade is the engine of economic growth. Although trade protection grew in the two decades after World War II, international trade has since grown dramatically. Where $62 billion in manufactured goods (in 2014 dollars) was exported worldwide in 1950, that figure was $18.8 trillion in 2013—more than 300 times larger. Even comparing today's trade levels to those of 1970, merchandise trade is sixty times greater, easily outpacing overall economic growth.

The third part of the Bretton Woods system was the stillborn International Trade Organization. The General Agreement on Tariffs and Trade took its place in 1948; its members (called contracting parties) were initially the largest developed countries, excluding the Eastern bloc and the Soviet Union as well as most less developed countries. Only gradually in the 1980s and 1990s did developing countries join GATT, and only in 1995 did a true global trade organization, the World Trade Organization, finally come into being. With the accession of China and Russia and others in this century, WTO membership has reached 160. Twenty-four states have observer status and are working toward membership. GATT had a loose link to the UN, but the WTO has none, although its director-general participates on the Chief Executives Board of UN agencies, chaired by the UNSG.

### GATT and WTO Principles and Operations

GATT and its successor, the WTO, are based on a number of important principles integral to the international trade regime, starting with support for trade liberalizaton, as outlined in Figure 8.4. At the heart of the GATT-based trading system were eight rounds of multilateral negotiations, between 1948 and 1994, that gradually reduced various types of trade barriers. Because GATT was not a formal organization, voting and formal decisions were not normal features of the rounds. Most decisions were taken bilaterally, then multilateralized. While it did have dispute settlement procedures, there were few ways to enforce decisions. The small bureaucracy (a staff of 200) was insulated and did not consult with businesses or NGOs, or review members' trade policies.

GATT negotiations in the 1960s were concerned with adapting the system to the European Community's creation and providing preferential access to Northern markets for the less developed countries to stimulate economic development. Average tariff cuts amounted to 10 percent and

---

**Figure 8.4 The World Trade Organization: Central Principles**

---

1. Nondiscrimination:
   a. Most-favored-nation treatment—products made in one member must be treated as favorably as like-products originating in another state
   b. National treatment—foreign-made products must be treated as favorably as like-products made domestically
2. Reciprocity: members try to make equivalent changes in policies; protection through tariffs only; members cannot use quotas
3. Transparency: members must publish their trade regulations and have procedures for review of administrative regulations
4. Safety valves for states to attain noneconomic objectives:
   a. Protect public health and national security
   b. Protect domestic industries from serious injury
5. Enforcement of obligations: mechanism for member states to bring cases before the WTO for dispute settlement

*Source:* Hoekman and Mavroidis 2007: 15–20.

---

then 35 percent on a volume of $40 billion in trade. The Tokyo Round, which concluded in 1979, resulted in still better treatment for LDCs and agreements on the elimination of subsidies and rules governing such non-tariff trade barriers as government procurement and technical barriers and standards. Average tariff cuts were 35 percent on $100 billion of trade. Although these enhanced the GATT-based trade system and made it fairer from the perspective of the LDCs, they did not significantly reduce growing protectionism.

The eighth round, or Uruguay Round, was concluded in 1993 after seven years of negotiations. It resulted in a 400-page trade agreement, the most comprehensive ever, covering everything from paperclips to computer chips. The 128 participants found the process difficult, as negotiations were affected by slower economic growth in the 1980s and 1990s, the complexity of many issues, and increased support for protectionism, especially in the United States. The Uruguay Round covered new items such as services (insurance, tourism, banking), intellectual property rights (copyrights, patents, trade markets), and, for the first time, agriculture and textiles. Previously, agriculture was seen as too contentious an issue, complicated by both US agricultural subsidies and the EU's protectionist Common Agricultural Policy. Average tariff cuts of 39 percent were negotiated on $3.7 trillion of trade. GATT established rules for the international trade regime, and trade among participating states expanded significantly, although GATT itself could not claim all the credit. Perhaps the most important outcome of the Uruguay Round, though, was the agreement to create the World Trade Organization.

In 1995, the WTO replaced GATT as the arbiter of trade rules, providing a formal organization for trade for the first time. It incorporated the general areas of GATT's jurisdiction, as well as expanded jurisdiction in intellectual property and services through the Agreement on Trade-Related Aspects of Intellectual Property Rights (TRIPS) and the General Agreement on Trade in Services (GATS). In all, WTO trade rules include over sixty agreements and decisions.

## WTO Governance Innovations and Dispute Settlement Procedures

The WTO has introduced several changes in governing procedures. Its top decisionmaking body, the Ministerial Council, meets at least every two years. The General Council, open to all members, meets several times a year. There is nothing in the WTO comparable to the IMF's or World Bank's executive boards. Council meetings, along with ministerial meetings, give the WTO a political prominence that GATT lacked. The WTO is a one-state, one-vote organization, unlike the World Bank or IMF, but decisionmaking is generally by consensus: each member has the right to make a motion, introduce and withdraw proposals, or block consensus. The tiny Republic of Georgia, for example, was able to block Russia's WTO membership for several months in 2013. Relative market size is the primary source of bargaining power, and weaker states are coerced by the powerful into agreeing with the consensus. Should the powerful not get their way, they can threaten to move the issue to another forum or create a new organization, and the proposals by the weak are often ignored (Steinberg 2002). The emergence since 2003 of the G-20 and of the Group of 90 (G-90), an umbrella alliance of the poorest and smallest states, makes it far more difficult to get agreement. Yet the presence of these groups has given greater representativeness to the decisionmaking process.

Based in Geneva, the WTO Secretariat has increased in size from the GATT days, but is still small (more than 600 individuals) compared to other major international economic institutions. It also has quite limited powers: the director-general cannot set the agenda for WTO meetings and cannot initiate a dispute settlement case. The secretariat cannot interpret GATT rules and is generally not permitted to chair committees. Thus the director-general is more a broker who tries to build a consensus for free trade through personal and political skills. Since trade policy is highly politicized at the national level, there is fear of giving more power to the WTO Secretariat. Despite these limitations, the secretariat does have influence through its analysis of world trade, technical assistance to developing countries, and interactions with members in developing approaches on particular issues. As a concession to shifts in global economic power, the first director-general from a developing nation, Roberto Azevedo of Brazil, was appointed in 2013.

The WTO's most important organizational innovations are the Trade Policy Review Mechanism and the Dispute Settlement Unit. The former conducts periodic surveillance of members' trade practices based on states' periodic reports. In this forum states can question each other about trade practices and learn how to draft trade regulations.

The Dispute Settlement Unit has two distinct bodies. The first is the Dispute Settlement Body, composed of representatives from all WTO members. This body tries to find diplomatic options to resolving disputes; when those options are exhausted, an ad hoc panel composed of three experts chosen by the parties is convened. Its report is due after six months. The second component is the Appellate Body, a standing organ composed of seven persons (appeals normally take sixty to ninety days). Its decisions are only binding when adopted by consensus in the Dispute Settlement Body. After this two-step procedure, the parties are obligated to implement the recommendations. Compliance panels evaluate whether compliance actually occurs and whether equivalent countermeasures (i.e., equivalent to the damages suffered) have been taken.

The Dispute Settlement Unit has become one of the busiest international adjudicatory bodies. As of 2014, 479 requests had been made, about one-third leading to a panel report and a quarter leading to "out of court" settlement or withdrawal, with about seventy Appellate Body decisions. The EU and United States are either the complainants or the respondents or third party in an overwhelming number of cases, but China's share, especially as a third party, has rapidly grown. Other developing countries are virtually absent (Hoekman and Mavroidis 2007: 82). The barriers for developing countries are both economic and political. Gathering the information for a case and actually bringing a case are costly, typically around $500,000. Politically, weaker states may fear jeopardizing relationships with more powerful states, especially if they find it impossible to coerce a settlement (Woods 2008: 5–6). The International Trade Centre—a joint undertaking by the WTO and UNCTAD—provides technical assistance to developing countries and emerging economies in trade policy.

China is now a regular party to disputes, having acted as a complainant in 12 cases, a respondent in 33, and a third party in 116 as of early 2015. It has "lost" a majority of the cases. The United States has brought more than 15 cases against China since the latter's accession in 2001—more than any other WTO member. US concerns center on China's adherence to WTO rules, the continuing heavy state role in its economy, and the incomplete adoption of rule of law (US Trade Representative 2013). Of cases involving the United States and China, for example, WTO panels have ruled against

China on cases involving Chinese tire imports to the United States and US exports of auto parts to China, as well as on Chinese export restrictions on rare earths. China's compliance with WTO decisions is still regarded as weak, although it has expressed a willingness to comply.

WTO cases have generated a number of ongoing controversies. One major issue concerns the distinction between product and process. GATT/WTO rules prohibit countries from banning a product because of the process by which it is produced. Thus, in 1989, when the EU banned the sale of hormone-treated beef for health reasons, the United States objected. A WTO panel in 1996 ruled in favor of the United States, holding that there was not enough scientific evidence about the connection between beef hormones and human health. When the EU refused to lift the ban, the WTO authorized the United States to retaliate, and it did so in 1999, increasing tariffs on imports from the EU in the amount of $116.8 million per year. Four years later, the EU amended its ban on hormone-treated beef, but a 2008 WTO panel upheld the US position that the revised ban was not justified scientifically and therefore was not consistent with WTO rules.

The WTO dispute settlement system has been hailed as a major advance in trade governance, as its legalization "decreases uncertainty and increases convergence of actors' expectations about international outcomes" (Kim 2008: 678–679). Still, given the complex and costly procedures, there may be adverse consequences for future trade cooperation and a rise in more limited and streamlined regional trade agreements.

## Trade Policy Areas

There are a number of key trade policy areas that have posed particular challenges since the WTO's creation. Among them are intellectual property, trade in services, government procurement, and agricultural subsidies. We look here at the first two. Neither are new issues, but negotiations over both have been particularly contentious.

The 1994 TRIPS agreement introduced intellectual property rules into the trade system for the first time—an important concern for the developed countries and MNCs. It is designed to protect intellectual property such as patents, trademarks, creative materials (books, CDs, videos), and software. TRIPS requires members to take provisional measures, award damages, and prevent entry of counterfeit goods. While the developed countries had one year to implement the new rules, less developed countries had until 2006, and until 2016 for pharmaceuticals. To protect profits and market shares, MNCs have fought not only for harmonization of international intellectual property standards, but also for raising those protections. The World Intellectual Property Organization (WIPO), a UN specialized agency, exists for this purpose. It administers twenty-one international treaties covering the field of industrial property and copyright and related rights, providing protection for the international business community. Three registration systems—for patents, trademarks, and industrial design—are of particular import, as they are the focus of 85 percent of the WIPO's budget. The WIPO, however, lacks binding and effective dispute resolution procedures. Many national judicial bodies, where enforcement actually occurs, also lack the capacity to enforce the rules. It is for this reason that MNCs and the United States have strongly supported using TRIPS and the WTO framework to force noncompliant countries to pass laws strengthening protection of intellectual property and to enforce them.

One intellectual property issue that has triggered particular controversy is antiretroviral drugs for treating HIV/AIDS and the provision of these drugs, patented by developed-country pharmaceutical MNCs, to the poor in developing countries. Beginning in the 1990s, AIDS activists and developing-country drug companies pushed to make low-cost generic drugs available to HIV-infected poor people. In 2003, a compromise was reached that permitted an interim waiver under TRIPS, allowing states to export generic pharmaceuticals made under license to developing countries in cases of national emergency. Despite the compromise, developed countries and their pharmaceutical companies worry that generics produced under compulsory licensing for poor-country markets will end up in the markets of developed countries, thus undercutting intellectual property protections. The WTO and TRIPS are the locus for addressing this problem.

Trade in services has been a key trade issue since the 1970s. With the 1994 General Agreement on Trade in Services, the WTO was charged with extending the multilateral trading system to the services sector, which includes public services often considered as government responsibilities, such as provision of education and water, as well as private services such as maritime transport, banking, tourism, and the legal profession. Negotiations are complex and laborious, as members send proposals directly to each other requesting greater access to markets for services and negotiate these requests bilaterally and multilaterally. The GATS agreement has so far not resulted in much added liberalization, as negotiations since 2000 have focused on locking in previous agreements.

*Expanding the global trade system: Complex WTO negotiations.* The Doha Round of WTO negotiations—labeled the "development" round—illustrates the challenges of contemporary trade negotiations that aim to expand the current global trade system. Begun in 2001 as the first round under the WTO, the talks aimed to produce major reform of the system by lowering various trade barriers and revising trade rules. The talks were supposed to serve the interests of developing countries in areas where prior GATT negotiations were thought to have disregarded them. The talks reached an impasse, however, in 2008 between the United States, Japan, and the EU on the one hand, and the G-20 emerging countries on the other. One of the main sticking points was the opening up of developed-country agricultural markets. Instead of meeting the demand to eliminate, or significantly reduce, farm subsidies, the United States proposed capping them. Although both the United States and the EU also offered an increase in the number of temporary work visas for professional workers, India and China, in particular, sought, if not an end to farm subsidies, then special safeguard mechanisms for their own poor farmers, essentially on the grounds of ensuring food security. Despite the dogged efforts of Pascal Lamy, then director-general of the WTO, no compromise was achieved and the talks collapsed. More generally, the Doha Round appeared to have failed over the perception of fairness in trade. The developing countries sought more advantages in the politically sensitive areas of agriculture and other labor-intensive sectors than the United States and EU were ready to negotiate. They were already dissatisfied with new rules that opened competition in investment and government procurement. Many placed blame on the WTO's director-general, Roberto Azevedo, for not exercising more leadership to iron out disagreements as his GATT predecessors had sometimes done.

At talks in Bali in 2013, negotiators thought they had broken the impasse. To pave the way for an expansive trade facilitation agreement to streamline customs procedures and upgrade border and port infrastructure, negotiators devised a temporary solution to the issue of food subsidies and stockpiles, which was of major concern to India and other developing countries. The latter would not be penalized for imposing subsidies greater than 10 percent—the WTO cap—on grain produced for food in a country, nor for stockpiling grain to ensure food security for millions of impoverished citizens. In mid-2014, however, India said it would veto any global deal that did not protect its food security program—potentially jeopardizing the Bali agreement. Then, in late 2014, India and the United States reached agreement on a timeline for negotiations on stockpiling, assuring India that the issue would not be sidelined. Director-General Azevedo reported, "This breakthrough represents a significant step in efforts to get the Bali package and the multilateral trading system back on track" (Bagri 2014: B3). As a result, WTO members agreed to move forward with the Bali agreement, including adoption of the Trade Facilitation Agreement—the first trade reform pact since the creation of the WTO itself in 1995.

In short, reaching agreement among 161 countries is a challenge. The complexities of new trade issues in a world of globalized production networks for automobiles and a host of other products remain. Meanwhile, the United States and European Union (and others) are pursuing regional and bilateral trade agreements, often with mutually incompatible rules, that will make future global agreements even harder to conclude. This trend rouses major debate among trade experts about the future of the WTO and the global trading system.

Another way to understand the challenges of WTO negotiations is to look at the negotiation process involved in bringing countries into the organization. China and Russia offer excellent examples. It is important to stress that membership in GATT and now the WTO involves adhesion to the core principles and all existing trade rules. This requires applicant countries to make changes in their own trade regulations and often in their economies. The complex negotiations concern how much they must change and how much time they have to come into full compliance.

China's formal accession to the WTO in 2001 after fifteen years of negotiations was complicated by the large size of its economy and its transition to a more open market economy. A 900-page accession document set the terms of China's membership. The Chinese cabinet, or state council, had to revise laws to permit foreign ventures in telecommunications, tourism, and banking. The agreement called for a continuous dismantling of barriers to trade, including eliminating restrictions on foreign law firms, opening the insurance market to foreign companies, and substantially reducing tariffs on foreign automobiles.

The difficulties, however, have been enormous. Laws governing foreign investment and particularly joint ventures were rudimentary; the Chinese security markets were not prepared for liberalization. WTO rules had to be incorporated into domestic legislation, and laws inconsistent with WTO rules had to be clarified. To monitor and enforce its WTO membership, China created a new WTO department, inquiry centers in major cities to provide trade-related information, a fair trade bureau to deal with complaints, and special courts where judges have the expertise to hear WTO-related disputes. Teams of Chinese trade officials were sent to local areas to enforce compliance with WTO rules.

Russia joined the WTO in 2012, following a record eighteen years of negotiations. In this case much of the opposition came from Russian domestic actors—businesses and ministries—that did not want to operate in a more competitive economic environment. Georgia raised political objections, seeking assurance that Russia would not provide weapons to the breakaway regions of South Ossetia and Abkhazia. The US Congress also tied Russian human rights violations to trade concessions, holding up the WTO negotiations.

With the Doha Round in doubt and regional trade agreements proliferating, clearly the future of WTO-based global trade governance is uncertain. Much will depend on whether major trading powers such as the United States, European Union, and China decide to push for a new agreement; whether India and other emerging countries can be accommodated; and on whether the WTO itself provides more leadership to bridge the differences.

## Macroeconomic Policy Coordination:
## The Roles of the OECD, G-7, and G-20

As international economic interdependence has grown, the need for coordinating the economic policies, especially of major economic powers, has increased. Coordination takes place in many settings, from the WTO, IMF, World Bank, and BIS to summits, the OECD, and various "Gs." It can also take a number of forms, including information-sharing regarding current and future policies, consultations about decisions being considered, establishing rules for acceptable policies, creating norms and expectations, and regular interactions among national policymakers. Coordination works best when countries enjoy good relations, and when problems are technical and can be delegated to specialists who have similar outlooks and are insulated from politics (Eichengreen 2011). Here we look briefly at the roles the OECD, G-7, and G-20 play in this process.

### *The Organization of Economic Cooperation and Development*

The OECD was the successor to the Organization for European Economic Cooperation, which was established to help funnel US Marshall Plan aid to European countries after World War II. In 1960, with Europe's recovery complete, it was enlarged to include the United States, Canada, Turkey, and Japan and retooled as an economic policy forum for the world's major industrial countries. Much of the impetus came from the United States, which was concerned about sharing the burden of aid to newly independent countries in Asia and Africa. The OECD's agenda over time has included promoting economic growth and financial stability based on reviews of members' economic policies, employment problems, education, energy policy, East-West trade, restrictive business practices, and aid to less developed regions. In short, almost everything but military matters has been on the OECD's agenda at some point. Its institutional procedures include small working groups of experts that are tasked with devising solutions to problems; consensus decisionmaking; annual closed sessions to review and critique the economic policies; and the involvement of high-level officials from member countries. The objective is collaboration and coordination based on information and exchange.

The OECD's staff has grown both in numbers and in expertise, and as a result the organization is seen as a reliable source of information on various economic issues. The organization's membership has also grown, from twenty to thirty-four, including South Korea, Mexico, Israel, and Chile among other graduates to the "rich countries' club."

Although not well known, the OECD has proved of considerable value over time as a venue for coordinating the policies of developed countries, even issuing guidelines to be adopted by non-OECD states in such areas as taxation policy and money laundering. And, since 1960, its Development Assistance Committee (DAC) has provided a forum for aid-giving countries to coordinate their spending levels and strategies (see Chapter 9).

The OECD has played an especially important role with respect to regulation of MNCs in the developed world. Its members have agreed to voluntary guidelines giving MNCs the same treatment as domestic corporations. Thus, host-country policies on employment and labor practices, environment, and combating bribery apply to both domestic and foreign corporations. Although the text of the guidelines never defines what a multinational corporation is, the principles and standards for conduct of business are designed to encourage MNC activity. Should disputes arise between host countries and MNCs, they are encouraged to utilize international dispute settlement mechanisms such as the World Bank's International Centre for the Settlement of Investment Disputes.

### The G-7

The power and dominance of the North and liberalism in the governance of global economic relations are evident in the G-7. This is truly the "club of the rich," an informal institution with no charter, a limited bureaucratic structure, and no permanent secretariat. Its members (see Figure 8.1) function as the self-appointed leaders of global economic governance.

The practice of convening annual summit meetings of heads of state and government of these seven leading industrial countries began in 1975 with an invitation from then–French president Valéry Giscard d'Estaing at a time of financial crisis. The United States had delinked the dollar from gold; OPEC had dramatically raised oil prices; and developing countries sought to create a new international economic order. The initial sessions were informal meetings of the leaders alone and there was no vision of permanence. Gradually, the leaders appointed representatives, known as "sherpas," (named after the Himalayan guides) to handle summit preparations and took steps toward the gradual institutionalization of the G-7. Among them were the 1977 decision to make the summits annual, having representatives lay the necessary groundwork for discussions, and expanding summits to include regular meetings of foreign, finance, and trade ministers. The result is "a complex network of close relationships" in a process that runs 365 days a year, twenty-four hours a day (Gstöhl 2007: 2).

What roles does the G-7 play in international economic governance? Those who follow it closely emphasize the value of high-level consultations to manage crises, to address new issues at an early stage, to prod other institutions such as the IMF and World Bank to take action, and to create new institutions when needed. It has also proven valuable for establishing personal relationships among leaders and learning from each other's experiences.

Like the OECD, the G-7 has addressed a wide range of issues, including the consequences of globalization, job loss, cross-border crimes, financial panic, debt relief, world poverty, terrorism, and drug smuggling. Dealing with Russia and its economic transition was also a major topic in the early 1990s. Debt and financial instability were prominent issues after the 1997–1998 Asian financial crisis. In 2002, leaders of several African nations were invited to discuss the New Partnership for Africa's Development, an African-developed initiative for sustainable economic growth, discussed in Chapter 9. This set a pattern for regularly inviting leaders from other countries to participate in some part of the annual G-7 summits. The 2005 G-7 summit, in Gleneagles, Scotland, resulted in agreement to cancel all debt for the poorest countries. In 2007 and 2008, global climate change and the Doha Round were major topics of discussion.

During the period from 1998 to 2014, when Russia joined the group for noneconomic discussions, some analysts referred to the G-8 as the center of global governance more generally, as the G-7/8 created groups to deal with issues like terrorism and drugs that had no IGO "homes."

The G-7 was also responsible for creating the Financial Stability Forum in the aftermath of the 1997–1998 Asian financial crisis, with the BIS providing secretariat services. The forum's task was to promote financial stability through information exchanges and cooperation in financial market supervisions and surveillance. This included strengthening international financial codes and standards, generally reflecting the "best practices" in advanced countries. The twelve financial codes that the forum unveiled in 2000 include corporate governance practices of the OECD, accounting standards of the International Accounting Standards Board, banking supervision of the Basel Committee on Banking Supervision, and money laundering activities of the FATF. Virtually all these standards were designed for the developing world, even though those states either were not included or were underrepresented when the codes were conceived. Nevertheless, the IMF and G-7 expected compliance and were prepared to use resource allocations and economic sanctions to enforce the standards (Drezner 2007: 136–145).

At the G-20 summit in 2009, the forum was reestablished as the Financial Stability Board; G-20 countries that were not already members were invited to join, and Spain and the European Commission were added. With the expanded membership has come a broader mandate and a more institutionalized structure.

Although the G-7 has been supplanted on several issues, the G-7 finance ministers continue to meet. In the spring of 2014, two leaders' summits were convened hastily to condemn Russia's annexation of Crimea and its violation of Ukraine's sovereignty, and to expel it from the G-8.

## The G-20

The 2008–2009 global financial crisis made it clear, as discussed in the opening case of this chapter, that many of the standards in banking, accounting, insurance, and securities were either inadequate or not being enforced. The crisis also made it evident that the G-7 members no longer dominated the world economy and therefore could not continue to make the rules without more consultation with all the new actors.

Recognition of the limitations of the G-7 actually became apparent much earlier, during the 1998 Asian financial crisis. At that time, US treasury secretary Lawrence Summers and Canadian finance minister Paul Martin convened a group of nineteen finance ministers from leading industrial and developing economies plus the EU. The G-20 was born. The finance ministers have met annually since 1999, but not until the 2008 financial crisis was a leaders' summit convened. The G-20 replicates much of the G-7 structure in that the association is informal, consisting of multiple working groups and periodic summits of heads of state, as well as meetings of senior ministers or their representatives. Like the G-7, the G-20 functions without a headquarters or permanent staff. The leadership rotates among the various member states, and the rotating chair is responsible for providing secretariat functions.

Since 2008, the G-20 has met at least annually to address financial crises, economic growth, trade, and employment. It has also adopted rules on tax havens and money laundering that parallel those of the OECD.

While it may be too soon to assess the G-20, it has greater diversity of membership and hence legitimacy. There is no veto power, weighted voting, or presumption that leadership will be monopolized by major powers. As Andrew Cooper and Ramesh Thakur (2013: 16) note, its size makes it difficult to manage. Therefore, much will depend on "whether or not leaders and their advisors could work together and make the commitments, big deals and concessions required not only to solve problems on an issue-specific basis but to maintain the momentum for the G20 as a pivotal and innovative forum of global governance."

Given the larger voice for developing countries, it is not surprising that the G-20 has consistently advocated national prerogatives to promote growth rather than submit to the rigors of market discipline. Yet some important economic players are not members of the G-20. Switzerland, for example, famous for its bankers' discretion, is not part of the G-20 discussion on banking secrecy. The absence of Israel and Iran, both major economic actors, also suggests the group's desire to avoid ugly political debates. And Pakistan, Nigeria, and Bangladesh, despite having a combined population of more than half a billion people, were not invited to join.

The G-20, like the OECD and G-7, has an ambitious agenda of coordinating the macroeconomic policies of a large number of major actors.

Another approach is to bring economic governance to the functional level or even the region.

## The Key Roles of Functional Institutions and Regimes

Functional organizations have been around longer than any other type of IGO, as discussed in Chapter 3. They are known for adopting a problem-solving, apolitical approach aimed at working with stakeholders such as states, citizens, corporations, professional associations, and social movements. While the list of functional organizations is long and many are addressed elsewhere in the book, two types are directly related to international trade and commerce: intergovernmental regimes in transportation (aviation and maritime transport) and the nongovernmental institution governing product standards, the International Organization for Standardization (ISO).

### Functional Regimes in Transportation

International trade and development and the international monetary system are lubricated by a network of international functional regimes. Trade cannot occur without a physical means to transport goods. Hence there are strong international rules and norms in ocean shipping and air transport, negotiated among relevant parties.

Ocean shipping and air transport are two areas that have had a direct impact on expanding economic relations. Thanks to technological improvements, both means of transport have become faster, more efficient, and cheaper. About 95 percent of international trade by weight, or about two-thirds of all international trade by value, occurs through ocean shipping.

The most important norms concerning shipping date back to the nineteenth century—namely freedom of the high seas and innocent passage through territorial waters, the right of the state to control entry of foreign ships, and flag-state jurisdiction over ships operating on the high seas. The myriad other norms, rules, and regulations have been the product of both public and private international organizations.

The International Maritime Organization (IMO) is the UN specialized agency designed to facilitate technical cooperation in shipping, through various committees that approve technical standards and regulations on such issues as accidents, pollution, and compensation. Until the 1960s, enforcement was centered on flag states (a few developing countries with little interest in regulation) and insurers or bankers with economic interests. As ocean shipping grew and safety standards came under attack, traditional maritime nations like Great Britain and the United States expanded their powers as coastal states under the 1972 International Convention for the Prevention of Pollution from Ships, and the IMO developed procedures that solidified it as the center for maritime regulations. That trend accelerated during the 1990s when IMO member states both helped flag states develop capacity to follow regulations and privately pressured them to follow international standards. Initiatives by both the United States after 9/11 and the EU's European Maritime Safety Agency to rank specific ships and flag states on the extent that they followed the rules and conducted container inspections enhanced the IMO's involvement (Anianova 2006).

Private initiatives are also important. The International Maritime Bureau collects data on pirate attacks and provides these updates to shipping firms, insurance companies, and the IMO. It is the responsibility of states, not the IMO, however, to police their own waters. Data compiled by the bureau suggest that states have actively responded to piracy attacks only 16 percent of the time, a figure that has not varied with the rise in piracy. Thus, with the rash of attacks off the coast of Somalia in 2007–2009, it fell to the UN Security Council to authorize enforcement under Chapter VII of the UN Charter, as discussed in Chapter 7 (Stiles 2009). But piracy has now shifted to Southeast Asia and the West African coast, motivated by petroleum cargo transported in small ships. Attacks in the Gulf of Guinea (West Africa) accounted for 19 percent of all maritime attacks in 2013.

During the latter half of the twentieth century, comparable norms evolved for air transport, as states recognized freedom of air transport above the oceans, while requiring state consent for passage over sovereign territory. For both air transport and ocean shipping, states have accepted norms governing damage control, accident prevention, and crimes such as piracy and hijacking, as well as norms to prevent pollution and environmental harm. Most of the airline and air transport norms were established through the International Civil Aviation Organization (ICAO), a specialized agency of the UN created in 1944, and the International Association of Transport Airlines (IATA), created by the airlines in 1945. At the outset, it was intended that the IATA would provide technical information to the ICAO and that the two would work closely together. The dominance of the US airline industry as supplier of aircraft, however, has meant that the United States plays a more hegemonic role in setting safety standards and norms. The IATA is most concerned with facilitating the flow of travelers and luggage, exchange of tickets, and fare-setting. The ICAO and IATA have made positive contributions to standardizing transport regulations and enhancing airline safety and efficiency.

In particular, the ICAO's inspection of its members' aviation administration systems—complete with a public "scorecard"—went far to push members toward improved safety and training. These efforts are ongoing. And after Malaysian Air Flight MH370 disappeared in 2014, there was renewed pressure on the ICAO to improve communication blind spots over the world's oceans.

### The International Organization for Standardization

The ISO is a unique, nongovernmental umbrella organization composed of 165 national standards-setting bodies that since 1946 has created technical specifications for products and services for most industries, spanning technology and manufacturing to food safety, agriculture, and health care. Experts from around the world develop the standards for different sectors based on their knowledge and experience. Some 19,500 international standards as of 2014 specify the chemical content of batteries, software found in credit card–reading machines, manufacturing of smokestack scrubbers, and the like. The ISO and its partner institution, the International Electrotechnical Commission, together promulgate 85 percent of the world's product standards. More than 1,500 new international industrial standards are set each year, some of which are later incorporated into domestic law (Büthe and Mattli 2011: 7).

Setting these standards allows consumers to trust the reliability of "ISO certified" goods and services and increases the chances that companies that comply will be able to market their goods and services worldwide. Yet standard-setting is inherently a political process. Firms that are unable to satisfy the requirements are by and large excluded from the marketplace. In some cases, the technology and capital investment required to meet the standards is beyond the capacity of many firms. Likewise, standards calling for certain levels of training of workers and staff may only be available abroad, making the meeting of the standard unrealistic. Even attending meetings may be too costly.

Since noncompliance is most likely to affect firms in developing countries, the ISO has developed outreach and training programs to help them achieve the standards. Despite questions about the legitimacy of the process, more and more firms have adopted ISO standards for their sector. And there can be a spillover effect. For example, when the ISO adopted a standard on environmental protection, firms that act as suppliers to companies that have embraced the standard have significantly reduced their own pollution, despite weak state laws on the subject (Prakash and Potoski 2014).

## Private Governance

For many years, but especially since the 1980s, governments, international organizations, and a variety of private entities (including for-profit and not-for-profit actors) have formed associative arrangements. But sometimes, private actors act independently in what is referred to as private governance.

Private economic governance takes a number of different forms. Production alliances or producer cartels are one form of private governance.

One example is the diamond cartel, which purports to control about 80 percent of the world's diamond trade. Largely controlled by the De Beers companies along with Russia, it makes a conscious effort to sustain the illusion that diamonds are scarce, therefore justifying high prices. The cartel works principally through a central selling organization to control the volume of diamonds on the international market, their classification, and advertising. Since 2003, the Kimberley Process Certification Scheme, a multistakeholder process, has sought to curb the flow of "conflict" or "blood" diamonds—diamonds whose sale fuels civil conflicts particularly in Africa. Organized through the World Diamond Council and monitored by independent groups, including Global Witness and Partnership Africa Canada, the Kimberley Process was successful for several years. In 2011, Global Witness pulled out, citing the ineffectiveness of the certification process.

Businesses or trade associations sometimes unite, sometimes cross-nationally, to develop industry-wide standards or enforce particular practices. The OECD has analyzed over 230 such corporate codes of conduct. Some are applicable only to a specific firm; others are in force among firms committing competitors to certain standards of conduct, such as the Code of Conduct for the Tea Sector or the Common Code for the Coffee Community.

Self-regulation is largely a response to informal and formal pressures from shareholders (under the rubric of socially responsible investing), from NGOs, and even from governments threatening stronger regulatory action. Such pressures have led corporations to impose self-restrictions governing purchasing agreements, labor conditions, and environmental standards. Since 2005, Walmart has demanded that its suppliers follow increasingly stringent environmental standards or have their contracts suspended. In most cases this means firms exceed the requirements of their own domestic law. Dozens of Chinese firms have, in fact, adopted Walmart's high standards, despite Beijing's weak environmental rules. The Rugmark Foundation and the Clean Clothes Campaign involve two NGO-inspired codes of conduct to improve labor conditions in respective industries. For firms to adopt such standards and still be competitive, however, it behooves them to cooperate with others for a joint industry standard. Many of these have developed partnerships among companies, labor groups, and NGOs, and are discussed in Chapters 10 and 11. The UN Global Compact on Corporate Responsibility represents such an approach and is discussed in Chapter 9.

There are advantages and disadvantages to private governance over state and IGO governance. On the positive side, firms develop relationships with each other over time and are often able to respond to changing conditions faster than could a government or international bureaucracy. Even though the decisions are not what could be considered democratic, it may not matter if the result better fits the demands and needs of ordinary people in places where their governments are unconcerned about their well-being. Perhaps Walmart and ISO environmental standards may be doing more for the health of Chinese people than the government. Yet there is the possibility that private actors are only accountable to themselves and that too much power is concentrated in their hands, while the interests of states and ordinary individuals are neglected (Papadopoulos 2013).

There are critics of all these approaches and no direct evidence that self-regulation works. Nevertheless, certification and monitoring programs have proliferated, with NGOs putting pressure on companies through sophisticated mass-marketing techniques. Sometimes private and governmental actors decide that an international arrangement may be too difficult to arrange and inefficient, and hence turn to regional arrangements and organizations.

## The Regionalization of Economic Governance

Regional governance has proliferated with the expansion of the EU and the creation of AFTA, NAFTA, the Asia-Pacific Economic Cooperation, Mercosur, ECOWAS, and other regional and subregional economic groups, discussed in Chapter 5. Indeed, since the Doha Round of WTO negotiations stalled in 2008, a hundred new regional trade agreements have come into force, for a total of nearly 380 as of mid-2014.

Regional or preferential trade agreements are predicated on the belief that members will experience economic benefits by taking advantage of economies of scale, spreading costs over larger regional markets, and increasing political cooperation. Two debates regarding regional trade agreements have emerged. First is the question of whether they improve the economic welfare of their members through trade creation or whether trade is actually diverted and thus reduces economic welfare. With regional trade agreements, some trade is created in goods produced efficiently relative to the rest of the world. Trade is also diverted from efficient nonmembers because of the preferences states grant to each other, and hence state welfare is reduced.

Second is the question of whether regional trade agreements are a steppingstone or a stumbling block to global trade arrangements. On the one hand, they clearly involve fewer parties in negotiations and enhance the competitiveness of some domestic industries, making it easier to argue for liberalization. Some see them as a steppingstone toward integration on a larger scale, since they allow states to gradually improve their competitiveness. On the other hand, under regional trade agreements, larger economies can impose their will more easily and interest groups may find it easier to lobby for their interests, inhibiting freer global trade. Jagdish Bhagwati (2008), a prominent opponent of regional trade agreements, calls this collection of agreements "termites in the trading system." Regional agreements make states less likely to agree to global tariff cuts; freer trade may erode the narrow gains already won. Both of these issues are prominent in the debate over the oldest and most extensive regional trade group, the European Union.

### The European Union's Single Market

The EU's evolution into a single regional market occurred in three distinct phases. In the first phase, from 1958 to 1968, members worked to eliminate internal tariffs, dismantle quantitative import restrictions among the six original members, and establish a common external tariff and the Common Agricultural Policy. Thereafter, members negotiated as a single entity in international trade negotiations. In the second phase, during the 1970s and early 1980s, membership was enlarged in two waves and key institutional changes were undertaken, as discussed in Chapter 5, but deeper integration stalled. In the third stage, members implemented the Single European Act to stimulate new economic growth by completing their single market and introducing the common currency (euro) to achieve monetary union.

*Breaking down the trade barriers.* The Single European Act (SEA) of 1987 provided the foundation for major economic changes and a deepening of the integration process. European economic growth had been sluggish since the mid-1970s and Japan and the United States were becoming increasingly competitive. Completing the single market would provide the needed boost. So in 1985 the European Commission issued a white paper on completing the internal market. When approved, the Single European Act amended the Treaty of Rome and gave new impetus to European integration.

The SEA's goal was to achieve a single market by December 1992 and to strengthen community institutions. This would ensure the free movement of goods, persons, and capital throughout the EU. The process was complicated, involving removal of all physical, fiscal, and technical barriers to trade, and harmonization of national standards through over 300 community directives. To eliminate restrictions on movement of goods and persons, it was necessary to eliminate customs duties, quantitative restrictions, and measures having equivalent effect. Customs barriers were abolished at the end of 1992, but the movement of persons proved more difficult. Since 1993, residents of EU member states have had the right to live and work in any other EU member state, although some restrictions were placed on citizens of Eastern European countries that joined the EU in 2004 and 2006. Most countries eliminated passport controls and adopted common visa regulations, but Britain, Ireland, and Denmark refused. States have gradually begun to recognize each other's educational and professional qualifications, a requirement for the free movement of labor.

Abolishing technical barriers to trade has proven more difficult. Although the European Court of Justice ruled in 1979, in the *Cassis de Dijon* case, that products meeting the standards of one member state could be legally sold in another (see ECJ 1979), states continue to assert health and safety standards as legitimate restrictions on trade. Since harmonizing technical standards had proven difficult, the SEA adopted the less rigid approach of mutual recognition, acknowledging that states could have different standards and requirements as long as those standards approximated each other.

Competition policy has also proved to be a significant technical barrier to trade. The Maastricht Treaty prohibits EU member states from giving preferences to home companies in government contracts, even though certain areas of economic activity, such as road transport, water, and financial services, are often under the control or management of state enterprises. Breaking long-standing state monopolies and prohibiting state aid to specific sectors are politically difficult, although most recognize that such practices do distort trade. The European Commission is now more actively examining malfeasance and initiating actions against states that provide uncompetitive (and therefore unfair) state aid. In addition, the Council of Ministers more carefully examines mergers for anticompetitive implications. Antitrust regulations have been expanded to eliminate monopolistic sales agreements, discrimination by nationality, and predatory pricing. In one controversial case that began in 2004 and dragged on until 2012, the EU found Microsoft guilty of anticompetitive behavior and fined it $794 million for failing to respect the settlement. This marked the first time a company had been fined for that reason, but, in fact, the fine had been significantly reduced from the original judgment of $2.7 billion.

A de facto single market exists today among the EU's twenty-eight members, with most restrictions eliminated. This has resulted in increased wealth and productivity as trade and foreign investment have grown; European corporations have become more competitive, and integration of transportation and energy networks has proceeded, although unemployment remains comparatively high, especially since the global financial crisis and the eurozone crisis that followed.

*The special problem of agriculture.* Of the EU's economic policies, none is more complicated than those that fall under the Common Agricultural and Rural Development Commission. Agriculture is the most integrated of the EU's economic sectors, receiving just over 42 percent of the EU's total budget. Foodstuffs are vital for national security, and no country wants to be dependent on other states for essentials.

A complicated and expensive system of subsidies to farmers was established under the CAP, whereby the EU purchases the surplus from farms at a guaranteed price and either stores it, donates it to food aid programs, or absorbs the loss. Significant reforms in effect since 2013 have simplified the regulations. The reforms eliminate intervention price supports for certain crops, provide added benefits to smaller active farmers, support sustainable farming practices, and boost rural employment opportunities.

Not only are EU members deeply attached to retaining the CAP, but the EU has also adopted very strict regulations on food imports, including a ban on many genetically modified foods, which particularly affects US-EU trade. These regulations and the remaining price supports have been and will continue to be an impediment in WTO negotiations.

*Monetary integration.* In the 1960s, members of the European Economic Community declared their interest not only in an economic union, but also in a monetary union, though not much progress was made for many years. The formation of the European Monetary System in 1979 created some structure for coordinating financial policy; the European Currency Unit served as a means of settling accounts; and the Exchange-Rate Mechanism provided fixed, though adjustable, bands of currency exchange. But these were weak instruments. In the late 1980s, during the discussions of the single market, provisions were made for greater cooperation in monetary policy.

The Maastricht Treaty of 1992 delineated the features and timetable for movement toward forming the European Monetary Union, which included establishing a single currency, the euro, and common monetary policies. The euro was realized for businesses in 1998 and for consumers in 2002. Not only does the single monetary unit serve as a powerful symbol of community unity (and loss of state sovereignty over currency), but member states have also agreed to relinquish their right to use exchange rates and interest rates as instruments of national economic policy.

The euro quickly established itself as a safe and stable currency worthy of use around the world. By reducing "transaction costs"—the costs of entering into a deal—it helped facilitate cross-border trade and investment. Many EU members, including Greece, Ireland, and Spain, experienced high growth rates during the 1990s and early 2000s. In Greece, public sector borrowing was fueled by high public sector wages. In Ireland and Spain, private sector borrowing was fueled by the construction and housing sector, all facilitated by low interest rates set by the European Central Bank (ECB).

When the global financial crisis hit, governments dependent on borrowing in international markets were unable to meet debt obligations, weak and loosely regulated banks were unable to cover liabilities, and individuals whose net worth had declined were confronted with declining wages and unemployment. Meanwhile, Germany, the strongest eurozone member, continued to enjoy trade surpluses because of high productivity and wage restraint. With German exports even more competitive, other eurozone countries had worsening balance-of-payments positions. But German, French, and Scandinavian banks had made substantial loans to states in trouble and were therefore vulnerable.

As problems worsened, critics questioned how the euro could work with no fiscal union and with each state having different tax and pension rules. How could the eurozone work with no strong central bank with bank regulatory oversight?

The response to the crisis was found in coordinated actions. Ireland took the first step at restoring fiscal stability with an austerity plan, then in 2010 turned to the EU and IMF for a financial bailout package of 85 billion euros, to be combined with tax increases and spending cuts. Greece required multiple bailouts from the EU, ECB, and IMF, as the government took multiple steps to slash public spending, improve tax collection, and renegotiate labor contracts, all of which were highly unpopular. By 2013, there had been more than twenty summits to address the eurozone crisis, involving the major leaders, and representatives from the European Central Bank, EU, IMF, as well as the private banks.

Questions remain, however, about the wisdom of imposing such severe austerity measures. For example, Germany became the target of considerable criticism by 2014 for its strict adherence to austerity. Even the ECB and IMF called for stimulus measures to invest in growth and reverse the high unemployment levels in many EU countries. With anti-austerity sentiments strong in many countries, alongside the growing strength of Euroskeptic parties, European leaders have become divided on the appropriate measures to address their economic problems. Indeed, Greece elected a leftist government in 2015 espousing an anti-austerity policy, widening the divide among EU members.

As a result of the eurozone crisis, major reforms have been instituted and others proposed. The Stability and Growth Pact, controlling national budgetary policies, has been strengthened, and fines have been levied for deviant policies. The European Financial Stability Forum, an IMF-like institution established in 2010, provides funding to facilitate structural adjustment among its members. The Macroeconomic Imbalance Procedure identifies risks, which then facilitates policy coordination. In 2012 the European Central Bank was reorganized to be a bank regulator, with deposit insurance programs to augment national programs and authority to examine bank balance sheets. In 2014 after the first review, it identified twenty-five failing banks and thirteen others that needed strengthening. Calls for some form of common governance, including a possible fiscal union, persist. Yet there also remains the possibility that Greece and other eurozone members may be forced to leave the zone, with unknown consequences for the EU.

## The ASEAN Free Trade Area

The ASEAN countries have been working toward their own free trade area since concluding AFTA in 1992. The four newer members were required to sign the agreement as a condition of joining ASEAN, but given longer time periods to meet the tariff reduction obligations. The AFTA agreement is relatively brief and contains no binding commitments, ironic given the fact that ASEAN members' prosperity depends heavily on trade. It is designed to eliminate all tariffs among members, but unlike in the EU, members do not aim to create a common external tariff. The exception to these reductions is rice, the regional food staple, along with certain other "highly sensitive products." By the end of 2014, 70 percent of ASEAN intraregional trade incurred no tariffs, and the average tariff rate was less than 5 percent.

AFTA has primarily focused on tariff reductions, but has begun to work also on nontariff barriers, which are now the primary protective measures, as well on quantitative restrictions and harmonization of customs rules. As of 2010, one study showed "positive and significant" trade creation effects on a wide range of products, particularly for the original six ASEAN members. Overall, the study showed an expansion of intra-ASEAN trade, especially imports of parts, components, and capital goods, which pointed to the formation of regional production networks. Exports to China had expanded more than intra-ASEAN exports, likewise indicating the formation of ASEAN-China production networks (Okabe and Urata 2013).

As discussed in Chapter 5, AFTA members signed agreements in 2009 to form an integrated ASEAN Economic Community by 2015 (minus a common currency) to boost growth. Whether ASEAN members can bridge their large differences in levels of development and national standards, however, remains to be seen. Most analysts say achieving the single market envisioned in the AEC is still a long way off. China has voiced its interest in joining AFTA—a step that would further complicate regional economic integration.

With the ASEAN Charter adopted in 2007 giving the organization legal personality, ASEAN had a basis for concluding trade agreements with countries, regional, subregional, and international organizations. As of 2014, it had six such agreements, with India, Australia and New Zealand, Japan, China, South Korea, and the EU. Like other preferential agreements, these violate the most-favored-nation principle by favoring only those that are parties, and illustrate the further splintering of the WTO-based global trade system.

Beyond AFTA, ASEAN has taken steps since the 1997–1998 Asian financial crisis to create mechanisms to prevent and address any future financial crises. In 2000, the ASEAN Plus Three established the ASEAN Surveillance Process to monitor capital flows, the Chiang Mai Initiative to provide a currency-swap arrangement supplementing the IMF, and a network of training institutions to strengthen banking capacity. These were clearly reactions to the harsh and inappropriate measures imposed by the IMF during the 1997–1998 crisis and subsequent scuttling by the United States of a proposed Asian monetary fund. In 2010, the Chiang Mai Initiative was "multilateralized" to create a reserve of pooled funds, then doubled in size in 2012 when a stability fund was created—all in response to adverse effects of the 2008 global financial crisis. In addition, ASEAN Plus Three finance ministerial meetings now include central bank governors.

Although there is considerable debate about how effective AFTA and the Chiang Mai Initiative are, ASEAN has clearly broadened the scope of regional economic governance beyond trade alone.

### The Proliferation of Regional Trade Agreements

To say that regional trade agreements (RTAs) have become popular since the end of the Cold War would be an understatement. As Figure 8.5 shows, the number of these agreements rose from roughly 50 in 1990 to nearly 400 less than twenty-five years later, with an average of over a dozen new agreements a year. If all the RTAs that have been agreed to enter into force, there will soon be nearly 600 of them.

With many governments skeptical about concluding a new WTO agreement and of the capacity of the WTO to meet all their needs, regional trade

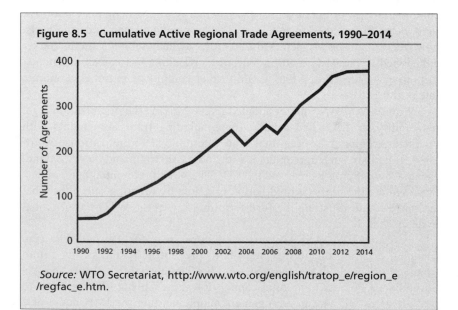

**Figure 8.5    Cumulative Active Regional Trade Agreements, 1990–2014**

*Source:* WTO Secretariat, http://www.wto.org/english/tratop_e/region_e/regfac_e.htm.

agreements are seen as a practical alternative, involving less risk, variable commitments, more familiar partners, and rapid enactment. But they may be far easier to create than to put into practice. Actual implementation depends mostly on whether the signatories are closely intertwined economically and have the resources to enforce new rules. Further, once multilateral trade agreements are in place, they are likely to expand to include more members—something that is rare with respect to bilateral deals (Mansfield and Pevehouse 2013).

Although RTAs have proliferated, in most cases they link a variety of countries with each other but they are not exclusive. In Africa, Latin America, as well as Europe, states belong to multiple bilateral, subregional, and regional agreements, leading many pundits to refer to a "spaghetti bowl" of state commitments. These crisscrossing commitments may limit the capacity of states to resort to protectionism when times get tough and should therefore help sustain international liberalism, but regional trade agreements may also work at cross-purposes and undermine overall effectiveness.

We look briefly at two major RTAs that have been under negotiation for a number of years: the Transatlantic Trade and Investment Partnership, between the United States and the European Union, and the Trans-Pacific Partnership.

*The proposed Transatlantic Trade and Investment Partnership (TTIP).* The United States and the European Union are negotiating a series of trade and investment agreements that would knit together their economies even more closely. In 2013, one-fifth of US exports went to the EU, while the EU exported one-eighth of its goods to the United States. The proposed TTIP is intended to reduce obstacles to trade and investment, such as EU barriers to genetically modified foods, and empower US firms to sue in local European courts. Some Europeans are concerned about granting more rights to US firms, which could lead to weakened worker protections, but some economists predict the deal could result in economic gains equivalent to an extra $700 per year for each European family of four (Francois et al. 2013). The negotiations are scheduled to conclude in 2015.

*The proposed Trans-Pacific Partnership (TPP).* Since 2011 the United States has also been involved in talks on a partnership that would more closely link twelve Pacific Rim nations, including both developed and developing states such as Canada, Chile, Mexico, Vietnam, Japan, and Australia. China, however, is not included in the negotiations, leading some analysts to see the TPP as part of US efforts to contain China's rise. One goal is regulatory harmonization, meaning that governments would adopt increasingly similar rules governing production and trade. This may lead to stricter rules for many countries, such as much stronger protection of copyrights and patents. In other cases it could lead to weakening of regulations, especially where foreign companies are able to sue local governments. More than for the TTIP, however, secrecy surrounding the talks for the TPP has prompted skepticism in the US Congress about negotiators' intentions. Senator Ron Wyden, for example, complained in 2012: "The majority of Congress is being kept in the dark as to the substance of the TPP negotiations, while representatives of U.S. corporations are being consulted and made privy to details of the agreement" (Edsall 2014).

## Critics of Governance Institutions in Finance and Trade

Developing countries have long been critics of the international liberal economic system and expressed this dissatisfaction through the UN. Along with a few developed states, they have criticized the central actors in economic governance, sought to regulate MNCs, and offered reform proposals. These criticisms have been rooted both in politics (the domination of the rich) and in economic theory (particularly Marxist and dependency theory). Still other criticisms have been rooted in concerns for equity, fairness, and social justice. Many critics of the liberal economic model have focused on the MNCs, believing that they occupy a position of preeminence without being subject to adequate international or state controls, as explored in depth in Chapter 9. Yet determining what is to be regulated, even defining what MNCs are, as well as the scope of regulations, has always been problematic. IGOs are easier to identify, making the IMF and WTO subject to criticisms from every ideological position. We look at critics of the IMF and WTO therefore, along with antiglobalization critics.

### The IMF and Its Critics

Developed-country critics of economic liberalism generally have targeted a number of specific deficiencies at the IMF, many of which were introduced earlier in this chapter. Interestingly, those critiques come from different ideological directions. Conservative critics say that the IMF is too interventionist in economies; they see the free market economy working efficiently without interference. Rescuing countries that have followed profligate economic policies—whether Thailand, Russia, Ukraine, Argentina, or Greece—poses a moral hazard.

Most liberal critics generally want reforms within the established frameworks. The 2008 global financial crisis resulted in calls for a new "architecture" of institutions and rules to govern, reinforcing banking regulations, modifying voting within the IMF, and enhancing surveillance mechanisms. Liberal feminists call for more women in policymaking positions, since only a quarter of the Fund's staff are women. When IMF managing director Dominique Strauss-Kahn resigned in 2011 amid a sex scandal, the Fund's female staff issued an open letter calling for a woman to run the organization. The appointment of Christine Lagarde as managing director was designed to improve the Fund's working environment and reputation. Still, only one woman sat on the IMF Executive Board in 2014, and fewer than 10 percent of the European Central Bank's leadership and senior staff are women.

A few radical critics from developed countries would join the critics from the developing countries of the IMF as an outmoded, Western-dominated institution failing to reflect changes in world affairs. Many of these positions are similar in their approach to the critiques of the WTO.

## The WTO and Its Critics

With a wide range of goods and services under its jurisdiction and strengthened dispute settlement mechanisms, the WTO has become a lightning rod for groups from both developed and developing countries who see the organization as the culprit in the negative consequences of economic globalization, usurping state sovereignty and domestic interests and favoring the interests of major developed countries over poor countries. Even though each WTO member has a voice through the consensus procedure, decisions often involve "unequally matched states against one another in chaotic bouts of negotiating which has seen developed countries secure more of the economic opportunities they already have while offering developing countries very little of what they actually need" (Wilkinson 2014: 2). Still others point out that although some developing states participate in the WTO's dispute settlement system, the vast majority do not, because of the considerable cost of proving injury from the trade policies of another country and the reluctance to retaliate against a major power should a decision be rendered in their favor.

At a more general level, many are critical of the effects of reducing barriers to trade and making the world more "globalized." Scholars sometimes question whether the world is globalizing and even more so whether it should be (Veseth 2010).

Among activists, antiglobalization NGOs are major opponents of WTO activity, charging that the WTO's power to make regulations that have consequences and settle disputes with authoritative measures is an intrusion on national sovereignty. They are also critical of the lack of transparency in WTO procedures. In addition, there is a widely held perception that the organization is captive to the demands of rich governments and big MNCs.

To other NGOs, the WTO's adherence to the interests of free trade undermines the application of labor and environmental standards, discussed in Chapters 10 and 11. Thus, labor movements and environmental groups have joined the opposition, believing that the WTO privileges economic liberalization over social values. The environmental groups argue that the trade rules need to be more environmentally friendly and urge the examination of environmental implications before WTO accords are passed. In 1996, the WTO rejected negotiations with labor groups, referring the promotion of labor standards to the ILO instead, where compliance procedures are generally loosely enforced. In contrast, labor groups from the developed world have lobbied for the WTO to take up the labor-friendly agenda, since the WTO has the power to institute trade sanctions for labor violations. Labor groups joined with other opponents of the WTO in the 1990s in mass protests against the organization.

### Antiglobalization Critics

In the late 1990s, opponents of economic globalization formed a broad movement of workers, environmentalists, farmers, religious activists, women, and human rights advocates seeking greater economic justice. Many of these groups have found common cause in the streets of Seattle, Prague, Washington, DC, and Calgary by staging mass protests in conjunction with meetings of the international financial institutions and G-7/8 since the late 1990s. Although groups have had their own agendas, they have been united in denouncing globalization and seeking a return to governance at the local (or national) level. To many, goals of economic efficiency and being able to buy the cheapest goods need to be replaced by support for local economies through providing local employment rather than exporting jobs, and by fair and environmentally friendly conditions for workers.

While demonstrators continue to march in the streets of Europe, antiglobalization protests have moved to the marketplace—supporting local agriculture, buying fair trade products, pressuring the giant multinational Walmart to reform its purchasing, labor, and other practices—in an effort to roll back economic globalization at the local level. The question, however, is no longer "Are you for or against globalization?" Now the question is "What should the rules of globalization be?" (Rodrik 2008: xx).

Decisions about free trade, stable currencies, and macroeconomic coordination, despite efforts by some to paint them as apolitical, are quintessential political decisions, since they shape who gets what. Many of those involved in global economic governance want us to believe that they are operating on the basis of technical, apolitical principles. Yet evidence from the IMF, WTO, MNCs, international banks, and large investment firms does not bear that out. The links between ideas, politics, and economics are even more clear when we examine global governance relating to human development.

## Suggested Further Reading

Cooper, Andrew F., and Ramesh Thakur. (2013) *The Group of Twenty*. London: Routledge.

Copelovitch, Mark S. (2010) *The International Monetary Fund in the Global Economy: Banks, Bonds, and Bailouts*. New York: Cambridge University Press.

Dobson, Hugo. (2006) *The Group of 7/8*. New York: Routledge.

Drezner, Daniel W. (2014) *The System Worked: How the World Stopped Another Great Depression*. Oxford: Oxford University Press.

Hoekman, Bernard M., and Michel M. Kostecki. (2009) *The Political Economy of the World Trading System: The WTO and Beyond*. 3rd ed. Oxford: Oxford University Press.

Murphy, Craig N., and JoAnne Yates. (2008) *The International Organization for Standardization (ISO)*. New York: Routledge.

Stone, Randall. (2011) *Controlling Institutions: International Organizations and the Global Economy*. New York: Cambridge University Press.

Vreeland, James Raymond. (2015) *The International Monetary Fund (IMF): Politics of Conditional Lending*. 2nd ed. New York: Routledge.

Woodward, Richard. (2009) *The Organisation for Economic Co-operation and Development (OECD)*. New York: Routledge.

## Internet Resources:

ASEAN Free Trade Area: www.asean.org
Bank for International Settlements: www.bis.org
Basel Committee on Banking Supervision: www.bis.org/bcbs
Corporate Accountability International: www.stopcorporateabuse.org
European Union: http://europa.eu
Financial Action Task Force: www.fatf-gafi.org
Financial Stability Board: www.financialstabilityboard.org
Group of Seven: www.g7.utoronto.ca
Group of 20: www.g20.utoronto.ca
International Association of Transport Airlines: www.iata.org
International Centre for the Settlement of Investment Disputes: http://icsid.world bank.org
International Civil Aviation Organization: www.icao.org
International Maritime Organization: www.imo.org
International Monetary Fund: www.imf.org
International Organization for Standardization: www.iso.org
North American Free Trade Agreement: www.nafta-sec-alena.org
Organization for Economic Cooperation and Development: www.oecd.org
World Bank: www.worldbank.org
World Intellectual Property Organization: www.wipo.int/portal/en/index
World Trade Organization: www.wto.org

# 9

# Promoting Economic Well-Being and Human Development

## Case Study: Economic Globalization and Africa

Economic globalization has had tremendous effects—both positive and negative—around the world since the early 1990s, when it became a fact of life for most states and people. It has led to a significant decline in the percentage of people living in extreme poverty worldwide from over 50 percent in 1981 to 22 percent by 2015, although over 1.4 billion people were still living on less than $1.25 a day. The South's share of the global middle class expanded from 26 percent to 58 percent between 1990 and 2010. Virtually all states had achieved improvement on the UN Development Programme's Human Development Index in 2014 compared to 1990.

While Africa remains the least-developed continent, it too has made significant strides in economic and human development. Despite the presence of many armed conflicts, there has been strong economic growth in many parts of the continent, with twenty non-oil-producing states in Africa experiencing growth of over 4 percent annually between 1998 and 2008. The reforms initiated by the Bretton Woods institutions, including structural adjustment programs and debt reduction initiatives (the Heavily Indebted Poor Countries Initiative [HIPC] and the Multilateral Debt Relief Initiative [MDRI]), have yielded growth in some cases. Africa also weathered the storm of the 2008 financial crisis due to the boom in primary commodities and greater economic diversification. Since 2000, real income has increased by more than 30 percent. Individual lives in many countries have improved. There has been a 30 percent reduction in deaths from malaria and a 74 percent reduction in the incidence of HIV/AIDS. Life expectancy has increased by 10 percent and child mortality rates have fallen steeply, all key indicators of an expanded view of development, namely human development. Africa is unusual, however, in that population growth has not dropped along with its economic growth as has happened in Latin America and Asia. Total fertility rate—the number of children a woman can expect

425

to have—is still 4.7. At that rate, the continent's population will top 2.4 billion by 2050, raising questions about whether future economic growth, food supply, education, health care, and infrastructure will match population growth.

These advances have been possible, in part, because both foreign direct investment (FDI) and development aid to African countries have increased. Since 2000, FDI to the continent increased from $33.5 billion to $246.4 billion in 2012. The amount supplied by the EU, China, Japan, and the United States grew by nearly five times during that time period, driven primarily by China. China's FDI grew at an annual rate of 53 percent, while Japan's increased by 29 percent, the EU's by 16 percent, and the United States's by 14 percent. Trade between China and Africa grew from $10 billion to $200 billion between 1990 and 2013, an average annual increase of 19 percent. Other countries, such as Malaysia and South Korea, are likewise turning to Africa, particularly for natural resources, contributing to their own and Africa's development. Major international banks also now see a number of African countries as stable enough to be attractive investment opportunities. Under the auspices of the Millennium Development Goals, US aid too has again been flowing to Africa. In 2004 the United States established the Millennium Challenge Corporation (MCC), promising funds to deserving countries. Of the twenty-six signed MCC compacts, fourteen are with African states, amounting to $5.5 billion in aid.

Governance in Africa has improved as well, in part a reflection of the donor community's emphasis on "good governance." Although only a few African countries have achieved Western standards of democratic governance, many of the more authoritarian regimes have trended toward broadly better governance, with more efficient tax collection systems and increased emphasis on rooting out corruption. Twenty-five out of fifty-three countries in Africa have some form of democratic government.

Civil society in Africa has expanded. Perhaps most critically, the number of civil conflicts has dropped precipitously, from a high of sixteen in 1999 to around seven in the 2000s, and these conflicts have not been as deadly in terms of battlefield deaths. All of these developments have led to a proliferation of articles with headlines such as "Emerging Africa" (*The Economist* 2013) and "Africa's Economic Boom: Why the Pessimists and the Optimists Are Both Right" (Devarajan and Fengler 2013).

These changes have not happened overnight. They reflect efforts by IGOs such as the World Bank, the African Development Bank, and the UN Economic Commission for Africa, and efforts by Africans themselves. The New Partnership for Africa's Development (NEPAD) was unveiled at the G-7/8 meeting in 2001, the first African-generated self-help plan. African leaders, reflecting the views of legislators, lawyers, and other groups across the continent, agreed to five priority areas: institutional capacity building for security, economic and corporate governance, infrastructure and communication technologies, bank financial standards, and agriculture and market access. They agreed that capital mobilization must be domestic; external aid should serve as a complement to Africa's own efforts. And they agreed to police themselves and other African leaders, promoting good governance in return for investment capital in the priority areas.

Despite this optimism, Africa remains the continent most needing development. Countries with the highest concentration of people living in extreme poverty in the world are all African, including Ethiopia, Liberia, Mozambique, and Sierra Leone. While economic growth has occurred, it has not resulted in enough jobs to support the growing youth population and efficient social services to protect the vulnerable. High rural-urban inequalities have undermined the relationship between growth and poverty reduction. Although child mortality has dropped, the rate in Africa is still twice that in the developing world as a whole. The probability of an African woman dying from pregnancy or birth remains high. Africa's rural population still lacks access to clean water and basic sanitation, affecting health and individual well being. Changes in climate are projected to further diminish Africa's water resources and alter agricultural production. In at least ten African countries, more than 75 percent of government expenditures are still funded by aid, which is indicative of the continent's dependency on external actors.

Africa's mixed experience illustrates that economic growth does not necessarily lead to human development for either all states or all individuals. Thus, the debate over economic globalization itself and over the liberal economic system as an engine for that globalization continues. So what is development? How has this idea evolved over time? And what is the best strategy to achieve its objectives?

## Evolution of the Idea of Development

Historically, the literature on development has been dominated by economists who "have focused overwhelmingly on the process of economic development rather than the broader processes of economic, social, cultural, and political advance" (Jolly et al. 2004: 9). Economic growth and measures of rising living standards, then, have long been the primary measures. Over time, however, thinking has evolved to include questions of human rights, sustainability, and gender, with much of that debate occurring within the UN. Ongoing debates on other issues such as how best to achieve development, and the role of the state, the relationship between trade and development, the effectiveness of various tools such as foreign aid and technology transfer have occurred in multiple forums, posing major challenges to the liberal economic model.

## Liberal Economic Theory and Development

Liberal economic theory, as described in Chapter 8, emphasizes the role of the market in stimulating both individual and collective economic growth, namely economic growth of the state. Government institutions perform critical functions of providing order and stability and in facilitating the free flow of trade. If markets are permitted to allocate resources efficiently, then increasing interdependence among economies will lead to greater economic development for all states.

For economic liberals, MNCs represent the most efficient mechanism for economic development and improved well-being. As described in Chapter 8, they are the transmission belts for growth, which is a prerequisite for development. If investment from MNCs or domestic savings is insufficient, grants and loans from other states and international organizations may be needed to jump-start the economic development process, which will eventually filter down to all the population.

The emphasis in the liberal economic view of development has historically been on state development, measured by growth of gross national product (GNP) or gross domestic product (GDP) per capita. This simplistic indicator shows strong differentiation between the developed North, where the richest countries enjoy an average GNP per capita of $40,307, and the developing South, where the poorest states average a GNP per capita of $2,830 (2013 figures) and where 1.4 billion people live on less than $1.25 a day. Proponents of economic liberalism point out that average per capita income in developing countries has doubled over a fifty-year period, with the GNPs of some economies growing more than fivefold. That trend will continue, they contend, and economic growth will lead to development.

## Challenge to Economic Liberalism: The Dependency School and the New International Economic Order

Beginning in the early 1950s, economists in the UN's Economic Commission for Latin America (ECLA) began to challenge the liberal economic model. They were proponents of the dependency school, discussed in Chapter 2, which argued that the developing world was permanently mired in poverty and unable to grow. Since capitalist economic systems are inherently expansionary, they require new resources from the developing world to generate growth. Yet the prices of primary commodity exports from the developing world do not keep pace with the prices of imported manufacturing goods. So if the developing countries are to improve their position economically, fundamental change in the international system is necessary. Otherwise, inequality between the developed North and the developing South will remain relatively permanent, irrespective of the domestic policies pursued or external assistance received.

ECLA's critique and its prescription for extricating countries from dependency became the basis for the establishment of the UN Conference on Trade and Development (UNCTAD) in the 1960s and for the proposed New International Economic Order (NIEO) in the 1970s. When UNCTAD was founded in 1964, many newly independent states from Africa, Asia, and Latin America formed the Group of 77. In their view, the inherently unequal international liberal trading system could not be made more equal without major changes. Because of the limited expertise of many governments, however, UNCTAD's secretariat played a key role in shaping the work of the G-77 in challenging predominant liberal thinking about economic development. In 1974, using its numerical voting majority in the UN General Assembly, the G-77 secured adoption of the Declaration on the Establishment of a New International Economic Order and the Charter of Economic Rights and Duties of States, marking the peak of confrontation between North and South, a divide that would affect every UN body for several years, as discussed in Chapter 4.

The G-77 sought changes in five major areas of international economic relations: commodity pricing, regulation of MNCs, improved means of technology transfer, increased foreign aid, and improved trading provisions. Although they won some concessions in trade relations, including recognition of the principle of preferential treatment for developing country exports, on most issues the North refused to negotiate.

Two issues shaped by the G-77 persist four decades later—debt relief and restructuring of the international financial institutions. The G-77 has sought changes in the weighted voting structures of the World Bank and IMF, and in the developed-country bias within the GATT/WTO. They have sought to alter basic power relationships that would lead to different economic policies. Realignment of voting shares has been negotiated, with China, Mexico, South Korea, and Turkeygaining more power, as discussed in Chapter 8, although in the eyes of most G-77 members fundamental power has not shifted.

Although the G-77 gradually splintered following the general acceptance (some say triumph) of economic liberalism in the 1980s and the diverging interests of many members, the leadership of the G-77 within the UN system provided the first fundamental and sustained challenge to the dominant liberal economic ideology. The group still enjoys legitimacy among many developing countries and has resisted the efforts of developed countries to terminate UNCTAD.

## Modifying Economic Liberalism

While the proposed NIEO proved too radical a critique to gain acceptance, there was recognition by the late 1970s that development defined as economic growth was too narrowly construed, leading to unanticipated detrimental effects, including environmental degradation and unsustainable growth. The book *The Limits to Growth* (Meadows et al. 1972) modeled exponential economic and population growth rates coupled with finite resource supplies, generating a vibrant public debate about the possibility of unsustainable and limited growth. With the 1982 adoption of the World Charter for Nature, the UN General Assembly began to articulate a newer approach to development, namely sustainable development. In 1983 the General Assembly established the World Commission on Environment and Development (WCED), headed by Prime Minister Gro Harlem Brundtland of Norway and composed of eminent persons. In the commission's 1987 report (WCED 1987), titled *Our Common Future,* the Brundtland Commission called for the adoption of the concept of sustainable development, defined as development that meets the needs of the present, alleviating poverty, supporting marginalized populations, and promoting environmentally sound projects, without compromising the ability of future generations to do the same. That approach subsequently was adopted by a number of IGOs, NGOs, and national development agencies in Canada, Sweden, and the United States. It was the underlying theme for the 1992 UN Conference on the Environment and Development, discussed in Chapter 11, and has become a constant theme in development discourse.

Still another modification occurred in the 1990s with the UN Development Programme's introduction of the concept of human development. The annual *Human Development Reports* put "people at the centre of development," applying the concept to provide "an integrated intellectual framework for catalyzing a new system-wide approach to economic and social development." The reports introduced a more sensitive measure of human development with the Human Development Index (HDI), which underscores that development is about improving the quality of life for human beings, not just promoting economic growth. The index is based on a composite of indicators, including health (infant mortality, life expectancy), education (years of schooling), and GNP per capita (on a logarithmic scale). Even more nuanced measures have been introduced, with the Multidimensional Poverty Index (MPI) reports in 2014 showing that about 1.6 billion people in the 104 countries covered live in multidimensional poverty; that is, they suffer from acute deprivation in health, education, and living standards. According to this view, development should be measured by how well people are doing on a variety of measures as well as on whether that development is sustainable.

Human development ideas continue to be expanded, debated, and refined. Among the most influential contemporary thinkers is Amartya Sen, one of the authors of the HDI and 1998 recipient of the Nobel Prize in Economics. Sen (1999) sees development as freedom. Governments need to remove barriers so that their citizens have the capability and hence the freedom to choose the course of their lives for themselves. Subsequent *Human Development Reports,* each of which has a different theme and lead authors, have refined and expanded these ideas, strengthening the notion of capabilities.

## Alternative Strategies to Achieve Development

Not only has development been an evolving concept, but how to achieve development continues to be widely debated, particularly the role of the state. To those in the liberal economic tradition, the role of the state is to provide a level playing field, including law and order, so that the private sector and individuals can unleash their productive energies.

Since the East Asian "tigers" such as South Korea, Singapore, and Taiwan successfully used a statist approach to their rapid development during the 1980s and early 1990s, there has been a revival of thinking embedded in statist mercantilism, namely that the state should actively support key industries through subsidies to enhance their international competitiveness and that internationally strong industries will bring economic wealth to the state. Indeed, mercantilism emphasizes the subordination of all economic activities to the goal of statebuilding.

More recently, a variation on this thinking has been labeled the Beijing Consensus, pointing to China's rapid, state-driven growth as a model. While there is no precise definition, the Beijing Consensus implies experimenting with policies that may be compatible with a state's political structure and cultural experience. In this perspective, state-owned or state-managed corporations may be used to invest capital in their own markets and abroad. At the same time, private companies are permitted to function. This approach has been viewed more favorably since the global economic crisis and China's success in weathering that crisis.

Economists and political scientists have also linked success to particular types of economic and political institutions. Daron Acemoglu and James Robinson (2012) argue, for example, that successful development demands strong economic and political institutions. States can escape from poverty when there are institutions protecting private property and competition as well as ensuring the rule of law to prevent corruption and extractive rents. In short, the current thinking is that institutions play a more critical role in successful development than the liberal economic model suggests.

A second debate is over the relationship between trade and development. There is no doubt that economic globalization has occurred in large part because of the expansion of trade, as noted in Chapter 8. But does development necessarily follow from economic growth? The WTO's Doha Round was named the "development round," but as one commentator cynically noted, "affixing the label 'development' . . . may have warmed a few hearts, but it has not filled any bellies" (Christy 2008: 24). That assessment reflects the position that states may develop gradually behind trade barriers before trade liberalization is instituted. Eliminating trade barriers, as liberal economists propose, may increase trade, but it does not necessarily lead to development (Rodrik 2007).

There are also debates about specific development tools such as private investment and foreign aid and their relative effectiveness. And, how effective are other tools such as technology transfer and technical assistance? Most liberal economists view market-driven private investment as the most effective, while still others acknowledge that foreign aid and technical assistance may be necessary to jump-start the process. Dependency theorists are skeptical of both private investment and foreign aid, as both bind dependent states to wealthy states. Proponents of human development are more agnostic about what tools will work. What is critical is to utilize all available tools to advance well-being.

Having explored the evolution of these ideas about development, sustainable development, and human development, we turn to examine how various actors, global and regional, formal and informal, public and private, as well as new forms of governance, have emerged to meet the challenges of human development.

## Actors in Promoting Development

The actors involved in promoting human development have become increasingly diverse. States are clearly important, because traditionally they have been responsible for their own growth and development as sovereign entities. Since the end of World War II, as described in Chapters 3 and 4, the UN, World Bank, and regional development banks have taken on new responsibilities, as have many other UN specialized agencies. Many developed countries became contributors to development through bilateral assistance programs or official development assistance during the Cold War, and the continuation of these programs is a political and moral imperative. MNCs, too, have filled a critical role. And with the emergence of the human development agenda, many NGOs have taken on new responsibilities to meet the needs of individuals and often marginalized populations. Other nonstate actors, including philanthropic organizations and foundations, diasporas, and even individual celebrities such as Bono, are now part of the panoply of development actors.

As noted in Chapter 4, the United Nations Charter says very little about how the institution should fulfill its mandate to promote economic and social well-being. The General Assembly provides overall direction; ECOSOC is tasked with coordination and the specialized agencies with operational activities. The World Bank has become the focal point for financing major development initiatives, with the IMF becoming important more recently as debt relief became an issue beginning in the 1980s. For linking trade and development, UNCTAD has served as the forum for developing countries, as GATT was viewed as serving developed countries' interests. And as human development has gained currency, other UN specialized agencies such as the WHO and FAO, in the areas of health and agriculture respectively, have gained prominence.

## The Bretton Woods Institutions

*The World Bank and development financing.* During the 1950s the World Bank shifted its focus from postwar reconstruction in Europe to development in Latin America, Asia, and later Africa, lending funds with interest to states proposing major economic development projects. The Bank generates these funds from member-state contributions and from borrowing in international financial markets. The loans are designed to complement private capital by funding projects that private banks would not support, such as infrastructure (dams, bridges, highways), social services (education, health care), and government restructuring. Unlike private banks, the World Bank attaches conditions to its loans in the form of policy changes it would like to see states make to promote economic development and alleviate poverty.

To aid the Bank in meeting the needs of developing countries, the International Finance Corporation (IFC) was created in 1956, the first of four subsidiary organizations of the World Bank Group. The IFC provides loans to promote the growth of private enterprises in over 100 developing countries, providing typically no more than 25 percent of the total estimated costs. Working with over 750 financial institutions, its 184 members provide about a third of the financing provided by international institutions to the private sector. Another Bank family member, the Multilateral Investment Guarantee Agency (MIGA), established in 1988, was meant to further augment private capital's contribution to less developed countries by insuring investments against losses. Such losses may include expropriation, governmental currency restrictions, and losses stemming from civil war or ethnic conflict. In 1960, the establishment of the International Development Association (IDA) provided no-interest "soft" (concessional) loans to the poorest countries, with repayment schedules of fifty years. Today, about eighty countries are eligible for this concessional lending based upon GNP per capita below an established threshold. IDA funds have to be continually replenished or added to by major donor countries.

Currently, the World Bank's 188 members together with its affiliates such as the IDA provide over $30 billion annually to 100 countries for more than 300 projects. Until the 1990s, loans were granted exclusively to governments and often were combined with loans from the principal bilateral donors (United States, Japan, Germany, United Kingdom) and other IGOs. This restriction now has been relaxed and private groups and NGOs can also be loan recipients.

Since the 1950s, there have been major shifts in development strategies that are reflected in money allocated to different sectors such as agriculture, transportation, or education. At times the World Bank, the IMF, and the UN itself have been at the forefront of articulating new strategies, and at other times they have responded to changes initiated by both the bilateral donor community and NGOs.

During the 1950s and 1960s, the World Bank emphasized large infra-structure projects (dams, electric facilities, telecommunications). In the 1970s, under the leadership of President Robert McNamara, the Bank shifted to a "basic needs" orientation, funding projects in health, education, and housing geared to improve the economic needs of the masses. During the 1980s, the mantra became private sector involvement, followed by sustainable economic development. In the 1990s, the focus shifted to "good governance."

Of these various changes, two trends have had the most profound impact. First is the reorientation toward support of the private sector in the 1980s. While the World Bank's founding Articles of Agreement supported private investment, the Bank was prohibited from making loans without government guarantees until the IFC was established. The Bank now strongly supports private sector involvement and privatization of government-owned industries in the expectation that growth will trickle down and everyone will eventually benefit.

Second are the changes consistent with the sustainable development goals. As discussed later, the Bank became more open to involving NGOs in planning and executing projects in the 1990s in order to change individual lives. And the Bank began to recognize that sustainable development, whether through public or private funds, requires good governance. But in the early 1990s, the term "governance" was left purposefully vague or defined very narrowly because of fear that the Bank's neutrality and apolitical mandate would be jeopardized. Not until 1995, under the leadership of President James Wolfensohn, was governmental corruption mentioned as an inhibitor of development. When the staff framed the issue in economic terms—that corruption had negative effects on development—they were able to establish their case. But developing good governance and rooting out systemic corruption require a long-term commitment that the Bank has had difficulty sustaining, since it has a history of making disbursements even when there is evidence of corruption in its own projects (Weaver 2008: 108–113). Thus the World Bank has increasingly addressed political issues, promoting sound governmental management and anticorruption measures.

*The International Monetary Fund and debt relief.* Although the IMF was not designed to be an aid agency, its role in development has grown, particularly since the 1980s, insofar as stable currency values and currency convertibility are necessary for trade and development. While some states' balance-of-payments shortfalls are temporary and can be accommodated through standby arrangements, other states experience long-term structural economic problems. And with heavy indebtedness, states would never be able to repay loans, much less amass capital for development. Thus the IMF, together with the World Bank and the G-7/8, became involved in the persistent issue of debt relief.

In 1980 the debt of all developing countries was $567 billion; by 2000 it had reached $2.2 trillion. In 1996 the IMF and World Bank undertook the Heavily Indebted Poor Countries Initiative. Bringing together various creditors, including the multilateral development banks, the Paris Club (official creditors) proposed to provide the most indebted with a means to achieving sustainable levels of debt. Never before had countries' debt been canceled or substantially rescheduled. A second initiative, the Multilateral Debt Relief Initiative, was undertaken in 2005. For the poorest countries that had already reached completion points under the HIPC, their external debt would be canceled in full. By the end of 2013, the HIPC and MDRI were completed for thirty-five countries at a cost of $114 billion. Countries receiving such relief had to submit plans to channel debt savings into poverty reduction programs. These programs have substantially alleviated debt burdens in recipient countries and enabled them to increase their poverty-reducing expenditures by 3.5 percent of GDP.

Reducing debt was only part of the IMF approach, however. It had become increasingly clear that states that suffered from chronic balance-of-payments difficulties and heavy debt would be unable to extricate themselves from these obligations, much less develop. The short-term remedies were not effective. For development assistance to be used effectively, major structural changes needed to be made.

*The Bank and Fund collaboration in structural adjustment.* In the 1980s the IMF helped forge the Washington Consensus, discussed in Chapter 8. States suffering from balance-of-payments problems and heavy debt, mainly in the developing world, were required to institute economic policy reforms in return for financial and developmental assistance (see Figure 8.3). These structural adjustment programs (SAPs) were carried out through cross-conditionality between the Fund, the Bank, and many bilateral donors.

Academic studies are divided over the effects of the structural adjustment programs. There is clear evidence that SAPs were successful in improving countries' balance of payments and in reducing inflationary pressures. Some of the Fund's studies suggest that SAPs had a positive effect on countries' economic growth (IMF 2007; Harrigan and el-Said 2010), but critics challenge those claims. For example, William Easterly (2006: 67–68, 218) found that African countries under structural adjustment actually experienced negative or zero growth, leading to a higher probability of state collapse. Many scholarly articles and NGOs hold SAPs responsible for disproportionately hurting the poor by cutting public expenditures, reducing subsidies on food, devaluing the currency (Nooruddin and Simmons 2006), and adversely affecting the environment.

Unquestionably, SAPs and particularly cross-conditionality led to some of the most devastating critiques of the Bank and Fund. They also inspired mass public demonstrations at the annual meetings of the Bank and Fund, as noted in Chapter 8, and critics blamed the institutions for everything from food and urban riots to government failures. They were also blamed for cuts in public health expenditures that contributed to worsening the 2014 Ebola outbreak in West Africa. Some, but not all, of these critiques have been consistent with neo-Marxist dependency theory, which calls for fundamental change.

As pressures intensified for change in the 1990s and academic studies as well as studies within the IMF and Bank showed questionable outcomes, the general consensus on SAPs unraveled. In 2006 the World Bank established the Commission on Growth and Development to reassess the effectiveness of the Washington Consensus and related policies. Its report, issued during the 2008 global financial crisis, made quite clear that a broad intellectual shift away from universalistic solutions to development is imperative (World Bank 2008). Instead, the report called for far more policy experimentation and targeted initiatives aimed at solving local problems, based on local initiatives. Solutions are to be found in greater investment in infrastructure, job creation, social protections, and equity (Birdsall and Fukuyama 2011). Governments should play a key role in setting priorities that are country- and context-specific.

The Commission on Growth and Development's report solidified changes that had been brewing. Beginning in 2009, the IMF discontinued structural performance criteria for loans to low-income countries. This represented a substantial overhaul of the IMF lending framework. The amount of the loans can be greater, and they are to be tailored according to the respective state's needs. Monitoring is done more quietly, to reduce the stigma attached to conditionality. Also, the IMF has urged lending to programs that encourage social safety nets for the most vulnerable within the population. It has even suggested that capital flows may need regulation and that states might take a proactive role in coordinating economic development. In these new emphases, cross-conditionality has been severed and the Bank and the Fund are working more closely with civil society organizations ("CSOs" in the Bank's lexicon) and other donors.

*Comparing Bank and Fund governance.* There are many similarities in the governance of these two institutions (on decisionmaking in the IMF, see Figure 8.2). By convention, both are led by individuals from the developed world—an American for the Bank presidency and a European for the position of IMF managing director. In both, a limited-member executive board decides everyday policies. Both executive boards operate under weighted voting systems that guarantee the voting power of the major donors commensurate with their contributions. Economists compose the majority of staff in both organizations, most of whom have been trained in Western universities in the liberal economic tradition.

Still, there are major differences. The Bank has about 9,000 professional staff and the Fund 2,600. The Bank's bureaucracy has been studied in depth due to its more open policies. It has a strong organizational culture and an ideology that is traditionally characterized as "an apolitical, technocratic, and economic rationality" (Weaver 2007: 504). Yet that culture has been described by the Bank's own internal evaluators in more negative terms such as the "disbursement imperative" and the "Washington-centric approval culture" (cited in Weaver 2007: 506). A 2013 survey by the Bank of its own employees revealed a "culture of fear," with a pervasive "fear of risk" and a "terrible" environment for collaboration (Lowrey 2013).

*The need for Bank and Fund reform.* Because the United States, Canada, European countries, and Japan still command more than 60 percent of the votes in the weighted voting systems of the IMF and the World Bank (magnified by special majorities [70–80 percent] of votes on certain issues), critics assert that they are a tool of the major developed countries. Although both were originally designed to be economic institutions, politics does intervene in the process of who gets financing and when. During the Cold War, funds were denied to leftist regimes in Vietnam, Cuba, Afghanistan, Nicaragua, Grenada, Chile, and Laos, among others. In all cases, the United States opposed funding because it disapproved of the regime in power. Domination by the few opens both institutions to criticism from developing countries that have less formal power within them.

Both institutions now face governance crises marked by outdated processes for selecting institutional heads. As discussed in Chapter 8, there is also a need to reform voting rights, with the BRICS growing in economic power but not yet given commensurate voting power, and the United States retaining power despite its declining relative economic status. Leadership in both institutions has been weakened by the scandals that led to the resignations of Bank president Paul Wolfowitz in 2007 and IMF managing director Dominique Strauss-Kahn in 2009. Critics consider both to have dysfunctional cultures.

Against this backdrop, World Bank president Jim Yong Kim announced a sweeping reorganization of the Bank in 2013 to address its ineffectiveness. Along with a $400 million budget cut, the Bank's reorganization is designed to reduce staff, streamline rules, and increase collaboration by creating fourteen "global practice" areas, such as agriculture, education, poverty, water, energy, and extractives, and by moving social development staff into those specific areas. This change, billed as the "biggest reorganization of the Bank in about two decades," has been criticized by those worried about the downgrading of the human development focus (Lowery 2013). Yet reorganization of such a large bureaucracy takes time to implement and it is unclear how the changes will impact programs. Just as the Bank and Fund have undergone changes in how they have addressed development, so too has the UN system.

## The United Nations and Development

The UN's approach to economic development has differed in some key ways from that of the Bretton Woods institutions, in part because, in relative terms, its budgetary allocations remain modest compared to those of either the World Bank institutions or the bilateral donors. But since the late 1990s there has been a considerable convergence of views. Here we discuss five major contributions of the UN to development.

*Ideas and goal-setting, from the Development Decades to the Millennium Development Goals and Sustainable Development Goals.* The UN has been a source of innovative ideas about development, namely that development does not happen automatically, that technical skills are necessary and cannot always be found domestically, that economic growth does not necessarily result in equity among different socioeconomic groups, and that development must be reoriented to human and sustainable development. Indeed, in the evolution of ideas from economic growth to sustainable development, charted earlier, it was the UN that played a key role in elucidating sustainable development and human development.

Along with the formulation of key ideas, the UN has set goals for the development community, beginning with the 1961 UN General Assembly's designation of the 1960s as the "United Nations Development Decade" to mobilize support for the steps both developed and developing nations needed to take to accelerate progress. In three subsequent Development Decades, various targets were announced, such as targets for annual aid to developing states and goals for increasing annual growth rates, domestic savings, and agricultural production. In addition, the UN set goals in a number of issue areas related to human development, including eradication of smallpox, expansion of education, reductions in child mortality, and increases in life expectancy, which became the operational responsibility of specialized agencies such as UNESCO, UNICEF, and the WHO. Many of these goals coalesced into the Millennium Development Goals in 2000.

The Millennium Declaration, adopted at the UN-sponsored Millennium Summit in 2000, was an outgrowth of the global conferences in the 1990s, discussed in Chapter 4, as well as fifty years of UN development practice that highlighted the interrelated nature of many development issues. The Millennium Development Goals (MDGs) incorporated a set of eight goals that represented a "compact among nations" to reduce poverty and promote sustainable human development in response to globalization. The mutually reinforcing and intertwined MDGs included halving world poverty and hunger, reducing infant mortality by two-thirds, and achieving universal primary education. The eighth goal calls for partnerships among various actors as a means to achieving the other seven goals. The goals were disaggregated into twenty-one specific targets and sixty performance indicators, with an elaborate implementation plan involving ten global task forces, MDG report cards for each developing country, regular monitoring, and a public information campaign to keep pressure on governments and international agencies.

The MDGs and the agenda they represented involved commitment not only from across the UN system, including the Bretton Woods institutions, but also from bilateral donors and NGOs. In the words of John Ruggie (2003: 305), setting those goals was "unprecedented for the UN and its agencies, let alone also the Bretton Woods institutions, to align their operational activities behind a unifying substantive framework."

But have the goals of the MDGs been achieved? Data are now available to evaluate progress. Figure 9.1 outlines some of the results achieved as of 2014. Three key goals have been met: both the number of individuals in extreme poverty and the poverty rates have fallen in every developing region including sub-Saharan Africa. The percentage of the population having completed primary education increased by 98 percent and infant mortality has been halved since 1990. Yet challenges remain. Much of the improvement is attributed, in fact, to major gains in China and India, while sub-Saharan Africa still lags on virtually every indicator. In 2015, 1.4 billion people still live on less than $1.25 a day and 600 million still lack access to clean water. But can the improvements in some categories be attributed to the MDGs? John McArthur (2014: 1) points to the methodological problem that many of the improvements predated the MDGs, noting that "progress toward the Goals is not the same as progress because of the Goals."

Even as work toward the MDGs continued, diplomats and experts began to hammer out the goals for the next fifteen years. The Sustainable Development Goals (SDGs) are designed to address some of the weaknesses of the MDGs, including not enough focus on the poorest of the poor and on jobs, insufficient attention to conflict and good governance, and the lack of targets on sustainability. The process for developing the new goals,

**Figure 9.1 The Millennium Development Goals:**
**Results Achieved as of 2014**

Goal 1: Eradicate extreme poverty and hunger
Halve proportion of people living on less than $1.25 a day and proportion
who suffer chronic hunger.
Results: 22 percent of people in developing countries live on less than $1.25
a day, down from 50 percent in 1990. Proportion of undernourished
decreased from 24 percent to 15 percent, but progress slowed. Virtually
all gains in China and Southeast Asia, not Africa.

Goal 2: Achieve universal primary education
Ensure that all children complete full course of primary education.
Results: 90 percent of children attending primary school, but progress
stagnated since 2012. Out-of-school children are in conflict zones.

Goal 3: Promote gender equality and empower women
Eliminate gender disparity in primary, secondary, and tertiary education.
Results: All regions closed, or near to closing, gender gap in primary
education. Gender disparity persists in higher levels of education and in
labor market.

Goal 4: Reduce child mortality
Reduce by two-thirds the mortality rate of children younger than five years.
Results: Child mortality decreased 50 percent. Four out of five child deaths
are in Africa.

Goal 5: Improve maternal health
Reduce by three-quarters the maternal mortality rate.
Results: Maternal mortality decreased 48 percent to 210 deaths per 100,000
live births. In Africa, number of maternal deaths decreased from 990 to
510 deaths per 100,000 live births.

Goal 6: Combat HIV/AIDS, malaria, and other diseases
Halt and reverse the spread of HIV/AIDS. Slow spread of malaria and other
diseases.
Results: 9.5 million people in developing countries have access to
antiretrovirals. 3.3 million deaths from malaria averted. 22 million lives
saved in fight against tuberculosis.

Goal 7: Ensure environmental sustainability
Reverse the loss of environmental resources. Halve the proportion of people
without sustainable access to safe drinking water and basic sanitation.
Results: 13 million hectares of forest lost. 50 percent increase in $CO_2$
emissions. 89 percent of population have access to improved source of
drinking water. 2 billion people have improved access to sanitation.

Goal 8: Develop a global partnership for development
Address special needs of least-developed countries, including more
generous development assistance.
Results: In 2013, global official development assistance was $134.8 billion,
highest ever recorded, but some shift away from the poorest countries.
Debt burden for developing countries was stable, at 3 percent of
revenue.

*Source:* UN 2014a.

however, is very different from that for the MDGs. While the latter were largely the work of then UN Secretary-General Kofi Annan, the SDG process was set in motion by the Rio Plus 20 conference in 2012, with the creation of an open working group. There is also a high-level panel of eminent persons overseeing the post-2015 development agenda, composed of stakeholders from civil society, the scientific community, and UN system, plus a UN-system task team composed of representatives from sixty UN agencies and other international organizations. The process includes both national consultations and a global conversation via MyWorld that invites users to select six priorities from a list of sixteen themes ranging from "honest and responsive government" to "action taken on climate change." "The tent is very large, and everyone is in it," one diplomat admits. Yet "priorities differ, agendas differ. The willingness to take on commitments differs" (quoted in Porter 2014: B2). As of late 2014, the process had produced seventeen goals and 269 tarets compared with eight MDGs, and there was still no convergence on measures to be used for assessing progress.

*Institutionalization of development in the UN.* The UN has developed a number of key institutions to facilitate its work, differentiating itself from the World Bank by making technical assistance—the provision of training programs and expert advice—its primary contribution to promoting development. The UN awards fellowships for advanced training, supplies equipment for training purposes, and provides experts for many projects jointly funded by other donors.

In 1965, the General Assembly established the UNDP as the lead organization in the provision of technical assistance. UNDP resident representatives are expected to assess local needs and priorities, coordinate programs, function as country representatives for some of the specialized agencies, and serve as the focal point between the UN and the recipient governments. Although the significance of resident representatives has grown, the resources at their disposal are dwarfed by those of the World Bank and major bilateral aid donors. While limited in their power to coordinate country-based activities, UNDP representatives have reached out to civil society organizations, regional institutions, and other stakeholders, leading often to the partnerships described later.

The UNDP has also played an important role in institutionalizing core development ideas, among them the annual *Human Development Reports.* These draw attention to core ideas reflecting UN system-wide priorities: "Making New Technologies Work for Human Development" (2001), "Human Mobility and Development" (2009), and "Sustaining Human Progress: Reducing Vulnerabilities and Building Resilience" (2014). And in addition to the global reports, there are now national and regional reports.

Beyond the emphasis on technical assistance, the five regional commissions under ECOSOC are designed to stimulate regional approaches to development. All have produced high-quality economic surveys of their respective regions as well as country plans used by national governments. ECLA served a vital role in opposing liberal economic thinking as described earlier; some of the commissions, most notably the Economic Commission for Western Asia, which encompasses the Middle Eastern countries, and the Economic Commission for Africa, have been hampered by disputes among members and lack of resources and expertise.

*The UN and women's roles in development.* The UN has played a special role with respect to promoting the roles of women in development, a process that took decades (Jain 2005). Eleanor Roosevelt and her Latin American colleagues failed to get gender equality included in the 1948 Universal Declaration of Human Rights. The UN Commission on the Status of Women gave priority to the political status of women in its earliest work. During the 1960s and 1970s, increased attention was paid to women's economic and social rights. Beginning with the sponsorship of International Women's Year in 1975 and followed by four UN women's conferences in 1975, 1980, 1985, and 1995, the UN made a contribution to reshaping the development agenda with women in mind.

The liberal economic tradition had assumed that all individuals, including women, would participate in and benefit equally from the economic development process. Yet the data charting women's economic position did not exist. The UN, with strong support from key donor states in northern Europe, began in the 1980s to collect data on women, resulting in the publication in 1990 of *The World's Women*—the first ever compilation of data on women and analysis of their situation relative to men across a range of fields. The UN also developed programs to expand women's productive roles in agriculture, small business, and industry, and to encourage microcredit for poor women. Activists put minimum standards of social security, maternity protection, and nondiscrimination in the workplace on the UN's agenda. Special UN programs have trained and mobilized women in the development process and provided financial assistance to projects run by women. Thus, the UN's women-in-development approach allocates funds for projects aimed at women and supports a greater role for women in development planning. Over time, these efforts have been mainstreamed throughout the UN system and, as a result, gender will be an integral part of the SDGs.

In 2010, in an effort to improve the effectiveness of women's programs, UN Women (officially the United Nations Entity for Gender Equality and the Empowerment of Women) was created, a merger of various parts of the UN. It brings together the human rights dimension (gender equality as a basic human right), the political (underrepresentation in decisionmaking), and the economic (empowering women in the economy), and is designed to help UN bodies formulate policy and standards, advise states with technical and financial support, and monitor the progress of each.

In 2014, both the MDG results (see Figure 9.1) and UN Women reports showed that girls have made significant progress in primary and lower secondary education, with regional variations; gender equality has been reached in primary education; and there has been progress in reducing child mortality, although girls' survival continues to be threatened in southern Asia. Persisting, however, are large gender gaps in employment. Simply having these data available is itself an important contribution of the UN.

*The UN and data-gathering.* The UN system has played an essential role in gathering and disseminating data to aid development planning. This includes setting international standards for gathering statistics, standardizing social statistics, and developing innovative indicators (Ward 2004). The HDI and the MPI are but two examples, now widely used by the development community. There are several other valuable indices, including the Gender Empowerment Index, the Gender Inequality Index, which is directly related to the UN's work on women, and the UN World Income Inequality Index, which is particularly useful with the IMF's new emphasis on income inequality.

As innovative as these indices are, they are only as useful as the original data on which they are based. Morten Jerven (2013) has begun a long-overdue discussion of the quality of the data that the UN and other IGOs gather and disseminate. Not only are there problems with the construction of the indices, but there are also inaccuracies and inconsistencies in the data provided, particularly by African countries, which tend to have underfunded statistical bureaus and lack technical expertise. Good human development programs depend on accurate data for goal-setting and assessment.

## The UN Functional Agencies and Development

The various UN specialized, functional agencies introduced in Chapter 3 were designed to address specific issues. Virtually all of them have adopted some kind of development agenda, even if it was not part of their original mandate. Technical agencies such as the ICAO, ITU, and WMO have created capacity-building components for programs to improve the capability of developing countries in their respective areas of expertise. UNIDO, for example, has particular responsibility for fostering industrialization, while UNESCO supports educational, scientific, and cultural programs, most of which target developing countries. Two of the specialized agencies introduced in Chapter 3, the WHO and the FAO, along with the related organizations in the food regime complex, have particularly important missions in human development. And because development issues have dominated the UN's economic and social agenda since the 1960s, tying health and food to development became the modus operandi.

*Health and the WHO.* Human well-being is directly tied to health. Both communicable and noncommunicable diseases decrease quality of life and often life expectancy. Inadequate health facilities and lack of trained medical personnel result in higher infant mortality and more maternal deaths—all directly and adversely affecting human development. The MDGs specifically targeted HIV/AIDS, malaria, and other diseases, recognizing how adversely they can affect development.

By the late 1970s, the World Health Organization had expanded its agenda from stopping the spread of communicable diseases to a more holistic view of health. In the 1978 Declaration of Alma Ata, the World Health Assembly declared the "Health for All" agenda. That emphasis included helping states improve their health infrastructure, supporting regional and local primary health clinics, and supplying necessary drugs. In the same year, the World Health Assembly mandated the development of a code of marketing practices under the Action Program on Essential Drugs. Countries were encouraged to develop national drug lists citing pharmaceuticals deemed essential to health needs, excluding dangerous pharmaceuticals or products that might represent a misallocation of health budgets. Such initiatives to improve accessibility to drugs were designed to improve the health of individuals. And with WHO support of rural health clinics and pharmacies, the health status of a particularly vulnerable population would improve.

Internationally supported efforts to eradicate particular diseases affecting less developed countries have long been integral to promoting health for all. The WHO's smallpox eradication program was widely acclaimed as a major success. And with the active support of Rotary International and the Bill and Melinda Gates Foundation, the goal of polio eradication is closer to realization, although outbreaks continue to occur, including in Nigeria, Pakistan, and Syria. The WHO's targeting of specific diseases has been criticized by some public health officials on the grounds that funds could better be used in improving primary health infrastructure. Clearly, both types of programs are critical for human development. What is optimum is integrating health prevention measures into local health clinics and programs.

The 2014 Ebola outbreak in West Africa severely challenged the WHO and the global community and demonstrated how intimately linked health (or disease) and development are. The WHO itself was hampered by budget and staff cuts as well as incompetent staff at the regional level and lack of reliable information to alert the world community. Indeed, the WHO did not issue its Public Health Emergency of International Concern until over four months after the outbreak! With broken local health systems unable to contain the outbreak, Doctors Without Borders found itself the primary international medical group organizing assistance on the ground. They benefited from having well-organized stockpiles of protective gear and well-trained personnel available immediately. In addition to the human costs, the economic costs are substantial. The World Bank estimated that the regional economic drain might be as high as $3.8 billion by the end of 2015, with particularly severe effects on the economies of Liberia, Sierra Leone, and Guinea—all of which are still recovering from civil wars in the 1990s and had enjoyed strong growth in recent years. Liberia's economy is likely to decline by at least 12 percent and the effects are apt to continue after the epidemic is contained.

Assessments of lessons learned during the 2014 Ebola outbreak led the WHO Executive Board in January 2015 to call for long overdue institutional reforms to bolster the agency's rapid response capacity. These include creating a reserve of public health workers to be supported by a $100 million contingency fund, which WHO could tap in a public health emergency. Because of significant budget cuts since 2012 that particularly affected outbreak- and crisis-response programs, the agency has become increasingly reliant on voluntary contributions that are often earmarked for specific projects. WHO's failures, however, have also been attributed to its decentralized structure of seven regional offices, which underscores the need for major reforms to enable the organization to better respond to future global health emergencies.

Aiding states on health-related issues is not the exclusive preserve of the WHO. Other IGOs and NGOs have become increasingly involved. UNICEF, for example, has played a major role in immunization programs against polio and other childhood diseases. In the 1980s, the World Bank emerged as the largest external financier of health programs in developing countries and, coincidentally, its president at the time of the Ebola outbreak in 2014 was a medical doctor, Jim Yong Kim, who drove the Bank to act on Ebola "with uncharacteristic speed" (Tavernise 2014). Since 2000, however, international funding has increasingly been funneled through major research institutes and foundations such as the Gates Foundation. NGOs are involved not only in providing emergency medical assistance, as Doctors Without Borders has done with the Ebola outbreak in West Africa, but also in training indigenous health professionals to help states develop the necessary technical expertise for viable health infrastructure. Indeed, it is these various actors that eventually created a new form of governance, as illustrated by the Global Fund and the GAVI Alliance described later.

*Agriculture, Food, and the FAO, IFAD, and WFP.* Agriculture and food supply are clearly crucial elements of human development, and therefore it is not surprising that the Food and Agriculture Organization came into being even before the UN itself—the first of three UN specialized agencies that form the food regime as well as the larger food regime complex. As discussed in Chapter 3, FAO support of high-yield strains of grain and rice, as well as fertilizers and pesticides, led to a "green revolution" in the 1950s and 1960s. That provided the foundation for the FAO's emphasis on food security, which entails ensuring not only adequate supplies through higher yields, but also efficient and secure distribution in times of shortage.

The second agency, the International Fund for Agricultural Development created in 1977, finances and cofinances projects to improve agricultural methods in rural areas, including ancillary financial services and off-farm employment. With adequate financial services, farmers have access to credit to purchase needed inputs and off-farm employment opportunities provide an alternative stable income, given the vagaries of farm incomes. As poverty rates have dropped in East Asia, more than 50 percent of IFAD funding goes to address African rural development.

The third agency, the World Food Programme, supplies not only emergency food aid but also development project aid. For example, its Food-for-Assets projects provide food in return for work on schools, wells, or roads. Providing food to schoolchildren encourages them to stay in school and improve future employment prospects.

Thus, since the 1980s, the programmatic thrust of the UN system's food and agricultural organizations has been to promote sustainable agricultural practices, rural development, and alleviation of acute and chronic hunger—all key elements of human development. Undergirding the attainment of these goals has been the "feed the hungry" norm, the core of the food regime, and the goal of increasing productivity so that all persons have access to a safe and sustainable food supply. A variety of other actors are part of the regime, including the regional development banks, the OECD, and the WTO, as well as nonstate actors such as Action Against Hunger, World Vision, Oxfam, private foundations, and even large private international companies.

### The Regional Multilateral Development Banks

In the late 1950s, 1960s, and 1970s, dissatisfaction with World Bank lending and scarcity of development funds for regional projects led developing countries in Asia, Latin America, Africa, the Middle East, and the Caribbean to create regional development banks. The European Bank for Reconstruction and Development was established in 1991, after the fall of communist regimes, to aid former Soviet-bloc countries transitioning to market economies. These banks are designed to promote regional programs and be more sensitive to regional needs and concerns. We look at four of them.

*The Inter-American Development Bank.* The oldest and among the most active of the regional development banks is the Inter-American Development Bank (IDB), with forty-six members and twenty-six of the borrowing members having just over 50 percent of the voting power. Founded in 1959, the IDB became a leader in social sector lending (health and education) and in lending to the smaller poor countries during the 1960s and 1970s. In the 1980s, the IDB aligned itself more with the World Bank's economic liberalization agenda. Since the 1990s, it has adopted the broader approach of the World Bank, working not only to reduce poverty and inequality by financing microentrepreneurs and small-scale farmers, but also to improve governance through promotion of democracy and regional integration.

Like the World Bank, the IDB currently consists of several separate agencies that emphasize different aspects of lending. The Inter-American Investment Corporation finances small- and medium-scale private interests; the Multilateral Investment Fund promotes reforms in investment practices to stimulate private sector involvement; the Fund for Special Operations lends to the least-developed countries on concessional terms. These various mechanisms lend over $11 billion annually.

The IDB has assumed a leadership position in the region because it chairs and convenes donor meetings. For example, it convened the 1994 Summit of the Americas, hosting the UNDP, regional NGOs, and governments in an effort to consolidate democracy (Nelson 2000). It has drawn NGOs into the consultation process, working, for example, with the Latin American Association of Popular Organizations, a regional network of development NGOs. NGOs, in turn, have pressured the IDB for greater flexibility and transparency.

The IDB's advantage has always been its close relationship with states and its specialized knowledge of the region. It maintains resident representatives in each of its borrowing countries, resulting in a steady flow of information concerning needs. As one government official put it, "The IDB is the Bank that respects our creativity" (www.idb.org). Yet the institution's close relationships with governments may also be a liability. Its president (always a Latin American) is closely scrutinized by the US and international banking community, as the United States still holds one-third of the total voting power, thereby limiting the IDB's autonomy. China joined the bank in 2009.

*The Asian Development Bank.* The Asian Development Bank (ADB) has also assumed a major leadership position in its respective region. Established in 1966 with headquarters in Manila, the bank currently has sixty-seven members (forty-eight regional and nineteen nonregional states). The ADB's almost 3,000 employees work in offices around the world (including major banking centers such as Tokyo and Frankfurt) and have made loans totaling more than $20 billion since 1966, most of them to the public sector.

Five core areas of operation are part of the ADB's Strategy 2020. These include infrastructure (currently half of all lending), environment including climate change, regional cooperation, financial sector development, and education. Funded projects include the Greater Mekong subregional initiatives in transportation, power, agricultural science, and technology in the river basin, and another focusing on the special needs of Bangladesh, Bhutan, India, and Nepal in energy, investment, transport, and water resource management.

Japan is one of the ADB's two largest shareholders, along with the United States; each controls 12.8 percent of shares. Long a strong financial backer of the ADB, Japan is the top contributor to the bank's special funds, including the concessional arm of the Asian Development Fund.

The Asian Development Fund, established in 2000, signaled to the international community that the ADB was refocusing on the goal of eliminating poverty and on working with civil society to accomplish its objectives. As of 2014, twenty-nine ADB member countries had access to the Asian Development Fund; seventeen had access only to those funds that are provided either with very low interest rates or as grants. The fund targets inclusive growth, with programs in education and health, environmental sustainability, and regional integration, many cofinanced with NGOs. This emphasis represents a significant departure from traditional multilateral development bank funding of state-supported, large infrastructure projects.

The ADB also has a new rival, as does the World Bank, in the Asian Infrastructure Investment Bank (AIIB), launched with China's leadership in 2015 and scheduled to be initially capitalized with $50 billion from China. Despite intense lobbying from the United States, many US allies, including Britain, France, Germany, Italy, Australia, and South Korea, and fifty other countries were accepted as charter members. One observer noted, "There is little dispute that the World Bank and the Asian Development Bank have been unable to fulfill the infrastructure needs in the region. . . . [Furthermore] China was upset that after the 2008 financial crisis, [the US] Congress rebuffed legislation intended to increase Beijing's voice in the World Bank and the International Monetary Fund" (Perlez 2015: A11). Having one or more wealthy donor countries within Asia, whether for the ADB or the new regional investment bank, provides a distinct advantage. Such is not the case in Africa.

*The African Development Bank.* The African Development Bank (AfDB) was founded in 1966 by African states, but agreed to admit nonregional members less than twenty years later in order to augment its economic resources. Fifty-three African states are now joined by twenty-five nonregional members, with the regional members holding 60 percent of the voting power and the nonregionals 40 percent. No state or even small group of states has veto power. Not only are the AfDB's president and more than 1,500 employees almost all African, but the organization has also tried to bring a uniquely African perspective to development problems, seeing itself as the repository of African knowledge and the voice of Africa in external organizations.

Originally defining itself as an economic development institution, the AfDB established only economic conditions for its loans, believing that the imposition of political criteria constituted unwarranted interference in the internal affairs of member states. AfDB officials, however, were pushed toward attaching conditionality to loans in the 1980s, suggesting that if a government did not move toward a market pricing system, it would have difficulty obtaining future loans (Mingst 1990). Over time, project-based lending has been accompanied by program and sector lending, and loans are made not only to governments but also to the private sector.

In the 1990s the AfDB lost its credit rating just as the continent itself was experiencing economic decline, creating a crisis. Following several restructurings, the bank strengthened top management, upgraded staff resources, made the institution more client-responsive, and increased support for many initiatives of others in the development community. From a policy perspective, this has resulted in a renewed emphasis on poverty reduction consistent with NEPAD as well as with the MDGs. It also increased lending for infrastructure, which in 2012 amounted to almost half of its spending, as well as increasing attention to regional projects and to systematically evaluating the results.

*The European Bank for Reconstruction and Development.* The European Bank for Reconstruction and Development (EBRD) was founded in 1991 to aid transitions to market economies in over thirty states, from Central Europe to Central Asia and now the Mediterranean littoral. There are sixty-four members, plus the EU and the European Investment Bank. The EBRD supports risky private projects in cooperation with commercial partners. It monitors recipients' progress in price and trade liberalization, competition policy, enterprise restructuring, and establishing new legal frameworks. It has helped states move to full market economies, while promoting safeguards for the environment and a commitment to sustainable energy. The EBRD administers between 350 and 400 projects annually, totaling 8–9 billion euros. Projects range from support for agriculture and agribusiness in Moldova and Georgia to provision of credit for small businesses in Serbia and Kazakhstan.

Several features distinguish the EBRD from its counterpart institutions. It was the first regional development bank to impose explicit political criteria: borrowing countries must be applying principles of multiparty democracy and pluralism. Thus the bank has explicitly promoted both capitalist economic development and democratization. Second, the EBRD promotes the private sector. Third, it operates with a greater range of financial instruments at its disposal, since like the World Bank it borrows funds in international capital markets. Fourth, since 2012, as a result of the Arab Spring, the bank has developed programs to facilitate private investment in Egypt, Morocco, Tunisia, and Jordan.

\* \* \*

Regional development banks, as well as the more localized development banks, enjoy a closer relationship with their constituencies than do other IGOs. With fewer members and more similar needs, development programs can theoretically be more closely tailored to national and local needs. While each of these regional development banks is committed to the liberal economic paradigm in general, they, like the Bretton Woods institutions and the rest of the UN system, have also converged in development thinking, recognizing the necessity of sustainable and human development and of incorporating NGOs and private actors as development partners.

### The Key Role of States: Official Development Assistance

Government-to-government bilateral aid, known as official development assistance (ODA), has long been another important source of capital for developing countries. Its importance underscores one key role of states in global governance relating to development. States have transferred over half a trillion dollars since World War II, with 95 percent of that coming from the twenty-nine members of the OECD's Development Assistance Committee (DAC). In 2013, that aid rose to a record $134.8 billion with increases from seventeen DAC countries, plus increases from Turkey, Russia, and the United Arab Emirates.

The amount of this aid, however, must be weighed against other considerations that reduce the effectiveness of ODA in bridging the finance gap for developing countries. Bilateral aid is often tied to political considerations, for example. In 2013, the United States, through the US Agency for International Development (USAID) and the US Department of State, allocated about one-third of its assistance to peace and security concerns and about one-half to human development, including economic development, education, health, and humanitarian assistance. The major recipient was

Afghanistan, in all categories. By region, sub-Saharan Africa received the largest share (25 percent), with Ethiopia and Kenya receiving the most; Afghanistan and Pakistan, Colombia and Haiti, and Jordan and Iraq topped the lists in other regions. In short, US development assistance serves multiple functions, not all related to development.

As part of its goal-setting role, and in response to G-77 pressure in the 1960s, the UN has set a target for donor countries. Initially, it was 1.0 percent of gross national income; when it was evident that this was unrealistic, the goal was reduced to 0.7 percent. In actuality, donors contribute between 0.1 percent of national income (Greece and Korea) and 1.0 percent (Norway and Sweden). Although the United States is the largest donor in absolute amounts (followed by Germany, Britain, France, and Japan), its ODA amounts to only 0.2 percent of US national income. In 2013, the UK increased its spending by 27.8 percent to hit the international target for the first time. These official assistance data do not tell the whole story. Non-DAC donors such as China, Brazil, India, Indonesia, and South Africa do not report data to the DAC, while other non-DAC countries like Kuwait, Russia, Saudi Arabia, and Turkey do report their ODA. The fact that Africa receives substantial aid from non-DAC sources such as China, and the fact that China's aid is often, by design, a mixture of aid, direct investment, service contracts, labor cooperation agreements, and long-term loans, mean that it is almost impossible to assess data on its ODA.

Despite these limitations, ODA is important and, since the early 1990s, DAC donors, the World Bank, and the IMF have agreed to promote private sector development, privatization, business training, microenterprise development, and an improved institutional environment for business. The G-7/8 provided one venue for giving impetus to coordinating aid policies as well addressing debt relief and global food supply. The OECD's DAC provided another. Until 2003 the DAC consisted only of major Western donor states. While they continue to drive the agenda, low- and middle-income countries and civil society are now included in discussions, in recognition of the need for greater local ownership of aid programs and better measures for evaluating the effectiveness of aid in view of recipient-country development strategies. Many of the newly emerging economies, including the BRICS, have not participated, even though those countries are both recipients in some cases and donors in others. Thus there has been increasing consistency in approaches between bilateral aid agencies and the multilateral development institutions.

The MDGs have also helped to focus aid efforts and even spur new approaches. For example, the United States created a "new compact for development" by promising to increase core assistance to less developed countries through the Millennium Challenge Corporation, operational since

2004. While the goals of the MDGs and the United States were similar, how the United States institutionalized its commitment was different and controversial. The United States would fund states to reduce poverty when recipients could show that they had already adopted "sound policies." These included good governance (stopping corruption, supporting human rights and rule of law); health and education of the citizenry; and economic policies promoting private enterprise and free trade. Countries have competed for the grants (not loans) according to how well they meet seventeen policy indicators of good governance.

The underlying idea is that only countries with good governance will be able to attract private investors and likely succeed; those countries should be rewarded. As of 2013, Millennium Challenge Compacts, large five-year grants, had been negotiated with twenty-five countries, fourteen of which were in Africa. Threshold programs, smaller grants to countries just short of meeting the criteria, were negotiated for twenty countries. In total, $8.4 billion was allocated. The use of specific criteria, including governance criteria, while compatible with newer thinking about the importance of strong institutions free of corruption, has nonetheless generated a heated debate. Questions include whether the criteria for eligibility are appropriate. Do countries that meet the strict criteria really need assistance in the first place? Is there sufficient empirical evidence to link meeting these criteria with development success?

The number of aid projects financed by the United States and other bilateral donors has escalated over time. A country, for example, may receive development aid from over thirty-eight different bilateral donors, a situation that has led to efforts to improve cooperation among the various donors and with the recipient countries, as discussed later. Multilateral donors have also expanded in number and have different preferences and procedures. This raises the question of whether fragmentation leads to ineffectiveness or promotes diversity in approaches that may, in the long term, bring better results.

There is a long-running, vigorous academic and policy debate on the question of aid effectiveness (Deaton 2013). The aid optimists, such as Jeffrey Sachs (2005), believe that there needs to be a "big push" to move people out of poverty. The pessimists, such as Dambisa Moyo (2009), claim that aid to African states has resulted in aid dependency, market distortion, and more poverty. Others, like William Easterly (2006), claim that aid needs to be targeted in narrower projects with measurable goals, and Paul Collier (2007) urges small amounts of aid to nudge those states that are home to "the bottom billion" of the poor in the right direction. Years of empirical work suggest that aid boosts growth, but despite all the studies, there is little consensus on the relative costs and on how aid leads to human development.

## Private International Finance

Despite the lack of empirical evidence about the effectiveness of public foreign aid in development, there is a widespread consensus that private international finance has played and continues to play an increasing role in international development, gradually exceeding official multilateral and bilateral channels. Since the mid-1980s, capital flows to developing countries have increased dramatically, to over $1 trillion as of 2010, while ODA has evened off, illustrating the private sector's growing importance in development. Private international capital was essential to the success of the Asian "tigers," although statist policies were crucial in harnessing that capital and making it productive. Africa currently is benefiting from heavy Chinese investment around the continent through both official and private channels. Between 2003 and 2012, that investment jumped from $500 million to $15 billion, much of it going to build infrastructure such as airports, dams, highways, and hospitals, as well as to mineral extraction. The downside is that China has also been importing Chinese workers for many of its projects and been oblivious to environmental consequences, generating critical assessments and concerns about a new form of colonialism (French 2014).

Yet only about 20 percent of private international finance actually goes to the least-developed countries. And for many of them, reliance on private capital is risky and potentially limiting. Most of this investment goes to just a few countries. Africa, the most capital-poor region, receives a small portion, but even that is targeted at a few countries, notably South Africa and Nigeria, not at the least-developed. Only since 2005 have other countries found themselves on the receiving end of significant private investment. Another problem is that private capital flows are highly volatile. After the 2010 peak in private international finance, the figure dropped to $775 billion two years later. In 2000, Mexico attracted $17.1 billion in foreign direct investment. A year later that investment reached $27.7 billion before dropping to $12.3 billion in 2003. South Africa attracted only $1.0 billion in 2000; investment rose to $7.3 billion a year later, then leveled off at around $0.7 billion for several years before bouncing back to $6.3 billion in 2005. Thus, while private capital flows are significantly greater than official development assistance, and at times have been key for certain developing countries, for others these flows have provided little to bridge the financing gap, and their very volatility makes them problematic for sustained development.

## NGOs and Development Assistance

NGOs are key actors in the development puzzle, but they have struggled to acquire more roles and to enhance their legitimacy. Incorporating them into the World Bank and IMF has been particularly difficult, because both institutions from their inception have been elite-run, dealing exclusively with borrowing governments, central banks, finance ministries, and international private lenders. In their first four decades, neither had direct relations with civil society actors in general nor with NGOs specifically.

Beginning in the mid-1980s, there was strong external pressure from donor governments and NGOs themselves for greater Bank and Fund accountability; NGOs' participation was one approach for improving both accountability and effectiveness (O'Brien et al. 2000). Following the 1988 annual meetings of the Bank and Fund, with renewed pressure from NGOs and Bank staff who were critical of the environmental and social consequences of the Bank's lending, the Bank began to use NGOs in different ways. Also, like bilateral development agencies, the Bank began to channel more funds through NGOs, as discussed in Chapter 6. By 1990, civil society organizations (the broader term preferred by the Bank, the Fund, and the EU, as it encompasses not only NGOs but also trade unions, faith-based organizations, movements of indigenous peoples, and foundations) were involved in 21 percent of projects. By 2010, fully 86 percent of Bank projects involved CSOs. In addition, CSO specialists have been hired at Bank field offices since 2001 to coordinate participation in projects ranging from project design and preparation to implementation and monitoring.

CSOs have gradually gained a voice in broader policy dialogues at the Bank, serving as instruments of accountability and securing the creation of various entities. For example, while a Women in Development Office was established in 1977, there was pressure for more. A unit on sustainable development was formed in the mid-1980s and subsequently renamed several times. The Bank's independent Inspection Panel was established in 1993 to hear complaints from people and communities impacted by Bank projects. In 2001 a gender mainstreaming strategy was approved. Several NGOs, including the Bank Information Center, Environmental Defense, and the Bretton Woods Project, are dedicated to monitoring World Bank activities and whistle-blowing when necessary. Thus, although governments are still formally charged with implementation of World Bank projects, the Bank has built CSO participation into projects and programs, encouraging greater grassroots participation.

The IMF, in contrast, has had a rockier relationship with CSOs, but in the late 1990s, bowing to the same pressures exerted on the World Bank, the Fund initiated more regular meetings and consultations. Parallel to its annual meetings, a Civil Society Policy Forum is now institutionalized. CSOs provide comments on IMF papers and are consulted in member-country negotiations. The IMF changed because of realization that "secrecy and aloofness from civil society negatively affected the IMF's reputation— thus risking far reaching consequences to the organization's effectiveness" (Belloni and Moschella 2013: 535). One empirical study of the IMF's relationship with CSOs in six sub-Saharan African countries suggests, however, that while the IMF now enjoys closer contacts with publics, those contacts have been "skewed toward urban, professional, propertied, male, and culturally Western circles." They have not provided entry for "rural dwellers, underclasses, women, and people living outside modern rationalist culture." In short, "the IMF 'opening' to civil society has been quite uneven" (Scholte 2012: 187).

By 2000, NGOs had become important channels for assistance, both serving their own missions and as subcontractors for donor governments, and increasingly working in partnerships with the World Bank, UNDP, and other IGOs. As important as NGOs are to the human development agenda, net grants by NGOs amount to only about 6 percent of the total assistance, according to an OECD estimate, although subcontracts amount to much more.

NGOs have also been innovators. One particularly effective approach to poverty alleviation developed by grassroots NGOs and nonprofit organizations is microcredit. The Grameen Bank, created in 1983 by a Bangladeshi academic turned banker, Muhammad Yunus (2006 recipient of the Nobel Peace Prize), provides small amounts of capital to people who cannot qualify for regular bank loans. Loans average $100, although some may be as little as $10 to $20. Its more than 2,000 branches have made loans to more than 7.5 million borrowers, governments, and private banks. The purpose is to empower women, who are typically ignored by multilateral institutions.

Microfinance institutions have grown exponentially, becoming bigger, more competitive, and more diverse. Some are not-for-profit organizations like the Grameen Bank, while others are for-profit institutions; some offer just credit, while increasingly others offer a variety of savings and insurance alternatives. Some have real physical buildings, others are a person, or even an Internet site like Kiva, which facilitates person-to-person microfinance opportunities.

There is a vigorous debate over whether NGOs in general (large NGOs such as Save the Children, Oxfam, and CARE or the hundreds of small grassroots NGOs) and microfinance institutions in particular lift people out of poverty. The Grameen Bank continues to report that more than half of its borrowers have moved above the poverty line, but empirical studies of multiple institutions have begun to refute Grameen's anecdotal evidence. There appears to be no overall impact on borrowers' household welfare after eighteen months, measured by income, spending, or school attendance. When the borrower already owned a small business, however, then the new credit infusion improved income and spending. In addition, new financial institutions serving the poor have been formed and their financial instruments have expanded from loans to savings accounts and microinsurance (Roodman 2012).

So, the actors in the multifaceted governance of human development are diverse and often overlapping. Virtually every development program includes contributions from the Bretton Woods institutions, the UNDP, a regional commission, some of the specialized agencies, whether the IFAD, FAO, or WHO, and bilateral donors. Increasingly, private actors are involved as well. Thus a number of unique governance arrangements have emerged. These include collaborations among states; partnerships among states, multiple IGOs, NGOs and other nonstate actors, including MNCs; and in a few cases some unique hybrid organizational forms.

## Evolving Varieties of Development-Related Governance

Much as governments have added new agencies or ministries to deal with new types of domestic issues, so too have specialized, functional organizations been created at the regional or global level to address new areas of global governance. Yet because issues do not always fall into neat "silos" and because particular IGOs may not have the full array of resources and actors, new varieties of governance have emerged, often involving different types of partnerships. Although various partners may not agree on the nature of the problem or the best way to approach the issues, and may have conflicting interests and be competitors for donor funding, development actors are increasingly recognizing the need to pool resources and expertise, to manage risk, and to collaborate to bring about the desired results.

### Partnerships: From the MDGs to the Global Compact and Beyond

Partnerships in development have gained more currency as human development agendas have broadened. Multifaceted development requires organizations with different skills and expertise in lobbying, agenda-setting, policy formulation, and implementation. Yet partnerships are not all the same: some are rather loose forms of organization, while others are highly institutionalized legal entities, with a unified budget and shared personnel (see Jönsson 2013; Schaferhoff, Campe, and Kaan 2009).

The World Bank, in a 2011 report on the effectiveness of its own aid, differentiated among types of partnerships. Traditional partnerships focus on harmonization of indicators and targets, joint missions to the field, and joint analytical work. Other partnerships focus on country-level integration, coordinating country needs, management processes, and donor activities (World Bank 2011a). Representatives from both the UNDP and the World Bank acknowledge the criticality of these partnerships and the problems arising from differing mandates and policy frameworks. Still another kind of partnership builds upon a wider array of stakeholders, including civil society, parliaments, and the private sector. The World Bank itself is involved in nearly 120 global partnership programs and 50 regional partnerships.

*The Millennium Development Goals and partnerships.* Beginning in 2004, the MDGs spawned an experimental partnership called the Millennium Village project. The project has been led by the UNDP, the New York–based nonprofit Millennium Promise, and the Earth Institute at Columbia University, with financing from Japan, philanthropist George Soros, private companies, and domestic sources. It has identified fourteen clusters of villages in ten African countries, including Ghana, Ethiopia, Malawi, and Nigeria. Village assistance, equivalent to annual investments of $110 person, is based on the idea that concentrated but inexpensive changes in health, water, agriculture, and roads can lift the 400,000 people in these villages out of severe poverty relatively rapidly.

Periodic assessments have shown strong results in improving agricultural outputs and health and education outcomes. But questions remain. Are these results sustainable without external assistance? Will there be unintended outcomes such as undue reliance on fertilizer or irrigation to improve agricultural productivity as Bill Hinchberger (2011) contends? Most damaging to the credibility of the Millennium Village is the failure to design the project so that reliable evaluation would be possible. No baseline data were collected; the sites were not randomized; matched sites were not identified; and assessment measures were not proposed (Clemens and Demombynes 2010).

Other partnerships have sprung up to provide services essential to achieving the MDGs, such as the distribution of antiretroviral therapies to fight against HIV/AIDS and supplying bed nets to fight against mosquitoes (through the Global Fund to Fight AIDS, Tuberculosis, and Malaria), and the construction of safe water systems (through the Water and Sanitation for the Urban Poor program). Studies on transnational health partnerships have shown them to be particularly effective in implementation of the health-related MDGs, but other partnerships, such as in water and sanitation, have been less successful (Liese and Beisheim 2011).

The SDG planning process outlined earlier includes efforts to develop indicators to evaluate specific partnerships. And as described, it involves a wide variety of groups, with Beyond 2015 (see www.beyond2015.org) playing a major role in making this process participatory and inclusive. The goals will undoubtedly be more ambitious; there will be more targets; and the SDGs will not only help the poor, but also tackle issues to save the planet.

*Collaboration through the OECD's Development Assistance Committee.* In 2011, the DAC convened the Fourth High-Level Forum on Aid Effectiveness in Busan, Korea, with a goal of reinvigorating efforts to achieve the Millennium Development Goals by broadening participation. This time, however, the traditional DAC donors were joined by representatives from 160 states (including the BRICS), CSOs, the UN system (the UNDP and specialized agencies), regional development banks, and private sector actors. The goal was to create a partnership among these various actors to promote a coordinated aid effort. The challenge post-Busan was to "construct a 'global-light,' and 'country-focused' system that provided room for 'differential commitments' and adequate monitoring to ensure compliance" (Atwood 2012: 24). Under the partnership, after a recipient government's development plans were clearly articulated, various donors were to coordinate which groups would work in specific areas. No longer would donors compete for the best projects, and only projects compatible with the recipient's development objectives would be supported. Thus, what began as an OECD-led effort to collect data on development aid, became the Global Partnership for Development—a nascent attempt at multi-actor collaboration.

*MNCs: From regulating to partnering.* The MDGs did not specifically incorporate MNCs, although many eventually bought into the goals. The reason for that omission has historical origins, in the story of how MNCs transformed from pariahs to be regulated into partners in human development.

Critics of the liberal economic model have long been dissatisfied with the roles multinational corporations play in economic affairs, as described earlier. Yet determining what is to be regulated, even defining what MNCs are, as well as the scope of regulations, has always been problematic.

The UN Commission on Transnational Corporations spearheaded the first effort, beginning in 1974 under the NIEO, by developing information systems about MNCs to help countries negotiate restrictions and by creating an international code of conduct to govern their behavior. Yet by the mid-1980s, economic liberalism had triumphed and privatization and deregulation were prominent on the international agenda. Discussions of regulating MNCs were quietly abandoned. The search for an international code of conduct officially met its demise in 1994 when the work of the commission was integrated into UNCTAD. The mandate changed dramatically: to provide governments interested in attracting foreign investment with the support to do so.

The thirty-four members of the OECD agreed on the clearest and the simplest model for regulation, namely voluntary guidelines, as outlined in Chapter 8. That approach has been effective because the members have all supported the right of MNCs to invest as they see fit, and all have strong functioning legal systems capable of enforcing restrictions on MNCs. Few developing countries, however, have strong rule-based systems, and some have been ideologically opposed to MNC activities. Furthermore, some MNCs have clearly engaged in behaviors that negatively affect developing countries, such as hiding profits and not paying taxes, fostering corrupt practices by allying themselves with unsavory officials, degrading the environment, and abusing the human rights of their workers.

NGOs have stepped in to monitor MNC behavior with the aid of technologies that enhance their organizational and communication abilities. Transparency International, for example, combats corruption worldwide, especially in business transactions. Its annual Corruption Perceptions Index is widely used by the public and private sectors. Key to its success is its network or coalition approach with businesses, governments, the OECD, and international financial institutions. Corporate Accountability International, previously known as Infact, is a grassroots organization that since 1977 has been educating the public about the abuses of power by large corporations and organizing for change. The organization enjoyed notoriety and success in the infant formula campaign against Nestlé Corporation between 1977 and 1986, and more recently spearheaded a campaign against the tobacco industry that resulted in the WHO Framework Convention on Tobacco Control, as discussed in Chapter 6.

As useful as NGOs are in monitoring harmful and illegal MNC behavior, the international efforts to regulate MNCs failed and the international community began to talk about bringing MNCs to the table as a way to monitor behavior. MNCs' role in health governance illustrates both the problems with MNCs that the developing world has encountered and the benefits of the newer partnership approach.

No one can doubt the key role that the pharmaceutical industry has played in fostering better health around the world. Still, beginning in 1963, less developed WHO member countries sought assurances that imported drugs were of sufficient quality, and sought technical assistance in monitoring quality control. The international drug companies largely opposed these efforts. Yet in 1970 the WHO approved guidelines for drug-manufacturing quality control, covering such issues as labeling, self-inspection, and reporting of adverse reactions. But the relationship has remained rocky.

In the late 1990s, the accessibility and affordability of drugs in developing countries appeared on the WHO's agenda. The antiretroviral "cocktail" of drugs used to treat HIV/AIDS has been of particular concern because the therapy has been far too costly for use in regions such as Africa. AIDS activists and health professionals raised the difficult economic and ethical issues these drug therapies pose: the high cost, reflecting research costs, high profit margins, and patents that give producers a monopoly on pricing, versus the humanitarian need to make these drugs available and affordable to the sick in developing countries. Much of that discussion over generics and protection of patents occurred within the World Trade Organization's TRIPS, as described in Chapter 8.

Under intense international pressure, the pharmaceutical companies offered concessions, but these proved unacceptable. Meanwhile, NGOs such as Oxfam, ACT UP (AIDS Coalition to Unleash Power), and Africa Action created the transnational Treatment Action Campaign in 1998 to exert pressure on the pharmaceutical companies to reduce prices of anti-retrovirals for developing countries and for African states in particular. The issue of profiteering pharmaceutical companies and the immorality of the high cost of drugs resonated around the world, and the work of these NGOs continues to put low-cost drugs into the hands of people who need them. Quiet diplomacy, mounting global activist pressures, and increasing competition from generic drugs have forced the pharmaceutical manufacturers to alter pricing strategies in poor countries and stop thwarting the sale of generics. As a result, the drugs have become cheaper and more affordable. This partnership has endured for more than a decade due to continuing strong international pressure.

Another example from the health area is a unique legal entity known as the Health in Africa Fund, which brings together the International Finance Corporation of the Bretton Woods institutions, the African Development Bank, the Bill and Melinda Gates Foundation, and Germany's national development finance agency. Managed by Aureos Capital, the Health in Africa Fund is a private equity fund established in 2009 that invests in small and medium-sized African companies, private health clinics, and diagnostic centers serving low-income populations.

Still another initiative is the 2013 partnership between the Bill and Melinda Gates Foundation and JP Morgan Chase. Their Global Health Investment Fund is designed to finance late-stage technology, including drugs, vaccines, and diagnostic tools for diseases that disproportionately burden low-income countries. This fund is designed to benefit developing countries struggling with high rates of maternal and child mortality and to generate profits for investors. Evidence suggests that these and other partnerships in health involving MNCs have been among the most effective partnerships.

*The Global Compact.* In 1999, UN Secretary-General Kofi Annan proposed a more comprehensive global approach to partnerships between corporations and the UN system at the World Economic Forum in Davos, Switzerland. He hoped to create a partnership among the UN, relevant UN agencies, research centers, corporations, and NGOs, including environmental, human rights, and labor groups represented by the International Confederation of Free Trade Unions. The purpose was to provide the social foundations for a sustainable global economy, encourage private sector investment in developing countries, and promote good corporate practices.

The Global Compact on Corporate Responsibility incorporates ten principles that participating companies agree to uphold. These include adherence to international human rights law, rejection of child and forced labor, abolition of discrimination in employment, and promotion of greater environmental responsibility. In 2013, there were more than 10,000 participants in the compact, 7,000 of which were businesses. Ruggie (2001, 2003) describes the compact as a set of nested networks in which participants learn how other companies have addressed the principles, learn which practices work and which fail, and increase corporate social responsibility. The Global Compact, he says (2003: 313), "is also an experiment in devising fundamentally new forms of global governance."

Critics of the Global Compact, including a US-based NGO, Corp-Watch, point to the lack of mechanisms for compliance. Companies can pick and choose which provisions apply, and enhance their public images without fundamentally changing corporate practice. The only requirement is that companies provide a "communication on progress" annually to show how the principles are being incorporated into business strategies and operations. Obviously, many MNCs are not members of the compact, and MNCs from North America are less represented (Kell, Slaughter, and Hale 2007). Yet the Global Compact can speak with a loud voice against a participating corporation. In 2014, for example, the body asked the InterContinental Hotels Group to respond to complaints from supporters of an independent Tibet about its plan to open a hotel in Llasa, a project alleged to be incompatible with the compact. Such public campaigns are designed to alter corporate behavior.

Public-private partnerships have proliferated, but not necessarily always for the good. As Marco Schaferhoff, Sabine Campe, and Christopher Kaan (2009: 465) note, their rise "has led to a more fragmented and uncoordinated global arena, wherein authority is exerted by a multitude of state and nonstate actors." Research has shown some to be effective, but others have yielded unintended side effects, one of which is to overwhelm the limited capacity of developing countries (464). With regard to the corporate social responsibility norms associated with the Global Compact, partnerships have promoted the norms, but "the empirical evidence is often illustrative and not conclusive" (461). Partnerships are also subject to the same questions that have to be asked about other varieties of global governance: What institutional design has been shown to be best? Are the partnerships legitimate, inclusive, and accountable?

*Partnerships in health and new governance forms.* HIV/AIDS provides a unique example of the limitations of conventional forms of international organization governance, weak public-private partnerships, and the evolution to new forms of more inclusive governance. The Global Fund to Fight

AIDS, Tuberculosis, and Malaria (the Global Fund), formed in 2001, and the Global Alliance for Vaccines and Immunizations (GAVI), formed in 2000, are examples of initiatives taken when the WHO's responses proved insufficient and new partnerships were needed to address problems.

Initially, in 1986, five years after AIDS was identified as a threat, the WHO took the lead in trying to convince member states to acknowledge HIV/AIDS as a major problem and commit resources. Many states, however, failed to act, and fewer still had the necessary resources. Other UN agencies gradually became involved when it became evident that the effects of AIDS reached beyond health. In 1996, the UN Joint Programme on HIV/AIDS (UNAIDS) was created by UNICEF, the UNDP, the UN Fund for Population Activities, UNESCO, and the WHO. The World Bank was the lead agency for global action, with the UN International Drug Control Programme (UNDCP), WFP, and ILO subsequently joining. This arrangement was a classic multi-institutional approach. The UN convened global AIDS conferences every two years to raise awareness and mobilize responses. Both the UN General Assembly and the UN Security Council held special sessions to address the issue, with the Council identifying the AIDS pandemic as a threat to global security in 2000, the first time a health issue was elevated to such status.

UNAIDS has proved unsatisfactory, however. The lack of local ownership of programs, inadequate institutional accountability measures, politicization of some programs, and the need for a steady stream of financial resources resulted in the creation of the Global Fund—a new kind of legal entity (Smyth and Triponel 2013). As an independent entity under Swiss law, it is designed to work explicitly at the grassroots level. While the World Bank manages the fund's resources, it does not decide how they are allocated. Rather, funding decisions are taken by an international board consisting of donors, recipients, NGOs, private sector actors, including business and foundations, and representatives from affected communities. The WHO, UNAIDS, public-private partnerships such as Roll Back Malaria and Stop TB, as well as the World Bank are involved. At the country level, proposals come through local governance structures involving all those working on the diseases within the country, including academic institutions, private business, and people living with the diseases. A highly legal process regulates who receives funding and how the funds are allocated and disbursed. It includes an extensive verification of performance and impact, which is made possible by the fund's unique status as an independent agency.

As of 2013, the Global Fund had allocated more than $28 billion for three programs: supplying 6.6 million people with antiretroviral treatments, 11.9 million with tuberculosis treatments, and 410 million people with insecticide-treated nets. Despite some problems, it has received high marks for its independence and professionalism, but achieving those marks has necessitated establishing a very different, more inclusive partnership.

GAVI, too, evolved in a similar fashion. In the early 1980s, the WHO established several separate vaccination programs aimed at delivering vaccines to children in developing countries, although the pharmaceutical companies were unable to provide vaccines in sufficient quantities. In the 1990s, the WHO, along with UNICEF and the UNDP, the World Bank, and the Rockefeller Foundation, formed a new Children's Vaccine Initiative, but the initiative was not successful, in part due to the WHO's rocky relationships with MNCs. GAVI was formed outside of the WHO structure, with major financial support from the Gates Foundation. It works with NGOs, other civil society actors, and the pharmaceutical industry, and is funded by state donors, the World Bank, private foundations, and capital markets. GAVI has regularized the relationship between the manufacturers of vaccines, developing-country health authorities, and the various sources of funding. GAVI's twenty-eight-member board is heavily weighted toward technical experts, while country-level committees review proposals for immunization services and proposals for strengthening health systems and civil society support systems.

In grading health governance, the Council on Foreign Relations (2014), in its Global Governance Report Card, gave its only "good" rating to the continuing battle against HIV/AIDS. It gave "average" ratings to the WHO's traditional functions, including targeting of noncommunicable diseases and managing of acute pandemics and infectious diseases generally, and to global health financing. Most disappointing is the "poor" rating given to efforts at improving health systems in developing countries. For many less developed countries, it is this weakness that most directly affects human development, as evidenced in the collapse of local health systems in the West African countries affected by the 2014 Ebola outbreak.

### A Regime Complex in Food

The multiplicity of organizations in the food regime, as discussed earlier, has resulted in considerable overlap in responsibilities and rules as well as divergent norms. This divergence has widened even further with the emergence of a global regime complex for food security—a shift in orientation from the earlier focus on expanding agricultural consumption, production, trade, and food aid. The WTO's 1995 Agreement on Agriculture and Agreement on the Application of Sanitary and Phytosanitary Measures form binding rules and emphasize liberalizing world agriculture in line with market principles. Added to this is the definition of food security negotiated at the 1996 World Food Summit, which introduced the concept of food security as a human right. Thus, the food security regime complex—a network of regimes that overlap and contain inherent contradictions consists of three overlapping regimes—agriculture and food, international trade, and human rights—each with different institutions, rules, and norms on food security. Memberships overlap, as most states are members of the FAO and the WTO as well as having ratified the major international human rights treaties (Margulis 2013).

Global demands for increased production of food have in fact been met with an increase in production, in absolute and per capita terms, as well as with greater food security for many. Yet a variety of factors pushed food prices to historic highs in 2008 and raised the number of hungry people to 1 billion. Food prices and markets have fluctuated significantly since then and were among the factors motivating the 2011 Arab Spring—a reminder that food prices are a factor in both economic growth and social stability. While the MDG target on reducing by half the proportion of people who are hungry may be met in 2015, there will still likely be about 800 million people globally who are undernourished. There are controversies within the food regime itself. Humanitarians might say the hungry should be fed whatever the cost and long-term consequences; developmentalists might stress the need to construct related infrastructure for the long term (Ross 2011). But the food regime is also affected by other regimes in both trade and human rights, complicating efforts to meet the expectations of all.

The increased use of biofuels for energy is one of the factors affecting food supplies and prices and illustrates the complexity of food security governance. Deemed valuable for the international energy regime, it has the effect of raising grain prices, creating shortages, and reducing surpluses available for food to feed the hungry. Likewise, genetically modified foods may increase the productivity of crops, but they increase costs and may adversely affect human health. Climate change is affecting agricultural production in many areas due to more frequent and extreme weather events, desertification, and temperature shifts, undermining agricultural productivity in some areas and resulting in geographic shifts in agricultural production. Agricultural trade policy in the WTO and the EU may support agricultural interests in developed countries, but is widely seen by the G-20 and developing countries more generally as detrimental to their food security, as discussed in Chapter 8. In short, the emergence of the regime complex for food security is evidence of a significant shift in governance, one where overlapping institutional responsibilities and conflicts among diverging norms and rules are likely to make it more difficult to reach consensus and to improve international cooperation to reduce hunger.

The new forms of development governance tend to be more inclusive and provide greater accountability and are perhaps more legitimate. Whether they are as effective or more effective than the older approaches remains to be seen. Evaluating effectiveness of diverse actors and approaches across the multiple dimensions of human development is a vexing problem. Equally difficult is evaluating the effectiveness and legitimacy of the multiplicity of approaches to enhancing human rights, the subject of the next chapter.

## Suggested Further Reading

Jolly, Richard, Louis Emmerij, Dharam Ghai, and Frédéric Lapeyne. (2004) *UN Contributions to Development Thinking and Practice.* Bloomington: Indiana University Press.

Park, Susan, and Jonathan R. Strand, eds. (2015) *Global Economic Governance and the Development Practices of the Multilateral Development Banks.* New York: Routledge.

Pattberg, Philipp, Frank Biermann, Sander Chan, and Ayşem Mert, eds. (2013) *Public-Private Partnerships for Sustainable Development: Emergence, Influence, and Legitimacy.* Cheltenham: Elgar.

Roodman, David (2012) *Due Diligence: An Impertinent Inquiry into Microfinance.* Washington, DC: Center for Global Development.

Weaver, Catherine E. (2008) *Hypocrisy Trap: The World Bank and the Poverty of Reform.* Princeton: Princeton University Press.

## Internet Resources

African Development Bank: www.afdb.org
Asian Development Bank: www.adb.org
Center for Global Development: www.cgd.org
Corp Watch: www.corpwatch.org
Corporate Accountability International: www.stopcorporateabuse.org
Doctors Without Borders: www.doctorswithoutborders.org
European Bank for Reconstruction and Development: www.ebrd.com
Food and Agriculture Organization: www.fao.org
Global Alliance on Vaccines and Initiative: www.gavi.org
Global Compact: www.unglobalcompact.org
Global Fund to Fight AIDS, Tuberculosis, and Malaria: www.theglobalfund.org
Group of 77: www.g77.org
*Human Development Reports:* www.hdr.undp.org/
Inter-American Development Bank: www.iadb.org
International Centre for Settlement of Investment Disputes: icsid.worldbank.org
International Monetary Fund: www.imf.org
Kiva: www.kiva.org
Millennium Challenge Corporation: www.mcc.gov
Millennium Development Goals: www.un.org/millenniumgoals
*My World: The United Nations Global Survey for a Better World:* http://vote.my world2015.org
Organization for Economic Cooperation and Development: www.oecd.org
UN Conference on Trade and Development: www.unctad.org
UN Development Programme: www.undp.org
UN Sustainable Development Knowledge Platform: http://sustainabledevelopment .un.org
UN Women: www.unwomen.org
US Agency for International Development: www.usaid.gov
World Bank: www.worldbank.org
World Food Program: www.wfp.org
*The World's Women* reports: http://unstats.un.org/unsd/demographic/products/Worlds women/WWreports.htm

# 10

# Protecting Human Rights

## Case Study: Human Trafficking

While institutionalized slavery disappeared at the end of the nineteenth century due to the efforts of the first human rights advocates—the anti-slavery groups—slave-like practices of forced labor and trafficking in persons continue today. The scope of human trafficking owes much to the rapid pace of globalization that opened doors to the free flow of capital and trade as well as to illicit industries like human trafficking. Many of those trafficked are women and children lured by promises of a better life and held against their will only to work long hours and suffer other abuses.

It is estimated that around 12 million people worldwide may be victims of human trafficking. The varying definitions of what constitutes trafficking and the clandestine nature of the problem make the number uncertain, however. Among the more reliable data sources is the Database on Human Trafficking Trends developed by the UN Office on Drugs and Crime (UNODC). Drawing on human trafficking incidences recorded by 113 major institutions between 1996 and 2003 in 161 countries, the data show that the majority are females, three-quarters are trafficked for sexual exploitation, and one-quarter are trafficked for forced labor and domestic servitude. Many are illegal migrants (Cho 2013: 687).

Trafficking is framed as both a human rights issue and a transnational crime, with profits in the billions annually. This dual framing has produced two separate lines of action. Human rights framing means setting standards and securing victims' rights to legal and rehabilitative remedies where the UN system has long been involved. The Universal Declaration on Human Rights included the right to be free from slavery or servitude. In 1951, the Convention for the Suppression of Traffic in Persons went into effect, prohibiting trafficking in persons for the purpose of prostitution (even with their consent). In 1956, the General Assembly explicitly identified contemporary practices that were considered "slave-like," among them serfdom, forced marriage, child labor, debt bondage, and trafficking in human beings, when it approved the Supplementary Convention on the Abolition of Slavery, Slave Trade, and Institutions and Practices Similar to Slavery. The ILO banned forced labor in a 1957 convention and addressed abuses of migrant workers in a 1975 convention. Other related UN actions include the conventions on women, children, and migrant workers; the Optional Protocol on Children in Armed Conflict and the Optional Protocol on the Sale of Children, Child Prostitution, and Child Pornography (2002); and the appointment of a special rapporteur to study the issues (see Table 10.1 later in the chapter).

Framing policy formulation under the rationale and language of criminal justice means ensuring aggressive prevention and prosecution of traffickers. Several actions have been taken, including the establishment of the Commission on Crime Prevention and Justice under ECOSOC, a global conference on transnational crime, and discussion of the possibility of a new convention on transnational organized crime. The consensus was that existing UN legal instruments were insufficient. Thus, in 1997, the General Assembly authorized the drafting of a new treaty.

Early in the drafting of the Convention Against Transnational Organized Crime, work began on a separate protocol on trafficking in persons. The drafting process for the protocol, which lasted from late 1998 through 2000, was highly contentious and drew active NGO advocacy. The most heated tug-of-war concerned the definition of sex trafficking. One camp, supported by the Coalition Against Trafficking in Women, insisted that prostitution in all its forms was exploitive and should be criminalized. The opposing view, advanced by the Human Rights Caucus, posited that non-coerced, consensual migrant sex work should not be prohibited by the protocol. The debate hinged on the definition of sex trafficking and "force" as a required element, as well as on whether "consent" should serve as a delineating concept between noncoerced sex work and sex trafficking. Both camps sought to influence the delegates directly as well as national governments. The final language maintains a distinction between consensual sex work and sex trafficking, but does not permit the consent of victims to be used as a shield for prosecution if other elements of exploitation are apparent.

The Convention Against Transnational Organized Crime, with the additional protocol on trafficking in persons as well as protocols on migrant smuggling and arms trafficking, was adopted by the General Assembly in 2000 and entered into force in 2003. All three are often referred to as the Palermo convention and protocols. According to the protocol on trafficking—officially titled the Protocol to Prevent, Suppress, and Punish Trafficking in Persons, Especially Women and Children—human trafficking is defined as follows:

> The recruitment, transportation, transfer, harbouring or receipt of persons, by means of the threat or use of force or other forms of coercion, of abduction, of fraud, of deception, of the abuse of power or of a position of vulnerability or of the giving or receiving of payments or benefits to achieve the consent of a person having control over another person, for the purpose of exploitation. Exploitation shall include, at a minimum, the exploitation of the prostitution of others or other forms of sexual exploitation, forced labour or services, slavery or practices similar to slavery, servitude or the removal of organs.

By 2014, 163 states had become party to the protocol. Because of its link to the transnational crime convention, the protocol uses the language of criminal law rather than of human rights. This means that the focus of implementation is not so much monitoring and promotion but law enforcement. UNODC works to combat trafficking under the convention, assisting states in drafting policies and providing training resources.

The Geneva-based UN human rights organs have continued their anti-trafficking work. The Human Rights Council (HRC) supports the special rapporteurs for these contemporary forms of slavery. These rapporteurs monitor and promote specific human rights by conducting country visits, receiving complaints from individuals, issuing reports to UN bodies, and communicating with governments. To generate publicity about slave-like practices, the UN General Assembly declared the year 2004 as the International Year to Commemorate the Struggle Against Slavery and Its Abolition and sponsored programs, exhibits, and educational programs. Likewise, the ILO undertook major studies in 2001 and 2005 of forced labor, including human trafficking, calling for its elimination within a decade.

In 1991, the General Assembly established the UN Voluntary Trust Fund on Contemporary Forms of Slavery to provide financial assistance to victims and to NGOs dealing with these issues. The aid to individuals is based on needs for security, education, independence, and reintegration and can include various supports such as legal aid, medical care, food, and counseling.

A second source of assistance for all stakeholders, including governments, business, civil society, and the media, is the United Nations Global Initiative to Fight Human Trafficking, better known as UN.GIFT. It was established in 2007 with funding from several UN agencies, the International Organization for Migration (IOM), the OSCE, and concerned states, among others. UN.GIFT's primary focus is on eradicating human trafficking by supporting partnerships and capacity building of state and nonstate stakeholders.

Particularly striking about efforts to deal with human trafficking is the absence of a single, dominant NGO coalition such as that formed to deal with violence against women or that formed to support the International

Criminal Court. The two coalitions active during the drafting of the Palermo protocol have not formed a single network to coordinate and facilitate anti-trafficking efforts. Anti-Slavery International includes human trafficking among its activities and works to raise awareness, lobbying countries to ratify conventions and strengthen their anti-trafficking efforts. Yet many NGOs prefer to operate independently and often see other NGOs as competitors for funding and attention, focusing on a particular group being trafficked. Yet, human trafficking remains a highly lucrative form of transnational organized crime. The scope of the problem continues to increase. Lack of public awareness of the problem in countries where trafficking originates (particularly many Southeast Asian and Eastern European countries) as well as in destination countries, including the United States, is an obstacle to these anti-trafficking efforts. In 2014, traffickers became increasingly active in the Middle East and North Africa in moving refugees, asylum-seekers, and migrants into Europe, posing major challenges for the EU and its members.

The focus on human trafficking reflects increased attention to human rights issues since World War II, a trend that Zbigniew Brzezinski (1989: 256) has called "the single most magnetic political idea of the contemporary time." That idea and attention have spurred the development of a broad range of international rights norms and global human rights governance initiatives.

## The Roots of Human Rights and Humanitarian Norms

The question of who should be protected—who is human—and how they should be protected has broadened over the centuries. Beginning with the nineteenth-century abolition of the slave trade, former slaves were granted nominal rights and protections. Christians were viewed as a special group needing protection from mistreatment by the Ottoman Turks, and the rights of those wounded during war were articulated with the establishment of the International Committee of the Red Cross, as described in Chapter 6. In the mid–twentieth century, colonialism came to an end. As Martha Finnemore (1996a: 173) describes: "Humanity was no longer something one could create by bringing savages to civilization. Rather, humanity was inherent in individual human beings." Asians and Africans now had human "rights," including the collective right to self-determination, as well as individual rights.

The Holocaust—Nazi Germany's campaign of genocide against Jews, Gypsies, and other "undesirables"—was a powerful impetus to the development of the contemporary human rights movement. In the 1970s, human rights violations in the Soviet Union and Eastern Europe drew public condemnation, as did the "disappearances" of individuals under the authoritarian regimes of Chile and Argentina. South Africa's egregious policy of apartheid—systematic repression and violence against the majority of the country's population solely on the basis of race—had a similar mobilizing effect. The dissolution of the Soviet Union and the downfall of other communist regimes in the early 1990s liberated international efforts to promote human rights from the ideological conflict of the Cold War. Events in Bosnia and Rwanda prompted pressure for prosecution of those responsible for war crimes, crimes against humanity, and genocide, and television pictures of starving children in Somalia provoked public demands that something be done.

In each case, the revolution in communication technologies has magnified the horror of the events by broadcasting pictures of genocide, ethnic violence, the use of child soldiers, and starving populations. In a twenty-four-hour news cycle, the media report the abuses of governments and suppressed groups, and the Internet, Facebook, and Twitter are used to mobilize responses. Technology has led to pressure by states and individuals for a variety of governance activities. The fact that over 100 of the 193 member states of the UN are now democracies magnifies the pressure for human rights governance. The forces of liberalization and globalization have also contributed to the erosion of Westphalian state sovereignty and the gradual acceptance of international accountability for how states treat their citizens. The roots of human rights and humanitarian norms can be found in all major religions and in widely divergent philosophical traditions.

### Religious Traditions

Hinduism, Judaism, Christianity, Buddhism, Islam, and Confucianism all assert both the dignity of individuals and people's responsibility to their fellow humans. Hindus prohibit infliction of physical or mental pain on others. Jews support the sacredness of individuals, as well as the responsibility of the individual to help those in need. Buddhism's Eight-Fold Path includes right thought and action toward all beings. Islam teaches equality of races and racial tolerance. While the relative importance of these values may vary, Paul Gordon Lauren (1998: 11) notes that "early ideas about general human rights . . . did not originate exclusively in one location like the West or even with any particular form of government like liberal democracy, but were shared throughout the ages by visionaries from many cultures in many lands who expressed themselves in different ways."

### The Philosophers and Political Theorists

Like the world's religious thinkers, philosophers and political theorists have conceptualized human rights, although they differ on many specific issues and ideas. Human rights philosophers from the liberal persuasion traditionally have emphasized individual rights that the state can neither usurp nor undermine. John Locke (1632–1704), among others, asserted that individuals are equal and autonomous beings whose natural rights predate both national and international law. Public authority is designed to secure these rights.

Key historical documents detail these rights, beginning with the English Magna Carta in 1215, the French Declaration of the Rights of Man in 1789, and the US Bill of Rights in 1791. For example, no individual should be "deprived of life, liberty, or property, without due process of law." Political and civil rights, including free speech, free assembly, free press, and freedom of religion, deserve utmost protection according to liberal theories. By custom, these rights have been referred to as first-generation human rights. To some theorists and many US pundits, these are not only the key human rights but also the only recognized human rights.

Theorists influenced by Karl Marx and other socialist thinkers concentrate on those rights that the state is responsible for providing. Emerging from Marx's concern for the welfare of industrialized labor, the duty of states is to advance the well-being of their citizens; the right of the citizens is to benefit from these socioeconomic advances. This view emphasizes minimum material rights that the state must provide to individuals. Referred to as second-generation human rights, these include the right to education, health care, social security, and housing, although the amount guaranteed is unspecified. Without those guarantees, socialist theorists believe that political and civil rights are meaningless.

Some contemporary writers have focused on human rights for specific groups. Indigenous peoples have been given special consideration, as have children, women, migrant workers, the disabled, refugees, and most recently gay, lesbian, bisexual, and transgender persons. Several UN resolutions also affirm certain collective rights, including the rights to development, a clean environment, and democracy. There is much more controversy over these emergent third-generation human rights. Does the expansion of fundamental human rights actually dilute the very rights that others are trying to protect?

The contemporary debate revolves around the relative priority attached to these three generations of rights. In Western liberal thinking, political and civil rights are clearly given higher status, while in many other parts of the world, priority goes to economic and social rights or to collective rights such as the right to development. Such disagreements help explain the lack of political will for international human rights enforcement and implementation. Just as the West has dominated economic relations, it has dominated human rights standard-setting. Thus the strongest part of both international and regional human rights governance mechanisms protects civil and political rights, while the other two generations of human rights have received less attention, in part because it is more difficult to establish standards of compliance for economic, social, and collective rights.

## The Debate over Universalism and Cultural Relativism

Are all these human rights truly universal—that is, applicable to all peoples, in all states, religions, and cultures? Are they inalienable—that is, fundamental to every person? Are they necessary to life? Are they nonnegotiable—so essential that they cannot be taken away? Or are rights dependent on culture? Since the 1970s, some Islamists have questioned the notion of universal human rights. Two issues—the rights of Muslims versus non-Muslims and the rights of men versus women—have posed the most problems, reflecting conflicting interpretations of Islamic teachings and practice. One approach is to accept the notion of equality but offer reasons why the principle of equality is not undermined by different rules protecting one group over another (Mayer 2013). Another was evident at a 2003 conference in Beirut where Islamic human rights activists, NGOs, and some governments proclaimed the universality of human rights and rejected the use of either culture or Islam to restrict those rights.

In the early 1990s, a number of Asian states argued that the principles in the Universal Declaration and other documents represented Western values that were being imposed on them and that the West was interfering in their internal affairs with its own definition of human rights. They also argued that advocating the rights of the individual over the welfare of the community is not only unsound but also contrary to different cultural traditions.

Much of the debate has been clearly political, taking place between authoritarian states concerned about human rights intervention in their domestic affairs, and Western democratic states eager to promote political change. The debate over universality versus cultural relativism is particularly sensitive, however, with respect to issues of religion, women's status, child protection, family planning, divorce, and practices such as female circumcision.

The Vienna Declaration and Programme of Action, adopted at the 1993 World Conference on Human Rights, stated: "All human rights are universal, indivisible and interdependent and interrelated." Regional arrangements, the declaration stated, "should reinforce universal human rights standards." Yet even that document included the qualification that "the significance of national and regional particularities and various historical, cultural and religious backgrounds must be borne in mind." Thus, Stephen Hopgood (2013) argues that while universalism has been the promise of the past, today it is ill adapted to the diversity of the multipolar world.

## The Evolution of Humanitarian Norms

Just as human rights norms have emerged and changed over time, so too have humanitarian norms. Originating in the nineteenth century, humanitarian norms were developed to save lives and alleviate pain in zones of conflict, without regard to the underlying beliefs or political allegiance of individuals. Thus humanitarian principles were apolitical, their proponents maintained, providing relief in an impartial, independent, and neutral way. Yet as Michael Barnett (2005: 724) argues, during the 1990s those core principles "crumbled . . . as humanitarianism's agenda ventured beyond relief and into the political world and agencies began working alongside, and with, states." We explore the relationship between humanitarianism and human rights in more detail later.

## The Key Role of States:
## Protectors and Abusers of Human Rights

States, as the Westphalian tradition and realists posit, are primarily responsible for protecting human rights standards within their own jurisdiction. Many liberal democratic states have based human rights practices on political and civil liberties, while socialist states have developed socioeconomic protections. Since the late 1970s, more than a hundred states have created national and subnational human rights institutions, independent bodies with the power to promote and protect human rights domestically. While these institutions have taken different forms (national commissions, ombudsmen, special commissions), they empower local actors and help embed human rights norms domestically (Kim 2013). States are also responsible for protecting against human rights abuses committed by private actors, including business enterprises acting in their jurisdiction, and for providing redress for those whose human rights have been abridged.

Some Western states also attempt to take their domestic commitment to human rights and internationalize it by supporting similar human rights provisions elsewhere. At US insistence, support for human rights guarantees was written into the new constitutions in both Iraq and Afghanistan. The EU has required candidate members to show significant progress toward improving their records on political and civil liberties prior to accession. These states believe that it is in their national interest to promote human rights abroad, that states sharing those values are better positioned to trade with, and less likely to go to war with, each other.

States are not just protectors, however; they are also the primary violators of individual human rights. Both regime type and real or perceived threats to the state are explanations for states' abuse of their own citizens. In general, authoritarian or autocratic states are more likely to abuse political and civil rights, while less developed states, even liberal democratic ones, may be unable to meet basic obligations of social and economic rights or collective rights due to scarce resources.

All states threatened by civil strife or terrorist activity, including democratic ones, are apt to use repression against foes, domestic and foreign.

State security prevails over individual rights in such situations. In fact, the International Covenant on Civil and Political Rights acknowledges that heads of state may revoke some political and civil liberties when national security is threatened. The United States, for example, has faced allegations of human rights violations concerning the continued detention at Guantanamo Bay of persons linked to the 9/11 attacks, and China has faced regular criticism for infringements of freedoms of assembly and expression as well as for its suppression of Uighurs and Tibetans. Poor states or states experiencing deteriorating economic conditions are apt to repress these rights, in an effort by the elite to maintain power and divert attention from economic disintegration. Economically developed states may also have difficulty meeting the demands of economic and social rights for all citizens. And in some cases, those rights may be deliberately undermined or denied due to discrimination on the basis of race, creed, national origin, or gender. Finally, high degrees of fractionalization along ethnic, religious, or ideological lines in societies tend to bring out the worst abuses. For example, Iraq's Shiite-dominated government has been accused of actions against the country's Sunni Arabs, Kurds, Turkmens, Christians, and other minorities.

## International Human Rights Institutions and Mechanisms

IGOs, in particular the UN, and NGOs have played key roles in the process of globalizing human rights. They have been central to establishing the norms, institutions, and activities for giving effect to the idea of universal rights. The international human rights movement—a dense network of human rights–oriented NGOs and dedicated individuals—has been responsible for drafting much of the language of human rights conventions and for mounting transnational campaigns to promote human rights norms. These groups and individuals and the processes by which they have persuaded governments to adopt human rights norms demonstrate the power of ideas to reshape definitions of national interests, a process best explained by social constructivist theorizing.

### NGOs and the Human Rights Movement

Nongovernmental organizations have long been active in human rights activities, with anti-slavery groups being among the first and most active. In the late eighteenth century, abolitionists in the United States (Society for the Relief of Free Negroes Unlawfully Held in Bondage), Great Britain (Society for Effecting the Abolition of the Slave Trade in Britain), and France (Société des Amis des Noirs) organized to promote ending the slave trade. Although these groups were not powerful enough to effect immediate international change, the group in Great Britain was strong enough to force

Parliament in 1807 to ban the slave trade for British citizens. Less than a decade later, in 1815, the Final Act of the Congress of Vienna included an Eight Power Declaration that the slave trade was "repugnant to the principles of humanity and universal morality" (Lauren 1996: 27). Willingness to sign a statement of principles, however, did not mean states were ready to take specific measures to abolish the practice.

Many human rights and humanitarian NGOs formed around specific issues either during or immediately following wars. The ICRC was established in the 1860s to protect wounded soldiers, prisoners of war, and civilians caught in war. During and after World War I, numerous NGOs formed to protect women and children from the devastation. With World War II, humanitarian relief organizations grew in number, including groups like Catholic Relief Services, originally formed in 1943 as War Relief Services, to provide emergency aid to refugees fleeing conflict in Europe. Later its mandate expanded to include providing humanitarian relief to the poor, the displaced, and individuals suffering from natural disasters. CARE and Oxfam followed.

In the late 1970s, after the two international human rights covenants went into effect, the 1975 Helsinki Accords were signed to promote human rights in Eastern Europe and the Soviet Union. The 1976 riots in Soweto and murder of black South African leader Steve Biko and the growing number of "disappearances" and other human rights abuses in Latin America were widely publicized. US president Jimmy Carter made human rights a priority in US foreign policy and Amnesty International was awarded the 1977 Nobel Peace Prize. These events gave a boost to the establishment of a new generation of human rights NGO groups, including Helsinki Watch, the Mothers (and Grandmothers) of the Plaza de Mayo, and the National Endowment for Democracy, a quasi-NGO. With the Cold War's end and the rise of democratic states in the 1980s and 1990s, another generation of NGOs developed, including the Open Society Institute. Today there are thousands of human rights groups at the international, national, subnational, and grassroots levels. Amnesty International and Human Rights Watch are by far the largest, best-known, and most influential groups. Over time, discrete human rights NGOs have together forged the international human rights movement, due in part to the rise of investigative journalism and the attention it has brought to human rights issues (Neier 2012: 5). The information revolution has facilitated the movement's ability to transmit such information across borders.

Despite their diversity, human rights NGOs perform a variety of functions and roles, both independently and in conjunction with IGOs, in international human rights governance. These include educating the public, providing expertise in drafting human rights conventions, monitoring violations, shaming violators, and mobilizing public support for changes in national policies. They may also undertake operational tasks such as providing aid for victims of human rights abuses, training police and judges, and running programs to rehabilitate former child soldiers. In addition, NGOs provided much of the momentum for the UN human rights conferences of the 1990s, including the 1993 World Conference on Human Rights (Vienna) and the 1995 Fourth World Conference on Women (Beijing).

As discussed in Chapter 6, a major strategy used by NGOs generally involves organizing transnational campaigns on specific issues. In the human rights field, there have been a variety of such campaigns, including those against apartheid, child labor, and sweatshops, as well as those promoting the rights of indigenous peoples and migrant workers. Many of these campaigns have involved both local groups and transnational coalitions. With the Internet and social media, individuals and groups are able to voice their grievances swiftly to a worldwide audience and to solicit sympathizers to take direct actions. As constructivists have shown, these campaigns shape discourse and ideas, leading to learning across multiple constituencies and to norm creation.

One example of a media-driven effort illustrates the promise and problems of the campaign approach. Since the late 1980s, the Lord's Resistance Army in Uganda and its leader Joseph Kony have been kidnapping children in northern Uganda, using them as child soldiers and creating fear and intimidation among the population. Invisible Children, founded in 2004, is an NGO organized to call attention to this abuse through film and organized political activity. Over the years, it has presented a simplistic but graphic message aimed at Western audiences to fight against Kony. In 2012, a half-hour video piece titled "Kony2012" went viral, attracting 80 million hits. While all agree that this abuse represents an egregious violation of human rights, not everyone, including many in Uganda itself, agree with Invisible Children's solution—military action. So in constructivist discourse, NGOs can aid in the spread of ideas and they can use material resources for effect, but NGOs and campaigns in general also have the power to distort messages, to oversimplify complex problems, and to offer slick solutions. As discussed in Chapter 6, this can undermine NGOs' credibility and human rights campaigns in the long run.

As strong and vocal as the human rights NGOs are, they do not always get their way. At the 1993 Vienna Conference, for example, a number of key NGO demands were not included in the final document, such as rights of the disabled, AIDS victims, and indigenous peoples. NGOs were also restricted from participating in the drafting of documents.

Thus, NGOs are still not equal partners with states in human rights governance. Much of their success, however, has been due to opportunities presented by the League of Nations and the UN.

## The League of Nations

The League of Nations Covenant made little mention of human rights, despite persistent efforts by some delegates to include principles of racial equality and religious freedom. One fascinating story concerns the efforts by representatives of the Japanese government to convince the principals, including US president Woodrow Wilson, to adopt a statement on human rights and racial equality. As a victorious and economically advanced power, Japan felt it had a credible claim and that such basic rights would not be rejected. Yet the initiative was blocked, with the US representatives recognizing that such a provision would doom Senate passage of the peace treaty (Lauren 1996: 82–93). The League's Covenant did, however, include specific provision for protection of minorities and dependent peoples in colonies held by Turkey and Germany, the defeated powers of World War I. These were placed under the mandate system, whereby a designated victor nation would administer the territory and supervise it through the Mandates Commission until independence.

The Mandates Commission, despite having no right of inspections, acquired a reputation of being thorough and neutral in its administration. Britain administered Palestine, Transjordan, Iraq, and Tanganyika; France assumed the same role for Syria and Lebanon. They divided responsibility for the Cameroons and Togoland; Belgium administered Rwanda-Urundi; South Africa administered South West Africa; and Japan administered several Pacific islands. Between 1932 and 1947, pressure from the Mandates Commission led to independence for the Arab mandates of Lebanon, Syria, Iraq, and Transjordan, with Palestine a glaring exception. The mandates in Africa (Cameroons, Togoland, and Rwanda-Urundi) and in the Pacific were transferred to the United Nations trusteeship system in 1946, with South West Africa being the sole exception. South Africa continued to administer the territory as its own, despite several legal challenges, and a long campaign through the UN led by African states. South West Africa (Namibia) did not attain independence until 1989, as discussed in Chapter 7.

The idea of the mandate system was a triumph, giving those under its supervision a greater degree of protection from abuses than they would have enjoyed otherwise. The system reflected the growing sentiment that territories were not to be annexed following wars, that the international community had responsibilities over dependent peoples, and that the eventual goal was self-determination.

In addition, US president Woodrow Wilson's powerful promise of a right to self-determination brought groups from all over the world to the 1919 Paris Peace Conference. As a result, the rights of minorities and the corollary responsibilities of states were a major topic. Five agreements, known as the Minority Treaties, required beneficiaries of the peace settlement, such as Poland and Czechoslovakia, among others, "to assure full and complete protection" to all their inhabitants "without distinction of birth, nationality, language, race, or religion." These agreements also provided for civil and political rights and imposed similar obligations on remnants of defeated states to be guaranteed by the League of Nations. Later, the League made admission of new members contingent on a pledge to protect minority rights. Minority rights were a major agenda item for the League bodies, creating "significant precedents for increased international protection of human rights" (Lauren 1998: 117).

In other human rights activities, the League conducted a study of slavery after intensive lobbying by the British Anti-Slavery and Aborigines Protection Society and established the Temporary Slavery Commission, whose report led to the 1926 International Convention on the Abolition of Slavery and the Slave Trade. While not listing specific practices or including monitoring provisions, the treaty was pathbreaking in setting the standard regarding slavery.

The League also established principles for assisting refugees and created the first organization dedicated to refugee relief, the Refugee Organization. Pressed by NGOs, it devoted attention to the issues of women's and children's rights, as well as the right to a minimum level of health, and in 1924 approved the Declaration on the Rights of the Child. In the 1930s, the League Assembly even discussed the possibility of an international human rights document, but no action was ever taken.

Rights of workers were an integral part of the International Labour Organization's agenda, as discussed in Chapter 3. The ILO's mandate to work for the improvement of workers' living conditions, health, safety, and livelihood was (and remains) clearly consistent with concepts of economic and social rights. Because it did not die with the League, the ILO's work provided a foundation for other UN human rights activities.

### The United Nations

A very different climate shaped the drafting of the UN Charter. US president Franklin Roosevelt's famous "Four Freedoms" speech in 1941 called for "a world founded upon four essential freedoms," and his vision of "the moral order" formed a normative base for the Allies in World War II (Roosevelt 1941). The chilling revelation of Nazi concentration camps drew attention to human rights as an international issue. Thus, at the founding UN conference in San Francisco, a broad spectrum of groups, from churches to peace societies, along with delegates from a number of small states, pushed for the inclusion of human rights language. The Preamble reaffirmed "faith in fundamental human rights, in the dignity and worth of the human person, in the equal rights of men and women and of nations large and small." Although references to human rights were more weakly worded than advocates had hoped, there were seven such references in the

UN Charter, placing the promotion of human rights among the central purposes of the new organization.

The UN Charter adopted a broad view of human rights, going far beyond the view of the League of Nations. Included in Article 1 is the statement that the organization would be responsible for organizing cooperation in areas of a "humanitarian character," and "in promoting and encouraging respect for human rights and for fundamental freedoms for all without distinction as to race, sex, language, or religion." Articles 55(c) and 56 amplify the UN's responsibility to promote "universal respect for, and observance of, human rights and fundamental freedoms for all" and the obligation of member states to "take joint and separate action in cooperation with the Organization for the achievement of the purposes set forth in Article 55."

These provisions did not define what was meant by "human rights and fundamental freedoms," but they established that human rights were a matter of international concern and that states had assumed some as-yet-undefined international obligation relating to them. Despite the inherent tension between establishing international standards and Article 2(7)'s principle of noninterference in a state's domestic affairs, these provided the UN with the legal authority to undertake the definition and codification of human rights. The first step in this direction was laid by the General Assembly's passage on December 10, 1948, of the Universal Declaration of Human Rights. Taken together, the UN Charter and the Universal Declaration of Human Rights represented a watershed moment.

In 1946 and 1947, ECOSOC established the Commission on Human Rights, the Commission on the Status of Women, and the Sub-Commission on the Prevention of Discrimination and Protection of Minorities. Between 1946 and 2006, the Commission on Human Rights was the hub of the UN system's human rights activity. It was largely responsible for drafting and negotiating the major documents that elaborate and define human rights norms, including the Universal Declaration of Human Rights and the international covenants. It conducted studies and issued reports. Only in 1970, however, did the commission gain the authority to review complaints of human rights violations, and since it met just once a year, its sessions included hearing complaints and individual petitions as well as addressing major human rights themes such as racism and violations of human rights in Israeli-occupied Arab territories.

Beginning in the 1970s, the Human Rights Commission became the subject of intense criticism for targeting some countries while ignoring the records of other egregious violators. Between 1970 and 1991, a few cases, namely South Africa, Israel, and Chile (under Augusto Pinochet), received significant attention, while other violators were ignored. Nonetheless, an empirical study of the commission's actions from 1979 to 2001 found that "targeting and punishment were driven to a considerable degree by the actual human rights records of potential targets" (Lebovic and Voeten 2006: 863). By the mid-1990s, some 60 percent of the more egregious violators had been examined by the commission, a finding consistent with the 2002–2005 period. Still, there was a growing tendency to avoid direct criticisms of states (Forsythe 2009). In 2001, the United States lost its commission seat for the first time and a few well-known human rights abusers such as Sudan, Zimbabwe, Saudi Arabia, Pakistan, and Cuba were elected members and Libya was elected chair (2002), causing the criticism of the commission to intensify.

In 2006, the Human Rights Commission was replaced by the Human Rights Council, whose forty-seven members are elected by secret ballot by a majority of members of the General Assembly for three-year renewable terms distributed among the five recognized regional groups. The HRC meets at least ten weeks throughout the year and reports to the General Assembly. To address the problem of having human rights violators among the membership, the human rights records of all potential council members are subject to scrutiny, and the council can suspend actual members suspected of abuses with a two-thirds vote—a provision that has failed to remedy the problem.

The council responds to complaints by appointing either individual experts or working groups to address specific concerns or thematic issues (known as Special Procedures 1235 and 1503). For example, the HRC has a number of special rapporteurs for specific human rights issues, including one for the Palestinian territories. These are individuals who investigate abuses with the consent of the state concerned. Another tool is the Universal Periodic Review, whereby each UN member state's record is reviewed every four years based on three documents: a written national report prepared by the state itself; a summary prepared by the Office of the UN High Commissioner for Human Rights (UNHCHR) with input from other UN bodies; and a summary report by international human rights groups and other stakeholders. The process includes dialogue among several HRC members, representatives from the state under review, and national and subnational human rights institutions (Wolman 2014). In 2008, the HRC established a new Advisory Committee, a human rights think tank of eighteen experts that conducts studies for the council employing a variety of governmental and independent sources. The UN human rights system is illustrated in Figure 10.1.

Some of the HRC's work has attracted public attention. In 2013, for example, the council established the Commission of Inquiry on Human Rights in the Democratic People's Republic of Korea, and a year later this commission's 400-page report was released. With testimony from 80 witnesses and 240 confidential interviews, it cataloged in detail evidence of

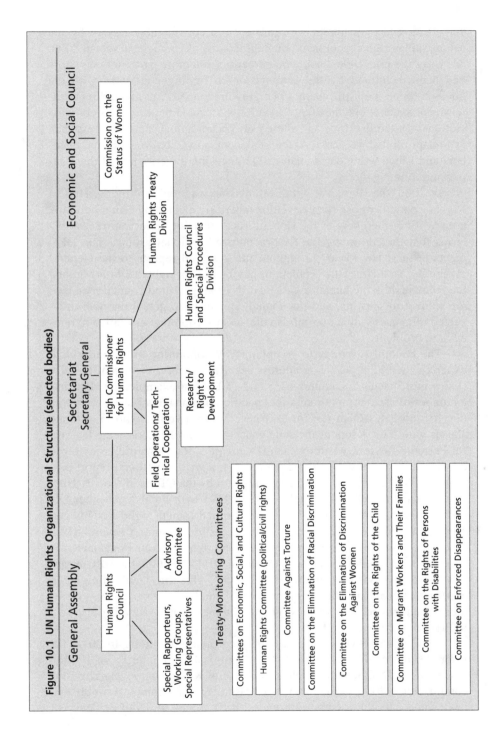

**Figure 10.1 UN Human Rights Organizational Structure (selected bodies)**

General Assembly

Secretariat
Secretary-General

Economic and Social Council

Human Rights
Council

Special Rapporteurs,
Working Groups,
Special Representatives

Advisory
Committee

High Commissioner
for Human Rights

Field Operations/Tech-
nical Cooperation

Research/
Right to
Development

Human Rights Treaty
Division

Human Rights Council
and Special Procedures
Division

Commission on the
Status of Women

Treaty-Monitoring Committees

Committees on Economic, Social, and Cultural Rights

Human Rights Committee (political/civil rights)

Committee Against Torture

Committee on the Elimination of Racial Discrimination

Committee on the Elimination of Discrimination
Against Women

Committee on the Rights of the Child

Committee on Migrant Workers and Their Families

Committee on the Rights of Persons
with Disabilities

Committee on Enforced Disappearances

systematic human rights abuses by the North Korean regime against its own citizens. North Korea vehemently denied the allegations. In late 2014, however, prompted by the report, the Security Council took up the subject of North Korea's human rights violations and the report's recommendation that the Security Council refer the problem to the ICC.

The Human Rights Council has legitimized an effort to consolidate an approach to businesses and human rights. In 2011 the council approved the "Guiding Principles on Business and Human Rights," a strong normative statement on how governments and businesses are expected to behave to protect human rights in a commercial setting, captured by the slogan "Protect, Respect, Remedy." The story of how that norm was created across various UN bodies and legitimated by the council is told by John Gerard Ruggie (2013), one of the architects, in the book *Just Business: Multinational Corporations and Human Rights.*

Despite these well-publicized actions of the HRC, we must ask: is the HRC less politicized than its predecessor, the Commission on Human Rights? One empirical study of four years of council decisions finds that the most controversial and polarizing resolutions are, indeed, sponsored by countries with blemished human rights records, including most notably Cuba, Egypt, and Pakistan (Hug and Lukacs 2014). A 2013 study of the P-5 and the first round of the Universal Periodic Review showed that France, the United Kingdom, the United States, and Russia all received many negative comments on their records while China primarily received positive ones, with all P-5 members participating. States accepted the recommendations and agreed to review the issues raised (Smith 2013: 13–14, 25). As transparent as the process was, the balance of comments clearly suggests a degree of politicization in the process.

The HRC shares its preeminent position with the UNHCHR, created in 1993. The latter provides a visible international advocate for human rights in the same way that the UN High Commissioner for Refugees focuses international attention on that problem. The office is responsible for mainstreaming human rights into the UN system, furnishing information to relevant UN bodies, promotion, and coordination. Increasingly, the UNHCHR is assuming an operational role, providing technical assistance to countries in the form of training courses for judges and prison officials, electoral assistance, and advisory services on constitutional and legislative reform, among other things (Mertus 2009b). With field offices in many countries, the UNHCHR is able not only to help strengthen domestic institutions, but also to promote compliance with international human rights standards and to report directly to the high commissioner on abuses.

The strength of the commissioner as an effective and vocal spokesperson depends on the individual personality of the officeholder. Both Mary Robinson, former president of Ireland, and Louise Arbour, former member of Canada's Supreme Court and chief prosecutor in the international ad hoc tribunals for Yugoslavia and Rwanda, elevated the effectiveness and prestige of the office. Likewise, South African judge Navanethem (Navi) Pillay, who served as high commissioner from 2008 to 2014, had a history of participation in human rights NGOs and was a strong and vocal commissioner, using her bully pulpit in 2014 to impose a deadline for the Sri Lankan government to initiate an inquiry into human rights violations during its civil war and to condemn the anti-LGBT legislation passed by Nigeria and Uganda. Yet the office, handicapped by its relatively small budget allocation (just 2 percent of the total UN budget), has had to appeal for voluntary contributions to perform essential tasks.

Although the former Commission on Human Rights and now the Human Rights Council have been the hubs for human rights activity in the UN, the General Assembly, by virtue of its central role for all issues, has also been important. In the General Assembly's first session in 1946, India and other countries introduced the issue of South Africa's treatment of its Indian population, beginning debate over what would become the UN's longest-running human rights issue: apartheid in South Africa. Colonialism was another prominent human rights issue during the UN's first twenty years, with debates over various colonial issues emerging out of the right to self-determination. Yet the General Assembly's role was circumscribed, because its members were seen as exercising a blatantly double standard. In the 1970s, for example, many third world states criticized white racism, Zionism, and neocolonialism, while at the same time ignoring issues of black racism, sexism in Muslim countries, and violations of human rights in the Soviet Union and Eastern European countries. That politicization of human rights undermined the General Assembly's legitimacy and effectiveness as a forum for human rights issues. Occasionally, however, the General Assembly has played a legitimizing role in introducing a new human rights issue, as illustrated in the LGBT case examined later in the chapter.

Neither the Security Council nor the International Court of Justice traditionally had significant involvement with human rights issues. In the case of the Security Council, this changed, however, in 1990. During the Cold War years, the Council linked security threats with human rights violations in only two instances: the unilateral declaration of independence by a white minority regime in Southern Rhodesia (now Zimbabwe) in 1965, and the white minority apartheid regime in South Africa. Both were treated as situations that threatened international peace and security, and sanctions were applied under Chapter VII of the UN Charter.

Since 1990, the Security Council has repeatedly been faced with threats to peace connected to large-scale humanitarian crises and demands for intervention under Chapter VII. Ethnic cleansing, genocide, and other crimes against humanity led it not only to authorize interventions and peacekeeping, as discussed in Chapter 7, but also to include human rights activities in the mandates for peacekeeping operations and to create two ad hoc war crimes tribunals. Peacebuilding operations have increasingly needed to address human rights protection. Thus the Security Council has embraced human rights norms and, in response to the push by human rights NGOs, routinely issues declarations on issues ranging from child soldiers to the role of women in promoting international peace and security.

The Rome Statute, which created the International Criminal Court, also gave the Security Council a role in referring situations involving war crimes and crimes against humanity to the ICC, used in two cases as of 2014—the situation in Darfur in 2005 and the situation in Libya in 2011. And the Security Council has the power to defer an ICC investigation or prosecution for up to twelve months. Yet Council referrals and deferrals risk fueling politicization of the ICC and undermining the legal principles on which international criminal justice is based because of the Council's selectivity in deciding what to refer (Arbour 2014: 198). The Security Council, however, is still hampered from addressing human rights issues when the interests of the P-5 or their allies are directly affected. In 2007, China and Russia vetoed a resolution on violations in Myanmar, and in 2008 they voted not to impose sanctions on Zimbabwe for its government's human rights violations. They claimed in both cases that such measures represented excessive interference in the country's domestic affairs. Yet in 2014 the Security Council unanimously condemned the violations of human rights and international humanitarian law by the Syrian government and authorized delivery of relief across the conflict lines, a major step, given Russian and Chinese opposition to all previous draft resolutions on the Syrian conflict.

The ICJ's role in human rights has also generally been minimal. It did confirm the principle of self-determination in the case regarding Western Sahara, noting that "self-determination requires a free and genuine expression of the will of the peoples concerned" (ICJ Advisory Opinion 1975). And it concluded that South Africa had violated its obligations toward South West Africa (Namibia) under the Universal Declaration of Human Rights (ICJ Advisory Opinion 1971). In 1993, the first case under the Genocide Convention was brought to the ICJ. It concerned the ongoing ethnic cleansing in Bosnia-Herzegovina. Indicative of the court's slow procedures, the case was decided only in 2007; a similar case involving Croatia and Serbia was begun in 2009 and concluded in 2015.

As legal scholar Louis Henkin (1998: 512) noted, "The purpose of international concern with human rights is to make national rights effective under national laws and through national institutions." If that is true, then the task of international organizations like the UN is particularly problematic, because it poses the possibility of interfering in the domestic affairs of states, which violates of the hallmark principles of state sovereignty. Yet the UN and regional organizations have undertaken a variety of functions and roles in creating processes for human rights governance, and states, too, are key players.

## The Processes of Human Rights Governance

Over seven decades, an international human rights regime has emerged that has articulated human rights norms and codified these standards in treaties, legal decisions, and practices. IGOs and NGOs have engaged in monitoring the human rights records of states, receiving reports of abuses and compliance, promoting norms of the regime, and enforcing compliance when states have committed gross violations of those norms.

### Setting Human Rights Standards and Norms

The prominent role of NGOs, transnational advocacy networks, and social movements in pushing for domestic laws and international treaties that set human rights standards has already been discussed. We can best illustrate NGOs' role here with a critical case. That role is well illustrated by the case of the anti-slavery movement. The UN and several regional IGOs have also played central roles in setting human rights standards.

*NGOs.* The nineteenth-century anti-slavery movement not only was one of the first examples of NGO activity, but also, as discussed earlier, helped create the norm prohibiting slavery. Supported by a diverse constituency in Great Britain, including religious groups (Quakers, Methodists, and Baptists), textile workers, rural housewives, and wealthy businessmen, the movement caught the attention of like-minded individuals in France and the Americas, forming what may be called the first transnational advocacy network. They worked tirelessly to abolish slavery, using a variety of tactics, including letter-writing, petitions, popular theater, and public speeches. They networked with others across the Atlantic, sending freed slaves on public speaking tours and exchanging strategies and information (Hochchild 2005). Later, the Anti-Slavery and Aborigines Protection Society played a key role in lobbying the League of Nations and in writing the 1926 International Convention on the Abolition of Slavery, as well as the 1956 Supplementary Convention on the Abolition of Slavery, Slave Trade, and Institutions and Practices Similar to Slavery. In the intervening quarter century, the group had expanded its agenda to include practices such as child labor, trafficking in human beings, and forced labor. In 1990, with a broadened orientation, the group changed its name to Anti-Slavery International. It and other NGOs continue to play key roles in setting human rights standards in many areas, since slavery in various forms, including human trafficking, continues to be a significant problem, as discussed in the opening case.

*The key role of the United Nations and treaty-making.* The UN's core role in the international human rights regime is its activity in defining and elaborating what constitutes internationally protected rights, initially in the Universal Declaration of Human Rights and the Convention on the Prevention and Punishment of the Crime of Genocide, both concluded in 1948. Under the leadership of Eleanor Roosevelt, who at that time was chair of the Commission on Human Rights, these documents articulated a far-reaching rights agenda. In particular, the Universal Declaration elucidated innovative principles: that people have these rights by virtue of being human; that they apply universally; that human rights include both political and civil rights and social and economic rights; and that advancement of these rights includes legislation, public discussion, and social monitoring. Almost seven decades later, the declaration continues to serve as a "rallying banner for the young, the poor, and the oppressed in their quest for a more just world" (Ramcharan 2008: 1). The expectation was that these rights would be set forth in treaties.

Although other human rights conventions were approved in the 1950s, it took until 1966 for the General Assembly to approve the International Covenant on Economic, Social, and Cultural Rights and the International Covenant on Civil and Political Rights. Both became operative in 1976 following the necessary number of ratifications. Together with the Universal Declaration, they are known as the "international bill of rights." That it took almost thirty years to define these legal standards suggests the difficulty of the task in a world where states jealously guard their national sovereignty. Indeed, not all states have ratified the covenants. The United States, for example, did not ratify the Covenant on Civil and Political Rights until 1992, and has yet to ratify the Covenant on Economic, Social, and Cultural Rights. Other states have ratified the covenants but attached reservations, declarations, or interpretative statements that in some cases undercut the whole intent. The same pattern is found with other human rights treaties such as the Convention on the Elimination of Discrimination Against Women (CEDAW). As of 2014, of the 188 parties to this convention, 62 had ratified with specific reservations, some on procedural issues and others on broader, more substantive issues such as provisions that conflict with sharia law. The price of ratification, therefore, has often been highly qualified, weaker conventions.

The covenants and the other human rights treaties exemplify the standard-setting character of the UN's role in human rights. Table 10.1 lists selected conventions by topic. These same standards are also found in national constitutions, legal documents, and court cases, as well as in regional human rights documents.

*Regional human rights standards.* Regional human rights bodies are also involved in the standard-setting process. Most have adopted similar stan-

**Table 10.1    Selected UN Human Rights Conventions**

| Treaty | Year Opened for Ratification | Year of Accessions | Number of Countries Ratified (2014) |
|---|---|---|---|
| **General human rights** | | | |
| International Covenant on Civil and Political Rights | 1966 | 1976 | 168 |
| International Covenant on Economic, Social, and Cultural Rights | 1966 | 1976 | 162 |
| **Racial discrimination** | | | |
| International Convention on the Elimination of All Forms of Racial Discrimination | 1966 | 1969 | 177 |
| International Convention on the Suppression and Punishment on the Crime of Apartheid | 1973 | 1976 | 109 |
| **Rights of women** | | | |
| Convention on the Elimination of All Forms of Discrimination Against Women | 1979 | 1981 | 188 |
| **Human trafficking and slave-like practices** | | | |
| Supplementary Convention on the Abolition of Slavery and the Slave Trade (1926) | As amended in 1957 | 1957 | 123 |
| Supplementary Convention on the Abolition of Slavery, the Slave Trade, and Institutions and Practices Similar to Slavery | 1956 | 1957 | 123 |
| UN Convention Against Transnational Organized Crime | 2000 | 2003 | 147 |
| **Refugees and stateless persons** | | | |
| Convention Relating to the Status of Refugees | 1951 | 1954 | 145 |
| Protocol Relating to the Status of Refugees | 1967 | 1967 | 146 |
| **Children** | | | |
| Convention on the Rights of the Child | 1989 | 1990 | 194 |
| Optional Protocol on the Involvement of Children in Armed Conflicts | 2000 | 2002 | 156 |
| Optional Protocol on the Sale of Children, Child Prostitution, and Child Pornography | 2000 | 2002 | 167 |
| **Other** | | | |
| Convention on the Prevention and Punishment of the Crime of Genocide | 1948 | 1951 | 146 |
| Convention Against Torture and Other Cruel, Inhuman, or Degrading Treatment or Punishment | 1984 | 1987 | 155 |
| Convention Concerning Indigenous and Tribal Peoples in Independent Countries | 1989 | 1991 | 22 |
| International Convention on the Protection of the Rights of All Migrant Workers and Members of Their Families | 1990 | 2003 | 47 |
| International Convention for the Protection of All Persons from Enforced Disappearance | 2006 | 2010 | 93 |
| Convention on the Rights of Persons with Disabilities | 2006 | 2008 | 147 |

*Sources:* University of Minnesota Human Rights Library, www.umn.edu/humanrts; UN High Commissioner for Human Rights, www.ohchr.org.

dards, although the relative importance attached to different kinds of rights has varied. The European system is viewed as the most successful system of human rights protection in terms of the consensus attained and the strength of the procedures established. The 1961 European Social Charter incorporates economic and social rights, including protections against poverty and sexual harassment. The 1953 European Convention on Human Rights and Fundamental Freedoms covers political and civil rights. The charter was revised in 1996 and all forty-seven members of the Council of Europe have ratified it.

The inter-American human rights regime, embedded in the Organization of American States and Inter-American Convention on Human Rights, highlights political and civil rights, although widespread abuses, including state-sanctioned disappearances in the 1970s and 1980s, undermined the regime. In the 1980s, Latin America experienced what has been called a "norms cascade," a rapid shift toward recognizing the legitimacy of human rights norms elucidated in the regional and international conventions (Lutz and Sikkink 2000: 638). In the 1990s, the OAS incorporated protection of democratic governments into its mandate, as discussed in Chapter 5.

The African Charter on Human and Peoples Rights, which was approved in 1981 and entered into force in 1986, is of special interest for two reasons. First, specific attention is given to third-generation rights—group and collective rights that are compatible with African traditions, including the right to development, to self-determination, and to full sovereignty over natural resources. Second, the African Charter is unique because of numerous "clawback clauses" that qualify or limit specific standards. For example, fundamental civil and political liberties are guaranteed except for reasons of law and order or for national security. Such clauses permit states to suspend fundamental rights with little protection and undermine the standards articulated in the African Charter (Mutua 1999: 358).

Conspicuously absent from the regional picture are Asian and Middle Eastern norms, standards, and institutions, although this is now changing in Southeast Asia. The ASEAN Charter, approved in 2008, included human rights for the first time. In 2009, the ASEAN Intergovernmental Commission on Human Rights was established, followed in 2010 by the ASEAN Commission on the Promotion and Protection of the Rights of Women and Children and in 2012 by the ASEAN Declaration on Human Rights. Even though civil society groups were critical of flaws in the declaration, these are major steps in a region where any discussion of international human rights norms has been considered inconsistent with the norm of noninterference. The mix of authoritarian, military, and democratic governments in the region, however, still makes it unlikely that there will be major progress in developing regional standards.

*States' commitment to and compliance with human rights treaties.* Why do states sign and ratify international human rights treaties? Do human rights standards and treaties actually change state behavior? The evidence is mixed on both questions.

Beth Simmons's study (2009: 28) of international law in domestic politics identifies three categories of governments on the question of why they ratify human rights agreements: the "sincere ratifiers," the "false negatives," and the "strategic ratifiers." The first and third are fairly self-evident; some governments genuinely support the rights covered by a particular treaty and expect to comply; others figure that by ratifying they may avoid criticism or improve their reputations at least in the short run. The United States illustrates the case of the "false negatives" in its long-standing pattern of refusing (or being unable) to ratify a number of conventions such as CEDAW and the Convention on the Rights of the Child despite its support for these rights on account of domestic political or institutional challenges that prevent ratification. The US federal system complicates implementation of international rights treaties because the national government's authority is constitutionally limited. The death penalty, for example, is a matter for state courts in the United States.

With regard to commitment, it is useful to study the wide variations in patterns of ratification of the various human rights treaties listed in Table 10.1. The Convention on the Rights of the Child has been ratified by all countries except the United States and Somalia; the Convention on the Rights of Migrant Workers has been signed by only thirty-eight countries and ratified by forty-seven as of 2014, more than a decade after it came into force. Furthermore, what the table does not show are the numbers and types of reservations that states have attached to their ratifications. Although more than 150 governments have ratified the Convention Against Torture, a significant number of them did so with reservations; the same is true for CEDAW. Not surprisingly perhaps, there are significant regional variations in the patterns of ratification, with the European countries having the strongest records, since commitment to democratic values and Western cultural mores are among the factors that tend to strengthen commitment to human rights (Simmons 2009: 65–66).

The ability of treaties to contribute to changes in states' behavior depends in large part on domestic politics. Compliance may therefore take place through domestic litigation and domestic executive and legislative processes by groups, including human rights NGOs, lawyers, and civil society activists, to translate treaty legal obligations into domestic law and practice and to aid the process of mobilizing support for change (Simmons 2009: 129–149). Compliance may depend on the presence of sympathetic NGOs. Emilie Hafner-Burton and Kiyoteru Tsutsui (2005), for example, have found that state ratification of six core international human rights treaties has led to changes in state practice if the issues covered by treaties are taken up by local NGOs that mobilize around the new standards and can use the treaty obligations to pressure governments. What both Hafner-Burton and Tsutsui (2005) and Simmons (2009), among others, have demonstrated is that increased NGO activity within a country, whether by local or transnational groups, or national and subnational human rights institutions such as provincial human rights councils and municipal ombudspersons, increases the likelihood that human rights treaties will have a positive effect on local human rights practices.

State judicial practices also matter. Milli Lake (2014), for example, shows how domestic and international actors have taken advantage of judicial processes in the eastern provinces of the Democratic Republic of Congo to compile a startlingly successful record in addressing rape and other sexual and gender-based violence in that fragile state. Other studies point to cases where ratification of treaties has led to significant changes in state behavior. Efforts by Turkey and Eastern European states to comply with European human rights conventions to boost their applications for EU membership illustrate the pull of compliance. As David Weissbrodt (2003: 89) aptly put it, "Getting countries to toe the mark is only possible when there is a mark to toe." Over time, the UN and some regional bodies have moved incrementally from articulating the standards to monitoring states' behavior.

## Monitoring Human Rights

Monitoring the implementation of human rights standards requires procedures for receiving complaints of violations from affected individuals or interested groups and reports of state practice. It may also be accompanied by the power to comment on reports, appoint working groups, and vote on resolutions of condemnation. Publicity and public shaming are key tools.

*UN approach.* The ILO was the first IGO to establish procedures for monitoring human rights within states, particularly workers' rights, as outlined in Chapter 3. The ILO's experience with monitoring is similar to the experience of other UN bodies. With only states represented in the UN and on the HRC, monitoring has had a checkered history. Only in 1967, for example, was the Commission of Human Rights empowered to examine gross violations in South Africa and Southern Rhodesia; three years later that authority was extended to include confidential investigations of individual complaints. Although this so-called 1503 procedure proved weak, during the 1970s the commission expanded its activities, creating working groups to study specific civil rights problems such as forced disappearances, torture, and religious discrimination. In its first report, in 1981, for example, the Working Group on Disappearances reported about 11,000–13,000 cases of disappearances from fifteen countries, ten of them in Latin America. By 1996, the same working group reported the virtual end of disappearances in the Western Hemisphere (Lutz and Sikkink 2000: 637). The 1503 procedure remains a way to pressure offending governments. Thematic and country rapporteurs as well as independent experts have been limited by minimal publicity, however. The Universal Periodic Reviews, described earlier, provide another monitoring mechanism. As states have fallen behind in meeting their obligations under the periodic review, however, in part because the process is burdensome, the reality of regular monitoring weakens.

Further initiatives in UN monitoring activities have accompanied the entry into force of specific treaties, many of which require states to submit periodic reports of their progress toward implementation. The General Assembly has established nine committees of independent experts, elected by the parties to each treaty and known as human rights treaty bodies, that review the reports and monitor treaty implementation. One of the most thorough is the Human Rights Committee, designed to process state reports under the International Covenant on Civil and Political Rights. It conducts open meetings, exposing states' human rights practices and its own actions to publicity by the media. These periodic reports are reviewed and discussed with states by the treaty committees. Human rights NGOs and national and subnational human rights institutions may also provide input.

Since the 1990s, there have been several significant developments in UN monitoring. These include the first human rights monitoring in conjunction with a peacekeeping mission, following the end of civil wars in El Salvador and Guatemala, as well as extensive involvement in election monitoring in conjunction with complex peacekeeping. Beginning in 1992, the Human Rights Committee removed the veil of secrecy and now publishes its conclusions. It has also appointed rapporteurs and special missions to address massive human rights violations in countries from Georgia and Colombia to the DRC.

Does UN monitoring make a difference? One argument contends that, over time, repeated condemnations can change attitudes, as was true, in part, in the case of South Africa. But that case is not entirely clear, since the repeated condemnations were subsequently coupled with more coercive sanctions. Another point of view holds that public monitoring, including naming and shaming, can antagonize states and harden their positions, leading to precisely the opposite of the intended effect. One study examined the question of monitoring by compiling data on efforts by the UN, NGOs, and news media between 1975 and 2000 to name and shame the human rights practices of 145 states. The data suggest that "governments put in the global spotlight for violations often adopt better protections for political rights afterward, but they rarely stop or appear to lessen acts of terror. Worse, terror sometimes increases after publicity" (Hafner-Burton 2008: 706).

In short, although UN human rights monitoring has increased, its impact is limited. Changing procedures does not necessarily result in changes in states' attitudes and behavior. The case of China suggests the difficulties. Following the 1989 Tiananmen Square massacre, the UN's Sub-Commission on the Prevention of Discrimination approved the first resolution ever directed against a P-5 member. Subsequently China became a target of attention, NGO interventions, and pressure from Western nations. Yet China fought back by challenging the independence of commission members, the secret voting, and NGO involvement. In 1991 it persuaded the United States and European Union to drop a resolution in return for China's offer not to veto a Security Council resolution on Iraq's invasion of Kuwait (Kinzelbach 2013: 168). China failed to block a resolution in 1995, but narrowly avoided condemnation when the vote failed. Its response was to offer to hold regular human rights dialogues, demonstrating the limits of UN monitoring of ongoing, systematic abuse of human rights by a powerful state. Ten years later, the UN Special Rapporteur on Torture made an official visit, only to find abuse "still widespread." Although China files required reports to treaty bodies, it continues to block efforts to examine its human rights record outside the Universal Periodic Review. Still, NGOs and other states have used that process to target China's actions in Tibet, against Muslim Uighurs in western China, and against other religious minorities as well as its restrictions on freedom of expression (Smith 2013: 16).

*European and other regional experiences with monitoring.* Of the regional human rights regimes, the European regime is the most effective for human rights monitoring. Under the European Convention on Human Rights, the European Commission of Human Rights is responsible for monitoring the general human rights situation, researching problem areas, conducting on-site visits, and engaging in promotional activities. Today the commission focuses on broader human rights issues, working directly with member states of the Council of Europe to improve human rights records.

The 1978 Inter-American Convention on Human Rights also established a dual commission and court system. The Inter-American Commission on Human Rights has monitoring responsibilities that include analyzing and investigating petitions from individuals who claim their rights have been violated by a member government. It receives about 1,500 petitions annually. The commission also issues requests to governments to adopt "precautionary measures" in cases where an individual is in harm's way. In 2013, among several hundred requests, requests to governments occurred in twenty-two cases. The commission decides whether the cases go to the Inter-American Court of Human Rights. Just over 1 percent of these petitions have been referred to the court.

The Inter-American Commission has also been active in issuing reports that outline human rights abuses. For example, it issued several reports on torture and arbitrary detention in Uruguay during the mid-1970s. Later in the 1970s and in the 1980s, it reported on abuses in Paraguay and conducted on-site investigations in Argentina and Nicaragua (Lutz and Sikkink 2000). Although final authority rested with domestic authorities, the monitoring and public condemnation of an abusive regime was a breakthrough. Still, the case of Ecuador illustrates the challenges. Ecuador's president Rafael Correa had a history of attacks on the press, and the OAS special rapporteur for freedom of expression had cited Ecuador for a number of incidents of infringement of press freedom. In 2012, Ecuador introduced recommendations to the commission that called for severe cuts to the special rapporteur's budget and for elimination of country reports, highlighting the difficulties of monitoring bodies calling attention to domestic abuses. In 2014, the commission visited the southern-border region of the United States as part of a monitoring report on the status of unaccompanied minors.

In Africa, the Commission on Human and Peoples Rights has had limited monitoring functions. It can consider state reports, collect documents, initiate studies, and disseminate information, but has no real monitoring or enforcement power. It has been hindered by the poor quality of the state reports submitted (Mutua 1999: 348–349). Thus, while the commission has had the authority to monitor behavior, in practice it cannot.

So the regional picture is a mixed one. The region where the human rights record is the best (Europe) is the one with the most active regional body involved in monitoring, but it is also the same region that is the most economically developed, has the most democracies, and has the strongest civil societies, all strong predictors of better human rights practices. Where abuses are greater, the monitoring system is weaker. Is it weak monitoring or underlying political and economic conditions that explain variations in human rights records among regions? In Asia and the Middle East, the lack of regional organizations with a human rights mandate means that human rights monitoring is left either to international institutions like the UN or to civil society or NGOs.

*NGO monitoring: Amnesty International and Human Rights Watch.* Given the relative weakness of regional IGO monitoring, a number of NGOs have stepped in to fill the gap. Amnesty International (AI), founded in 1961, was until 1981 the only NGO continuously monitoring human rights abuses and is perhaps the most well-known human rights NGO and among the most respected (Clark 2001). Emphasizing impartial and independent research, the AI secretariat, based in London, was traditionally organized along national lines, with individual researchers following specific cases over time. That information was utilized by individual chapters, which used the media and letter-writing campaigns to protect prisoners of conscience across all types of political systems. The approach facilitated direct links between those individuals and their supporters. Amnesty International often worked with sitting governments to advocate for the release of prisoners. High-profile cases maintained the momentum of the organization as "keepers of the flame" (Hopgood 2006). Its credibility as an independent and reliable information source and as an NGO with no political affiliation earned the organization the 1977 Nobel Peace Prize.

During the 1970s, Amnesty International, overwhelmed by the number of individual cases, began to move to support campaigns on broader cross-national issues. Although that change was controversial within the secretariat, AI mounted campaigns against torture and inhumane treatment of prisoners, the death penalty, violence against women, and, more recently, discrimination based on sexual orientation. In these situations, it has acted strategically, finding issues and states where there is reasonable likelihood of success. One empirical study of Amnesty International's background reports and press releases covering 148 countries between 1986 and 2000 found the organization concentrating on high-profile powerful countries, such as China, Russia, Indonesia, and the United States, while some of the most repressive states, including Afghanistan, Somalia, Myanmar, and Burundi, received considerably less attention (Ron, Ramos, and Rodgers 2005). Still, Amnesty International has maintained its credibility. There is evidence that it does not exaggerate human rights abuses in crisis situations, although it might be in their strategic interest for fund-raising purposes (Hill, Moore, and Mukherjee 2013). That credibility has led the US Department of State and various UN bodies to use AI information in their reports on states' human rights records.

Human Rights Watch (HRW), founded in 1978 following the Final Act of the Conference on Security and Cooperation in Europe, was designed to monitor progress in liberalizing Eastern Europe under the so-called Helsinki Accords. Originally named Helsinki Watch, it was also formed to mobilize the US government to take a more active stand on civil and political rights. The timing was auspicious, as then–US president Jimmy Carter was a vocal supporter of human rights. Transformed into Human Rights Watch, its reach became global and its focus expanded to all generations of human rights. It was Aryeh Neier, executive director of Human Rights Watch, who in 1992 proposed creating the ad hoc war crimes tribunal for Yugoslavia. Without his initiative, supported by a number of other NGOs, the tribunal would have never been established. And thanks to the courageous reporting and meticulous research of Alison Des Forges, HRW's representative in Rwanda, the organization was able to alert the international community to the cause of the Rwandan genocide.

While both Amnesty International and Human Rights Watch have expanded coverage of human rights issues, the two organizations differ. AI is a mass-membership organization (3 million individuals strong) with offices in eighty countries. Mobilization of its constituencies and networking are critical to its success, along with its attention to research. HRW relies more on the financial support of powerful foundations, in addition to individual contributions. With a smaller membership, it works to shame abusers by publicizing actions and working through governments.

Both organizations' monitoring, as well as that of other human rights organizations, is legitimized by their accurate documentation of abuses. On-site investigations are key, as is meticulous research. Armed with this information, human rights organizations have acquired sufficient legitimacy to pressure governments and international organizations and to develop networks with like-minded NGOs.

Grassroots and international NGOs, as well as IGOs, have taken full advantage of communication technologies since the UNHCHR launched its website in 1996. For the first time, NGOs had access to both official documents and government reports to the treaty bodies. As access to official information has become easier, the NGOs have become adept at using the Internet and social media. Whether in southern Mexico, Liberia, East Timor, Myanmar, or Tibet, grassroots NGOs have been able to get their messages out and form networks with like-minded groups. Through such networks, NGOs are able to articulate a moral consciousness, empower domestic opposition, and pressure governments themselves to pay attention to issues and situations (Risse, Ropp, and Sikkink 1999). In short, the change in communications used by both NGOs and IGOs has propelled human rights to the forefront of the international agenda in a way never before envisioned.

The experts that make up the UN human rights treaty bodies depend heavily on information compiled by NGOs, since many state reports are self-serving and rarely disclose treaty violations. So NGOs, with their unique local information base, along with national and subnational human rights institutions, have undertaken the task of evaluating such reports, gathering additional information, pushing states for compliance, and publicizing abuses. The relationships between NGOs and the treaty bodies vary, however. The Committee on the Rights of the Child enjoys the closest working relationship with NGOs, which regularly review state reports, maintain dialogue with local NGOs, and help to disseminate information. The Committee Against Torture calls upon concerned NGOs only on an ad hoc basis, while the Committee on the Elimination of Discrimination Against Women does not formally solicit information from NGOs. So while NGOs may enjoy a unique capacity to engage in monitoring, part of their ability to carry out this function depends on the political space provided by each separate treaty body.

National human rights institutions now have access to participate in the work of the Human Rights Council independent of their national delegations, while subnational institutions generally lack such access. Both the disabilities convention and the optional protocol to the torture convention, however, contain provisions that require state parties to set up, designate, or maintain mechanisms for implementation at subnational levels. This has led to subnational human rights institutions playing key roles as independent mechanisms for monitoring and reporting (Wolman 2014: 445–446).

Thus, IGOs and NGOs have developed unanticipated capacities for monitoring, but their measurable impact is still limited. Does naming and shaming work as a strategy? Amanda Murdie and David Davis (2012) examine the effects of human rights organizations' shaming on state behavior. Drawing on data from over 400 human rights organizations on shaming governments between 1992 and 2004, the authors find that states targeted by NGOs do improve their human rights practices. Shaming by international NGOs, however, proved not to be enough. Consistent with earlier findings, shaming is effective when there are both domestic NGOs present on the ground and advocacy by other third parties and individuals.

Changes in attitudes and behavior, however, also require proactive efforts to educate government officials, police, judges, and ordinary citizens about international human rights norms—tasks that promote human rights.

## Promoting Human Rights

Translating norms and rhetoric into actions that go beyond stopping violations and also change long-term attitudes and behavior is the challenge of promoting human rights. These efforts have been increasingly shared by the various actors in human rights governance.

*UN role.* The UN has played a far more active role in human rights promotion since the early 1990s. It has promoted democratization through its electoral assistance programs, both in conjunction with postconflict peacebuilding missions such as in Kosovo, Iraq, East Timor, and Afghanistan, and at the request of states needing assistance in reforming electoral and judicial institutions. The UN Electoral Assistance Division, created in 1992, provides technical assistance to states regarding political rights and democratization. More than a hundred member states have requested assistance in organizing and conducting democratic elections.

The UN role varies. Sometimes it involves certifying electoral processes, as it did in the contested Côte d'Ivoire election in 2010; sometimes it involves expert monitoring using personnel from the UN as well as regional organizations such as the OSCE and the OAS, or from NGOs like the Carter Center and the National Endowment for Democracy. Sometimes the UN shares that responsibility with states, as in Afghanistan in 2004–2005 and again in 2014, Iraq in 2005, and South Sudan in 2011. The UN provides technical assistance to states in developing credible, sustainable national electoral systems. In Afghanistan's 2014 presidential election, the UN was also responsible for overseeing the recount of all votes. Although international monitoring does not necessarily eliminate cheating or fraud, states gain legitimacy by having external monitors and are viewed as illegitimate if monitors are not present (Kelley 2008).

Since the early 1990s, the language of second- and third-generation human rights has increasingly been linked to development activities and programs across the entire UN system. Secretary-General Boutros-Ghali's *Agenda for Development* (1995) helped to make this connection through its emphasis on the right to development. Since the mid-1990s, the World Bank has promoted "good governance" in its development programs, including attention to the recipient's political and civil rights record and the empowerment of women and civil society actors. The UN is geared operationally to promoting those rights in a proactive way by integrating human rights norms, standards, and principles into policies and processes of development. The UNHCHR, as discussed earlier, has primary responsibility for overseeing the UN's promotional activities, supported by many of the specialized agencies.

In the case of the Democratic Republic of Congo, the Security Council's initial (1999) mandate for the UN mission there (MONUC and later MONUSCO, discussed in Chapter 7) recognized the need to "assist in the protection of human rights" and included creation of a technical assistance program and a rule-of-law section for judicial capacity-building. Support came from both the UN and the EU Commission. The UNDP has been a key partner in this process, launching a $390 million program in 2008. Part of the reform included the creation of a special police unit for the protection of women and children, with funding from USAID, the American Bar Association, CARE, and Save the Children. The NGO Avocats Sans Frontières, along with the UNDP, the EU, NGOs, and other governments, initiated a mobile courts program to spur a rapid legal response of investigations into crimes, hearings, and court decisions. Congolese authorities, including judges, retain jurisdiction over sentencing and enforcement (Lake 2014: 520–522). Clearly, the DRC case highlights the interaction between the UN and NGOs as well as other actors in promoting human rights.

*NGO role.* NGOs have been active in providing education on human rights in Cambodia, Central America, Kosovo, Afghanistan, and elsewhere. The Unrepresented Nations and Peoples Organization, for example, assists and empowers indigenous peoples such as Australia's Aborigines, circumpolar groups in the Arctic, and Native Americans to represent themselves more effectively by providing training in international and human rights law among other things. The NGO Cultural Survival has an extensive education and outreach program to raise awareness about indigenous peoples, ethnic minorities, and human rights. Through its publications, it has helped to shape the debate on the third-generation rights affecting indigenous peoples. And Amnesty International–USA, the National Endowment for Democracy, and the Open Society Institute have sponsored the development of human rights educational curricula and lobbied state and local educational boards for their adoption.

In the DRC case, international NGOs coordinate the schedules for the mobile courts program, collect evidence, recruit witnesses, and perform a number of other tasks that normally might fall to branches of the government. Congolese NGOs such as HEAL Africa conduct legal education as well as capacity-building for Congolese courts and legal practitioners and operate support structures for victims and witnesses that have facilitated their participation in legal processes. The availability of international grants to support such activities facilitates the process (Lake 2014: 522).

*Regional organizations.* Many of the regional IGOs in Europe, Latin America, and Africa undertake relatively noncontroversial and similar educational promotional activities with respect to human rights. For newly created states, or states wishing to join an organization, seminars are given regarding human rights and how to incorporate provisions for their protection into constitutions. For special groups, such as women, educational programs detailing specific rights are undertaken. There are training programs for judges, police, and teachers. Promotional activities are by their nature long-term solutions to human rights problems. They do not mitigate current abuses to enforce human rights compliance.

### Enforcing International Human Rights Norms
Of the various governance tasks in human rights, enforcement is the most problematic, since states generally have low stakes in enforcing other states' compliance and international institutions have limited capacity to compel compliance. Although the international community has increasingly undertaken various enforcement activities, states continue to be the major enforcers of human rights norms. States seeking to enforce human rights in other countries can generally take two approaches to enforcement: national courts and coercive measures.

*National courts.* Two cases illustrate the ways in which judicial action through national courts may be used to enforce international norms. Under the US Alien Tort Claims Act of 1789, federal courts in the United States have jurisdiction in civil cases filed by individuals of any nationality who are present in the country, for egregious acts committed in violation of the law of nations (i.e., international law) or a US treaty. In one much publicized case, *Doe v. UNOCAL* (2002), the US-based oil company was accused of complicity in using forced labor provided by the Burmese military government and of rape and murder during the construction of a gas pipeline in that country (Myanmar). The case was eventually settled in 2005 when the company agreed to compensate Burmese villagers and work to improve the quality of life for people in the pipeline region. Use of the Alien Tort Claims Act is increasingly controversial, however. In 2013, the US Supreme Court, in *Kiobel v. Royal Dutch Petroleum,* announced in a unanimous decision that the Nigerian plaintiffs could not sue in US courts on the grounds that they had only a minimal presence in the United States and the human rights abuses had occurred abroad. This case may provide a "chilling effect" on efforts to use US courts for relief of human rights violations abroad.

Another example of using national courts relying on international law to enforce human rights involves the case of former Chilean dictator Augusto Pinochet. Under a warrant issued by a Spanish judge seeking to extradite him, Pinochet was detained in Great Britain in 1998 for crimes allegedly committed while head of state. While some of those crimes were committed against Spanish nationals living in Chile, Spain also claimed universal jurisdiction on the basis of crimes against humanity, which any state can legitimately do. The Judicial Committee of Britain's House of Lords upheld Pinochet's arrest on the basis of international prohibitions against torture and murder and rejected his claim of sovereign immunity. Pinochet's ill health, however, was used as justification for turning him over to Chilean authorities and hence avoiding political repercussions. Although Pinochet was subsequently stripped of his immunity and indicted, his death in 2006 ended the prosecution. Spanish magistrates have continued to invoke universal jurisdiction, issuing arrest warrants in 2013 against several Chinese leaders for human rights violations in Tibet. As in the United States, however, this approach is increasingly controversial and the Spanish government is trying to limit the power of the judiciary to prevent judges from investigating crimes of genocide committed abroad. Still, the precedent has been set that under universal jurisdiction individual leaders can be held accountable in other jurisdictions for major human rights violations committed against their own people, thus loosening the Westphalian hold on sovereignty.

*Coercive measures.* Whereas national courts are used by individual plaintiffs, NGOs, or activist judges, governments and groups of states may take coercive actions. The international community may impose sanctions through the UN or regional IGO, authorize other enforcement measures, or initiate action through the Security Council to refer a case involving war crimes or crimes against humanity to the International Criminal Court. The case of apartheid in South Africa illustrates how governments themselves may take unilateral coercive measures against other states. While the UN General Assembly recommended international sanctions against that country for its apartheid policy, little happened until the 1980s, when key states changed their policies. Responding to a public campaign of civil disobedience, the US Congress called for a review of US policy and for sanctions and, in 1986, approved the Comprehensive Anti-Apartheid Act over a presidential veto. Other powerful states followed suit, including Great Britain. The imposition of sanctions boosted the morale of apartheid opponents and inflicted pain on the South African business community and, through it, the government. The sanctions, along with the persistent campaign by the international community, were partly responsible for ending apartheid in the early 1990s and the installation of a majority democratic government in 1994.

A second instance illustrates the difficulty of sustaining sanctions. Following China's crackdown on dissidents and the Tiananmen Square massacre in June 1989, the United States along with Japan and EU members instituted an arms embargo against China, suspended export credits and official visits, and got the World Bank and Asian Development Bank to cancel new lending to China. Some estimate that the coercive actions may have cost China over $11 billion in bilateral aid over a four-year period. By 1990 Japan had ended its sanctions, and in 1994 the United States granted most-favored-nation status to China without human rights conditions attached (Donnelly 1998: 120–124), each bowing to economic pressures.

Studies of foreign aid donors' use of sanctions to punish repressive states suggest that donors use negative sanctions for human rights abuses selectively and that an aid recipient's human rights record plays at best a limited role in aid allocation. Richard Nielson (2013), for example, found that aid sanctions are used when the donor has few close ties with the violator, when violations negatively affect the donor, and when violations are widely publicized. Furthermore, donors are likely to cut aid to economic sectors yet continue aid for basic social services. Countries with strong human rights traditions, however, are "*less* likely to sanction rights violations," leading Nielson (2013: 800–801) to suggest that "supposedly moral policies may be adopted for amoral reasons: to pursue state interests."

*UN enforcement.* The UN's enforcement authority, as discussed in Chapters 4 and 7, is found in Chapter VII of the UN Charter. Under that provision, if the Security Council determines that human rights violations threaten or breach international peace, it has the authority to take enforcement actions. Yet in the two Cold War cases of enforcement discussed earlier, the Security Council failed to make an explicit linkage between human rights violations and security threats. The sanctions weakened the minority regimes, but did not directly change their policies.

Whether UN sanctions should be instituted against governments responsible for gross violations of human rights is still highly controversial, as the case of Zimbabwe illustrates. Since 2000, the regime of Robert Mugabe has engaged in systematic human rights abuses against its citizens and undermined the democratic process. In 2008, the United States and EU proposed targeted UN sanctions against Mugabe and other Zimbabwean officials (specifically travel bans and asset freezes), but Russia and China vetoed the draft resolution. The EU had instituted sanctions in 2002 and the United States in 2003, each targeting individual members of the regime, but not the government as a whole or the business community. Gradually each has relaxed the sanctions, reducing the number of individuals on the list, in hopes of encouraging political reform.

Enforcement action may also involve the use of military force. Since the Cold War's end, enforcement actions have been authorized under Chapter VII to deal with numerous ethnic conflicts that have produced egregious human rights violations and tough policy dilemmas for states, IGOs, and NGOs. Ethnic cleansing in Bosnia and Kosovo, genocide in Rwanda and Darfur, famine and state collapse in Somalia, systematic rape and chaos in the DRC, and Qaddafi's threats against his own people in Libya have all led to humanitarian interventions involving UN or regional peacekeeping forces to protect individuals from abuse. As discussed in Chapter 7 and illustrated by the discussion of genocide later in this chapter, humanitarian intervention, particularly R2P, is still a contested norm. When applied, however, it demonstrates international will to use the UN to enforce human rights and humanitarian norms.

A major step in human rights enforcement has involved the expansion of international criminal law with trials of individuals charged with war crimes and crimes against humanity in ad hoc tribunals, in hybrid courts, and through the International Criminal Court.

*Ad hoc war crimes tribunals.* The desire to punish individuals responsible for war crimes during World War II led to the establishment of the first war crimes tribunals. Because the Nuremberg and Tokyo trials were the victor's punishment, they were not regarded as precedents for future wartime crimes, however. Yet in the 1990s, the idea of individual responsibility for war crimes and crimes against humanity was revived in the face of the atrocities committed during conflicts in the former Yugoslavia and Rwanda. Frustrated by the international community's inability to bring to justice those responsible for crimes and prodded by human rights activists, the UN Security Council established the International Criminal Tribunal for the Former Yugoslavia (ICTY) in 1993, followed by the International Criminal Tribunal for Rwanda (ICTR) in 1994, and facilitated the creation of other hybrid courts. Each of these courts began slowly, developing structures and procedures, hiring personnel, and winning the cooperation of states.

The ICTY, employing twenty permanent judges and three separate proceedings, as well as over 750 staff members from seventy-six countries, developed answers to questions of authority, jurisdiction, evidence, sentencing, and imprisonment. As of 2014, the court had completed proceedings for 141 out of 161 persons indicted. Of those cases, seventy-four individuals were sentenced, thirteen were transferred to countries in the former Yugoslavia for trial, while thirty-six cases were terminated or indictments withdrawn, including that of former Yugoslav president Slobodan Milosevic, who died during the trial in 2006. Eighteen individuals were acquitted. The 2008 capture of Radovan Karadzic, wartime leader of the Bosnian Serbs, followed in 2011 by that of former Serb general Ratko Mladic, led to their indictment for the 1995 killing of almost 8,000 Bosnian Muslim men and boys in Srebrenica and torturing and sexually assaulting non-Serbs. Their capture, transfer to The Hague, and prosecution added two high-profile cases to the ICTY docket, which as of 2014 still had eighteen other cases in process. The accomplishments of the ICTY include developing procedures for establishing the relevant facts, providing victims a forum in which to be heard, and fleshing out international laws on war crimes, genocide, and torture. Some accountability has been achieved and the rule of law strengthened. While its proceedings have bogged down in technicalities and the costs have escalated to $250 million as of 2012–2013, the ICTY has developed a body of jurisprudence and its procedures have paved the way for the ICTR and other tribunals, including the ICC.

The ICTR has also been criticized for its slow proceedings and high cost, attributed in part to its location in Arusha, Tanzania. Nonetheless, by the end of 2014, all the trial work had been completed for the ninety-four accused; fifty-two individuals had been convicted; an additional eleven cases remained on appeal; twelve individuals had been acquitted; two persons had been released; two had died before their trials were completed; and ten were transferred to national jurisdiction. The very first trial, of Jean-Paul Akayesu, set a key precedent when the court concluded that rape (a strategy used against Tutsi women) is a crime of genocide. Among those convicted are a former prime minister and the highest authority in the Rwandan defense ministry, convicted in 2008 for the killing of the Rwandan prime minister, the president of the constitutional court, and three top opposition leaders.

These two tribunals had set 2014 as termination dates. The ICTR was closer to conclusion, however, than the ICTY at that point. Both have elaborated on the Geneva Conventions, established many precedents in procedure, and applied international humanitarian law to internal armed conflicts.

*Hybrid courts.* In 2002 and 2008, two courts employing national and international law, procedures, and jurists were established by agreements between the UN and the governments of Sierra Leone and Cambodia to judge individual criminal responsibility for crimes against humanity and war crimes. In theory, such courts, because of their proximity, may have greater cultural sensitivity and hence more legitimacy, although because they operate with voluntary contributions, they have fewer resources. The Special Court for Sierra Leone tried individuals for crimes against civilians and UN peacekeepers during that country's civil war (1991–2002). Of ten persons tried, nine were convicted and sentenced; two others died before proceedings commenced; a third escaped. The most well-known defendant was Charles Taylor, the former Liberian president, who was convicted in 2012 of terrorism, participation in a joint criminal enterprise, planning attacks on three cities, war crimes, and crimes against humanity in aiding the two rebel groups in the Sierra Leone civil war. This made him the first former head of state found guilty by an international criminal tribunal. His trial was held in The Hague and he is serving his sentence in a UK prison. The Sierra Leone tribunal concluded its work at the end of 2013.

The Khmer Rouge Tribunal (Extraordinary Chambers in the Courts of Cambodia) has faced significant difficulties in its trials of individuals charged for their roles in the Khmer Rouge regime and the deaths of 1.7 million Cambodians by starvation, torture, forced labor, and execution between 1975 and 1979. The length of time that has passed makes gathering evidence difficult. The first trial, against "Duch," the former chair of the central prison in Phnom Penh, concluded in 2010 and his conviction was upheld on appeal in 2012. Trials of two other survivors from the Khmer leadership concluded in 2014 with their conviction and sentencing; another two trials were terminated by death and illness; five additional suspects were still under investigation in late 2014; and three suspects were charged in early 2015. The Cambodian government has repeatedly tried to block the court proceedings. The question of whether these trials are, in fact, achieving the goal of bringing justice to Cambodia and promoting national reconciliation remains an open one.

There are a number of other hybrid, mixed, or internationalized courts now that vary in makeup and procedures as well as in how they link national and international law. These include programs in Kosovo, Lebanon, and Timor Leste. Clearly, however, efforts to find ways to hold individuals accountable for various types of crimes under international humanitarian law continue. How well these courts serve justice is another question.

*The International Criminal Court.* In 1998, in light of the difficulties posed by the ad hoc nature of the tribunals for Yugoslavia and Rwanda and a long-standing movement to create a permanent international criminal court, UN members concluded the Rome Statute for the International Criminal Court. The Coalition for the International Criminal Court, an umbrella group of 2,000 NGOs, mobilized international support for the ICC and promoted ratification of the statute, and today continues with promotional activities. The ICC is officially recognized as an independent permanent judicial institution, but it reports its activities to the UN Secretary-General, has observer status in the General Assembly, and may address the Security Council.

The ICC began to function in 2002 and its first judges (eighteen) and prosecutors were chosen in 2003. As of 2014, 122 states had ratified the Rome Statute, including all European and South American states, but still representing only a minority of the world's peoples. Prominent among the absentees are China, India, Iraq, Turkey, and the United States. Perhaps most controversial was Palestine's decision to join the court in 2015.

When inaugurated, the ICC was called "the most ambitious initiative in the history of modern international law" (Simons 2003: A9). It enjoys both compulsory jurisdiction and jurisdiction over individuals, in contrast to the jurisdiction of the ICJ. The court has jurisdiction over "serious" war crimes that represent a "policy or plan," rather than just random acts in wartime. Abuses must be "systematic or widespread." Four types of crimes are covered: genocide (attacking a group of people and killing them because of race, ethnicity, religion); crimes against humanity (murder, enslavement, forcible transfer of population, torture); war crimes; and crimes of aggression (initially undefined). No individuals (save those under eighteen years of age) are immune from jurisdiction, including heads of state and military leaders. The ICC functions as a court of last resort in that it can hear cases only when national courts are unwilling or unable to deal with grave atrocities. Prosecution is forbidden for crimes committed before July 1, 2002, when the court came into being, and individuals must be present during the trial. Anyone—an individual, government, group, or the UN Security Council—can bring a case before the ICC.

As of early 2015, there were twenty-two cases on the ICC docket addressing war crimes or crimes against humanity in nine "situations," all African cases, including individuals in the Central African Republic, Côte d'Ivoire, Darfur, the Democratic Republic of Congo, Kenya, Libya, and Mali. Four states had referred cases; those in Côte d'Ivoire and Kenya were initiated by the ICC prosecutor; and the two others were referred by the UN Security Council. Preliminary examinations of other potential cases in Afghanistan, Colombia, Georgia, Guinea, Honduras, Iraq, Nigeria, Palestine, and Ukraine were at various stages of investigation in early 2015.

The ICC initiated its first trials in 2009 after almost seven years of preparatory work ranging from the selection of initial judges and appointment of the chief prosecutor to developing the processes for investigations and selecting cases, establishing court regulations, and evaluating issues of jurisdiction and admissibility (Schiff 2008: 102–143). For the two ad hoc criminal tribunals, whose missions were much clearer than that of the ICC, these processes had taken about two years. As of late 2014, the ICC had tried, convicted, and sentenced two defendants, both Congolese warlords, and acquitted a third individual. Thomas Lubanga Dyilo was convicted of war crimes in recruiting child soldiers, while Germain Katanga was found guilty of both war crimes and crimes against humanity in attacking a village in eastern DRC, but acquitted of rape and using child soldiers. In 2009, the ICC, in its first indictment against a sitting president, charged Sudan's Omar Hassan al-Bashir and three associates with war crimes and crimes against humanity. In 2011, an indictment was issued against Uhuru Kenyatta and two other Kenyans for their role in the interethnic violence following the 2007 presidential election. Although it had initiated the ICC proceeding, the Kenyan government sought to defer the trials. Kenyatta became president in 2013 and efforts to postpone the trial or change court procedures continued until late 2014 when the case was dropped for lack of evidence. Still, President Kenyatta set an important precedent when he appeared in person before the court. In the Sudanese case, the ICC prosecutor suspended investigations in late 2014 because no arrests had been made in a decade and the Security Council and member states had been unwilling to take further action. In March 2015, the ICC asked the Security Council to take steps to enforce compliance. Many international jurists view the case and the court's ability to carry out prosecution as a test of the court's credibility.

The prevalence of African cases at the ICC and the high-profile cases of Presidents Bashir and Kenyatta has sparked a strong backlash against the ICC in Africa. The UN Security Council rejected Kenya's request to delay proceedings, nonetheless, while the African Union, Organisation of Islamic Cooperation, and Arab League accused the court of racism and neocolonialism. President Bashir himself openly defied the court, while some African leaders mounted a campaign to press African states to withdraw from the ICC. A counter-movement has also been launched by an international advocacy group, Avaaz, calling on African leaders to stay in the ICC.

Even Western advocates for the ICC are becoming increasingly disillusioned. Is the $1 billion cost for just two convictions worth the price? Is the annual budget of $166 million justified? As one reporter (D. Davenport 2014) remarked, "small fish, few cases, fewer convictions, arrest warrants ignored, all while the Court burns through millions of dollars a year in The Hague. It seems evident that something is wrong with this picture."

Consider the case of the United States and the ICC. Historically, the United States supported international accountability for war crimes, but ended up opposing the ICC and "unsigning" the Rome Statute in 2001. One major concern was the possibility that the ICC might prosecute US military personnel or even the US president without US approval. More generally, the United States asserted that the ICC infringes on its sovereignty and, as a world power, it has "exceptional" international responsibilities that should make its military and civilian leaders immune from the ICC's jurisdiction. It would have preferred an international court whose powers depended upon approval by the UN Security Council. To shield itself from ICC juris-diction, the United States negotiated bilateral immunity and impunity agreements with over a hundred countries that promised not to turn over indicted US nationals, as permitted under Article 98 of the ICC statute. Economic aid to countries not signing such agreements can be suspended. The 2003 American Service-Members Protection Act offers another mea-sure of protection.

In reality, the United States has ended up taking a more pragmatic approach. In 2005 it abstained on the Security Council resolution referring Darfur/Sudan to the court, and in 2011 it voted in favor of referring Libya. It has sent US troops to assist in capturing Joseph Kony. In 2014, the US pushed a Security Council draft resolution to refer Syria to the court, know-ing full well that it would fail, but also inserting language to block any investigation into the Golan Heights occupied by Israel, any prosecution of US soldiers, and any US financial support for the court. Clearly, the United States supports the ICC "only when it suits the administration's foreign pol-icy agenda, using the threat of prosecution to skewer its foes while protect-ing its friends from its reach." The danger, however, in such a selective approach is that international criminal justice and the ICC could become increasingly politicized, undermining their credibility (Sengupta 2014b).

These international criminal proceedings raise key dilemmas, since the ICC, ad hoc courts, and hybrid courts are not just judicial bodies, but also political entities whose decisions affect interstate relations. If states like Cambodia try to limit a court's reach and the court accepts the limitations, its legitimacy as an independent judiciary may be undermined. If states reject a court's indictment, as Sudan has done, and its president openly defies the ICC's order to arrest him, then the court's legitimacy is tarnished. And if states cooperate out of purely political motives, like Serbia and the United States, then a court's credibility as a judicial body may likewise be undermined.

Perhaps even more vexing is the tension between peace and justice. The jurisdiction of the international criminal courts extends to crimes committed during time of wars or conflict. Yet seeking to hold key individuals responsible for those crimes might jeopardize the possibility of securing long-term peace. Thus, is it more critical to try individuals for wrongdoing or to ensure a peace? Might international prosecution actually prolong ongoing conflicts if key individuals refuse to negotiate peace out of fear of punishment? The 2005 ICC indictment of Joseph Kony just when a peace agreement seemed possible may explain his disappearance. Likewise, the indictment of the Sudanese president and his defiance of the court have contributed to the failure of efforts to secure peaceful resolution of the Darfur conflict. Unquestionably, civilians in the region have suffered still more, as the government expelled humanitarian aid agencies in 2009 and 2010 in retaliation for the arrest warrant for President Bashir. Thus, international criminal courts may punish the responsible in the name of justice, but jeopardize the possibilities of achieving peace and stability in a country or region (Schiff 2008; Snyder and Vinjamuri 2003–2004). Regional human rights courts do not face these same dilemmas, since their jurisdiction covers different types of human rights violations.

*Regional enforcement.* With mandatory jurisdiction over forty-seven member states and 800 million people, the European Court of Human Rights (ECHR) is the only regional court that has enforcement mechanisms. In the European Convention on Human Rights, two-thirds of the articles deal with enforcement. Over time, the ECHR's caseload has increased exponentially, with 91 percent of the judgments occurring since 1998. Over 50,000 applications are submitted annually, although 90 percent are ultimately proclaimed inadmissible. Between 1958 and 2011, the court issued 14,940 binding rulings (Alter 2014: 73). The subjects include controversial issues in political and civil rights such as challenges to Great Britain's policy of collecting and keeping fingerprint and DNA samples of all criminal suspects (even those later found innocent); Bulgaria's procedures for fair trials and sentencing; and Poland's permitting of US Central Intelligence Agency "black sites" where prisoners were mistreated and tortured during the US-led global war on terror.

The ECHR's judgments are directly enforced in the national courts of states that are parties to the European Convention on Human Rights. States are obligated to inform the Council of Europe of actions taken to comply with the court's judgment. Sometimes that means paying compensation, which is relatively easy to enforce. National laws or practices may need to be changed, making it more difficult to ensure enforcement. Bulgaria, for example, had to strengthen its laws after a 1998 decision found its legal procedures inadequate for investigating charges of wrongdoing by police and other officials. While occasionally states choose not to enforce the court's decisions, the European system exhibits the only case of states yielding sovereignty to an international human rights court that can enforce its judgments.

Among the other regional courts, the Inter-American Court of Human Rights is the most active, hearing appeals from the twenty member states of the Inter-American Commission on Human Rights, as well as from individuals, totaling roughly 1,500 petitions annually. It also issues several hundred requests to states each year to adopt "precautionary measures" where individuals are at risk of harm. Twenty-two of its thirty-five members have accepted compulsory jurisdiction. Between the court's founding in 1979 and 2011, it had issued 239 binding rulings and 20 advisory opinions (Alter 2014: 73). In 2011, the Inter-American Court issued a landmark ruling requiring states to investigate human rights violations and punish those responsible, regardless of amnesty laws that had been passed to protect former officials of military regimes. As part of the efforts to enforce human rights standards, the Inter-American Commission also conducts on-site visits and reports on human rights situations.

As discussed in Chapter 5, the 2001 Inter-American Democratic Charter helped broaden the conditions under which the OAS may act in the event of an unconstitutional regime change in a Latin American state that undermines the regional commitment to democracy. While not legally binding, the charter has been used on several occasions to apply diplomatic pressure on Haiti, Honduras, Venezuela, Ecuador, Bolivia, and Nicaragua (Hawkins 2008). Together, the commission and the court have increasingly taken on the "pivotal role of condemnation and early warning in response to situations that undermine the consolidation of democracy and rule of law" in the hemisphere (Dilitzky 2012: 11).

The African Court of Human and Peoples Rights became operational in 2006, following the entry into force in 2004 of the Protocol to the African Charter on Human and Peoples Rights. It has its seat in Arusha, Tanzania, and is composed of eleven judges serving six-year terms. Between receipt of its first case in 2008 and 2014, the court handled twenty-eight cases, finalizing twenty-three of them, with five contentious cases pending in 2014. A 2013 judgment, for example, found Tanzania had violated several articles of the African Charter, including rights to freedom of association. The court directed Tanzania to take constitutional, legislative, and other measures to remedy the violations.

Limiting the reach of the African court, however, is the fact that only half of the AU's fifty-four members have ratified the protocol and become parties, despite the AU's encouraging of member states to use the court rather than the ICC. In a further indication of many African states' desire to keep human rights enforcement within Africa, the 2008 AU summit approved a protocol to merge the African Court of Human and Peoples Rights with a yet-to-be-established African Court of Justice, to form the African Court of Justice and Human Rights. The court's jurisdiction would extend to cases of genocide. A 2014 amendment to the protocol, if ratified, will give heads of state and other senior officials immunity from prosecution. This would make the proposed court a very different entity, as the jurisdiction of all other international criminal courts has applied equally to all persons. As of early 2014, only five countries had ratified the protocol, however.

*Nonstate enforcement efforts.* Nonstate actors, strictly speaking, lack capacity to compel compliance with human rights norms through coercive measures. Debate among NGOs, for example, has focused on whether or not to join with states and IGOs in supporting sanctions and boycotts against offending states. Many NGOs have feared that taking sides by supporting sanctions might jeopardize neutrality and hence their effectiveness and legitimacy. The World Council of Churches confronted this dilemma beginning in the late 1960s. The council adopted two enforcement approaches: money disbursed to liberation groups in southern Africa to support their struggle against white minority regimes, and participation in a global campaign to pressure MNCs to change behavior or withdraw investment from the region. Their strategy resonated with most but not all of the council's membership and was one part of the global campaign to end racial discrimination in southern Africa.

As a result of the creation of the UN Global Compact and other initiatives regarding corporate behavior, MNCs and international businesses, while not technically enforcers, increasingly are viewed as having the duty to respect human rights, meaning not infringing on the rights of others and addressing harms that do occur (Ruggie 2013). Thus, businesses have the responsibility to establish expectations of adherence to human rights norms and to work to ensure that those policies are reflected in corporate operations.

## Global Human Rights and Humanitarian Governance in Action

Of the many human rights and humanitarian issues, four in particular—genocide and ethnic cleansing, violence against women, LGBT rights, and refugees—help to illustrate the strengths and successes, and the weaknesses and failures, of global human rights governance in action.

## Genocide and Ethnic Cleansing

Despite the rhetoric of "never again," genocide continues to take the lives of millions. The Holocaust of World War II was a key event, but genocides occurred before (the Belgian Congo in the late nineteenth century, Armenia in 1915) and after (East Pakistan, Cambodia, Iraq, Rwanda, Darfur, and South Sudan). Yet prior to 1944, the term *genocide* did not exist. It was coined by a Polish lawyer, Raphael Lemkin, a tireless advocate for recognition of the crime, although he did not live long enough to see the UN's Convention on the Prevention and Punishment of Genocide ratified by his adopted country, the United States (Frieze 2013). The convention was drafted after a laborious two-year process in ECOSOC's Ad Hoc Committee on Genocide, and unanimously adopted by the UN General Assembly in 1948. The convention defines the crime of genocide, lists the prohibited acts, and calls for punishment of the perpetrators (see Figure 10.2 for key provisions).

The Genocide Convention was rapidly signed and ratified and widely recognized as a major advance in international human rights law. Yet how would it be interpreted and enforced? For example, it does not specify how many people have to be killed to constitute genocide, but only addresses the intention on the part of the perpetrators to destroy a group of people "in whole or in part." The convention created no permanent treaty body to monitor situations or provide early warnings of impending or actual genocide. And for many years it seemed to have little effect. The international community ignored several situations that appeared to be genocide, such as the "killing fields" of Cambodia, where almost one-third of the country's population died in the mid-1970s.

Three post–Cold War cases, Bosnia, Rwanda, and Darfur, illustrate the dilemmas associated with application of the Genocide Convention. Were these cases genocide? Was there a systematic attempt by one group to exterminate another group? Or were these just brutal civil wars? If genocide was committed, the parties to the convention were obligated to respond under Article I, but proving genocide is problematic. Few perpetrators leave behind conclusive evidence of intent. In all of these cases, the UN member states failed to act decisively to stop the killing.

During the Yugoslav civil war, the term *ethnic cleansing* was coined to refer to systematic efforts by Croatia, the Bosnian Serbs, and Serbia itself to remove peoples of another group from their territory, but not necessarily to wipe out the entire group or part of it as specified in the Genocide Convention. In Bosnia, Muslim civilians were forced by Serb troops to flee towns for Muslim areas within Bosnia or for neighboring countries. Some were deported to neighboring Macedonia, while others were placed in concentration camps. Sixty thousand Bosnian women were raped by Serb

**Figure 10.2  The Genocide Convention (key provisions)**

Article I    Genocide, whether committed in time of peace or in time of war, is a crime under international law which they undertake to prevent and punish.

Article II    Genocide means any of the following acts committed with intent to destroy, in whole or in part, a national, ethnical, racial or religious group, as such:
   (a)  Killing members of the group;
   (b)  Causing serious bodily or mental harm to members of the group;
   (c)  Deliberately inflicting on the group conditions of life calculated to bring about its physical destruction in whole or in part;
   (d)  Imposing measures intended to prevent births within the group;
   (e)  Forcibly transferring children of the group to another group.

Article III    The following acts shall be punishable:
   (a)  Genocide;
   (b)  Conspiracy to commit genocide;
   (c)  Direct and public incitement to commit genocide;
   (d)  Attempt to commit genocide;
   (e)  Complicity in genocide.

Article IV   Persons committing genocide or any of the other acts enumerated in Article III shall be punished, whether they are constitutionally responsible rulers, public officials or private individuals.

Article V    The Contracting Parties undertake to enact . . . the necessary legislation to give effect to the provisions of the present Convention and to provide effective penalties for persons guilty of genocide or any of the other acts enumerated in Article III.

forces. Croatia expelled Serbs from its territory, and Serbia expelled Kosovar Albanians from Kosovo.

Investigators from the UN Commission on Human Rights, beginning in 1992, reported "massive and grave violations of human rights" against the Bosnian Muslim population. In the same year, the General Assembly condemned Serbia's ethnic cleansing of Bosnia's Muslims as a form of genocide, while the ICJ began to consider the specific case in 1993. A Commission of Experts created by the Security Council in 1993 conducted further investigations. Before its report was issued in 1995, the Security Council established the ICTY, instituted an arms embargo on all parties, and imposed trade sanctions on Serbia, condemning it for human rights violations. By December 1995, when the Dayton Peace Accords were signed, the war had resulted in 200,000 deaths and millions of homeless, missing, or internally displaced persons.

Why didn't the Security Council undertake more direct action? Was ethnic cleansing in Bosnia equivalent to genocide? The UN Commission of Experts and the Commission on Human Rights both said that Serbia had a conscious policy of systematic genocide. Some states and NGOs, such as Doctors Without Borders, disagreed. Still others maintained that all sides were guilty. The fact was that Security Council members lacked the political will to stop the killing. In 2007, the ICJ concluded that although Serbia failed to prevent the 1995 Srebrenica genocide, Serbia neither committed genocide nor conspired nor was complicit in the act of genocide. The judges pointed to insufficient proof of intentionality to destroy the Bosnians as a whole or in part. The controversy continues, however. In 1999, Croatia filed suit against Serbia over the genocide claims, and Serbia filed a countersuit in 2010. Hearings finally began in 2014 and a decision was announced in 2015 that neither Croatia nor Serbia had committed genocide against each other's population during the Balkan wars that followed the collapse of Yugoslavia in the early 1990s. Crimes were committed by both countries, but the intent to commit genocide had not been proven against either, the court decided (ICJ Contentious Case 2015). The ICTY, however, has long since ruled that genocide was committed in Bosnia when the UN safe haven of Srebrenica was overrun by Bosnian Serb forces in 1995. And, in 2015, prosecutors in Serbia began arresting persons suspected of having participated in the Srebrenica massacre, widening the focus beyond high-level personnel. These trials will be held in Serbia itself—a first.

The evidence of genocide in Rwanda is much more definitive. In April 1994, following the death of the Rwandan and Burundian presidents in a mysterious plane crash, Hutu extremists in the Rwandan military and police began systematically slaughtering the minority Tutsis as well as moderate Hutus in a campaign of violence orchestrated by Radio Libres des Milles Collines. In a ten-week period, over 800,000 were killed out of a total Rwandan population of 7 million. Even before the plane crash, reports from NGOs and UN peacekeepers warned that there were plans to target the Tutsi population. In January 1994, General Romeo Dallaire's warnings of an impending genocide went unheeded at UN headquarters and his request for additional UN troops to augment his small, 2,500-member peacekeeping force was denied. Instead, he was forced to confine his activities to evacuating foreigners.

Why did the international community fail to respond? Samantha Power (2002) traces the reasons for the US failure to take any action to self-serving caution and the belief at first that the killings were merely "random tribal slaughter." When evidence mounted to the contrary, it was ignored and officials avoided using the term *genocide,* knowing full well that if it was invoked, they would be forced to take action under the terms of the Genocide Convention. Philip Gourevitch (1998) and Michael Barnett

(2002) place harshest blame on the UN, which they maintain should not have withdrawn its peacekeepers when it did. Virtually all the key Security Council members preferred taking no military action, and the Secretariat misunderstood and ignored the problem. Other scholars have suggested that the genocide occurred so fast, beginning in outlying areas, that the world could not have reliably known enough or had the time to prevent it (Kuperman 2001).

Beginning in 2003, thousands of people fled their homes in the western region of Darfur in Sudan after attacks from government-backed Arab militias (the Janjaweed) on a rebel uprising. Although the international community and UN provided humanitarian relief, the Security Council issued only weak warnings to Sudan, despite the efforts of some, including then–US secretary of state Colin Powell, who labeled Darfur a case of genocide in 2004. Exact figures are hard to come by, but estimates are that between 2003 and 2008, over 300,000 people were killed in Darfur, 2.3 million were displaced within the country, and another 250,000 fled, mostly to neighboring Chad. Large numbers of villages were destroyed and more than 3 million people were dependent on international humanitarian aid. The situation drew the attention of celebrities such as George Clooney and sparked a "Save Darfur" media campaign to raise awareness of the little-known region and to press governments to act. With both China and Russia opposing coercive measures against Sudan, the Security Council referred the case to the ICC in 2005 and supported a small AU monitoring force. Only in 2007, with Sudan's consent, was the stronger hybrid UN-AU peacekeeping force (UNAMID) approved, and until 2009 it looked like conflict had diminished and displaced people were returning home. While levels of violence in Darfur did diminish for a time, when the ICC in 2010 issued a second arrest warrant against Sudan's President Bashir, violence flared in retaliation against humanitarian aid groups and workers. Neither the peace agreement between North and South Sudan nor the 2011 referendum supporting the South's secession have led to the permanent cessation of violence.

As discussed in Chapter 7, UNAMID has had serious problems and been routinely hampered by the Sudanese government, its peacekeepers often subject to attack (a crime under the ICC Rome Statute). More serious, however, are charges contained in a 2014 report that the mission failed to protect Darfur civilians, and the peacekeepers' "presence didn't deter either the government or the rebels from attacking the civilians." More damning perhaps are revelations that the UN withheld evidence collected by UNAMID linking Sudanese authorities to serious crimes and that UNAMID itself often failed to report attacks on civilians. One former UN official is quoted as saying, "We can't say all what we see in Darfur" (Lynch 2014a).

All three cases demonstrate the failure to enforce the international norm prohibiting genocide despite the evidence that genocide was occurring. The fact that two of the cases occurred in Africa, a continent already rife with ethnic and racial strife, provides some explanation. Were these just examples of brutal civil wars or were they truly genocides? Was racism itself a factor in the failures to respond adequately? The cases also point to the practical limitations to taking action against massive human rights violations. Timing (close to the Somalia debacle) and location proved critical in the Rwanda case; remoteness has been a factor in the Darfur case, as it has in the case of interethnic violence bordering on genocide in the newly independent South Sudan and in the Central African Republic in 2014. In all three cases, the UN Security Council's P-5 had competing priorities and therefore lacked the political will to act. To compensate for the UN's own institutional weaknesses and lack of an early warning mechanism, the UN Office of the Special Adviser on the Prevention of Genocide was established in 2004 to collect information on potential future genocides and make recommendations to the Security Council on actions to prevent or halt genocide, albeit too late to prevent "never again" in any of these cases. And other cases of possible genocide continue to occur. In early 2015, for example, the UNHCHR reported that ISIS may have committed genocide and war crimes against the minority Yazidi community in Iraq and called for the Security Council to refer the case to the ICC.

## Violence Against Women

Violence against women has been a problem for centuries, much like the problem of human trafficking discussed at the beginning of this chapter. Until recently, these issues were hidden in the private sphere of family and communal life, where local authorities and national governments did not intervene and to which the international community turned a blind eye. Forced marriages at a young age, physical abuse by spouses including disfigurement and rape, crippling dowry payments, female genital mutilation, and honor killings all occur within the home and family. A gendered division of labor forces women into sweatshop labor, prostitution, and trafficking in their bodies; and in civil and international wars, women are raped, tortured, and forced into providing sexual services for troops. Yet only since the 1990s have these abuses against women come to be viewed as human rights issues.

Although the UN and its specialized agencies took up women's issues beginning in 1946, discussion was not framed in terms of women's rights as human rights until the 1980s and 1990s. NGO work on this issue dates from 1976, when a group of women from developed countries organized the International Tribunal on Crimes Against Women, gathering 2,000 women activists from forty different countries. The tribunal was ironically a reaction to the 1975 UN Conference on Women, which failed to address the issue of violence against women. It heard testimonials from those who had suffered from domestic violence (dowry-death) or community violence (rape and sexual slavery). It provided a major impetus to publicizing gender violence and to networking, opening up an issue that had theretofore been regarded as private. The tribunal contributed also to the adoption of the Convention on the Elimination of All Forms of Discrimination Against Women (CEDAW) in 1979, yet that convention did not address violence against women.

During the 1980s, small groups of experts based in agencies within the UN system convened intergovernmental meetings. The first UN survey on violence against women was published in 1989. Yet the UN itself still separated women's rights and human rights conceptually and bureaucratically, with the Commission on Human Rights located in Geneva and the Commission on the Status of Women located in New York. Activist Charlotte Bunch's 1990 article "Women's Rights Are Human Rights" helped establish the conceptual link between the two. The 1993 World Conference on Human Rights, in Vienna, endorsed this concept and put the issue on the agenda. The success of the Vienna Conference in marrying human rights and women's rights can be attributed to the ninety or so human rights and women's NGOs that organized the Global Campaign for Women's Human Rights. A key element in that campaign was the focus on gender-based violence. Feminist organizations demanded institutional changes, engaged in lobbying, brought lawsuits, and networked across international and regional organizations (Htun and Weldon 2012). The Global Campaign also organized the Global Tribunal on Violations of Women's Human Rights at the parallel NGO forum, hearing testimony of abused women and putting a human face on the related problems. The joint efforts of women's and human rights groups produced Article 18 of the Vienna Declaration and Programme of Action, which declared: "The human rights of women and of the girl-child are an inalienable, integral and indivisible part of universal human rights." Violence against women and other abuses in situations of war, peace, and domestic family life were identified as breaches of both human rights and humanitarian norms.

In 1993, the UN General Assembly approved the United Nations Declaration on the Elimination of Violence Against Women. It also called for a special rapporteur on violence against women as well as for states to take steps to combat violence against women (Joachim 2007).

The UN system was not the only locus of activity. Activists in the Americas also introduced violence-against-women issues in the OAS, which concluded the Inter-American Convention on Violence Against Women in 1994. Members of the EU likewise undertook to combat gender violence as a result of the interest of states that had strong domestic feminist lobbies, including Germany, Sweden, Finland, and Austria. Both the Maastricht Treaty (1993) and the Amsterdam Treaty (1997) expanded EU legal competence and highlighted respect for human rights and the rule of law. In 1996, a widely publicized Belgian case of sexual abuse of young girls drew attention to the fact that gender violence was occurring not just "out there in the developing world" but also right at home. The European Women's Lobby, with its 2,700 affiliates, brought the issue to the public agenda through its Policy Action Center on Violence Against Women. This precipitated a response from the European Parliament's activist Women's Rights Committee. With enlargement to the east and the Schengen Agreement opening the EU's internal borders, trafficking in women and violence emerging from that practice became a broader European issue.

Getting women's issues on the European agenda was not without controversy, as activists questioned the competence of the European Women's Lobby. The European Commission itself was slow to take up the issues until pushed by activist female commissioners. And there has been an ongoing dispute about prostitution, as discussed in the opening case of this chapter. The EU established the Daphne program in 1997 to address gender violence, helping to expand the capacity of states and local organizations to aid victims (Montoya 2008).

A comparative study of seventy countries over four decades by Mala Htun and Laurel Weldon (2012) found that strong advocacy and mobilization by autonomous domestic feminist groups and gradual regional diffusion of norms addressing violence against women rather than ratification of CEDAW, leftist parties, women in government, or national wealth best explained variations in states' policy development. Over time, then, states began to take a variety of actions such as funding domestic violence shelters, creating rape crisis centers, adopting specialized legislation, targeting vulnerable populations of women like immigrants, minority groups, and refugees, training professionals who respond to victims, and funding prevention and public education programs. These women's groups "articulate the social perspective of marginalized groups, transform social practice, and change public opinion . . . [and] drive sweeping change" (Htun and Weldon 2012: 564).

The issue of female genital mutilation (FGM) has garnered significant attention and effort. NGOs like Tostan framed the issue as one of women's health and human rights. UNICEF and UNESCO have provided educational materials and financial support for a human rights–based curriculum addressing the issue. A 2013 UNICEF report found that the practice, which has affected as many as 125 million girls and women, was in decline in about half of the twenty-nine states in Africa and the Middle East where it has been prevalent. The study suggests that changes in attitudes of the rising generation offer the best explanation for this trend. Nevertheless, in states where Tostan has been most active, such as Senegal, the practice continues, and remains prevalent also in Djibouti, Egypt, Eritrea, Guinea, Mali, and Somalia (UNICEF 2013).

In 2014, a four-day Global Summit to End Sexual Violence in Conflict was convened in London by Britain's foreign secretary and Special Envoy for the UNHCR Angelina Jolie. The summit drew 123 government delegations, along with 1,700 activists and survivors of conflict zones. Among the outcomes of the summit was the International Protocol on the Documentation and Investigation of Sexual Violence in Conflict, which sets standards for collecting information, evidence, and witness protection. The efforts of activists and sentences delivered by international tribunals and the ICC have begun to make those responsible for committing sexual violence accountable. Still, UN Secretary-General Ban Ki-moon called attention to a UN report in March 2015 that indicated one in three women today are subject to physical violence. The report also drew attention to the rise of extremism and conservatism as a factor in the persistence of the problem of violence against women (Sengupta 2015a).

Ultimately, the solution to addressing violence against women, indeed all discrimination against women, is to elevate women from their historically subordinate status to men. Liberal feminists see that progress has been made, because both public and private abuses are the subject of media attention, concerted NGO activities, and states' actions. Critical feminists, however, point to the economic forces that continue to place women in a disadvantaged position. Virtually all condemn the various forms of both public and private violence against women, though their remedies for relief vary.

### The Quest for LGBT Rights

Rights based on sexual orientation and gender identity of lesbian, gay, bisexual, and transgender persons have gained increasing prominence, even though they remain highly controversial. While the first gay organization dates from 1892 in Germany, that movement peaked during the 1930s in Germany, the Netherlands, and Sweden. The Society for Human Rights, the first formally organized gay group in the United States, was established in 1924. The Nazi suppression of homosexual groups during the World War II, however, had a chilling effect on public activities for several decades. During the 1970s and 1980s, organizations in the United States, Canada, Australia, and Western Europe connected, using the language of civil rights, much like African Americans and women before them. First in Norway in 1981, then several years later in the English-speaking world, the groups met with success by building on grassroots activities in voluntary associations and labor unions, then lobbying municipal and state or provincial administrations for legalization of gay rights. Since that time, some European states (the Netherlands, France), several Latin American states (Brazil, Argentina, Uruguay), Canada, and South Africa have accepted LGBT rights as human rights and even legalized marriage; the Indian Supreme Court recognized transgender persons as a third gender and acknowledged their equal rights. Still others have legalized LGBT civil and political rights, although laws prohibiting sexual relations between consenting adults of the same gender remain on the books.

The challenge has been greater in the developing world and in nations where traditional religious and social structures are dominant. In those cases, national laws permitting discrimination on the basis of sexual orientation with respect to employment, movement, housing, and government services are common, generally supported by their publics. Such laws are especially common in the Islamic world. In addition, harassment, assault, and even murder of gays and lesbians continue to be widespread; in 2014, seventy-six countries still criminalized homosexual behavior; ten countries made it punishable by death or life imprisonment. For example, Nigeria passed a law in 2014 stipulating fourteen years imprisonment for entering a same sex union and Uganda passed a law punishing homosexual acts by life in prison. In five countries, the penalty for engaging in homosexual behavior is death. In Bolivia, Russia, and South Africa, LGBT demands have actually provoked a backlash. Some anti-gay rights NGOs have formed coalitions of their own and shared information and strategies to block reforms. This has led some to advise gay activists to limit their objectives, consistent with the relatively conservative Yogyakarta Principles discussed below (Mittelstaedt 2008).

The goal of the International Lesbian, Gay, Bisexual, Trans, and Intersex Association (ILGA), an umbrella group of hundreds of LGBT advocacy groups formed in 1978, has been to internationalize the struggle for LGBT rights. But getting access to the UN and other international bodies has been an uphill battle. Even Human Rights Watch and Amnesty International were reluctant to endorse LGBT rights. Only after contentious debate did AI agree in 1991 to defend people imprisoned because of homosexuality. In its 1994 report on LGBT rights, AI noted rather cautiously that no international treaty explicitly defended these rights. Amnesty International provided encouragement for Human Rights Watch to take up the issue a few years later (Hagland 1997; Mertus 2009a).

Participation of LGBT groups in UN human rights forums came slowly. Lesbian groups participated in the UN women's conference in 1985 and two gay organizations attended the Vienna conference on human rights in 1993. The ILGA was granted consultative status to the UN in 1992, but that status was subsequently suspended in 1994 after the United States and a number of conservative NGOs objected on the grounds that one of the ILGA's affiliates advocated sex between adults and minors. After the ILGA expelled the group in question, it reapplied for NGO consultative status, which was granted in 2011 (ILGA 2013).

LGBT success in changing policy also has come slowly. The ILGA's first success was persuading the WHO to drop homosexuality from its International Classification of Diseases in 1993. In 1992 the Commission on Human Rights declared that the right against discrimination on the basis of sex declared in the International Covenant on Civil and Political Rights should be read to also mean "sexual orientation." In 2003, a proposal before the Commission on Human Rights to condemn discrimination on the basis of sexual orientation was narrowly accepted. Those opposed then threatened to add innumerable amendments, prompting the delegates to agree to delaying action. By 2006 support had grown and the resolution passed (O'Flaherty and Fisher 2008).

LGBT groups have carved a message and a successful strategy that has proven compelling to their international audience. In 2007, twenty-nine legal scholars from twenty-five countries (with the support of the International Commission of Jurists and the International Service for Human Rights) drafted the Yogyakarta Principles on the Application of Human Rights Law in Relation to Sexual Orientation and Gender Identity. Rather than develop new rules to govern policies on LGBT issues or propose a new convention, they instead scoured the existing international human rights agreements and showed how they applied to gay rights. For example, where a human rights treaty forbids discrimination on the basis of gender, it is contended under these principles that this also refers to sexual orientation. Likewise, where treaties endorse the right to privacy, they are implicitly endorsing the right to partnering between consenting adults (Principles 2 and 6). CEDAW has been interpreted to endorse nondiscrimination on the basis of sexual orientation, although many states have appended reservations that nullify this interpretation (Mittelstaedt 2008: 362).

The UN General Assembly in 2008 broke the taboo on the subject of homosexual rights in major UN bodies. With support from the UNHCHR and European and Latin American states, the Assembly issued a declaration seeking to decriminalize homosexuality. Two years later, the UN Special Rapporteur on the Right to Education, Vernor Muñoz, drafted a proposal calling for teaching that same-sex relations are valid, prompting a reply from Malawi's representative that the special rapporteur had "sought to: introduce 'controversial concepts' that were not recognized under international law; create new human rights; and . . . propagate controversial principles [the Yogyakarta Principles] that were not endorsed at the international level" (International Service for Human Rights 2010).

Despite such opposition, both the High Commissioner for Human Rights, Navi Pillay, and the UN Secretary-General, Ban Ki-moon, began to speak out publicly. In 2010, the Secretary-General, rejecting discrimination based on sexual orientation and gender identity, affirmed: "Where there is a tension between cultural attitudes and universal human rights, universal rights must carry the day" (United Nations Secretary-General 2010). In 2011, the Human Rights Council adopted the first UN resolution (Resolution 17/19) on sexual orientation, expressing "grave concern" at violence and discrimination against individuals based on sexual orientation and gender identity. That was followed by the first UN report on the issue, written by the office the UNHCHR. The Human Rights Council in 2012 became the first UN intergovernmental body to hold a formal debate on the subject, and High Commissioner Pillay launched a public information campaign to promote greater respect for the rights of LGBT people a year later.

The struggle for LGBT rights continues in other forums. Decisions taken by the European Court of Human Rights in support of LGBT rights are increasing the probability of policy change in Council of Europe member states. National courts are using the European court's precedents to rule domestic laws invalid, if the governing regime at the time those laws were passed was not opposed to LGBT equality (Helfer and Voeten 2014). The issue will not be ignored, even if it remains highly controversial.

## The Humanitarian Challenges of Refugees and IDPs

Once thought to be a temporary problem at the end of World War II, the refugee problem worldwide has increased dramatically, with people fleeing war, civil unrest, genocide, famine, and dire economic conditions. The scale of the problem now poses a severe global governance challenge, highlighting both the shortcomings of the existing legal regime and the practical questions of how to serve both the short- and long-term needs of individuals.

By the end of 2014, the total number of persons "of concern" was 51.2 million—the highest since the end of World War II—including 16.7 million refugees and 33.3 million internally displaced persons. There were also 4.9 million Palestinians under the care of the UN Relief and Works Agency (UNRWA), created in 1949 specifically to serve their needs. The largest numbers of refugees were from Afghanistan, Syria, Iraq, Somalia, the DRC, and Sudan. Much of the increase was driven by the conflict in Syria, as well as violence in the Central African Republic and South Sudan (UNHCR 2014). Eighty percent of the refugees and IDPs were hosted by developing countries, and children made up 46 percent of the refugee population. Yet only 526,000 refugees were voluntarily repatriated in 2012, and 88,600 were resettled in twenty-two countries, illustrating what has become a problem of protracted situations. It is compounded by a "crisis of asylum" as states have adopted restrictive asylum policies and Western states have sought to keep refugees in their region of origin (Loescher and Milner 2011: 196). Yet the numbers of asylum-seekers soared more than 45 percent in 2014 over 2013 as more than 850,000 new applications for asylum were filed, most of them in Europe (Sengupta 2015c: A5). The problem is both a humanitarian and a human rights problem.

Key to understanding the work and limitations of the UNHCR is the definition of "refugee" in the 1951 Convention Relating to the Status of Refugees: a person who because of a "well-founded fear of being perse-cuted for reasons of race, religion, nationality, membership of a particular social group or political opinion, is outside the country of his nationality and is unable or, owing to such fear, is unwilling to avail himself of the protection of that country." The UNHCR's responsibility is to protect peo-ple who are certified as refugees by providing temporary refuge until another state grants them asylum or they can return home. The most signif-icant right of a refugee is "non-refoulement"—the principle that refugees cannot be forced to return to their country of origin. The UNHCR's man-date, therefore, is to provide administrative assistance and identity papers, and protect refugees from forced repatriation and from exploitation in the host state. This legal protection mandate has become increasingly difficult to implement as the numbers of refugees have surged.

Originally, the 1951 convention only applied to Europe, but it was made universal by the 1967 protocol. And the definition of refugee has been broadened through regional agreements in both Africa and Central America to include those displaced by internal conflicts. These regional documents now correspond more to actual causes of flight, but they also respond to the reality that it is "often impossible for asylum seekers to gen-erate documented evidence of individual persecution required by the 1951 Convention . . . [since] most contemporary mass exoduses occur when political violence is of a generalized nature rather than a direct individual threat" (Loescher and Milner 2011: 191–192). Thus the UNHCR has adapted its own mandate to address this reality, shifting from legal protec-tion to providing assistance to refugees in camps, while potential countries of asylum focus more on individuals and on persecution rather than on groups of people at risk from violence.

Internally displaced persons, people forced to move or relocate within their own country due to violence, development projects, or natural disas-ters (but not poverty or unemployment), are not considered refugees under the convention. They present particular challenges since they remain within the boundaries of ostensibly sovereign states and hence are subject to domestic jurisdiction. Until the early 2000s, there was no international legal basis for providing assistance. The largest numbers of IDPs (over 1 million each) are found in Colombia, the DRC, Iraq, Nigeria, South Sudan, Sudan, and Syria (see the website of the Internal Displacement Monitoring Centre, www.internal-displacement.org). Their numbers have increased dramatically because of changes in the nature of warfare, ethnic cleansing, and even more accurate data (Weiss and Korn 2006: 12).

Attention to the issue of IDPs came primarily as a result of the work of two individuals in the 1990s—Francis Deng and Roberta Cohen—as well as the concerns of NGOs such as the World Council of Churches, the Refugee Policy Group, and Quakers. The initial step was getting the UN Commission on Human Rights to identify existing laws and mechanisms for their protection. Deng, a former Sudanese diplomat and expert on African anthropology, was named Special Representative of the UN Secretary-General in 1992. He provided intellectual leadership through a combination of personality, his framing of an idea regarding international protection for IDPs, his position as a temporary civil servant, and his stature as a person of prominence outside the UN bureaucracy (Bode 2014). Cohen had been active with the Refugee Policy Group in Geneva, which had been lobbying on the issue; she had also written the first paper articulating the idea of sovereignty as "responsibility on the part of governments to protect their citizens" (Weiss and Korn 2006: 24). Throughout the 1990s, Deng and Cohen led the Project on Internal Displacement at the Brookings Institution, and Deng served as SRSG (1992–2004), urging states to incorporate IDP principles into domestic law. The roles of Deng and Cohen illustrate how important key individuals can be in bringing attention to a human rights issue.

The culmination of Cohen and Deng's efforts came when the 2005 World Summit endorsed the Guiding Principles on Internal Displacement, which state that national governments have the primary responsibility for protection and assistance to IDPs within their jurisdiction and that international assistance to IDPs is not to be considered interference in a state's internal affairs. In 2009, the AU adopted the Convention for the Protection and Assistance of Internally Displaced Persons in Africa.

Since the mid-1990s, the UNHCR has gradually taken on responsibility for assisting a significant portion of IDPs worldwide, along with refugees and asylum seekers. As Cohen (2009: 589) points out, "their status is often interchangeable . . . [and] IDPs are potential refugees while returning refugees often become IDPs." In part, however, to remedy the problem of so called "protection gaps" for IDPs, the UN established a system in late 2005 of appointing different UN agencies as leads in various areas of humanitarian action. As discussed in Chapter 3, the UNHCR works with the World Food Programme, UNICEF, and UNESCO, and the International Organization for Migration (IOM), as well as with regional organizations. The IOM, founded to facilitate the settlement of the displaced after World War II, provides a wide range of services in migrant, refugee, and disaster relief camps and tracks migration trends as part of its mandate to support orderly and humane migration. Among the NGOs serving refugees and IDPs are the International Committee of the Red Cross and Doctors without Borders.

The Syrian civil war illustrates the scale of the problems of internal displacement and the governance challenges they present. As of the beginning of 2015, over 9.3 million people needed assistance inside Syria, including 6.5 million IDPs and perhaps as many as 5 million children. There were more than 3 million refugees in the neighboring countries of Turkey, Lebanon, Jordan, and Iraq. In just one weekend in late September 2014, more than 130,000 Syrians fled into southern Turkey to escape the advance of ISIS.

The handling of the situation is different in each host country, but the UNHCR generally serves as the lead agency because of its responsibility for registering all persons. In providing relief, it works with IGOs, NGOs, and local groups. For example, the Turkish Disaster and Emergency Management Authority is the lead agency in Turkey, coordinating all the agencies, including Turkish NGOs and IGOs. More than twenty-two refugee camps have been constructed, but these serve only about 30 percent of the refugees in Turkey, providing education, health care, banking, translation, communication, religious services, security, and social activities. Working alongside Turkish NGOs like the Foundation for Human Rights and Freedoms and Humanitarian Relief are a few international NGOs. The Turkish government's position is that these individuals are "guests" and Turkey is providing "temporary protection" until the individuals return to Syria.

While the specific situations are different in Lebanon, Jordan, and Iraq, the challenges are the same. How can the states provide housing and sustain the large number of refugees? While some refugees in Jordan, for example, are housed in UNHCR-organized camps, many are dispersed, staying with family members and friends. Can Lebanon remain stable given that the growing number of refugees are becoming a burden on the local population? Fearing that danger, in early 2015, Lebanon began limiting the number of Syrians who could enter the country. International financial contributions, coordinated in part by the UN through the 2014 Syria Regional Refugee Response Plan, have been slow to arrive, despite the desperate pleas of the humanitarian community. Little is known about Syrian refugees in Iraq since ISIS's seizure of territory in 2014. In 2014, the needs were estimated at a cost of $2.3 billion, yet as of midyear less than half that amount had been received in donations, underscoring the chronic problem of resources for international agencies totally dependent on voluntary donations.

Referring to some of the dilemmas in refugee aid, Sadako Ogata (2005: 25), head of the UNHCR from 1990 to 2000—a period of massive refugee flows—concludes in her book *The Turbulent Decade* that, ultimately, although the UNHCR saves lives and protects people from flagrant abuses, "there are no humanitarian solutions to humanitarian problems." Refugee problems "are essentially political in origin and therefore have to be addressed through political action. Humanitarian action may create space for political action but on its own can never substitute for it." Syria's refugee problem, like that in many other conflict situations, awaits a political solution.

## The Globalization of Human Rights and the Role of the United States

States remain key actors in the globalized world of human rights, although IGOs, NGOs, experts, and networks play critical roles in norm creation, monitoring, promotion, and in some cases enforcement. No state may be as crucial as the United States.

Historically, the United States was a leader in supporting human rights and international mechanisms for accountability. Founded on liberal principles guaranteeing the political and civil rights of individuals, it has long been a beacon for others. Yet its record is a mixed one. The United States has failed to sign many human rights conventions. It has signed but never ratified many others, including the Convention Relating to the Status of Refugees, the International Covenant on Economic, Social, and Cultural Rights, CEDAW, the Convention on the Rights of the Child, and the Rome Statute of the ICC. That trend continued in 2012 when the US Senate failed to ratify the UN Convention on the Rights of Persons with Disabilities.

In short, the United States has a record of not committing itself to international human rights standards. Although the specific reasons may vary, both realist and liberal institutionalist explanations are relevant. The United States may work to reinterpret or thwart treaties already in force, consistent with what is deemed in the national interest. Its human rights record since 9/11 has been under particular scrutiny, as discussed earlier. While US abuses are not as widespread or as degrading as those in other countries, they have tarnished America's reputation "because they were carried out by a powerful democratic state with great influence on other states" and because both transnational campaigns and domestic pressure by the courts and civil society proved ineffective at changing US policy, at least in the short run (Sikkink 2013: 145–146).

Consistent with liberal institutionalist theory, domestic structure and politics provide major explanations for US policy. The United States opposes or has attached reservations to treaties that it deems to be contrary to the US Constitution or inconsistent with the principles of federalism, such as the death penalty, which is a prerogative for states. An understanding was attached to the Convention on the Elimination of All Forms of Racial Discrimination, for example, saying that the provisions would be implemented by the federal government to the extent that it had jurisdiction in such matters. In virtually every case, the United States also adds the declaration that the particular treaty is not self-executing—that is, it does not create rights that are directly enforceable (Buergenthal 1995: 290–298). Julie Mertus (2008: 2) calls the US approach a "bait and switch," arguing that "human rights are something the United States encourages for other countries, whereas the same standards do not apply in the same manner in the United States."

Why is the United States so ambivalent about committing itself to the international human rights regime? Stewart Patrick (2002), Andrew Moravcsik (2002), and others explain this ambivalence by referring to US exceptionalism. This idea has led to the claim that the United States does not have to be accountable for human rights protections in the same way that other countries are accountable, and the stance that it will not be circumscribed by the actions of others. The United States also is very sensitive to the possibility of losing its authority to what some Americans view as an unelected and unaccountable global bureaucracy.

Has US ambivalence toward the international human rights regime made a difference? At one level, the answer is "of course." When international institutions clash with a superpower that controls essential financial resources, it makes a difference. Yet at another level, adherence to human rights norms is firmly established in a strong network of NGOs and democratic states, supported by public opinion. As constructivists argue, the norms are firmly implanted and this explains why the deviant behavior of the United States has generated such vigorous debate and condemnation both inside and outside the country. The jury on the long-term impact of this behavior may still be out, however, particularly as shifts in global power mean more influence for China and other emerging states that are far less devoted to human rights norms than is the United States.

There has been remarkable progress in human rights governance since World War II. Globalization of communication and ideas has been a powerful stimulus to the development of international human rights and humanitarian activities. Just as there has been a backlash against economic and cultural globalization, however, so too there may be a backlash against political globalization implicit in human rights governance. Environmental issues, the subject of the next chapter, have become globalized in many of the same ways.

## Suggested Further Reading

Barnett, Michael. (2011) *Empire of Humanity: A History of Humanitarianism.* Ithaca: Cornell University Press.
Brysk, Alison, and Austin Choi-Fitzpatrick, eds. (2012) *From Human Trafficking to Human Rights: Reframing Contemporary Slavery.* Philadelphia: University of Pennsylvania Press.

Lauren, Paul Gordon. (2011) *The Evolution of International Human Rights: Visions Seen.* 3rd ed. Philadelphia: University of Pennsylvania Press.

Loescher, Gil, Alexander Betts, and James Milner. (2008) *The United Nations High Commissioner for Refugees (UNHCR): The Politics and Practice of Refugee Protection Into the Twenty-First Century.* New York: Routledge.

Mertus, Julie A. (2009) *The United Nations and Human Rights: A Guide for a New Era.* 2nd ed. London: Routledge.

Neier, Aryeh. (2012) *The International Human Rights Movement: A History.* Princeton: Princeton University Press.

Schiff, Benjamin. (2008) *Building the International Criminal Court.* New York: Cambridge University Press.

Sikkink, Kathryn. (2011) *The Justice Cascade: How Human Rights Prosecutions Are Changing World Politics.* New York: Norton.

Simmons, Beth A. (2009) *Mobilizing for Human Rights: International Law in Domestic Politics.* New York: Cambridge University Press.

## Important Databases

International Displacement Monitoring Centre: www.internal-displacement.org
University of Minnesota International Human Rights Instruments. www1.umn.edu/humanrts/instree/ainstls1.htm

## Internet Resources

Amnesty International: www.amnesty.org
Anti-Slavery International: www.antislavery.org
Avocats sans Frontières: http://en.asf-network.org
Coalition for an International Criminal Court: www.iccnow.org
European Court of Human Rights: www.echr.coe.int
Extraordinary Chambers in the Courts of Cambodia: www.eccc.gov.kh/en
Feminist Majority Foundation: www.feminist.org
Human Rights Watch: www.hrw.org
Inter-American Commission on Human Rights: www.oas.org/en/iachr
Inter-American Court of Human Rights; Inter-American Convention on Human Rights: www.umn.edu/humanrts
International Commission of Jurists: www.icj.org
International Committee of the Red Cross: www.icrc.org
International Criminal Court: www.icc-cpi.int
International Criminal Tribunal for Rwanda: www.ictr.org
International Criminal Tribunal for the Former Yugoslavia: www.un.org/icty
International Lesbian, Gay, Bisexual, Trans, and Intersex Association: http://ilga.org
International Organization for Migration: www.iom.int
Open Society Initiative: www.opensocietyfoundations.org
Special Court for Sierra Leone: www.sc-sl.org
UN High Commissioner for Human Rights: www.ohchr.org
UN High Commissioner for Refugees: www.unhcr.org
World Council of Churches: www.wcc-coe.org

# 11

# Protecting
# the Environment

## Case Study: Climate Change

"Warming of the climate system is unequivocal, and since the 1950s, many of the observed changes are unprecedented over decades to millennia. The atmosphere and ocean have warmed, the amounts of snow and ice have diminished, sea level has risen, and the concentrations of greenhouse gases have increased" (IPCC 2013). Thus opens the 2013 report on the physical basis of climate change by Working Group I of the Intergovernmental Panel on Climate Change (IPCC). Other parts of this Fifth Assessment Report issued in early 2014 underscore that the human influence on climate change is clear and the rate of change is accelerating, but mitigation is still possible and averting catastrophe is still affordable (IPCC 2014). Although other recent studies have found that there may be a pause in the upward trend in temperature, the long-term effects of the trend are widespread: glaciers and sea ice are melting, the oceans are becoming acidified, hurricanes are strengthening, deserts are expanding, and weather patterns are becoming more extreme, affecting land use, most notably in Africa, coastal zones, island states, the Arctic, and Antarctica. The two greenhouse gases blamed for atmospheric heat retention, carbon dioxide ($CO_2$) and methane, have experienced sharp spikes after 12,000 years of relative consistency. Consensus among scientists on the extent of the problem and its link to human activity has taken almost two decades to achieve, yet debates among citizens and policymakers still continue. How much is Earth heating up? The estimates vary between 1.9 and 3 degrees centigrade. What policies need to be instituted? The burning of fossil fuel for energy, the major culprit, has long been viewed as essential for maintaining high rates of economic growth, and only slowly are sufficient supplies of alternative energy sources at affordable cost being developed.

Recognition of the problem of climate change dates back to 1988 when the IPCC was formed at the urging of bureaucrats in the World Meteorological Organization (WMO) and the United Nations Environment Programme (UNEP). Its purpose was to synthesize the state of knowledge about climate change and recommend possible responses. Over time, the IPCC has helped to generate attention by the scientific community and create an epistemic community around the issue. Participants in the IPCC process include experts in the physical and natural sciences, engineering, social sciences, public policy, and management. Some 1,250 individuals participated in the fifth review process, completed in 2014, along with representatives of 194 governments, organized into three working groups. The 2013 scientific report, for example, synthesized some 9,200 scientific works from around the world. The IPCC process, therefore, forms a core part of climate change governance, a role that was recognized by the awarding of the 2007 Nobel Peace Prize to the IPCC and former US vice president Al Gore.

At the 1992 UN Conference on the Environment and Development, held in Rio de Janeiro, more than a hundred countries signed the UN Framework Convention on Climate Change (UNFCC)—the first step toward creating a regime to govern climate change. Framework conventions are used in situations where negotiators can agree that a problem exists and on some principles, but not on any legally binding obligations. In 1997, the UNFCC was supplemented by the Kyoto Protocol, which aimed to stabilize the concentration of greenhouse gases and required developed countries to reduce their overall greenhouse-gas emissions according to a timetable. While developing countries, including China and India, were not included in the emission limitation requirement, the norm of "common but differentiated responsibility"—that states take appropriate actions within their means—was accepted. States have several ways to meet the international targets besides just reducing emissions, for example by earning credits for carbon sinks such as forests. A Joint Implementation Mechanism was designed to enable developed countries to work with developing states to reduce emissions or enhance sinks and obtain credit for emission reductions. A market-based emissions trading system permits states, local jurisdictions, and private companies to reduce greenhouse-gas emissions below what is required or to trade the excess reductions in order to offset other types of emissions. The protocol also created the Clean Development Mechanism, which developed states and private companies can use to meet domestic emission targets by financing greenhouse-gas abatement projects in developing countries.

The Kyoto Protocol came into force in 2005, ratified by 156 states representing 55 percent of greenhouse-gas emissions, including the EU member states, Russia, Canada, China, India, and Japan. The protocol itself created very little institutional structure to aid in implementation. Authority was given to the Global Environmental Facility (GEF, discussed later) to finance projects for increasing energy efficiency and energy conservation.

From the outset, the United States raised serious objections to the Kyoto Protocol and is not a party. US concerns centered particularly on the two-tier system that excuses developing countries from obligations to reduce emissions and on the economic costs that the United States would incur in implementation. As an energy-intensive economy, the United States, which emits more than two times the average per capita $CO_2$ emissions of European states, proposed using its vast carbon sinks to offset the preponderance of its emission reductions, a position rejected by the Europeans. US private industry, too, initially opposed the regulatory approach of the protocol and formed the Global Climate Coalition, which opposed all mandatory limitations on greenhouse-gas emissions and sponsored publicity campaigns in support of that position. By 2001, however, views began to change, as some companies realized that climate change was affecting their operations and that the move to more energy-saving technologies could itself be profitable. Many US businesses, once opposed to Kyoto, now assert the need to go beyond Kyoto and support a successor agreement. US military analysts in 2014 acknowledged increased scientific certainty about climate change and growing evidence of the link between it and security threats such as conflicts over food and water in Africa and vulnerability of people and food supplies to rising sea levels (C. Davenport 2014).

In contrast to the United States, support for the Kyoto Protocol and steps to address climate change have been much greater within the European Union, whose then fifteen members ratified the protocol in 2002. They have created their own regulatory systems with legally binding targets and timetables. In 2005, they launched the EU Emissions Trading System, the cornerstone of EU policy and the key tool for reducing industrial greenhouse-gas emissions. States that use less than their allowance may sell credits to others that are having difficulty meeting their obligations, with fines assessed for states that fail to meet those obligations. As of 2014, the system covers more than 11,000 power stations and industrial plants, but has encountered difficulties. Economic recession in the eurozone has decreased demand for the permits and there is major overcapacity in the carbon market. EU member states utilize Kyoto mechanisms for reductions and have been strong proponents of developing renewable energy sources. For example, the Carbon Fund for Europe is a trust fund administered by the World Bank and the European Investment Bank, established to pool money for climate-friendly projects in other countries and hence earn emission credits under Kyoto's Joint Implementation Mechanism.

Still, the fifteen EU member states that originally ratified the protocol more than met their targets for emission reductions by 2012, and the EU accounts for only 10 percent of greenhouse-gas emissions worldwide. In late 2014, EU leaders agreed on a new climate and energy framework that commits members to reducing greenhouse-gas emissions by at least 40 percent by 2030, which will increase the share of renewables in the energy mix, increase energy savings, and enhance the EU's energy infrastructure. This commitment, however, may be reviewed after the 2015 negotiations described later.

The Kyoto Protocol was intended as a relatively short-term step in the process of addressing climate change and scheduled to expire in 2012. Consequently, the UN has convened a series of annual conferences since 2007 with the initial goal of renegotiating and extending Kyoto. As negotiations dragged on, the goal became a new agreement under the UNFCC-based regime by the end of 2015. The process has been marked by the continuing North-South divide, with developing countries arguing as they have since 1997 that they should not bear the costs to their economic growth of adapting to climate change and that the developed countries who are responsible for much of the problem must demonstrate their commitment to reductions first, as well as provide financing for developing countries.

One of the major challenges is bringing the top three emitters—China (number one since 2008), the United States, and India—on board with any agreement. In 2014, China accounted for one-quarter of global greenhouse-gas emissions, and over the next twenty years those emissions are expected to grow by an amount equivalent to total US emissions (Porter 2014). China has continued to argue that as a developing country it should not have to take steps to cut its carbon emissions, although, in fact, it is doing so on its own. India's emissions are also projected at least to double over coming decades, and it has refused to offer a plan to cut them, since its priority is poverty alleviation and economic growth. In late 2014 the United States and China signed a "landmark agreement" whereby China agreed for the first time to stop its emissions from growing by 2030 and the United States announced new targets for reducing carbon emissions. As one journalist claimed, "A climate deal between China and the United States, the world's No. 1 and No. 2 carbon polluters, is viewed as essential to concluding a new global accord" (Lander 2014: A1). Another important step in the negotiations was the agreement in Lima, Peru, in late 2014 that every country—rich and poor—must take steps to reduce the burning of oil, gas, and coal by some amount, and announce how much it will cut by mid-2015. The agreement relies heavily on global peer pressure to get countries to act.

One group of states that are among the strongest advocates of urgent action on climate change is the Alliance of Small Island States. This coalition of forty-four island and low-lying coastal states and observers ranging from Antigua to Vanuatu has come together around their shared development challenges given the adverse effects of rising sea levels. They have no formal charter or institutions, and function primarily through their New

York–based UN missions, with major policy decisions being taken by their ambassadors. They have, however, been a forceful lobbying group pushing for concrete action, since many of them are already experiencing effects of climate change.

The annual conferences of UNFCC parties have produced only modest steps so far. For example, at the 2007 conference in Bali, agreement was secured that China and India should be included in any follow-on agreement, but what that meant was unclear. It was agreed in 2008 meetings that states should be given credit for saving forests and expand a fund to help poorer countries adapt. In Copenhagen, the following year, the parties agreed to provide both technology and financing ($30 billion annually) to mitigate the effects of climate change. But the gap between projected need and pledges for mitigation for the developing countries remained wide. With the Kyoto Protocol already extended, the target date for concluding a new agreement is the conference in Paris in 2015. Given this history, a consensus has emerged on the dysfunctionality of the process of trying to accomplish all the goals simultaneously. One scholar describes the negotiations as having led to "sub-optimal diplomatic and environmental outcomes" in which "procedural issues frequently take precedence over substantive ones" (Elliott 2013: 848).

As one would expect, environmental NGOs have been active throughout this process. Greenpeace and the World Wildlife Fund have provided leadership on the issue, and the Climate Action Network is now a worldwide network of over 900 NGOs in 100 countries supporting the transition to a low- or zero-carbon economy, with the goal of phasing out net greenhouse-gas emissions by 2050, while promoting adaptation in the most vulnerable communities. Seeing climate change as a crosscutting issue, the network has worked to link the negotiations for a Kyoto successor agreement with the process of developing new the Sustainable Development Goals (SDGs), discussed in Chapter 9, pushing to mainstream climate action across these goals.

Since the treaty-based regulatory approach of Kyoto has not worked as anticipated, what other actions have been taken to address climate change? The reality is that quite a lot has happened at different levels of governance. To see that, however, it helps to apply the concept of a regime complex, described in Chapters 1 and 9.

Robert Keohane and David Victor (2011: 9) describe the climate change regime complex as "a loosely coupled system of institutions; it has no clear hierarchy or core. . . . [Its] elements are loosely linked to one another." The UNFCC and Kyoto Protocol form one constituent part; other parts include climate change initiatives taken by the G-8, G-20, EU, and World Bank; the Nuclear Suppliers Group; regional pollution control institutions; the US Climate Action Partnership (an alliance of firms and

NGOs); the Montreal Protocol on Substances that Deplete the Ozone Layer; and a wide array of national and subnational activities.

In Europe and the United States, subnational entities have emerged as important actors in global-warming initiatives. In Europe, for example, four transnational municipal networks have steered member cities toward adoption of climate strategies. Lacking coercive power, the networks use communications, project funding, and certification to push for change (Hakelberg 2014). The EU also channels funding to municipalities. Similar networks exist in the United States. The International Council for Local Environmental Initiatives coordinates the Cities for Climate Protection, a network of over a thousand cities in more than thirty countries, including the United States. These transnational networks represent a new form of environmental governance, taking action in cities, where most greenhouse-gases are emitted (Betsill and Bulkeley 2006). In the United States, individual states have taken initiatives, often working with other states in a region or with neighboring Canadian provinces. Examples include the New England Governors–Eastern Canadian Premiers Climate Change Action Plan and the Western Regional Climate Action Initiative (Arizona, California, New Mexico, Oregon, and Washington), both of which call for regional targets for reduction and mechanisms for monitoring and managing emissions. In 2008, under the Regional Greenhouse Gas Initiative, ten states participated in the first-ever auction of pollution rights, establishing caps on $CO_2$ emissions and calling for utilities to buy allowances to pollute.

Various other transnational groups are experimenting with climate change initiatives, many only loosely connected to official UN negotiations. Matthew Hoffmann (2011) analyzes these various experiments, including the Climate Group, Climate Wise, and the Carbon Disclosure Project. Since 2004, the Climate Group, for example, has brought together both government authorities (Germany, California, Connecticut, state of Victoria, Australia, London) and corporate leaders (British Petroleum, HSBC, Shell). It is seen as a way to learn best practices, exercise corporate social responsibility, and deploy climate-friendly technologies.

There are now a plethora of such transnational governance initiatives—private as well as public-private in various combinations of business, government, and civil society groups. An empirical study of over sixty of such initiatives (Bulkeley et al. 2012) shows that most begin at the local level and are joined by NGOs and then states and IGOs. Most are devoted to capacity-building and information-sharing; the overwhelming number lack formal organizational structure.

These developments are all compatible with what Keohane and Victor and others have argued: the need to focus on parts of the climate change problem rather than the whole, to recognize the existence of a regime complex rather than just a single climate change regime centered on the

UNFCC and Kyoto Protocol. "Both political reality and the need for flexibility and diversity suggest that it is preferable to work for a loosely linked
but effective regime complex for climate change" (Keohane and Victor
2011: 20).

The long debate over whether climate change is real and human-caused
illustrates the distinct challenge for governance created by scientific uncertainty surrounding many environmental issues. The IPCC's role illustrates
the importance of scientific expertise to environmental governance, and
also the importance of a variety of actors other than states. The climate
change issues illustrate the evolution of many different types of governance
mechanisms. Changing behaviors over the long term is difficult and costly,
yet the threat to human security is severe and the need for multilevel global
governance has never been greater.

## Relating Environmental Problems
## to Security, Economics, and Human Rights

A contemporary ecosystem perspective confirms that various environmental issues are integrally related to each other and have critical economic
repercussions. The case of climate change illustrates these connections, as
economic downturns may make it more difficult to pay the costs of reducing emissions. Development issues, discussed in Chapter 9, also illustrate
the connections, as higher levels of economic development mean increased
demands for natural resources and energy. Economic growth at any cost
may also lead to unsound decisions or negative externalities, costly unintended consequences that adversely affect the quality of the environment.

Environmental issues have a connection not only to economics, but
also to human rights. Leading environmentalists have met stiff opposition,
harassment, and violent ends. The leader of the Greenbelt movement in
Kenya, female activist and 2004 Nobel Peace Prize winner Wangari
Maathai, was imprisoned for her activities in seeking to protect open spaces
in Nairobi. Ken Saro-Wiwa, environmental activist of the Movement for the
Survival of Ogoni People, the leader of the fight against exploitation by the
Nigerian government and Royal Dutch Shell, was killed for that cause. It
is Saro-Wiwa who claimed that the environment is humanity's first right.

Finally, lack of critical resources poses a threat to states' security, and
unsustainable environmental practices pose a threat to human security,
potentially leading to resource-motivated violence and intrastate and interstate wars. The search to guarantee supply of nonrenewable natural
resources such as petroleum motivated Japan's aggression in China and
Southeast Asia and Germany's invasion of southern Russia's oil fields during World War II. The same search today fuels conflicts in the Caspian Sea
basin and the South and East China Seas. The need for usable water for

agricultural productivity and human needs has led to major disputes in the Middle East over access to the water of the Jordan, Tigris-Euphrates, Nile, and Indus Rivers. Mass migrations, deforestation, desertification, flooding, loss of water supplies, collapse of agricultural production, and hunger burden neighboring states with refugees and in some cases threaten regional peace and stability, as conditions in Mali, Indonesia, and the Philippines confirm. As Jared Diamond (2005) warns in *Collapse,* the struggle for scarce resources can and has led to the collapse of states and empires.

In short, issues once perceived as "merely environmental" have far-reaching economic, human rights, and security implications. As the destructive Superstorm Sandy (2013) in the United States, extreme heat in Australia, and typhoons in Myanmar (2008), Japan (2014), and the Philippines (2013) remind us, we live in a fragile and vulnerable environment.

## Emergence of the Environment as an Issue Area

International environmental issues have become part of the public agenda only in the past five decades, in large part as a result of two major long-term trends (Meyer et al. 1997). The first is the gradual expansion of scientific knowledge that has enabled people to collect data that monitors environmental trends. The second is the rise of environment-oriented civil society associations, first national NGOs such as the Society for the Protection of Birds (1889) and the Sierra Club (1892), then international NGOs such as the Society for the Preservation of the Wild Fauna of the Empire (1903) and the Commission for the International Protection of Nature (1913, subsequently renamed the International Union for the Conservation of Nature [IUCN] in 1956).

During the 1960s, increased interest in the environment resulted in broader public responses. Rachel Carson's book *Silent Spring* (1962) and Jacques-Yves Cousteau's book *The Living Sea* (1963) galvanized environmental activists and helped to cement in the public consciousness the notion of the interdependence of all living things. Individual events, such as the Torrey Canyon oil spill in 1967 and the photographs of Earth from space taken by astronauts in 1969, also proved to be catalysts for a view of the planet as a single ecosystem. Over the following decades, interest in environmental issues broadened in scope to include both protection of the natural environment and curbing of the destructive effects of industrialization.

Biologist Garrett Hardin's article "The Tragedy of the Commons," published in 1968, set the stage for the theoretical and practical collective goods dilemmas posed by many environmental issues, as discussed in Chapter 2. Hardin suggested some simplistic strategies to overcome this tragedy of the commons. Yet almost five decades after Hardin's article was published, the effort to create multilevel environmental governance for a wide range of problems continues.

## The Evolution of Global Environmental Governance

International conferences sponsored by the UN have played a major role in the evolution of global environmental governance, as have NGOs and epistemic communities. They have put environmental issues on the international agenda and provided frameworks for negotiations and subsequent institutionalization. Although the UN Charter itself contains no mention of environmental protection, UN-sponsored conferences filled a critical gap in the evolution of environmental governance.

### UN Global Conferences and the Articulation of Norms: From Stockholm to Johannesburg

*The Stockholm Conference.* In the late 1960s, Sweden and other Nordic states proposed an international environmental conference on the environment, resulting in the 1972 UN Conference on the Human Environment (UNCHE), in Stockholm. The conference effectively put environmental issues on the agenda of the UN and many governments, initiating the piecemeal construction of international environmental institutions, expansion of the environmental agenda, increasing acceptance of international environmental standards, and extensive involvement of NGOs and scientific and technical groups in policymaking efforts. Thrust into the popular consciousness was the notion of "Spaceship Earth" and the slogan "Think Globally, Act Locally."

During the preparatory meetings for the 1972 conference, UNCHE secretary-general Maurice Strong, a Canadian businessman, provided the leadership to bridge the divergent interests of North and South by forging the conceptual links between development and environment. The North emphasized issues such as preservation of species and the need to curb environmental and transborder pollution. The South, however, feared that environmental regulation could hamper economic growth and divert resources from economic development. While many developing countries were reluctant to attend the conference, those that did had to be persuaded that environmental problems were a concern for everyone, not a plot to keep them underdeveloped.

The Stockholm Declaration, a soft-law statement of twenty-six principles, called on states and international organizations to coordinate activities. It endorsed states' obligation to protect the environment and not to damage the environment of others. It also recognized the principle that environmental policies should enhance developing countries' economic potential and not hamper the attainment of better living conditions. The Stockholm participants agreed not to use environmental concerns as justification for discriminatory trade practices or as a way to decrease access to markets. Conferees called for creation of a new UN body to coordinate environmental activities and promote governmental cooperation—the United Nations Environment Programme. The Stockholm Conference also inaugurated the practice of a parallel NGO forum, run simultaneously with the official conference, as discussed in Chapter 6. Almost 250 NGOs participated, setting an important precedent. At the state level, environmental ministries began to be formed to improve national capacity and signal commitment to addressing the issues. That trend toward state institutionalization has continued, accelerating even more over the subsequent two decades (Aklin and Urpelainen 2014).

*Moving to sustainable development.* The consensus forged at Stockholm on integrating the environment and development was met with some skepticism by the less developed countries, who argued that environmental concerns diverted attention from the need to pursue economic growth. That tension led the UN General Assembly in 1983 to establish the World Commission on Environment and Development (or Brundtland Commission), discussed in Chapter 9, to develop the concept of sustainable development. Its report, *Our Common Future,* called for "development that meets the needs of the present without compromising the ability of future generations to meet their own needs" (WCED 1987: 8). It sought to balance ecological concerns with the economic growth necessary to reduce poverty. The report underscored that the South could not develop in the same way the industrialized countries did, because humanity could not survive a similarly radical transformation in the environment.

The Brundtland Commission's approach was adopted in 1987 by UNEP and later by the World Bank, NGOs, and many national development agencies. It became the rallying cry of the environmental movement and a concept articulated by academics, state officials, and leading scientists. It acknowledged that poverty is a critical source of environmental degradation; it encouraged people to begin to think about critical links among agriculture, trade, transportation, energy, and the environment; and it called attention to the long-term view (Esty 2001).

*The Rio Conference.* Twenty years after Stockholm, the 1992 UN Conference on the Environment and Development (UNCED), or Earth Summit, held in Rio de Janeiro, convened in the aftermath of a series of key scientific findings during the 1980s: the discovery of the ozone hole over Antarctica, the growing evidence of global warming, and the accumulating data on loss of biodiversity and depletion of fisheries. These developments shaped the Rio Conference agenda.

The Earth Summit was the largest of the UN-sponsored global conferences at that time, both in the number of participants and in the scope of the agenda. Preparatory meetings were used to articulate positions, resolve basic issues, and negotiate the text for all conference documents. NGOs played key roles in the preparatory process and the conference. The 1,400 accredited environmental organizations included not only traditional, large, well-financed NGOs, such as the World Wide Fund for Nature and the IUCN, but also many new grassroots groups that typically were poorly financed and had few previous transnational linkages.

The final outcomes of the Earth Summit were the 800-page Agenda 21, the UN Convention on Biological Diversity, and the UN Framework Convention on Climate Change. The South succeeded in integrating issues of economic reform into Agenda 21 and reaffirming the principle of sovereignty over natural resources. Yet it also accepted the propositions that degradation of those resources was a threat to global security and that states must be responsible stewards. Second, the linkage between development and the environment was expanded to the issue of trade in GATT and to the gradual "greening" of World Bank programs. UNCED's third outcome was the acceptance of direct NGO participation in dealing with environmental issues. NGOs were given the capability of participating at all levels, from policy- and decisionmaking to implementation. What began as a parallel informal process of participation within the UN system evolved into a more formal role. Indeed, NGOs' participation at the Earth Summit stimulated a review of their relationship with the UN overall, as discussed in Chapter 6.

Finally, just as Stockholm led to the establishment of UNEP, Rio led to the creation in 1993 of the Commission on Sustainable Development to encourage and monitor the implementation of Agenda 21. It also led to the restructuring of the Global Environmental Facility, both of which are discussed later.

The two framework conventions concluded at the Earth Summit illustrate critical dilemmas that environmental issues pose. For example, the Convention on Biological Diversity includes both the principles of national sovereignty over domestic resources and the obligation of states to conserve biological diversity. States commit themselves to developing national preservation plans, and wealthy states pledge to provide funding for states unable to pay. Follow-up, however, was voluntary, and many states were unwilling to take action. The same was true of the UNFCC, as discussed in the opening case study of this chapter.

Several UN conferences that followed the Earth Summit, including the 1995 Social Summit, the 1995 Fourth Women's Conference, and the 1996

Habitat II Conference, reinforced the discourse of sustainable development. For example, the 1994 International Conference on Population and Development built on Rio's foundations to emphasize the need to slow population growth rates as part of sustainable development. Likewise, the seventh Millennium Development Goal dealt with ensuring environmental sustainability, although specific operational indicators were not established.

*Rio Plus 10: The Johannesburg Summit.* The purpose of the 2002 UN World Summit on Sustainable Development, also known as Rio Plus 10, was to build on the ambitious yet poorly executed agenda of Rio. The change of name to "summit" reflected the opposition from some states to continuing the pattern of UN global conferences, as discussed in Chapter 4. Participants hoped to stem the rising toll of poverty and curb pollution and deforestation, which had only accelerated during the 1990s. The South wanted more aid for economic growth. The Europeans wanted targets and timetables, while the United States found targets unnecessary. The divisions were profound. Few states did the necessary preparatory groundwork. By the time the summit convened, there was also increasing disillusionment with the notion of sustainable development, seeing it as a "buzzword largely devoid of content" (Esty 2001: 74).

The major outcome of the summit, its implementation plan, included some targets in the areas of access to clean water and proper sanitation, reduction of biodiversity loss, better use of chemicals, and more renewable energy. These goals were to be achieved through partnerships among governments, citizen groups, and business (called action coalitions)—the governance approach for human development as discussed in Chapter 9. Overall, Rio Plus 10 was generally seen as disappointing compared to previous gatherings, yet that disappointment led to a ten-year social science–based research program, the Earth System Governance Project, to provide a roadmap for major institutional changes, proposals that would be made in a follow-up conference a decade later (Biermann 2012).

*Back to Rio: Rio Plus 20.* In 2012, The UN Conference on Sustainable Development reconvened. Its final document, *The Future We Want,* reaffirmed past commitments, but as Maria Ivanova (2013: 4) describes, "offers no targets, timelines, or specific objectives. Inclusive of every possible topic within sustainable development, it does not prioritize any areas or express a particular sense of urgency. Its most important achievement, some observers lamented, was simply that it did not regress." But in keeping with the recommendations of Frank Biermann (2012), it confirmed institutional changes, including strengthening the structure and financing of UNEP, abolishing the Commission on Sustainable Development, and pledging to set the global Sustainable Development Goals to replace the MDGs.

Thus, while the mega-conference approach may have outlived its usefulness, Rio Plus 20, like the other summits before it, forced states to adopt national agendas, socialized them to accept new norms of behavior, and brought together the scientific community and environmental NGOs to learn from each other. As constructivists argue, this process over time has led to significant shifts in perceptions and behavior that created the foundations of global environmental governance (Haas 2002).

## NGO Roles in Environmental Governance

NGOs have played important roles in environmental affairs since the nineteenth century. Since the 1960s, however, with the emergence of a global environmental movement and especially following the 1972 Stockholm Conference, the number and scope of both internationally based NGOs and small, locally based environmental NGOs in less developed countries have expanded. Environmental organizations now number in the tens of thousands. The European Environmental Bureau, the liaison office between the EU organs and NGOs, lists 140 European environmental citizen organizations, for example. The bureau has offices in Brussels, receives funding from the European Commission, operates through a set of well-organized working groups on major issues, and enjoys consultative status in EU institutions and routine contacts with the European Environmental Agency. It has mounted recent campaigns focusing on banning mercury and adopting energy-saving "Coolproducts." Most NGOs have neither the same levels of funding nor the same access to decisionmakers.

Environmental NGOs are rarely united in either approach or ideological orientation; some prefer to work within the status quo, others oppose any change, while others seek radical change. They have given individual citizens a voice in environmental governance and many names are well-known, including Earthwatch, the Environmental Defense Fund, the Nature Conservancy, Greenpeace, the Sierra Club, the World Wide Fund for Nature, the Rainforest Action Network, and the Earth Island Institute.

Environmental NGOs, among other roles, serve as generalized international critics. Because they are not attached to nation-states and do not depend on states for funds, they are able to take critical positions. For example, Greenpeace publishes the "Waste Trade Update," the authoritative source for information relating to the 1989 Basel Convention on the Control of Transboundary Movements of Hazardous Wastes and Their Disposal. Some NGOs offer even more targeted criticism. The Rainforest Action Network, for example, launched an initiative against Amazon deforestation precipitated by cattle ranching by targeting Burger King for buying Brazilian beef. It also targeted Home Depot for selling old-growth wood. Groups use a variety of means ranging from boycotts to media campaigns, but their impact is often limited. Some groups engage in direct, confrontational actions—"direct enforcement" or, to some, ecoterrorism—to stop purportedly illegal practices by states and private actors (Eilstrup-Sangiovanni and Bondaroff 2014). Greenpeace and Friends of the Earth initiated environmental direct action in the 1970s in efforts to halt nuclear testing in the South Pacific and Japanese and Soviet whaling, including sinking or disabling ships. Such actions are examples of "*direct* pressure on perpetrators as opposed to indirectly pressuring states to change their policy through an appeal to public opinion" (Eilstrup-Sangiovanni and Bondaroff 2014: 351).

Second, NGOs are sometimes linked to epistemic communities. Individual experts from NGOs, along with their counterparts in IGOs and government agencies, may well form part of an epistemic community. Sometimes the epistemic communities try to change the way people think about issues in the interest of environmental preservation. The World Wide Fund for Nature, for example, uses its expertise to try to convince consumers and medical practitioners in Asia to try to end the use of endangered species like bears and rhinos for medicinal purposes. The International Water Resources Association and several NGOs have worked to get policymakers to adopt a more integrated resource management perspective in their thinking about water and rivers (Conca 2006: 123–140).

Third, NGOs often work through environmental IGOs, particularly UNEP, to which 174 NGOs are accredited, because that is where they get access to states. They participate along with other nonstate stakeholders (business and industry, farmers, indigenous peoples, scientific/technical groups) in virtually every area of UNEP activity. In cooperation with state parties to the Convention to Regulate International Trade in Endangered Species of Wild Fauna and Flora (CITES), the WWF and IUCN formed a network called TRAFFIC to monitor trade in endangered species and wildlife. It performs on-site inspections and trains state officials and legal professionals, as discussed below. NGOs use their access to states through IGOs as a lever or boomerang to influence states' domestic policies, as US-based NGOs have tried to do to change attitudes on climate change.

Finally, and perhaps most important, NGOs attempt to influence states' environmental policies directly. Some NGOs, like the World Resource Institute, have extensive research staffs and provide valuable information for policymakers. The US–based World Wildlife Fund (a branch of the WWF) has worked directly with the Chinese Ministry of Forestry to manage the endangered panda bear, for example. Together with the US Agency for International Development (USAID), NGOs have helped fund Zambia's national game preserves, including training locals in anti-poaching strategies and using funds earned from the tourist trade for local development projects. Some NGOs may initiate formal legal proceedings against states for noncompliance. The Earth Island Institute used this approach in the tuna/dolphin controversy, appealing to US courts to enforce the 1972

Marine Mammal Protection Act. They may work through states' legislative or bureaucratic processes to pressure authorities to impose sanctions against other parties. NGOs may also work with local-level organizations. The WWF, for example, trains local villagers as wildlife conservationists and helps fund nurseries for restoration and reintroduction of indigenous crops. NGO-provided training is a particularly important function, as many governments may not have the technical capacity and resources to provide it without external assistance.

NGOs may work directly with states to package issues in ways that enhance the possibility of compliance with sets of obligations stemming from treaties or other commitments, including providing financial resources. Debt-for-nature swaps—the acquisition of debt, usually by a conservation NGO, followed by redemption of that debt in local currency to be used for conservation purposes—are one such example. Beginning in 1987, NGOs such as Conservation International and the Nature Conservancy arranged such swaps in Bolivia, Costa Rica, Ecuador, Zambia, Madagascar, and the Philippines, with local NGOs obtaining title to the preserved land. Another example is the use of conservation trust funds created with money from grants, donations, and earmarked fees to fund projects such as the WWF has undertaken in Central Africa, Brazil, Peru, and elsewhere to provide technical support for carbon finance mechanisms to reduce greenhouse-gas emissions. Projects in states are widely recognized as NGO funding opportunities, for it is in states that environmental policy is made and implemented.

Still, the overall impact of NGOs on environmental governance is a matter of dispute and not easily evaluated. They have had particular impact on treaty-negotiating processes, by working behind the scenes to reframe issues and influence the positions of state negotiators, and sometimes their proposals have found their way into treaty texts (Betsill and Corell 2008). They have had major impacts on monitoring environmental quality and national compliance, with Greenpeace keeping track of national compliance for many treaties, for example, and the World Conservation Union tracking compliance with species conservation treaties. NGOs have also played a key role in "greening" the international financial institutions, including most notably the World Bank, as discussed below, and in activating environmental constituencies around the world, using social media and the Internet to provide information and mobilize action groups.

## The Role of Epistemic Communities

Epistemic communities also perform a vital role in global environmental governance processes. In the 1970s, the dominant epistemic community concerned with the international environment comprised resource managers and liberal economists. Gradually, as environmental issues gained attention, ecologists and other environmental scientists in various specialized fields formed issue-specific epistemic communities. Scientists are the linchpins of these epistemic communities, serving as networks of professionals who can provide the vital data and analysis needed to expose problems and consult with governments and international agencies about policy options.

The Intergovernmental Panel on Climate Change is one such epistemic community, as discussed earlier. When scientific information is unclear or when members of the epistemic community disagree, as they did for many years on the climate change issue, then they too become a key part of the political process. When there is agreement among scientific experts, as there now is in the IPCC, then international action is more likely to be forthcoming, as uncertainty is reduced.

UNEP's Mediterranean Action Plan, for example, was developed with the help of an epistemic community of ecological experts from around the Mediterranean basin. Beginning in 1972, the experts participated in meetings in a professional but unofficial capacity; UNEP administrators relied on the epistemic community for obtaining the data needed to establish the monitoring program and modify it accordingly. These experts were also active in the domestic bargaining processes within Mediterranean littoral states, fostering learning among governmental officials and elites. As Peter Haas (1990: 188) concludes, "The transnational alliance between the ecological epistemic community and national marine scientists led governments to define their interests, so that they accepted a collective program that was increasingly comprehensive and complied with such arrangements domestically."

To be successful, epistemic communities have to be continually nurtured, new research opportunities presented, and new networks developed. For a global epistemic community to be legitimate, members have to come from both developing and developed countries, a difficult task given the more limited number of scientific specialists from the South.

## Global Environmental Regimes and Institutions
UN-sponsored global conferences have resulted not only in the formation of epistemic communities and the proliferation of NGOs, but also in the establishment of key principles, new norms, and programs of action. In many cases, those principles have been translated into specific standards and incorporated into environmental treaties and specific global institutions.

### Principles of Environmental Governance
The core principles and norms governing the environment have evolved over more than a century and certain ones are generally recognized as customary law. The first is the principle of "no significant harm." This came

from the 1941 *Trail Smelter Arbitration* between the United States and Canada and from Principle 21 of the Stockholm Declaration. States have the responsibility to ensure that activities within their jurisdiction do not cause environmental damage to others. The second is the principle of "good neighbor" cooperation. According to Stockholm's Principle 27, states agree to cooperate should environmental problems arise. There are also emerging principles that are not yet recognized as binding international law. Many of these were incorporated in the Rio Declaration on Environment and Development, including the "polluter pays" principle, the precautionary principle (take action on the basis of scientific warning), and the preventive action principle (take action within one's own state). The nondiscrimination principle obligates states to treat domestic and international environmental concerns in the same way. Finally, the principles of sustainable development and intergenerational equity suggest that no policies should obligate future generations or incur costs that are then transferred to subsequent generations.

Because most of these are emerging principles, environmental law is mostly soft law. Although nonbinding, it is useful because it offers a starting point for getting agreement on more ambitious norms. Furthermore, soft law often foreshadows hard law of the future, describing acceptable norms of behavior and codifying developing rules of customary practice.

Law-creating conventions, embodying principles, norms, and where possible rules, form the foundations for environmental governance.

### Global Environmental Agreements

There were almost 1,200 multilateral environmental agreements and 1,500 bilateral agreements as of 2013. In the fifteen years after Stockholm, for example, more agreements were concluded than ever before. In general, these agreements articulate the normative content of a specific issue, initiate information-gathering activities, and call for voluntary restrictions on domestic activities that result in transnational harm. Much less attention is given to spelling out means of implementation and compliance. With the growing number of such treaties, there have been changes in subject and scope. Prior to the 1970s, most agreements were very specific, applying to one species or a particular local or regional problem. Since the 1970s, the agreements have broadened to deal with activities negatively affecting the global or regional commons. In recent years, many agreements are amendments to existing conventions.

Table 11.1 provides a selective list of both global and regional agreements. Some of these are linked to specific organizations while others are freestanding, autonomous arrangements. Most call for a conference or meeting of the parties that has decisionmaking powers, a small secretariat, and one or more specialized subsidiary bodies, often convened on an ad hoc

**Table 11.1    Selected Global and Regional Environmental Agreements**

| Treaty | Year Opened for Ratification | Year Entered into Force | Number of Ratifications, Accessions (2014) |
|---|---|---|---|
| Global environmental agreements | | | |
| International Convention for the Regulation of Whaling | 1946 | 1948 | 38 |
| Convention for the Protection of the World Cultural and Natural Heritage | 1972 | 1975 | 189 |
| Convention on the Prevention of Marine Pollution by the Dumping of Wastes and Other Matter | 1972 | 1975 | 80 |
| Convention on the International Trade in Endangered Species of Wild Fauna and Flora | 1973 | 1975 | 175 |
| Convention on Long-Range Transboundary Air Pollution | 1979 | 1983 | 51 |
| Convention on the Conservation of Antarctic Marine Living Resources | 1980 | 1982 | 34 |
| Vienna Convention for the Protection of the Ozone Layer | 1985 | 1988 | 197 |
| Montreal Protocol on Substances That Deplete the Ozone Layer | 1987 | 1989 | 197 |
| Convention on the Control of Transboundary Movements of Hazardous Wastes and Their Disposal | 1989 | 1992 | 172 |
| UN Convention on Biological Diversity | 1992 | 1993 | 193 |
| UN Framework Convention on Climate Change | 1992 | 1994 | 195 |
| UN Convention to Combat Desertification in Those Countries Experiencing Serious Drought and/or Desertification, Particularly in Africa | 1994 | 1996 | 198 |
| Kyoto Protocol to UN Framework Convention on Climate Change | 1997 | 2005 | 192 |
| Convention on the Conservation and Management of the Highly Migratory Fish Stocks of the Western and Central Pacific | 2000 | 2004 | 25 |
| Convention on Persistent Organic Pollutants | 2001 | 2004 | 176 |
| International Tropical Timber Agreement | 2006 | 2011 | 63 |
| Minamata Convention on Mercury | 2013 | pending | 11 |

*(continues)*

basis. While few include provisions for dispute settlement, there is evidence that states are more likely to participate in environmental treaties when there are provisions for dispute settlement and when assistance is provided for building state capacity (Bernauer et al. 2013).

The Convention on International Trade in Endangered Species, covering about 34,000 specific species, provides an example of a flexible agreement. Species that are threatened with extinction receive the greatest degree of protection, and trade is prohibited, as it was for the African elephant (and ivory) in 1989. For species needing intermediate levels of protection including polar bears and grizzly bears, trade is permitted but highly regu-

Table 11.1     continued

| Treaty | Year Opened for Ratification | Year Entered into Force | Number of Ratifications, Accessions (2014) |
|---|---|---|---|
| Regional environmental agreements | | | |
| Convention for the Protection of the Mediterranean Sea Against Pollution | 1976 | 1978 | 22 |
| Convention on Long-Range Transboundary Air Pollution in Europe | 1979 | 1983 | 51 |
| North American Agreement on Environmental Cooperation (Canada, Mexico, United States) | 1993 | 1994 | 3 |
| Convention for the Protection of the Black Sea Against Pollution | 1992 | 1994 | 6 |
| Convention on Cooperation for Protection and Sustainable Use of the Danube River | 1994 | 1998 | 15 |
| ASEAN Agreement on Transboundary Haze Pollution | 2002 | 2003 | 9 |
| Treaty on the Conservation and Sustainable Development of the Forest Ecosystems of Central Africa | 2005 | 2006 | 8 |
| Agreement on the Conservation of Gorillas and Their Habitats | 2007 | 2008 | 5 |
| Agreement on the Nile River Basin Cooperative Framework | 2010 | pending | 10 |
| Agreement on Cooperation on Marine Oil Pollution, Preparedness, and Response in the Arctic | 2013 | pending | 4 |

*Note:* For additional information, see International Environmental Agreements Database Project, http://iea.uoregon.edu.

lated. For still another group, regulation is domestic. Parties meet every two years to determine whether to add, delete, or transfer species from one list to another. State and regional variations in levels of protection enhance that flexibility. CITES proved especially effective in the early years, but the highly publicized cases of the African elephant and the rhino are particularly vexing, as high demand in Asia has fueled extensive poaching in Africa.

CITES implementation mechanisms are unique. As discussed earlier, TRAFFIC verifies compliance with CITES rulings, working directly with governments to provide information, monitoring, training, and education programs for wildlife-trade enforcement officers. It also works on the demand side, organizing campaigns to reduce demand for the products in East Asian countries. The flexible arrangements and cooperation with NGOs engendered by CITES are more the exception than the rule among environmental regimes. WildAid, another NGO, is trying to do the same specifically in China, enlisting celebrities such as basketball player Yao Ming to endorse the campaign to reduce demand for ivory and rhino horn. On the supply side, states like Kenya and South Africa have expanded anti-poaching units and increased penalties for abuses. At one time, these combined measures pointed to an estimated twofold increase in the African elephant population, but 2013 reports estimate a 50–67 percent decline in the number of elephants in some parts of East Africa (Levin 2014: A14).

### International Environmental Institutions

The creation and subsequent strengthening of international environmental institutions have been a permanent legacy of the UN-sponsored conferences. These institutions play key roles in the process of global environmental governance, helping to set standards and participating in the negotiation of the treaties listed in Table 11.1. They monitor state behavior. They aid state members, NGOs, and other IGOs in the promotion of environmental standards. And occasionally these institutions enforce environmental law. Five institutions stand out, three of which were created specifically to address environmental problems and two of which, while originally tasked with development and trade, have been pressured to respond to environmental issues.

*The United Nations Environment Programme.* While many older IGOs had an environmental component to their responsibility (such as the WMO's monitoring of air pollution and the FAO's researching of environmental effects on water and fisheries), there was no agency or program devoted to environmental issues until the creation of UNEP after the 1972 Stockholm Conference. With Maurice Strong as its first executive director, UNEP championed the new environmental agenda and, with its headquarters in Nairobi, Kenya, became the first UN agency based in a developing country. Its mandate is to promote international cooperation in the field of the environment, serve as an early warning system to alert the international community to environmental dangers, provide guidance for the direction of environmental programs in the UN system, and review implementation of these programs. Its responsibilities are both "normative and catalytic" (Ivanova 2010: 33). Until 2013, its Governing Council set general policy and reported to the UN General Assembly through ECOSOC. For its relatively small size and budget (originally all raised through voluntary contributions), UNEP has a large agenda (DeSombre 2006: 14–20).

UNEP has four major responsibilities. First, it plays a key role in negotiating international environmental agreements and in providing the secretariat and oversight for treaty bodies. CITES, the Basel Convention on the Transboundary Movement of Hazardous Wastes, the Montreal Protocol Multilateral Fund, and the Convention on Migratory Species are among those covered. In some cases, it has been a catalyst for negotiations, as when UNEP executive director Mustafa Tolba provided leadership for the negotiation of the Montreal Protocol on Substances That Deplete the Ozone

Layer in the 1980s, convening interested constituencies, applying pressure, and floating proposals.

Second, UNEP is charged with monitoring the international environment. For actual research, it commissions outside experts. Its Division of Early Warning Assessment coordinates information on water under the Global Environmental Monitoring System and on toxic substances under the International Registry of Potentially Toxic Chemicals. Often it works in close collaboration with other IGOs. To monitor atmospheric and ocean quality, UNEP works with the WMO and the International Oceanographic Council respectively. The monitoring and assessments enable UNEP to play an agenda-setting role on specific issues, as it has on chemical pollutants, hazardous wastes, and marine pollution.

Third, UNEP oversees the Regional Seas Program to protect thirteen regional seas. That responsibility was an expansion of UNEP's initial work in the Mediterranean Sea. Although that program is often seen as one of UNEP's major successes, the plans for various seas have faced critical problems, including contentious political relationships among participating states and lack of adequate funding. And fourth, UNEP manages the Dams and Development Program, a multistakeholder project, which is discussed later.

During its early years, UNEP was strengthened by the dynamic leadership of its first two executive directors, Maurice Strong and Mustapha Tolba. Yet it has always been handicapped by its limited leverage over UN specialized agencies and national governments, its location outside other UN centers, and the limited engagement of government stakeholders in its projects. Most limiting is its small budget (around $200 million), which reflects, in part, the dissatisfaction of major UN donors such as the United States, the United Kingdom, and Spain, which perceive that the UNEP bureaucracy has been captured by LDC interests.

Critics of UNEP's performance note its major shortcomings: its absence from the climate change debate; its inability to coordinate international environmental action or even provide for greater harmonization of reporting requirements for various conventions; and its inability to respond to the needs of states to enhance national environmental capacity. It is also important to note that UNEP was designed as a program, not a specialized UN agency; its leadership needs key negotiating skills, but its isolated location in Africa hampers that activity and makes it difficult to hire expert personnel (Ivanova 2010).

Partially in response to this critique as well as to the need to strengthen it as an organization, UNEP's Governing Council was upgraded to become the United Nations Environment Assembly in 2013. This was seen by then–UNEP executive director Achim Steiner as "a watershed moment." He added: "Universal membership establishes a new, fully-representative platform to strengthen the environmental dimension of sustainable development, and provides all governments with an equal voice on the decisions and action needed to support the global environment, and ensure a fairer share of the world's resources for all" (UNEP 2012). Other reforms brought greater stability in finances, with a portion of the budget coming from assessed contributions (earlier, all funding was from voluntary contributions), and more formal authority to aid states in capacity-building and implement environmental commitments (Ivanova 2013).

*The Global Environmental Facility.* Created in 1991, the GEF is the most prominent international funder of environmental projects in low- and middle-income countries. Originally housed within the World Bank, in the mid-1990s it was restructured and became a separate institution. While the Bank continues to serve as a trustee of the funding facility and provides administration services, that separation enhanced the organization's legitimacy for the developing countries who are skeptical of the Bank's liberal economic orientation. UNEP provides scientific oversight and helps in selecting priorities, and the UNDP coordinates with other bilateral donors. NGOs are involved in the planning and execution of projects. The GEF has emerged as a useful complement to other sources of financial assistance for environmental projects in developing countries.

GEF funds cover the cost differential between a project initiated with environmental objectives and an alternative project undertaken without attention to global environmental concerns. Most importantly, its funds help leverage other funding for projects, so that by 2013 it had disbursed some $12.5 billion in grants, supplemented by $58 billion in cofinancing. In addition, through 16,000 small grants ($50,000–$250,000 each), the facility subsidizes grassroots groups, thereby building on its commitment to NGO participation.

GEF's priorities include financing the commitments under the UN Convention on Biological Diversity and UNFCC, with small grants for energy efficiency, renewable energy, emissions inventories, and adaptation projects, as well as commitments under the Stockholm Convention on Persistent Organic Pollutants, the UN Convention to Combat Desertification, and the Minamata Convention on Mercury. Most ozone-related funding is handled through the Montreal Protocol Multilateral Fund, not the Global Environmental Facility.

The Global Environmental Facility's 183 member governments are represented in the facility's assembly; its council is composed of thirty-two states, with sixteen from developing countries, fourteen from developed countries, and two from the former Soviet bloc, and meets twice a year to approve work programs and projects. Decisions require double majorities of the funder and developing member states. Every three years, the affected parties review general policies and approve any changes to the GEF agreement. Funds are replenished by the donors every four years and programmatic initiatives have become more cohesive. NGOs enjoy an open invitation to participate.

The GEF, like UNEP, fills a critical niche with almost 90 percent of its funding supporting climate change and biodiversity activities. Two main criticisms persist: not having its own social safeguards in place, relying instead on those of its implementing agencies, and not working closely enough with state-level and civil society actors to reflect local priorities. As is evident with all development partnerships, working relationships within the Global Environmental Facility need to be constantly renegotiated.

*From Commission to High-Level Political Forum.* The Commission on Sustainable Development was created following the 1992 Rio Conference to monitor implementation of Agenda 21, give policy guidance on future initiatives, and promote partnerships for sustainable development. Located in New York, the commission served for twenty years as the venue for discussion of issues related to sustainable development; whether it was more than just a "talk-shop," however, is debatable (Kaasa 2007: 112–116). It carried out its monitoring role by receiving reports from states, other UN bodies, and NGOs, but the content, formatting, and timing of states' reports was up to them, with no baselines and hence no way to assess progress or make cross-national comparisons. The commission did have some success relating to forests, oceans, and freshwater as well as in promoting multistakeholder dialogues thanks in large part to the EU's priority on environmental issues (Kaasa 2007: 116–119).

The 2012 Rio Plus 20 Summit made the decision to replace the Commission on Sustainable Development with the High-Level Political Forum on Sustainable Development, which convenes every four years at the heads-of-state level under UN General Assembly auspices and annually under ECOSOC. The hope is that the forum will prove more capable of meeting the challenges of sustainable development, given the role of high-level officials in reviewing progress and suggesting an actionable agenda (Ivanova 2013). The intention is to make this new body a more equal match to the World Bank and WTO, which are far more powerful with respect to environmental issues.

*The World Bank: A rocky road to becoming green.* The World Bank is the largest multilateral donor for economic development and, as such, has been under the most pressure to make its economic development policies compatible with environmental sustainability. Yet its record has been a mixed one. In fact, it was during the 1960s and 1970s, when Bank funding focused on major infrastructure projects, that the emerging transnational environmental advocacy networks targeted Bank development projects that hurt the environment. Such high-profile projects as Brazil's Amazon basin development project, Indonesia's population relocation from Java to neighboring islands, and dam projects in India came under intense scrutiny. Opposition to dam construction, for example, was led by the International Rivers Network, which beginning in the mid-1980s campaigned against China's Three Gorges Dam, Malaysia's Bakun Dam, and India's Sardar Sarovar-Narmada project, among others (Khagram 2000). The coalition claimed that such projects diverted rivers, accelerated deforestation, changed ecosystems, forced people to move to environmentally fragile areas, and had unanticipated negative effects on both the local population and the indigenous peoples. The same arguments were made about the Amazon basin project, which brought the Bank adverse publicity for failing to provide environmental safeguards.

Susan Park (2010: 2) contends that the transnational environmental advocacy networks "*informed and helped shape* member states' decisions to implement new environmental standards." The Bank's response to this pressure came slowly. In the 1970s, environmental advisers were appointed, but their concerns were not integrated into the mainstream of Bank projects. By the end of the 1980s, Bank officials began to acknowledge environmental problems and work more closely with environmental NGOs. In 1993, again in response to NGO pressure, the World Bank established the independent Inspection Panel to investigate specific projects in response to citizens' claims of harm. Only in a few cases, such as Nepal's Arun III Dam, was the project subsequently canceled, however. Since 1993, lending for environmental programs has increased. Between 2004 and 2013, loans amounted to $31.8 billion, with most going to climate change projects, followed by water resource management and pollution projects. The number of staff addressing sustainable development and environmental issues has expanded. The Bank has published ten social and environmental safeguard policies, showing how it promotes inclusive and environmentally sustainable development and how its compliance procedures ensure that safeguard policies are followed in the sensitive areas of forestry, waterways, natural habitat, and dams. The Bank's annual *World Development Report* now includes considerable coverage of environmental issues in the context of sustainable development. Other Bank reports and meetings also reflect "green" language.

The depth of the Bank's commitment to environmental sustainability is still questioned, however. In 2008, the Bank's Independent Evaluation Group conducted its first systematic study of the environmental effects Bank projects, numbering 7,000 for the period 1990–2007. The report found that at each step of the lending process there was a lack of environmental focus and monitoring. The results may not be surprising, given that the environmental units of the Bank employ far fewer staff than do the administrative or economic divisions, and given that their staff have had a difficult time making the case for environmental policies solely based on economic analysis—the Bank's dominant culture. Whether environmental plans and concerns are actually integrated into projects depends too often on the interests of individual country directors (Weaver 2008: chap. 5). Another evaluation of 274 Bank environmental projects using the Bank's own evaluation process found that projects that addressed local priorities, namely water and sanitation projects, were more successful than those that addressed global issues such as climate change or protecting biodiversity, because the former were subject to greater accountability from local constituencies (Buntaine and Parks 2013: 77).

So as Catherine Weaver (2008: 21) asks, has the Bank become "green," or has it just been "greenwashed"? Although some practices have changed, the real question is whether the Bank has fundamentally altered its attitude toward development and whether new norms have been internalized. Weaver points to the "incongruence of sustainable development goals with the intellectual and operational cultures of the Bank" (24). One of the harshest critics of World Bank environmental policies argues that the Bank has actually hastened environmental destruction and that the Bank's culture may not be able to change (Rich 2013). Others disagree.

The same question is also relevant to the regional development banks, as they have followed the World Bank's lead and gradually adopted an environmental agenda, safeguards, and implementing mechanisms. Although adoption of an environmental agenda in these banks has generally lagged the World Bank's adoption, in some cases, such as that of the AfDB, environmental issues have gained urgency as the effects of climate change on the planet have become apparent. The AfDB serves as the implementing agency for the Global Environmental Facility in Africa, managing twenty-three projects across the continent, and more than half of these in 2013 alone. And "green growth" rhetoric is central to its 2013 strategy commitment to building resilience to climate shocks with infrastructure and natural resource protection.

*The greening of trade: From GATT to the WTO.* GATT was as reluctant as the World Bank and regional development banks to embrace environmental initiatives. In fact, when members of GATT were invited to work on the preparatory meeting for the 1972 Stockholm Conference, they feared that world market competitiveness would decline should anti-pollution standards be passed. GATT's Trade and Environment Working Group sought to avoid situations where pollution control systems would interfere with international trade. As Michel Damian and Jean-Christophe Graz (2001: 600) remind us, "The guiding principle at GATT was above all to prevent distortions and hindrances to trade, and to keep the environment on the margins of trade."

Yet GATT and later its successor, the WTO, as well as other trade organizations, had to adjust to a new reality. Many of the multilateral environmental agreements listed in Table 11.1 include provisions that could restrict trade. The concept of sustainable development carries with it recognition that restrictions on trade may serve environmental objectives. Thus, GATT, the WTO, and other trade organizations have gradually been forced to address the tensions among trade, development, and environmental objectives and resulting legal disputes. The 1972 US Marine Mammal Protection Act, for example, prohibited the importation of Mexican tuna because tuna were caught with nets that entangled threatened (but not endangered) dolphins. In 1991, a GATT dispute panel ruled in favor of Mexico, declaring that environmental concerns over a foreign industry could not be used to bar imports. Despite protests from environmentalists, the decision was never formally approved by GATT's governing body and thus set no precedent. The United States and Mexico negotiated a bilateral settlement. GATT rules at the time required states to treat all like-products equally, without regard to process or how a product was made. Only gradually have environmental concerns been taken into account.

The 1994 agreement that established the WTO recognized the "objective of sustainable development, seeking both to protect and preserve the environment." Although that agreement incorporates GATT's Article XX, which requires states to treat all like-products as national equivalents, it also provides for protection of human, animal, and plant life or health, and for conservation of exhaustible natural resources. If those conditions arise, then countries can ban the products, so long as they do not protect only their own industries and do not unfairly discriminate. The WTO established its Committee on Trade and Environment under pressure from the European Union and the United States. Its responsibility has included clarifying the relationship between the multilateral environmental agreements and WTO rules, protecting market access for developing countries, and addressing the legality of eco-labeling to bring the practice under WTO rules. On the first issue, no specific provisions under multilateral environmental agreements have been challenged in the WTO, suggesting that such agreements may be the more effective way of addressing environmental problems. On the second issue, developing countries have been given more rights to participate in standard-setting, thus enabling them to protect their access to markets. On the third, the WTO has not mandated environmental labeling that gives full information to consumers. But the WTO has ruled that labeling requirements and practices should not discriminate, whether between trading partners (i.e., most-favored-nation treatment) or between domestically produced goods (national treatment).

If a dispute occurs over a trade action taken under an environmental agreement, then disputants should try to use the environmental agreement to settle the case. But the WTO will not ignore environmental issues and the organization's Dispute Settlement Body has made several decisions relating to environment/trade issues. In one 1998 case, for example, the panel upheld the US ban on imports of shrimp that were harvested in a way that harmed sea turtles, basing the decision on Article XX's general exceptions clause. Furthermore, the panel pushed the members to protect the sea turtles, resulting in the 2001 Memorandum of Understanding on the Conservation and Management of Marine Turtles and Their Habitats in the Indian Ocean. The WTO panel opened the door to an environmental justification for banning trade in a product when the purpose is to safeguard an endangered species, assuming that proper procedures are followed, including nondiscrimination (Weinstein and Charnovitz 2001: 151–152).

The WTO is far from a green institution. It still has no organizational commitment to environmental protection, nor has it accepted the precautionary principle as grounds for restricting trade as the EU has done. Instead, the WTO has given greater weight to scientific proof over the precautionary principle, and its legal decisions, while moving in the direction of accepting trade restrictions for the purposes of environmental protection, are very narrowly constructed. Many of the WTO's sessions are held behind closed doors, but it does permit *amicus curiae* briefs from citizens and NGOs, and over time more hearings have been held in public, adding transparency to its process.

One of the objectives of the WTO's Doha Round of trade negotiations has been to enhance the relationship between trade and the environment, including the reduction or elimination of tariff and nontariff barriers on environmental goods and services. But defining what is an environmental good or service has proved to be a stumbling block, and with the collapse of negotiations in 2008, as discussed in Chapter 8, the WTO's Trade and Environmental Committee has been relegated to maintaining contacts between the WTO Secretariat and the secretariats of the various multilateral environmental agreements.

## Public-Private Partnerships and Environmental Governance

Just as private actors, businesses, and associations have played an increasingly important role in economic governance, private and other types of initiatives have expanded in the environmental arena. The Global Environmental Facility's Small Grants Program is one of the early public-private partnerships. The World Commission on Dams (WCD) provides a good illustration.

In 1998, the WCD was created as an independent international body composed of twelve commissioners representing affected peoples' groups, research institutes, hydropower companies, multilateral development banks, river basin authorities, and governments directly involved with construction of large hydroelectric dams. The commission's mandate was to conduct a review of the development effectiveness of 125 dams and establish social, economic, and environmental criteria for future construction. Although its recommendations were not legally binding, it provided a knowledge base for evaluation and a normative framework. The commission issued its report in 2000 and was disbanded in 2001, with its tasks being assumed by UNEP's Dams and Development Project and its campaigns folded into work by the World Conservation Union and World Wide Fund for Nature. The commission, however, provided an important model for public-private governance. It succeeded in shifting the focus toward a comprehensive view of water and energy needs and in establishing "'core values' of equity, efficiency, participatory decision making, sustainability, and accountability in all decisions related to dams and their alternatives" (Conca 2006: 198). The WCD has been called "the most innovative international institutional experiment" (Khagram 2000: 105). It clearly encouraged the formation of other partnerships, as over 4,000 public-private partnerships were registered with the UN Commission on Sustainable Development following the Johannesburg Summit of 2002.

Why have public-private partnerships been so critical in international environmental governance? Several factors account for this development: IGOs frequently adopt new programs without providing funds for implementation. As the idea of public-private partnerships has taken hold, they have provided a way of tapping other sources of funding and responding to pressure from NGOs. And as Liliana Andonova (2010: 31) notes, partnerships have provided a way "to engage nonstate actors in dialogue and co-governance on the basis of soft, experimental agreements, which at the same time can deflect pressure, co-opt critics, and increase the flow of information and expertise."

Public-private partnerships have been called a new form of global governance. They are not just replacing state authority with participation of NGOs and other representatives of global civil society. They are a form of hybridization, in which there is "retention of some traditional foundations of state authority" and also the growth of nonstate authority "grounded in a blend of expertise and moral claims" (Conca 2006: 211).

## Private Governance and Rule-Setting

The Forest Stewardship Council (FSC) provides an excellent example of private environmental governance and rule-setting. Protection of endangered tropical forests has long been on the international agenda. Since the

1970s in UNCTAD and the 1980s with the International Tropical Timber Organization, resource management issues have included the goal of certifying that all tropical timber traded internationally comes from sustainably managed sources. Yet by the early 1990s it was clear that tropical deforestation had become a major problem. The rates of deforestation were doubling in the Amazon basin during the early 1990s, although by 2012 that had declined dramatically. Indonesia in 2014 achieved the dubious distinction of having the highest rate of deforestation in the world. That has led over the past two decades to massive fires and air pollution, threatening soil productivity and endangering species, in order to promote timber and palm oil exports. Economic downturns such as the 1998 Asian financial crisis create even more incentives to increase exports. Yet conflicting interests between producers of tropical timber (developing states, local communities, timber companies) and consumers (mainly in developed countries) who seek low prices have led to a deadlock, despite the goals of the 1992 Rio Conference.

The FSC was formed in 1993 by a group of 300 individuals brought together by the World Wide Fund for Nature (and its US affiliate, also the WWF) and Greenpeace and includes labor unions, indigenous peoples' groups, retailers, the consultancy sector, and the timber industry, as well as environmental NGOs. Based in Bonn, Germany, it is an independent voluntary arrangement designed to set environmentally sound, sustainable standards for the forest products industry. Its certification is intended to permit consumers to make environmentally informed purchasing decisions.

The FSC uses a combination of strategies to encourage compliance. It uses social pressure on retailers of timber products and on consumers to persuade them to refrain from buying wood from nonsustainable sources. It offers producers a certificate stating that sustainable forest management practices are being used (Dingwerth and Pattberg 2009: 712). To put this into operation, highly detailed technical information on both forest management practices and a "chain of custody" as wood moves from forest to consumer is required. Only wood receiving a certification carries the FSC logo. Major stakeholders meet in two chambers to discuss economic, environmental, and social issues and to monitor compliance. What is unique about this private governance arrangement is the provision of separate subchambers for representatives from the North and from the South, giving the South greater participation opportunities than found in most arrangements, even though groups from the North are better resourced (Dingwerth 2008: 617–619).

Several criteria and questions can be used to evaluate the FSC (Pattberg 2011: 269–271). Has certification aided in biodiversity conservation? Based on a study of almost 130 certification reports from twenty-one countries, positive biodiversity impacts have been noted in aquatic and riparian zones, high-value forests, and endangered species (Newsom and Hewitt 2005). Has logging of certified forests resulted in preservation of endangered species? A case study from Malaysia found that to be true (Mannan et al. 2008). Have deforestation and wildfires been reduced? Research from Guatemala finds this to be the case (Hughell and Butterfield 2008). The FSC's own reports indicate that 180 million hectares have been FSC-certified in eighty-one countries. However, most of the land is in North and South America, while Africa and Southeast Asia lag far behind. Still, at least in early 2000, there was evidence that financial markets were paying more attention to these corporate practices, to the benefit of firms that became leaders, while punishing those that lagged behind (Conroy 2002: 215).

The FSC has also expanded the discussion of deforestation to include not only sustainability, but also tenure rights, indigenous peoples, and community rights. In short, the FSC is an innovative instrument of private voluntary regulation that has served as a model for alternative certification schemes, not only in the area of forestry but also in the sustainable management of fisheries.

Another private governance organization that sets standards and includes a monitoring and enforcement mechanism to evaluate whether firms are complying with their obligations is the International Organization for Standardization 14001 (Potoski and Elwakeil 2011). ISO 14001 was developed in the 1990s as an extension of the ISO (see Chapter 8), designed to provide participating industrial plants with an environmental management system for internal operations. The process for certification is extensive and costly (upward of $100,000), requiring specialized training and documentation. Not only does it help plants meet national environmental guidelines, but it also encourages members to take additional steps in the interests of environmental compliance. Independent external audits are conducted to ensure compliance. Judged by the number of participants, ISO 14001 has been successful, but nearly 80 percent of the adopters are in Europe or Asia, where the approach is widely used. Matthew Potoski and Elizabeth Elwakeil (2011: 298) explain these cross-national differences: "firms adopt ISO 14001 to signal their environmental activities in export markets and when their domestic markets have more experience with management-based standards," and firms are less likely to adopt "when their domestic regulatory environment is less flexible and more adversarial," as in North America and Latin America. The hope is to improve environmental conditions through voluntary actions of certified firms.

## Global Environmental Governance in Action

The case of global warming discussed at the beginning of this chapter illustrates unique challenges for global governance. Contrasting efforts to address climate change with what is widely regarded as the successful case of reducing ozone depletion shows how global governance was achieved in the latter, while it has proved so difficult in the former. In both cases, the global commons are threatened.

## Ozone Depletion: Anatomy of Success

Ozone depletion was thrust onto the international agenda in 1975, following a report submitted by two US scientists attributing depletion of the ozone layer to use of chlorofluorocarbons (CFCs), which are widely used in refrigeration systems. The correlation between use of CFCs and ozone depletion was a contested one among scientists for several years. But in a little less than a decade, following publication of new data confirming a widening ozone hole over Antarctica, most states and scientific experts acknowledged the scope of the problem. The United States and European states were both the major producers of CFCs and the major consumers, although usage in the newly industrializing countries such as India, China, Brazil, and Mexico was rising at about 10 percent annually.

The success of the international approach to governance of ozone can be attributed to several factors. Most important may have been the role of leadership on the issue from the United States, Canada, and Norway. The support of those countries rested on a mobilized public who articulated the issue and on supportive NGOs. In particular, the US government became active due to several catalytic events. Multilateral institutions were also critical, particularly UNEP, whose executive director, Mustafa Tolba, mobilized an international constituency and initiated consultations with key governments, private interest groups, and IGOs. He argued for flexibility, applied pressure, and floated his own proposals as a stimulus to participants (Benedick 1998). Scientists provided convincing data on the extent of the problem and on monitoring it, giving the process scientific validation. Multinational corporations that produced CFCs, including Dow Chemical and DupPont, found suitable substitutes at acceptable cost for most uses. Since only a small percentage of their business depended on this one product, they were able to accept a compromise with little effect on their profitability. The conditions proved ripe for a negotiated approach.

Furthermore, the negotiating process and procedures were handled expeditiously. The process was subdivided into smaller problems and the treaty was a flexible instrument that could be made stricter should the scientific evidence warrant change, or loosened, had the ozone hole problem been shown to be less severe. The parties agreed to compliance mechanisms that were independent of any formal dispute settlement procedures. An ad hoc working group of legal experts on noncompliance was established. It was to offer conciliatory measures to encourage full compliance in a cooperative, nonjudicial, and nonconfrontational way. Finally, the UNEP secretariat was at the center of the implementation process.

In the first phase, states promised to cooperate on research and data acquisition as agreed in the 1985 Vienna Convention. The second phase was the 1987 Montreal Protocol on Substances That Deplete the Ozone Layer, together with the 1990 London Agreement, which further tightened states' commitment to phase out ozone-depleting chemicals. While the negotiations were not easy, at the end of the process states agreed to permanent, quantitative emission limits on five CFCs for all countries, although some international trading in emission entitlements was permitted. The industrialized countries agreed to pay for the incremental costs of compliance for developing countries and the Global Environmental Facility offered financial assistance to help economies in transition—both key elements for reaching agreement.

The Ozone Secretariat, served by UNEP, is an example of a small secretariat with authority to oversee the various treaties and protocols, which along with a working group of the parties, a variety of expert panels, and a multilateral implementation fund forms the ozone regime (Bauer 2006: 34). The secretariat is the hub of a network of over a hundred national ozone units that provide services to developing countries' ministries, as well as draft initiatives for amendments and adjustments to the Montreal Protocol, in keeping with recommendations from the Technology and Economic Assessment Panel. Since passage of the Montreal Protocol, subsequent conferences have expanded regulations to include almost a hundred different ozone-depleting substances. A 2014 study identified several new ozone-depleting substances that are being evaluated by the secretariat's advisory panel. Over time, the Ozone Secretariat has acquired a solid reputation for its technical expertise, transparency, and strong diplomatic skills. It has found the "balance between being an active player behind the scenes and being perceived as a neutral and 'passive' tool from the viewpoint of governments" (Bauer 2006: 43–44).

Although the Global Environmental Facility was originally to serve as the principal source of funding for developing countries, in fact the Multilateral Fund for the Implementation of the Montreal Protocol has played that role in assisting developing countries in controlling ozone-depleting substances. The GEF has also provided financial assistance to Central and Eastern European countries. The Implementation Committee handles cases of noncompliance with the rules on consumption and production of controlled substances and provides both technical assistance to analyze the reasons for noncompliance and additional funding. Over $3 billion in funds were allocated for specific projects between 1991 and 2013.

Worldwide consumption of ozone-depleting substances has declined more than 75 percent since the Montreal Protocol came into force in the late 1980s, even while production has grown slightly in the developing world. In 2014, UNEP scientists concluded that Earth's ozone layer was "well on the way to recovery" thanks to action against the ozone-depleting substances. Also, as noted in the climate change case study, they reported that the Montreal Protocol has made a large contribution to the reduction of greenhouse gases—which constitute some 90 percent of the emissions linked to ozone-depleting substances (UNEP 2014). Demand for products using CFC-like compounds continues to grow, however, as growing middle classes in China, India, and other developing countries demand refrigerators and air conditioners, but research for substitutes has been promising. States have instituted measures compatible with the regulatory provisions. In all likelihood, the global stratosphere has already experienced its highest levels of ozone depletion. But whether this will result in a permanent change in the ozone layer remains an open question. Outside of the polar regions, the ozone layer shows signs of recovery, while polar ozone loss remains large and variable. If current trends continue, scientists predict the recovery of the ozone layer by 2050.

## Regional Environmental Governance

Many environmental issues require regional rather than global responses, and some issues, such as climate change, have seen strong regional initiatives. A number of regional IGOs, including the EU, NAFTA, and ASEAN, are involved with environmental issues, often responding to problems with differing approaches and degrees of institutionalization. There are also a large number of regional environmental agreements, as shown in Table 11.1, some with an entirely environmental emphasis, others linked to other issues. Most date from after the Stockholm Conference, where regional activities were highlighted and UNEP was charged with monitoring regional activities.

Yet *region* in environmental affairs may be defined by ecological systems such as the Mediterranean Sea or the Mekong River basin, or the transboundary flow of pollution such as the haze from forest fires in Indonesia. In other words, where regional institutional mechanisms have been created for environmental governance, they may be outside established regional IGOs. Generally, regional governance is founded on the subsidiarity principle: decisions are most effective when taken at the lowest possible level (Betsill 2007: 12–13). We look here at environmental governance in three regional organizations: the EU, NAFTA, and ASEAN.

### The European Union

Among the regions, the EU has the strongest, most extensive, and most innovative environmental policies and has been a strong proponent of addressing climate change and global environmental governance. But it did not start out that way. There was no mention of the environment in the

European Community's original Treaty of Rome. It was not until the Single European Act of 1987 called for accelerated integration of a single economic market that the environment was mentioned for the first time. Balanced growth meant integrating environmental policies. Ten years later, in the Treaty of Amsterdam, signatories agreed that harmonizing environmental standards within the EU meant leveling the economic playing field and ensuring fair competition. Under the Lisbon Treaty, the EU committed itself to "sustainable development . . . based on . . . a high level of protection and improvement of the quality of the environment" (Article 2.3). That commitment also reflects strong public opinion in favor of environmental regulations, the emergence of green political parties in most EU member states, and the development of effective domestic environmental agencies at the national and local levels.

EU environmental principles are based on two key general principles: the notion that the polluter should pay to restore the environment, and the notion that preventive action should be taken when faced with an environmental threat. What differentiates the EU from other regional IGOs is the increasing reliance on the precautionary principle. The EU has also set environmental standards at all stages of the process, from production and distribution to consumption (eco-labeling), and has made access to information and transparency essential to a notion of justice in environmental matters.

EU environmental law now includes more than six environmental action programs and over 300 legislative acts with over 80 directives (Vogler 2011: 19) covering such issues as air, water, soil, waste disposal, genetically modified organisms (GMOs), biosafety, coastal-zone management, and hazardous chemicals. For example, in the area of air pollution, the EU has adopted increasingly strict directives on air pollution by vehicles, large plants, power stations, and aircraft, the phasing out of CFCs, prohibitions against various forms of noise pollution, and an energy tax on carbon dioxide emissions. On water pollution, the EU has common standards for surface and underground water, drinking water, and toxic substances. Environmental impact assessments have been mandatory since 1985 for all public and private projects above a certain size, and consultation with the public is required. As Henrik Selin (2007: 64) reports, not only is the environment "where national policy has been harmonized the furthest," but much "policy-making competence has been transferred from the national governments to the EU level." Indeed, the EU Commission has been the initiator, even though states themselves are the implementers.

Since the mid-1980s, the pace of community environmental legislation has slowed and the emphasis has changed with greater institutionalization. First, there has been a movement toward passage of directives over regulations. With directives, the EU sets out the framework with comprehensive long-term objectives, but it is left to the member states to decide the specific methods to be employed and to pass the appropriate legislation. For example, the EU passed the Integrated Pollution Prevention and Control Directive in 1996, a directive aimed at instituting permit requirements for large industrial users to take specific measures to minimize air, water, and land pollution. States themselves have discretion for establishing specific standards in keeping with technical requirements and local environmental circumstances. Similarly, in 1996, the EU passed the Ambient Air Quality and Auto Emissions Standards. Although the directive does not establish specific standards for all parameters, some are established for thirteen of the major pollutants, tightening standards for sulfur dioxide, nitrogen dioxide, and lead, among others. This approach to governance gives space for local and national variation, but establishes overall EU standards that help to level the economic playing field.

Second, the EU has taken steps to give consumers the power to make informed choices. In 1992, the Council of Ministers initiated rules for granting EU eco-labels for environmentally friendly products, enabling the consumer to choose those types of goods. Labeling of products from production to consumption phases is a prominent EU approach.

Third, in 1993 the European Environment Agency was established as an independent body to collect data that are comparable across member states so that appropriate policies are developed. That agency is weaker than anticipated, although one task has been to compile the EU's reports under the UN Framework Convention on Climate Change. The European Environmental Bureau has enabled NGOs to form active coalitions and gain access to all the EU institutions, though their relative impact varies by issue area and group. The major responsibility for environmental policy rests with the Commission's Directorate-General for the Environment, with detailed work falling to the Committee of Permanent Representatives. Their approach, and the probable explanation for the EU's comparative success, is to combine both management and enforcement strategies in order to achieve a binding common policy, utilizing allies in the scientific and NGO communities. The most controversial issues, like climate change, however, go to the heads of state in the European Council. It was the Council that announced the new EU climate change targets in 2014.

Fourth, several mechanisms have been developed to back up environmental policies with financing. These include the Financial Instrument for the Environment (LIFE), which aids states in complying with environmental guidelines and has financed over almost 4,000 projects, at a value of 3 billion euros, since its establishment. Funds from LIFE may jump-start a project. States may be given extra time to comply with EU rules and directives in order to improve domestic government capacity; national administrators from one jurisdiction may be sent to another to aid their government officials. The Commission monitors implementation and issues summary reports on violations, although it may not make on-site inspections nor may it investigate direct violations. The Commission may interpret guidelines when uncertainty exists. "This twinning of cooperative and coercive instruments in a 'management-enforcement ladder' makes the EU exceedingly effective in combating detected violations, thereby reducing noncompliance to a temporal phenomenon" (Tallberg 2002: 610).

Finally, another key to the EU's success in pushing environmental regulation is the role of the European Court of Justice. More often than not, the court has upheld EU environmental law. In a 2007 case, for example, the ECJ imposed a temporary measure on Poland to suspend work on a highway that traversed an environmentally sensitive zone that had been protected by the EU's Directorate-General for the Environment in 2000. Eventually an alternate route was found.

As environmentally sensitive and technically advanced as the EU is in terms of environmental issues, political differences and implementation problems are still prevalent. Austria, Denmark, Germany, Finland, the Netherlands, and Sweden are very strong supporters of environmental protection. Having adopted higher national standards, these countries have pushed for stronger EU-wide regulations. The relatively less developed states such as Greece, Portugal, and Spain have more lax standards and have been laggards in meeting the framework directives. The EU's newer members from Eastern Europe are at a lower level of economic development and have weaker environmental regulations, but since they joined they have had to implement EU policies and approaches. The European Commission projected in 2001 that the 2004 enlargement process might prove to be "the biggest single contribution to global sustainable development that the EU can make" (European Commission 2001: 13). That has also proven to be the case for states that are current candidates for EU membership. They have to meet rigorous environmental requirements by the time of accession. Funds have been established to help this group of countries, which includes Albania, Iceland, Macedonia, Montenegro, Serbia, and Turkey, implement the EU standards.

Within the core EU states, it is clear that there has been a profound transformation. As the mayor of one Ruhr town in the late 1990s put it: "Twenty years ago, this city didn't have anybody who dealt with environmental issues. Today, we have a whole department and they get involved in everything—construction, industrial development, noise abatement. . . . But what has changed even more intensively is the attitudes of the people. They want something done for environmental protection, and they know environmental protection doesn't stop at the border" (quoted in Andrews 2001: A3).

But while the EU has become a strong advocate on environmental issues in other IGOs and has supported multilateral environmental treaties across a range of issue areas, the European commitment has waned with regard to climate change, as discussed earlier.

## The North American Free Trade Agreement

The 1995 North American Free Trade Agreement approached environmental protection from two different angles. First, NAFTA addressed sanitary and phytosanitary measures (animal and plant health). Each country is entitled to establish its own level of protection in these areas and prohibit the importation of products that do not meet these sanitary or health standards. Second, NAFTA developed an explicit linkage between trade and the environment. The debate over inclusion of this linkage pitted trade economists against environmentalists. The former argued that if Mexican prosperity resulted from the trade agreement, then environmental regulations would follow. There was little need to directly incorporate environmental provisions. Environmentalists, on the other hand, using the language of sustainable development, argued for enforcement of environmental laws and regulations.

In the final agreement, provisions to promote sustainable development as well as to strengthen and enforce environmental laws and regulations were included, making NAFTA more environmentally friendly than most other trade agreements or the WTO. Each party is able to maintain its own level of environmental protection and ban imports produced in violation of those standards. The conditions for such bans are carefully specified: there can be no discrimination between domestic and foreign suppliers, nor can they create unnecessary obstacles to trade. Only legitimate objectives can be served by environmental restrictions. And environmental measures cannot be "applied in an arbitrary or unjustifiable manner" or "constitute a disguised restriction on international trade or investment." When disputes arise over the application of the standard, the burden is to prove that it is contrary to NAFTA. Expert environmental advice is sought in such cases.

The North American Commission for Environmental Cooperation addresses regional issues. Unlike the EU approach, NAFTA does not set common standards, but encourages compliance with domestic law and facilitates capacity-building in member states. Thus the commission has addressed several environmental issues, including chemicals management, freshwater conservation, maize and biodiversity, and climate change in a limited way. An example of capacity-building is the commission's development of an online training course for customs officials and border inspectors on the illegal trade in ozone-depleting substances. More generally, it issues periodic overviews of environmental conditions in NAFTA's three countries—Canada, Mexico, and the United States.

Although NAFTA is the first international trade agreement to incorporate strong environmental actions and provide for NGO consultations,

MNCs are also guaranteed clear and transparent rules to protect investor rights. They have the right to sue host governments under NAFTA's Chapter 11, with the World Bank's International Centre for Settlement of Investment Disputes handling these claims. Chapter 11 is controversial, for several reasons. First, discussions are conducted in private. The decisions have been ambiguous, weighed down in jurisdictional and procedural issues, with no method for clarification. Second, Chapter 11 decisions have tended to support the interests of the MNCs against state environmental regulation, angering some states and the NGO community. For example, Mexico has lost at least five disputes under Chapter 11, with the government having to pay $200 million in penalties to corporations. Canada has also lost or settled the same number of Chapter 11 cases, awarding $157 million in compensation to foreign companies. Third, it is still unclear how the decisions can be enforced. But as one study asserts: "The 'chilling effect' that these rules put on governments is now undeniable. The mere threat of an investment lawsuit can be enough to discourage new public interest legislation that could interfere with a corporation's expected profits" (Perez-Rocha and Trew 2014).

While to a few observers NAFTA represents the greenest-ever trade agreement, others disagree. NAFTA has done little to curb the destructive activities of some companies and prevent the export of hazardous wastes to Mexico. Corporations are winning many disputes under Chapter 11, as mentioned, but often on narrow procedural grounds. Environmental issues along the US-Mexico border are not covered by NAFTA, but are handled through a binational commission that hears complaints yet has no enforcement powers. The increasing number of such environmental cases and the publicity suggest, however, that environmental protection is gaining support. Thus, agreement on issues like air and water quality is likely to be joined by greater agreement on climate change.

### The Association of Southeast Asian Nations

Not all regions have successfully dealt with specific environmental governance issues. ASEAN provides an example of a regional IGO whose agenda has broadened to include environmental issues and that has increasingly incorporated NGOs into its activity. Yet its core norm of nonintervention and its members' diverse levels of development hamper its ability to respond. External actors including UNEP, the Asian Development Bank, and the UN Economic and Social Commission for Asia and the Pacific have helped to move the process forward.

ASEAN countries began cooperating on environmental policy in 1977; by 1989, annual meetings of governmental environmental specialists were being held; and in the 1990s, NGOs within the region, aided by US or European NGOs, developed regional networks and participated in consultations forged during the Rio Conference. Yet environmental cooperation has never been a priority, and the rhetoric of ASEAN's Strategic Plan of Action on the Environment of the 1990s was not matched with actions. Economic growth remained the main concern and the Asian financial crisis in the late 1990s prompted states to set aside environmental goals in favor of economic recovery. ASEAN's preference for weak institutionalism, nonbinding agreements, reliance on national institutions, and noninterference in the affairs of other states also impeded regional action (Elliott 2011). Additionally, states in the region have lacked the capacity for monitoring and implementation and are hindered by poor coordination between jurisdictions (both interstate and intrastate).

Over time, ASEAN's environmental concerns have become more urgent, including calls for greater institutionalization, better harmonization of goals, and better operational and technical cooperation. What is called the "haze problem" provided a key impetus to action.

The haze problem in Southeast Asia, caused by deforestation and land practices in Indonesia, has been a persistent problem since the mid-1980s. It is estimated that nearly 60 percent of the country's forests have been burned or logged. This includes land cleared by small-scale subsistence farmers and by commercial plantations, notably for palm oil used for biofuel, as well as logging for pulp and paper production. Because the majority of the activity is illegal, estimates of the scale of the problem vary widely, but it is generally agreed that the rate of loss has at least doubled since 1990. In 2014, Indonesia achieved the dubious distinction of having the highest rate of deforestation in the world. The deforestation itself is a major problem and contributes to Indonesia being among the top contributors to greenhouse-gas emissions. The problem first reached extreme levels in 1997–1998, when thick toxic haze from burning forests affected Singapore and Malaysia as well as Indonesia, making it a regional problem. It has grown in recent years, with 2013 being judged the most extreme to date.

In addition to the haze, the excessive grazing, overuse of chemical fertilizers, and urban pollution are making the region one of the most environmentally fragile in the world. Local NGOs challenged government policy by publicizing abuses and instituting legal action against the government of Indonesia. They enlisted the support of international NGOs such as the World Wide Fund for Nature, which was already involved in Indonesia's national parks and biodiversity initiatives. These activities challenged the ASEAN norm of nonintervention and put NGOs at center stage.

In 2003, ASEAN concluded the Agreement on Transboundary Haze Pollution—its first regional environmental agreement. It included new laws with penalties for noncompliance and a monitoring fund. Only in 2014, however, did Indonesia ratify the agreement—the last ASEAN member to do so. Its lax enforcement of a 2011 moratorium on new licenses for logging has only fueled more illegal logging, indicating that effective enforcement of the regional agreement will be difficult.

Between 2003 and 2009, ASEAN set a number of ambitious environmental goals as part of the effort to create the ASEAN Community, discussed in Chapter 5. ASEAN's Vision 2020 calls for a "clean and Green ASEAN" and delineates a wide-ranging agenda, including specific projects in forestry, coastal environments, water management, and peatland management.

In 2007, ASEAN members issued the Singapore Declaration on Climate Change, Energy, and the Environment—a first step in developing a regional approach to climate change in recognition of the region's vulnerability to major weather events and coastal flooding. Developing a network approach on the related issues as well as partnerships with the private sector and the UN, ASEAN has laid out a position that includes cooperation for cleaner energy, an emphasis on adaptation and mitigation, and international agreements that are consistent with "common and differentiated responsibilities." There is still considerable skepticism, however, about whether and to what extent ASEAN and its members will support and sustain this commitment to addressing environmental issues (Elliott 2011). As discussed in Chapter 5, it has a history of being strong on rhetoric and weak on commitment.

### Regional Environmental Agreements

Many environmental agreements are focused on a specific issue in a specific region. In several parts of the world, states have grappled with problems of river basin development and related environmental issues, including for the Nile River, affecting Egypt, Ethiopia, and Sudan; the Jordan River, shared by Israel, Jordan, Lebanon, and Syria; the Indus River, shared by Afghanistan, India, and Pakistan; the Mekong River, shared by Cambodia, China, Laos, Thailand, Vietnam, among others; and the Colorado River and Rio Grande, shared by the United States and Mexico. In many of these cases, countries have signed agreements for the allocation of available water supplies and for protecting water quality, but some have left out key participants. For example, the Mekong River Commission includes Cambodia, Laos, Thailand, and Vietnam, but the two upper–river basin countries—China and Myanmar—are only dialogue partners. In other cases, parties to agreements have refused to follow through with treaty obligations; and still others have not yet begun to address the extant environmental dimension.

Regional treaties have led to international litigation in several cases. A prominent one involves a dam project on the Danube River. The Gabcikovo-Nagymaros hydroelectric project was begun under a treaty signed by

Czechoslovakia and Hungary in 1977. Opposition by NGOs and actions by Slovakia (a successor state to Czechoslovakia) in the early 1990s resulted in a case before the ICJ in 1993, the first environmental case for the court. Hungary sued for environmental damage under the precautionary principle, while Slovakia cited Hungary for violations of the original treaty. The 1997 judgment held that both Hungary and Slovakia had breached their obligations under the treaty. The court argued that an integrated joint project had been constructed and that negotiations on the multiple issues needed to continue using current environmental standards, not 1977 standards, to protect water quality and nature (ICJ Contentious Case 1997). The decision was narrowly construed and the details were left to the parties to implement (Deets 2009).

Another case concerns the 1960 Indus Waters Treaty between India and Pakistan. The case arose from an Indian proposal to build a major hydroelectric project on a tributary river in the Indian-administered part of Jammu and Kashmir. Pakistan was concerned about the dam's effects on its water supply and requested the first-ever arbitration, as provided by the treaty. The Permanent Court of Arbitration, in The Hague, in its 2013 decision, recognized India's right to divert water for the project, but "tempered" its ruling by acknowledging Pakistan's right to a minimum flow of water (Permanent Court of Arbitration 2013). Most interesting from the perspective of environmental law, the court found that a state is obligated to take "environmental protection" into consideration when its activities may harm a bordering state. As in the ICJ case regarding the Gabcikovo-Nagymaros hydroelectric project, the Permanent Court of Arbitration applied current customary environmental principles (Kumar 2013).

The ICJ and other international courts have not generally addressed environmental issues, but as illustrated earlier this is changing. In 2008, Ecuador brought Colombia before the ICJ, claiming that Colombia's aerial spraying of toxic herbicides near their shared border was having adverse environmental and economic effects on its territory (ICJ Contentious Case 2008). Ecuador's case placed heavy weight on ecological arguments. In 2010, Australia brought suit against Japan in the ICJ, arguing that Japan was not complying with the 1986 moratorium on commercial whaling. In 2014, the ICJ ordered Japan to halt its whale hunt, concluding that it had breached its international obligations. Japan had argued it needed data to monitor the effects of overfishing on whale population and, hence, that its whaling was for scientific purposes, an argument the court rejected (ICJ Contentious Case 2014). The decision was celebrated by the environmental community and NGOs; Japan initially indicated it would comply, but announced in 2014 that it would resume its scientific whaling program.

* * *

Regimes, regime complexes, IGOs, agreements, public-private partnerships, and private governance arrangements at the global, regional, and local levels all contribute to global environmental governance, creating an increasingly dense network. As discussed in Chapter 1, however, it is essential to examine the extent to which states and nonstate actors implement and comply with environmental rules. It is also essential to utilize scientific research to ascertain whether these actions have been effective—whether they have contributed to reducing environmental degradation in its various manifestations.

## The Challenges of Implementation, Compliance, and Effectiveness

There has been lively debate among academics and policymakers in the pages of journals such as *Global Environmental Politics* and *Global Governance* regarding the need for substantial restructuring of environmental governance institutions. On one side are those who argue for greater centralization in a global environmental organization. Lack of resources and poor coordination, some suggest, can be resolved by creating a World Environment Organization (see Biermann and Bauer 2005). Others argue that creating a new architecture will divert attention from the major institutional and policy issues. They can point to the urgency of the climate change issue, and the evidence that a multilevel, decentralized approach has emerged from both top-down initiatives of states and IGOs and bottom-up activities of epistemic communities, NGOs, and local governments. Peter Haas (2007), for example, sees "a broader decentralized network of environmental governance, where UNEP serves as a hub linking together spokes connecting to additional policy networks of scientists, NGOs, MNCs, IO secretariats, and state actors." He advocates strengthening UNEP's ability to receive and transmit information to a variety of recipients, with compliance left to development agencies. Ken Conca's hybridization concept (2006: 67–69) is a much more bottom-up approach, drawing upon a constructivist analysis of the water issue. In this view, governance emerges at numerous sites where values and rules are contested and where nonstate actors can take on substantive roles. Such bottom-up alternatives perhaps come closer to achieving democratic environmental governance.

Beyond the issue of institutional architecture, however, there are critical questions to be addressed. Have the parties (i.e., states) taken measures to implement existing international accords? Have the parties complied with the provisions of the accords? Especially for developing countries, failure to implement and comply is often a failure of state capacity, as in the case of Indonesia's lax enforcement of its moratorium on new logging licenses. Thus, enhancing state capacities can be a crucial requirement for environmental implementation and compliance. On some environmental issues, local, subnational, and private nongovernmental responses are required, and hence compliance and implementation depend on national enforcement capabilities.

More generally, are the various environmental arrangements effective? For a long time, states' compliance with and implementation of international agreements was used as the primary measure of effectiveness (Weiss and Jacobson 2000). As Oran Young (1999) has noted, however, effectiveness is a complex, multidimensional concept. Subsequent studies have demonstrated the need for both qualitative and quantitative analysis to determine changes in behavior by various actors, and determine effects on the environment itself, that can be linked to specific agreements or rules. Helmut Breitmeier, Arild Underdal, and Young (2011) compare the findings of two major multinational studies: the Oslo-Seattle project, with fourteen cases, and the International Regimes Database Project, with twenty-four cases. Although the studies are not exactly comparable, both come to the conclusion that environmental regimes do matter; their contributions vary by the nature of the problem and the character of the regime, but the regimes have a strong or a moderate causal effect in terms of programmatic activities and in improving data and reducing uncertainty. They found that some of the determinants of effectiveness included the distribution of power, the roles of "pushers and laggards," the influence of decision rules, and the degree of available knowledge of the problem. In terms of solving particular environmental problems, Hiroshi Ohta and Atsuchi Ishii (2014: 582) note, however, that there are "very few cases that clearly show any improvement of the environment except for the ozone regime and the international regulation of oil pollution of the sea." Undoubtedly, extensive further study will be required to answer the question of the effectiveness of environment governance in reducing environmental degradation.

The questions of effectiveness and how best to address particular issues apply across all global governance issues addressed in this book. We turn to them and issues of legitimacy, accountability, effectiveness, and leadership in the final chapter.

## Suggested Further Reading

Benedick, Richard Elliot. (1998) *Ozone Diplomacy: New Directions in Safeguarding the Planet.* Enlarged ed. Cambridge: Harvard University Press.

Conca, Ken. (2006) *Governing Water: Contentious Transnational Politics and Global Institution Building.* Cambridge: MIT Press.

Elliott, Lorraine, and Shaun Breslin, eds. (2011). *Comparative Environmental Regionalism.* London: Routledge.

Green, Jessica. (2014) *Rethinking Private Authority: Agents and Entrepreneurs in Global Environmental Governance*. Princeton: Princeton University Press.

Hoffmann, Matthew J. (2011) *Climate Governance at the Crossroads: Experiments with a Global Response After Kyoto*. Oxford: Oxford University Press.

Park, Susan. (2010) *The World Bank Group and Environmentalists: Changing International Organization Identities*. London: Manchester University Press.

Prakash, Aseem, and Matthew Potoski (2006). *The Voluntary Environmentalists: Green Clubs, ISO 14001, and Voluntary Regulations*. Cambridge: Cambridge University Press.

## Important Databases

International Environmental Agreements Database Project: http://iea.uoregon.edu
International Regimes Database Project: www.fernuni-hagen.de/polis/lg2/projekte/InternationalRegimesDatabase.shtml

## Internet Resources

Clean Development Mechanism: http://cdm.unfccc.int
Climate Action Network: www.climatenetwork.org
Commission on Sustainable Development: www.un.org/esa/sustdev/csd.htm
Convention on Biological Diversity: www.biodiv.org
Convention on International Trade in Endangered Species: www.cites.org
European Environmental Bureau: www.eeb.org
Forest Stewardship Council: www.fsc.org
Friends of the Earth International (Netherlands): www.foei.org
Global Environmental Facility: www.gefweb.org
Intergovernmental Panel on Climate Change: www.ipcc.ch
International Commission for the Protection of the Danube River: www.icpdr.org
Montreal Protocol: www.unep.org/ozone/montreal.html
Multilateral Fund for the Implementation of the Montreal Protocol: www.multilateralfund.org
The Nature Conservancy: www.nature.org
North American Commission on Environmental Cooperation: www.cec.org
Rainforest Action Network: www.ran.org
TRAFFIC: www.traffic.org
UN Climate Change Gateway: www.un.org/climatechange
UN Environment Programme: www.unep.org
UN Framework Convention on Climate Change; Kyoto Protocol: www.unfccc.int
UN Johannesburg Summit (2002): www.johannesburgsummit.org
World Wide Fund for Nature: www.panda.org
World Wildlife Fund (US affiliate of World Wide Fund for Nature): www.worldwildlife.org

# 12

# Dilemmas in Global Governance

## What Makes Global Governance Different?

Global governance issues defy easy categorization. Trafficking in women and children, like the older problems of piracy and slavery, may be economically motivated, but it violates core human rights norms. The issue of refugees is an issue of human rights, but the problem is closely linked to the dynamics of failed states and ethnic conflicts, civil wars, deepening poverty, and government weakness. Climate change and loss of rainforest biodiversity are fundamentally environmental issues, yet any action or inaction has critical economic and political ramifications. Issues of human development not only are economic issues, but also have social and political ramifications. HIV/AIDS and Ebola are not just health issues, but also humanitarian problems that threaten economic and social development in the world's poorest regions and hence are threats to human security. There are no neat categories, even though traditional IGOs are often organized as if there were.

The conventional strategies of adding responsibilities to already-existing organizations and of creating new IGOs to address new dimensions of problems have each been used. For example, in the early 1990s, when the UN first undertook peacebuilding responsibilities and election monitoring, both were handled by the Departments of Political Affairs and Peacekeeping Operations. By 1992, the Electoral Assistance Unit was created; only in 2006 were the Peacebuilding Commission and the Department of Field Support established. With HIV/AIDS, the World Health Organization took the lead, but gradually other UN agencies became involved as the multifaceted nature of the problem became evident: UNICEF to address mother-to-child transmission; the UNDP as high mortality affected national development agendas; UNESCO, the World Bank, and ILO as labor and employment were affected. What began as a health issue became a security issue when the UN Security Council adopted the topic.

States and IGOs are no longer the only important actors in dealing with these international problems. Civil society, NGOs, transnational advocacy networks, and social movements demand inclusion in governance efforts across a range of different issues. Expert groups and epistemic communities are essential for the knowledge and expertise they can provide. Private corporations have become increasingly important partners and suppliers of resources that governments and IGOs are less able to provide, resulting in a variety of public-private partnerships as discussed throughout the book.

Proliferation of actors has generated much controversy about the roles of states in global governance. Certainly states remain key actors in traditional IGOs, where they hold the purse strings and where dominant states (or coalitions) tend to control agendas, as seen in the international financial and security institutions. With respect to threats to peace and security, states have always assumed a controlling position and continue to do so. Yet even in security issues, as noted in Chapter 7, emerging norms of human security make responsibility to protect people a new expectation of statehood.

The proliferation of nonstate actors has unquestionably diminished the power of states to shape international policy outcomes. The concepts of sustainable development and human rights challenge sovereignty and the principle of nonintervention. Still, major powers such as the United States, Russia, and China, among others, may resist having their power and sovereignty undermined across a broad range of issues. The puzzle for students of global governance is how much importance to accord to states versus nonstate actors and how much authority is delegated to each.

Finally, there is no single model of global governance to fit all issues and policy problems, just as there is no single structure of global governance but a multitude of approaches that do not fit together in an elegant way. As Stewart Patrick (2014b: 59) predicts, "The future will see not the renovation or the construction of a glistening new international architecture but rather the continued spread of an unattractive but adaptable multilateral sprawl that delivers a partial measure of international cooperation through a welter of informal arrangements and piecemeal approaches."

Groups of actors coalesce in various ways over time to confront new governance challenges. Not only do such coalitions shift, as evidenced by the emergence of the G-20 during the 2008–2009 global financial crisis, but the proliferation of other actors relevant to various issues has led to new partnerships in global governance that blur the boundaries between public and private actors and between domestic and international actors. The Global Compact on Corporate Responsibility illustrates such a partnership approach among the UN, multinational corporations, and NGOs, as do the multistakeholder World Commission on Dams and multistakeholder Forest Stewardship Council, discussed in Chapter 11.

For human development, discussed in Chapter 9, there are multiple and strong development institutions at both the international and the regional level that provide the foundation for governance, but depend on state cooperation and increasingly delegate delivery of development aid to NGOs. In international finance, financial markets and networks make private actors central to governance, limiting the authority and control of states and even of the International Monetary Fund. NGO coalitions, too, have shown their influence, whether by organizing on behalf of disabled people or uniting to save an endangered species. For peace and security, there is enhanced collaboration among and between the UN and regional organizations as well as ad hoc contact and friends groups and the multinational anti-piracy maritime force, as discussed in Chapter 7. That has challenged the secretariats of the UN and many regional organizations to improve ways of structuring cooperation and partnerships.

Another approach to new governance challenges is more targeted initiatives, limited to a very specific problem and involving only the most relevant actors. Both private and private-public governance schemes provide relevant examples, including bond-rating agencies, the ISO 14001, and the Financial Action Task Force.

Sometimes the various constituencies have such different interests that one governance approach may be impractical. Internet governance is a case in point, where interests are sharply differentiated among governments, private businesses, and traditional Net users, making any universal regulatory framework impractical. States want some degree of control to protect citizens and in the interest of national security. Private businesses need rules of property, currency, and enforcement to advance their commercial interests. NGOs are concerned with access and privacy issues. One governance institution cannot meet the needs of all—and certainly no existing IGO can do so.

The result is several different governance approaches. Private companies working with states, the UN, and the International Telecommunication Union have taken steps to narrow the digital divide among states, for example. Since 1998, the Internet Corporation for Assigned Names and Numbers (ICANN), a group of California-based private actors (under contract from the US Department of Commerce until 2014), has allocated domain names, established rules for reallocation of names, and set regulations for selling domain names. Regulating specific activities on the Internet remains largely a state responsibility (for example, China's "Great Firewall"), but to deal with use of the Internet for illegal activities like online money laundering requires both state and international governance such as through the Financial Action Task Force. And in Western countries, private companies such as Symantec and Intel, with their technological expertise, have been primary actors in developing firewalls and encryption to protect online transmissions.

To enhance legitimacy with multiple stakeholders, the Internet Governance Forum (IGF), convened for the first time in 2006, is now the focal point for initiatives relating to Internet governance. This multistakeholder process is an open forum of all public and private actors organized around informal workshops on relevant Internet issues. Though the IGF is not a decisionmaking body itself, its recommendations are taken to relevant bodies such as the ITU. The IGF is now viewed as the venue for discussing all aspects of Internet governance. It convenes annually, with working groups addressing specific issues. Participants include government officials, academics, civil society members, and any interested parties. While a small permanent secretariat is based at the UN's Geneva headquarters, actual authority is dispersed to other entities, including ICANN and the FATF among others. Yet inherent tensions remain, for as Debora Spar (1999: 47) reminded us many years ago, "on the Internet, some degree of anarchy is acceptable, even desirable. In fact, many users came to cyberspace precisely because of its anarchy, its anonymity, its secretiveness, and lack of rules." No one model of global governance is likely to work across all issues.

If James Rosenau (1995: 13) is right that global governance constitutes "systems of rule at all levels of human activity—from the family to the international organization—in which the pursuit of goals through exercise of control has transnational repercussions," then we need to be prepared for much more complex, multilayered, and crosscutting processes and interactions that are constantly changing. There is no global supranational authority now, any more than there was in 1945 when the UN was founded. But realistically, what can the various actors in global governance do well? What can they not do in terms of meeting the challenges of global governance?

## What Can Global Governance Actors Do?

Actors in global governance can perform many tasks quite well. We identify six areas where these actors have made significant contributions to global governance.

### Developing New Ideas

The United Nations, as discussed in Chapter 4, has traditionally been described as the center of global governance. The United Nations Intellectual History Project concludes in its final volume with a list of ideas that are among the UN's most significant contributions (Jolly, Emmerij, and Weiss 2009). These ideas have come from member states, from the UN Secretariat and major bodies, as well as from NGOs, experts, and consultants. UN bodies have provided forums for debate; Secretariat officials and experts have promoted adoption of policy ideas; member states and NGOs have implemented or tested ideas and policies at the country level, and provided resources for implementing, monitoring progress, and sometimes burying ideas.

Among the ideas advanced by the UN is *peacekeeping,* the idea that the military personnel, police, and civilians from states acting on behalf of the international community could insert themselves into conflict situations. It represents an institutional innovation that was not explicit in the UN Charter. The UN has also been instrumental in expanding the very concept of security from state security to *human security.* Humans, too, need to be secure, from violence, from economic deprivation, from poverty, infectious diseases, human rights violations by states, and environmental degradation, as illustrated in Chapters 7, 9, 10, and 11.

In the area of economic development, the UN has benefited from the creativity of innovative economists who have at one time or another been employed by the UN or served as consultants and who have contributed to key UN ideas. *Sustainability,* as enunciated in the General Assembly-commissioned Brundtland Report discussed in Chapter 9, clearly showed that economic development cannot occur without assurances that resources will not be exploited and that unintended consequences will be considered, and showed that resource uses need to be managed for future generations. As a result, the UN and other development institutions began to weigh development needs with environmental imperatives. And just as security has been redefined as human security, development too has been reconceived as *human development.* This idea represents a sea change in thinking, from traditional economic theory that measured development in terms of growth in a state's GNP over time and in comparison to that of other states. Thinking about human development led to the Millennium Development Goals and is continuing to evolve in the search for the Sustainable Development Goals for the next decade.

While universalizing *human rights for all* represents a key normative idea for which the UN deserves major credit, NGOs, in particular, played an important role in getting protections into the UN Charter, and they continue to play critical roles in the promotion and monitoring of human rights for all vulnerable people. On several issues, the UN alone did not act independently or even initiate discussion. In enhancing the status of women and in espousing the relationship between the environment and development, key Northern states and NGOs played that role. Likewise, in universalizing human rights such as protection of LGBT rights, key NGOs acted, taking their demands to both sympathetic states and various UN bodies.

The idea of microfinance, supplying small amounts of financial assistance to individuals and groups who are unable to access resources through regular banking systems, emerged from the Grameen Bank experience, an idea that has been subsequently adopted and modified by other nonprofit groups as well as by for-profit banks and even the World Bank. Some ideas like microfinance have been mainstreamed and taken hold; others have not.

### Filling Knowledge Gaps, Gathering Data

Translating ideas into agenda items requires collection of data, both to highlight problem areas and to identify data that need to be collected. In the early years, the UN and the Bretton Woods institutions played a key role in helping states gather basic data, reflecting the experience of dominant states and the methods of liberal economists located in the international economic institutions.

As new issues emerged, new kinds of data needed to be collected. We did not know whether economic development affected everyone equally, as liberal economists predicted, until data were collected comparing women and men on various development indicators. If protection of women from violence includes abuses in both the public sphere and the private sphere, then data on the latter need to be collected. Yet sometimes the data are too controversial, either because a particular activity such as violence in the home, terrorism, or corruption lacks an agreed definition, or because such data may implicate member states for not preventing the activity or even actively promoting it, or because it may offend cultural norms. But after Transparency International introduced corruption indices, for example, the door was opened for gathering some cross-national statistics that reflect, even obliquely, the costs of corruption.

Sometimes it is an epistemic community that is most responsible for initiating data-collection activities. Environmental scientists based in different institutions stressed the need for collecting baseline data so that environmental change could better be assessed. Now all the major environmental organizations—public, private, international, regional, and local—collect such data. Yet as the response to the climate change data has illustrated, this does not mean that there is immediate agreement on what the data mean or what policies need to be implemented, especially over the long term. In the case of climate change, it took almost twenty years for the scientific community to reach consensus on the link between human activity and changes evident in the data.

Thus, we now have a variety of indicators and data that help us to link numbers to the ideas and enable us to set goals, another key contribution of global governance actors.

### Setting, Promoting, and Monitoring Goals

Virtually all global governance actors set and promote goals. Among IGOs, the UN is often criticized as a forum for declarations that make no difference and for setting goals, like eliminating extreme poverty worldwide, that are impossible to meet. Yet one of the surprising conclusions from the UN Intellectual History Project is the importance of UN goal-setting. Indeed, setting targets for economic and social development is seen as a "singular UN achievement" (Jolly, Emmerij, and Weiss 2009: 43). Some fifty economic and social goals in all, beginning with the First Development Decade in 1960 and including the MDGs for poverty reduction, have been set and promoted. The MDGs have been accompanied by systematic monitoring and reporting on an annual basis, a process that states have accepted. The long list of human rights treaties negotiated under UN auspices established the normative foundation for global human rights for all. The UN has established international machinery for their promotion through the office of the UNHCHR, as well as mechanisms for monitoring states' human rights records and compliance with treaties, as discussed in Chapter 10. In the area of health, the "Health for All" goals in the late 1970s moved the WHO and other health actors to focus on improving the state health infrastructure to meet the goals. In short, goals have provided a focus "for mobilizing interests, especially the interests of NGOs, and for generating pressures for action" (Jolly, Emmerij, and Weiss 2009: 44).

### Agenda-Setting in International Arenas

Few doubt the value of the UN as a general forum, and particularly the General Assembly as a voice of the "peoples of the world," enabling member states to raise and act on new issues, thereby setting agendas for the UN itself, for other IGOs, for NGOs, and for states themselves. No one has any doubts about the forum's value over time for promoting self-determination and decolonization; for calling attention to apartheid and pressuring South Africa to change; for negotiating the comprehensive Law of the Sea Convention and recognizing the unique position of small island states in the global climate change debate; or for putting on the agenda the rights of the disabled, migrant workers, and LGBT community. In virtually all cases, years of hard work occurred before the agenda was accepted.

Certainly in the eyes of some, the UN as a forum has been abused, such as when majorities repeatedly linked Zionism with racism in General Assembly resolutions. Yet for others such as the Palestinians, the forum provided the venue in 2012 for recognition of Palestine and its admission as a nonmember observer state. When the Security Council was blocked by Russian and Chinese vetoes from referring the Syrian government to the International Criminal Court in 2014 for its massive crimes against its own citizens, the General Assembly could at least serve as a forum to mobilize global sentiment on that crisis. Thus, the value of having a place where issues can be raised, resolutions can be put forward, and consensus built or votes taken is to serve both agenda-setting and tension-releasing functions for the international community. No other IGO or global governance venue can substitute for the UN's agenda-setting potential and its forum function.

Yet the emergence of more IGOs has provided more forums—whether it be the World Bank, one of the regional multilateral development banks, the recently created China-led Asian Infrastructure Investment Bank, or the Latin American Development Bank. These provide opportunities for states and nonstate actors to forum-shop, as discussed in Chapter 1. Thus, for states with labor issues, the ILO, the WTO, and the EU are all potential venues. Environmental issues may find sympathetic voices in UNEP, the World Bank, or major NGOs. Intellectual property issues may find a forum in the WTO's TRIPS or the World Intellectual Property Organization. And the growth of foundations and NGOs with technical expertise and resources has meant that urgent health issues may find forums in specialized bureaucracies like the US Centers for Disease Control, the WHO, NGOs such as International Partners in Health or Doctors Without Borders, or foundations like the Gates Foundation.

### Ability to Adapt and Reform

If organizations do not adapt or change, they lose their relevance, decline, or die. Despite the arduous process for UN Charter reform requiring the concurrence of the P-5, the UN has found other ways to adapt to changing circumstances: creating new bodies such as the Office of the High Commissioner for Human Rights or the Peacebuilding Commission or bringing all UN development agencies and programs together in the field. Where it has failed to reform, particularly with Security Council membership, the legitimacy of the organization has been substantially challenged, since it does not adequately represent the world today. The international financial institutions, however, have made some accommodations to rising economic powers, giving them more of a voting voice, albeit stymied for the time being by domestic politics in the United States. Nevertheless, for many, and especially for emerging powers, those changes do not go far enough and new forums, such as the AIIB and BRICS New Development Bank, may be created.

Regional organizations have often successfully shifted focus with changes in the international setting, national interests, and new actors. Some examples include the EU's evolution from an economic union to a political and nascent security community; the SCO's shift from a security organization to one concerned with expanding trade and economic ties; and the OAU/AU transition from its anticolonial underpinnings to a positive agenda in support of regional security and democratization. In the words of one analyst, regional organizations are "giving universal membership bodies a run for their money," leading to the discussion in Chapter 7 of how to "harmonize and complement the UN system rather than undermine it" (Patrick 2014b: 65).

## Innovation: New Varieties of Governance

In the first decades after World War II, neither the United Nations system nor the Bretton Woods institutions recognized how other actors might be mobilized to enhance their own programs. UN funding came from state assessments and voluntary contributions. Funding for World Bank projects and projects emanating from bilateral lending institutions went directly to governments. Private corporations' resources were harnessed on behalf of international goals and programs only in the 1980s.

Several key trends resulted in changes to the traditional model. Funding was too limited to meet global needs; MNCs were recognized as key sources of international capital to be harnessed not regulated; programs aimed at local communities required local expertise, and NGOs were better positioned on the ground. Even in international peacekeeping operations, the UN and regional organizations have learned the value of involving locals on the ground.

New varieties of global governance have grown: partnerships, networks, private governance, rule-based governance, and public-private partnerships. Yet these are not all the same. Some have been granted significant autonomy and authority by states through formal or informal agreements. Institutions having such authority can "make legally binding decisions on matters relating to a state's domestic jurisdiction, even if those decisions are contrary to a state's own policies and preferences" (Cooper et al. 2008: 505). Others involve both public actors (global and regional IGOs) and private actors (NGOs, MNCs, and foundations), as illustrated by the examples of UNAIDS and the Global Fund to Fight AIDS, Tuberculosis, and Malaria. Such partnerships are essential for augmenting financial resources and marshalling expertise; in providing broader participation from donors; and for improving "buy-in" and, hence, legitimacy for recipient states and individuals. Others have not been granted such authority, do not have such broad participation, and struggle to define the limits of their actions.

Still, much as these innovations in global governance seem to have made a difference, the evidence is still anecdotal and circumstantial. It appears as if "learning" has taken place as constructivists suggest. Lessons learned from one actor are often diffused to others. States have learned from the success of NGOs in framing issues for public consumption and using the Internet and social media to create networks, mobilize support, organize advocacy campaigns, and get issues such as landmines, cluster munitions, child soldiers, violence against women, or species-loss onto the international agenda. They have accepted the need for intensive on-site inspections for arms control, monitoring compliance with sanctions, and explicit efforts to promote human and gender security, and have established the mechanisms for such activities.

International development institutions have learned from NGO experiences that reaching out to people in local communities, to those affected, and involving them in the planning and execution of projects, will lead to greater project success. Some IGOs have learned that decisions are better if they are taken at the lowest possible level, based on the EU's experience with subsidiarity. Thus the poverty reduction programs tied to IMF debt relief have called for local groups to propose development projects best suited to the locale. The Global Fund also calls for local initiatives and local accountability. Partnerships and multistakeholder initiatives provide a venue for learning to occur. But learning may not occur and some tasks required by global governance issues may not be possible.

## What Global Governance Actors Cannot Do

Global governance actors are unable at this point, either singularly or together, to do at least five tasks well. As John Ruggie reminds us, "international organizations remain anchored in the state system. . . . Their role in actual enforcement remains tightly constrained by states" (quoted in Weiss and Thakur 2010: xvii). Indeed, it is in the area of enforcement where global governance falls short.

### Enforcement

The UN and other IGOs can generally only make recommendations. As Thomas Weiss and Ramesh Thakur (2010: 21) acknowledge, "no ways exist to enforce decisions and no mechanisms exist to compel states to comply with decisions." There is no international executive with an international military at its disposal; there is no international legislature; there is no international judiciary with compulsory jurisdiction. The European Union is a prominent exception in those areas of common policies where sovereignty has been delegated to the EU and where the decisions of the EU Court of Justice are directly enforceable in member states. But even in the EU, policy areas such as foreign policy remain intergovernmental and require unanimous approval from member states.

The UN Security Council, under Chapter VII, clearly can authorize sanctions and coercive military action if the P-5 concur (or do not exercise their vetoes). Although sanctions have been extensively used since the Cold War's end, military enforcement action is still rare, despite the greater use of Chapter VII authority in mandates for peace operations, as discussed in Chapter 7. Even if there is consensus on some type of enforcement, it may be for a relatively brief period of time and member states may not back up that commitment with sufficient resources to ensure success. With sanctions, the possibility of cheating is always present and the longer they are in place, the greater the possibility of leakage. For military enforcement, a clear lesson of the early post–Cold War years is that the UN must rely on major powers, on a coalition of the willing, or on NATO with its military alliance capabilities for joint action. States simply are unwilling to grant the UN direct control over the types of military resources necessary for major coercive action. They are also very often reluctant to see the UN intervene in some situations—sometimes because of their own national interests, be they economic or political, as one would predict from a realist view of what IGOs can do.

In March 2015 as the Syrian civil war entered its fifth year, the UN's own reputation and that of the Security Council in particular was clearly suffering. A political solution continued to elude the UN's third special envoy; despite Council authorization to deliver food and medicine, aid agencies continued to be stymied; and a litany of torture, rape, executions, bombing of civilian targets, and displacement continued with no one held accountable. Jan Egeland, former UN relief coordinator noted, "I fear the Syrian war will become one of the darkest chapters in the history of the United Nations. . . . The organization was founded on the ruins of World War II precisely to avoid conflicts like this one engulfing a whole region" (Sengupta 2015b: A4).

Still, other "softer" forms of enforcement are possible in other contexts. In economic issues, both "carrots" and "sticks" can be utilized— carrots meaning financial rewards for taking certain mandated actions, and sticks meaning the withholding of aid for failure to meet demands, as both the IMF and World Bank have done. But strict conditionality was not always imposed as agreements were renegotiated and conditions modified over time.

In human rights, enforcement has included bringing individuals to justice under the ICC or ad hoc courts. For the most part, however, to punish state noncompliance, various actors must rely on "naming and shaming." If accompanied by strong domestic measures for compliance from NGOs, then that may be effective. On other issues, however, publicly naming and shaming states for noncompliance may not yield the desired results, especially when the target does not care about its reputation for following the rules.

When international enforcement is pitted against the national interests of a great power, then none of the global governance actors may be able to respond without endangering international peace and security. Consider the case of China's challenge to the UN Law of the Sea Convention. The treaty was concluded in 1982, came into effect in 1994, and was ratified by China in 1996. It establishes legal boundaries for the territorial sea, the exclusive economic zone, and support for the principle of open and free navigation. China's extensive claims in the South China Sea are not compatible with the treaty and overlap the claims of five other states in the region (Brunei, Indonesia, Malaysia, the Philippines, and Vietnam, as well as Taiwan). In 2014, the Philippines, with US support, filed a claim with the International Tribunal for the Law of the Sea to settle the dispute by arbitration. China has refused to participate, continues to violate key principles, and is constructing new land forms, airstrips, and other facilities on disputed reefs and islets to bolster its claims. Yet, is the United States, which has not ratified the treaty, ready to enforce the principles and support its allies in the region as well as its own interests? If China continues to thwart the international legal regime, no other country is capable of enforcement. Such are the limitations of global governance in the realist world.

### Reacting Quickly in a Crisis

Virtually none of the global governance actors, save a few powerful states, have the administrative, logistical, or financial resources to react rapidly in crisis situations. Major natural disasters such as Typhoon Haiyan (2013) are a test of rapid response. The UN humanitarian relief system and relief NGOs including the ICRC responded, but much of the work was carried out by the US military, which has the capacity (and willingness) to undertake rapid responses in almost all areas of the world. In contrast, China was roundly criticized in 2013 when it failed to provide much financial assistance or to send its hospital ship to the Philippines after Typhoon Haiyan.

The rapid acceleration of the Ebola outbreak from a health threat in isolated West African locales to a full-blown international emergency tested the capacity of health governance actors to respond rapidly in 2014. There are no NATO-like health troops! The WHO was designed to establish guidelines to stop the spread of communicable diseases and provide limited technical assistance, as discussed in Chapter 3. Its mandate has expanded to include noncommunicable diseases and health lifestyle issues, while its budget has been cut in recent years, necessitating cuts that actually split the duties of the pandemic-response department at headquarters. NGOs like Doctors Without Borders are designed to respond rapidly in a crisis like the Ebola outbreak, but never on such a scale and with the number of trained medical volunteers needed. And even the most developed states like the United States did not have the procedures, protocols, or equipment to react rapidly in the crisis and took weeks to provide assistance. If Ebola is serving as a "test of multilateralism," as Jan Eliasson, deputy secretary-general of the UN asserted, the system is failing. Neither the WHO nor governments are in charge (quoted in Patrick 2014a). Therefore, as discussed in Chapter 9, WHO reform is critical if global health governance actors are going to be better prepared for the next health emergency.

Responses to human-made humanitarian crises are also hamstrung due to the inability to ramp up operations in a short period of time. As many times as the UNHCR and partner NGOs have responded to refugee crises, they have been overwhelmed in their Middle East operations since 2011, especially with the huge numbers of refugees and displaced persons in the Syrian civil war as well as following the 2014 ISIS advances in Syria and Iraq, as discussed in Chapters 7 and 10.

Similar limitations are true when the need for a rapid international military response is needed. As emphasized in Chapter 7, multilateral military interventions, be they organized under the UN, under NATO, or under the EU, require time: time to get the consent of the P-5 in the case of the UN, or the approval of NATO or EU member states; time to organize the dedicated military units from member states; time to transport troops and equipment to the crisis area. France was able to intervene rapidly as the situation deteriorated in Côte d'Ivoire, Mali, and Niger in recent years. French troops served as a stopgap measure until AU/ECOWAS forces were mobilized and deployed. Often in such situations, the US military provides transport and logistical support. Time does not stand still in crisis situations.

## Managing Large, Long-Term Projects on Behalf of Broad Goals

Many of *the actions* needed for global governance initiatives, whether they be sanctioning, peacebuilding, statebuilding, or economic development, demand long-term commitments. The IAEA's role in the nuclear nonproliferation regime illustrates this well, as discussed in Chapter 7. Inspections must be done at periodic intervals indefinitely, with particular vigilance in those instances where states such as Iran or North Korea are suspected of developing weapons programs. Complex multidimensional peace operations with large numbers of personnel and varied responsibilities—keeping the peace, organizing elections, rebuilding the local police, creating a new judicial system, stimulating economic development, and even serving as an interim government—require a long-term commitment.

Economic development and especially human development are even longer-term undertakings that the UN was never designed to address. As noted in Chapter 9, both the UN and the World Bank changed approaches over time, making it impossible to evaluate whether they had any positive effect in the long term. The reality is that no one knows precisely how to achieve development—what combination of factors and steps will yield positive results in each unique setting. Those commitments to activities requiring years demand that member states not waiver from their commitments; that a steady stream of the "right" kind of resources be provided; that those receiving the aid put the funds to good use and manage the programs to achieve their objectives. Even then, the problem remains of how to define success. And, if many different instruments are employed, how do we know what has worked? It may take years for institutional changes to show actual results.

## Coordinating the Activities of a Variety of Agencies

With all global governance innovations, multiple actors are involved. In the late 1990s, Jessica Mathews (1997: 61) wrote of "the new medievalism" to capture the variety of arrangements and authorities operating without a clear hierarchy, much as characterized the Middle Ages. Whether the needs are long-term or in a crisis, all initiatives require coordination among various actors, agencies, funds, and programs. Yet as numerous UN staff and NGOs have remarked, "Everyone is for coordination but nobody wants to be coordinated" (quoted in Weiss 2009: 81). This has been a chronic problem, as seen in ECOSOC's long-term inability to coordinate the multiple, overlapping UN economic and social programs and agencies discussed in Chapter 4. It can also be seen in the problems of uncoordinated responses to complex humanitarian crises. Weiss (2012: 14) refers to the "spaghetti junction" of the UN organizational chart (see Figure 4.2) and suggests that it creates either "productive clashes over institutional turf and competition for resources, or paralysis. . . [rather than] more integrated, mutually reinforcing, and collaborative partnerships among the various moving parts of the United Nations." The proliferation of regional trade agreements discussed in Chapter 8, with many states belonging to several agreements, each with different rules and regulations, is another example where coordination is needed but too often lacking.

## The Struggle to Deal with the Dark Side Within States

As discussed in Chapter 1, global governance threats are now transnational, but the roots of many threats are within states. Many states with weak governments lack the capacity to meet these problems, while other states lack the willingness to address them. The transnational movement of illicit drugs, people, and money requires actions within states to enforce laws and monitor borders. While the EU under its criminal justice procedures has established a structure to deal with this "dark side" and provides funds to improve the capacity of states, some of the most affected states (even within the EU) are overwhelmed and enforcement efforts lag far behind, as the January 2015 terrorist attack in Paris made clear. Still other states are unwilling to address the problem, as their own authorities may be complicit and corrupt or because they are afraid of the negative repercussions from domestic constituencies as illustrated by the Nigerian government's failure to address the attacks by Boko Haram in 2014 and 2015.

The rise of ISIS well illustrates the problem: a group funded by illegal seizures of oil wells and bank assets and occupying large swaths of territory and major cities; a crippled Iraqi government and military struggling to respond effectively because of sectarian conflicts; a Syrian government, viewed by many as a terrorist regime in itself, caught in a long civil war and fighting for its survival; the international community, personified by the UN Security Council, unable to agree on multilateral action.

## Challenges for the Future

The challenges of legitimacy, accountability, effectiveness, and leadership are found in all governance arrangements. Absent any single structure or set of structures, there can be no single standard for legitimacy or accountability, no single set of prescriptions for enhancing democratic representation of civil society in international institutions and policymaking processes, no single standard for measuring effectiveness, and no agreed-upon algorithm for leadership. These challenges arise at two levels: individual actors in global governance need to be legitimate, accountable, and effective; and global governance generally must be legitimate, accountable, and effective, having positive impacts on people's lives, improving living standards, while meeting standards of equity, fairness, and justice. These are dilemmas for global governance more broadly.

### The Challenge of Legitimacy

To be accepted as legitimate by the international community, various structures and processes of global governance must accommodate the participation of civil society in some fashion, since one of the distinctive characteristics of global governance is ensuring that various actors have a voice. The challenge of democratizing and therefore legitimizing global governance structures is not just one of having access to formal procedures, but also one of having "the broadest possible participation on a global scale," writes Fred Dallmayr (2002: 154–155). Widening or globalizing political participation, he continues, also contributes to "fostering of a genuine sense of global or cosmopolitan justice," and the "democratic process is the best means for changing conditions of injustice and promoting justice." Hence, legitimacy depends in large part on the diversity and breadth of support for various elements of global governance.

Participation gives people a sense of ownership and a stake in outcomes of policymaking. An important part of the story of this book is how nongovernmental organizations and other civil society actors have broadened participation in particular institutions and how newer global governance arrangements have expanded participation to the local level. In peacekeeping, this means being cognizant of how operations affect local conditions and people, as well as of unintended side effects such as skewing local economies and employment structures or undermining traditional gender relations. In development, this means listening to local needs; in human rights, this means activating local networks; in health governance, this requires bringing in those populations most affected. And, multilayered governance approaches provide multiple venues for participation by transnational actors.

Given the global norm of democratic governance, however, an additional aspect of the legitimacy challenge is that individual actors must be democratized. This is a particular challenge because globalization has undermined some aspects of liberal democracy in states, and UN targeted sanctions, for example, have been shown to unintentionally strengthen authoritarian rule. States that are not currently democratic will face continuing pressures for political change, as will IGOs and NGOs that are perceived to suffer from "democratic deficits," including the European Union, the international financial institutions, and even NGOs themselves who may only represent self-selected elites, as discussed in Chapter 6. Calling for the abolition of organizations judged undemocratic does not solve the problem. Rather, an approach that systematically examines "where, to what extent, and which international organizations are undemocratic, with the aim to derive a nuanced assessment of their level of democracy and recommendations for improvements," is needed (Zweifel 2006: 14). Incremental changes to the structure will not do.

To be considered legitimate, global governance cannot be seen as a US, Western, or liberal economic project that is only compatible with the power and preferences of the United States, large Western-based multinational corporations, Northern NGOs, and Western-trained experts. Nor can it be considered an activity that the United States can control. International institutions, be they the United Nations, the International Monetary Fund, the Global Environmental Facility, or Human Rights Watch, cannot be controlled by the preferences of a dominant state if they are to remain legitimate in a globalized world. The UN Security Council maintains its legitimacy indefinitely even if there is no revision of its membership. As Ngaire Woods (1999: 43) reminds us, "A symmetry of power must exist within the institution because it is unlikely to endure over time if powerful states or groups of states can simply flout the rules." In addition, global governance must represent wider liberal, social, and political values like those that human security, human development, poverty alleviation, and sustainable development embody.

Finally, global governance will not be widely regarded as legitimate unless its pieces combat the gross inequalities of power, wealth, and knowledge in today's world. These inequalities have profound implications for promoting justice in the international community. Democratization requires accountability. Legitimacy and justice also require effectiveness.

## The Challenge of Accountability

Who watches the governors? Who is accountable, to whom, for what, and by what mechanism are critical questions for global (and other) governors (Avant, Finnemore, and Sell 2010a: 363–364). In a perfectly functioning democracy, the people, through electoral processes, provide a semblance of accountability, but that will never be possible at the international level. Thus, accountability must be built into global governance in different ways, as discussed in Chapter 1 and in the work of Ruth Grant and Robert Keohane (2005). One of those is by enhancing the transparency of decisionmaking within institutions. States' own accountability and transparency have been significantly enhanced through requirements for reporting the status of human rights or trade-law implementation of counterterrorism activities and of on-site weapons inspections, as well as by the vigilance of NGO monitoring. While IGOs must inform members of activities and decisions, as well as the grounds on which decisions are taken, closed IMF or Security Council meetings and consensus decisionmaking often limit accountability, because there is no published record of activity and states' positions. The P-5, the WTO's Quadrilateral Group, the G 7, and other exclusive group consultations exclude large numbers of other interested actors. Unanimous voting, while probably the best way to ensure accountability, proved impractical as a decisionmaking procedure for international collective action in the League of Nations. Yet as Woods (1999: 45) warns, "Accountability needs to reflect [*sic*] not just in formal representation but equally in decisionmaking procedures and rules and also in the implementation of decisions."

Improving accountability in international actors has been difficult, but steps have been taken in the right direction. The UN itself has developed many forms of budgetary control to improve its accountability to the major contributors. The World Bank's Inspection Panel investigates allegations by NGOs, states, and private actors who assert that the Bank is not following its own procedures. One study found, in fact, that accountability mechanisms were first developed by the IGOs with larger budgets (UN), where principal members contributed large portions of the budget (UN, World Bank), decision processes involved majority rule or weighted voting (UN, World Bank, IMF), and member states had strong democratic norms (EU). Once the first ones were established, however, they spread rapidly by processes of diffusion across IGOs that interacted with one another. This may explain why even states lacking domestic oversight provisions "have nevertheless adopted such mechanisms in IGOs" (Grigorescu 2010: 884).

Ensuring the accountability of NGOs is also important because their numbers and reach can be extensive and their organizational structure can often be obscure. Often it is assumed that NGOs are more accountable to people in general, yet they rarely, in fact, have internal democratic mechanisms for the selection of officers, and many might better be seen as elite groups rather than representative groups. In few cases are there mechanisms to guarantee the transparency of their actions, especially to those most affected by their work or on whose behalf they make claims. One mechanism of NGO accountability is money. Since NGOs depend on private contributions, if they are perceived as not responsive to their donors, contributions will likely diminish and they will be unable to function.

MNCs and international business coalitions are difficult to make accountable to the international community. The FATF and OECD regulations on bribery of foreign officials are two effective examples. NGOs like Corporate Accountability International and Transparency International provide accountability for the private business sector, using publicity and public pressure to ensure accountability for a broader constituency.

Lack of transparency in some situations is an essential ingredient for ensuring that participants in decisionmaking can reach decisions without the outside political pressures that openness would make impossible. The dual challenge for making global governance accountable is one of balancing the needs for transparency and openness with the need for efficacy.

### The Challenge of Effectiveness

Good global governance needs to be effective, actually addressing and sometimes resolving global governance problems. Has human security been enhanced? Has human development been improved? Has extreme poverty been alleviated? Are more human rights being respected for more people? Has environmental degradation been curbed and steps been taken that will slow climate change? Amartya Sen (2001) puts it in broader terms: "The central issue, directly, or indirectly, is inequality: between peoples as well as between nations. The relevant inequalities include disparities in affluence, but also gross asymmetries in political, social, and economic power. A crucial question concerns the sharing of potential gains from globalization between rich and poor countries, and between different groups within countries." These disparities have critical ramifications, as a UN panel warned several months before the 9/11 attacks: "In the global village, someone else's poverty very soon becomes one's own problem: of lack of markets for one's products, illegal immigration, pollution, contagious disease, insecurity, fanaticism, terrorism" (UN 2001: 3). Addressing inequality effectively becomes imperative not only for reasons of global security, but also for reasons of equity, fairness, and justice.

### The Dilemma of Leadership: Bringing States Back In?

None of these challenges can be effectively met without leadership. Is it possible to have diffusion of power and leaders coming from diverse sources, as described in Chapter 1? Or perhaps, is it time to bring states back into our thinking about global governance? Domestic political factors will always put limits on state leaders—be they the failure of the United States to approve changes in IMF quotas, the "culture of reticence" that has constricted German and Japanese use of force in peace operations, or China's need for energy to support its continuing economic growth even when it conflicts with addressing climate change.

Following World War II, the United States provided the vision and the resources to create the postwar liberal order based on the UN system, the Bretton Woods institutions, and the rule of law. Can the United States today as a superpower in relative decline provide the necessary leadership when it has so often thwarted international rules over the years, acted without UN Security Council authorization in Iraq in 2003, failed to ratify key human rights treaties, and reinterpreted other conventions in its own national interest? The United States itself is now so significantly hampered by domestic political divisions and government paralysis that it is hard to imagine it providing much leadership for elements of global governance. Furthermore, US leadership sometimes comes with the risk of undermining the legitimacy of global governance. Yet, absent US willingness and ability to lead in some areas and to bear the material and nonmaterial costs, effectiveness is often jeopardized.

Can China play a leadership role? This would be an "about face" from its record in the 1980s and 1990s of playing a low-key role, showing "little interest in, or respect for the norms, principles, and even rules of the international organizations it joined" (Kent 2007: 63). There is increasing evidence of China's "selective multilateralism," in its relationship to ASEAN and its initiatives in the SCO and with the BRICS, as discussed in Chapter 5. There is also clear evidence since 2013 of China's assertiveness as a rising power, its flouting of the law of the sea, and its thwarting of efforts to impose standards of good governance and sustainability in development aid and investment. Its leadership role in the creation of new international economic and financial institutions such as the Asian Infrastructure Investment Bank and the New Development Bank clearly challenges the dominance of the Bretton Woods institutions and the United States.

And what about the EU—could it play a more decisive leadership role in global governance? Although economic integration continues to proceed, the eurozone crisis gives us pause about considering an expanded EU role while reduced military expenditures by member states limit the EU's ability to mount significant military operations. Strains within the EU over immigration and even over its supranational character—witness recent election results in several EU countries and the United Kingdom's planned 2017 vote on membership—inevitably undercut its ability to function as a unitary entity. Certainly, the EU has aspirations to be a normative great power, promoting a set of core values, but outside the EU it is not necessarily seen that way, as Russia's hostile reaction to the EU-Ukraine agreement in 2013–2014 showed (Bengtsson and Elgstrom 2012). And while the EU boasts of providing over half of the world's humanitarian assistance, its slow response to the Ebola outbreak tarnished that positive image. Influencing the thinking of others and promoting values like peace, human rights, and democracy may not be enough. Diplomatic and economic instruments may not be sufficient. There are times when hard military power matters!

The reality is that in today's world, no single state or other actor will dominate or provide leadership in the manner in which the United States did after World War II. Leadership will come from many quarters—from individual states (large and small or middle-sized) or new "Gs"; from NGOs, especially transnational advocacy groups; from public-private partnerships; from corporations; and perhaps even from prominent individuals. As Deborah Avant, Martha Finnemore, and Susan Sell (2010a: 357) argue, there are multiple authorities in global politics that "draw their authority from expertise, morality, competence, and other sources that are independent of the state." It may be that a more robust, universal-membership body will replace the UN, as Thomas Weiss (2014b) suggests, should a global crisis of sufficient magnitude provide the impetus. He and others would go even further by arguing that good global governance can only come from world government. Yet we should note, in closing this account of global governance, the words of Inis Claude (1988: 108) many years ago: "Multilateralism has no magic that transforms states or enables them to create composite entities better endowed than themselves with political virtue." In short, there is no assurance that any particular form of global governance is or will be inherently "good," and any assessment surely depends on the purposes it serves, its effectiveness in making a real difference, and who benefits.

## Suggested Further Reading

Dingwerth, Klaus. (2007) *The New Transnationalism: Transnational Governance and Democratic Legitimacy.* New York: Palgrave Macmillan.

Koppell, Jonathan G. S. (2011) *World Rule: Accountability, Legitimacy, and the Design of Global Governance.* Chicago: University of Chicago Press.

Weiss, Thomas G. (2012) *What's Wrong with the United Nations and How to Fix It.* 2nd ed. Cambridge: Polity.

———. (2014) *Governing the World? Addressing "Problems Without Passports."* Boulder: Paradigm.

Zweifel, Thomas D. (2006) *International Organizations and Democracy: Accountability, Politics, and Power.* Boulder: Lynne Rienner.

# Acronyms

| | |
|---|---|
| ADB | Asian Development Bank |
| AEC | ASEAN Economic Community |
| AfDB | African Development Bank |
| AFTA | ASEAN Free Trade Area |
| AI | Amnesty International |
| AIDS | acquired immunodeficiency syndrome |
| AIIB | Asian Infrastructure Investment Bank |
| ALBA | Bolivarian Alliance for the Peoples of Our America |
| AMIS | AU Mission in Sudan |
| AMISOM | AU Mission in Somalia |
| APEC | Asia-Pacific Economic Cooperation |
| APT | ASEAN Plus Three |
| AQIM | al-Qaeda in the Islamic Maghreb |
| ARF | ASEAN Regional Forum |
| ASEAN | Association of Southeast Asian Nations |
| ASEAN-ISIS | ASEAN Institutes for Strategic and International Studies |
| AU | African Union |
| BINGO | business or industry NGO |
| BIS | Bank for International Settlements |
| BRICS | Brazil, Russia, India, China, and South Africa |
| BWC | Biological Weapons Convention |
| CACM | Central American Common Market |
| CAP | Common Agricultural Policy (EU) |
| CAR | Central African Republic |
| CARICOM | Caribbean Community |
| CEDAW | Convention on the Elimination of All Forms of Discrimination Against Women |
| CEMAC | Economic and Monetary Community of Central Africa |
| CFC | chlorofluorocarbon |
| CFSP | Common Foreign and Security Policy (EU) |
| CGIAR | Consultative Group on International Agricultural Research |
| CITES | Convention on International Trade in Endangered Species of Wild Fauna and Flora |
| CoCom | Coordinating Committee for Multilateral Export Controls |
| COMECON | Council of Mutual Economic Assistance |

| | |
|---|---|
| COMESA | Common Market for Eastern and Southern Africa |
| CoNGO | Conference of Non-Governmental Organizations in Consultative Relationship with the United Nations |
| COREPER | Committee of Permanent Representatives (EU) |
| CSCAP | Council for Security Cooperation in the Asia-Pacific |
| CSCE | Conference on Security and Cooperation in Europe (now OSCE) |
| CSO | civil society organization |
| CTBT | Comprehensive Test Ban Treaty |
| CTC | Counter-Terrorism Committee (UN) |
| CTED | Counter-Terrorism Executive Directorate (UN) |
| CWC | Chemical Weapons Convention |
| DAC | Development Assistance Committee (OECD) |
| DAWN | Development Alternatives with Women for a New Era |
| DONGO | donor-dominated NGO |
| DPKO | Department of Peacekeeping Operations (UN) |
| DRC | Democratic Republic of Congo (formerly Zaire) |
| EAC | East African Community |
| EAS | East Asia Summit |
| EBRD | European Bank for Reconstruction and Development |
| EC | European Community (also known as European Economic Community [EEC]; now known as European Union [EU]) |
| ECB | European Central Bank |
| ECHR | European Court of Human Rights |
| ECJ | European Court of Justice (also known as Court of Justice of the European Communities, and Court of Justice of the European Union) |
| ECLA | Economic Commission for Latin America (CEPAL in Spanish) |
| ECLAC | Economic Commission for Latin America and the Caribbean (UN) |
| ECOMOG | ECOWAS Cease-Fire Monitoring Group |
| ECOSOC | Economic and Social Council (UN) |
| ECOWAS | Economic Community of West African States |
| ECSC | European Coal and Steel Community |
| EEC | European Economic Community (also known as European Community [EC] or Common Market; now known as European Union[EU]) |
| EFTA | European Free Trade Association |
| EMU | European Monetary Union |
| EP | European Parliament |
| EPC | European Political Cooperation |
| ESDP | European Security and Defense Policy |
| EU | European Union (previously known as European Community [EC] or European Economic Community [EEC]) |
| EULEX | EU Rule of Law Mission in Kosovo |
| Euratom | European Atomic Energy Community |
| Eurojust | European Judicial Cooperation Unit (EU) |
| Europol | European Police Office (EU) |
| FAO | Food and Agriculture Organization |
| FATF | Financial Action Task Force |
| FDI | foreign direct investment |
| FGM | female genital mutilation |
| FSC | Forest Stewardship Council |
| FTAA | Free Trade Agreement of the Americas |

| | |
|---|---|
| G-7 | Group of Seven |
| G-8 | Group of Eight |
| G-20 | Group of 20 |
| G-77 | Group of 77 |
| G-90 | Group of 90 (developing-country WTO members) |
| GATS | General Agreement on Trade in Services |
| GATT | General Agreement on Tariffs and Trade |
| GAVI | Global Alliance for Vaccines and Immunizations |
| GCC | Gulf Cooperation Council |
| GDP | gross domestic product |
| GEF | Global Environmental Facility |
| GMO | genetically modified organism |
| GNP | gross national product |
| GONGO | government-organized nongovernmental organization |
| HDI | Human Development Index |
| HIPC | Heavily Indebted Poor Countries Initiative |
| HIV | human immunodeficiency syndrome |
| HLPF | High-Level Political Forum on Sustainable Development |
| HRC | Human Rights Council (UN) |
| HRW | Human Rights Watch |
| IAEA | International Atomic Energy Agency |
| IATA | International Association of Transport Airlines |
| IBRD | International Bank for Reconstruction and Development (also known as World Bank) |
| ICANN | Internet Corporation for Assigned Names and Numbers |
| ICAO | International Civil Aviation Organization |
| ICBL | International Campaign to Ban Landmines |
| ICC | International Criminal Court |
| ICG | International Crisis Group |
| ICISS | International Commission on Intervention and State Sovereignty |
| ICJ | International Court of Justice |
| ICRC | International Committee of the Red Cross |
| ICSID | International Centre for the Settlement of Investment Disputes (World Bank) |
| ICTR | International Criminal Tribunal for Rwanda |
| ICTY | International Criminal Tribunal for the Former Yugoslavia |
| IDA | International Development Association |
| IDB | Inter-American Development Bank |
| IDP | internally displaced person |
| IFAD | International Fund for Agricultural Development |
| IFC | International Finance Corporation |
| IFOR | Implementation Force (NATO force in former Yugoslavia) |
| IGAD | Intergovernmental Authority for Development (Africa) |
| IGF | Internet Governance Forum |
| IGO | intergovernmental organization |
| ILGA | International Lesbian, Gay, Bisexual, Trans, and Intersex Association |
| ILO | International Labour Organization |
| IMF | International Monetary Fund |
| IMO | International Maritime Organization |
| INGO | international nongovernmental organization |
| Interpol | International Criminal Police Organization |
| IO | international organization |

| | |
|---|---|
| IOM | International Organization for Migration |
| IPCC | Intergovernmental Panel on Climate Change (UN) |
| IPI | International Peace Institute |
| IR | international relations |
| ISAF | International Security Assistance Force (NATO force in Afghanistan) |
| ISIL | Islamic State of Iraq and the Levant |
| ISIS | Islamic State of Iraq and Syria |
| ISO | International Organization for Standardization |
| ITU | International Telecommunication Union (formerly International Telegraph Union) |
| IUCN | International Union for the Conservation of Nature and Natural Resources (now known as IUCN–World Conservation Union) |
| KFOR | Kosovo Force (NATO) |
| LAFTA | Latin American Free Trade Association |
| LDC | less developed country |
| LGBT | lesbian, gay, bisexual, and transgender |
| LIFE | Financial Instrument for the Environment (EU) |
| MCC | Millennium Challenge Corporation |
| MDGs | Millennium Development Goals |
| MDRI | Multilateral Debt Relief Initiative |
| MEP | member of European Parliament |
| Mercosur | Common Market of the South (Mercado Común del Sur; also known as Southern Cone Common Market) |
| MIGA | Multilateral Investment Guarantee Agency |
| MINUSMA | Multidimensional Integrated Stabilization Mission in Mali |
| MNC | multinational corporation |
| MONUC | UN Organization Mission in the Democratic Republic of Congo |
| MONUSCO | UN Organization Stabilization Mission in the Democratic Republic of Congo |
| MPI | Multidimensional Poverty Index |
| NAFTA | North American Free Trade Agreement |
| NAM | Non-Aligned Movement |
| NATO | North Atlantic Treaty Organization |
| NEPAD | New Partnership for Africa's Development |
| NGO | nongovernmental organization |
| NIEO | New International Economic Order |
| NPT | Nuclear Non-Proliferation Treaty |
| NSA | nonstate actor |
| OAS | Organization of American States |
| OAU | Organization of African Unity |
| OCHA | Office for Coordination of Humanitarian Affairs (UN) |
| ODA | official development assistance |
| OECD | Organization for Economic Cooperation and Development |
| OEEC | Organization for European Economic Cooperation |
| OIC | Organisation of Islamic Cooperation (formerly Organisation of the Islamic Conference) |
| OIHP | Office International d'Hygiène Publique |
| OPCW | Organization for the Prohibition of Chemical Weapons |
| OPEC | Organization of Petroleum Exporting Countries |
| OSCE | Organization for Security and Cooperation in Europe (formerly CSCE) |
| P-5 | five permanent members of the UN Security Council |

| | |
|---|---|
| PBC | Peacebuilding Commission (UN) |
| PCIJ | Permanent Court of International Justice |
| PLO | Palestine Liberation Organization |
| POC | protection of civilians |
| PRC | People's Republic of China |
| ProMED | Program for Monitoring Emerging Diseases |
| PSC | Peace and Security Council (AU) |
| R2P | responsibility to protect |
| RTA | regional trade agreement |
| RUF | Revolutionary United Front (Sierra Leone) |
| SAARC | South Asian Association of Regional Cooperation |
| SACEUR | Supreme Allied Commander Europe (NATO) |
| SACU | Southern African Customs Union |
| SADC | Southern African Development Community |
| SADCC | Southern African Development Coordination Conference |
| SALT | Strategic Arms Limitation Talks |
| SAP | structural adjustment program (IMF) |
| SARS | severe acute respiratory syndrome |
| SCO | Shanghai Cooperation Organization |
| SDGs | Sustainable Development Goals |
| SEA | Single European Act (EU) |
| SEATO | Southeast Asian Treaty Organization |
| SFOR | Stabilization Force (NATO force in former Yugoslavia) |
| SHAPE | Supreme Headquarters Allied Powers Europe (NATO) |
| SIPRI | Stockholm International Peace Research Institute |
| SRSG | Special Representative of the Secretary-General (UN) |
| START | Strategic Arms Reduction Treaty |
| SWAPO | South West Africa People's Organization (Namibia) |
| TAN | transnational advocacy network |
| TNC | transnational corporation |
| TRAFFIC | Trade Records Analysis of Flora and Fauna in Commerce |
| TRIPS | Agreement on Trade-Related Aspects of Intellectual Property Rights (WTO) |
| TTIP | Transatlantic Trade and Investment Partnership |
| TPP | Trans-Pacific Partnership |
| UIA | Union of International Associations |
| UIC | Union of Islamic Courts (Somalia) |
| UK | United Kingdom |
| UN | United Nations |
| UN.GIFT | UN Global Initiative to Fight Human Trafficking |
| UNAIDS | UN Joint Programme on HIV/AIDS |
| UNAMID | UN-AU Hybrid Mission in Darfur |
| UNASUR | Union of South American Nations |
| UNA-USA | United Nations Association of the United States of America |
| UNCED | UN Conference on the Environment and Development (Rio Conference) |
| UNCHE | UN Conference on the Human Environment (Stockholm Conference) |
| UNCTAD | UN Conference on Trade and Development |
| UNDCP | UN International Drug Control Programme |
| UNDOF | UN Disengagement Observer Force |
| UNDP | UN Development Programme |
| UNEF | UN Emergency Force |

| | |
|---|---|
| UNEP | UN Environment Programme |
| UNESCO | UN Educational, Scientific, and Cultural Organization |
| UNFCC | UN Framework Convention on Climate Change |
| UNFICYP | UN Peacekeeping Force in Cyprus |
| UNFPA | UN Fund for Population Activities |
| UNHCHR | UN High Commissioner for Human Rights |
| UNHCR | UN High Commissioner for Refugees |
| UNICEF | UN Children's Fund |
| UNIDO | UN Industrial Development Organization |
| UNIFEM | UN Development Fund for Women |
| UNIFIL | UN Interim Force in Lebanon |
| UNIHP | UN Intellectual History Project |
| UNIIMOG | UN Iran-Iraq Military Observer Group |
| UNIKOM | UN Iraq-Kuwait Observer Mission |
| UNITA | National Union for the Total Independence of Angola |
| UNITAF | United Task Force on Somalia (also known as Operation Restore Hope) |
| UNMEE | UN Mission in Ethiopia and Eritrea |
| UNMIK | UN Mission in Kosovo |
| UNMISS | UN Mission in South Sudan |
| UNMIT | UN Integrated Mission in Timor |
| UNMOVIC | UN Monitoring, Verification, and Inspection Commission |
| UNOCHA | UN Office for the Coordination of Humanitarian Affairs |
| UNOCI | UN Operation in Côte d'Ivoire |
| UNODC | UN Office on Drugs and Crime |
| UNOSOM | UN Operation in Somalia |
| UNPROFOR | UN Protection Force for Yugoslavia |
| UNRRA | UN Relief and Rehabilitation Administration |
| UNRWA | UN Relief and Works Agency for Palestine Refugees in the Near East |
| UNSCOM | UN Special Commission for the Disarmament of Iraq |
| UNSG | UN Secretary-General |
| UNTAC | UN Transitional Authority in Cambodia |
| UNTAET | UN Transitional Administration in East Timor |
| UNTAG | UN Transition Assistance Group in Namibia |
| UPU | Universal Postal Union |
| USAID | US Agency for International Development |
| WCD | World Commission on Dams |
| WCED | World Commission on Environment and Development (also known as the Brundtland Commission) |
| WFP | World Food Programme |
| WHA | World Health Assembly |
| WHO | World Health Organization |
| WIPO | World Intellectual Property Organization |
| WMD | weapons of mass destruction |
| WMO | World Meteorological Organization |
| WSIS | World Summit on the Information Society |
| WTO | World Trade Organization |
| WWF | World Wide Fund for Nature (and its US affiliate, World Wildlife Fund) |

# References

Abbott, Kenneth W., Robert O. Keohane, Andrew Moravcsik, Anne-Marie Slaughter, and Duncan Snidal. (2000) "The Concept of Legalization." *International Organization* 54:3 (Summer): 401–419.

Abbott, Kenneth W., and Duncan Snidal. (1998) "Why States Act Through Formal International Organizations." *Journal of Conflict Resolution* 42:1 (February): 3–32.

Abdulla, Abdul Kahleq. (1999) "Gulf Cooperation Council: Origin, Nature, and Process." In *Middle East Dilemma,* edited by Michael Hudson. Washington, DC: Taurus. www.ciaonet.org/book/hudson/hudson07.html.

Acemoglu, Daron, and James Robinson. (2012) *Why Nations Fail: The Origins of Power, Prosperity, and Poverty.* New York: Crown.

Acharya, Amitav. (1997) "Ideas, Identity, and Institution-Building: From the 'ASEAN Way' to the 'Asia-Pacific Way'?" *Pacific Review* 10:3: 319–346.

———. (2001) *Constructing a Security Community in Southeast Asia: ASEAN and the Problem of Regional Order.* New York: Routledge.

———. (2007a) "The Emerging Regional Architecture of World Politics." *World Politics* 59 (July): 629–652.

———. (2007b) "Regional Institutions and Security in the Asia-Pacific: Evolution, Adaptation, and Prospects for Transformation." In *Reassessing Security Cooperation in the Asia-Pacific: Competition, Congruence, and Transformation,* edited by Amitav Acharya and Evelyn Goh. Cambridge: MIT Press, pp. 19–40.

———. (2012) *The Making of Southeast Asia: International Relations of a Region.* Ithaca: Cornell University Press.

———. (2013) "Power Shift or Paradigm Shift? China's Rise and Asia's Emerging Security Order." *International Studies Quarterly* 58:1 (March): 158–173.

Acharya, Amitav, and Alastair Ian Johnston, eds. (2007) "Conclusion: Institutional Features, Cooperation Effects, and the Agenda for Further Research on Comparative Regionalism." In *Crafting Cooperation: Regional International Institutions in Comparative Perspective,* edited by Amitav Acharya and Alastair Ian Johnston. Cambridge: Cambridge University Press, pp. 244–278.

Adebajo, Adekeye. (2014) "UN Peacekeeping and the Quest for a Pax Africana." *Current History* 113:763 (May): 178–184.

Adler, Emmanuel, and Steven Bernstein. (2005) "Knowledge in Power: The Epistemic Construction of Global Governance." In *Power in Global Governance,* edited by Michael Barnett and Raymond Duvall. New York: Cambridge University Press, pp. 294–318.

Akbarzadeh, Shadram, and Kylie Connor. (2005) "The Organization of the Islamic Conference: Sharing an Illusion." *Middle East Policy* 12:2 (May): 79–92.

Aklin, Michael, and Johannes Urpelainen. (2014) "The Global Spread of Environmental Ministries: Domestic-International Interactions." *International Studies Quarterly* 58:4 (December): 764–780.

Aldrich, George H., and Christine M. Chinkin. (2000) "A Century of Achievement and Unfinished Work." *American Journal of International Law* 94:1 (January): 90–98.

Alger, Chadwick F. (2002) "The Emerging Roles of NGOs in the UN System: From Article 71 to a People's Millennium Assembly." *Global Governance* 8:1 (January–March): 93–117.

———. (2007) "Widening Participation." In *The Oxford Handbook on the United Nations,* edited by Thomas G. Weiss and Sam Daws. New York: Oxford University Press, pp. 701–715.

Alter, Karen J. (2000) "The European Union's Legal System and Domestic Policy: Spillover or Backlash?" *International Organization* 54:3 (Summer): 489–518.

———. (2014) *The New Terrain of International Law: Courts, Politics, Rights.* Princeton: Princeton University Press.

Andonova, Liliana B. (2010) "Public-Private Partnerships for the Earth: Politics and Patterns of Hybrid Authority in the Multilateral System." *Global Environmental Politics* 10:2 (May): 25–53.

Andrews, Edmund L. (2001) "Frustrated Europeans Set to Battle US on Climate." *New York Times* (July 16): A3.

Anianova, Ekaterina. (2006) "The International Maritime Organization: Tanker or Speedboat?" In *International Maritime Organizations and Their Contribution Towards a Sustainable Marine Development,* edited by Peter Ehlers and Rainer Lagoni. Hamburg: LIT, pp. 77–103.

Annan, Kofi. (1999) *Annual Report of the Secretary-General to the General Assembly.* SG/SM/7136 GA/9596 (20 September).

———. (2000) "We the Peoples: The Role of the United Nations in the 21st Century." www.un.org/millennium/sg/report/full.htm.

———. (2005) *In Larger Freedom: Towards Development, Security, and Human Rights for All.* Report of the UN Secretary-General. www.un.org/largerfreedom /contents.htm.

———. (2006) "Address to the Opening of the 61st General Assembly Session." UN News Centre (September 19). http://huwu.org/apps/news/story.asp?newsid =19889&cr=general&cr1=debate.

Arbour, Louise. (2014) "The Relationship Between the ICC and the UN Security Council." *Global Governance* 20:2 (April–June): 195–201.

Arceneaux, Craig L., and David Pion-Berlin. (2007) "Issues, Threats, and Institutions: Explaining OAS Responses to Democratic Dilemmas in Latin America." *Latin American Politics and Society* 49:2 (May 23): 1–31.

Aris, Stephen. (2013) *Shanghai Cooperation Organization: Mapping Multilateralism in Transition.* New York: International Peace Institute.

Atwood, David C. (1997) "Mobilizing Around the United Nations Special Sessions on Disarmament." In *Transnational Social Movements and Global Politics: Solidarity Beyond the State,* edited by Jackie Smith, Charles Chatfield, and Ron Pagnucco. Syracuse: Syracuse University Press, pp. 141–158.

Atwood, J. Brian. (2012) *Creating a Global Partnership for Effective Development Cooperation.* Washington, DC: Center for Global Development.

Autesserre, Séverine. (2010) *The Trouble with the Congo: Local Violence and the Failure of International Peacebuilding.* New York: Cambridge University Press.

———. (2014) *Peaceland: Conflict Resolution and the Everyday Politics of International Intervention.* New York: Cambridge University Press.

Avant, Deborah D., Martha Finnemore, and Susan K. Sell. (2010a) "Conclusion: Authority, Legitimacy, and Accountability in Global Politics." In *Who Governs the Globe?* edited by Deborah D. Avant, Martha Finnemore, and Susan K. Sell. New York: Cambridge University Press, pp. 356–370.

————, eds. (2010b) *Who Governs the Globe?* New York: Cambridge University Press.

————. (2010c) "Who Governs the Globe?" In *Who Governs the Globe?* edited by Deborah D. Avant, Martha Finnemore, and Susan K. Sell. New York: Cambridge University Press, pp. 1–34.

Axelrod, Robert, and Robert O. Keohane. (1986) "Achieving Cooperation Under Anarchy: Strategies and Institutions." In *Cooperation Under Anarchy,* edited by Kenneth Oye. Princeton: Princeton University Press, pp. 226–254.

Ayangafac, Chrysantus, and Jakkie Cilliers. (2011) "African Solutions to African Problems." In *Rewiring Regional Security in a Fragmented World,* edited by Chester A. Crocker, Fen Osler Hampson, and Pamela Aall. Washington, DC: US Institute of Peace, pp. 115–148.

Ba, Alice D. (2006) "Who's Socializing Whom? Complex Engagement in Sino-ASEAN Relations." *Pacific Review* 19:2: 157–179.

————. (2014) "Institutional Divergence and Convergence in the Asia-Pacific? ASEAN in Practice and Theory." *Cambridge Review of International Affairs* 27:2 (June): 295–318.

Backer, David A., and Paul K. Huth. (2014) "Global Trends in Armed Conflict, 1946–2012." In *Peace and Conflict 2014,* edited by David A. Backer, Jonathan Wilkenfeld, and Paul K. Huth. Boulder: Paradigm, pp. 18–22.

Backer, David A., Jonathan Wilkenfeld, and Paul K. Huth. (2014) *Peace and Conflict, 2014.* Boulder: Paradigm.

Bagri, Nehra Thirani. (2014) "U.S.-India Agreement on Stockpiles of Food Revives a Trade Deal." *New York Times* (November 14): B3.

Ball, Desmond, and Kwa Chong Guan. (2010) *Assessing Track 2 Diplomacy in the Asia Pacific Region: A CSCAP Reader.* Malaysia: Council for Security Cooperation in the Asia Pacific (CSCAP).

Barnett, Michael. (2002) *Eyewitness to a Genocide: The United Nations and Rwanda.* Ithaca: Cornell University Press.

————. (2005) "Humanitarianism Transformed." *Perspectives on Politics* 3:4 (December): 723–740.

————. (2011) *Empire of Humanity: A History of Humanitarianism.* Ithaca: Cornell University Press.

Barnett, Michael, and Raymond Duvall. (2005) "Power in Global Governance." In *Power in Global Governance,* edited by Michael Barnett and Raymond Duvall. New York: Cambridge University Press, pp. 1–32.

Barnett, Michael, Songying Fang, and Christoph Zürcher. (2014) "Compromised Peacebuilding." *International Studies Quarterly* 58:3 (September): 608–620.

Barnett, Michael, and Martha Finnemore. (1999) "The Politics, Power, and Pathologies of International Organizations." *International Organization* 53:4 (Autumn): 699–732.

————. (2004) *Rules for the World: International Organizations in Global Politics.* Ithaca: Cornell University Press.

————. (2005) "The Power of Liberal International Organizations." In *Power in Global Governance,* edited by Michael Barnett and Raymond Duvall. New York: Cambridge University Press, pp. 161–184.

Barnett, Michael, Hunjoon Kim, Madalene O'Donnell, and Laura Sitea. (2007) "Peacebuilding: What Is in a Name?" *Global Governance* 13:1 (January– March): 35–58.

Barnett, Michael, and Etel Solingen. (2007) "Designed to Fail or Failure of Design? The Origins and Legacy of the Arab League." In *Crafting Cooperation: Regional International Institutions in Comparative Perspective,* edited by Amitav Acharya and Alastair Ian Johnston. Cambridge: Cambridge University Press, pp. 180–220.

Bauer, Steffen. (2006) "Does Bureaucracy Really Matter? The Authority of Intergovernmental Treaty Secretariats in Global Environmental Politics." *Global Environmental Politics* 6:1 (February): 23–49.

Beigbeder, Yves. (2000) "The United Nations Secretariat: Reform in Progress." In *The United Nations at the Millennium: The Principal Organs,* edited by Paul Taylor and A. J. R. Groom. New York: Continuum, pp. 196–223.

Bellamy, Alex J., and Paul D. Williams. (2011) "The New Politics of Protection? Côte d'Ivoire, Libya, and the Responsibility to Protect." *International Affairs* 87:4 (July): 825–850.

Belloni, Roberto, and Manuela Moschella. (2013) "The IMF and Civil Society." *International Politics* 50:4: 532–552.

Benedick, Richard Elliot. (1998) *Ozone Diplomacy: New Directions in Safeguarding the Planet.* Enlarged ed. Cambridge: Harvard University Press.

Bengtsson, Rikard, and Ole Elgstrom. (2012) "Conflicting Role Conceptions? The European Union in Global Politics." *Foreign Policy Analysis* 8:1 (January): 93–108.

Bennett, A. LeRoy. (1995) *International Organizations: Principles and Issues.* 6th ed. Englewood Cliffs, NJ: Prentice Hall.

Bernauer, Thomas, Anna Kalbhenn, Vally Koubi, and Gabriele Spilker. (2013) "Is There a 'Depth Versus Participation' Dilemma in International Cooperation?" *Review of International Organizations* 8: 477–497.

Betsill, Michele M. (2007) "Regional Governance of Global Climate Change: The North American Commission for Environmental Cooperation." *Global Environmental Politics* 7:2 (May): 11–27.

Betsill, Michele M., and Harriet Bulkeley. (2006) "Cities and the Multilateral Governance of Global Climate Change." *Global Governance* 12:2 (April–June): 141–159.

Betsill, Michele M., and Elisabeth Corell, eds. (2008) *NGO Diplomacy: The Influence of Nongovernmental Organizations in International Environmental Negotiations.* Cambridge: MIT Press.

Bhagwati, Jagdish. (2004) *In Defense of Globalization.* New York: Oxford University Press.

———. (2008) *Termites in the Trading System: How Preferential Agreements Undermine Free Trade.* New York: Oxford University Press.

Biermann, Frank. (2012) "Navigating the Antropocene: Improving Earth System Governance." *Science* 335 (16 March): 1306–1307.

Biermann, Frank, and Steffen Bauer, eds. (2005) *A World Environment Organization: Solution or Threat for Effective International Environmental Governance?* Aldershot: Ashgate.

Biermann, Frank, and Philipp Pattberg. (2012) "Global Environmental Governance Revisited." In *Global Environmental Governance Revisited,* edited by Frank Biermann and Philipp Pattberg. Cambridge: MIT Press, pp. 1–23.

Biermann, Frank, and Bernd Siebenhüner, eds. (2009) *Managers of Global Change: The Influence of International Environmental Bureaucracies.* Cambridge: MIT Press.

———. (2013) "Problem Solving by International Bureaucracies: The Influence of International Secretariats on World Politics." In *Routledge Handbook of International Organization,* edited by Bob Reinalda. New York: Routledge, pp. 149–161.

Biersteker, Thomas, Sue E. Eckert, Marcos Tourinho, and Zuzana Hudáková. (2013) *The Effectiveness of United Nations Targeted Sanctions: Findings from the Targeted Sanctions Consortium (TSC).* http://graduateinstitute.ch/un-sanctions.

Bilder, Richard B. (1997) "Adjudication: International Arbitral Tribunals and Courts." In *Peacemaking in International Conflict: Methods and Techniques,* edited by I. William Zartman and J. Lewis Rasmussen. Washington, DC: US Institute of Peace, pp. 155–190.

Birdsall, Nancy, and Francis Fukuyama. (2011) "The Post–Washington Consensus: Development After the Crisis." *Foreign Affairs* 90:2: 45–53.

Bob, Clifford. (2005) *The Marketing of Rebellion: Insurgents, Media, and International Activism.* New York: Cambridge University Press.

———. (2010) "Packing Heat: Pro-Gun Groups and the Governance of Small Arms." In *Who Governs the Globe?* edited by Deborah D. Avant, Martha Finnemore, and Susan K. Sell. New York: Cambridge University Press, pp. 183–201.

Bode, Ingvild. (2014) "Francis Deng and the Concern for Internally Displaced Persons: Intellectual Leadership in the United Nations." *Global Governance* 20:2 (April–June): 277–295.

Bodin, Jean. (1967) *Six Books on the Commonwealth*. Oxford: Blackwell.

Bosch, Olivia, and Peter van Ham. (2007) "UNSCR 1520: Its Future and Contribution to Global Non-Proliferation and Counter-Terrorism." In *Global Non-Proliferation and Counter-Terrorism: The Impact of UNSCR 1540*, edited by Olivia Bosch and Peter van Ham. London: Chatham, pp. 207–226.

Boutros-Ghali, Boutros. (1992) *An Agenda for Peace: Preventive Diplomacy, Peacemaking, and Peacekeeping*. New York: United Nations.

———. (1995) *An Agenda for Development*. New York: United Nations.

Braithwaite, John. (2013) "Evaluating the Timor-Leste Peace Operation." In *Peace Operation Success: A Comparative Analysis*, edited by Daniel Druckman and Paul F. Diehl. Leiden: Martinus Nijhoff, pp. 85–110.

Breitmeier, Helmut, Arild Underdal, and Oran R. Young. (2011) "The Effectiveness of International Environmental Regimes: Comparing and Contrasting Findings from Quantitative Research." *International Studies Review* 134 (December): 579–605.

Brown, Mark Malloch. (2008) "The John W. Holmes Lecture: Can the UN Be Reformed?" *Global Governance* 14:1 (January–March): 1–12.

Brown, Michael E., and Richard N. Rosecrance. (1999) *The Costs of Conflict: Prevention and Cure in the Global Arena*. Lanham: Rowman and Littlefield.

Brzezinski, Zbigniew. (1989) *The Grand Failure: The Birth and Death of Communism in the Twentieth Century*. New York: Scribner's.

Buergenthal, Thomas. (1995) *International Human Rights in a Nutshell*. 2nd ed. St. Paul: West.

Bulkeley, Harriet, et al. (2012) "Governing Climate Change Transnationally: Assessing the Evidence from a Database of Sixty Initiatives." *Environment and Planning C: Government and Policy* 30:4: 591–612.

Bull, Hedley. (1977) *The Anarchical Society: A Study of Order in World Politics*. New York: Columbia University Press.

Bunch, Charlotte. (1990) "Women's Rights Are Human Rights: Toward a Re-Vision of Human Rights." *Human Rights Quarterly* 12:4: 486–500.

Bures, Oldrich, and Stephanie Ahern. (2007) "The European Model of Building Regional Cooperation Against Terrorism." In *Uniting Against Terror: Cooperative Nonmilitary Responses to the Global Terrorist Threat*, edited by David Cortright and George A. Lopez. Cambridge: MIT Press, pp. 187–236.

Buntaine, Mark T., and Bradley C. Parks. (2013) "When Do Environmentally Focused Assistance Projects Achieve Their Objectives? Evidence from World Bank Post-Project Evaluations." *Global Governmental Politics* 13:2 (May): 65–88.

Büthe, Tim, and Walter Mattli. (2011) *The New Global Rulers: The Privatization of Regulation in the World Economy*. Princeton: Princeton University Press.

Butler, Michael J. (2012) "Ten Years After: (Re)assessing Neo-Trusteeship and UN State-Building in Timor-Leste." *International Studies Perspectives* 13:1 (February): 85–104.

Buzan, Barry. (2004) *From International to World Society? English School Theory and the Social Structure of Globalisation*. Cambridge: Cambridge University Press.

Buzan, Barry, and Ole Waever. (2009) "Macrosecuritisation and Security Constellations: Reconsidering the Scale in Securitisation Theory." *Review of International Studies* 35:2 (April): 253–276.

Buzan, Barry, Ole Waever, and Jaap de Wilde. (1998) *Security: A New Framework for Analysis*. Boulder: Lynne Rienner.

Caballero-Anthony, Mely. (2014) "Understanding ASEAN's Centrality: Bases and Prospects in an Evolving Regional Architecture." *Pacific Review* 27:4 (September): 563–584.

Call, Charles T., and Elizabeth M. Cousens. (2008) "Ending Wars and Building Peace: International Responses to War-Torn Societies." *International Studies Perspectives* 9:1 (February): 1–21.

Caporaso, James A. (1993) "International Relations Theory and Multilateralism: The Search for Foundations." In *Multilateralism Matters: The Theory and Praxis of an International Form,* edited by John Gerard Ruggie. New York: Columbia University Press, pp. 51–90.

Carson, Rachel. (1962) *Silent Spring.* Cambridge, MA: Houghton Mifflin.

Casaburi, Gabriel, Maria Pia Riggirozzi, Maria Fernanda Tuozzo, and Diana Tussie. (2000) "Multilateral Development Banks, Governments, and Civil Society: Chiaroscuros in a Triangular Relationship." *Global Governance* 6:4 (October–December): 493–517.

Castañeda, Jorge G. (2014) "NAFTA's Mixed Record: The View from Mexico." *Foreign Affairs* 93:1 (January–February): 134–141.

Center on International Cooperation at New York University. (2013) *Annual Review of Global Peace Operations 2013.* Boulder: Lynne Rienner.

Charnovitz, Steve. (1997) "Two Centuries of Participation: NGOs and International Governance." *Michigan Journal of International Law* 18:183 (Winter): 184–286.

———. (2006) "Nongovernmental Organizations and International Law." *American Journal of International Law* 100:2 (April): 348–372.

Chayes, Abram, and Antonia Handler Chayes. (1995) *The New Sovereignty: Compliance with International Regulatory Agreements.* Cambridge: Harvard University Press.

Checkel, Jeffrey T., ed. (2005) *International Institutions and Socialization in Europe.* Special Issue: *International Organization* 59:4 (Fall).

———. (2007) "Social Mechanisms and Regional Cooperation: Are Europe and the EU Really All That Different?" In *Crafting Cooperation: Regional International Institutions in Comparative Perspective,* edited by Amitav Acharya and Alastair Ian Johnston. Cambridge: Cambridge University Press, pp. 221–243.

Chesterman, Simon, ed. (2007) *Secretary or General? The UN Secretary-General in World Politics.* Cambridge: Cambridge University Press.

Cho, Seo-Young. (2013) "Integrating Equality: Globalization, Women's Rights, and Human Trafficking." *International Studies Quarterly* 57:4 (December): 683–697.

Christy, David S. J. (2008) "Round and Round We Go." *World Policy Journal* 25:2 (Summer): 19–27.

Clark, Ann Marie. (2001) *Diplomacy of Conscience: Amnesty International and Changing Human Rights Norms.* Princeton: Princeton University Press.

Clark, Ann Marie, Elisabeth J. Friedman, and Kathryn Hochstetler. (1998) "The Sovereign Limits of Global Civil Society: A Comparison of NGO Participation in UN World Conferences on the Environment, Human Rights, and Women." *World Politics* 51:1 (October): 1–35.

Clarke, Walter, and Jeffrey Herbst. (1996) "Somalia and the Future of Humanitarian Intervention." *Foreign Affairs* 75:2 (March–April): 70–85.

Claude, Inis L., Jr. (1964) *Swords Into Plowshares: The Problems and Progress of International Organization.* 3rd ed. New York: Random House.

———. (1967) *The Changing United Nations.* New York: Random House.

———. (1988) "The Vogue of Collectivism in Inbternational Relations." In *States and the Global System: Politics, Law, and Organization,* edited by Inis L. Claude Jr. New York: St. Martin's, pp. 133–144.

Clemens, Michael A., and Gabriel Demombynes. (2010) "When Does Rigorous Impact Evaluation Make a Difference? The Case of the Millennium Villages." Working Paper no. 225. Washington, DC: Center for Global Development.

Cohen, Roberta. (2009) "Up Close and From the Tower: Two Views of Refugee and Internally Displaced Populations." *International Studies Review* 11:3 (September): 585–591.

Coll, Charles T. (2008) "Knowing Peace When You See It: Setting Standards for Peace-building Success." *Civil Wars* 10:2 (Spring): 173–194.

Collier, Paul. (2007) *The Bottom Billion: Why the Poorest Countries Are Failing and What Can Be Done About It.* New York: Oxford University Press.

Commission on Global Governance. (1995) *Our Global Neighbourhood: Report of the Commission on Global Governance.* Oxford: Oxford University Press.

Conca, Ken. (2006) *Governing Water: Contentious Transnational Politics and Global Institution Building.* Cambridge: MIT Press.

Conroy, Michael E. (2002) "Can Advocacy-Led Certification Systems Transform Global Corporate Practices?" In *Global Backlash: Citizen Initiatives for a Just World Economy,* edited by Robin Broad. Lanham: Rowman and Littlefield, pp. 210–215.

Conroy, Richard. (1994) "Peacekeeping and Peace Enforcement in Somalia." Paper presented at the annual meeting of the International Studies Association, Washington, DC (March 30–April 2).

Cooley, Alexander, and James Ron. (2002) "The NGO Scramble: Organizational Insecurity and the Political Economy of Transnational Action." *International Security* 27:1 (Summer): 5–39.

Cooper, Andrew F. (2004) "The Making of the Inter-American Democratic Charter: A Case of Complex Multilateralism." *International Studies Perspectives* 5:1 (February): 92–113.

Cooper, Andrew F., and Ramesh Thakur. (2013) *The Group of Twenty (G20).* London: Routledge.

———. (2014) "The BRICS in the New Global Economic Geography." In *International Organizations and Global Governance,* edited by Thomas G. Weiss and Rorden Wilkinson. New York: Routledge, pp. 265–278.

Cooper, Scott, Darren Hawkins, Wade Jacoby, and Daniel Nielson. (2008) "Yielding Sovereignty to International Institutions: Bringing System Structure Back In." *International Studies Review* 10:3 (September): 501–524.

Copelovitch, Mark S. (2010) *The International Monetary Fund in the Global Economy: Banks, Bonds, and Bailouts.* New York: Cambridge University Press.

Cortright, David, and George A. Lopez. (2000) *The Sanctions Decade: Assessing UN Strategies in the 1990s.* Boulder: Lynne Rienner.

———. (2002) *Sanctions and the Search for Security.* Boulder: Lynne Rienner.

Cortright, David, and Ron Pagnucco. (1997) "Limits to Transnationalism: The 1980s Freeze Campaign." In *Transnational Social Movements and Global Politics: Solidarity Beyond the State,* edited by Jackie Smith, Charles Chatfield, and Ron Pagnucco. Syracuse: Syracuse University Press, pp. 159–174.

Council on Foreign Relations. (2013) "Issue Brief: The Global Regime for Terrorism." www.cfr.org/terrorism/global-regime-terrorism/p25729.

———. (2014) *Global Governance Report Card on International Health.*

Cousens, Elizabeth, and David Harland. (2006) "Post-Dayton Bosnia and Herzegovina." In *Twenty-First-Century Peace Operations,* edited by William J. Durch. Washington, DC: US Institute of Peace, pp. 49–140.

Cousteau, Jacques-Yves, with James Dugan. (1963) *The Living Sea.* New York: Harper and Row.

Cox, Robert W. (1986) "Social Forces, States, and World Orders: Beyond International Relations Theory." In *Neorealism and Its Critics,* edited by Robert O. Keohane. New York: Columbia University Press, pp. 204–254.

———. (1992a) "Globalization, Multilateralism and Democracy." John W. Holmes Memorial Lecture. Academic Council on the United Nations System (ACUNS), Reports and Papers no. 2.

———. (1992b) "Toward a Post-Hegemonic Conceptualization of World Order: Reflections on the Relevancy of Ibn Khaldun." In *Governance Without Government: Order and Change in World Politics,* edited by James N. Rosenau and Ernst-Otto Czempiel. New York: Cambridge University Press, pp. 132–159.

Crocker, Chester A., Fen Osler Hampson, and Pamela Aall, eds. (1999) *Herding Cats: Multiparty Mediation in a Complex World*. Washington, DC: US Institute of Peace.
———. (2004) *Taming Intractable Conflicts: Mediation in the Hardest Cases*. Washington, DC: US Institute of Peace.
———. (2011) *Rewiring Regional Security in a Fragmented World*. Washington, DC: US Institute of Peace.
Cronin, Bruce, and Ian Hurd, eds. (2008) *The UN Security Council and the Politics of International Authority*. New York: Routledge.
Crossette, Barbara. (1999) "Kofi Annan Unsettles People, As He Believes U.N. Should Do." *New York Times* (December 31): A1, A8.
Cupitt, Richard, Rodney Whitlock, and Lynn Williams Whitlock. (1997) "The (Im)mortality of International Governmental Organizations." In *The Politics of Global Governance: International Organizations in an Interdependent World*, edited by Paul F. Diehl. Boulder: Lynne Rienner, pp. 7–23.
Daalder, Ivo H., and James G. Stavridis. (2012) "NATO's Victory in Libya: The Right Way to Run an Intervention." *Foreign Affairs* 91:2 (March–April): 2–7.
Dallmayr, Fred R. (2002) "Globalization and Inequality: A Plea for Global Justice." *International Studies Review* 4:2 (Summer): 137–156.
Damian, Michel, and Jean-Christophe Graz. (2001) "The World Trade Organization, the Environment, and the Ecological Critique." *International Social Science Journal* 170 (December): 597–610.
Dany, Charlotte. (2014) "Janus-Faced NGO Participation in Global Governance: Structural Constraints for NGO Influence." *Global Governance* 20:3 (July–September): 419–436.
Davenport, Coral. (2014) "Climate Change Deemed Growing Security Threat by Military Researchers." *New York Times* (May 14): A18.
Davenport, David. (2014) "International Criminal Court: 12 Years, 1 Billion, 2 Convictions." *Forbes* (March 12): A18.
Deaton, Angus. (2013) *The Great Escape: Health, Wealth, and the Origins of Inequality*. Princeton: Princeton University Press.
de Beaufort Wijnholds, Onno. (2011) *Fighting Financial Fires: An IMF Insider Account*. Houndmills: Palgrave Macmillan.
Deets, Stephen. (2009) "Constituting Interests and Identities in a Two-Level Game: Understanding the Gabcikovo-Nagymaros Dam Conflict." *Foreign Policy Analysis* 5:1 (January): 37–56.
DeMars, William. (2005) *NGOs and Transnational Networks: Wild Cards in World Politics*. London: Pluto.
DeSombre, Elizabeth R. (2006) *Global Environmental Institutions*. London: Routledge.
Devarajan, Shantayanan, and Wilfgang Fengler. (2013) "Africa's Economic Boom: Why the Pessimists and the Optimists Are Both Right." *Foreign Affairs* 92:3 (May–June): 68–81.
Dharmapuri, Sahana. (2013) "Not Just a Numbers Game: Increasing Women's Participation in UN Peacekeeping." Providing for Peacekeeping no. 4. New York: International Peace Institute.
Diamond, Jarod. (2005) *Collapse: How Societies Choose to Fail or Collapse*. New York: Penguin.
Diehl, Paul F. (2000) "Forks in the Road: Theoretical and Policy Concerns for 21st Century Peacekeeping." *Global Society* 14:3: 337–360.
———. (2008) *Peace Operations*. Malden, MA: Polity.
Diehl, Paul, and Alexandru Balas. (2014) *Peace Operations*. 2nd ed. Malden, MA: Polity.
Diehl, Paul, and Daniel Druckman. (2010) *Evaluating Peace Operations*. Boulder: Lynne Rienner.

Dilitzky, Ariel E. (2012) "Twenty Reflections on the Process of Reflection." *Aportes: Magazine of the Due Process of Law Foundation* 5:16 (June): 11–13.

Dimitrov, Radoslav S., Detlef Sprinz, Gerald M. Digiusto, and Alexander Kelle. (2007) "International Nonregimes: A Research Agenda." *International Studies Review* 9:2 (Spring): 230–258.

Dingwerth, Klaus. (2008) "Private Transnational Governance and the Developing World: A Comparative Perspective." *International Studies Quarterly* 52:3 (September): 607–634.

Dingwerth, Klaus, and Philipp Pattberg. (2006) "Global Governance as a Perspective on World Politics." *Global Governance* 12:2 (April–June): 185–203.

———. (2009) "World Politics and Organizational Fields: The Case of Transnational Sustainability Governance." *European Journal of International Relations* 15 (November): 707–744.

Dobbins, James, et al. (2005) *The UN's Role in Nation-Building: From the Congo to Iraq*. Santa Monica: RAND.

Dominguez, Jorge I. (2007) "International Cooperation in Latin America: The Design of Regional Institutions by Slow Accretion." In *Crafting Cooperation: Regional International Institutions in Comparative Perspective*, edited by Amitav Acharya and Alastair Ian Johnston. New York: Cambridge University Press, pp. 83–128.

Donnelly, Jack. (1998) *International Human Rights*. 2nd ed. Boulder: Westview.

Dosch, Jörn. (2008) "ASEAN's Reluctant Liberal Turn and the Thorny Road to Democracy Promotion." *Pacific Review* 21:4: 527–545.

Doxey, Margaret. (2007) *United Nations Sanctions: Trends and Problems*. Halifax: Centre for Foreign Policy Studies.

Doyle, Michael W. (1995) *UN Peacekeeping in Cambodia: UNTAC's Civil Mandate*. Boulder: Lynne Rienner.

Doyle, Michael W., and Nicholas Sambanis. (2006) *Making War and Building Peace*. Princeton: Princeton University Press.

Drezner, Daniel W. (2007) *All Politics Is Global: Explaining International Regulatory Regimes*. Princeton: Princeton University Press.

———. (2012) "The Irony of Global Economic Governance: The System Worked." Working paper. New York: Council on Foreign Relations.

———. (2014) *The System Worked: How the World Stopped Another Great Depression*. Oxford: Oxford University Press.

Drezner, Daniel, and Kathleen R. McNamara. (2013) "International Political Economy, Global Financial Orders and the 2008 Financial Crisis." *Perspectives on Politics* 11:1 (March): 155–166.

Dryzek, John S. (2012) "Global Civil Society: The Progress of Post-Westphalian Politics." *Annual Review of Political Science* 15: 101–119.

Duffield, John. (2003) "The Limits of 'Rational Design.'" *International Organization* 57:2 (Spring): 411–430.

———. (2007) "What Are International Institutions?" *International Studies Review* 9:1 (Spring): 1–22.

Easterly, William. (2006) *The White Man's Burden: Why the West's Efforts to Aid the Rest Have Done So Much Ill and So Little Good*. New York: Penguin.

*The Economist*. (2013) "Emerging Africa: A Hopeful Continent." (March 2): 3–16.

———. (2014a) "Elected, Yet Strangely Unaccountable." (May 17): 21–24.

———. (2014b) "South-East Asia Finds the Decorum of Its Regional Club Rather Rudely Shattered." (May 17): 42.

Edsall, Thomas B. (2014) "Free Trade Disagreement." *International New York Times* (February 4). www.nytimes.com/2014/02/05/opinion/edsall-free-trade-disagreement.

Eichengreen, Barry. (2011) "International Policy Coordination: The Long View." Unpublished conference paper. http://eml.berkeley.edu/~eichengr/intl_policy_coord_9-19-11.pdf.

Eilstrup-Sangiovanni, Mette, and Teale N. Phelps Bondaroff. (2014) "From Advocacy to Confrontation: Direct Enforcement by Environmental NGOs." *International Studies Quarterly* 58:2 (June): 348–361.

Elliott, Kimberly Ann. (2000) "Getting Beyond No . . . ! Promoting Worker Rights and Trade." In *The WTO After Seattle,* edited by Jeffrey J. Schott. Washington, DC: Institute for International Economics, pp. 187–204.

Elliott, Lorraine. (2011) "East Asia and Sub-Regional Diversity: Initiatives, Institutions, and Identity." In *Comparative Environmental Regionalism,* edited by Lorraine Elliott and Shaun Breslin. London: Routledge, pp.56–75.

———. (2013) "Climate Diplomacy." In *The Oxford Handbook of Modern Diplomacy,* edited by Andrew F. Cooper, Jorge Heine, and Ramesh Thakur. Oxford: Oxford University Press, pp. 840–856.

Emmerij, Louis, Richard Jolly, and Thomas G. Weiss. (2001) *Ahead of the Curve: UN Ideas and Global Challenges.* Bloomington: Indiana University Press.

Enloe, Cynthia. (2004) *The Curious Feminist: Searching for Women in a New Age of Empire.* Berkeley: University of California Press.

Essoungou, André-Michel. (2011) "Foreign Investors Eye African Consumers." *Africa Renewal* 25:1 (April): 13–15.

Esty, Daniel C. (2001) "A Term's Limits." *Foreign Policy* 126 (September–October): 74–75.

European Commission. (2001) "Ten Years After Rio: Preparing for the World Summit on Sustainable Development in 2002." Com (2001) 53 Final.

European Court of Justice (ECJ). (1964) *Flaminio Costa v. Enel.* Case 6/64 in the Court of Justice of the European Communities, *Reports of Cases Before the Court.*

———. (1979) *Cassis de Dijon.* Officially, *Rewe-Zentral AG v. Bundesmonopolverwaltung für Branntwein.* Case 120/78 in the Court of Justice of the European Communities, *Reports of Cases Before the Court.*

———. (1995) *Union Royale Belge des Sociétés de Football Association, ASBL v. Bosman.* Court of Justice of the European Union, *Reports of Cases Before the Court.*

———. (2014) *Digital Rights Ireland Ltd C-293/12 and Karntner Landesregierung C-594/12* (April).

Evans, Gareth. (2012) "The Responsibility to Protect After Libya and Syria." Address to annual Castan Centre Human Rights Law Conference, Melbourne (20 July). www.gevans.org/speeches/speech476.html.

Evans, Paul. (2005) "Between Regionalism and Regionalization: Policy Networks and the Nascent East Asian Institutional Identity." In *Remapping East Asia: The Construction of a Region,* edited by T. J. Pempel. Ithaca: Cornell University Press, pp. 195–215.

Fasulo, Linda. (2009) *An Insider's Guide to the United Nations.* 2nd ed. New Haven: Yale University Press.

Fawcett, Louise. (2003) "The Evolving Architecture of Regionalization." In *The United Nations and Regional Security: Europe and Beyond,* edited by Michael Pugh and Waheguru Pal Singh Sidhu. Boulder: Lynne Rienner, pp. 11–30.

Fearon, James, and Alexander Wendt. (2002) "Rationalism vs. Constructivism: A Skeptical View." In *The Handbook of International Relations,* edited by Walter Carlsnaes, Thomas Risse, and Beth Simmons. London: Sage, pp. 52–72.

Fidler, David. (2007) "How Dr. Chan Intends to Defend the Planet from Pandemics." *The Economist* (June 16): 67–68.

Findley, Michael, Daniel Nielson, and J. C. Sharman. (2014) *Global Shell Games: Experiments in Transnational Relations, Crime, and Terrorism.* New York: Cambridge University Press.

Finnemore, Martha. (1996a) "Constructing Norms of Humanitarian Intervention." In *The Culture of National Security: Norms and Identity in World Politics,* edited by Peter J. Katzenstein. New York: Columbia University Press, pp. 153–185.

———. (1996b) *National Interests in International Society.* Ithaca: Cornell University Press.

———. (2003) *The Purpose of Intervention: Changing Beliefs About the Use of Force.* Ithaca: Cornell University Press.

———. (2014) "Dynamics of Global Governance: Building on What We Know?" *International Studies Quarterly* 58:1 (March): 221–224.

Finnemore, Martha, and Kathryn Sikkink. (1998) "Norms and International Relations Theory." *International Organizations* 52:4 (Fall): 887–917.

———. (2001) "Taking Stock: The Constructivist Research Program in International Relations and Comparative Politics." *Annual Review of Political Science* 4: 391–416.

Fomerand, Jacques. (1996) "UN Conferences: Media Events or Genuine Diplomacy?" *Global Governance* 2:3 (September–December): 361–375.

Forsythe, David P. (2005) *The Humanitarians: The International Committee of the Red Cross.* Cambridge: Cambridge University Press, pp. 85–110.

———. (2006) *Human Rights in International Relations.* 2nd ed. Cambridge: Cambridge University Press.

Forsythe, David P., with Baekkwan Park. (2009) "Turbulent Transition: From the UN Human Rights Commission to the Council." In *The United Nations: Past, Present, and Future—Proceedings of the 2007 Frances Marion University UN Symposium,* edited by Scott Kaufman and Alissa Waters. New York: Nova Science, pp. 85–110.

Fortna, Virginia Page. (2004a) "Does Peacekeeping Keep Peace? International Intervention and the Duration of Peace After Civil War." *International Studies Quarterly* 48:2 (June): 269–292.

———. (2004b) *Peace Time: Cease-Fire Arrangements and the Durability of Peace.* Princeton: Princeton University Press.

———. (2008) *Does Peacekeeping Work? Shaping Belligerents Choices After Civil War.* Princeton: Princeton University Press.

Franck, Thomas M. (1990) *The Power of Legitimacy Among Nations.* New York: Oxford University Press.

Francois, Joseph et al. (2013) *Reducing Transatlantic Barriers to Trade and Investment: An Economic Assessment. Final Project Report (March).* London: Center for Economic Policy Research. http://trade.ec.europa.eu/doclib/docs/2013/march/tradoc_150737.pdf.

French, Howard W. (2014) *China's Second Continent: How a Million Migrants Are Building a New Empire in Africa.* New York: Random House.

Friedman, Elisabeth Jay, Kathryn Hochstetler, and Ann Marie Clark. (2005) *Sovereignty, Democracy, and Global Civil Society: State-Society Relations at UN World Conferences.* Albany: SUNY Press.

Frieze, Donna-Lee. (2013) *Totally Unofficial: The Autobiography of Raphael Lemkin.* New Haven: Yale University Press.

Fröhlich, Manuel. (2013) "The Special Representatives of the UN Secretary-General." In *Routledge Handbook of International Organizations,* edited by Bob Reinalda. New York: Routledge, pp. 231–243.

———. (2014) "The John Holmes Memorial Lecture: Representing the United Nations—Individual Actors, International Agency, and Leadership." *Global Governance* 20:2 (April–June): 169–193.

Gardini, Gian Luca. (2010) *The Origins of Mercosur: Democracy and Regionalism in South America.* New York: Palgrave Macmillan.

Gardner, Kathryn L. (2007) "Task Force and International Efforts to Capture Terrorist Finances." In *Uniting Against Terror: Cooperative Nonmilitary Responses to the Global Terrorist Threat,* edited by David Cortright and George A. Lopez. Cambridge: MIT Press, pp. 157–186.

Garfield, Richard. (1999) "Morbidity and Mortality Among Iraqi Children from 1990–1998: Assessing the Impact of Economic Sanctions." Occasional Paper no. 16:OP:3. Kroc Institute for International Peace Studies, University of Notre Dame, and Fourth Freedom Forum. www.fourthfreedom.org/php/t-si-index.php?hinc+garf.hinc.

Ghébali, Victor-Yves. (2005) "The OSCE Between Crisis and Reform: Towards a New Lease on Life." Policy Paper no. 10. Geneva: Centre for the Democratic Control of Armed Forces.

Gill, Stephen. (1994) "Structural Change and Global Political Economy: Globalizing Elites and the Emerging World Order." In *Global Transformation: Challenges to the State System,* edited by Yoshikazu Sakamoto. Tokyo: UN University Press.

Gilpin, Robert. (1975) "Three Models of the Future." *International Organization* 29:1 (Winter): 37–60.

———. (1987) *The Political Economy of International Relations.* Princeton: Princeton University Press.

———. (2001) *Global Political Economy: Understanding the International Economic Order.* Princeton: Princeton University Press.

Ginsberg, Roy H. (2007) *Demystifying the European Union: The Enduring Logic of Regional Integration.* Lanham: Rowman and Littlefield.

Glanville, Luke. (2014) "Syria Teaches Us Little About Questions of Military Intervention." In *Into the Eleventh Hour: R2P, Syria, and Humanitarianism in Crisis,* edited by E–International Relations. www.e-ir.info/2014/02/07/syria-teaches-us-little-about-questions-of-military-intervention.

Goldstein, Joshua S. (2011) *Winning the War on War: The Decline of Armed Conflict Worldwide.* New York: Dutton.

Goodhand, Jonathan. (2006) *Aiding Peace? The Role of NGOs in Armed Conflict.* Boulder: Lynne Rienner.

Gourevitch, Peter, and David Lake. (2012) "Beyond Virtue: Evaluating and Enhancing Credibility of Non-Governmental Organizations." In *The Credibility of Transnational NGOs: When Virtue Is Not Enough,* edited by Peter A. Gourevitch and David A. Lake. New York: Cambridge University Press, pp. 3–34.

Gourevitch, Philip. (1998) *We Wish to Inform You That Tomorrow We Will Be Killed with Our Families: Stories from Rwanda.* New York: Farrar, Straus, and Giroux.

———. (2003) "The Optimist: Kofi Annan's U.N. Has Never Been More Important and More Imperiled." *New Yorker* (March 3): 50–73.

Gowan, Richard. (2011) "Multilateral Political Missions and Preventive Diplomacy." Special Report no. 299. Washington, DC: US Institute of Peace.

Gowan, Richard, and Franziska Brantner. (2008) "A Global Force for Human Rights? An Audit of European Power at the UN." European Council on Foreign Relations. http://ecfr.en/paper/~documents/un-report.pdf.

Grant, Ruth W., and Robert O. Keohane. (2005) "Accountability and Abuses of Power in World Politics." *American Political Science Review* 99:1 (February): 29–43.

Greenhouse, Steven. (2013) "Major Retailers Agree to Inspection Standards in Bangladesh." *New York Times* (November 20): B3.

Gregoratti, Catia. (2014) "UN-Business Partnerships." In *International Organization and Global Governance,* edited by Thomas G. Weiss and Rorden Wilkinson. New York: Routledge, pp. 309–321.

Greig, J. Michael, and Paul F. Diehl. (2005) "The Peacekeeping-Peacemaking Dilemma." *International Studies Quarterly* 49:4 (December): 621–645.

Grieco, Joseph M. (1993) "Anarchy and the Limits of Cooperation: A Realist Critique of the Newest Liberal Institutionalism." In *Neorealism and Neoliberalism: The Contemporary Debate,* edited by David A. Baldwin. New York: Columbia University Press, pp. 116–140.

Grigorescu, Alexandru. (2005) "Mapping the UN–League of Nations Analogy: Are There Still Lessons to Be Learned from the League?" *Global Governance* 11:1 (January–March): 25–42.

———. (2007) "Transparency of Intergovernmental Organizations: The Roles of Member States, International Bureaucracies, and Nongovernmental Organizations." *International Studies Quarterly* 51:3 (September): 625–648.

———. (2010) "The Spread of Bureaucratic Oversight Mechanisms Across Intergovernmental Organizations." *International Studies Quarterly* 54: 3 (September): 871–886.

Gruber, Lloyd. (2000) *Ruling the World: Power Politics and the Rise of Supranational Institutions.* Princeton: Princeton University Press.

Gstöhl, Sieglinde. (2007) "Governance Through Government Networks: The G8 and International Organizations." *Review of International Organizations* 2:1 (January): 1–37.

Gutner, Tamar. (2010) "When 'Doing Good' Does Not: The IMF and the Millennium Development Goals." In *Who Governs the Globe?* edited by Deborah D. Avant, Martha Finnemore, and Susan K. Sell. New York: Cambridge University Press, pp. 266–291.

Haack, Kirsten. (2014) "Breaking Barriers? Women's Representation and Leadership at the United Nations." *Global Governance* 20:1 (Jan.–Mar.): 37–54.

Haack, Kirsten, and Kent J. Kille. (2012) "The UN Secretary-General and Self-Directed Leadership: Development of the Democracy Agenda." In *International Organizations as Self-Directed Actors: A Framework for Analysis,* edited by Joel B. Oestreich. New York: Routledge, pp. 29–59.

Haas, Ernst B. (1964) *Beyond the Nation-State: Functionalism and International Organization.* Stanford: Stanford University Press.

———. (1990) *When Knowledge Is Power: Three Models of Change in International Organizations.* Berkeley: University of California Press.

Haas, Peter M. (1990) *Saving the Mediterranean: The Politics of International Environmental Cooperation.* New York: Columbia University Press.

———. (1992) "Introduction: Epistemic Communities and International Policy Coordination." *International Organization* 46:1 (Winter): 1–35.

———. (2002) "UN Conferences and Constructivist Governance of the Environment." *Global Governance* 8:1 (January–March): 73–91.

———. (2007) "Turning Up the Heat on Global Environmental Governance." *The Forum* 5:2. www.bepress.com/forum/vol5/iss2/art8.

Hafner-Burton, Emilie. (2008) "Sticks and Stones: Naming and Shaming the Human Rights Enforcement Problem." *International Organization* 62:4 (Fall): 689–716.

Hafner-Burton, Emilie, and Kiyoteru Tsutsui. (2005) "Human Rights in a Globalized World: The Paradox of Empty Promises." *American Journal of Sociology* 110:5 (March): 1373–1411.

Hagland, Paul EeNam Park. (1997) "International Theory and LGBT Politics: Testing the limits of a Human Rights–Based Strategy." *GLQ: A Journal of Lesbian and Gay Studies* 3:4 (May): 357–384.

Hakelberg, Lukas. (2014) "Governance by Diffusion: Transnational Municipal Networks and the Spread of Local Climate Strategies in Europe." *Global Environmental Politics* 14:1 (February): 107–129.

Hall, Brian. (1994) "Blue Helmets." *New York Times Magazine* (January 2): 22.

Hampson, Fen Osler. (2001) "Parent, Midwife, or Accidental Executioner? The Role of Third Parties in Ending Violent Conflict." In *Turbulent Peace: The Challenges of Managing International Conflict,* edited by Chester A. Crocker, Fen Osler Hampson, and Pamela Aall. Washington, DC: US Institute Peace, pp. 387–406.

Hampson, Fen Osler, with Michael Hart. (1995) *Multilateral Negotiations: Lessons from Arms Control, Trade, and the Environment.* Baltimore: Johns Hopkins University Press.

Hara, Fabienne. (2011) "Preventive Diplomacy in Africa: Adapting to New Realities." In *Preventive Diplomacy: Regions in Focus,* edited by Francesco Mancini. New York: International Peace Institute, pp. 4–14.

Hardin, Garrett. (1968) "The Tragedy of the Commons." *Science* 162 (December 13): 1243–1248.

Hardt, Heidi. (2013) "Keep Friends Close, but Colleagues Closer: Efficiency in the Establishment of Peace Operations." *Global Governance* 19:3 (July–September): 377–399.

Harrigan, Jane R., and Hamed el-Said. (2010) "The Economic Impact of IMF and World Bank Programs in the Middle East and North Africa: A Case Study of Jordan, Egypt, Morocco, and Tunisia, 1983–2004." *Review of Middle East Economics and Finance* 6:2: 1–25.

Hasenclever, Andreas, Peter Mayer, and Volker Rittberger. (2000) "Integrating Theories of International Regimes." *Review of International Studies* 26: 3–33.

Hawkins, Darren. (2008) "Protecting Democracy in Europe and the Americas." *International Organization* 62:3 (Summer): 373–403.

Hawkins, Darren G., David A. Lake, Daniel L. Nielson, and Michael J. Tierney, eds. (2006) *Delegation and Agency in International Organizations.* Cambridge: Cambridge University Press.

Hawkins, Peter. (1997) "Organizational Culture: Sailing Between Evangelism and Complexity." *Human Relations* 50:4: 417–440.

Hehir, Aidan. (2013) "The Permanence of Inconsistency: Libya, the Security Council, and the Responsibility to Protect." *International Security* 38:1 (Summer): 137–159.

———. (2014) "Syria and the Dawn of a New Era." In *Into the Eleventh Hour: R2P, Syria, and Humanitarianism in Crisis,* edited by E–International Relations. www.e-ir.info/2014/02/23/syria-and-the-dawn-of-a-new-era.

Heine, Jorge. (2013) "From Club to Network Diplomacy." In *The Oxford Handbook of Modern Diplomacy,* edited by Andrew F. Cooper, Jorge Heine, and Ramesh Thakur. Oxford: Oxford University Press, pp. 54–69.

Heins, Volker. (2008) *Nongovernmental Organizations in International Society: Struggles over Recognition.* New York: Palgrave Macmillan.

Helfer, Laurence R., and Erik Voeten. (2014) "International Courts as Agents of Legal Change: Evidence from LGBT Rights in Europe." *International Organization* 68:1 (Winter): 77–110.

Helleiner, Eric. (2014) "Southern Pioneers of International Development." *Global Governance* 20:3 (July–Sept.): 375–388.

Hemmer, Christopher, and Peter J. Katzenstein. (2002) "Why Is There No NATO in Asia? Collective Identity, Regionalism, and the Origins of Multilateralism." *International Organization* 56:3 (Summer): 575–607.

Henkin, Louis. (1979) *How Nations Behave: Law and Foreign Policy.* 2nd ed. New York: Columbia University Press.

———. (1998) "The Universal Declaration and the US Constitution." *PS: Political Science and Politics* 31:3 (September): 512.

Hentz, James J. (2005) "South Africa and the Political Economy of Regional Cooperation in Southern Africa." *Journal of Modern African Studies* 43:1: 21–51.

Hewitt, J. Joseph. (2008) "Trends in Global Conflict, 1946–2005." In *Peace and Conflict 2008,* edited by J. Joseph Hewitt, Jonathan Wilkenfeld, and Ted Robert Gurr. Boulder: Paradigm, pp. 21–26.

Hill, Daniel W., Jr., Will H. Moore, and Bumba Mukherjee. (2013) "Information Politics Versus Organizational Incentives: When Are Amnesty International's 'Naming and Shaming' Reports Biased?" *International Studies Quarterly* 57:2 (June): 219–232.

Hinchberger, Bill. (2011) "Millennium Development Villages: A Lasting Impact?" *Africa Renewal* (December): 6–8.

Hirst, Monica. (1999) "Mercosur's Complex Political Agenda." In *Mercosur: Regional Integration, World Markets,* edited by Riordan Roett. Boulder: Lynne Rienner, pp. 35–48.

Hochchild, Adam. (2005) *Bury the Chains: Prophets and Rebels in the Fight to Free an Empire's Slaves.* Boston: Houghton Mifflin.

Hoekman, Bernard M., and Petros C. Mavroidis. (2007) *The World Trade Organization: Law, Economics, and Politics.* London: Routledge.

Hoffmann, Matthew J. (2011) *Climate Governance at the Crossroads: Experimenting with a Global Response After Kyoto.* Oxford: Oxford University Press.

Holsti, Kalevi. (2004) *Taming the Sovereigns: Institutional Change in International Politics.* New York: Cambridge University Press.

Hopgood, Stephen. (2006) *Keepers of the Flame: Understanding Amnesty International.* Ithaca: Cornell University Press.

——. (2013) *The Endtimes of Human Rights.* Ithaca: Cornell University Press.

Hopmann, P. Terrence. (2000) "The Organization for Security and Cooperation in Europe: Its Contribution to Conflict Prevention and Resolution." In *International Conflict Resolution After the Cold War,* edited by Paul C. Stern and Daniel Druckman. Washington, DC: National Academy Press, pp. 569–615.

Hossain, Ishtiaq. (2012) "The Organization of Islamic Conference (OIC): Nature, Role, and the Issues." *Journal of Third World Studies* 29:1: 287–314.

Howard, Lise Morjé. (2008) *UN Peacekeeping in Civil Wars.* New York: Cambridge University Press.

Howard, Philip N., Aiden Duffy, Deen Freelon, Muzammil Hussain, Will Mari, and Marwa Mazaid. (2011) "Opening Closed Regimes: What Was the Role of Social Media During the Arab Spring?" Working Paper no. 2011.1. Seattle: Project on Information Technology and Political Islam.

Htun, Mala, and S. Laurel Weldon. (2012) "The Civic Origins of Progressive Policy Change: Combating Violence Against Women in Global Perspective, 1975–2005." *American Political Science Review* 106:3 (August): 548–569.

Hudson, Natalie Florea. (2009) *Gender, Human Security, and the UN: Security Language as a Political Framework.* New York: Routledge.

Hufbauer, Gary Clyde, Cathleen Cimino, and Tyler Moran. (2014) *NAFTA at 20: Misleading Charges and Positive Achievements.* Washington, DC: Peterson Institute for International Economics.

Hufbauer, Gary Clyde, and Jeffrey Schott. (2005) *NAFTA Revisited: Achievements and Challenges.* Washington, DC: Peterson Institute for International Economics.

Hufbauer, Gary Clyde, Jeffrey J. Schott, Kimberly Ann Elliott, and Barbara Oegg. (2007) *Economic Sanctions Reconsidered.* 3rd ed. Washington, DC: Peterson Institute for International Economics.

Hug, Simon. (2012) "What's in a Vote?" Paper prepared for presentation at the annual meeting of the American Political Science Association, New Orleans (August 30–September 2). www.un.org/Depts/dhl/resguide/gavote.htm.

Hug, Simon, and Richard Lukacs. (2014) "Preferences or Blocs? Voting in the United Nations Human Rights Council." *Review of International Organizations* 9:1 (March): 83–106.

Hughell, D., and R. Butterfield. (2008) "Impact of FSC Certification on Deforestation and the Incidence of Wildfires in the Maya Biosphere Reserve." www.rainforest-alliance.org/forestry/documents/peten_study.pdf.

Human Security Report Project. (2013) *Human Security Report 2013: The Decline in Global Violence: Evidence, Explanation, and Contestation.* Vancouver: Human Security Press.

Hurd, Ian. (2002) "Legitimacy, Power, and the Symbolic Life of the UN Security Council." *Global Governance* 8:1 (January–March): 35–51.

——. (2007) *After Anarchy: Legitimacy and Power in the United Nations Security Council.* Princeton: Princeton University Press.

——. (2008a) "Myths of Membership: The Politics of Legitimation in UN Security Council Reform." *Global Governance* 14:2 (April–June): 199–217.

——. (2008b) "Theories and Tests of International Authority." In *The UN Security Council and the Politics of International Authority,* edited by Bruce Cronin and Ian Hurd. New York: Routledge, pp. 23–39.

Hurrell, Andrew. (1995) "Regionalism in the Americas." In *Regionalism in World Politics: Regional Organization and International Order,* edited by Louise Fawcett and Andrew Hurrell. New York: Oxford University Press, pp. 250–282.

——. (2007) "One World? Many Worlds? The Place of Regions in the Study of International Society." *International Affairs* 83:1: 127–146.

Institute for Economics and Peace. (2014) *Global Terrorism Index 2014: Measuring and Understanding the Impact of Terrorism.* http://economicsandpeace.org/research/iep -indices-data/global-terrorism-index.

Intergovernmental Panel on Climate Change (IPCC). (2013) Working Group I "Summary for Policymakers." www.climatechange2013.org/images/report /WG1AR5_SPM _FINAL.pdf.

———. (2014) Working Group II "Summary for Policymakers." http://ipcc-wg2.gov /AR5/.

International Commission on Intervention and State Sovereignty (ICISS). (2001) *The Responsibility to Protect: Report of the International Commission on Intervention and State Sovereignty.* Ottawa: International Development Research Centre for ICISS.

International Court of Justice (ICJ), Advisory Opinions. (1949) "Reparation for Injuries Suffered in the Service of the United Nations." *ICJ Reports,* 174.

———. (1951) "Reservations to the Convention on the Prevention and Punishment of the Crime of Genocide." *ICJ Reports,* 15.

———. (1962) "Certain Expenses of the United Nations." *ICJ Reports,* 168.

———. (1971) "Legal Consequences for States of the Continued Presence of South Africa in Namibia." *ICJ Reports,* 144.

———. (1975) "Western Sahara *(Spain v. Morocco)."* *ICJ Reports,* 12.

———. (1999) "Difference Relating to Immunity from Legal Process of a Special Rapporteur of the Commission on Human Rights." *ICJ Reports* 62.

———. (2004) "Legal Consequences Arising from the Construction of a Wall in the Occupied Palestinian Territories." *ICJ Reports,* 136.

———. (2010) "Accordance with International Law of the Unilateral Declaration of Independence in Respect of Kosovo." *ICJ Reports,* 403.

International Court of Justice (ICJ), Contentious Cases. (1969) North Sea Continental Shelf cases *(Federal Republic of Germany v. Denmark; Federal Republic of Germany v. Netherlands). ICJ Reports,* 3.

———. (1974) Nuclear-test cases *(New Zealand v. France). ICJ Reports,* 253.

———. (1980) Case concerning US diplomatic and consular staff in Tehran *(United States of America v. Iran). ICJ Reports,* 3.

———. (1984a) Case concerning Gulf of Maine area *(Canada v. United States of America). ICJ Reports,* 246.

———. (1984b) Case concerning military and paramilitary activities in and against Nicaragua *(Nicaragua v. United States). ICJ Reports,* 292.

———. (1986) Case concerning military and paramilitary activities in and against Nicaragua *(Nicaragua v. United States). ICJ Reports,* 14.

———. (1992) Questions of interpretation and application of the 1971 Montreal Convention arising from the aerial incident at Lockerbie *(Libyan Arab Jamahiriya v. United Kingdom). ICJ Reports,* 3.

———. (1997) Case concerning Gabcikovo-Nagymaros project *(Hungary v. Slovakia). ICJ Reports,* 1.

———. (2002) Case concerning land and maritime boundary between Cameroon and Nigeria *(Cameroon v. Nigeria). ICJ Reports,* 303.

———. (2007) Case concerning application of Convention on the Prevention and Punishment of the Crime of Genocide *(Bosnia and Herzegovina v. Serbia and Montenegro). ICJ Reports* 43.

———. (2008) Application of Republic of Ecuador: Case concerning aerial herbicide spraying *(Ecuador v. Colombia). ICJ Reports* 174.

———. (2014) Case concerning whaling in the Antarctic *(Australia v. Japan: New Zealand Intervening).* www.icj-cij.rg/docket/files/148/18136.pdf.

———. (2015) Application of the Convention on the Prevention and Punishment of the Crime of Genocide *(Croatia v. Serbia).* www.icj-cij.org/docket/files /118/18422.pdf.

International Crisis Group (ICG). (2008) "Timor-Leste: Security Sector Reform." Asia Report no. 143 (January 17). www.crisisgroup.org/home/index.cfm?id =5264&l =1.

———. (2013) "Understanding Conflict in Eastern Congo (I): The Ruzizi Plain." ICG Africa Report no. 206 (July). www.crisisgroup.org/en/regions/africa/central-africa /dr-congo/206-comprendre-les-conflits-dans-lest-du-congo-i-la-plaine-de-la-ruzizi .aspx.

———. (2014) "South Sudan: A Civil War by Any Other Name." ICG Africa Report no. 217 (April). www.crisisgroup.org/en/regions/africa/horn-of-africa /south-sudan/217 -south-sudan-a-civil-war-by-any-other-name.aspx.

International Lesbian, Gay, Bisexual, Trans, and Intersex Association (ILGA). (2013) "ECOSOC: LGBT Voices at the United Nations/ECOSOC Council Vote Grants Consultative Status to ILGA." http://ilga.org/ilga/en/article/n5Geb HB1PY.

International Monetary Fund (IMF) Independent Evaluation Office. (2007) *Evaluation Report: The IMF and Aid to Sub-Saharan Africa.* Washington, DC: IMF.

———. (2014) "Quota Factsheet." https://www.imf.org/external/np/exr/facts/quotas.htm.

International Service for Human Rights. (2010) "Majority of GA Third Committee Unable to Accept Report on the Human Right to Sexual Education." www.ishr.ch /archive-general-assembly/933-majority-of-ga-third-committee-unable-to-accept -report-on-the-human-right-to-sexual-education.

Ivanova, Maria. (2010) "UNEP in Global Environmental Governance: Design, Leadership, and Location." *Global Environmental Politics* 10:1 (February): 30–59.

———. (2013) "The Contested Legacy of Rio + 20." *Global Environmental Politics* 13:4 (November): 1–11.

Jackson, Nicole. (2006) "International Organizations, Security Dichotomies, and the Trafficking of Persons and Narcotics in Post-Soviet Central Asia: A Critique of the Securitization Framework." *Security Dialogue* 38 (September): 299–317.

Jacobson, Harold K. (1984) *Networks of Interdependence: International Organizations and the Global Political System.* 2nd ed. New York: Knopf.

Jacobson, Harold K., William M. Reisinger, and Todd Mathers. (1986) "National Entanglements in International Governmental Organizations." *American Political Science Review* 80:1 (March): 141–160.

Jacobson, Harold K., and Edith Brown Weiss. (1995) "Strengthening Compliance with International Environmental Accords: Preliminary Observations from a Collaborative Project." *Global Governance* 1:2 (May–August): 119–148.

Jain, Devaki. (2005) *Women, Development, and the UN: A Sixty-Year Quest for Equality and Justice.* Bloomington: Indiana University Press.

Jentleson, Bruce W. (1999) *Opportunities Missed, Opportunities Seized: Preventive Diplomacy in the Post–Cold War World.* Lanham: Rowman and Littlefield.

———. (2012) "The John Holmes Memorial Lecture: Global Governance in a Copernican World." *Global Governance* 18:2 (April–June): 133–148.

Jerven, Morten. (2013) *Poor Numbers: How We Are Misled by African Development Statistics and What to Do About It.* Ithaca: Cornell University Press.

Joachim, Jutta. (2007) *Agenda Setting, the UN, and NGOs: Gender Violence and Reproductive Rights.* Washington, DC: Georgetown University Press.

Johnston, Alastair Ian. (2003) "Socialization in International Institutions: The ASEAN Way and International Relations Theory." In *International Relations Theory and the Asia-Pacific,* edited by G. John Ikenberry and Michael Mastunduno. New York: Columbia University Press, pp. 107–162.

Johnston, Douglas. (1997) *Consent and Commitment in the World Community.* Irvington-on-Hudson: Transnational.

Johnstone, Ian. (2007) "The Secretary-General as Norm Entrepreneur." In *Secretary or General? The UN Secretary-General in World Politics,* edited by Simon Chesterman. Cambridge: Cambridge University Press, pp. 123–138.

————. (2008) "The Security Council as Legislature." In *The UN Security Council and the Politics of International Authority,* edited by Bruce Cronin and Ian Hurd. New York: Routledge, pp. 80–104.

Jolly, Richard, Louis Emmerij, Dharam Ghai, and Frédéric Lapeyne. (2004) *UN Contributions to Developing Thinking and Practice.* Bloomington: Indiana University Press.

Jolly, Richard, Louis Emmerij, and Thomas G. Weiss. (2009) *UN Ideas That Changed the World.* Bloomington: Indiana University Press.

Jonah, James O. C. (2007) "Secretariat Independence and Reform." In *The Oxford Handbook on the United Nations,* edited by Thomas G. Weiss and Sam Daws. Oxford: Oxford University Press, pp. 160–174.

Jönsson, Christer. (1986) "Interorganization Theory and International Organization." *International Studies Quarterly* 30:1: 39–57.

————. (2013) "International Organizations at the Moving Public-Private Borderline." *Global Governance* 19:1 (January–March): 1–18.

Kaasa, Stine Madland. (2007) "The UN Commission on Sustainable Development: Which Mechanisms Explain Its Accomplishments?" *Global Environmental Politics* 7:3 (August): 107–129.

Kahler, Miles. (2009) "Networked Politics: Agency, Power, and Governance." In *Networked Politics: Agency, Power, and Governance,* edited by Miles Kahler. Ithaca: Cornell University Press, pp. 1–22.

Kaldor, Mary. (2003) "The Idea of Global Civil Society." *International Affairs* 79:3 (May): 583–593.

Karlsrud, John. (2015) "The UN at War: Examining the Consequences of Peace-Enforcement Mandates for the UN Peace-Keeping Operations in the CAR, the DRC, and Mali." *Third World Quarterly* 36:1: 40–54.

Karns, Margaret P. (1987) "Ad Hoc Multilateral Diplomacy: The United States, the Contact Group, and Namibia." *International Organization* 41:1 (Winter): 93–123.

————. (2009) "The Challenges of Maintaining Peace and Security in the 21st Century: The United Nations and Regional Organizations." In *The United Nations: Past, Present, and Future—Proceedings of the 2007 Francis Marion University UN Symposium,* edited by Scott Kaufman and Alissa Warters. New York: Nova Science, pp. 115–146.

————. (2012) "The Roots of UN Post-Conflict Peacebuilding." In *International Organizations as Self-Directed Actors,* edited by Joel E. Oestreich. New York: Routledge, pp. 60–88.

Karns, Margaret P., and Karen A. Mingst. (2002) "The United States as 'Deadbeat'? US Policy and the UN Financial Crisis." In *Multilateralism and US Foreign Policy: Ambivalent Engagement,* edited by Stewart Patrick and Shepard Forman. Boulder: Lynne Rienner, pp. 267–294.

Katsumata, Hiro. (2006) "Establishment of the ASEAN Regional Forum: Constructing a 'Talking Shop' or a 'New Brewery'?" *Pacific Review* 19:2: 181–198.

Katzenstein, Peter J. (2005) *A World of Regions: Asia and Europe in the American Imperium.* Ithaca: Cornell University Press.

Kaul, Inge. (2000) "Governing Global Public Goods in a Multi-Actor World: The Role of the United Nations." In *New Millennium, New Perspectives: The United Nations, Security, and Governance,* edited by Ramesh Thakur and Edward Newman. Tokyo: UN University Press, pp. 296–315.

Keck, Margaret E., and Kathryn Sikkink. (1998) *Activists Beyond Borders: Advocacy Networks in International Politics.* Ithaca: Cornell University Press.

Kell, Georg, Anne-Marie Slaughter, and Thomas Hale. (2007) "Silent Reform Through the Global Compact." *UN Chronicle* 44:1 (March): 26–30.

Kelley, Judith. (2008) "Assessing the Complex Evolution of Norms: The Rise of International Election Monitoring." *International Organization* 62:2 (Spring): 221–255.

Kent, Ann. (2007) *Beyond Compliance: China, International Organizations, and Global Security.* Stanford: Stanford University Press.

Keohane, Robert O. (1984) *After Hegemony: Cooperation and Discord in the World Political Economy.* Princeton: Princeton University Press.

———. (1993) "Institutional Theory and the Realist Challenge After the Cold War." In *Neorealism and Neoliberalism: The Contemporary Debate,* edited by David A. Baldwin. New York: Columbia University Press, pp. 269–300.

Keohane, Robert O., and Lisa L. Martin. (1995) "The Promise of Institutionalist Theory." *International Security* 20:1 (Summer): 39–51.

Keohane, Robert O., and Joseph S. Nye Jr. (1971) *Transnational Relations and World Politics.* Cambridge: Harvard University Press.

———. (1977) *Power and Interdependence: World Politics in Transition.* Boston: Little, Brown.

Keohane, Robert O., and David G. Victor. (2011) "The Regime Complex for Climate Change." *Perspectives on Politics* 9:1: 7–23.

Khagram, Sanjeev. (2000) "Toward Democratic Governance for Sustainable Development: Transnational Civil Society Organizing Around Big Dams." In *The Third Force: The Rise of Transnational Civil Society,* edited by Ann M. Florini. Tokyo: Japan Center for International Exchange, pp. 83–114.

Khong, Yuen Foong, and Helen E. S. Nesadurai. (2007) "Hanging Together, Institutional Design, and Cooperation in Southeast Asia: AFTA and the ARF." In *Crafting Cooperation: Regional International Institutions in Comparative Perspective,* edited by Amitav Acharya and Alastair Ian Johnston. New York: Cambridge University Press, pp. 32–82.

Kille, Kent J. (2006) *From Manager to Visionary: The Secretary-General of the United Nations.* New York: Palgrave Macmillan.

Kim, Dongwook. (2013) "International Nongovernmental Organizations and the Global Diffusion of National Human Rights Institutions." *International Organization* 67:3 (Summer): 505–539.

Kim, Moonhawk. (2008) "Costly Procedures: Divergent Effects of Legalization in the GATT/WTO Dispute Settlement Procedures." *International Studies Quarterly* 52:3 (September): 657–686.

Kindleberger, Charles P. (1973) *The World in Depression, 1929–39.* Berkeley: University of California Press.

———. (1986) "International Public Goods Without International Government." *American Economic Review* 76:1 (March): 1–13.

Kinzelbach, Katrin. (2013) "Resisting the Power of Human Rights: the People's Republic of China." In *The Persistent Power of Human Rights: From Commitment to Compliance,* edited by Thomas Risse, Stephen C. Ropp, and Kathryn Sikkink. New York: Cambridge University Press, pp. 164–181.

Klotz, Audie. (1995) *Norms in International Relations: The Struggle Against Apartheid.* Ithaca: Cornell University Press.

Koppell, Jonathan G. S. (2011) "Accountability for Global Governance Organizations." In *Accountable Governance: Problems and Promises,* edited by Melvin J. Dubnick and H. George Frederickson. Armonk, NY: Sharpe, pp. 55–77.

Koremenos, Barbara, Charles Lipson, and Duncan Snidal. (2001) "The Rational Design of International Institutions." *International Organization* 55 (Autumn): 761–799.

Krasner, Stephen D. (1982) "Structural Causes and Regime Consequences: Regimes as Intervening Variables." In *International Regimes,* edited by Stephen D. Krasner. Ithaca: Cornell University Press, pp. 1–21.

———. (1993) "Westphalia and All That." In *Ideas and Foreign Policy,* edited by Judith Goldstein and Robert O. Keohane. Ithaca: Cornell University Press, pp. 235–264.

Kristoff, Madeline, and Liz Panarelli. (2010) "Haiti: A Republic of NGOs?" *Peace Brief* no. 23 (April 26). US Institute of Peace. www.usip.org/sites/default/files/PB%2023%20Haiti%20a%20Republic %20of%20NGOs.pdf.

Ku, Charlotte. (2001) "Global Governance and the Changing Face of International Law." John W. Holmes Memorial Lecture. Academic Council on the United Nations System (ACUNS), Reports and Papers no. 2.

Ku, Charlotte, and Paul F. Diehl. (2006) "Filling in the Gaps: Extrasystemic Mechanisms for Addressing Imbalances Between the International Legal Operating System and the Normative System." *Global Governance* 12:2 (April–June): 161–183.

Kulish, Nicholas, and Somini Sengupta. (2013) "New U.N.'s Brigade's Aggressive Stance in Africa Brings Success, and Risks." *New York Times* (November 13): A10.

Kumar, Shashank P. (2013) "The Indus Waters Kishenganga Arbitration (*Pakistan v. India*)." *American Society of International Law Insights* 17:13 (May 13). srn.com /abstract+2264464.

Kuperman, Alan J. (2001) *The Limits of Humanitarian Intervention: Genocide in Rwanda.* Washington, DC: Brookings Institution.

Kurlantzick, Joshua. (2012) "ASEAN's Future and Asian Integration." Working paper. New York: Council on Foreign Relations.

Kydd, Andrew H. (2005) *Trust and Mistrust in International Relations.* Princeton: Princeton University Press.

Laatikainen, Katie Verlin. (2006) "Pushing Soft Power: Middle Power Diplomacy at the UN." In *The European Union at the United Nations: Intersecting Multilateralisms,* edited by Katie Verlin Laatikainen and Karen E. Smith. New York: Palgrave Macmillan, pp. 70–91.

LaFree, Gary, and Laura Dugan. (2014) "Global Trends in Terrorism, 1970–2011." In *Peace and Conflict 2014,* edited by David A. Backer, Jonathan Wilkenfeld, and Paul K. Huth. Boulder: Paradigm, pp. 29–42.

Lake, David A. (2010) "Rightful Rules: Authority, Order, and the Foundations of Global Governance." *International Studies Quarterly* 54:3 (September): 587–613.

Lake, David A., and Matthew D. McCubbins. (2006) "The Logic of Delegation to International Organizations." In *Delegation and Agency in International Organizations,* edited by Darren Hawkins et al. Cambridge: Cambridge University Press, pp. 341–368.

Lake, Milli. (2014) "Organizing Hypocrisy: Providing Legal Accountability for Human Rights Violations in Areas of Limited Statehood." *International Studies Quarterly* 58:3 (September): 515–526.

Lander, Mark. (2014) "U.S. and China Reach Climate Accord After Months of Talks." *New York Times* (November 11): A1.

Lasswell, Harold D. (1941) "The Garrison State." *American Journal of Sociology* 46 (January): 455–468.

Lauren, Paul Gordon. (1996) *Power and Prejudice: The Politics and Diplomacy of Racial Discrimination.* 2nd ed. Boulder: Westview.

———. (1998) *The Evolution of International Human Rights: Visions Seen.* Philadelphia: University of Pennsylvania Press.

Laurenti, Jeffrey. (2007) "Financing." In *The Oxford Handbook on the United Nations,* edited by Thomas G. Weiss and Sam Daws. New York: Oxford University Press, pp. 675–700.

Lawson, Fred. (2012) *Transformations of Regional Economic Governance in the Gulf Cooperation Council.* Qatar: Center for International and Regional Studies, Georgetown University School of Foreign Service in Qatar.

Lebovic, James H., and Eric Voeten. (2006) "The Politics of Shame: The Condemnation of Country Human Rights Practices in the UNHCHR." *International Studies Quarterly* 50:4 (December): 861–888.

Legrenzi, Matteo, and Marina Calculli. (2013) "Regionalism and Regionalization in the Middle East: Options and Challenges." New York: International Peace Institute.

Levin, Dan. (2014) "Report Implicates Chinese Officials in Smuggled Tanzanian Ivory." *New York Times* (November 6): A14.

Liese, Andrea, and Marianne Beisheim. (2011) "Transnational Public-Private Partnerships and the Provision of Collective Good in Developing Countries." In *Governance Without a State? Policies and Politics in Areas of Limited Statehood,* edited by Thomas Risse. New York: Columbia University Press, pp. 115–143.

Linklater, Andrew, and Hisemi Suganami. (2006) *The English School of International Relations: A Contemporary Reassessment.* Cambridge: Cambridge University Press.

Lipschutz, Ronnie D. (1997) "From Place to Planet: Local Knowledge and Global Environmental Governance." *Global Governance* 3:1 (January–April): 83–102.

Lipson, Charles. (1984) "International Cooperation in Economic and Security Affairs." *World Politics* 37 (October): 1–23.

Lischer, Sarah Kenyon. (2007) "Military Intervention and the Humanitarian 'Force Multiplier.'" *Global Governance* 13:1 (January–March): 99–118.

Loescher, Gil, Alexander Betts, and James Milner. (2008) *The United Nations High Commissioner for Refugees (UNHCR): The Politics and Practice of Refugee Protection Into the Twenty-First Century.* New York: Routledge.

Loescher, Gil, and James Milner. (2011) "UNHCR and the Global Governance of Refugees." In *Global Migration Governance,* edited by Alexander Betts. New York: Oxford University Press, pp. 189–209.

Lowrey, Annie. (2013) "World Bank, Rooted in Bureaucracy, Proposes a Sweeping Reorganization." *New York Times* (October 7): B2.

Luck, Edward C. (2005) "How Not to Reform the United Nations." *Global Governance* 11:4 (October–December): 407–414.

———. (2006) "The Uninvited Challenge: Terrorism Targets the United Nations." In *Multilateralism Under Challenge? Power, International Order, and Structural Change,* edited by Edward Newman, Ramesh Thakur, and John Tirman. New York: UN University Press, pp. 336–355.

———. (2007) "Principal Organs." In *The Oxford Handbook on the United Nations,* edited by Thomas G. Weiss and Sam Daws. Oxford: Oxford University Press, pp. 653–674.

Lutz, Ellen L., and Kathryn Sikkink. (2000) "International Human Rights Law and Practice in Latin America." *International Organization* 54:3 (Summer): 633–659.

Lynch, Colum. (2010) "Departing U.N. Official Calls Ban's Leadership 'Deplorable' in 50-Page Memo." *Washington Post* (July 20): A14.

———. (2014a) "They Just Stood Watching." *Foreign Policy* (April 7). http://foreignpolicy.com/2014/04/07/they-just-stood-watching-2/.

———. (2014b) "A Mission That Was Set Up to Fail." *Foreign Policy* (April 8). http://foreignpolicy.com/2014/04/08/a-mission-that-was-set-up-to-fail/.

Mace, Gordon, et al. (1999) *The Americas in Transition: The Contours of Regionalism.* Boulder: Lynne Rienner.

MacKay, Judith. (2003) "The Making of a Convention on Tobacco Control." *Bulletin of the World Health Organization* 81:8 (January): 551.

Maddy-Weitzman, Bruce. (2012) "The Arab League Comes Alive." *Middle East Quarterly* 19:3 (Summer): 71–78.

Madsen, Frank G. (2014) "Transnational Criminal Networks." In *International Organization and Global Governance,* edited by Thomas G. Weiss and Rorden Wilkinson. New York: Routledge, pp. 397–410.

Mahbubani, Kishore. (2013) "Multilateral Diplomacy." In *The Oxford Handbook of Modern Diplomacy,* edited by Andrew F. Cooper, Jorge Heine, and Ramesh Thakur. Oxford: Oxford University Press, pp. 248–262.

Makinda, Samuel M., and F. Wafula Okumu. (2008) *The African Union: Challenges of Globalization, Security, and Governance.* New York: Routledge.

Malone, David M. (2006) *The International Struggle over Iraq: Politics in the UN Security Council, 1980–2005.* New York: Oxford University Press.

Mannan, S., et al. (2008) "Deramakot Forest Shows Positive Conservation Impacts of RIL." *ITTO Tropical Forest Update* 18:2: 7–9.

Mansfield, Edward D., and Helen V. Milner. (1999) "The New Wave of Regionalism." *International Organization* 53:3 (Summer): 589–627.

Mansfield, Edward D., and Jon C. W. Pevehouse. (2013) "The Expansion of Preferential Trading Arrangements." *International Studies Quarterly* 57:3 (September): 592–604.

Margulis, Matias E. (2013) "The Regime Complex for Food Security: Implications for the Global Hunger Challenge." *Global Governance* 19:1 (January–March): 53–67.

Mathews, Jessica T. (1997) "Power Shift." *Foreign Affairs* 76:1 (January–February): 50–66.

Mathiason, John. (2007) *Invisible Governance: International Secretariats in Global Politics.* Bloomfield, CT: Kumarian.

Mayall, James. (1982) *The Community of States: A Study in International Political Theory.* New York: Allen and Unwin.

Mayer, Ann Elizabeth. (2013) *Islam and Human Rights: Tradition and Politics.* 5th ed. Boulder: Westview.

McArthur, John. (2014) "Seven Million Lives Saved: Under-5 Mortality Since the Launch of the Millennium Development Goals." Brookings Institution. www.brookings.edu /research/papers/2014/09/under-five-child-mortality-mcarthur.

McCandless, Erin. (2013) "Wicked Problems in Peacebuilding and Statebuilding: Making Progress in Measuring Progress Through the New Deal." *Global Governance* 19:2 (April–June): 227–248.

McCormick, John, and Jonathan Olsen. (2014) *The European Union: Politics and Policies.* Boulder: Westview.

McDermott, Roger N. (2012) "The Shanghai Cooperation Organization's Impact on Central Asian Security: A View from Kazakhstan." *Problems of Post-Communism* 59:4 (July–August): 56–65.

McGann, James G. (2014) "Think Tanks and Global Policy Networks." In *International Organization and Global Governance,* edited by Thomas G. Weiss and Rorden Wilkinson. New York: Routledge, pp. 360–371.

McGrew, Anthony. (2008) "Globalization and Global Politics." In *The Globalization of World Politics: An Introduction to International Relations,* 4th ed., edited by John Baylis, Steve Smith, and Patricia Owens. New York: Oxford University Press, pp. 16–33.

McKeon, Nora. (2009) *The United Nations and Civil Society: Legitimating Global Governance—Whose Voice?* London: Zed.

Meadows, Donella, et al. (1972) *The Limits to Growth.* New York: Universe.

Mearsheimer, John J. (1994–1995) "The False Promise of International Institutions." *International Security* 19:3 (Winter): 5–49.

Mera, Laura Gomez. (2005) "Explaining Mercosur's Survival: Strategic Sources of Argentine-Brazilian Convergence." *Journal of Latin American Studies* 37: 109–140.

Merrills, J. G. (2011) *International Dispute Settlement.* 5th ed. Cambridge: Cambridge University Press.

Mertus, Julie A. (2008) *Bait and Switch: Human Rights and U.S. Foreign Policy.* 2nd ed. New York: Routledge.

———. (2009a) "Applying the Gatekeeper Model of Human Rights Activism: The U.S.-Based Movement for LGBT Rights." In *The International Struggle for New Human Rights,* edited by Clifford Bob. Philadelphia: University of Pennsylvania Press, pp. 52–67.

———. (2009b). *The United Nations and Human Rights. A Guide for a New Era.* 2nd ed. London: Routledge.

Meyer, John W., David John Frank, Ann Hironaka, Evan Schofer, and Nancy Brandon Tuma. (1997) "The Structuring of a World Environmental Regime, 1870–1990." *International Organization* 51:4 (Autumn): 623–651.

Meyer, Peter J. (2014) *Organization of American States: Background and Issues for Congress.* Washington, DC: Congressional Research Service.

Minear, Larry. (1994) "Humanitarian Action in the Former Yugoslavia: The U.N.'s Role, 1991–1993." Occasional Paper no. 18. Providence, RI: Thomas J. Watson Institute for International Studies.

Mingst, Karen A. (1987) "Inter-Organizational Politics: The World Bank and the African Development Bank." *Review of International Studies* 13: 281–293.

———. (1990) *Politics and the African Development Bank*. Lexington: University of Kentucky Press.

Mitrany, David. (1946) *A Working Peace System*. London: Royal Institute of International Affairs.

Mittelstaedt, Emma. (2008) "Safeguarding the Rights of Sexual Minorities: The Incremental and Legal Approaches to Enforcing International Human Rights Obligations." *Chicago Journal of International Law* 9:1 (Summer): 353–386.

Montoya, Celeste. (2008) "The European Union, Capacity Building, and Transnational Networks: Combating Violence Against Women Through the Daphne Program." *International Organization* 62:2 (Spring): 359–372.

Moon, Chung-In, and Jongryn Mo. (2000) *Economic Crisis and Structural Reforms in South Korea: Assessments and Implications*. Washington, DC: Economic Strategy Institution.

Moravcsik, Andrew. (1997) "Taking Preferences Seriously: A Liberal Theory of International Politics." *International Organization* 51:4 (Autumn): 513–553.

———. (1998) *The Choice for Europe: Social Purpose and State Power from Messina to Maastricht*. Ithaca: Cornell University Press.

———. (2002) "Why Is US Human Rights Policy So Unilateralist?" In *Multilateralism and US Foreign Policy: Ambivalent Engagement*, edited by Stewart Patrick and Shepard Forman. Boulder: Lynne Rienner, pp. 345–376.

Morelli, Vincent, and Paul Gallis. (2008) *NATO in Afghanistan: A Test of the Transatlantic Alliance*. Washington, DC: Congressional Research Service.

Morgenthau, Hans. (1967) *Politics Among Nations*. 4th ed. New York: Knopf.

Morris, Justin. (2013) "Libya and Syria: R2P and the Spectre of the Swinging Pendulum." *International Affairs* 39:5 (September): 1265–1283.

Moyo, Dambisa. (2009) *Dead Aid: Why Aid Is Not Working and How There Is a Better Way for Africa*. New York: Farrar, Straus, and Giroux.

Murdie, Amanda M., and David R. Davis. (2012) "Shaming and Blaming: Using Events Data to Assess the Impact of Human Rights INGOs." *International Studies Quarterly* 56:1 (March): 1–16.

Murphy, Craig. (1994) *International Organization and Industrial Change*. New York: Oxford University Press.

———. (2000) "Global Governance: Poorly Done and Poorly Understood." *International Affairs* 75:4 (October–December): 789–803.

Murphy, Hannah. (2010) *The Making of International Trade Policy: NGOs, Agenda-Setting and the WTO*. Cheltenham: Elgar.

Mutua, Makau. (1999) "The African Human Rights Court: A Two-Legged Stool?" *Human Rights Quarterly* 21:2: 342–363.

Narine, Shaun. (2004) "State Sovereignty, Political Legitimacy, and Regional Institutionalism in the Asia-Pacific." *Pacific Review* 17:3: 423–450.

———. (2008) "Forty Years of ASEAN: A Historical Review." *Pacific Review* 21:4: 411–429.

Neier, Aryeh. (2012) *The International Human Rights Movement: A History*. Princeton: Princeton University Press.

Nelson, Paul. (2000) "Whose Civil Society? Whose Governance? Decisionmaking and Practice in the New Agenda of the Inter-American Development Bank and the World Bank." *Global Governance* 6:4 (October–December): 405–432.

Newman, Edward. (2001) "Human Security and Constructivism." *International Studies Perspectives* 2:3 (August): 239–251.

Newsom, D., and D. Hewitt. (2005) "The Global Impacts of SmartWood Certification: Final Report of the TREES Program for the Rainforest Alliance." www.rainforest-alliance.org/forestry/documents/sw_impacts.pdf.

Nielson, Richard. (2013) "Rewarding Human Rights? Selective Aid Sanctions Against Repressive States." *International Studies Quarterly* 57:4 (December): 791–803.

Nooruddin, Irfan, and Joel W. Simmons. (2006) "The Politics of Hard Choices: IMF Programs and Government Spending." *International Organization* 60:4: 1001–1033.

Oatley, Thomas. (2001) "Multilateralizing Trade and Payments in Postwar Europe." *International Organization* 55:4 (Autumn): 949–969.

Obama, Barack. (2007) "Remarks of Senator Obama to the Chicago Council on Global Affairs." www.cfr.org/elections/remarks-senator-barack-obama-chicago-council -global-affairs/p13172.

O'Brien, Robert, Anne Marie Goetz, Jan Aart Scholte, and Marc Williams. (2000) *Contesting Global Governance: Multilateral Economic Institutions and Global Social Movements.* Cambridge: Cambridge University Press.

Oelsner, Andrea. (2013) "The Institutional Identity of Regional Organizations, or Mercosur's Identity Crisis." *International Studies Quarterly* 57:1 (March): 115–127.

Oestreich, Joel E. (2012) "Introduction." In *International Organizations as Self-Directed Actors,* edited by Joel E. Oestrich. New York: Routledge, pp. 1–25.

O'Flaherty, Michael, and John Fisher. (2008) "Sexual Orientation, Gender Identity, and International Human Rights Law: Contextualizing the Yogyakarta Principles." *Human Rights Law Review* 8:2: 207–248.

Ogata, Sadako. (2005) *The Turbulent Decade: Confronting the Refugee Crises of the 1990s.* New York: Norton.

Ohanyan, Anna. (2012) "Network Institutionalism and NGO Studies." *International Studies Perspectives* 13:4 (November): 366–389.

Ohta, Hiroshi, and Atsuchi Ishii. (2014) "The Forum: Disaggregating Effectiveness." *International Studies Review* 15:4 (December): 581–583.

Okabe, Misa, and Shujiro Urata. (2013) "The Impact of AFTA on Intra-AFTA Trade." ERIA Discussion Paper Series. Economic Research Institute for ASEAN and East Asia. www.eria.org/ERIA-DP-2013-05.pdf.

Olson, Mancur. (1968) *The Logic of Collective Action.* New York: Schocken.

One World Trust. (2011) *Pathways to Accountability: The Revised Global Accountability Framework.* www.oneworldtrust.org/globalaccountability/pathways.

Orsini, Amandine, Jean-Fréderic Morin, and Oran Young. (2013) "Regime Complexes: A Buzz, a Boom, or a Boost for Global Governance?" *Global Governance* 19:1 (January–March): 27–40.

Ostrom, Elinor. (1990) *Governing the Commons: The Evolution of Institutions for Collective Action.* Cambridge: Cambridge University Press.

Padelford, Norman J. (1945) Unpublished letter to family and friends (June 26).

Papadopoulos, Yannis. (2013) "The Challenge of Transnational Private Governance: Evaluating Authorization, Representation, and Accountability." Working Paper no. 8 (February). Paris: SciencesPo/LIEPP (Laboratoire Interdisciplinaire d'évaluation des politiques publiques.

Paris, Roland. (2004) *At War's End: Building Peace After Civil Conflict.* New York: Cambridge University Press.

Park, Susan. (2010) *The World Bank Group and Environmentalists: Changing International Organization Identities.* London: Manchester University Press.

Pastor, Robert A. (2005) "North America and the Americas: Integration Among Unequal Partners." In *Global Politics of Regionalism: Theory and Practice,* edited by Mary Farrell, Björn Hettne, and Luk Van Langenhove. London: Pluto, pp. 202–221.

Patrick, Stewart. (2002) "Multilateralism and Its Discontents: The Causes and Consequences of US Ambivalence." In *Multilateralism and US Foreign Policy: Ambivalent Engagement,* edited by Stewart Patrick and Shepard Forman. Boulder: Lynne Rienner, pp. 1–44.

———. (2014a) "Ebola Reveals Gaps in Global Epidemic Response." *The Internationalist* (September 10). Council on Foreign Relations. http://blogs.cfr.org/patrick /2014/09/10/ebola-revals-gaps-in-global.

———. (2014b) "The Unruled World: The Case for Good Enough Global Governance." *Foreign Affairs* 93:1 (January–February): 58–73.

Pattberg, Philipp. (2011) "Forest Stewardship Council." In *Handbook of Transnational Governance: Institutions and Innovations,* edited by Thomas Hale and David Held. Cambridge: Polity, pp. 265–273.

Paul, James A. (1999) "NGO Access at the UN." www.globalpolicy.org/ngos/analysis /jap-accs.htm.

Pempel, T. J., ed. (2005) *Remapping East Asia: The Construction of a Region.* Ithaca: Cornell University Press.

Perez-Rocha, Manuel, and Stuart Trew. (2014) "NAFTA at 20: A Model for Corporate Rule." *Foreign Policy in Focus* (January 14). fpif.org/nafta-20-model-corporate -rule/.

Perlez, Jane. (2015) "Hostility from U.S. as China Lures Allies to New Bank." *New York Times* (March 20): A11.

Permanent Court of Arbitration. (2013) *In the Matter of the Indus Waters Kishenganga Arbitration.* www.pca-cpa.org/showfile.asp?fil_id=2471.

Peterson, V. Spike. (2003) *A Critical Rewriting of Global Political Economy: Integrating Reproductive, Productive, and Virtual Economies.* RIPE Studies in Global Political Economy. London: Routledge.

Phelan, William. (2012) "What Is *Sui Generis* About the European Union? Costly International Cooperation in a Self-Contained Regime." *International Studies Review* 14:3 (September): 367–385.

Popovski, Vesselin. (2011) "The Concepts of Responsibility to Protect and Protection of Civilians: 'Sisters, but Not Twins.'" *Security Challenges* 7:4 (Summer): 1–12.

Porter, Eduardo. (2014) "At the U.N., A Free for All on Setting Global Goals." *New York Times* (May 7): B1–B2.

Potoski, Matthew, and Elizabeth Elwakeil. (2011) "International Organization for Standardization 14001." In *Handbook of Transnational Governance: Institutions and Innovations,* edited by Thomas Hale and David Held. Cambridge: Polity, pp. 295–302.

Power, Samantha. (2002) *"A Problem from Hell": America and the Age of Genocide.* New York: Basic.

Prakash, Aseem, and Matthew Potoski. (2014) "Global Private Regimes, Domestic Public Law: ISO 14001 and Pollution Reduction." *Comparative Political Studies* 47:3 (March): 369–394.

Preston, Julia. (1994) "Boutros-Ghali Rushes in . . . in a Violent World: The U.N. Secretary-General Has an Activist's Agenda." *Washington Post National Weekly Edition* (January 10–16): 10–11.

Price, Richard, and Nina Tannenwald. (1996) "Norms and Deterrence: The Nuclear and Chemical Weapons Taboo." In *The Culture of National Security: Norms and Identity in World Politics,* edited by Peter J. Katzenstein. New York: Columbia University Press, pp. 114–152.

Princen, Thomas. (1995) "Ivory, Conservation, and Environmental Transnational Coalitions." In *Bringing Transnational Relations Back In: Non-State Actors, Domestic Structures, and International Institutions,* edited by Thomas Risse-Kappen. New York: Cambridge University Press, pp. 227–256.

Puchala, Donald J., and Roger A. Coate. (1989) "The Challenge of Relevance: The United Nations in a Changing World Environment." Academic Council on the United Nations System (ACUNS), Reports and Papers no. 5.

Rachman, Gideon. (2011) "Think Again: American Decline. This Time It's for Real." *Foreign Policy* (January–February): 59–63.

Ramcharan, B. G. (2000) "The International Court of Justice." In *The United Nations at the Millennium: The Principal Organs,* edited by Paul Taylor and A. J. R. Groom. New York: Continuum, pp. 177–195.

———. (2008) "The Universal Declaration of Human Rights at Sixty." Academic Council on the United Nations System (ACUNS), *In Memorandum* 76 (Fall): 1–3.

Ravenhill, John. (2001) *APEC and the Construction of Pacific Rim Regionalism.* Cambridge: Cambridge University Press.

———. (2007a) "In Search of an East Asian Region: Beyond Network Power." *Journal of East Asian Studies* 7 (Roundtable: Peter J. Katzenstein's Contributions to the Study of East Asian Regionalism): 387–394.

———. (2007b) "Mission Creep or Mission Impossible? APEC and Security." In *Reassessing Security Cooperation in the Asia-Pacific: Competition, Congruence, and Transformation,* edited by Amitav Acharya and Evelyn Goh. Cambridge: MIT Press, pp. 135–154.

———. (2008) "Fighting Irrelevance: An Economic Community 'with ASEAN Characteristics.'" *Pacific Review* 21:4: 469–487.

Reimann, Kim D. (2006) "A View from the Top: International Politics, Norms, and the Worldwide Growth of NGOs." *International Studies Quarterly* 50:1 (March): 45–67.

Reincke, Wolfgang H. (1999–2000) "The Other World Wide Web: Global Public Policy Networks." *Foreign Policy* 117 (Winter) 44–57.

Rich, Bruce. (2013) *Foreclosing the Future: The World Bank and the Politics of Environmental Destruction.* Washington, DC: Island Press.

Richter, Paul, and Henry Chu. (2009) "Middle East Envoy George Mitchell No Stranger to Conflicts." *Los Angeles Times* (January 24). www.latimes.com/news/nation world/world/middleeast/la-fg-mitchell24-2009jan24,0,4541587.story.

Riggs, Robert E., and Jack C. Plano. (1994) *The United Nations: International Organization of World Politics.* 2nd ed. Belmont, CA: Wadsworth.

Risse, Thomas, Stephen C. Ropp, and Kathryn Sikkink, eds. (1999) *The Power of Human Rights: International Norms and Domestic Change.* New York: Cambridge University Press.

Risse-Kappen, Thomas, ed. (1995) *Bringing Transnational Relations Back In: Non-State Actors, Domestic Structures, and International Institutions.* New York: Cambridge University Press.

Rittberger, Volker, ed., with Peter Mayer. (1993) *Regime Theory and International Relations.* Oxford: Clarendon.

Roberge, Ian. (2011) "Financial Action Task Force." In *Handbook of Transnational Governance: Institutions and Innovations,* edited by Thomas Hale and David Held. London: Polity, pp. 45–50.

Roberts, Adam. (1999) "NATO's 'Humanitarian War' over Kosovo." *Survival* 41:2 (Spring): 102–123.

Rodrik, Dani. (2007) "The Global Governance of Trade As If Development Really Mattered." In *One Economics, Many Recipes: Globalization, Institutions, and Economic Growth,* edited by Dani Rodrik. Princeton: Princeton University Press, pp. 213–236.

———. (2008) "The Death of the Globalization Consensus." Policy Innovations paper. Carnegie Council. www.policyinnovations.org/ideas/commentary/data /000072.

Roemer, Ruth, Allyn Taylor, and Jean Lariviere. (2005) "Origins of the WHO Framework Convention on Tobacco Control." *American Journal of Public Health* 95:6 (June): 936–938.

Romano, Cesare P. R. (1999) "The Proliferation of International Judicial Bodies: The Pieces of the Puzzle." *International Law and Politics* 31: 709–751.

Ron, James, Howard Ramos, and Kathleen Rodgers. (2005) "Transnational Information Politics: NGO Human Rights Reporting, 1986–2000." *International Studies Quarterly* 49:3 (September): 557–587.

Roodman, David. (2012) *Due Diligence: An Impertinent Inquiry into Microfinance.* Washington, DC: Center for Global Development.

Roosevelt, Franklin. (1941) "Address by the President." 87th Congress. *Congressional Record* 44: 46–47.

Rosand, Eric, and Alistair Millar. (2007) "Strengthening International Law and Global Implementation." In *Uniting Against Terror: Cooperative Nonmilitary Responses to the Global Terrorist Threat,* edited by David Cortright and George A. Lopez. Cambridge: MIT Press, pp. 51–82.

Rosenau, James N. (1992) "Governance, Order, and Change in World Politics." In *Governance Without Government: Order and Change in World Politics,* edited by James N. Rosenau and E. O. Czempiel. Cambridge: Cambridge University Press, pp. 1–29.

———. (1995) "Governance in the Twenty-First Century." *Global Governance* 1:1 (Winter): 13–43.

———. (1997) *Along the Domestic-Foreign Frontier: Exploring Governance in a Turbulent World.* Cambridge: Cambridge University Press.

Rosenberg, Robin L. (2001) "The OAS and the Summit of the Americas: Coexistence or Integration of Forces for Multilateralism?" *Latin American Politics and Society* 43:1 (Spring): 79–101.

Ross, Sandy. (2011) *The World Food Programme in Global Politics.* Boulder: First-Forum.

Rothkopf, David. (2014) "We Are Losing the War on Terror." *Foreign Policy* (June 10). www.foreignpolicy.com/articles/2014/06/10/we_are_losing_the_war_on_terror _mosul_karachi_9_11.

Ruane, Abigail. (2011) "Pursuing Inclusive Interests, Both Deep and Wide: Women's Human Rights and the United Nations." In *Feminism and International Relations: Conversations About the Past, Present, and Future,* edited by J. Ann Tickner and Laura Sjoberg. London: Routledge, pp. 48–67.

Ruggie, John Gerard. (1982) "International Regimes, Transactions, and Change: Embedded Liberalism in the Postwar Economic Order." *International Organization* 36:2 (Spring): 379–415.

———. (1993) "Multilateralism: The Anatomy of an Institution." In *Multilateralism Matters: The Theory and Praxis of an Institutional Form,* edited by John Gerard Ruggie. New York: Columbia University Press, pp. 3–47.

———. (2001) "Global_Governance.net: The Global Compact as Learning Network." *Global Governance* 7:4 (October–December): 371–378.

———. (2003) "The United Nations and Globalization: Patterns and Limits of Institutional Adaptation." *Global Governance* 9:3 (July–September): 301–321.

———. (2013) *Just Business: Multinational Corporations and Human Rights.* New York: Norton.

Sachs, Jeffrey D. (2005) *The End of Poverty: Economic Possibilities for Our Time.* New York: Penguin.

Sahnoun, Mohamed. (1994) *Somalia: The Missed Opportunities.* Washington, DC: US Institute of Peace.

Sanderson, John. (2001) "Cambodia." In *United Nations Peacekeeping Operations: Ad Hoc Missions, Permanent Engagement,* edited by Albrecht Schnabel and Ramesh Thakur. Tokyo: UN University Press, pp. 155–166.

Sandholtz, Wayne, and Kendall Stiles. (2009) *International Norms and Cycles of Change.* New York: Oxford University Press.

Schaferhoff, Marco, Sabine Campe, and Christopher Kaan. (2009) "Transnational Public-Private Partnerships in International Relations: Making Sense of Concepts, Research Frameworks, and Results." *International Studies Review* 11:3 (September): 451–474.

Schechter, Michael. (2001) "Making Meaningful UN-Sponsored World Conferences of the 1990s: NGOs to the Rescue?" In *United Nations–Sponsored World Conferences: Focus on Impact and Follow-Up,* edited by Michael G. Schechter. Tokyo: UN University Press, pp. 184–217.

———. (2005) *United Nations Global Conferences.* New York: Routledge.

Schiff, Benjamin N. (2008) *Building the International Criminal Court.* New York: Cambridge University Press.

Schillemans, Thomas, and Mark Bovens. (2011) "The Challenge of Multiple Accountability: Does Redundancy Lead to Overload?" In *Accountable Governance: Problems and Promises,* edited by Melvin J. Dubnick and H. George Frederickson. Armonk, NY: Sharpe, pp. 3–21.

Schimmelfennig, Frank. (2007) "Functional Form, Identity-Driven Cooperation: Institutional Designs and Effects in Post–Cold War NATO." In *Crafting Cooperation: Regional International Institutions in Comparative Perspective,* edited by Amitav Acharya and Alastair Ian Johnston. Cambridge: Cambridge University Press, pp. 145–179.

Scholte, Jan Art. (2012) "A More Inclusive Global Governance? The IMF and Civil Society in Africa." *Global Governance* 18:2 (April–June): 185–206.

Schulenburg, Michael von der. (2014) "Rethinking Peacebuilding: Transforming the UN Approach." International Peace Academy Policy Papers. www.ipinst.org/publication /policy-papers/detail/436-new-report-transforming-the-un-approach-to-peace building-.html?tmpl=component&print=1.

*Security Council Report.* (2013a) "The Security Council and the UN Peacebuilding Commission." *Special Research Report* (18 April). www.securitycouncilreport.org/special -research-report/the-security-council-and-the-un-peacebuilding-commission.php.

———. (2013b) "UN Sanctions." *Special Research Report* (November 25). www .securitycouncilreport.org/special-research-report/un-sanctions.php.

———. (2014a) "In Hindsight: Consensus in the Security Council." *Monthly Forecast* (January). www.securitycouncilreport.org/monthly-forecast/2014-01/in_hindsight _consensus_in_the_security_council.php.

———. (2014b) "Security Council Working Methods: A Tale of Two Councils?" *Special Research Report* (March 25). www.securitycouncilreport.org/special-research -report/security-council-working-methods-a-tale-of-two-councils.php.

———. (2015) "April 2015 Monthly Forecast. 'Status Update.'" www.securitycouncil report.org/monthly-forecast/2015-04/status_update_29.php.

Selin, Henrik. (2007) "Coalition Politics and Chemicals Management in a Regulatory Ambitious Europe." *Global Environmental Politics* 7:3 (August): 63–93.

Sen, Amartya. (1999) *Development as Freedom.* New York: Knopf.

———. (2001) "A World of Extremes: Ten Theses on Globalization." *Los Angeles Times* (July 17).

Sengupta, Somini. (2014a) "In Dealings on Syria, Security Council Exposes Its Failings." *New York Times* (May 9): A12.

———. (2014b) "Politics Seen Undercutting Credibility of a Court." *New York Times* (June 3): A1, A4.

———. (2015a) "U.N. Reveals 'Alarmingly High' Levels of Violence Against Women." *New York Times* (March 10): A4

———. (2015b) "United Nations' Reputation Slips as Four-Year War in Syria Drags On." *New York Times* (March 13): A4.

———. (2015c) "Applications for Asylum Are Surging." *New York Times* (March 26): A5.

Shaw, Timothy M. (2008) *Commonwealth Inter- and Non-State Contributions to Global Governance.* New York: Routledge.

Sheeran, Scott, and Stephanie Case. (2014) *The Intervention Brigade: Legal Issues for the UN in the Democratic Republic of the Congo.* New York: International Peace Institute. http://reliefweb.int/sites/reliefweb.int/files/resources/ipi_e_pub_legal_issues _ drc_brigade.pdf.

Shifter, Michael. (2012) "The Shifting Landscape of Latin American Regionalism." *Current History* (February): 56–61.

Sikkink, Kathryn. (2009) "The Power of Networks in International Politics." In *Networked Politics: Agency, Power, and Governance,* edited by Miles Kahler. Ithaca: Cornell University Press, pp. 228–247.

———. (2013) "The United States and Torture: Does the Spiral Model Work?" In *The Persistent Power of Human Rights: From Commitment to Compliance*, edited by Thomas Risse, Stephen C. Ropp, and Kathryn Sikkink. New York: Cambridge University Press, pp. 145–163.

Simmons, Beth A. (2002) "Capacity, Commitment, and Compliance: International Institutions and Territorial Disputes." *Journal of Conflict Resolution* 46:6 (December): 829–856.

———. (2009) *Mobilizing for Human Rights: International Law in Domestic Politics*. New York: Cambridge University Press.

———. (2011) "International Studies in the Global Information Age." *International Studies Quarterly* 55:3 (September): 589–600.

Simmons, P. J. (1998) "Learning to Live with NGOs." *Foreign Policy* 112 (Fall): 82–96.

Simmons, P. J., and Chantal de Jonge Oudraat. (2001) "Managing Global Issues: An Introduction." In *Managing Global Issues: Lessons Learned*, edited by P. J. Simmons and Chantal de Jonge Oudraat. Washington, DC: Carnegie Endowment for International Peace, pp. 3–24.

Simons, Marlise. (2003) "World Court for Crimes of War Opens in The Hague." *New York Times* (March 12): A9.

Sinclair, Timothy J. (2001) "The Infrastructure of Global Governance: Quasi-Regulatory Mechanisms and the New Global Finance." *Global Governance* 7:4 (October–December): 441–451.

Skendaj, Elton. (2014) "International Insulation from Politics and the Challenge of State Building: Learning from Kosovo." *Global Governance* 20:3 (July–September): 459–481.

Slaughter, Anne Marie. (2004) *A New World Order*. Princeton: Princeton University Press.

Smillie, Ian, and Larry Minear. (2004) *The Charity of Nations: Humanitarian Action in a Calculating World*. Bloomfield, CT: Kumarian.

Smith, Courtney B. (1999) "The Politics of Global Consensus Building: A Comparative Analysis." *Global Governance* 5:2 (April–June): 173–201.

———. (2006) *Politics and Process at the United Nations: The Global Dance*. Boulder: Lynne Rienner.

Smith, Jackie, and Dawn Wiest. (2012) *Social Movements in the World-System: The Politics of Crisis and Transformation*. New York: Russell Sage.

Smith, Rhona. (2013) "'To See Themselves As Others See Them': The Five Permanent Members of the Security Council and the Human Rights Council's Universal Periodic Review." *Human Rights Quarterly* 35:1 (February): 1–32.

Smyth, Sophia, and Anna Triponel. (2013) "Funding Global Health." *Health and Human Rights* 15:1 (June): 58–70.

Snyder, Jack, and Leslie Vinjamuri. (2003–2004) "Trials and Errors: Principle and Pragmatism in Strategies of International Justice." *International Security* 28:3 (Winter): 5–44.

Söderbaum, Fredrik. (2003) "Introduction: Theories of New Regionalism." In *Theories of New Regionalism: A Palgrave Reader*, edited by Fredrik Söderbaum and Timothy M. Shaw. London: Palgrave Macmillan, pp. 1–21.

Soesastro, Hadi, and Charles E. Morrison. (2001) "Rethinking the ASEAN Formula: The Way Forward for Southeast Asia." In *East Asia and the International System: Report of a Special Study Group*, edited by Charles E. Morrison. New York: Trilateral Commission, pp. 57–75.

Solingen, Etel. (1998) *Regional Orders at Century's Dawn: Global and Domestic Influences on Grand Strategy*. Princeton: Princeton University Press.

———. (2008) "The Genesis, Design, and Effects of Regional Institutions: Lessons from East Asia and the Middle East." *International Studies Quarterly* 52:2 (June): 261–294.

Spar, Debora L. (1994) *The Cooperative Edge: The Internal Politics of International Cartels.* Ithaca: Cornell University Press.

———. (1999) "Lost in (Cyber) Space: The Private Rules of Online Commerce." In *Private Authority and International Affairs,* edited by A. Claire Cutler, Virginia Haufler, and Tony Porter. Albany: SUNY Press, pp. 31–51.

Spiro, Peter J. (1996) "New Global Potentates: Nongovernmental Organizations and the 'Unregulated' Marketplace." *Cardozo Law Review* 18 (December): 957–969.

Stedman, Stephen John, Donald Rothchild, and Elizabeth M. Cousens. (2002) *Ending Civil Wars: The Implementation of Peace Agreements.* Boulder: Lynne Rienner.

Stein, Arthur A. (1982) "Coordination and Collaboration: Regimes in an Anarchic World." *International Organization* 36:2 (Spring): 299–324.

Steinberg, Richard H. (2002) "In the Shadow of Law or Power? Consensus-Based Bargaining and Outcomes in the GATT/WTO." *International Organization* 56:2 (Spring): 339–374.

Stiglitz, Joseph. (2002) *Globalization and Its Discontents.* New York: Norton.

Stiles, Kendall W. (1998) "Civil Society Empowerment and Multilateral Donors: International Institutions and New International Norms." *Global Governance* 4:2 (April–June): 199–216.

———. (2009) "Disaggregating Delegation: Multiplying Agents in the International Maritime Safety Regime." Paper presented at the annual meeting of the International Studies Association, New York (February 15–18).

Stone, Randall. (2011) *Controlling Institutions: International Organizations and the Global Economy.* New York: Cambridge University Press.

Tallberg, Jonas. (2002) "Paths to Compliance: Enforcement, Management, and the European Union." *International Organization* 56:3 (Summer): 609–643.

Tallberg, Jonas, Thomas Sommerer, Theresa Squatrito, and Christer Jönsson. (2013) *The Opening Up of International Organizations: Transnational Access in Global Governance.* Cambridge: Cambridge University Press.

Tan, See Seng. (2013) "Herding Cats: The Role of Persuasion in Political Change and Continuity in the Association of Southeast Asian Nations (ASEAN)." *International Relations of the Asia-Pacific* 13:2 (May): 233–265.

Tannenwald, Nina, ed. (2007) *The Nuclear Taboo: The United States and the Non-Use of Nuclear Weapons Since 1945.* New York: Cambridge University Press.

Tansey, Oisín. (2014) "Evaluating the Legacies of State-Building: Success, Failure, and the Role of Responsibility." *International Studies Quarterly* 58:1 (March): 174–186.

Tavernise, Sabrina. (2014) "A Bank Chief Makes Ebola His Mission." *New York Times* (October 14): D1–D2.

Taylor, Paul. (2000) "Managing the Economic and Social Activities of the United Nations System: Developing the Role of ECOSOC." In *The United Nations at the Millennium: The Principal Organs,* edited by Paul Taylor and A. J. R. Groom. New York: Continuum, pp. 100–141.

Tepperman, Jonathan. (2013) "Where Are You, Ban Ki-moon?" *International New York Times* (September 24). www.nytimes.com/2013/09/25/opinion/tepperman-where-are-you-ban-ki-moon.html.

Terry, Fiona. (2002) *Condemned to Repeat? The Paradox of Humanitarian Action.* Ithaca: Cornell University Press.

Thakur, Ramesh. (2006) *The United Nations, Peace, and Security.* New York: Cambridge University Press.

———. (2014) "Not Just Another Brick in the Geopolitical Wall." *Tehelka Magazine* 11:31 (2 August). www.tehelka.com/by-leveraging-its-ties-with-non-western-powers-brics-can-check-us-hegemony/.

Thakur, Ramesh, and William Maley. (1999) "The Ottawa Convention on Landmines: A Landmark Humanitarian Treaty in Arms Control." *Global Governance* 5:3 (July–September): 273–302.

Tickner, J. Ann. (2001) *Gendering World Politics: Issues and Approaches in the Post–Cold War Era*. New York: Columbia University Press.

Tilly, Charles. (2004) *Social Movements, 1768–2004*. Boulder: Paradigm.

Traub, James. (2006) *The Best Intentions: Kofi Annan and the UN in the Era of American World Power*. New York: Farrar, Straus, and Giroux.

True, Jacqui. (2011) "Feminist Problems with International Norms: Gender Mainstreaming in Global Governance." In *Feminism and International Relations: Conversations About the Past, Present, and Future*, edited by J. Ann Tickner and Laura Sjoberg. London: Routledge, pp. 73–88.

Union of International Associations. (various years) *Yearbook of International Organizations*. Brussels.

United Nations (UN). (1992) "Letter Dated 29 November 1992 from the Secretary-General Addressed to the President of the Security Council." S/24868.

———. (1993) "The 'Second Generation': Cambodia Elections 'Free and Fair,' but Challenges Remain." *UN Chronicle* 30:5 (November–December): 26.

———. (1996) *The Blue Helmets: A Review of United Nations Peace-Keeping*. 3rd ed. New York: UN Department of Public Information.

———. (1999a) "Address of the Secretary-General to the UN General Assembly, 20 September." GA/9596.

———. (1999b) Press release. SG/SM/6938 (March 24). www.un.org/docs/sg/sgsm .htm.

———. (1999c) Press release. SG/SM/7263, AFR/196 (December 16). www.un.org /docs/sg/sgsm.htm.

———. (1999d) *Report of the Secretary-General on the UN Preliminary Deployment in the Democratic Republic of Congo*. S/1999/790.

———. (2000) *Report of the Panel on United Nations Peace Operations* (Brahimi Report). A/55/305-S/2000/809 (August 21).

———. (2001) *Report of the High-Level Panel on Financing for Development Appointed by the United Nations Secretary-General*. 55th General Assembly Session, Agenda Item no. 101. A/55/1000 (June 26). www.un.org/esa/ffd/a55-1000.pdf.

———. (2004) *A More Secure World: Our Shared Responsibility*. Report of the Secretary-General's High-Level Panel on Threats, Challenges, and Change. New York. www.un.org/secureworld.

———. (2005) *World Summit Outcome*. A/60/L.1, sec. 81. www.un-ngls.org/un-summit -final-doc.pdf.

———. (2008) *Peacekeeping Operations: Principles and Guidelines*. New York: UN Department of Peacekeeping Operations, Department of Field Support.

———. (2014a) *The Millennium Development Goals Report 2014*. www.un.org /millen-niumgoals/2014%20MDG%20report/MDG.

———. (2014b) "Secretary-General's Remarks to Security Council High-Level Summit on Foreign Terrorist Fighters." (24 September). www.un.org/sg/statements /index.asp?nid=8040.

United Nations Children's Fund (UNICEF). (2013) *Female Genital Mutilation/Cutting: A Statistical Overview and Exploration of the Dynamics of Change*. New York.

United Nations Development Programme (UNDP) and Arab Fund for Economic and Social Development. (2002) *Arab Human Development Report: Creating Opportunities for Future Generations*. New York.

United Nations Environment Programme (UNEP). (2012) "United Nations Environment Programme Upgraded to Universal Membership Following Rio+20 Summit." www.unep.org/newscentre/default.aspx?DocumentID+2700&ArticleID =9363.

———. (2014) "Ozone Layer on Track to Recovery: Success Story Should Encourage Action on Climate." www.unep.org/newscentre/default.aspx?Document ID=2796& ArticleID=10978.

United Nations High Commissioner for Refugees (UNHCR). (2013) *Displacement: The New 21st Century Challenge—UNHCR Global Trends 2012*. www.unhcr.org/51 bacb0f9.html.

————. (2014) *War's Human Cost—UNHCR Global Trends 2013.* www.unhcr .org/5399a14f9.United Nations Secretary-General. (2010) *Remarks at Event on Ending Violence and Criminal Sanctions Based on Sexual Orientation and Gender Identity.* www.un.org/apps/news/infocus/sgspeeches/statements_full.asp?statID = 1034#.VKgmeXuZaXg.

————. (2011) *Preventive Diplomacy: Delivering Results.* S/2011/552 (26 August). www.un.org/wcm/webdav/site/undpa/shared/undpa/pdf/SG%20Report%20on%20Pr eventive%20Diplomacy.pdf.

UN Women. (2014) "Current Status of Women." www.unwomen.org/en/how-we-work /un-system-coordination/women-in-the-united-nations/current-status-of-women.

US Ninth Circuit Court of Appeals. (2002) *Doe v. UNOCAL.* 395 F.3d 932.

US Supreme Court. (2013) *Kiobel v. Royal Dutch Petroleum.* 133 S. Ct. 1659.

US Trade Representative. (2013) *2013 Report to Congress on China's WTO Compliance.* www.ustr.gov/sites/default/files/2013-Report-to-Congress-China-WTO -Compliance.pdf.

Uvin, Peter. (1998) *Aiding Violence: The Development Enterprise in Rwanda.* West Hartford, CT: Kumarian.

Väyrynen, Raimo. (2003) "Regionalism: Old and New." *International Studies Review* 5:1 (March): 25–51.

Veseth, Michael. (2010) *Globaloney 2.0: The Crash of 2008 and the Future of Globalization.* New York: Rowman and Littlefield.

Vieira de Mello, Sergio. (2001) "How Not to Run a Country: Lessons from Kosovo and East Timor." Paper presented at the UNITAR-IPS-JIIA Conference to Assess the Report on UN Peace Operations, Singapore (April 2–3).

Voeten, Erik. (2005) "The Political Origins of the UN Security Council's Ability to Legitimize the Use of Force." *International Organization* 59:3 (Summer): 527–557.

Vogler, John. (2011) "European Union Environmental Policy." In *Comparative Environmental Regionalism,* edited by Lorraine Elliott and Shaun Breslin. London: Routledge, pp. 19–36.

Waldman, Amy. (2003) "Helping Hand for Bangladesh's Poor." *New York Times* (March 25): A8.

Waltz, Kenneth N. (1979) *Theory of International Politics.* Reading: Addison-Wesley.

Wang, Jianwei. (2008) "China and SCO: Towards a New Type of Interstate Relations." In *China Turns to Multilateralism: Foreign Policy and Regional Security,* edited by Guoguang Wu and Helen Lansdowne. New York: Routledge, pp. 104–126.

Wapner, Paul. (1996) *Environmental Activism and World Civil Politics.* Albany: SUNY Press.

————. (2007) "The State or Else! Statism's Resilience in NGO Studies." *International Studies Review* 9:1 (Spring): 85–89.

Ward, Michael. (2004) *Quantifying the World: UN Contributions to Statistics.* Bloomington: Indiana University Press.

Warkentin, Craig. (2001) *Reshaping World Politics: NGOs, the Internet, and Global Civil Society.* Lanham: Rowman and Littlefield.

Weaver, Catherine E. (2007) "The World's Bank and the Bank's World." *Global Governance* 13:4 (October–December): 493–512.

————. (2008) *Hypocrisy Trap: The World Bank and the Poverty of Reform.* Princeton: Princeton University Press.

Weinberger, Naomi. (2002) "Civil-Military Coordination in Peacebuilding: The Challenge of Afghanistan." *Journal of International Affairs* 55:2 (Spring): 245–274.

Weinstein, Michael M., and Steve Charnovitz. (2001) "The Greening of the WTO." *Foreign Affairs* 80:6 (November–December): 147–156.

Weiss, Edith Brown, and Harold K. Jacobson, eds. (2000) *Engaging Countries: Strengthening Compliance with International Environmental Accords.* Cambridge: MIT Press.

Weiss, Thomas G. (2009) *What's Wrong with the United Nations and How to Fix It.* Cambridge: Polity.

——. (2014a) "After Syria, Whither R2P?" In *Into the Eleventh Hour: R2P, Syria, and Humanitarianism in Crisis,* E–International Relations. www.e-ir.info/2014/02/02 /after-syria-whither-r2p.

——. (2014b) "Reinvigorating the 'Second' United Nations: People Matter." In *Routledge Handbook of International Organizations,* edited by Bob Reinalda. New York: Routledge, pp. 299–311.

Weiss, Thomas G., and David A. Korn. (2006) *Internal Displacement: Conceptualization and Its Consequences.* New York: Routledge.

Weiss, Thomas G., and Ramesh Thakur. (2010) *Global Governance and the UN: An Unfinished Journey.* Bloomington: Indiana University Press.

Weiss, Thomas G., and Rorden Wilkinson. (2014) "Rethinking Global Governance? Complexity, Authority, Power, Change." *International Studies Quarterly* 58:1 (March): 207–215.

Weissbrodt, David. (2003) "Do Human Rights Treaties Make Things Worse?" *Foreign Policy* 134 (January–February): 88–89.

Welz, Martin. (2013) "The African Union Beyond Africa: Explaining the Limited Impact of Africa's Continental Organization on Global Governance." *Global Governance* 19:3 (July–September): 425–441.

Wendt, Alexander. (1995) "Constructing International Politics." *International Security* 20.1 (Summer): 71–81.

Whitfield, Teresa. (2007) *Friends Indeed? The United Nations, Groups of Friends, and Resolution of Conflict.* Washington, DC: US Institute of Peace.

Wilkinson, Rorden. (2014) "The WTO, the UN, and the Future of Global Development: What Matters and Why." *Future United Nations Development System,* briefing no. 15 (March).

Willetts, Peter. (2006) "The Cardoso Report on the UN and Civil Society: Functionalism, Global Corporatism, or Global Democracy?" *Global Governance* 12:3 (July–Sept.): 305–324.

——. (2010) *Non-Governmental Organizations in World Politics: The Construction of Global Governance.* London: Routledge.

Williams, Paul D. (2007) "From Non-Intervention to Non-Indifference: The Origins and Development of the African Union's Security Culture." *African Affairs* 106 (April): 253–279.

——. (2011) *War and Conflict in Africa.* Cambridge: Polity.

Williams, Paul D., and Solomon A. Dersso. (2015) "Saving Strangers and Neighbors: Advancing UN-AU Cooperation on Peace Operations." New York: International Peace Institute. http://reliefweb.int/sites/reliefweb.int/files/resources/ipi_e_pub _saving_strangers_and_neighbors.pdf.

Wilson, Peter. (2012) "The English School Meets the Chicago School: The Case for a Grounded Theory of International Institutions." *International Studies Review* 14:4 (December): 567–590.

Wolman, Andrew. (2014) "Welcoming a New International Human Rights Actor? The Participation of Subnational Human Rights Institutions at the UN." *Global Governance* 20:3 (July–September): 437–457.

Wong, Wendy H. (2012) "Becoming a Household Name: How Human Rights NGOs Establish Credibility Through Organizational Structure." In *The Credibility of Transnational NGOs: When Virtue Is Not Enough,* edited by Peter A. Gourevitch and David A. Lake. New York: Cambridge University Press, pp. 86–112.

Woods, Lawrence T. (1993) *Asia-Pacific Diplomacy: Nongovernmental Organizations and International Relations.* Vancouver: University of British Columbia Press.

Woods, Ngaire. (1999) "Good Governance in International Organizations." *Global Governance* 5:1 (January–March): 39–61.

————. (2008) "Governing the Global Economy: Strengthening Multilateral Institutions." New York: International Peace Institute.

World Bank. (2008) "The Growth Report: Strategies for Sustained Growth and Inclusive Development." Commission on Growth and Development. www.growthcommission.org.

————. (2011a) *The World Bank and Aid Effectiveness: Performance to Date and Agenda Ahead.* Washington, DC: World Bank.

————. (2011b) *World Development Report 2011: Conflict, Security, and Development.* Washington, DC: World Bank.

World Commission on Environment and Development (WCED). (1987) *Our Common Future* (Brundtland Commission Report). Oxford: Oxford University Press.

Wroughton, Lesley. (2008) "Gates, Buffett Back WFP Plan to Help Poor Farmers." *Reuters* (September 25).

Youde, Jeremy. (2012) *Global Health Governance.* Malden, MA: Polity.

Young, Kevin. (2011) "The Basel Committee on Banking Supervision." In *Handbook of Transnational Governance: Institutions and Innovations,* edited by Thomas Hale and David Held. London: Polity, pp. 39–45.

Young, Oran R. (1967) *The Intermediaries: Third Parties in International Crises.* Princeton: Princeton University Press.

————. (1989) *International Cooperation: Building Regimes for Natural Resources and the Environment.* Ithaca: Cornell University Press.

————. (1999) *The Effectiveness of International Environmental Regimes: Causal Connections and Behavioral Mechanisms.* Cambridge: MIT Press.

Yuan, Jing-Dong. (2010) "China's Role in Establishing and Building the Shanghai Cooperation Organization (SCO)." *Journal of Contemporary China* 19:67 (November): 855–869.

Zartman, I. William, and Saadia Touval. (1996) "International Mediation in the Post–Cold War Era." In *Managing Global Chaos: Sources of and Responses to International Conflict,* edited by Chester A. Crocker and Fen Osler Hampson, with Pamela Aall. Washington, DC: US Institute of Peace, pp. 445–462.

Zweifel, Thomas D. (2006) *International Organizations and Democracy: Accountability, Politics, and Power.* Boulder: Lynne Rienner.

# Index

# About the Book

The third edition of the award-winning *International Organizations* has been thoroughly revised and updated to take into account new developments and shifting power relations since 2009, as well as the most current scholarship.

As before, the authors provide a comprehensive, in-depth examination of the full range of international organizations. New features of the book include attention to a broader range of theoretical approaches, to the increasing importance of regional organizations, and to emerging forms of governance. And new case studies highlight the governance dilemmas posed by the Libyan and Syrian civil wars, human trafficking, LGBT rights, climate change, and more.

**Margaret P. Karns** is professor emerita of political science at the University of Dayton and external faculty fellow, Center for Governance and Sustainability, University of Massachusetts–Boston. **Karen A. Mingst** is Lockwood Chair Professor in the Patterson School of Diplomacy and International Commerce and professor of political science at the University of Kentucky. **Kendall W. Stiles** is professor of political science at Brigham Young University.